TEXAS

AND

OKLAHOMA

BIRTHS, DEATHS

AND

MARRIAGES

from the

FORT WORTH RECORD

November 1903 *to* November 1904

Abstracted and Compiled
by
Bruce Bumbalough

HERITAGE BOOKS
2008

HERITAGE BOOKS
AN IMPRINT OF HERITAGE BOOKS, INC.

Books, CDs, and more—Worldwide

For our listing of thousands of titles see our website
at
www.HeritageBooks.com

Published 2008 by
HERITAGE BOOKS, INC.
Publishing Division
100 Railroad Ave. #104
Westminster, Maryland 21157

Copyright © 2008 Bruce Bumbalough

All rights reserved. No part of this book may be reproduced or transmitted in any form or by any means, electronic or mechanical, including photocopying, recording or by any information storage and retrieval system without written permission from the author, except for the inclusion of brief quotations in a review.

International Standard Book Numbers
Paperbound: 978-0-7884-4782-2
Clothbound: 978-0-7884-7507-8

Table of Contents

Introduction	5
November, 1903	7
December, 1903	13
January, 1904	23
February, 1904	39
March, 1904	57
April, 1904	75
May, 1904	93
June, 1904	107
July, 1904	121
August, 1904	133
September, 1904	149
October, 1904	167
November, 1904	185
Index	199

Introduction

Fort Worth has had many newspapers during the more than 150 years it has existed as a place in Texas. Among the early ones were the *Fort Worth Tribune*, the *Democrat*, the *Democrat-Advance*, and the *Fort Worth Standard* and the *Fort Worth Register*. As the city began to grow dramatically in the first decade of the twentieth century, the number of newspapers increased.

The *Fort Worth Record* started in 1903 in competition with the *Fort Worth Register* as a morning paper in the city. The *Record* bought out the *Register* in 1904 and was known as the *Fort Worth Record and Register* for some time. Clarence Ousley was the editor of the *Record* from 1903 to 1917. The paper reported news from across Texas, Indian Territory, Oklahoma Territory, the nation, and the world. It provided coverage of the Russo - Japanese war, the presidential election of 1904 and the 1904 World's Fair. There was also extensive coverage of the railroads and their business activities.

William Capps bought the *Record and Register* about 1912. Ousley had been the president of the paper as well as editor and manager prior to its sale to Capps. He stayed on as editor until 1917 when W. H. Bagley bought it from William Capps. Bagley installed Hugh Nugent Fitzgerald as the editor. Jim Allison bought enough stock in the *Record* to become president and publisher in 1921. Allison sold the *Record* to William Randolph Hearst in 1923. Hearst named Dan D. Moore as editor and publisher. The *Fort Worth Star-Telegram* purchased the *Record* from Hearst on November 1, 1925 and renamed it the *Fort Worth Record-Telegram*. It continued as the *Record-Telegram* until 1931. The *Record-Telegram* remained as a morning paper with the *Star Telegram* as an evening paper. In 1931, the *Record-Telegram* was renamed the *Star-Telegram* and continues as a morning paper in Fort Worth to this day. The evening *Star-Telegram* suspended publication in 1995.[1]

The *Fort Worth Record and Register* is especially helpful to genealogists and family historians because it reported vital statistics, such as births and deaths, marriages, legal proceedings for cities and towns in Texas, Oklahoma Territory, and Indian Territory, school events, pension grants, appointments of postmasters, personals, society happenings, club news, lists of guests registered at hotels in Fort Worth, lists of letters being held at the post office, attendees at the 1904 World's Fair in St. Louis and others. The compiler elected to include only the births, marriages and deaths because of the sheer volume of information in a daily newspaper.

Journalistic style of the period often identified family members only by the relationship to the head of household. Many times a story reporting the death of a child would simply say, for example, "The three year old daughter of John SMITH was killed yesterday in Ardmore, Indian Territory."

Similarly, the journalistic style of the period was such that races of the people involved were often times named. Minority groups were often treated disparagingly in the stories. Racial designations are omitted from the abstracts.

The abstracts are arranged chronologically. In the interests of conserving space, cities that are well-known in Texas are listed without the state designator. The five cities that do not receive a state identification in Texas are Austin, Dallas, El Paso, Fort Worth and Houston. All other Texas communities are designated with the state. All cities and towns in Indian Territory or Oklahoma Territory will list the territory. Similarly, all cities and towns in states other than Texas or the two territories will be identified with the state in which they are located. The only other exceptions will be the rare instances in which the state or territory could not be determined by the compiler.

The compiler made every attempt to insure the accuracy of these abstracts. Any errors he made are not intentional and are solely his responsibility.

There were several small communities in Tarrant County mentioned in the *Fort Worth Record*. Many of these have been absorbed by Fort Worth. Communities such as Rosen Heights, Arlington Heights, Marine, Enon, Glenwood, North Fort Worth, Riverside and Handley are now a part of the City of Fort Worth.

---

[1] Much of the information about the history of newspapers in Fort Worth comes from *The Handbook of Texas* and from a speech given by Phillip Meeks to the Newcomen Society in 1981.

The Handbook of Texas is a good source for information about towns and cities in Texas. It is available online and in print format.

November, 1903

The microfilm begins with the issue of November 20, 1903.

Friday, November 20, 1903

J. A. AMMER died yesterday at Denison, Texas.

Maggie BECKNELL was convicted of murdering her six-week old infant and sentenced to life imprisonment. The trial took place in Sherman, Texas.

Two daughters, ages 8 and 10, of Perry VICKERS died in a house fire at Tyler, Texas. Their names were not listed.

Prominent citizen Gus REYMERSHOFFER died of a heart attack at Galveston, Texas.

Reverend W. F. MCDOWELL died at Ardmore, Indian Territory.

Railroad engineer J. C. ROBERTSON was killed at the Clear Fork bridge west of Fort Worth on Monday. His funeral was held in Marshall, Texas.

Josie GENICARTO, 5, died from injuries suffered when her clothing caught fire in Houston.

Pioneer "Grandpa" RELATOR died of natural causes in the Parker Community near McKinney, Texas.

Marriage licenses issued by Tarrant County Clerk: P. B. STAGGS and Lula HENRY, George JORDAN and Annie YOUNGS, A. J. WARBLOM and Bertha JONES, John W. FAIRAMA and Alice GRAY, and Claud O. GORDON and Christine BEGGS.

Births recorded at Tarrant County Clerk's Office: a boy to Mr. and Mrs. Jesse ESTES on November 12, a girl to Mr. and Mrs. John HUNTER on November 14, a boy to Mr. and Mrs. R. F. WOODSON on November 9, a girl to Mr. and Mrs. Leonard PAYNE on November 11, a girl to Mr. and Mrs. Alvin WATSON on November 14, a boy to Mr. and Mrs. C. M. ADAMS on November 15, and a girl to Mr. and Mrs. John L. GREEN on November 10.

Charles STATELER and Emma BROWN married yesterday south of Mineral Wells, Texas.

Wesley M. SUMNER and Rubye CRAIGO married yesterday in Paris, Texas.

Ernest MUMPOWER of Denison and Nancy FITZGERALD married yesterday west of Paris, Texas.

Frank F. REID and Angie PROCTOR married yesterday in Paris, Texas.

Mrs. A. M. VAN NEEF, Jr., died Tuesday in Marshall, Texas. Burial was in Greenwood Cemetery in Marshall.

A. S. TILLERY died and was buried yesterday at Forney, Texas.

A. B. COOPER, age about 50, died Tuesday in Texarkana.

R. H. CAMPBELL of Dallas and Hattie ALVIS married yesterday at Terrell, Texas.

Mrs. Files MALONE, 90, died at a neighbor's home in Ferris, Texas.

Saturday, November 21, 1903

The paper for this date did not appear on the microfilm

Sunday, November 22, 1903

Mittie ROBINSON and John SNEED married in El Paso recently. SNEED is the editor of the *El Paso Evening News*.

W. D. GALLAGHER and Lula C. CATO married yesterday in McKinney, Texas.

Mrs. SAXTON, 78, died yesterday suddenly at the home of her daughter, Mrs. HENDERSON, in Ennis, Texas. No given names were listed.

Judge Charles Chandler PARKER and Mrs. A. M. Clayton FARRIS married yesterday in South McAlester, Indian Territory.

Thomas Clayton FROST, president of Frost National Bank, died yesterday in San Antonio.

W. R. TOLER died yesterday of injuries sustained in a fall while working at Central School in Ennis, Texas.

Mrs. BATTLE died yesterday in a fire at the home of her son, Rev. Rofe BATTLE, in Ennis, Texas.

Jenny GOSS was shot to death at Miller Lumber Mill in Shepherd, Texas. Hinson DARBY was arrested.

Sam DODSON was convicted of manslaughter for the 1901 shooting death of Allen BROWN. DODSON was sentenced to five years in prison.

Jack COCOANUT died of injuries suffered in a fire at county jail in Austin yesterday.

L. P. KING was killed Thursday on the Texas and Pacific Railroad near Mesquite, Texas.

Judge Robert F. MOORE died in Fort Worth on Friday. He was buried in Oakwood Cemetery in Fort Worth.

Mrs. Elizabeth LINTHICUM died Friday in Garza, Texas. She had been a resident of Texas since 1833.

Polly Ann GREEN, 73, died Thursday in Stony, Texas. She was buried near Stony.

Katherine WEST, 76, died Friday in Terrell, Texas. She was buried in Pecan Cemetery in McKinney.

Dr. J. Hillary TAYLOR died yesterday in Marshall, Texas. He was buried in Longview.

James ADAMS died Thursday in Ferris, Texas.

Mrs. W. T. MOORE died of heart failure Friday in McKinney, Texas.

"Uncle Billie" HENDERSON died Friday in Longview, Texas.

Lois WHITE, the daughter of Mr. and Mrs. George C. WHITE, and Sam HENDERSON married Wednesday evening in Fort Worth.

Christine BEGGS and Claud GORDON married Thursday evening in Fort Worth.

Mary NEUMEGEN and M. A. ROSENTHAL married last Sunday in Fort Worth.

Maggie ROBINSON drowned yesterday after she suffered a seizure while washing at Beaumont, Texas.

Monday, November 23, 1903

Vera PLUMMER, about 20, committed suicide yesterday in East Vernon, Texas.

C. C. MAYDEN and Naomi STALLCUP married yesterday in McKinney, Texas.

Mrs. D. H. COLLINS died yesterday in Sanger, Texas. She was buried in Sanger Cemetery.

Mrs. H. M. WYNNE, 79, died yesterday in the home of A. M. WYNNE, her son, in Temple, Texas.

F. J. EVANS and Lillian THOMPSON married in Fort Worth yesterday.

Sam HANNA died yesterday in Denison, Texas. He was a former mayor of Denison.

James SHUCKEY, of St. Louis, Missouri, was killed in Beaver County, Indian Territory. His horse threw him while he was branding calves. No date was reported.

The two year old son of James SMITH died of eating matches at Binger, Oklahoma Territory.

The 13 year old son of Jonathan OSBORNE died when he was kicked and dragged by a mule at Olustee, Oklahoma Territory.

Tuesday, November 24, 1903

Emmett MITCHELL and Eva COLDBERG married in the home of her sister, Mrs. Sam LUCAS, in Palestine, Texas. Both the bride and groom were from Pittsburg.

Edgar WILLMON and Gertie May JOHNSON married Sunday in Cleburne, Texas.

Lem HOYL and Minnie REYNOLDS were married Wednesday by Rev. W. C. CARTER in Decatur, Texas.

Jimmie GREEN and May CRUTCHFIELD were married Sunday by Rev. F. O. MILLER in Bellevue, Texas.

Dr. H. S. FREEMAN died suddenly yesterday in his home in Sherman, Texas.

Rosa Yet LEE, 7, died in St. Joseph Infirmary in Fort Worth yesterday after a 16 day illness.

W. M. PATE, 74, was found dead in his cabin at Brownwood, Texas.

A. POTTER was held guiltless in the death of Charles ORR, a burglar killed while breaking into Harden Brothers Store at McGee, Oklahoma Territory. No dates were reported.

The funeral of Colonel Edwin Elias OVERALL was held yesterday in Fort Worth.

Marriage Licenses issued by the Tarrant County Clerk: F. J. EVANS and Lillian B. THOMPSON, W. H. THETFORD and Sue SHERLOCK, W. M. J. TURNER and Sallie BALCH, Ivey RICHARDS and Mamie HURD, Will ROSS and Minnie COFFEY, and John BELL and Mary CHRISTFER.

Jesse SMITH, 17, was killed in Houston when he was struck by a railroad car there. No date was reported.

Births reported to the Tarrant County Clerk: a boy to Mr. and Mrs. Charley BROWN on November 21, a boy to Mr. and Mrs. Phillips HAYES on November 15, a girl to Mr. and Mrs. J. J. TAYLOR on November 15, a boy to Mr. and Mrs. J. E. MORRIS on November 20, a boy to Mr. and Mrs. Daniel M. ROSE on November 12, and a girl to Mr. and Mrs. S. H. MCCLURE on August 3.

The body of W. E. WILLIS, a telegraph operator at Galveston, Texas, was found in the bay. He was believed to have been murdered.

Wednesday, November 25, 1903

John M. HAMPTON, of Bellevue, Texas, and Eva DERRICK were married last Sunday in Jacksboro.

C. Steele COVINGTON and Nora HARRELL were married by Rev. J. G. LANE in Hillsboro, Texas. No date was reported.

Ed PATTERSON and Julia FOWLER were married Sunday by Rev. S. H. SLAUGHTER in Ennis, Texas.

Mortimer L. KARY of Beaumont, Texas, and Adele DEUTSCHNER of Corsicana married in her parent's home. She is the daughter of Mr. and Mrs. David DEUTSCHNER.

J. W. SELLERS and Effie COCKRELL, married yesterday in McKinney, Texas. COCKRELL is from Blue Ridge, Texas.

William H. RICHARDSON of Malta, Montana, and Josie PARKER of McKinney, Texas, married Sunday. She is the daughter of Mr. and Mrs. R. L. PARKER.

E. L. SHIELDS and L. V. MCCARVER of near Wilmith, Texas, married at the home of Rev. J. A. HELD in McKinney, Texas.

J. A. STRANGE and Laura WHISENANT married at the home of Dr. E. E. KING in McKinney, Texas.

Carl Schwartz COBB, son of Mr. and Mrs. R. E. COBB, died Monday in Denton, Texas. He was buried in Odd Fellows' Cemetery.

John M. WILLIAMSON died Sunday night at Tuscola, Texas.

J. K. LEE died early Tuesday at his home in Temple, Texas.

Eva DEDMON, 2, died yesterday in McKinney, Texas. She was buried in Pecan Grove. She was the daughter of Mr. and Mrs. Charles DEDMON.

The baby of Mr. and Mrs. Will EMMINS, of Byron, Texas died yesterday.

Rufus BINCON was convicted of murdering his adopted daughter and sentenced to hang at Ardmore, Indian Territory.

Mrs. Lou EATON, 25, died suddenly at Springfield, Oklahoma Territory. She left a husband and two daughters.

J. W. RHODES of Navasota, Texas, was found dead in a lake in Kansas City, Missouri. He fled from a private sanitarium there.

Bailey IVEY shot and killed Frank CHAMBERS yesterday afternoon near Berryville, Texas.

Marriages licenses issued by Tarrant County Clerk: Peyton IRVING and Anita MCCORMICK, C. W. WEAVER and Claudia WISEMAN, Royal S. LOVING and Lillian S. PARKER, Zack J. CHILDRESS and Lillian ISBELL, and A. C. MCCULLOCH and Annie J. MILLER.

S. A. WRIGHT, a druggist from Pilot Point, Texas, and Mary JOHNSON were married yesterday at the Worth Hotel in Fort Worth by the Rev. R. R. HAMLIN.

Z. J. CHILDRESS and Lillian ISBELL were married by the Rev R. R. HAMLIN at the home of her parents in Fort Worth.

Claudia WISEMAN and Charlie WEAVER were married at her parent's home in Fort Worth by the Rev. J. D. YOUNG.

The bodies of Hiram R. PATTERSON and Gabe SMITH arrived from the Philippine Islands. They were will killed while serving in the Quartermaster Corps there.

Albert MCCOY married Emma HARTLEY in Dallas yesterday. The groom is from Ennis, Texas.

The funeral of Mrs. James M. INGRAM was held yesterday in Terrell, Texas.

Pete EMSERY shot and killed Oscar SIMPSON at a dance near Tucumcari, New Mexico Territory. No date was given.

John MALLOY was found dead at his father's ranch near San Angelo, Texas. He was from Eden. His horse may have thrown him.

Wednesday, November 26, 1903

J. E. BARTEK and Emily TOLES married Sunday in Temple, Texas. Justice WARD presided.

Jim JONES and Alice WATKINS were married by Justice WARD in Temple, Texas. John CONFAR and Matilda MOTT also married in the double ceremony.

William NICHOLS of Houston and Esther SNODGRASS married Monday in Ennis, Texas. Rev. R. T. PHILLIPS officiated.

R. B. CALDWELL and Ethel DOKE married Wednesday in Corsicana, Texas.

James ALLEN, 28, died yesterday of typhoid fever in McKinney, Texas.

Ike ARMSTRONG, who died in Dallas on Saturday, was buried yesterday in Van Alstyne, Texas.

Mrs. W. A. MERRITT died yesterday at her home near Ennis, Texas.

Samuel MITCHELL died at Medford, Oklahoma Territory. No date was reported.

Rose HAYES, 39, committed suicide in Enid, Oklahoma Territory.

Dr. A. I. CAMMACK died suddenly yesterday in Waco, Texas. He was 65 and died from the results of a Civil War wound.

Irma BURNETT, 4, died of burns suffered while playing near the fire grate at her home in Marshall, Texas. She was the daughter of Mr. and Mrs. S. R. BURNETT.

Marriage licenses issued by Tarrant County Clerk: F. A. WRIGHT and Mary B. JOHNSON, W. L. VAN ZANDT and Belle WILLIAMS, E. L. ANDREWS and Ethel A. NEWBILL, James D. WHITSELL and Rebecca M. BROCK, and B. L. ORRICK and A. L. CHAMBERS.

Births reported to the Tarrant County Clerk: a boy to Mr. and Mrs. J. A. KELLEY, Fort Worth, on November 19; a boy to Mr. and Mrs. Charles STEEMPF, Fort Worth, on November 21; a girl to Mr. and Mrs. Samuel BROWNING, Fort Worth, on November 20; a girl to Mr. and Mrs. George W. BELL, Birdville, on November 23; a boy to Mr. and Mrs. John DAWSON, Fort Worth, on November 16; a girl to Mr. and Mrs. John FLYNN on November 19; a boy to Mr. and Mrs. M. V. HERRINGTON, Fort Worth, on November 21; a girl to Mr. and Mrs. Jess CANTWELL, Johnson Station, on November 18; a girl to Mr. and Mrs. Homer CLARK, Johnson Station, on November 20; a boy to Mr. and Mrs. Russell G. MCDANIEL, Johnson Station, on November 18; a boy to Mr. and Mrs. P. F. SANDERS, Grapevine, on November 15; a girl to Mr. and Mrs. Thomas W. LIDESTER, Grapevine, on November 16; and a boy to Mr. and Mrs. G. T. LOWE, Johnson Station, on November 21.

Deaths reported to Tarrant County Clerk: Lucinda BYAS, 60, residing in Dove on November 12; and Clarence CATE, 1 month, residing in Grapevine on November 14.

Ernest ANDREWS married Lillian LAWRENCE Tuesday in Fort Worth. Rev. N. B. READ performed the ceremony.

Thursday, November 27, 1903

W. P. KAKEN died suddenly of heart failure in Dallas yesterday.

County attorney J. H. MCHANEY and Nora KENNARD married yesterday in Longview, Texas. Rev. W. M. ALLEN officiated.

C. A. ROTAN and Mrs. Mattie A. SANDERS married Wednesday in Hillsboro, Texas. Rev. E. T. HUBBARD performed the ceremony.

Henry PRICE married Fannie HALL Wednesday south of Paris, Texas. Rev. J. H. MYERS officiated.

John GUFFEE of Fort Worth and Mattie Sue TOM married in San Angelo, Texas. She is the daughter of Mr. and Mrs. Dudley TOM.

John GODSOE, 22, died Sunday at his home near Antelope, Texas. He weighed about 500 pounds at his death and had appeared at the Texas State Fair.

Solomon W. SANDERS was accidentally killed while returning from a hunting trip yesterday. He lived in Taylor, Texas.

Tobia NOVICH, 82, died Wednesday from burns suffered when a gas stove exploded at her home in Waco, Texas.

Munsey VAUGHAN, mortally wounded by his former father-in-law Bill RIDLEY, died Thursday morning in Lawton, Oklahoma Territory.

Dr. J. P. ANDERSON, a dentist, died in San Angelo, Texas. His remains were shipped to Greenwood, South Carolina.

Claude ISBELL and Audrey MEADOWS married at Jacksboro, Texas. Rev. Leland MALONE officiated.

Friday, November 28, 1903

The paper for this date did not appear on the microfilm.

Saturday, November 29, 1903

William SQUIRES, 65, of Dallas, died in jail while serving a sentence for being drunk.

Marriage licenses issued by Tarrant County Clerk: C. E. MARTIN and M. LITTLEFIELD, A. F. WHITE and Florence PRATTLER, James NEVITT and Emma LAWSON, and Austin P. MEDLEY and Mrs. Nannie COOK.

Births reported to the Tarrant County Clerk: a boy to Mr. and Mrs. Lee CANTWELL, Johnson Station, on November 25; a boy to Mr. and Mrs. Tom LAWLING on November 24; a girl to Mr. and Mrs. Fred MITCHELL, near Johnson Station, on November 24; a girl to Mr. and Mrs. Albert G. FURMAN, Grapevine, on November 22; a boy to Mr. and Mrs. Jack ROYSTER, Fort Worth, on November 24; and a boy to Mr. and Mrs. Rastburn GRAY, Fort Worth, with no date reported.

Death reported to the Tarrant County Clerk: Robert SLATER, 29, residing in Fort Worth died on November 28.

Joseph MAYER, 50, of Fort Worth, died yesterday in New York City.

K. REED, 82, died at the Fort Worth residence of his son, O. E. REED.

May GILLHAM married Tobe MURRAY on November 21 in Fort Worth.

T. B. STEVENSON and Emma PRICE married Wednesday in North Marshall, Texas.

H. BECHTOLD and Della BLALOCK married last Tuesday at Hallville, Texas.

Vernon ADAMS and Emma DAVIDSON married Thursday in the parsonage of the First Methodist Episcopal Church (South) in Marshall, Texas.

J. W. PLATT and Carrie GROVES married Thursday in Marshall, Texas.

Wieland Burwell LANICCA, of Chicago, Illinois, and Maude Gertrude LILLEY married Wednesday in Sherman (Texas) First Presbyterian Church. Rev. Ernest VERNON officiated.

C. L. HEATH and Mrs. Lena G. WAGNER married Wednesday in Cleburne, Texas.

J. M. NASH and Valley MEADOR married Wednesday in Cleburne, Texas.

James B. MURDOCK and Lettie BLAKELEY married Friday at Ennis, Texas. The Reverends T. J. DUNCAN and Fred GALBREATH officiated.

D. D. MEASURALL and Mrs. C. A. JONES married Thursday in Texarkana.

Dr. Orlando Steen HOLLIDAY and Jennie ROSEBOROUGH married Thursday in Texarkana. Rev. Percy T. FENN officiated.

C. F. BRUCE, son of D. C. BRUCE of Dallas, and Ida WINKLER married Thursday in Weatherford, Texas.

Courtland G. HARVEY and Rose WRIGHT married Wednesday in Mineral Wells, Texas. They will live in Denison, Texas.

W. D. MENTON, Jr., and Belle FRY married Thursday night in Marshall, Texas.

Dr. Roy S. LOVING of Fort Worth and Lillian S. PARKER married Thursday in Mexia, Texas.

Jim NICHOLS, 14, drowned in a weedy bayou near Houston when he fell into it while chasing a dog. No date was reported.

Henry JONES was robbed and killed in New Mexico. He had lived near Cleburne, Texas. No date was reported.

James H. EVANS was shot and killed while shucking corn near El Reno, Texas.

Ernest BOUTON was shot and killed by another man about two miles from Hempstead, Texas.

Tom HUBBARD, about 50, died near Marble Falls, Texas.

Mrs. Morris CHILDS's infant was fatally burned near Troupe, Texas. No other information about the child was reported.

R. R. SLATER, foreman at Swift and Company's glycerin plant in Fort Worth, was killed yesterday when a glycerin tank exploded.

Monday, November 30, 1903

The paper from this date did not appear on the microfilm.

December, 1903

Tuesday, December 1, 1903

W. B. CRAWFORD, 60, was accidentally shot and killed by his son near Elgin, Oklahoma Territory. The younger CRAWFORD was cleaning a pistol when it went off and struck the victim.

Mrs. BRAWLEY died suddenly yesterday in Hinkley, Indian Territory. Her husband managed a plumbing company in Hinkley. Her given name was not listed.

Dora WALKER and William JONES were jailed in Ardmore, Indian Territory on charges of assault to kill. WALKER is accused of shooting Green WALKER.

George BERNER, 37, a noted photographer, died yesterday in Austin.

Forrest CAMPBELL and Willie MABRY married Sunday in Austin.

The funeral of William B. FAULK took place yesterday in Austin. He was a member of Troop H, 15th US Cavalry. He died on a transport ship returning to the United States from the Philippine Islands.

Gay VIOLETTE of Gainesville, Texas, married Marvin TUNNERY of Philadelphia, Pennsylvania, in the Tarrant County Courthouse. They will live in Philadelphia.

The funeral of Charles B. HALL took place yesterday in Fort Worth. Hall, a member of the Cooks and Waiters Union, died Sunday.

Scottie B. AUTRY, 5, died Sunday of typhoid fever in Ennis, Texas.

The body of Dr. O. C. TODD was buried yesterday in Corsicana, Texas. He died last Saturday in Powell.

Isaac M. FUSTON died of pneumonia Saturday night in Waxahachie, Texas. He was the janitor at Park School there.

G. A. LADD and Rosa STUBBLEFIELD were married by Rev. B.M. Taylor in Loving's Valley, Texas. .

Wednesday, December 2, 1903

J. D. MURPHREE and Annie FITZPATRICK married yesterday in Midlothian, Texas. The bride is from Lancaster, Texas.

David GREENWOOD was stabbed and killed in a knife duel at Texarkana. Dick DELK was wounded by Greenwood, but survived and was arrested on a murder charge.

Mrs. R. H. HORN, already critically ill, died when she caught fire yesterday in Sanderson, Texas.

Octavia THORNTON died when she was shot by John BROWN in Manor, Texas.

William LEBEN died of gunshot wounds in Houston.

Frank W. WARREN, about 30, was found dead yesterday in Corpus Christi, Texas. His brother is E. F. WARREN of San Antonio.

Fred ARNOLD, Ira STRICKLAND and Mike WALKER were killed in a mine explosion at Bonanza, Arkansas. Frank and William ARNOLD of Cleburne, Texas, are brothers and brothers-in-law of the victims.

John SIMMLER was killed by an accidental gunshot in Adamsville, Texas. His own gun discharged while he was trying to stop his team from running away.

Juan PETTIS, about 40, killed his wife and then himself near Manor, Texas.

Mrs. Mary E. HUGHES, 74, widow of Dr. F. E. HUGHES, died in Dallas yesterday. She was a daughter of Paul C. VENABLE.

"Uncle John" HENSLEY, 83, a pioneer of Jack County, Texas, died at his ranch five miles west of Jacksboro Sunday. He came to Jack County in 1856, and married Katie SANDERS in 1862. Nine of their twelve children survive.

Albert MASSEY, 5, died Sunday night at his home near Terrell, Texas. He was the son of Mr. and Mrs. G.M. MASSEY.

Mrs. J. A. WILSON, 19, died of a stroke Sunday at her home four miles west of McKinney, Texas.

John H. HARTNESS and Birdie LEE married on November 30 at Mineral Wells, Texas.

Dr. Ed HARDIE and Mamie SMITH were married Sunday in Kaufman, Texas. Both the bride and groom are from Terrell.

James T. HOWELL and Birtle BOCK married on November 30 in Terrell, Texas. Rev. V. B. HOWARD officiated.

The infant daughter of Mr. and Mrs. F. W. THIESL died November 29 at Cleburne, Texas.

Mrs. Will EASTERMAN died on November 28 in Keene, Texas.

Mrs. Zenah STEVENS, who died Sunday at Cleburne, Texas, leaves five children: C. W. STEVENS, Belle STEVENS, Mrs. Dora BELL, Carrie STEVENS and Mrs. C. J. LOCKETT.

Marriage licenses issued by Tarrant County Clerk: Martin TUNNEY and Gaye VIOLETTE, T. W. MCPHERSON and Hettie WITHROW, and J. A. WHITSELL and Mary DANIELS.

Births recorded by Tarrant County Clerk: a boy to Mr. and Mrs. Thomas L. BLACKMON on November 19, a girl to Mr. and Mrs. Oscar KEUHN on November 26, a boy to Mr. and Mrs. G. W. STEPHENS on November 29, and a girl to Mr. and Mrs. J. P. PARKS, on November 28.

Deaths recorded by Tarrant County Clerk: M. E. GRAHAM, 31, residing in Fort Worth on November 27.

Thursday, December 3, 1903

Jennie EWING, 16, died yesterday in Ardmore, Indian Territory. She was killed trying to put out a fire at the telephone switchboard. Her clothing caught fire.

Friday, December 4, 1903

Mrs. Lydia Starr MCPHERSON died Wednesday in Sherman, Texas. She was the founder of the *Sherman Democrat*, now operated by her sons, G. O. and E. C. HUNTER.

H. P. HALL and Mattie SCOTT married Tuesday in McKinney, Texas.

W. L. WELCH and Mattie JENNINGS married Monday in Greenville, Texas. Rev. F. E. FINCHER officiated.

L. B. SPARKS and Laura WOODS married yesterday in Waxahachie, Texas. Rev J. N. IVEY officiated.

H. G. BISHOP and Mattie BISHOP married yesterday at the courthouse in Cleburne, Texas. There was no indication of whether the two were related.

F. E. EDWARDS and Bertha SELLERS married Monday of last week in Granbury, Texas.

H. T. JORDAN and Arie STEDHAM married Monday in Abilene, Texas.

G. C. BULLARD and Adaline ROACH married Tuesday night in Decatur, Texas.

Mrs. Elizabeth BUSHEY died at Denton, Texas. She was buried in City Cemetery today after a funeral at the Catholic Church. She was the widow of Joseph BUSHEY, Sr.

Caroline Ellis STEVENS, wife of Judge J. W. STEVENS, was buried yesterday in Hillsboro, Texas.

Mrs. George M. HUNT died on Wednesday of last week in Lubbock, Texas.

Charles D. SPARKS was killed when a wagon hit his buggy yesterday in Waco, Texas.

Charles CABINES and Manuel ALLAN died in a jail fire at Eagle Lake, Texas.

Sam TOMLIN of Tyler, Texas, died when he was thrown from his buggy and his neck broken.

A child of Hattie ROGERS died from burns suffered while playing around a fire in Pittsburg, Texas. A child of Will STRICKLAND died of burns the same day near the ROGERS child's death. The name of the neither child was given.

Mr. ESTES, father of Mrs. Simon GILBERT, killed himself near Brazos Station, Texas.

W. H. BUCHANAN died of a gunshot wound at Beaumont, Texas. Sid JOHNSON of Orange hit BUCHANAN while shooting at another man.

Marriage licenses issued by Tarrant County Clerk: Fred H. DOWDY and Nina LETTER; J. J. HUFFMAN and L. A. AUTRY; and C. A. HUDSON and Miss Clarence FLEET.

Births recorded by Tarrant County Clerk: a boy to Mr. and Mrs. Joe HUTT, near Mansfield, on November 28; a girl to Mr. and Mrs. Albert GAINES, Arlington, on November 19; and a girl to Mr. and Mrs. Thomas H. BLACKWELL with no date or place listed

Deaths recorded by Tarrant County Clerk: Mrs. George SHORT, 74, residing near Mansfield died on November 28; and Joseph NUGENT, 74, residing in Mansfield died on November 29.

Charles GIVENS, a boy, was killed by an accidental gunshot wound to the head at Houston Thursday. His father was buried the day before.

Saturday, December 5, 1903

Margareta REYNA was hanged yesterday at Halletsville, Texas. He had been convicted of sexual assault.

Fred G. HIRGLE, 20, died of pneumonia at Guthrie, Oklahoma Territory. He was a grocer.

Marriage licenses issued by Tarrant County Clerk: J. A. BOYD and Frances ARMSTRONG; Tom WILSON and Myrtle WRIGHT; and Horace MANN and Rebecca H. BEASLEY.

Deaths recorded by Tarrant County Clerk: Eugene LUCCACHE, 2 months, residing in Fort Worth on November 28; and Myrtle BURCH, 9 months, on November 27.

Sunday, December 6, 1903

G. W. WALTON, Sr. died Thursday at his home near Sparta, Texas.

The five year old son of Mr. and Mrs. K. W. JOHNSON died Tuesday night in Greenville, Texas.

J. A. NIXON of Killeen, Texas, and Linda WATSON married in Temple Thursday. Rev. C. B. WRIGHT officiated.

L. L. SPANN and Nellie CORNWELL married in Frost, Texas. The groom was from Ennis. The bride was from Mertens.

James A. GRIFFIN, of Frisco, Texas, and Ella HILL married Wednesday in Hillsboro.

John BONNER killed Noah DUFF last night. DUFF lived near Richardson, Texas. BONNER was arrested and placed in Dallas County Jail.

Willis JEFFERSON died of pneumonia in an ambulance in Dallas last night.

Willie HUDDLO, 14, died of an accidental gunshot wound in Dallas. He was wounded while hunting two weeks ago.

Jason SPENCE was killed by a tramp at South McAlester, Indian Territory. SPENCE was shot trying to evict some tramps from a train. He lived in Shawnee, Indian Territory.

Henry WHISTON killed Jim SPRATT in a knife fight in Ardmore, Indian Territory.

Rev. J. P. GROW, a noted evangelist, died in Gainesville, Texas.

Richard RATLIFF died when he was struck by pieces of a broken fly wheel at H.J. TRUMAN's wood yard in Corsicana, Texas.

The trial of Oscar FURGUSON, charged with the murder of Tom P. VARNELL, will be held in Cleburne, Texas.

Marriage licenses by Tarrant County Clerk: Cleveland ARCHER and Lela JOHNSTON, Walter ARCHER and Jennie JOHNSTON, and P. D. SELF and Mary SCROGGINS.

Births reported by Tarrant County Clerk: a girl to Mr. and Mrs. William MOORE, near Arlington, on November 17; a boy to Mr. and Mrs. Jasper CHURCH, Arlington, on November 16; a boy to Joe WALKER, Arlington, on November 13; a boy to Mr. and Mrs. Wade STUART, Arlington, on November 14; a boy to Mr. and Mrs. G. B. WHITE, Arlington, on November 13; a girl to Mr. and Mrs. Oscar BRYANT, Arlington, on November 10; a boy to Mr. and Mrs. W. HOUSTON on December 3 with no residence listed; a girl to Mr. and Mrs. Will HENDRICKS on November 3 with no residence listed; and a girl to Mr. and Mrs. Henry ROGERS, near Kennedale, on November 26.

Monday, December 7, 1903

No paper for this date appeared on the microfilm.

Tuesday, December 8, 1903

Ed TUBBS, 18 was accidentally killed by a gunshot at Brooksville, Texas.

Marriage licenses issued by Tarrant County Clerk: J. N. HELM and Beulah KERBY, J. B. NORMAN and Myrtle MERCER, and J. B. BLACKFORD and Mrs. Maggie H. CARVER

Archer PARKS, 40, died last Sunday after being run over by a wagon at Vernon, Texas.

Claud GOLDEN was shot and killed on the court square at Pilot Point, Texas. John MOODY was arrested and jailed for the shooting.

T. C. WALLACE was sentenced to die for killing J. P. AUSTIN on August 18, 1898. The trial took place in Mt. Vernon, Texas.

J. V. EDWARDS, about 70, was found dead in an abandoned flour mill at Houston yesterday.

Col. George W. HYNSON, 82, died in Dallas yesterday.

George BURTON pled guilty to first degree manslaughter in Tecumseh, Texas. BURTON killed Ray LOVE last winter.

The funeral of George R. WHITE was held yesterday in Fort Worth. He was born in Philadelphia, Pennsylvania, in 1855 and had lived in Fort Worth for 18 years. He leaves a wife and four children: May, Ethel, William, and George.

Wednesday, December 9, 1903 to
Saturday, December 12, 1903

The papers for these dates did not appear on the microfilm.

Sunday, December 13, 1903

Col. R. B. PARROTT died recently in Hot Springs, Arkansas. Friends in Dallas were notified yesterday.

A. F. SEVERT died in a hospital at Galveston, Texas. He was given incorrect medication.

Col. C. T. PROUTY, territorial grain inspector, died yesterday at Kingfisher, Oklahoma Territory. He was injured in a runaway accident last week.

Marriage licenses issued by Tarrant County Clerk: George PERROTT and Lou ROBERTSON, C. V. TUNNELL and Lola EDWARDS, M. C. WORTHY and Trisie PENICK, N. A. HAMMACH and Lovella NADRY, J. S. EASTERWOOD and Bennie SEAY, J. M. MANN and May BIGHAM, Mach FRAZIER and Ida DAVIS, Harris BRISTOW and Minnie STUBBS, and W. P. WHITE and Bessie REVES.

Births recorded by Tarrant County Clerk: a girl to Mr. and Mrs. J. G. GRIDER on December 9 with no residence listed.

Deaths recorded by Tarrant County Clerk: Nancy KELLY, 42, died on December 10; Mike JOHNSON, 78, residing near Fort Worth, died on December 10.

Avery CROCKETT, who lived near Thorp Springs, Texas, committed suicide by hanging Thursday night. He was a grandchild of Davy CROCKETT.

Ivey MATTHEWS died after he accidentally shot himself while hunting near Texarkana.

T. R. KINCAIDE and Lena RICE were married Friday near Paris, Texas.

H. N. MCKELLAR and Roxie TAYLOR, daughter of Col. T. R. TAYLOR, married Friday night in Pecos, Texas.

John PARLIER died yesterday in Ardmore, Indian Territory.

John Henry LOCHMAN, 94, died on December 5 at the home of Henry A. LOCHMAN, his son, in Pinoak, Texas.

Charlie FARRELL, 6, died at Terrell, Texas. He was the son of Mr. and Mrs. Alec FARRELL.

William BOND, about 30, died on December 10 in Gainesville, Texas. He was the stenographer for the Southern Judicial District, Indian Territory.

Mrs. L. MORRIS died Friday in Paris, Texas. She operated the Morris Hotel there.

Mrs. M. T. HALEY, 55, died of consumption this week in McKinney, Texas. Two days later her daughter, Mrs. Will MOSKEY, died of the same disease.

Monday, December 14, 1903 and
Tuesday, December 15, 1903

The paper for these dates did not appear on the microfilm.

Wednesday, December 16, 1903

Lem JOHNSON, about 20, died yesterday in Houston. He was burned in a fire last week at Angelina, Texas. He had a brother Harry and an aunt named Mrs. Alice OATS, who lived in Paris, Texas.

Mrs. William C. YOUNG, 64, died Monday in her home in South Dallas. She was the wife of Rev. W.C. YOUNG. She had lived in Dallas for 40 years.

The remains of W. R. SCROGIN are being returned to Terrell, Texas. He died Sunday in St. Louis, Missouri.

A. G. JONES, 49, died yesterday at Guthrie, Oklahoma Territory. He was born in Broadhead, Wisconsin. He served as a deputy U.S. Marshall before becoming a realtor.

William SWINEHART died Sunday at Pond Creek, Oklahoma Territory. He was an Oklahoma pioneer.

Marriage licenses issued by Tarrant County Clerk: J. H. WHITNER and Lula HIMES, G. M. BIGHAM and Minnie FRAZIER, L. ADELBERG and Ida LASKEY, William O'BRIEN and Mrs. Blanche DALTON, Charles E. FERRIS and Eliza Y. CHEATHAM, and Henry G. STEVENS and Florence O. ROBINSON.

Births recorded by Tarrant County Clerk: a girl to Mr. and Mrs. Walter C. BRADLEY on December 11; a boy to Mr. and Mrs. Emmel REDMAN on December 14; a boy to Mr. and Mrs. Charles VARIAN of Azle on December 8; and a boy to Mr. and Mrs. Frank FOWLER of Azle on December 10.

Jennie PLUMMER, daughter of Capt. and Mrs. O. T. PLUMMER, died yesterday at Cleburne, Texas.

Major A. J. ROSE, an early settler of Bell County, died Sunday at his home in Salado, Texas.

D. T. JARVIS died of Bright's disease yesterday at Lawton, Oklahoma Territory.

Mrs. F. M. SELF died on December 13 at Joshua, Texas. She was the mother of Dr. T. N. SELF.

Fauchon WILLIAMS and Philip RAY married in Dallas recently.

W. E. EARNEST and Miss S. A. ARMSTRONG were married Monday at Gainesville, Texas. Judge J. M. WRIGHT officiated.

Cotany CAGE and Lake Ern PARK were married in Dallas last Sunday.

Mary HOLLINGSWORTH and John WATSON were married Monday at Santa Anna, Texas. He is from Ballinger, Texas.

The funeral of Owen CONNOLLY was held yesterday at Ennis, Texas. CONNOLLY was killed by a Midland train.

J. H. RUTLAND died at Houston yesterday after being overcome by paint fumes while painting in an engine tank there.

Leonard WILSON, 16, was killed when he was kicked by a horse yesterday at Lawton, Oklahoma Territory.

Iron Martin JONES, 3, died of burns at Austin yesterday. He was the son of Mr. and Mrs. H. G. JONES.

Mrs. Nancy BLEWITT, 80, died yesterday at the home of her son, C. H. BLEWITT, in Richardson, Texas. She had lived in Dallas County since 1850 and was the widow of C. P. BLEWITT.

James E. JACKSON died on his farm 12 miles northeast of Dallas. He had lived on the farm since 1846.

Marriages licenses issued by Tarrant County Clerk: Harvey L. SHAW and Cora AUTREY; J. M. SCOTT, Jr. and Jessie GARRETT; E. C. SPEARMAN, Jr. and Gertrude PEARSON; and G. R. YANTIS and Susie WILLIAMS.

Births recorded by Tarrant County Clerk: a boy to Mr. and Mrs. R. C. HOUSTON on December 8; a boy to Mr. and Mrs. D. C. LAWRENCE on December 17; a girl to Mr. and Mrs. C. W. LUTT on December 14.

Deaths recorded by Tarrant County Clerk: E. L. STAGNER, 11 months, on December 14; Elizabeth P. HORD, 71, on December 15; and Mrs. A. M. CALBERT, 24, on December 13.

Leonard C. REAGIN and Zada YATES married yesterday in the Baptist Church at Forney, Texas.

Thursday, December 17, 1903 to
Saturday, December 19, 1903

The papers from these dates did not appear on the microfilm.

Sunday, December 20, 1903

F. D. COPING and Tennie SMITH married December 18 in Antler, Indian Territory. He is the editor of the *Hugo Husonian* at Hugo, Indian Territory.

John ARNAPEIGER and Delia WISEMAN were married on Thursday at Van Alstyne, Texas.

C. POLK, of Prairie Lea, Texas, was arrested and charged with the killing of Dr. W. D. BRANYON.

Mrs. W. A. DIXON received a payment of $1037 from the recent death of her husband at Crisp, Texas. She will pay the final note against her house.

The infant child of R. C. CALLAHAN died Friday of croup. The funeral was yesterday at the family home in Rhome, Texas.

C. R. BIGHAM and Julia WALLER were married Thursday at Campbell, Texas. Rev. F. L. YOUNG officiated.

Marriage licenses by Tarrant County Clerk: Frank ABERNATHIE and Edna CHEATHAM; S. J. TIDWELL and Lou DONOHO; R. W. ARP and Kate May FLANNERY; G. W. TOWNSHEND and Millie VOTAW; Albert LOPES and Eliza May HAWORTH; Charles WILLIAMS and Maude GOODNIGHT; U. J. POND and Leila May MCCARTHY; T. H. JONES and Bessie GHALESON; Louis JACKSON and Blanche COBLE; and Howard MITCHELL and Eliza SLAUGHTER.

Births recorded by Tarrant County Clerk: a girl to Mr. and Mrs. H. BROADKEY on December 16; a girl to Mr. and Mrs. Mat SHEA on December 17 a girl to Mr. and Mrs. Albert A. DAVIS on December 4.and a girl to Mr. and Mrs. Charles BENNETT on December 15.

Deaths recorded by Tarrant County Clerk: Mattie A. ABSTON, 56, on December 15.

Captain N. ANDERSON, pioneer of Greenville and Hunt County, died Friday in Greenville, Texas.

Mrs. H. L. ABSLOR died Friday night at Fort Worth. Her funeral will be today. She was born October 30, 1847 at Edgefield Junction, Tennessee. Surviving are her husband, four daughters and one son.

Monday, December 21, 1903

The paper for this date did not appear on the microfilm.

Tuesday, December 22, 1903

G. F. WINNINGHAM of Prairie Grove and Lizzie JOHNSON of Mt. Calm, Texas were married Sunday at Mt. Calm.

There were three marriages at Frisco, Texas, on December 20: Frank WITT and Angie PAINE of Little Elm; Robert CONKLIN and Stella EPSON; and Vinius HUSBAND and Lena RUDOLPH.

R. M. CONKLIN and S. M. EPERSON of Frisco were married Saturday night at McKinney, Texas.

J. W. SQUIRES died on December 12 at his home three miles north of Dickens, Texas.

Susan E. PRATT died suddenly at Durant, Indian Territory on December 20. She was buried there yesterday.

The body of Henry JONES, who was killed at Roswell, New Mexico Territory, will be buried today in Cleburne, Texas.

T. Bailey SLAYDEN, 28, died yesterday at Waco, Texas. He had been thrown from his buggy Saturday night.

George W. PECKHAM and Elsie MEYERS married yesterday afternoon in Fort Worth.

Marriage licenses issued by Tarrant County Clerk: J. W. EMBRY and Lena TURNER; L. LUTTLE and Miss D. WALKUP; O. A. METCALF and Miss T. R. ANDERSON; C. E. HALL and Dasie CLEMENT; G. W. PECKHAM and Elsie MEYERS; and F. M. GREER and Josie LUCAS.

Births recorded by Tarrant County Clerk: a boy to Mr. and Mrs. Charlie JACK on December 6; a girl to Mr. and Mrs. William LITTLE of near Fort Worth on December 16; a girl to Mr. and Mrs. Mat SHEA on December 17 and a girl to Mr. and Mrs. Albert DAVIS of near Fort Worth on December 6.

Death recorded by Tarrant County Clerk: Mary Anne WRIGHT, 66, on December 19.

Wednesday, December 23 to
Thursday, December 24, 1903

The papers from these dates did not appear on the microfilm

Friday, December 25, 1903

Leatine WILLIAMS and John HIXSON were married on December 16 at Jefferson, Texas. Judge T. D. ROWELL officiated.

J. F. LUTHER and Mary E. LOOMIS married Wednesday at Jefferson, Texas. Rev. C. R. POWELL officiated.

Ira TRICE and Rosa LANGDON married Sunday at Pittsburg, Texas.

H. P. HOUZELL and Kate CLEMENTS married Sunday at Pittsburg, Texas.

C. H. FERGUSON and Marcella MARTIN married Wednesday night south of Mt. Calm, Texas.

G. W. WALTERS and Elva REED married Wednesday north of Paris, Texas.

J. A. HAWORTH and Mrs. A. M. VAUGHAN married yesterday at Paris, Texas. Rev. Chase MANTON officiated.

William A. EVANS, a resident of Raymond, Virginia, and Cynthia R. RAINEY of Paris, Texas, were married Tuesday in the latter place. Rev. Chase MANTON officiated.

Sanford LITTLETON of died yesterday in Nashville, Tennessee. His brothers were Mace and Charley LITTLTON of Weatherford, Texas.

The funeral of Mrs. C. A. COE was held yesterday at Weatherford, Texas.

Ivy WHITTY shot and killed W. M. PRUE Wednesday at Groveton, Texas.

Bill MATTHEWS was found dead at Cameron, Texas. He had been thrown from his wagon.

Marriages licenses issued by Tarrant County Clerk: W. N. CASTLEBERRY and Anna BERRY; W. C. GILL and Mrs. W. C. KING; R. H. BONHAM and Bessie FITZGERALD; W. E. CHILDERS and Mrs. Dora QUINN; Sam MCGEE and Angie QUINN; John WILSON and Maude KERBE; A. H. O'NEAL and Miss M. B. SHARPE; William O. GATTON and Carrie L. ESTES; John E. JARVIS and Lizzie M. DUNWOODY; E. J. PALMER and Mary PAXTON; D. DANIELS and Alberta E. WOODS; Sam CARREL and Maggie SUTTON; G. M. LASSATER and Ada WILLIAMS ; Frank BELL and Sallie HAGOOD; and John SHELTON and Lillie CHRISTOPHER.

Births recorded by Tarrant County Clerk: a girl to Mr. and Mrs. J. T. LAWLESS on December 17; a girl to Mr. and Mrs. E. A. CRIMM of near Birdville on December 19; a girl to Mr. and Mrs. Robert HARRIS on December 21; and a girl to Mr. and Mrs. W. T. MAXEY of Marine on December 20.

Saturday, December 26, 1903

Otto KAUFMAN was killed when he was hit by a locomotive in Houston yesterday.

John MCDOWELL and Moselle ROBERTS married Wednesday at the home of the bride's parents in Temple, Texas.

W. P. SULLIVAN and Alta MARTIN married Wednesday at Greenville, Texas. Squire Tom MCDANIEL officiated.

J. F. CAPERTON and Lena Bell IRVIN married Wednesday night in Campbell, Texas.

Professor C. G. GREEN and Maud BUSH married Wednesday night in Wolfe City, Texas.

Professor Joseph HARRISON and Ellen STONE married Wednesday night in Wolfe City, Texas.

Tom SLAVEN and Miss M. B. SLAVEN married Sunday afternoon in Greenville, Texas. Rev. F. E. FINCHER officiated.

Nannie LONGENEUKER and E. L. WELCH married Thursday at Guthrie, Oklahoma Territory. They are both from Cushion, Oklahoma Territory.

W. D. RAINES and Myrtle O. WEAVER married Wednesday evening in the home of the bride's parents at Marshall, Texas. Rev. F. S. HALTON officiated.

Max MUNZESHEIMER, 55, died yesterday in Guthrie, Oklahoma Territory. He was buried in Gainesville, Texas.

Ed HUGHES died Wednesday of pneumonia at Timpson, Texas.

The two year old child of Mr. and Mrs. Clyde SHUFERT choked to death last Tuesday in Denton, Texas. Burial was in the city cemetery there.

Mrs. L. L. LEGTERS died in Albuquerque, New Mexico Territory. She was to be buried in Holland, Michigan.

J. W. HENSHAW, 60, died Wednesday at Waco, Texas.

Mrs. Mattie NORRIS died at the home of Mrs. C. L. DICKEY, her daughter, in Plano, Texas.

PILARSOTO was killed in San Antonio when he was hit by a train there yesterday.

Thomas H. CELLUM was killed while working as a brakeman for the Texas and Pacific Railroad at Reisor, Texas.

Henry BUDDE was killed Thursday in Lindenau, Texas.

Mr. and Mrs. L. G. ROBERTSON have returned to Dallas from Palestine, Texas. Parks ADDINGTON, their son-in-law was killed there eight days ago. Effie Robertson ADDINGTON returned to Dallas with her parents.

Mrs. J. S. LANGE died of pneumonia in Los Angeles, California. She will be buried in Dallas.

Sunday, December 27 to
Wednesday, December 30, 1903

Only the comic strips for December 27 appeared on the microfilm.

Thursday, December 31, 1903

The bodies of Juan VILLE and son were found on the railroad tracks at Eagle Lake, Texas. They may have been murdered.

Marriage licenses issued at Waxahachie, Texas: J. H. REYNOLDS and Belle MERRITT, R. A. CLOUGH and Annie ARDEN, G. B. RICHMOND and Clara O'BANION, H. H. WHEATLEY and Ida COX, T. J. LEHEW and Katie SHACKLEFORD, W. C. HOBBS and Fannie Lou TENNERY, Henry INGRAM and Bessie Joel CARR, E. MECHEN and Grace MCCAIN, O. S. HOLLABAUGH and Marie WALLIS, J. I. JEAN and Laura MAYNARD, J. H. ERBY and Carrie STUART, and R. G. SCANLON and Etta WEBB.

Minnie BRADLEY was arrested and charged with the Christmas Eve murder of Sam KNOX at Caldwell, Texas.

J. S. MILES gave bond of $1500 in the death of yardmaster William MASSENGILL at Lufkin, Texas.

Tom LIPSCOMB was killed when he was hit by a train Wednesday at Belleville, Texas.

Robert H. DENNIS and Annie GAIL married yesterday in Ardmore, Indian Territory.

Wallace B. DAVIS and Effie Montrose RODGERS married yesterday in Paris, Texas.

William B. PHIPPS and Mattie Belle STEPHENS married in Paris, Texas. They will live in South McAlester, Indian Territory. PHIPPS is a civil engineer with the Missouri, Kansas and Texas railroad there.

E. L. BRUCE and Evaline GRAHAM married Tuesday in Mineola, Texas.

Dan KING and Christine CARR married Christmas Eve in Greenville, Texas. Rev. F. L. YOUNG officiated.

Mrs. Bonnie Mattie WEBB and Theodore G. MOSELEY, both of Temple, Texas, were married by Rev. F. R. STABB at San Angelo, Texas.

H. T. LAIR and Delta WALDEN married Tuesday in Greenville, Texas. Rev. R. G. HORSELEY officiated.

Dr. Adolph J. LENGEL of Dallas died at his home yesterday.

Marriage licenses issued by Tarrant County Clerk: Charles W. WALKER and Allie VARNELL, A. E. JONES and Miss G. A. LABAUNE, and William O'NEAL and Johnnie BEARD.

Births recorded by Tarrant County Clerk: a girl to Mr. and Mrs. C. R. PAYNE on December 28 and a boy to Mr. and Mrs. James ABRAM on December 29.

Cap WILSON died yesterday at the county farm near Waxahachie, Texas.

George F. ELMO was buried yesterday in the Harris Creek cemetery at MacGregor, Texas.

Mrs. M. E. MCBRIDE died yesterday at the home of R. A. MCBRIDE in Ennis, Texas. R. A. MCBRIDE was the son of the deceased.

Dr. J. M. SHEGOG died yesterday at Ennis, Texas.

J.W. MCKINNEY and Ruby COCHRAN married yesterday in Gainesville, Texas.

J. B. EDWARDS made bond of $1000 in the death of Sam REISMANNET in Ennis, Texas.

Hers EVANS made bond of $5000 in the death of Jim LEAR at Cleburne, Texas.

Capt W. H. SLUDER died yesterday in Paris, Texas. He was a former mayor of the city.

Henry TOMLINSON died Saturday when he fell from his horse near Detroit, Texas.

Dan COLLINS died yesterday at his father's home in Alvarado, Texas.

Mrs. Carrie MCCONNELL died at Greenville, Texas.

W. F. HULL died Sunday in San Angelo, Texas.

January, 1904

Friday, January 1, 1904 to Sunday, January 3 1904

The papers from these dates did not appear on the microfilm.

Monday, January 4, 1904

Mrs. J. D. SEAY was accidentally shot and killed by her husband while celebrating the holidays with pistols near Alfalfa, Oklahoma Territory.

The body of Will JOHNSON, who was killed by a state ranger near El Paso a few days ago, will be returned to Weatherford, Texas.

D. LOTSPEICH died yesterday in Abilene, Texas. He was a cotton buyer.

Mrs. L. J. STRONG died in Clifton, Arizona Territory.

George T. RUSSELL died yesterday in Mangum, Oklahoma Territory.

Joseph SMITH married Elsie DODDS on December 19, 1903, in Henderson, Tennessee. They will live in Greenville, Texas.

C. C. BURDEN married Pearl WISELEY at Paris, Texas. She is the daughter of W. G. WISELEY.

Dr. L. B. STEVENS and Sallie WHOLTTEN married yesterday in Paris, Texas.

A. A. PITTUCK, editor of *Texas Farm and Ranch,* died in Dallas yesterday.

Mrs. E. L. ARMSTRONG died Sunday in Corsicana, Texas.

Sarah WINTEROWD, 35, died yesterday at Ennis, Texas. She was the spouse of C. W. WINTEROWD.

Mrs. W. E. STEWART died of pneumonia at Weatherford, Texas. She was buried there yesterday.

George BOYLE died Sunday night in Honey Grove, Texas.

W. S. PATE was stabbed to death yesterday in Cleburne, Texas. John A. BATESON surrendered to police and was jailed.

Marriages licenses issued by Tarrant County Clerk: C. M. BROCK and Eunice SOUSTRON, and L. C. GARDNER and Adalin Lillian TRAMPTON.

Births recorded by Tarrant County Clerk: a boy to Mr. and Mrs. W. W. HUBBARD, near Grapevine, on December 26; a boy to Mr. and Mrs. David REAVES on December 26 with no place listed; a girl to Mr. and Mrs. Walter LANDRUTH, Grapevine, on December 27; and a boy to Mr. and Mrs. Sam MCDOWELL, Grapevine, on December 25.

Death recorded by Tarrant County Clerk: Mona THOMPSON, 2, residing near Grapevine on December 30.

Tuesday, January 5, 1904

The paper for this date did not appear on the microfilm.

Wednesday, January 6, 1904

The infant of Mr. and Mrs. Benjamin GRIGGS died in Gainesville, Texas.

Jones FOSTER died Monday in Ennis, Texas.

A child of Mr. and Mrs. H. H. SWINK died Monday in Temple, Texas.

S. M. MCASHAN, 74, died in Houston. He was a native of Virginia and came to Texas when he was 15.

Joy CARPENTER, 4, died yesterday of burns in Austin. She was the daughter of S. P. CARPENTER.

Marriage licenses issued by Tarrant County Clerk: B. O. GRAY and May ELMO.

Births recorded by Tarrant County Clerk: a girl to Mr. and Mrs. A. W. WEATHERFORD on January 1 with no place listed; a girl to Mr. and Mrs. Louis NICHOLS on December 25 with no place listed; a girl to Mr. and Mrs. GRAHAM, White Settlement, on December 26.

Death recorded by Tarrant County Clerk: Simpson NOATON, 35, of Fort Worth with no date or cause listed.

Thursday, January 7, 1904

The remains of Mrs. M. R. AVINGER were taken to Avinger, Texas. She died in Sulphur Springs, Texas.

Mrs. W. J. GORDON died Tuesday in Corsicana, Texas.

Sam WYNNE died Saturday at Alvarado, Texas.

Dave GAY died in Fort Worth yesterday. He was shot by Eunice FERRELL on December 26, 1903.

J. M. MOORHEAD is on trial in Fort Worth for the October 12, 1903, death of D. C. CALDWELL near Handley, Texas.

Turner CHASE, 10, died of tetanus at Smithville, Texas.

Ensign Ashton BELDEN and Mary E. COLLOM married in Fort Worth yesterday. Rev. Barto B. RAMAGE officiated.

Marriage licenses issued by Tarrant County Clerk: H. V. BOOKER and Willie FULLER, and E. A. BELDEN and Mary Eldorn COLLOM.

Friday, January 8, 1904

H. D. MOSS and R. H. BAILEY killed themselves in separate incidents at Wynnewood, Oklahoma Territory. Moss died of a gunshot wound on Wednesday while BAILEY died of a gunshot wound Thursday.

Mrs. F. A. LANE died Friday night at Quinlan, Texas. She was buried in Atlanta.

J. H. RAINEY died yesterday in Waco, Texas.

Saturday, January 9, 1904

Richard COKER of Austin and Josephine JUHLIN were married Wednesday night in Lampasas, Texas. Rev. W. T. RENFRO performed the ceremony.

T. A. MACGREGOR and Mary MCGEE married Wednesday in Lampasas, Texas. Dr. W. A. WILSON officiated. The couple will live in Belton, Texas.

Lillie BARROW and Jim CYRUS married Wednesday in Cleburne, Texas.

John MCAFEE and Ethel GROVES married Sunday in Greenville, Texas. Rev. C. P. SIMPSON officiated.

John P. FUGITT and Beatrice YARBROUGH married Monday in Greenville, Texas.

Myrtle CHARLESVILLE and H. C. ELLIOTT married in Greenville, Texas.

Charlie AMACKER and Roe NORTHINGTON married Sunday at Abilene, Texas.

Joe C. LANGRAN and Florence PARVIN married Wednesday in Denton, Texas. Rev. T. J. BECKHAM officiated.

B. E. WEBB and Beatrice EASOY married Wednesday in Ennis, Texas. Rev. R. T. PHILLIPS officiated. They live near Garrett, Texas.

Joe KELLEY and Minnie HERRON married Thursday in Ennis, Texas. Rev. J. T. MALONE officiated.

R. D. TERRELL and Beatrice GRAHAM married Thursday in Paris, Texas. Rev. Charles MANTON officiated.

Col. Gus SHOW and Corrinne FOOTE married in Clarksville, Texas. Rev. L. S. BARTON officiated.

J. M. WRIGHT and Mattie BUTCHER married Thursday in Paris, Texas. Rev. L. L. PRICE performed the ceremony.

Frank SCOONOVER and Lucille MILLER married Thursday in Belton, Texas.

J.H. RAINEY died Thursday in Waco, Texas. His funeral was in Waco yesterday.

Mrs. Ruth HARGRAVES died in Fort Worth yesterday. She will be buried in Rhome, Texas.

Mrs. John E. BYRNES, 42, died in Fort Worth yesterday. She leaves a husband, six daughters and one son.

Edward F. CULLEN of Austin died yesterday in Richmond, Virginia.

Mrs. S. V. MOORE died of pneumonia yesterday in Terrell, Texas. Her children are Mrs. G. C. JONES of Arkadelphia, Arkansas; Mrs. Byron DREW of Ardmore, Indian Territory; Mrs. J. C. TRICE, Mrs. W. L. MARTIN, Annie MOORE and John MOORE.

Mrs. Phillip ROACH died Tuesday night in Terrell, Texas. She leaves her husband and five small children.

Mrs. Ida CANNON, 40, died of pneumonia in Terrell, Texas. She was the widowed mother of six children who will be sent to an orphanage.

Allen SWEARINGEN, 32, died at San Antonio of consumption Thursday.

R. W. INMAN died Thursday in Terrell, Texas.

C. B. SULLIVAN died Tuesday in Texarkana. He was buried in the Catholic cemetery there.

Robert BOYER died in Goldthwaite, Texas. His remains were shipped to Woodstock, Virginia.

R. J. BAGGS, about 50, died yesterday in Mineral Wells, Texas.

Mrs. Lurinda BULARD, 88, died in Ardmore, Indian Territory, while visiting her son, A. A. BULARD, there. She lived in Lake Wilson, Minnesota.

Mrs. C. E. ROYSTER, 56, died in Vineland, Texas. She was the mother of Mrs. Vick HANEY. She left her husband and three children.

Henry SHIELDS, 69, died Wednesday near McKinney, Texas. He had lived on his farm in the White's Grove Community for 53 years.

Marriage licenses issued by Tarrant County Clerk: Henry WRIGHT and Alice WHITE, Bob WALKER and Mary YOUNG, and Henry ROSS and Claudy THOMAS.

Births recorded by Tarrant County Clerk: a boy to Mr. and Mrs. Marshall CLARK, Arlington, on January 5; a girl to Mr. and Mrs. Dan YANKEY, Arlington, on December 24; a girl to Mr. and Mrs. Toby JOHNSON, Arlington, on December 25; a boy to Mr. and Mrs. Charles T. BROWN, Arlington, on December 12; a boy to Mr. and Mrs. Watt REAVIS, Arlington, on December 8; and a boy to Mr. and Mrs. Hill CARLISLE, Arlington, on December 10.

Deaths recorded by Tarrant County Clerk: Henry Randall HITT, 14, residing in Arlington, died on December 14.

Sunday, January 10, 1904

Dr. George P. HACKENBERG died Friday in Austin.

Rev. J. S. MCFARLANE died at Stillwell, Indian Territory. Born in 1818 in Crawfordsville, Indiana, he was noted as an evangelist.

Colonel William D. CRAIG, 86, died Friday night at Handley, Texas.

Dr. Edwin R. HAWKINS died Friday in Greenville, Texas. His funeral was held Saturday there.

Mrs. Albert MILLER, 35, died of burns in Aledo, Texas. She leaves two sons, aged 9 and 2. She will be buried in Garland, Texas.

Mrs. S. E. LEECROFT died yesterday in Denison, Texas.

Maggie HARMON died Friday of consumption near Poetry, Texas.

Charles F. BROWN, 83, died Friday in Sherman, Texas.

Dud ALLEN, accidentally shot and killed Wednesday, was buried Friday in East Hill cemetery at Gainesville, Texas.

Monday, January 11, 1904

John HARGRAVES was killed Saturday in an industrial accident at Denison, Texas.

A. J. EMIN died in Dallas Saturday.

Claude DONALDSON, 16, of Fayetteville, Arkansas, was killed when he fell from a moving train north of Summit, Indian Territory.

The two-year-old daughter of John ROSPESIL burned to death in Prague, Oklahoma Territory.

Peter DAVIS, of Fort Worth, was killed at Enid, Oklahoma Territory. He fell under the car he was coupling. He was a Rock Island railroad brakeman.

Samuel BENSON was killed yesterday in Port Arthur, Texas. He was crushed between two railroad cars.

Mrs. Al CLARK, 83, died Sunday in Guthrie, Oklahoma Territory.

Mrs. D. W. COOPER died Sunday in Chico, Texas. She will be buried in Pleasant Grove cemetery today.

Mrs. P. T. HUGHES died Saturday in Texarkana. She is survived by her husband and three children.

Marriage licenses issued at Greenville, Texas: Obie KIRKLAND and Sarah MCDONALD.

A. H. THORNTON, 83, died yesterday in Texarkana.

Tuesday, January 12, 1904

George D. BROOKS of Houston, his wife and son were killed in Central America. They were hit by a train between Colima and Manzanillo.

James DUGAN drowned in Galveston Bay while returning to the British steamship *Civilian*.

Harry E. RICHARDSON committed suicide at the Alamo Hotel in San Antonio on January 2.

J.W. MESSENGER died of heart failure yesterday in Dallas. He will be buried in Lameta, Texas.

Marriage licenses issued by Tarrant County Clerk: I. N. WEBSTER and Sallie Lee JOLLY, and A. A. CALLAWAY and Myrtle GREEN.

Births recorded by Tarrant County Clerk: a girl to Mr. and Mrs. J. M. WATTS, near Birdville, on January 8; a boy to Mr. and Mrs. J. E. KEYS on January 8 with no place listed; a girl to Mr. and Mrs. Charles H. KANE, North Fort Worth, on December 21; a boy to Mr. and Mrs. S. H. MACMURRAY, Arlington, on January 2; a boy to Mr. and Mrs. Sam D. TRIPLETT, Fort Worth, on January 4; and a boy to Mr. and Mrs. Charles D. CARTER, Fort Worth, on January 7.

Deaths recorded by Tarrant County Clerk: Lizzie BURNS, 53, on January 7; and Mrs. M. F. WHISENANT, 27, on January 9. No causes or places were provided.

Alfred TURNER shot and killed Rev. Mr. MOSS and his son in a land dispute near Elmore, Indian Territory.

Alvis PARNELL and Velma WILLIAMS married Sunday in Purcell, Indian Territory.

Wednesday, January 13, 1904

Funeral services of Mary Simmons WAUL, widow of General T. N. WAUL, will be held in the home of Mrs. W. B. HARRISON of Fort Worth. Mrs. WAUL died Monday in Greenville, Texas. Mrs. HARRISON was the niece of Mrs. WAUL.

John B. HUFF and Kate ROBERTSON married last night in Fort Worth. She was the sister of L. P. ROBERTSON.

William BOUNDS bled to death while shearing a mule near Purdun, Texas. The shears were knocked from his hand and cut his femoral artery.

A double wedding took place Tuesday morning in Gainesville, Texas. While William PELS married Annie ROEWE, Joseph FLEITMAN married Katie ROEWE. Rev. BONAVENTURA officiated.

Alonzo R. CUSHMAN died Monday in Mineral Wells, Texas. His funeral will be today in Greenville, Texas.

Mrs. A. A. TERHUNE died last night at her daughter's home in Greenville, Texas. She will be buried in Jefferson, Texas.

Fred NIBLING, Sr., 65, who lived near Moffat, Texas, died yesterday. He was the father of Mrs. W. C. HALBURT and Fred NIBLING, Jr.

W. F. LOREN, 75, died suddenly yesterday in Texarkana.

Carl HILL and Bertha HARGREAVE married at midnight last night in Ennis, Texas. The Rev. W. K. PENROD performed the ceremony.

Harry JACO and Myrtle FINLEY married in Dallas yesterday evening. They will live in Ennis, Texas.

H. WESTBROOK and Rebecca DICKINSON married in Ennis, Texas. Rev. W. K. PENROD officiated.

Charles SLOCUM and Laura SLATER married Sunday in Bristol, Texas.

Mrs. John GARNER died of burns today three miles south of Paris, Texas.

Rev. G. W. GRACE died in Greenville, Texas.

Miss Josephine MACKENZIE died yesterday in Corpus Christi, Texas.

Rev A. GOSSERT died last Thursday in Johnsonville, Tennessee. He lived in Ennis, Texas.

Marriage licenses issued at Cleburne, Texas: J. C. NEFF and Sadie ENGLISH, James C. _____ and Lillian FRANK, and Dr. Frank HOWELL and Cora LANDRUTH.

Births recorded by Tarrant County Clerk: a girl to Mr. and Mrs. Robert MCBEE on January 3; and a girl to Mr. and Mrs. Charles PREWETT on January 4. No places were provided.

Thursday, January 14, 1904

Maggie PORTER was shot and killed by Collier JONES in Dallas yesterday.

Mrs. Catherine BINGHAM, 89, died near Kingfisher, Oklahoma Territory. She left 69 descendents.

Larren T. GASTON, 78, died yesterday in Hackberry, Oklahoma Territory.

John HALK, about 40, was killed near Randolph, Texas. He fell under a rail car. He left a wife and son.

Ernest MEYERS, a native of Germany, became a naturalized citizen in Dallas yesterday. He then applied for a license to marry Miss Rosa MIERS.

Marriages licenses issued by Tarrant County Clerk: M. D. BROOKS and Mary FORGEY, and Lou TATUM and Emma YANCEY.

Births recorded by Tarrant County Clerk: a boy to Mr. and Mrs. W. HEADON, Fort Worth, on January 10; a girl to Mr. and Mrs. John STEPHENS, Mansfield, on December 29; a girl to Mr. and Mrs. Tom MEYERS, Mansfield, on January 2; a boy to Mr. and Mrs. O. R. SHARPE, Kennedale, on December 29; and a boy to Mr. and Mrs. James HELM, Peden, on January 2.

Ideifonso GARZA shot and mortally wounded Antonio GARZA, his brother, before eloping to San Antonio with his niece, Rosa GARZA. The shooting happened in Clear Springs, Texas.

Dr. H. W. NEWMAN and Dora ODEKIRK married Tuesday in Guthrie, Oklahoma Territory.

Leo M. LEVI, 47, died in New York City yesterday. He was a native of Victoria, Texas. He had lived in New York City for four years. He was an attorney.

Friday, January 15, 1904

H. F. BROWN, 70, died yesterday afternoon in his Fort Worth home. He was the brother of Dr. E. F. BROWN.

Marriage licenses issued by Tarrant County Clerk: W. W. HENDERSON and Elizabeth A. HARMON, and D. R. COX and Mrs. J. GANN.

Births recorded by Tarrant County Clerk: a boy to Mr. and Mrs. Albert WARREN, Arlington, on January 10; a girl to Mr. and Mrs. J. F. BRUMMETT, Arlington, on January 13; a girl to Mr. and Mrs. James GROGAN, Arlington, on January 7; and a boy to Mr. and Mrs. Joseph S. MYERS, Fort Worth, on January 13.

Ross MILLSAP was shot and killed Wednesday night by an unknown assailant while he sat in a hotel lobby in Abilene, Texas.

Lou PERKINS died yesterday in Corsicana, Texas.

Mrs. Will LAYFIELD died Tuesday five miles north of Rhome, Texas. She was buried in Fair View Cemetery.

Ludie KNIGHT, 22, died yesterday in Grandview, Texas.

Mrs. A. E. RICE, 73, died Wednesday in Belton, Texas. She was buried in the Moffat Cemetery. Surviving are Prof. RICE of Austin, Mrs. L. F. GRIMES and Mrs. T. C. CASKEY of Belton.

G. P. RELFE died in Springfield, Missouri. He was the nephew of W. W. CAMMACK of Cleburne, Texas.

Emory WILKINS married Brice SCROGGINS yesterday. He is the son of Denton pioneer Charles WILKINS.

William H. WATSON and Ola May MCCOY received a marriage license at Oklahoma City, Oklahoma Territory.

Fannie BERRY and Samuel WELLS married Tuesday in Abilene, Texas. Rev J. W. KEEBEL officiated.

Tucker FRANKS and Iva DAVIS married Wednesday in Cleburne, Texas.

A. P. BURKHALTER and Edna HILL married Thursday in the courthouse in Cleburne, Texas.

J. M. BROOKS and Mary AIKIN married Wednesday by in Waxahachie, Texas. Rev. O. F. SENSABAUGH officiated

C. H. LANEY and Laura DEATON married Sunday in Pittsburg, Texas. Rev. J. S. MATHIS officiated.

John KENT and Mittie PEACOCK married Sunday in Pittsburg, Texas. Rev. A. R. MORRIS officiated.

Saturday, January 16, 1904

J. J. QUINN and Mike MAHAFFEY died suddenly yesterday at Sour Lake, Texas. It is believed they died of natural gas poisoning.

Mrs. A. M. DOUGLAS died Thursday night at her home in Covington, Texas.

The remains of Dr. T. A. MITCHELL, 73, were shipped to Monroe, Louisiana.

James RICE died when he was hit by a rail car while crossing the Texas and Pacific tracks at Turber, Texas.

Emma HARRIS, 6, died of burns in the Rhea Mills community near McKinney, Texas. She was buried in the Walnut Grove cemetery. Emma was the daughter of Thomas HARRIS.

Thorpe ABBOTT, 15, died of blood poisoning in Woodville, Texas.

J. M. CHAPPELL is in a Dallas jail charged with killing William C. MCCAHAN yesterday.

Officer Howell COBB shot and killed Eduardo EMMA in El Paso yesterday. EMMA was resisting arrest when he was killed.

Lawrence POWELL died yesterday of heart failure in Galveston, Texas.

Paul OLDENBERG died yesterday of heart failure in Galveston, Texas.

Dr. James C. JOHNSTON and Lucy BOATWICK married Wednesday at Commerce, Texas. Rev. B. C. HICKS officiated.

Lon DOWELL and Lena CURRY married Thursday in Greenville, Texas.

Charlie JUSTIN, 24, died of consumption Wednesday in Durant, Indian Territory.

Sallie JEFFRIES died Thursday in Childress, Texas. She was the wife of J. H. JEFFRIES and was buried in Childress.

Mrs. Nancy C. CRAWFORD died Thursday at Cooper, Texas. She was the wife of J. W. CRAWFORD and daughter of S. H. LANE. LANE is a former county judge of Delta County and is now mayor of Cooper.

Gus HUDDLESTON was shot and killed Thursday in a saloon in Arapahoe, Indian Territory. Saloon owner John BINGHAM fled after he shot HUDDLESTON.

Births recorded by Tarrant County Clerk: a boy to Mr. and Mrs. Ed MORGAN, Fort Worth, on January 12; a boy to Mr. and Mrs. W. W. BRADY, Fort Worth, on January 14; a boy to Mr. and Mrs. W. A. JOHNSON, Kennedale, on January 7; a boy to Mr. and Mrs. Jim STRAIN, Marine, on January 8; and a girl to Mr. and Mrs. J. F. TEDLEY, Fort Worth, on January 13.

Death recorded by Tarrant County Clerk: Fannie ADAMSON, 1 month, died of pneumonia on January 14.

Henry TITUS, 23, died in Kansas City. He was livestock agent for the Panhandle territory on the Santa Fe railroad.

Sunday, January 17, 1904

Judge J. M. SKELTON died yesterday at his home in Dallas. He was born in east Tennessee on February 5, 1844, had resided in Dallas since 1878 and served as a justice of the peace from 1882 to 1903.

Mrs. J. C. DECKER, 70, died in the hospital portion of the county jail in Dallas Friday.

Fletcher D. GRANGER died in Austin yesterday.

August CAHN, 53, died yesterday at his home in Dallas.

Charles HOWELL died at his home north of Dallas. He was a pioneer of Dallas.

John HAYS and Addie EDDLEMAN married Sunday evening at Graham, Texas. She is the daughter of Mrs. H. B. EDDLEMAN. Rev R. V. COX officiated.

Marriage licenses issued by Hunt County Court Clerk's Office in Greenville, Texas: Dave RAINWATER and Eula MITCHELL, J. L. GOODWIN and Clota TURLEY, J. W. REESE and Malissa SMITH, W. H. VAUGHAN and Effie HADDON, W. H. BRADLEY and Mattie LANGFORD, Lonnie DUWELL and Lena CURRY, and John W. RAGAN and Ella PITTMAN.

Elsie MCCALL and Samuel LINDSAY married last February in Oklahoma City, Oklahoma Territory.

S. B. COATS and Virginia TATUM married Friday night in Corsicana, Texas. Rev. J. B. BERRY officiated.

Wilburn TODD and Mary WALKER married yesterday in Waxahachie, Texas.

Si AIKENS, about 80 and a former slave, died a few days ago in Waxahachie, Texas.

Rev. J. W. PORTER, 91, a Methodist minister, died Saturday in Sanger, Texas. He was buried in the Sanger Cemetery.

Dr. E. R. MANNING died Thursday at Elamford, Texas. He was buried Saturday in Albany, Texas. He was a Mason.

Professor F. H. SLOVER, principal of the Sunset school, died Friday. He was buried by the Woodman of the World lodge.

Captain John DYSART, 77, of Anna, Texas, died Saturday. He was injured in a runaway accident six weeks ago. He was a Confederate veteran and a pioneer settler of Collin County.

A little son of Frank ELWICK and wife was buried yesterday at Ennis, Texas.

A three months old baby of P. B. RICE and wife died yesterday at Ennis, Texas. It will be buried today.

Miss Gertrude WINTEROWD of Crisp, Texas, died of pneumonia Wednesday.

R. E. BARNWELL died of typhoid fever Friday in Pittsburg, Texas.

S. T. BARTLETT died Friday night in Chicago, Illinois. He was a partner in Bartlett and Keeler in Gainesville, Texas.

Taylor HOLLINS, died of pneumonia at his home in Corsicana, Texas Thursday.

The nine year old daughter of Albert NIOUS was killed by her younger brother who was playing with a handgun. The family lived two miles west of San Antonio.

John MACKEY, 15, was accidentally killed in a hunting accident at Katy Lake near Hillsboro, Texas. He was hunting with Willie DATO when the shotgun they used accidentally discharged while they were on an embankment.

Mrs. A. D. LINTON committed suicide yesterday in Paris, Texas.

W. T. TURNER was bound over to for trial in the deaths of W. C. MOSS and Al MOSS near Pauls Valley, Indian Territory Saturday. (See January 12, 1904).

Lon CRISMAN, 28, was killed in Fort Worth when he was crushed under the pilot of a locomotive in the railroad shops.

Mrs. Charles SCHWACKHAMMER was given a house and lot in Fort Worth by friends. Her late husband was murdered by Rufus MARTIN at Polytechnic College last fall. MARTIN received the death penalty for the crime.

Monday, January 18, 1904

The remains of Harry QUARLES, 31, arrived Saturday in Waco, Texas. His funeral was yesterday. He died Friday in Shreveport, Louisiana. He was a newspaperman and the brother of James Hays QUARLES. James Hays QUARLES is now the last surviving member of his family.

Dan COODY is on trial for the murder of his uncle Joseph COODY in Muskogee, Indian Territory.

Alonzo "Lon" CHRISMAN, a railroad brakeman who was killed in the railroad shops, was thrown from the pilot of a Frisco passenger locomotive. He was riding the pilot guiding the engineer through the yard when the pilot hit a frog on the track and threw Chrisman from the pilot and under the wheels of the locomotive. He will be buried in Springfield, Missouri.

Mrs. J. H. WOOD died Saturday in Temple, Texas. She was the mother of Mrs. J. B. BLACK.

C. C. JELINE, 50, died of Bright's disease in Mineral Wells, Texas. He lived in Wichita Falls, Texas.

Mrs. Frank STEVENS died Thursday of pneumonia at her home in Mineral Wells, Texas.

Mrs. Julia OSBORNE died of pneumonia Sunday at Cleburne, Texas. She was the wife of Dr. J. D. OSBORNE and a former vice-president of the Texas Federation of Women's Clubs.

Dr. C. B. WILLIAMS and Reba QUINN married last Tuesday in Rusk, Texas.

Marriage licenses issued at Hunt County Clerk's Office in Greenville, Texas F. M. BEAN and Maud MOORMAN, B. J. GRAVES and Mattie ANDERSON, and J. T. YOUNG and Mary FOX.

C. F. BOOTH and Laura EVANS married Saturday night in Merkel, Texas. She is a teacher and he is a businessman in El Paso, Arkansas.

John FISHER shot and killed Luther COLLINS in Dallas yesterday. COLLINS attacked FISHER with a knife after an argument. FISHER was jailed.

Kathleen SHARP, 5, daughter of Mr. and Mrs. Walter B. SHARP, died yesterday at her home in Dallas.

W. L. BROWN and Edith Gale HUNTER, both of Sherman, Texas, were married in Fort Worth by Rev. ___.E. CHANDLER yesterday.

W. M. PAYNE and Minnie BUSTER married yesterday at the home of the bride's parents in Emberson, Texas.

Ned CHEATHAM and Dale SLAUGHTER were married Sunday in Edgewood, Texas. The wedding took place in the home of the bride's father.

Frederick E. RAMSEY and Maggie L. ABBOTT married Sunday in Waxahachie, Texas. Rev. J. C. SMITH officiated.

Ed WILLIAMS and Minnie BERRIER married Sunday in Waxahachie, Texas. Rev. J. S. ELLIOTT performed the ceremony.

The funeral of Mrs. J. P. OSBORNE was held yesterday at the Church of the Holy Comforter in Cleburne, Texas. A large number of people attended. Her husband is a former mayor of Cleburne.

Charles O. JOLINE died Sunday morning in Mineral Wells, Texas. He was a former mayor of Wichita Falls, Texas and was buried there. He was a Mason.

Mrs. M. J. HARDIN died at the residence of Mrs. J. H. BROWN, her daughter, Sunday night in Paris, Texas. Mrs. HARDIN will be buried in Terrell, Texas.

Charles STANDIFER was found dead in Lampasas, Texas. He may have overdosed on morphine.

Ross MILLSAP, killed in a hotel lobby in Abilene, Texas, recently, was a cattleman from Roby, Texas. He is survived by his wife and one daughter. Millsap's daughter was recently married to Ross GREEN, a druggist in Roby.

Jesse P. PORTMAN was killed by Robert BROCK at Letot, 12 miles from Dallas. BROCK admits the shooting. BROCK fired into a party of which PORTMAN was a member after gunshots were fired into his home. BROCK was released on bond. PORTMAN lived in Denton County, Texas.

Marriage licenses issued by Tarrant County Clerk: T. F. MCKINNEY and Nome HOOT, D. M. WILSON, Jr. and Mrs. Lennie WILSON, and C. F. NELSON and Gertrude MORRIS.

Tuesday, January 19, 1904

The paper for this date did not appear on the microfilm.

Wednesday, January 20, 1904

Mrs. R. MITCHELL, 90, died in Bowie, Texas. She was the grandmother of Brice HOSKINS, assistant city editor of the *Dallas Times Herald*.

Sarah MCCAHAN and Anna MCCHAN, sister and niece of William C. MCCAHAN, who was killed last Thursday by J. M. CHAPPELL, arrived in Dallas to attend the funeral. Rev. John MCCAHAN and James MCCAHAN will arrive soon.

Mrs. Eliza APPLEWHITE, 81, died Tuesday morning in San Antonio. She was a native of Mississippi and had lived in San Antonio for 50 years before her death. She was the wife of Stephen APPLEWHITE and mother of T. C. APPLEWHITE.

The body of Mrs. Claud LOGSDEN was disinterred ten days after her death. Suspicions of poisoning led to the exhumation.

Ed SKILLERN, 44, died Tuesday in Nacogdoches, Texas. He was shot by Al SCOTT last Wednesday there.

The wife of Will DANIELS died yesterday from burn injuries in Edgewood, Texas. She leaves a small child and her husband, who is a well respected farmer in the New Hope community.

W. A. STANDIFER died from pneumonia at his home in Fort Worth at midnight last night. He leaves his wife and daughter, Mrs. B. L. WAGGOMAN.

Grant WILLIAMS was sentenced to die for the murders of Lee BURGHER and Ed DOLAN. The trial took place in South McAlester, Indian Territory.

Hubbard TURNER, 30, died Monday of yellow jaundice in Cooper, Texas.

Mrs. W. J. HARDIN was buried Monday in the city cemetery in Terrell, Texas. She died in Paris, Texas.

R. L. YEARWOOD died Sunday in North Marshall, Texas. He was buried in Greenwood Cemetery Tuesday.

Mrs. N. J. HARVEY, 74, died suddenly Monday in Hillsboro, Texas. She was a native of Kentucky and the mother of Hillsboro City Assessor and Collector Ed HARVEY.

Mrs. George BARNARD, 73, died Monday night in Del Rio, Texas. She was buried in Waco, Texas. She was the oldest sister of the late Governor L. S. ROSS.

Mrs. STRIBLING, mother of F. M. STRIBLING, died Monday and was buried Tuesday in Cleburne, Texas.

Marriage licenses issued by Tarrant County Clerk: Bert HUGHES and Della REAVES, and W. L. BROWN and Edith Gail HUNTER.

Mrs. Will DANIELS was buried yesterday in New Hope cemetery at Edgewood, Texas.

A. A. DUNNICA and Katherine M. KNIGHT married Tuesday in Guthrie, Oklahoma Territory. DUNNICA is a linotype operator for the *Guthrie Daily Leader*.

George L. ADAIR, 60, was found dead in the Mohawk Hotel in Fort Worth. He was from Ennis, Texas. The death was ruled suicide. He suffered from cancer. He had a brother named James H. ADAIR and a sister, Mrs. John T. LOCKMAN, in Houston.

Mary WEST died yesterday in San Antonio. She died at the home of her daughter, Mrs. H. H. SHINER. Three sons, George, Sol and Ike WEST, also survive.

The body of S. T. BARTLETT was buried in East Hill Cemetery in Gainesville, Texas.

T. J. WADLEY died yesterday of pneumonia in Ardmore, Indian Territory.

Mrs. Nannie HAWPE, wife of J. R. HAWPE, died yesterday in Cleburne, Texas.

M. D. RIDE, 89, died yesterday in Denison, Texas. He was a pioneer there.

Mrs. H. J. AIKEN, 48, died Tuesday at Salado, Texas.

J. L. LOVELESS, 45, died at home in Mineral Wells, Texas.

Dr. Scott MILAM died Monday in Glen Rose, Texas. He had lived in Somervell County since 1875. He leaves a wife and two daughters, Mrs. W. D. FELDER of Terrell, Texas, and Mrs. J. E. PEARCE of Georgetown, Texas.

Dr. Royal R. MULKEY, 27, died yesterday in Corsicana, Texas. He leaves a widow. Rev. Abe MULKEY is his father.

W. A. STANDIFER died in Fort Worth Thursday night of pneumonia. He leaves his wife, Mrs. Margaret Eleanor Armstrong STANDIFER, two sons, Charles A. STANDIFER and L. E. STANDIFER and a daughter, Mrs. B. L. WAGGOMAN. Mrs. WAGGOMAN is the wife of Fort Worth Alderman Ben L. WAGGOMAN. W. A. STANDIFER was a Mason, a member of the Knights of Honor and the United Confederate Veterans. He served with Terry's Texas Rangers during the Civil War.

Annie FOURNIER died Monday in Fort Worth and was buried in the city cemetery. Rev. Carrie M. HINSDALE officiated.

S. H. WALKER, 86, died yesterday in Mitchellsville, Iowa. He was the father of Colonel T. O. WALKER of the *Record and Register*.

Births recorded by Tarrant County Clerk's Office: a boy to Mr. and Mrs. L. J. CLAYPOOLE, Fort Worth on January 14; a boy to Mr. and Mrs. William HILLARD, Fort Worth, on January 19; a boy to Mr. and Mrs. J. W. TONNALE, Fort Worth, on January 15; a boy to Mr. and Mrs. J. O. IVEY, Marine, on January 15; a boy to Mr. and Mrs. V. R. HUNTER, Fort Worth, on January 17; a boy to Mr. and Mrs. James PINTO, Fort Worth, on January 19; and a girl to Mr. and Mrs. S. T. MCAFFEE on January 19 with no place listed.

Deaths recorded by Tarrant County Clerk: Luke CANTRELL, 24, residing in Fort Worth on January 16; and Mary WILLIAMS, 61, on January 16. No cause of death was listed.

Marriage licenses issued in Fort Worth: Charles T. STEVENSON and Mrs. Lena B. ROBINSON, A. S. ALBRIGHT and Hattie Lois OVERSTREET, C. S. JOINER and Anna WALKER, and David ALEXANDER and Bessie SCOTT.

Friday, January 22, 1904 and
Saturday, January 23, 1904

The papers from these dates did not appear on the microfilm.

Sunday, January 24, 1904

John HARPER, 15, stabbed and killed Jim MURCHISON, 14, in Dale, Texas. The fight followed an argument while the boys were playing.

J. F. HEIMER, 64, died Friday and was buried Saturday in Fort Worth.

George B. GAY, a farmer living nine miles northwest of Sanger, Texas, died Tuesday of accidental gunshot wounds suffered the previous Wednesday.

Mrs. Preston STAGGS, 62, died Friday at her home north of Weatherford, Texas.

Dr. ARNOLD, an aged hermit, died in a fire yesterday near Alvarado, Texas. He had no relatives and was buried by the county.

Enos COTHER, 61, committed suicide yesterday at Brenham, Texas.

J. W. PARSONS, about 58, died from an accidentally self-inflicted gunshot wound yesterday in Woodville, Texas.

Will HARRIS was found guilty of second degree murder and sentenced to five years in prison. He killed Felix CHENAULT.

Professor Frances C. OAKES and Myrtle GIBSON married yesterday in Yukon, Oklahoma Territory. OAKES is on the faculty of the Central Oklahoma Normal School.

Al LEWIS and Nannie DONIHOO married in McKinney, Texas yesterday.

Wilson MCBRIDE and Mattie HAMIL married Thursday in Paris, Texas. Rev. J. T. PINSON joined them in matrimony.

Grover WITT, 19, died at his father's home in the Allen community near McKinney, Texas. WITT's father was John WITT. Young WITT was a student at Grayson College in Whitewright, Texas.

Lucia E. LEE, 84, died at the home of W. A. ADAIR in Marshall, Texas. ADAIR was her nephew and the proprietor of the *Marshall Evening Messenger*.

C. RUTHERFORD, 95, died Tuesday in Graham, Texas.

J. K. NORTON died Wednesday in his home near Ivan in Stephens County, Texas. He suffered from pneumonia.

James BRYAN died Wednesday from measles in Wayland Springs, Tennessee. He lived near Graham, Texas.

Will ALDREDGE died Friday in Mineral Wells, Texas. He was a member of Woodsmen of the World and a brother of George N. ALDREDGE of Dallas

Lora ADDISON died Thursday in Denton, Texas. She resided with her sister, Mrs. William FRAZIER. She died of consumption and was buried in the Odd Fellows Cemetery.

Minter H. PARKER, 78, died Friday morning at his home in Blossom, Texas.

Mrs. BUGG, mother of B. N. BUGG, was buried yesterday at Gainesville, Texas.

Ben KNIGHT died Thursday night in Becton, Texas.

George B. EVANS, 24, died in San Antonio of tuberculosis yesterday. He was a resident of Chicago.

The body of W. M. LIEL, 52, who died Saturday morning, was shipped to St. Louis. His wife accompanied the remains.

Marriage licenses issued by Tarrant County Clerk: O. D. BALL and Fannie Bell COOK, and Charles LINDSAY and Ella WILLIAMS.

Monday, January 25, 1904

R. C. FRANCES, about 49, bookkeeper of the Grayson Oil Mills in Sherman, Texas, was stabbed to death Sunday night. He was survived by a wife and four children.

The three year old son of James TARWATERS was killed in Smithfield, Texas. He pulled a shotgun down from the wall, causing it to discharge and kill him.

Professor A. P. WHITNEY and Harriett Josephine METZGER were married Saturday in Fort Worth. He is the registrar at Trinity University in Waxahachie, Texas, and she is a professional nurse in the girls' dormitory at the University.

Marriage licenses issued at Greenville, Texas: Paul P. SHRAM and Luellen STEVENS, George W. BARR and Lillie WRIGHT, W. F. KELLEY and Eva GARRISON, and W. A. MCCRARY and Lillie MILLIGAN.

Mrs. L. B. COVINGTON died Friday at the residence of Mrs. J. F. BAILEY, her daughter, in Greenville, Texas

Mrs. N. C. HARGIS, 86, died Saturday in Denison, Texas.

Elder William ISOMS, longtime Methodist minister, died Saturday in Handley, Texas.

Will LILLARD died Saturday at his home in Paris, Texas.

George SHERIDAN died of consumption Saturday in Paris, Texas.

O. D. BALL and Fannie Bell COOK were married Saturday in Fort Worth. He is an employee of the Rock Island Railroad. She is from Bowie, Texas. Dr. Luther LITTLE officiated.

Tuesday, January 26, 1904

The paper for this date did not appear on the microfilm.

Wednesday, January 27, 1904

George RISER, of Meridian, Texas, died. He was the brother of Mrs. W. H. JAMES of Dallas.

Mrs. N. J. KLEEFER, 65, died in St. James Infirmary in Fort Worth yesterday.

Frank FITE and Geraldine SEWELL married Monday in Paris, Texas. Justice J. R. G. LANG officiated.

D. W. LEE and Beulah MORRIS married Sunday in the Methodist church parsonage in Covington, Texas.

Mrs. Jane CLAYTON, 80, died Sunday at the home of her daughter, Mrs. Kelley KENDAL, 65 miles from Pecos, Texas. She was buried in Pecos. She was born June 11, 1822 in St. Clair County, Missouri. She came to Texas in 1842. She was a Baptist.

Mrs. W. T. HALL, 60, died of pneumonia at her home four miles northwest of McKinney, Texas. She was buried in the Horn Cemetery yesterday. She is survived by her husband and six children.

George B. ROGERS, proprietor of the Gainesville Iron Works, died Monday at his home in Gainesville, Texas. Funeral will be held at the First Presbyterian Church tomorrow.

An infant child of Robert CENDER died Sunday of pneumonia in Frisco, Texas.

Ruth EARLEY, 18, died Monday in Frisco, Texas. She was buried in the Rowlett Cemetery yesterday. She was daughter of A. L. EARLEY.

L. H. BROWN, about 53, died at his home in Marshall, Oklahoma Territory. He is survived by his wife and eight children. Mrs. BROWN is the former Mary A. CHRISTMAN of Wisconsin.

The ten month old child of Frank THOMSON burned to death Monday in Sparks, Oklahoma Territory.

Albert WHITNEY, charged with the murder of R. C. FRANCIS, of Sherman, Texas, was arrested in Helen, Indian Territory.

Marriage licenses issued by Tarrant County Clerk in Fort Worth: C. L. PHENIX and Lucille WILSON, J. A. CONSTABLE and Nannie BRADLEY, Jack TIBBS and Ellen CALDWELL, Jim OGLE and Rosa L. HOLLIS, and H. L. ENTRIKEN and Sallie Mae SPENCER.

Births recorded by Tarrant County Clerk: a boy to Mr. and Mrs. J. F. BROWN, Fort Worth, on January 25; and a girl to Mr. and Mrs. Lee Andrew NULL, Fort Worth, on January 18.

Deaths recorded by Tarrant County Clerk: the infant son of Mr. and Mrs. R. A. BOBO on December 14; and Harry A. RANSOM, 36, of Mart, Texas on January 25.

Harry A. RANSOM will be buried today from Gause's undertaking establishment. RANSOM was found dead yesterday on a freight train north of Saginaw, was. His death was from unknown causes, according to the coroner.

Thursday, January 28, 1904

Leve BAKER, 104, died Monday night from burns suffered when her dress caught fire at Calvert, Texas.

B. S. FITZGERALD, 71, died at the residence of Mrs. J. L. BATES, his daughter, in Houston yesterday.

Rev. T. J. DUNCAN, pastor of the Methodist Church in Ennis, Texas, died yesterday at his home. He is survived by his wife and four children: Rev. Jerome DUNCAN of Hillsboro, Texas; Boaz DUNCAN of Los Angeles, Stark DUNCAN of Dallas and Miss Callie DUNCAN of Ennis, Texas.

S. H. REED died Tuesday in Longview, Texas. He was a former Confederate soldier.

Martha YOUNG died Tuesday in her home near Denton, Texas. She was buried yesterday. She had lived in Denton County since 1846.

Mrs. Harriet LEVINSON, 60, died yesterday in the home of Mrs. H. C. JOEKEL, her daughter, in Giddings, Texas.

J. H. BOOTH was found dead yesterday in his boarding house in Gainesville, Texas.

Fred CHRISTIAN, 18, died of peritonitis Tuesday in Lucas, Texas. He was the son of John W. CHRISTIAN

Mrs. Minnie HURDS died Tuesday in the home of her sister, Mrs. Dillard RUSHING in Roxton, Texas. Mrs. HURDS lived in Honey Grove, Texas.

A 14 year old son of B. B. MCDANIEL died Tuesday in Guthrie, Oklahoma Territory. The boy, his two brothers are father all caught pneumonia after fighting a prairie fire on Christmas Day.

Railroad fireman Amos COOK died Tuesday in Troupe, Texas.

Marriage licenses issued by Tarrant County Clerk: C. M. MCNEIL and Sindie WELCH, J. B. WHITE and Sally WIMBLEY, and Dave MOORE and Jennie BURTON.

Births recorded by Tarrant County Clerk: a girl to Mr. and Mrs. Tom BARBOOZA, Fort Worth, on January 23; a girl to Mr. and Mrs. J. DENARDS, North Fort Worth, on January 18; a boy to Mr. and Mrs. John DIEHL, Fort Worth, on January 17; a girl to Mr. and Mrs. J. H. HOFFMAN, Fort Worth, on January 16; a boy to Mr. and Mrs. J. F. BOBO, near Azle, with no date listed; a girl to Mr. and Mrs. Joseph JOHNSTON, Fort Worth, on January 22; a girl to Mr. and Mrs. Charles V. INGRAM, Fort Worth, on January 18; a boy to Mr. and Mrs. T. P. VERNON, Fort Worth, on January 24; and a girl to Mr. and Mrs. Will HIRST, Bedford, on January 16.

Deaths recorded by Tarrant County Clerk: Hugh F. BROWN, 79, residing in Fort Worth, died of pneumonia on January 14.

Owen LAWS and Bertha ANDERSON married Monday in West Paris, Texas. Rev. V. L. ROSE officiated.

Lon BLACKLOUPE and Ada GRESHAM married yesterday in Ennis, Texas. Rev. S. H. SLAUGHTER performed the ceremony.

Edgar E. HUNTER and Bena A. WARREN married Sunday in Joshua, Texas. Rev. J. P. MUSSETT officiated.

Marriage licenses issued by Hunt County Clerk in Greenville, Texas: W. A. MCCRARY and Lillie MILLIGAN, and H. A. WILLIAMS and Bennah BOXTER.

W. D. GLOVER and M. F. FAULK married Tuesday in Greenville, Texas. The ceremony was held in the home of Mrs. A. J. DANIEL and was performed by Rev. J. W. HOLSAPPLE.

Paul D. SHRAM and Luellen STEVENS married Sunday in the home of the bride's parents in Daingerfield, Texas. Rev. MORGAN officiated.

G. W. BARR and Lillie WRIGHT married last Friday in Kingston, Texas. The Rev. N. B. MCDANIEL officiated.

Mrs. Perthenia JOHNSON, a Brazos County pioneer, died Tuesday night at the home of Mrs. John JONES west of Bryan, Texas. She came to Brazos County in 1851.

Friday, January 29, 1904

M. MAYHEW and Virgie BURRAGE married yesterday in McKinney, Texas.

William LEATHERS and Lulu SNOW were married by Rev. J. L. MORRIS yesterday in Paris, Texas.

Visnie CLARK and Virgil SKEEN married yesterday in Pittsburg, Texas. The ceremony took place in the home of her parents, Mr. and Mrs. J. __. CLARK.

A twin daughter of W. F. MARTIN died Tuesday in Cleburne, Texas.

The remains of J. H. BOOTHE were shipped to Paris, Texas. He died Wednesday in Gainesville, Texas.

"Grandma" SKIFFLETT, about 70, died Monday in her home near Storey in Denton County, Texas.

Mrs. J. M. SUMMER, 48, died of pneumonia Wednesday in Paris, Texas.

Neer MCLOUD died suddenly while feeding his dogs in Guthrie, Oklahoma Territory.

Marriage licenses issued by Tarrant County Clerk: E. P. FREEMAN and Mary Elizabeth O'CONNOR, W. R. LUNK and Mrs. R. E. CAMPBELL, Frank POLLARD and Teresa STEGALL, and C. H. BORDIN and E. Lucille YOUNGBLOOD.

Saturday, January 30, 1904

W. H. STEIN, about 25 and a medical student, died of pneumonia in St. James Infirmary in Fort Worth.

C. H. BORDIN and E. Lucille YOUNGBLOOD were married in the Baptist parsonage Thursday. BORDIN is a deputy clerk in the prison at Huntsville, Texas. YOUNGBLOOD is a former schoolteacher at Thurber, Texas. She is from Mansfield, Texas.

Jesse GORDON was killed in an argument over prohibition at Delaware Bend in Cooke County, Texas. Sud YOUNG was arrested for murder.

Albert WHITTEN was remanded to jail yesterday for the murder of R. C. FRANCES in Sherman, Texas.

The son of Fred JARVIS was killed Tuesday when he was dragged by a pony in Wharton, Texas.

Willis CLARKE killed his wife yesterday in Orange, Texas. He then attempted to take his own life.

Mrs. Van KIRKPTRICK died yesterday in Hillsboro, Texas. While she was ill, her six month old son died, but she was never told of his death.

W. C. VANLANDINGHAM died Monday in the home of his son, W. T. VANLANDINGHAM, in Greenville, Texas.

J. M. CLYMER, 82, died Thursday at his home near Celeste in Hunt County, Texas. He had lived in Hunt County for 50 years and leaves a son and six daughters.

R.__.CRISP died Monday in Greenville, Texas. His 75-year-old wife survives. He was a pioneer of Greenville.

Abe SWANN, 50, died Tuesday at Swann's Gin, 8 miles north of Greenville, Texas.

H. A. BRYANT died Thursday in Cleburne, Texas. His children are Witt, John, Sam, Wallace and Annie BRYANT.

Mrs. J. G. HARDING, 40, died of heart failure Thursday at Weatherford, Texas. She was buried there yesterday.

T. D. SHAY died Thursday in Italy, Texas.

Marie LAMB, 4, died of diphtheria at the state orphanage in Corsicana, Texas.

The trial of Dr. J. H. HATCHER is underway in Ardmore, Indian Territory. He is accused of murdering Lizzie RISTON by poisoning her with aconite.

Bishop HOLMES, 29, committed suicide in Dallas yesterday. He was a recently married man who was out of work. He was the son of Capt. J. P. HOLMES of Greenville, Texas.

Mrs. Hannah VALENTI died yesterday in Dallas. Her funeral took place in the Central Congregational Church there.

G. M. ALLEN and Pearl WHITBECK married at the home of Mrs. N. B. PITTMAN, the bride's sister, in Ennis, Texas. Rev. S. H. SLAUGHTER officiated.

Robert R. COGSDELL and Rezi COVINGTON married Thursday at the Methodist parsonage in Cleburne, Texas. Rev. Charles BROWN officiated.

May DICKEY and M. R. FARMER were married near Blum, Texas on January 24.

Mrs. Antonio SANCHEZ died Wednesday of burns suffered Tuesday night at Eagle Pass, Texas. Her husband, when told of his wife's burns, accidentally fell into a coal mine shaft and broke his neck Tuesday night.

Births recorded by Tarrant County Clerk: a boy to Mr. and Mrs. R. C. GALBREATH, Fort Worth, on January 26; a boy to Mr. and Mrs. Whitley THWEATT, Grapevine, on January 20; twin girls to Mr. and Mrs. M. R. LOONEY, Forth Worth, on January 28; a girl to Mr. and Mrs. J. R. CRAWFORD, Grapevine, on January 4; a girl to Mr. and Mrs. J. AXELROD, Fort Worth, on January 27; a boy to Mr. and Mrs. C. R. MILLER, Keller, on January 19; a boy to Mr. and Mrs. George ERNEST, Handley, on January 4; a boy to Mr. and Mrs. Doug LEWIS, Newark, on January 23; and a girl to Mr. and Mrs. Thomas EVANS, Handley, on January 1.

Deaths recorded by Tarrant County Clerk: William BYARS, 22, residing in White Settlement, died of pneumonia on January 15; the infant son of _____ HERNDON, residing in Fort Worth, died of heart failure on January 18.

Marriage licenses issued by Tarrant County Clerk: William H. DOWDEN and Nancy Jane BRYANT, and J. L. WILEY and Mrs. A. M. BOID.

Mrs. Laura Johnston CLAYTON, widow of George Root CLAYTON, died yesterday at her home in Fort Worth. She is survived by her daughter, Lilly B. CLAYTON and a son, George R. CLAYTON.

Sunday, January 31, 1904

M. FINNEGAN, 62, was killed in the Santa Fe yards yesterday at Cleburne, Texas. He was hit by a passing train while crossing the tracks.

Sam BELL was killed in a well accident near Hewitt, Texas. Hewitt is located ten miles south of Waco.

The funeral of L. G. BYRNES, a cigar maker, was held at Gause's undertaking establishment in Fort Worth. BYRNES was a member of Local 245, CMIU of A.

Mrs. Elsie SMALL died yesterday in Muskogee, Indian Territory. She leaves a six year old daughter. Mrs. SMALL was the daughter of former Congressman [S. S.] KIRKPATRICK of Fredonia, Kansas, and the sister of Byron KIRKPATRICK of Pryor Creek, Indian Territory. Editor's note: The initials of Congressman Kirkpatrick were provided from another source.

Jack W. GALLAGHER died in Durant, Indian Territory. His remains were sent to Labell, Missouri. He was a druggist.

Houston WEAVER died at Wilmer, Texas after he was attacked by unknown parties.

A 13 month old son of W. L. SMITH died Friday night after being scalded in Haslet, Texas.

Cain KEMP, about 38, died of consumption Friday in Joshua, Texas. He was a merchant.

Dr. J. M. OWENSBY, a prominent physician, died yesterday in Denison, Texas.

Marriage licenses issued by Tarrant County Clerk: J. C. MORROW and Lottie HILLARD, J. W. TOMLIN and Minnie TEAGUE; L. HUEY and Mrs. George BERRY, and David HEWITT and Mrs. Cora HENDRICKS.

Births recorded by Tarrant County Clerk: a girl to Mr. and Mrs. J. W. DOOR, Handley, on January 5; a boy to Mr. and Mrs. Henry LEWIS, Handley, on January 5; a girl to Mr. and Mrs. W. S. CANNON, Arlington, on January 16; a girl to Mr. and Mrs. C. G. GRAHAM, Handley, on January 30; a girl to Mr. and Mrs. James BATES, White Settlement, on January 21; a boy to Mr. and Mrs. John R. HARLAN, Forrest Hill, on January 26; a girl to Mr. and Mrs.

Stephen UPSHUR, Mansfield, on January 7; a girl to Mr. and Mrs. W. W. HARRELL, Mansfield, on January 29; a boy to Mr. and Mrs. Odus HUNTER, Mansfield, on January 28; a boy to Mr. and Mrs. John TURNBO, Arlington, on January 24; a boy to Mr. and Mrs. James REILLY, Riverside, on January 24; and a boy to Mr. and Mrs. J. C. PULLEN, Fort Worth, on January 27.

Deaths recorded by Tarrant County Clerk: Annie WHITWORTH, 17, residing in Fort Worth, died of pneumonia with no date listed.

R. E. LYONS of Fort Worth and Carrie HOOVER married Wednesday in Chetopa, Kansas. The wedding took place in the home of Mr. and Mrs. M. V. HOOVER, the parents of the bride.

February, 1904

Monday, February 1, 1904

Henry MAGEL and his son Charles died when a gas explosion destroyed their home in Pittsburg, Texas.

Capt W. A. J. NICHOLSON, 68, died Saturday in Hillsboro, Texas. He served as an alderman in that city.

C. W. POLK accidentally shot and killed himself while cleaning a revolver in Holdersville, Indian Territory.

John JONES accidentally shot and killed George W. WILSON, his cousin, while hunting near Taloga, Indian Territory.

Roy SIMMONS, 7, was killed when a tree fell on him near Ahern, Oklahoma Territory.

The death of D. H. WEAVER near Wilmer, Texas created much interest. He was a prominent farmer who was active politically. Oso TIREE was arrested for murder in the case. WEAVER was buried in Lancaster, Texas.

John WALKER was acquitted Saturday in the death of Will CLINER on December 23, 1902, in Cisco, Texas.

Dan SURGNOR died Saturday of blood poisoning in Sherman, Texas.

Former county treasurer W. M. BAGLEY, 72, died of pneumonia Friday in McKinney, Texas.

John Q. WEST, 20, and Hubert HICKS, 21, died Saturday in Ardmore, Indian Territory.

Larry MCCARTNEY died Saturday four miles north of Waxahachie, Texas. He was buried in Waxahachie.

Mrs. Jane HOBSON, 82, died Saturday at her home southeast of Decatur, Texas. She had lived in Wise County for 56 years.

Mrs. S. C. CATNER, 69, wife of M. CATNER, died Thursday at her home in Decatur, Texas. She was buried Friday in Decatur City Cemetery.

William COOK died Thursday at his home north of Decatur, Texas. He was buried Sunday in Decatur City Cemetery.

G. W. TAYLOR, 54, died yesterday of heart failure in Mineral Wells, Texas. His body was shipped to Texarkana.

Mrs. E. M. GRAHAM died in Odessa, Texas. She was the mother of Ector County Sheriff GRAHAM.

Mrs. W. G. HULLY died Friday at her home near Godley in Johnson County, Texas.

J. R. NICKERSON and Annie MULLINS married Saturday in McKinney, Texas. The bride is from Branch, Texas.

William DICKENS and Minnie HUNT were married by Rev. PERTIE Saturday in Temple, Texas.

Saturday, February 2, 1904

Births recorded by Tarrant County Clerk: a boy to Mr. and Mrs. S. C. POWELL, Grapevine, on January 8; a girl to Mr. and Mrs. John W. CORNER, Grapevine, on January 28; a boy to Mr. and Mrs. T. W. POOR, Grapevine, on January 4; a girl to Mr. and Mrs. W. G. CANNON, Handley, on January 16; a boy to Mr. and Mrs. John R. HORTON, Forrest Hill, on January 26; a girl to Mr. and Mrs. James BATES, White Settlement, on January 30; a boy to Mr. and Mrs. Henry LEWIS, Handley, on January 5; a girl to Mr. and Mrs. J. W. DORR, Handley, on January 5; a boy to Mr. and Mrs. J. C. PULLEN, Fort Worth, with no date listed; and a boy to Mr. and Mrs. James RILEY, Riverside, on January 24.

Deaths recorded by Tarrant County Clerk: Laura WALLACE, 24, suicide, no date listed; Mary Ellen DAY, 42, residing in Grapevine with no date or cause listed; and M. L. LIPSCOMB, 87, residing in Grapevine with no date or cause listed.

Marriage licenses issued by Tarrant County Clerk: W. J. MAINS and Grace BOZARTH, and W. O. SCHULTZ and Winfred SANSOM.

Mrs. John RALSTON died when her dress caught fire Monday in Holland, Texas.

Mariah COULTER died from burns suffered when her dress caught fire Monday in Wellborn, Texas.

Abbie WRIGHT died when her house burned to the ground during the night Sunday at Mexia, Texas.

Rev. M. GLADSON died Sunday at his home in Weatherford, Texas. He was buried in Fort Worth.

George MCDONALD, father of black political leader Gooseneck Bill MCDONALD, died Sunday at Kaufman, Texas.

Marriage licenses issued by Johnson County Clerk in Cleburne, Texas: R. H. CAMERON and Iva Dan GRESHAM, Minton SMITH and Mrs. Ethel HAGGARD, and Oscar DAVIS and Daisye BRYANT.

Wednesday, February 3, 1904

W. J. LONG, 50, died of a self-inflicted gunshot wound Thursday in Wellington, Texas. He was buried in Wellington.

Mrs. A. H. LIGHTFOOT died Sunday in Rockdale, Texas. She previously lived at Pittsburg, Texas.

William KING died Monday night at his home in Marshall, Texas. He was an employee of the Texas and Pacific Railroad.

Mrs. D. O. DUNHAM died at her home Sunday in Covington, Texas. She was buried in the city cemetery Monday.

Mrs. J. A. HERMAN died Sunday in Graham, Texas. She was the wife of the proprietor of the Commerce Hotel in Graham.

Robert S. DANIEL died Sunday night at his home in Waxahachie, Texas. He suffered from Bright's disease.

R. D. OWEN, 25, died of pneumonia Monday in Waco, Texas. He was an attorney.

Capt. R. B. CAMPBELL died Sunday night in Corsicana, Texas.

Mrs. A. C. LONG, 71, died Monday in Corsicana, Texas. She was buried in Kaufman, Texas.

C. E. SIMMONS and Oaka JAMES married Monday in Marshall, Texas.

C. C. STEPHENSON and Mary CURRY married Sunday in Greenville, Texas. Rev N. C. LITTLE officiated. The groom is from Paris, Texas.

J. W. PAUL and Mollie PATTERSON married Monday in Greenville, Texas. Rev. N. C. LITTLE officiated.

J. S. PIERCE and Willie HANCOCK married in Greenville, Texas. Rev. N. C. LITTLE officiated.

Henry E. SMITH and Bessie WHEELER married Monday afternoon in Denton, Texas. He is principal of the public schools in Chico.

Walter BROWN, was shot Monday near Griffin, Texas. He died yesterday. He was from Troupe, Texas.

Two daughters of J. D. LAYFIELD burned to death last night in Justin, Texas. Their mother was badly burned and may not live. None of the victims were named.

Alex MCDONALD was injured in a railroad accident Sunday near Denison, Texas. He died Tuesday of his injuries.

Nellie May HAYSELE, 6, died yesterday in Sherman, Texas. She died from the effects of a rusty nail in her foot.

Bert WOLFE, of Greenville, Texas, was shot and killed west of Fort Worth Tuesday. He was the son of Rev. M. M. WOLFE.

Mrs. M. L. SIMMONS, 42, died in Dallas. Her brother, L. O. WAGONER was killed recently in Plano, Texas. His remains were disinterred and the remains of both shipped to Meridian, Mississippi.

Thursday, February 4, 1904

W. J. HALL died of pneumonia yesterday in Belton, Texas. He was cashier for the Santa Fe railroad and a member of the Knights of Pythias.

H. E. P. HOLLAND died of pneumonia in Springtown, Texas. He was the father of Mrs. W. C. COX and was buried in Peaster, Texas.

Mrs. W. C. COX, wife of the editor of the *Springtown Index*, died of pneumonia and was buried in the Springtown, Texas cemetery.

T. J. SLAYDEN died Monday night in Waxahachie, Texas.

W. S. SHEPHARD died Tuesday at his home three miles north of Corsicana, Texas.

Mrs. Martin L. LEWIS, 50, died of pneumonia at her home in Weatherford, Texas.

Dr. M. A. TAYLOR died of pneumonia Tuesday in Honey Grove, Texas. He was buried at Oakwood, Texas. He was a Methodist and a Mason.

J. M. BRYANT, 49, died of pneumonia in Ardmore, Indian Territory. He was well known in Grayson County, Texas and had lived in Duncan.

William RICHARDSON, 83, died of pneumonia Tuesday night at Durwood, Indian Territory.

The funeral of A. L. FAIRCHILD took place Tuesday in Gainesville, Texas. He died in Sherman earlier that day.

Marriages licenses issued by the Hunt County Clerk in Greenville, Texas: David GIVING and Frances LASATER, M. N. EVANS and Alice MCWHIRTER, Jimmie W. PAUL and Mollie PATTERSON, Morand SHULER and Leona KILLIAN, Reuben MARLER and Martha J. GRIFFITH, J. S. PIERCE and Willie HANCOCK, and Johnny WALKER and Daisy ANDREWS.

Dana BASS and Lawrence BRAMLETT married Tuesday night in Longview, Texas. They were childhood sweethearts.

Marriage licenses issued by the Johnson County Clerk in Cleburne, Texas: Arthur NORRIS and Edith VICK, F. W. MARSHALL and Mettie HUTCHINSON, and F. E. ARMSTRONG and Josie HALE.

John MILAM died yesterday in surgery to amputate his foot after an accident in Georgetown, Texas.

The two year old daughter of Mr. and Mrs. Hez EVANS died Tuesday near Caddo, Texas. EVANS was an inmate in the prison serving a sentence for manslaughter at the time of his daughter's death.

Grant WILLIAMS and Albert SCOTT were sentenced to death in South McAlester, Indian Territory. WILLIAMS killed two unnamed people. SCOTT killed Cash ELLIS.

A settlement was reached yesterday in the 17th District Court case of Mrs. Elizabeth WELLS v. Chicago, Rock Island and Pacific Railroad. The railroad will pay Mrs. WELLS $4000 in the death of her railroad fireman husband, George W. WELLS on December 12, 1902.

Marriage licenses issued by Tarrant County Clerk: Edward APPLEBY and Elmira Laura JOHNSTON, and Dr. H. W. JACKSON and Mary E. POWELL

N. V. DEDRICK died in Houston yesterday. He lived at Navasota, Texas.

Mrs. J. L. SEWELL died Tuesday in Texarkana. She was from Fairview, Texas.

Mrs. E. P. COMER, wife of C. H. COMER, died in Fort Worth early today. She leaves her husband, a son, H. M. COMER, and two daughters, Mrs. J. V. RANKIN and Mrs. A. T. MARSH.

Elmira Laura JOHNSTON, daughter of the late Dr. JOHNSTON, married Edward APPLEBY yesterday in Fort Worth. They will honeymoon in New York, Boston and Chicago.

Mrs. Annette A. NAGLE, widow of J. W. NAGLE, died and was buried yesterday in Austin.

The funeral of Harry MCALLISTER took place yesterday from his home in Fort Worth. Rev. Luther LITTLE officiated. Burial was in city cemetery.

Friday, February 5, 1904

The paper for this date did not appear on the microfilm.

Saturday, February 6, 1904

Mrs. Larkin ADAMSON, 82, died at her home in the Chambersville community near McKinney, Texas.

John HAMLETT died Thursday at his home in Roxton, Texas. He was a farmer and a Mason.

Levi BUMPUS, about 65, died Thursday at his home in Mineral Wells, Texas.

A. C. GLASGOW died Tuesday in Terrell, Texas. He was buried today in Center Point Cemetery at Alvarado, Texas. He was a Mason. Surviving are his wife and three children: A. J. GLASGOW of West, Texas; W. C. GLASGOW and Mrs. A. E. BILLINGSLEY in Alvarado.

George J. SEE, editor of the *Bandera Enterprise*, died yesterday of pneumonia in Bandera, Texas.

W. S. TEAGUE, a printer, died Thursday in Greenville, Texas. He leaves a wife in Corsicana, Texas, a daughter in Denison, Texas, and a son in Dallas.

Clide FOOTE and Ida WILLIAMS were married yesterday in Temple, Texas.

Rev. D. M. THOMAS, 75, was found dead in his room in San Antonio Friday afternoon. He was a Presbyterian minister.

Sam FRAZIER died suddenly yesterday in Ardmore, Indian Territory.

The three year old child of John BARBER burned to death near Norman, Indian Territory.

The three year old child of Edward REUTER died from burns near Ingalls, Indian Territory.

Frank TIERRY married Mary A. WALSH, in the Oriental Hotel in Dallas Friday afternoon. The bride is from Grand Saline, Texas.

John BEATY married his bride in the Oriental Hotel earlier in the week. Her name was not given. He is from Waxahachie, Texas.

Mrs. W. P. HARDWICK and O. P. HANEY are managing the Hotel Worth in Fort Worth.

Births recorded by Tarrant County Clerk: a girl to Mr. and Mrs. Dan SPEARMAN, Mansfield, on January 25; a boy to Mr. and Mrs. J. W. HILL, Fort Worth, on January 19; a boy to Mr. and Mrs. R. B. CHRISTIANSEN, Fort Worth, on February 3; a girl to Mr. and Mrs. W. M. TRAMMELL, Rosen Heights, on February 2; a boy to Mr. and Mrs. Charles GLINK, Fort Worth, on January 31; a boy to Mr. and Mrs. W. L. WOOD, Mansfield, on February 3; a boy to Mr. and Mrs. J. S. HUNTER, Kennedale, on January 31; and a boy to Mr. and Mrs. J. M. MARTIN, Marine, on January 5.

Deaths recorded by Tarrant County Clerk: Roy NELSON, 19, residing in Fort Worth, died of pneumonia on January 25 and Joseph L. LOVING, 35, residing in Fort Worth, died from a pistol shot on February 4.

George B. WILLIAMS, 40, died from appendicitis at the infirmary in Fort Worth Thursday.

The funeral of Joseph LOVING was held at the First Presbyterian Church in Fort Worth Friday. Rev. C. R. HYDE officiated. He was buried in the new cemetery.

Locomotive engineer William TROGLE was killed on January 19 when his train wrecked. No location was given.

Jeff DAVIS, a prominent planter, was shot and killed near Fort Towson, Indian Territory. Family troubles are believed to be the reason.

Mrs. L. H. STEPHENS died at the home of Mrs. W. M. CUNNINGHAM in Amarillo, Texas on January 11.

Sunday, February 7, 1904

A. LASNER, city salesman for Stewart and Currie, was found dead in his bed in Dallas yesterday. He was about 70 years old and died of heart failure. He had two sons and two daughters in Chicago. No names were listed for the children.

Mrs. Ola BAKER and T. L. VAN ZANDT married Friday at Van Alstyne, Texas. They took the train for Galveston and New Orleans.

Harry L. ANDERSON and Lula JACKSON married Friday in Kaufman, Texas. Rev. W. D. MONTCASTLE officiated.

Mayne MACON and Ed STOWE were married Thursday evening in San Angelo, Texas.

Earl COLES, 14, son of Mr. and Mrs. J. C. COLES, died Tuesday at Floyd, Texas.

A telegram was received in Marshall, Texas last evening stating that J. L. PERNET, a former resident in Marshall, had died in Nashville, Tennessee.

Edward M. UNDERHILL, 63, died yesterday in Austin. He was an expert railroad accountant.

Thomas PRUITT, an aged resident of Shawnee, fell from the Choctaw Bridge over Spaniard Creek and was killed in Guthrie, Oklahoma Territory.

Edna Eugene SOUTHERN died at Sherman, Texas on January 26 and was buried there the next day. She was the sister of Mrs. Manie THAYER of Fort Worth. She was also court stenographer of the 51st District Court.

Kettler MCWILLIAMS was killed by police in Navasota, Texas. MCWILLIAMS was resisting arrest and assaulted a police officer with a knife before being killed. Police were looking for MCWILLIAMS after he cut Baker STEPHENSON with a knife.

Mrs. M. R. LAMB, J. T. LAMB, R. W. LAMB and Mrs. Jennie ADAMSON placed a card of thanks following the death of M. R. LAMB, their husband and father.

Monday, February 8, 1904

Gus MCCOWEN committed suicide Saturday in Cleburne, Texas. He was found shot to death Sunday. A recent illness may have caused the suicide.

Perry TOWNE died Saturday of wounds inflicted by Frank WAFAER, his son-in-law, several days ago. TOWNE was shot in Hobart, Oklahoma Territory.

David DIEGEE, 67, died suddenly in Dodue, Oklahoma Territory. He was the postmaster and a resident of the strip since its opening. His date of death was not reported.

J. J. RAMSAY died yesterday in Cleburne, Texas. Surviving children are Colonel W. F. RAMSAY, Sam RAMSAY and John RAMSAY.

The remains of Mrs. Helen FRAZIER reached Marshall, Texas yesterday. She was buried in Greenwood Cemetery. She died in Fort Worth.

George W. CHAPMAN died Saturday in Starrville, Texas. He was a farmer and leaves his wife and two children.

News of the death of Ed DURRETT near Dallas a few days ago reached Waxahachie, Texas.

John BATESON was found guilty Saturday in Cleburne, Texas of killing W. S. PATE. He was sentenced to 35 years in prison.

Oscar BLACK, a railroad brakeman, accidentally drank carbolic acid and died in El Paso.

B. O. BARNES, formerly a railroad engineer and saloon keeper, was declared of unsound mind at a trial in Cleburne, Texas. He was ordered to the state asylum in Terrell, Texas.

Valentine VILLELA was killed in San Antonio when he fell under the wheels of a street car there yesterday.

Tuesday, February 9, 1904

Herman OTTO was placed on trial in Beaumont, Texas for the murder of Frank OBST last August.

Mrs. HARTNETT, mother of C. D. and Con D. HARTNETT, died Saturday at her home in Weatherford, Texas. She was 83. The funeral was held Monday at the Catholic Church.

Peter HARVEY died Saturday at his home near Phantom Hill in Jones County, Texas.

Mrs. T. C. KYLE, about 35, died Saturday in Texarkana. The funeral services were Sunday at Rose Hill Cemetery.

Young TAYLOR died yesterday in Keene, Texas. He died from injuries sustained when he jumped from a third floor window. He was undergoing treatment for mental illness. He was buried in Waxahachie, Texas.

Fannie WEAKLEY died of pneumonia yesterday in Milford, Texas. She was a pioneer of Ellis County.

J. W. WILBOURN, 85, died Friday in Gail, Texas. He was a pioneer of Hunt County but moved to Gail for his health.

Ruby JONES and Frank SHELLENBARGER married yesterday in Guthrie, Oklahoma Territory.

Births recorded by Tarrant County Clerk: a girl to Mr. and Mrs. G. S. MCTEER, Marine, on February 4; a girl to Mr. and Mrs. Gordon SLATURNE, Arlington, on February 2; a boy to Mr. and Mrs. R. E. GOREE, Marine, on

February 3; a girl to Mr. and Mrs. Hamp G. RICE, Johnson Station, on January 30; a girl to Mr. and Mrs. H. W. TATUM, Arlington, on February 4; a girl to Mr. and Mrs. J. A. BLASSO, Nine Mile Bridge, on February 3; a girl to Mr. and Mrs. John NASH, Riverside, on January 31; a boy to Mr. and Mrs. J. R. MCLARREN, Fort Worth, on January 4; a girl to Mr. and Mrs. John H. FRAZIER, Fort Worth, on January 26; a girl to Mr. and Mrs. E. E. TEAGUE, Azle, on January 30; a boy to Mr. and Mrs. M. CALLOWAY, Birdville, on February 2; a boy to Mr. and Mrs. J. E. MCBRAYER, Marine, on January 30; and a boy to Mr. and Mrs. George H. BULLARD, Fort Worth, on February 2.

Deaths recorded by Tarrant County Clerk: A. B. COOPER, 28, residing in Fort Worth, died of epilepsy on January 28; James PONDER residing in Keller, died of pneumonia on December 25; and Edward S. PARKER, 22, residing in Fort Worth died on February 2.

Henry LANG was shot to death yesterday in Batson, Texas. He was a bartender. He was shot when he tried to stop a fight in his bar.

Antoine WOTIPKA, a bartender, was found dead in his room in Houston yesterday. He had been shot.

Gertrude BOYLE died from poisoning at St. Joseph's Infirmary in Fort Worth yesterday. She swallowed the tablets last week. The funeral will be held at Gause's undertaking establishment in Fort Worth today.

Wednesday, February 10, 1904
The paper for this date did not appear on the microfilm.

Thursday, February 11, 1904
William EMMONS was fatally stabbed by M. BULLARD near Lawton, Oklahoma Territory. The two men argued over cattle. BULLARD was arrested.

America COFFEE, 98, died of cancer today in Ardmore, Indian Territory. She was a pioneer of Ardmore.

Charley TUGWELL died this morning. He had been shot yesterday by Otis PRIDY near Duncan, Indian Territory. PRIDY will be tried in Chickasha.

Rev. A. A. DUNCAN and Rosa HART married in Minneola, Texas. They will live in Lufkin, Texas. Rev. J. H. GAMBRELL of Tyler officiated.

Lt. A. C. OSBORN and Alma Kate BREWSTER married last night in Laredo, Texas. Rev. J. WARD officiated.

Mrs. May WILSON died yesterday of pneumonia in Corsicana, Texas. She was a widow and left three children. The children were placed in the state orphan asylum in Corsicana.

Mrs. Z. B. THOMASON died Monday in Haskell, Texas.

James CLOUD, 15 months, died Monday night. His funeral was yesterday.

A seven month old child of John PETRIL died Monday in Ennis, Texas.

Warren HOOKS, 6, died of burns in Towson, Texas. He was the son of W. B. HOOKS, a planter and merchant.

Friday, February 12, 1904
Apolicario HERNANDEZ shot and killed his wife Wednesday in Bluntzer, Texas. She was not named in the article. He killed her because she refused to live with him. The couple had been separated for several months.

John HARKEY, a young farmer of Lancaster, Texas, was fatally wounded while hunting yesterday.

Brant PAYNE and Estelle KEACH married Wednesday in Killeen, Texas.

Mrs. Dona BEALE and R. W. BEAUMONT were married at her home in Waxahachie, Texas. The Rev. C. R. WRIGHT officiated.

Mary MILLER and Mr. HILL of Fort Worth married Wednesday in Boyd, Texas. Rev. FRENCH officiated. First names for HILL and FRENCH were not given.

S. E. SPRADLIN, 79, died yesterday in Ardmore, Indian Territory. He was born in Kentucky and had lived in Ardmore for five years.

J. H. STEPHENSON, 72, died Wednesday night at his home near Mountain Park, Texas.

R. R. STILLWELL died yesterday in Corsicana, Texas. He leaves a widow, two sons and two daughters. Gono ADAMS, a step-son, is in the U.S. Coastal Artillery near San Francisco.

William WELCH, a railroad conductor, died yesterday in San Antonio.

John MONAGHEN was found dead yesterday at his home in Greenville, Texas.

Mrs. J. D. LAYFIELD and her five year old daughter died yesterday of burns suffered a week ago in Justin, Texas. Four of the five family members died from the fire.

Marriage licenses issued by Tarrant County Clerk in Fort Worth: Albert C. GEORGE and Nellie ROBERTS, and Sam A. WALDEN and Lillie M. KILLOUGH.

Homer L. REEVES, 5, died yesterday in Fort Worth. He was to be buried in Longview, Texas. He was the son of Texas and Pacific Railroad conductor E. R. REEVES.

Saturday, February 13, 1904

Marriage licenses issued in Greenville, Texas: C. B. HALE and Alice JOHNSON, W. T. YOUNG and Claudie WILLIAMS, and Ernest DANIEL and Vera CADE.

James AVERITT and Fannie RUSSELL married yesterday in McKinney, Texas. The bride is from Petersburg, Texas.

The remains of Capt. Lucian FLYNN arrived yesterday in Corsicana, Texas. His sister is Mrs. Eulalia SMITH. Capt. FLYNN graduated from the U.S. Naval Academy in 1872.

The funeral of John MONEGHAN took place in his home in Gainesville, Texas. Survivors include his wife and two children. Cause of death was a stroke of apoplexy.

Mrs. M. E. EDWARDS, 79, died Thursday at the home of her daughter in Greenville, Texas. Services were held yesterday.

Mr. C. ROSE, superintendent of the city school, died yesterday in Stanford, Texas.

The remains of Richard THOMAS, who died in Fort Worth Thursday, were buried yesterday in Ennis, Texas. The funeral was held at the Methodist Episcopal Church. THOMAS was a Texas and Pacific Railway mail clerk.

James G. MORRIS died yesterday in Denison, Texas. He was a veteran of the Civil War, serving in Colonel Morgan's Kentucky cavalry.

Mrs. Pearl BONNER, 22, died Thursday of heart disease in Ardmore, Indian Territory. She was the wife of druggist Mitch BONNER.

Mrs. W. P. MCMILLAN, 57, died Thursday in Greenville, Texas. She leaves six daughters. Rev. J. R. WAGES preached the funeral yesterday.

Mrs. Nellie KERR died in a fire yesterday in Sour Lake, Texas.

Mrs. C. DONNEY gave birth to triplets west of Springtown, Texas.

Corp. SNEE of the 26th Infantry died Thursday in Eagle Pass, Texas. He was injured when hit by a rock thrown by a Mexican citizen last Saturday night.

Marriage licenses issued at the Tarrant County Clerk's Office: Branch B. DUNHAM and Maud J. WEBSTER, and S. K. BANKS and D. J. BOOE.

Births recorded at the Tarrant County Clerk's office: a boy to Mr. and Mrs. R. L. MCCREIGHT, Fort Worth, on February 10; a girl to Mr. and Mrs. J. P. SCOTT, Euless, on February 1; a boy to Mr. and Mrs. J. D. POLLOCK, Kennedale, on February 8; a girl to Mr. and Mrs. W. C. PAYNE, Fort Worth, on January 20; a girl to Mr. and Mrs. W. V. MCCLURE, Fort Worth, on January 11; a girl to Mr. and Mrs. L. P. MAREN, Kennedale, on February 10; a girl Mr. and Mrs. B. I. TEAL, Kennedale, on February 3; a girl to Mr. and Mrs. C. C. WAGONER, Kennedale, on February 2; and a girl to Mr. and Mrs. John HUDSON, with no place listed, on February 2.

Deaths recorded at the Tarrant County Clerk's Office: Clara DAVIDSON, 1, residing near Birdville, died of erysipelas on February 8; and James T. WALCOTT, 35, residing in Rosen Heights, died of malignant endocarditis on February 9.

Leah RAGAN, 4, died in a barn fire at Pinkerton, Texas. She was the daughter of Dr. J. B. RAGAN. A two-year-old daughter of T. V. GORDON was also killed. Her name was not listed.

Lee CANNON, a saloon keeper in Dalhart, Texas, was killed in a fight Wednesday night.

Sunday, February 14, 1904

The body of Henry FUGETT, who was hanged Friday in Cleburne, Texas, was shipped to Mooreville in Falls County, Texas for interment.

The infant son of Mr. and Mrs. E. C. STALCUP died Thursday in Cleburne, Texas.

H. V. EVETTS, 44, died Friday night in Ardmore, Indian Territory. He had lived in Ardmore for 12 years, coming from Alabama. He was a member of the Woodmen of the World.

Mary ROBERTSON, 60, died Friday night at the home of J. H. BAKER, her brother-in-law, south of Van Alstyne, Texas. The cause of death was pneumonia.

DeMoore KOONCE, son of Mrs. Lula KOONCE, died Monday in Mount Vernon, Texas.

A. K. KING died Tuesday of pneumonia and measles in Mount Vernon, Texas.

Mrs. George W. BRYANT married J. HENRY in her home in south Franklin County, Texas. Rev. W. J. COWLEY officiated.

Dan BENNETT and Amanda GREENLEIGH married in Majors, Texas. Elder W. I. DAVIS officiated.

W. T. YOUNG and Claudie WILLIAMS married Thursday in the Hunt County Courthouse at Greenville, Texas. Esquire Tom MCDANIEL officiated.

Mrs. Blanche HILL married J. A. POSEY yesterday in Cleburne, Texas.

Robert POTTER and his wife recently remarried after being divorced for 35 years. They were in Denison, Texas yesterday, traveling to Kentucky to see a son Mrs. POTTER had not seen since the divorce. Her name was not listed.

The remains of Jack DAMRON were taken to Temple, Texas. He died in San Angelo, Texas. He was an employee of the First National Bank and the SW Telegraph and Telephone Company.

Florence H. BROWDER, badly burned last Saturday, died yesterday. She was four years old and the daughter of W. W. BROWDER. She lived at Calhoun, Texas, five miles from Dallas.

Births recorded by Tarrant County Clerk: a boy to Mr. and Mrs. Tony BOTFO, Fort Worth, on February 2; a boy to Mr. and Mrs. Collins BAKER, Fort Worth, on February 5; and a girl to Mr. and Mrs. James H. CANNON on February 7.

Deaths recorded by Tarrant County Clerk: Sallie Anne BROILES, 62, residing in Mansfield, died of old age on February 5; Homer REEVER, 5, residing in Fort Worth, died of croup on February 12; Willie S. COX, 18, residing in Fort Worth, died of pneumonia on February 12; and Luther L. FLETCHER, 32, residing in Fort Worth of pneumonia on February 7.

Marriage licenses issued by Tarrant County Clerk: J. S. GAUYTON and Miss A. M. PRIDDY, and Henry WALLACE and Mrs. Katie AYRES.

Monday, February 15, 1904

Col. J. M. HILL, 86, died in Austin yesterday. He was a hero of the Battle of San Jacinto.

Sidney SWINK, member of an old and prominent family in Dallas, committed suicide at the Oriental HOTEL in Dallas. He suffered from consumption.

T. W. HYDE and Mary WEAVER married Saturday in Belton, Texas.

Richard ALEXANDER died of lockjaw in Gainesville, Texas Friday night.

Tuesday, February 16, 1904

G. C. KERR was killed Saturday afternoon in the railroads yards at Chickasha, Texas. He leaves a wife and four children. They were not named. He was buried in Marlow, Texas.

Green FAULKNER, 60, was buried Sunday in Lancaster, Texas. He was a former slave.

The funeral of Col. J. M. HILL took place yesterday in Austin.

H. H. COLCLAZER, 52, died in San Antonio yesterday. He leaves a wife and will be buried in San Antonio. He served as special agent in Texas, Oklahoma, and Louisiana for rural free mail delivery.

Marriage licenses by Tarrant County Clerk: P. B. SMITH and Ruby WHITE, and A. L. SHELTON and Mrs. Eula ROGERS.

Births recorded by Tarrant County Clerk: a girl to Mr. and Mrs. A. J. MAYTON, Fort Worth, on February 7.

Deaths recorded by Tarrant County Clerk: Jacob BROWN, 14, residing near Ark Grove, died of meningitis on February 6; and Mrs. Annie GETSINGER, 44, residing in Fort Worth, died of pneumonia on February 13.

M. J. BROOKS and Ora PARSONS married Sunday afternoon in McGregor, Texas. Judge MIDDLETON performed the ceremony.

Marriage licenses issued by Hunt County Clerk in Greenville, Texas: J. M. NICHOLSON and Latha STRANGE, Henry REEVES and Alice HUDSON, and Thomas SMALLWOOD and Bessie GIBSON.

J. T. WATKINS and Rosa FARRISH were married by Rev. M. C. JOHNSON yesterday in Corsicana, Texas. The bride is from Cryer Creek, Texas.

Julian T. LOCKHARD, treasurer of the Central Trust Company, and Zebbie DOYLE were married in South McAlester, Indian Territory. Bishop BROOKE of Guthrie officiated.

J. Clifford HOENY and Lillian BOLLETER were married yesterday in Laredo, Texas. She was the daughter of T. J. BOLLETER, manager of the Western Union office in Laredo. He works for the *Dallas News*.

Murray HOWARD, of Valley Mills, Texas, and Nona DONAN married Sunday in Lampasas, Texas. Rev. W. T. RENFRO officiated. The marriage took place in the home of Henry YATES, the bride's stepfather.

Mrs. M. A. JOHNSON died this morning in the home of Mrs. R. Y. PRIGMORE in Fort Worth. Other survivors are Jake JOHNSON, her son, and Mrs. J. L. DEARING, her daughter. Mrs. JOHNSON was the widow of Dr. John JOHNSON and had lived in Fort Worth and Tarrant County for 20 years.

Lewis GRANTHAM, 5, died of poisoning after drinking lye at McGregor, Texas. He was the son of Mr. and Mrs. J. D. GRANTHAM.

Jonah AYERS, 60, died Saturday in his home near Ennis, Texas. He leaves a widow and a son.

Dave PILARD, 18, died of pneumonia Saturday in Ennis, Texas.

Mrs. Seymour LEMMON died Thursday in Shreveport, Louisiana. She was a former resident of Ennis, Texas. She was the daughter of Captain M. A. BELCHER.

Mrs. Nannie HOPPER died Sunday in Denison, Texas.

John WILLIAMS shot and killed John SWEAT Sunday in Lehigh, Indian Territory.

H. P. LITTLE of Fort Worth died Sunday morning of pneumonia. Rev. J. W. CALDWELL conducted the funeral.

Wednesday, February 17, 1904

Robert COOT died from an overdose of laudanum Monday in Berwyn, Indian Territory. He was a traveling salesman for Padgett Brothers in Waco, Texas.

Births recorded at the Tarrant County Clerk's office: a boy to Mr. and Mrs. John GRIFFIN, Fort Worth, on February 11.

Deaths recorded at the Tarrant County Clerk's office: Mrs. TRAVIS, 60, residing in Keller, died of dropsy on February 12; William Harney BURKE, 7, residing in Fort Worth, died of pneumonia on February 7; W.S. BENTON, 78, residing in Keller, died of the flu on February 10.

Marriage license issued at the Tarrant County Clerk's Office: H. M. CLARK and Lizzie WHITE.

Mrs. N. B. PORTER died Monday east of Albany, Texas.

Mrs. George W. TODD, 26, died at the Curtis House Monday night. Her remains were shipped to St. Louis for burial.

Mose SIMINGTON, 22, died from strychnine poisoning Sunday evening east of Temple, Texas.

Mrs. James DORRIS died in Denison, Texas yesterday.

Harry GILBERT died in El Paso Monday. He was an attorney.

The six year old daughter of Mr. and Mrs. G. A. OLIVER died Monday in Abbott, Texas. She was buried there. Her name was not reported.

Thursday, February 18, 1904

The remains of Mrs. Willie T. MANAHAN, who died in Pecos City, Texas, recently, reached Waco and were buried there yesterday. She had lived in Pecos City for 20 years, but had lived in Waco before that. Her only son, Charlie MANAHAN, survives her.

Horace GOOLSBY died of tuberculosis Wednesday in Greenville, Texas. His funeral will be today from the family home.

"Aunt Patsy" KIRBY, 86, died of old age at her home in the Grove community in Collin County, Texas. She had lived there for 60 years.

Mrs. A. J. HARRIS died of pneumonia yesterday in Belton, Texas.

Daisy CEFFERTY, an infant, died Tuesday in Ennis, Texas. She was buried there yesterday.

Mrs. Fannie CONNOR died Sunday of heart failure. She was buried yesterday in Abilene, Texas.

Captain J. W. SPARGENBURG died in DeKalb, Illinois. He was the father of Mrs. H. E. KINSLOE of Corsicana, Texas.

Joe HARRIS died on February 9 at Rio Vista in Johnson County, Texas. Mrs. S. W. REEVES, the grandmother of Joe HARRIS, died the preceding Saturday.

The funeral of C. A. LANKFORD, about 40, who died in Gainesville, Texas Monday, took place Tuesday in the Barnhart Cemetery, southwest of Gainesville. He is survived by his wife and adopted daughter.

Mrs. W. B. (or W. R.) WISE died yesterday morning of consumption at her home in Greenville, Texas.

W. H. KEMPER, formerly of Dallas, died Tuesday in Phoenix, Arizona. He was formerly associated with the Dallas firm of KEMPER and DODSON and will be buried in Dallas.

Charley WEBB, 12, died of lockjaw in Sherman, Texas yesterday.

Carl MCLYNN died in Sherman, Texas of an overdose of bromidia. He was the son-in-law of Judge D. K. BRYANT.

Ethel THOMPSON, 27, was killed in Waco, Texas. Her horse threw her.

George SHAW, 27, was killed three miles north of Valley Mills, Texas. He was struck by a train while crossing the tracks with a horse and wagon.

W. Z. WILKERSON, and Marie HUNLEY married Sunday in Lancaster, Texas. The groom is from Denison, Texas.

Lee CLAUNCH and Maude TERRY married Sunday in Noruna, Texas. Rev. B.E. HIGGINS officiated.

B. S. DOTY and Mary E. LOSEY married Tuesday in Graham, Texas. Rev. E. V. COX officiated.

Harry M. HEFFNER and Daisy HILLGER were married yesterday morning by Rev. W. Fred GALBRAITH in Fort Worth

J. A. JOURDAN, 35, died at his Fort Worth home yesterday of pneumonia. Dr. WHITEHURST of the Methodist Church officiated at the funeral. J. A. JOURDAN was a brother of Professor W. T. JOURDAN of Wichita Falls. T. H. HOWARD of Temple is a brother of Mrs. JOURDAN.

Births recorded at the Tarrant County Clerk's office: a boy to Mr. and Mrs. J. W. JENKINS, near Kennedale, on February 15; a boy to Mr. and Mrs. C. L. LANKLORD, Fort Worth, on February 13; a boy to Mr. and Mrs. S. D. FORD, Fort Worth, on February 6; and a girl to Mr. and Mrs. F. F. MULLINS, Fort Worth, on February 17.

Deaths recorded at the Tarrant County Clerk's office: Infant of Mr. and Mrs. M. R. LOONEY died of pneumonia on February 15 with no place given; Toyra CLARK, 38, residing in Arlington, died of pneumonia on February 15; Henry Richard SMITH, 6, residing near Arlington, died of peritonitis on February 9; and Robert GREER, 31, residing in Fort Worth, died of mitral lesion on February 15.

Marriage licenses issued by Tarrant County Clerk's office: G. W. GALBREATH and Lizzie DECKER, D. M. WEATHERFORD and Miss E. BENNETT, Clarence PIERCE and Myrandy COX, and Adam MCCLARY and Mary L. OLIVER.

Ella BERRY and T. E. MCKINNEY of Fort Worth were married in the Methodist parsonage by Dr. MONK yesterday. The bride is from Itasca, Texas.

Friday, February 19, 1904

H. H. SCURLOCK and May MCMICKLE married Wednesday in Texarkana. Rev. James THOMAS joined them in matrimony.

Captain W. E. BEST, 67, died at his home in Dallas yesterday. He was born in Ireland and served as a Captain in the Union Army during the Civil War. He married Isabell OTWAY in New Orleans 37 years ago. He is survived by his wife and ten children: P. K. BEST, G. M. BEST, Robert BEST and Mrs. J. H. FLORENCE of Dallas, Edward BEST, James BEST, Zoe BEST, Willie BEST and Mrs. E. B. BROWN of Greenwood and Mrs. E. G. BROWNING of Montana.

Walter ALTENBERG, 3, died in Dallas of scalds he received when he fell into a tub of hot water. He was the son of John and Mary ALTENBERG.

Mrs. F. J. JOHNSON, 28, committed suicide near Alpha, Texas Wednesday. She had been ill for some time. Justice John WARNER of Richardson ruled the death was due to a self-inflicted pistol wound to the head.

Richard T. BEAUREGARD died at his home in San Antonio. He was a well-known rancher, having lived in Wilson County for many years. He was born in New Orleans in 1845 and was a nephew of Confederate general P. G. T. BEAUREGARD.

J. A. FAIN, Sr., 64, died Wednesday in Denton, Texas. His funeral was yesterday with burial in Gribble Springs Cemetery.

A memorial service for Frances WILLARD will be held at the Baptist Church in Hillsboro, Texas.

Sarah ELY, a member of the Otoe nation, was smothered to death by the women of the nation yesterday. They followed an old custom of smothering those thought to be dying.

A body found in burning debris ten days ago near Stroud, Oklahoma Territory was identified as that of "Sporty" WHITLOW, who had lived near Bristow, Indian Territory. Robbery may have been the motive for the killing.

Mrs. W. E. REARDON died Tuesday in Pittsburg, Texas.

Mrs. J. M. DAVIS died in Belton, Texas.

The remains of Mrs. MARION, who died last Tuesday, were buried in the family burying ground near Dye school house Wednesday. The story was datelined in Gainesville, Texas.

D. J. CARLETON, 65, of Clinton, Iowa, died at the home of his son-in-law, H. W. DEAN, yesterday in Gainesville, Texas. The funeral was today. He was a Mason.

Charlie RICHARDS, a farmer living near Garrett, Texas, died yesterday. Burial was in Myrtle Cemetery in Ennis, Texas.

"Uncle Johnnie" BISHOP died Wednesday near Cleburne, Texas. He was the father of Charles BISHOP, Mrs. Lawrence PENNINGTON of Johnson County and Mrs. B. L. BROWN of Fort Worth

Addie STANLEY, 77, died Wednesday morning in Greenville, Texas. Her death occurred at the home of Dr. HILL, her nephew.

J. E. JANUARY, 78, former Fort Worth resident, died yesterday morning in Whitesboro, Texas. He is survived by a son, F. B. JANUARY.

Dr. I. M. FUNK, 76, died at his home in Fort Worth yesterday of blood poisoning. He is survived by his wife and two daughters, Kathy PATTERSON and Minnie BYRD.

Saturday, February 20, 1904

John B. CONRAD, 82, died in San Antonio Friday. He was a confederate veteran. He started the first furniture factory in San Antonio in 1852.

W.D. PHILLIPS and Tullie THALEN married Thursday in Greenville, Texas,. Justice Tom MCDANIEL presided.

The remains of Harry GILBERT, who died in El Paso Monday, arrived Wednesday in Duncan, Indian Territory. He was buried the same day in the city cemetery there. He was an attorney.

A. D. DENNY, who lived west of Chico, Texas, died Thursday and was buried in the Pleasant Grove Cemetery.

Mrs. Bird HUMPHREYS died Thursday in Sparta, Texas.

Mrs. Nancy NEWLIN, 62, died in Ardmore, Indian Territory Thursday night. The remains were shipped to Lamar, Missouri.

The two-year-old child of Mr. and Mrs. W. F. WOODWARD died yesterday in Denton, Texas. Burial will be today. The child's name was not given.

Mrs. Harry COCHRAN, died yesterday in Belton, Texas. She had been married less than a year.

J. K. CHRISTIAN died of cancer near Rosston, Texas. The funeral was yesterday at his home. He is survived by his wife and several grown children.

Edgar KIRBY, 9, died Thursday of bronchial pneumonia. He was the son of J. C. KIRBY of Forest Grove, Texas.

W. E. GATES died in Hedrick, Oklahoma Territory. He was buried in Cleburne, Texas. His wife survives him. She is a sister of Mrs. S. N. CLARK. He was an undertaker in Cleburne before going to Oklahoma Territory.

Elmo HOCKNEY died of pneumonia Wednesday at the residence of O. T. MATHES in Springtown, Texas.

Temp WEATHERFORD and Ernie BENNETT married in Fort Worth Thursday. They will live north of Terrell, Texas.

Willie MOODY and Gertie GRANDSTOFF married Thursday in Gainesville, Texas. Justice of the Peace PEARMAN officiated.

Mrs. Ruby KITTERMAN, 23, of Henry, South Dakota, died from exposure in a hospital in El Reno, Oklahoma Territory Thursday.

Deaths recorded at the Tarrant County Clerk's office: Mollie WALLACE, 16, residing in Fort Worth, died of Bright's disease on February 15; Gussie SUGART, 2, residing north of Grapevine, died of pneumonia on February 16; and J. A. JOURDAN, 38, residing in Fort Worth, died of pneumonia on February 16.

Births recorded at the Tarrant County Clerk's office: a boy to Mr. and Mrs. Jack BEALE, Fort Worth, on February 7; a boy to Mr. and Mrs. J. E. WEATHERBY, Fort Worth, on February 12; a girl to Mr. and Mrs. W. M. TRIMBLE, Marine, on February 11; a girl to Mr. and Mrs. D. O. HAYES, Riverside, on February 17; a boy to Mr. and Mrs. O. K. SHUMAN with no date or place listed; a girl to Mr. and Mrs. Wright DRISKELL, Grapevine, on February 15; a boy to Mr. and Mrs. E. T. WITHROW, near Grapevine, on February 5; a boy to Mr. and Mrs. A. BIDAUT, Bransford, on February 17; and a boy to Amanda HARE, Bransford, on February 8.

Marriage licenses issued at Tarrant County Clerk's office: W. L. DRISTELL and Fannie HALL.

Sunday, February 21, 1904

A daughter of Jack WASHBURN fell into an open fireplace Thursday at her home on the Clear Fork of the Trinity River in Young County. She was so badly burned that she died shortly afterward. Her name was not listed.

Eva BRITTON stabbed and killed Mamie SMITH yesterday in Beaumont, Texas.

Mrs. L. W. CLARK, 68, wife of W. F. CLARK, pastor of Clark's Chapel, died yesterday at her home in Dallas. She was a native of Georgia and a Dallas resident for 18 years.

Kid BARNETT, allegedly shot by Gus BADER last Friday, died in St. Joseph's Hospital yesterday. BADER surrendered to authorities and was released on $1250 bail.

Lem H. TRUE, 33, was killed instantly last night when a boxcar hit his shanty at the Texas and Pacific crossing on Main Street. He was a flagman for the Texas and Pacific at that crossing. Pat SHEA, a Texas and Pacific conductor, was injured in the accident.

Deaths recorded at the Tarrant County Clerk's office: Charles STORY, 2, residing in Marine, died of measles on February 16.

Births recorded at the Tarrant County Clerk's office: a boy to Mr. and Mrs. R. E. USELTON, Euless, on February 13.

Marriage licenses issued at the Tarrant County Clerk's office: J. T. SMITH and May WEATHERFORD, W. C. MCCALLUM and Annie MCKIBBEN, W. H. HOUSTON and Edna HUGHES, E. P. MOORE and Ethel BENNETT, and Charles C. CONE and Etta PRICE.

Miss Lutie SELKIRK and Jessie CHILDRESS married Monday night at Trinity Episcopal Church in Galveston, Texas. The bride is the daughter of Mr. and Mrs. William SELKIRK. The groom is the assistant engineer for the Santa Fe Railroad.

Monday, February 22, 1904

Mrs. Carrie E. SHIELDS, wife of Fred SHIELDS, committed suicide in San Antonio yesterday. In a letter to her brother A. WELL of New Orleans, she stated that death was preferable to a separation from her husband. The coupe had been married less than a year.

W. B. HIGGINS died of blood poisoning yesterday in Pittsburg, Texas. His remains were shipped to Livermore, England.

H. N. ANDERSON died Saturday at his home three miles south of Denton, Texas. He was buried in Argyle Cemetery. He was a farmer and had been a ship's carpenter.

C. H. HOWARD, 21, died of pneumonia Saturday. He lived in the Melissa community near McKinney, Texas.

Mrs. J. M. DAVIS of Superior, Wisconsin, died in Belton, Texas. She was visiting her parents.

Mrs. Harry T. COCHRAN died in Belton, Texas. Her funeral will be Tuesday. She was the daughter of Mr. and Mrs. Walton G. BARTLETT and had been married only 11 months.

J. T. JOHNSON, 53, died at his home south of Waxahachie, Texas yesterday.

Jeff OWENS, 16, died near Ennis, Texas Saturday. The cause of death was congestion of the brain.

Kelly KENDALL died at Toyah, Texas Saturday. His body will be shipped to Abilene, Texas.

J. F. JONES, 58, died Saturday in Ardmore, Indian Territory. He was the father of A. F. JONES, a grocer.

Mrs. W. H. ALLEN died in Honey Grove, Texas Thursday of consumption. She leaves a husband and three small children.

Mrs. Will BLAIR died at her home south of Honey Grove, Texas. She was buried Saturday at McGraw's Chapel.

R. G. BAKER died at the home of Willie BAKER, his brother, south of Gainesville, Texas. The cause of death was pneumonia. He leaves three small children. His wife died three weeks ago.

Joe L. CHANDLER and Julia Mae LANGLEY married in Denton County, Texas Thursday night. Rev. L.G. WHITE officiated. The couple will live in Krum, Texas.

Lee WILLIE and Bettie PERKINS married Wednesday night in Denton, Texas.

May WEATHERFORD and J. T. SMITH were married by Rev. J. D. YOUNG in Glenwood, Texas Sunday. She is the daughter of A. W. WEATHERFORD. He is associated with McNatt and Co., a cotton firm. The couple will live in Grand Prairie, Texas.

Tuesday, February 23, 1904

Ike DENTON, 35, was shot and killed by John FINLEY, 39, near Princeton, Texas yesterday. DENTON was a boarder in FINLEY's home. The two men were arguing over chickens and eggs. FINLEY shot DENTON while DENTON was chasing FINLEY with a butcher knife.

John H. BURNS died in jail at Cotulla, Texas. He fell from a bridge while drinking and sought the protection of the sheriff after his injury.

Capt. J. Ad DARBY, 74, died yesterday in West Point, Texas. He was a Civil War veteran serving in Green's Brigade.

The remains of J. H. SCOTT were sent from San Angelo, Texas to Lampasas, Texas for burial. He died in San Angelo Saturday.

J. N. WOOD died in Durwood, Indian Territory of pneumonia. He was buried there yesterday.

George ALEXANDER died suddenly Saturday in the Parlar Saloon in San Angelo, Texas. He was employed there.

Mrs. T. M. BLAKEMOORE died Sunday at her home near Caps, Texas.

Dick BRACKEN died in Abilene, Texas Sunday afternoon. He will be buried there tomorrow.

Mrs. Mary R. HARVEY, 79, died Saturday in Cooper, Texas. She was the mother of Richard HARVEY of Fort Worth and the mother-in-law of J. F. HOLMES, county judge of Delta County.

The infant daughter of Mr. and Mrs. Harry PENNEWELL died Friday night in Greenville, Texas. She will be buried Sunday there. Her name was not listed.

William T. WILSON died of tuberculosis Sunday in Abilene, Texas. He was an attorney.

J. E. TURNER, 75, died Saturday in Van Alstyne, Texas.

John WILLIAMS died yesterday in Bella, Texas.

The mother of Dr. R. S. FAIR died in Virginia after a fall. Dr. FAIR lives in Belton, Texas.

The five year old son of W. R. HOLLAND died Sunday evening at Bardwell, Texas of pneumonia and measles.

Royal FAULK, 3, died of measles at Byron, Texas.

W. A. ELLINGTON, 68, died of Bright's disease Saturday near Bristol, Texas. He was buried with Masonic honors yesterday.

The funeral of Louis Sherwood (Kid) BARRETT will take place this afternoon in Fort Worth.

The funeral of Lemuel (Lem) H. TRUE took place from the family home on Louisiana Street in Fort Worth. He was buried in Oakwood Cemetery. Rev. J. B. FRENCH conducted the services.

H. H. PUGH was acquitted of falsely swearing the age of his wife-to-be to obtain a marriage license. Mrs. PUGH, nee Maude GRIFFIN, was 14 at the time of the marriage last September 1. Her father brought the charges. Mrs. PUGH looks much older than her age.

Wednesday, February 24, 1904

Cart BROWN and Cyril HOGETT burned to death yesterday in jail fire at Mountain Valley, Indian Territory.

R. S. GARDNER died of paralysis of the heart yesterday in Palestine, Texas. He was an attorney.

N. R. HENDRICKS died Monday in Cleburne, Texas.

Eugene SPOONAMOORE died Monday in Cleburne, Texas. He was the 18 month old son of Mr. and Mrs. J. L. SPOONAMOORE.

Mrs. C. MCFARLAND died at Grandview, Texas Monday. She was the mother of Mrs. W. J. HURLEY and grandmother of Mrs. R. E. ALEXANDER and George HURLEY of Cleburne.

R. F. JONES, 70, will be buried in Walnut Grove Cemetery in Collin County today. He was a longtime resident of Collin County but moved to Haskell, Texas.

Major SEE died Sunday night at Trickham, Texas and was buried Monday by the Masons.

J. H. SCOTT, former athlete, died Saturday night in San Angelo, Texas. He was buried in Lampasas, Texas.

Mrs. R. E. YOAKUM died Monday in Ennis, Texas. She was the mother of B. F. YOAKUM.

Louis SMART and Ethel REEVES were married in Pittsburg, Texas. Rev. B. H. SIMS officiated.

Marriage licenses issued at the Hunt County Clerk's office in Greenville, Texas: R. B. CALLAHAN and Annie ONVER; Will WHITE and Delos MURRELL; J. C. COONRAD and Annie TOWNSEND; and W. G. GRASON and Millie E. UTT.

Mel HARGRAVE and Lelia SPRADLING married last Wednesday in Commerce, Texas. Rev. R. C. HICKS officiated. The couple will live in Mt. Vernon, Texas.

D. H. CONNOR and Mrs. Ida SAWYERS married in Gainesville, Texas.

S. H. WILFORD of Needles, California and Margaret E. MONTGOMERY were married in Denison, Texas. He was an electrician.

R. F. JONES, 71, died in Haskell, Texas of injuries sustained when he fell from the roof of his barn. He was sweeping snow from the roof.

Talmadge CAWTHRONE was accidentally shot and killed Monday while hunting near Huntsville, Texas.

Mrs. Paul SHEFFIELD, 17, shot and killed herself in San Augustine, Texas. She had been married three weeks.

Marriage license issued at Tarrant County Clerk's Office in Fort Worth: Pearlie REYNOLDS and Josephine CHERRY.

Births recorded at Tarrant County Clerk's office in Fort Worth: a girl to Mr. and Mrs. R. S. WANSLEY of Saginaw on February 13; a girl to Mr. and Mrs. Clarence YOUNG of Fort Worth on February 20; a boy to Mr. and Mrs. Martin GLOZE of Fort Worth on February 9; a girl to Mr. and Mrs. T. Z. LUCE of Fort Worth on February 14; a girl to Mr. and Mrs. John CLARK of Keller on February 19; a boy to J. H. SIDES of Fort Worth on February 22; and a girl to Mr. and Mrs. Walter JONES of Tarrant County on February 17.

Thursday, February 25, 1904

A. L. PRATHER killed himself yesterday after shooting J. Cullen STRINGER in Mount Vernon, Texas.

John KENNEY was killed yesterday in Woodville, Texas. He was killed by escaping steam from a Texas and New Orleans railroad locomotive.

Five members of the family of P. S. CRAWFORD died from eating poisoned bread at Cayuga, Indian Territory. Only Bert CRAWFORD survived. He didn't eat the bread.

The suit of Mrs. R.A. ERWIN against the Northern Texas Traction Company is on trial in 17th District Court. Mrs. ERWIN seeks $10,000 in damages from the death of Ruby ERWIN, 4, who was killed by a street car in North Fort Worth.

Births record at the Tarrant County Clerk's office: a boy to Mr. and Mrs. Ernest BANNER, of Fort Worth, on February 20; and a girl to Mr. and Mrs. G. R. HAYS, of Fort Worth, on February 22.

Deaths recorded at the Tarrant County Clerk's office: M. T. CULWELL, 41, residing in Fort Worth, died of cancer of the liver on February 22; and BiJone GLENN, 25, residing in Fort Worth, died of tuberculosis on February 22.

Marriage licenses issued at the Tarrant County Clerk's office: A. R. STEWART and Ellen HALE; and William HUDELSON and Mrs. G. A. BRESSLER.

Friday, February 26, 1904

W. C. ROGERS and Inez DAVENPORT married Wednesday at the home of F. J. R. DAVENPORT, the father of the bride, near Nash, Texas.

Pearl CHAMBERS, of Garden City, Texas, and Earl HARREMAN married at the home of the bride's parents. The groom is the son of Councilman HARREMAN of San Angelo, Texas.

Allen URQUHART and Mattie ROGERS married yesterday in Jefferson, Texas. Rev. W. K. JOHNSON of the Presbyterian Church officiated.

R. B. RICHARDSON and Alta ALLEN married in the county clerk's office in Denton, Texas Wednesday. The couple will live in Fort Worth.

Jim BURTON was sentenced to life in prison for the death of Charlie BUTLER at his trial in Dallas Wednesday. BUTLER was killed last December 12 in Dallas.

Dr. T. S. GALBRAITH, 62, died Wednesday night in Seymour, Indiana. He leaves a wife and three children. His brother is H. GALBRAITH of Terrell, Texas.

A meeting of the Abilene Bar Association was called to honor William T. WILSON, who died recently.

Mrs. J. P. SEVIER died Monday in Texarkana of pneumonia.

Walter HOIGWOOD, 32, died of pneumonia in Texarkana Wednesday.

M. J. HARRIS, 80 and a Confederate veteran, died at the home of his son, Capt. J. N. HARRIS, Monday in Texarkana.

Jerry BURNETT, a Denton County pioneer, died Wednesday in Denton, Texas. His funeral was yesterday with burial in the family cemetery on Denton Creek.

Mrs. Annie Laura MALKEY, wife of W. D. MALKEY, died Tuesday. She was buried in Oddfellows Cemetery in Denton, Texas. Cause of death was blood poisoning.

Albert DADNEY of Thorp Springs, Texas died yesterday. He was been accidentally shot by his brother on February 15.

"Aunt Sue" BARKER died of breast cancer at her home in Midlothian, Texas. She was the wife of Rev. Charles H. BARKER.

The funeral of Arthur L. TEMPLE took place in the home of his brother, W.C. TEMPLE, in Midlothian, Texas. Burial was in the Midlothian cemetery.

H. A. CASEY, 77, died yesterday at Belton, Texas. He was a pioneer of Belton and came to the area from Kentucky.

S. Morton ROBERTS died yesterday in Denton, Texas. The remains were shipped to Mexico, Missouri.

The two year old son of Mr. and Mrs. J. H. FLOYD died Wednesday of pneumonia in Cleburne, Texas. His name was not given.

The infant of Mr. and Mrs. Jack COFFMAN died Tuesday in Cleburne, Texas. COFFMAN was employed by the Santa Fe railroad. The baby's name was not given.

Mrs. Bud EAGER died Monday at Caps, Texas. She was buried at Border's Chapel.

The remains of S. K. KENDALL were buried Monday in Abilene, Texas,. He died Saturday in Toyah, Texas.

Mrs. W. D. STROUD died of consumption Monday in Springtown, Texas.

John SABINO, Jr., 18, died of appendicitis Wednesday in Texarkana and was buried yesterday.

Mr. A. BLAKER, a farmer living near Oscar, Texas, died yesterday of pneumonia.

Mrs. Addie LAMBRIGHT died Wednesday of pneumonia at the home of Mrs. William GLENN, her sister in McKinney, Texas.

Reuben HEDGES died at his home one mile northwest of Smithfield, Texas Monday. He was one of the oldest settlers of Tarrant Co.

Marriage licenses issued by Tarrant County Clerk yesterday: James T. PACE and Mary Magdalene GLOVER.

Deaths recorded at the Tarrant County Clerk's office yesterday: M. A. JOHNSON, 77, residing in Forth Worth died of cancer of February 16.

Births recorded at Tarrant County Clerk's office yesterday: a girl to Mr. and Mrs. William SANDERS of Marine on February 22; a girl to Mr. and Mrs. Mariano CONIGLIO of Fort Worth on February 24; a girl to Mr. and Mrs. Thomas H. HUFF of Fort Worth on February 19; a boy to Mr. and Mrs. J. T. HARNEY of Marine on February 25; and a girl to Mr. and Mrs. J. L. POINTER of Kennedale on February 20.

Jefferson A. MCANALLY died after being thrown from his horse in Fort Worth yesterday morning. His funeral took place yesterday from the home on Twelfth Street. Dr. Luther LITTLE officiated. The death of J. A. MCANALLY followed by only 25 days the death of his wife. She was not named. His death created calls for the city and county to improve the way they handle emergency victims.

Saturday, February 27, 1904

Lilly BOSLEY, wife of Will BOSLEY, was charged with accomplice to murder in the death of her husband some days ago. Will BOSLEY's body was found on the KATY track south of Dallas.

Frank W. BEACHUM, who lived in Waxahachie, Texas, died suddenly in Italy, Texas Thursday. He was buried in Waxahachie yesterday.

Judge J. L. L. MCCALL, 60, died at his home in Weatherford, Texas yesterday of flu. He was an attorney. He was survived by Judge George H. MCCALL, J. M. MCCALL and Mrs. C. C. BARTHOLD of Weatherford, Mrs. Ed ROTAN of Waco, Texas and Rev. John N. MCCALL of Cleburne, Texas . There were also three other unnamed surviving children.

Mrs. T. C. BOWEN died at the home of W. A. WHEELER, her son-in-law, in Gainesville, Texas Wednesday night. Her funeral was Thursday with burial in East Hill Cemetery. Elder John T. LAUDERDALE of St. Jo, Texas officiated.

H. H. EARP, 60, died in Wieland, Texas at the home of his son Alex EARP. Several married daughters also survived. They were not named.

Walter DAVIDSON, about 20, died three miles north of Weatherford, Texas Thursday.

Phil ADAMS, a member of the International Order of Odd Fellows from Taylor, Texas, died in Bartlett, Texas Thursday.

W.C. MOORE died near Waco, Texas yesterday. He was a pioneer of Texas. Among the survivors was Mrs. Stella OLENBUSH.

The two year-old child of Mr. and Mrs. Will KING died of pneumonia Thursday in Temple, Texas. He was not named.

R. C. FARQUHAR died in Mineral Wells, Texas Thursday. He had moved to Mineral Wells from Detroit, Michigan.

Mrs. J. R. MYRICK, John BACKE, Miss Grace BARLOW and Mrs. M. A. V. BARNETT died in Hillsboro, Texas Thursday. The first three were buried in the new cemetery in Hillsboro while the fourth was buried in Massey, Texas.

W. A. ALBERTHAL and Fannie DEVLIN were married in San Antonio Monday. They will live in San Angelo, Texas.

Dr. F. A. STEVENS, of Berwyn, Indian Territory, died in Gainesville, Texas yesterday of pneumonia.

Marriage licenses issued at the Tarrant County Clerk's office: S. D. LEWIS, aged 19 and R. F. LEWIS, aged 18.

Deaths recorded at the Tarrant County Clerk's office: Dora Elizabeth KELLY, 7 months, residing in Fort Worth, died of pneumonia on February 22.

Births recorded at the Tarrant County Clerk's Office: a boy to Mr. and Mrs. E. R. THURMAN, of Birdville, on February 25, a boy to Mr. and Mrs. S. M. FERGUSON, of Fort Worth, on February 22, and a girl to Mr. and Mrs. Walter CANNON, of Bedford, on February 13.

Roy J. LYNN settled his lawsuit against the Texas and Pacific Coal Company out of court. He accepted a payment of $5200. The suit was brought after LYNN lost a leg in a mining accident at Thurber, Texas.

Sunday, February 28, 1904

A. L. TAYLOR died in Dallas yesterday. He was a native of St. Louis and had resided in Dallas for ten years. He is survived by his wife, a sister in St. Louis and a brother, James M. TAYLOR. Burial will be in Oakland Cemetery.

Winfield WOODMANSEE, 17, died Friday after being accidentally shot by Thomas LUTTERELL at Hawley, Oklahoma Territory.

L. B. PERSON died Friday of an overdose of morphine near Nome, Texas.

Monday, February 29, 1904

R. CUNNINGHAM, 62, died Saturday after he fell from a windmill south of Terrell, Texas.

John HOVINGHORST died of cancer Saturday in Guthrie, Oklahoma Territory.

Mrs. J. D. MUCKLEROY, 47, died Saturday afternoon at the home of Mrs. Joe HARDIN, her sister, in Terrell, Texas. Other survivors include her husband, a son in Kaufman, and two brothers, J. D. GRAY and Dr. G. W. GRAY. Rev. W. E. GRAHAM officiated at the funeral. Burial was in Kaufman Cemetery.

Bishop Antoine DURIER died in Natchitoches, Louisiana. He had served as a bishop since 1883. The cause of death was paralysis.

The 18 month old baby of Mr. and Mrs. G. A. BARTELS died in Cleburne, Texas. The baby's name and date of death were omitted from the report.

Howard HIX died Saturday in Cleburne, Texas. Survivors include his wife Donaho HIX, his brother Roscoe HIX and four daughters: Mrs. Tee BROWN of Denton, Mrs. S. E. LONG of Fort Worth, Mrs. H. FRANK and Ollie HIX of Cleburne.

Z. W. DAVIDSON, 85, of Greenville, Texas, died suddenly Saturday at the home of R.L. DAVIDSON, his son. He was a Mason.

William "Uncle Billy" HUEY, 71, died at Mountain Springs in Cocke County, Texas Friday. Survivors include his wife and three grown children. They were not named.

Judge J. L. L. MCCALL was buried in Weatherford, Texas yesterday.

Colonel James F. TUCKER died at his home in Elysian Fields, Texas last Friday. He was a planter in Harrison County and had lived in the county since 1847.

Mrs. Louisa GILMORE, 80, died yesterday in Dallas. Her daughter is Mrs. W.D. KNOWLES.

Hortense MORGAN, 14, died of meningitis at Linden, Texas Saturday. She was the daughter of Mr. and Mrs. J. T. MORGAN.

Andrew ANDAY died Tuesday at his home near Caddo Mills, Texas. The cause of death was blood poisoning.

Ludwig AXE, 76, died in Dallas yesterday. He was a tailor and a native of Germany.

Solomon HOTUBBY, 101, died Saturday in Pickens County, Indian Territory.

H. T. WEATHERS, 76, died Saturday in Floyd, Texas.

Mrs. Mary DUNN, 68, died of tuberculosis Thursday at her home in the Attoga community near McKinney, Texas.

W. R. TOLAS and Mattie STASTNEY married Friday at the home of John BOTHA in Temple, Texas. Justice WARD officiated.

Paul MCCLELLAN, who died at police headquarters yesterday, boarded with Timothy MORARITY. MORARITY will bury him as MCCLELLAN had no Fort Worth relatives. He was Catholic.

March, 1904

Tuesday, March 1, 1904

Ben P. DRESSER of Texarkana was accidentally killed by a shotgun at his home yesterday.

The remains of Joe ROBERTSON, son of W. A. ROBERTSON, arrived in Denton, Texas from Abilene, Texas. He was a member of the Woodmen of the World. He was buried in Little Elm, Texas.

News of the death of W. H. TYSON in Alvarado, Texas was received at Cleburne, Texas today.

Henry B. MORRISON, a farmer, died in New Boston, Texas Sunday morning of pneumonia. He was a member of the Woodmen of the World. Survivors include his wife and four small children. They were not named.

James H. OTT, 25, died of pneumonia in Weatherford, Texas. He leaves a wife and a small child.

Mrs. Carrie BELL, sister-in-law of Bishop R. L. SELLE, died in Africa. SELLE is presiding bishop of the Methodist Episcopal Church in Fort Worth.

Professor E. W. WADE was killed in Grand Falls, Texas by Mr. KIMBERLAIN Monday. The dispute involved Professor WADE's children. His remains were returned to McColl, Mississippi. KIMBERLAIN was held without bail.

Marriage licenses issued at Cleburne, Texas: G. T. MURRAY and Lizzie REDINE; and Harry HOLLAND and Luella HOLLAND.

J. A. SMITH of Dallas and Miss Willie WELLS of Garrett, Texas were married by Rev. J. P. MAHANEY in Garrett Sunday afternoon.

Marriage licenses issued at the Hunt County Clerk's office in Greenville, Texas: J. H. WATSON and Minnie DENNIS; J. L. MCKEE and Nora MORROW; Fate REDDEN and Rachel RUSSELL; and James JONES and Emma TAVE.

Marriage licenses issued by Tarrant County Clerk: O. H. BETTES and Lizzie TIDWELL; Gregorio ORTIS and Esmeregilda VILLALON; and William SIMPSON and Nora JOHNSON.

Births recorded at Tarrant County Clerk's office: a boy to Mr. and Mrs. J. S. TRAMMEL of Tarrant County on February 20; a boy to Mr. and Mrs. James B. BAKER of Riverside on February 28; a girl to Mr. and Mrs. D. P. PINEOD of Arlington on February 19; a girl to Mr. and Mrs. James HICKERSON of Benbrook of February 22; and a girl to Mr. and Mrs. Hugh ELROD of Fort Worth on February 25.

Deaths recorded at Tarrant County Clerk's Office: Infant of J. H. TOWNSEND, residing in Fort Worth, died of measles on February 25; daughter of George PETTERS, 11, residing near Arlington, died of measles and pneumonia on February 24; and Ella HARRIS, 20, residing in North Fort Worth, died of measles and pneumonia on February 23.

R. N. MCCULLOUGH, who died at Childress, Texas last Sunday, will be buried from the home of Mrs. A. B. MILLER, the mother-in-law of the deceased in Fort Worth tomorrow.

Wednesday, March 2, 1904

Ed TATE, 20, a KATY brakeman, was killed at Hills Prairie, Texas when he was hit by a freight train yesterday. He was the son of Tom TATE, engineer on the Katy tap to Belton. Burial was in Smithville.

Mary GILMORE was sentenced to two years in prison for manslaughter in the death of Hanna SMITH last fall. The trial took place in Sherman, Texas.

W. H. GOODWIN committed suicide in Laredo, Texas yesterday. He shot himself through the heart.

Sturino GARZA died of the injuries he received when he fell from a freight train near Pettus, Texas Sunday.

At Ponca City, Indian Territory, Mrs. James OWENS was shot and killed by James ATCHESON as a result of jealousy. The date was not listed.

Tony BOONE died from gunshot wounds received in a saloon fight in Ponca City, Indian Territory Saturday night.

George Lewis RUNGE, 23, died of Bright's disease in Fort Worth yesterday. He will be buried in Austin. His parents are Mr. and Mrs. Julius RUNGE of Galveston. Young RUNGE worked for Armour and Company in Fort Worth.

Thursday, March 3, 1904

Ed DUNBAR of Liberty, Texas was killed by a Southern Pacific train on the edge of Houston. No date was listed.

George F. PIERSON, 44, well-known area newspaperman, died at the home of Mrs. G. W. MAGRUDER in Fort Worth yesterday.

A. T. BROWN died yesterday in Fort Worth. The cause of death was a tumor of the stomach. He was born in Murfreesboro, Tennessee, in 1823 and lived in Decatur, Texas before coming to Fort Worth.

Marriage licenses issued by the Tarrant County Clerk's office: Patrick BLUNT and Zola WARRICK; and T. J. BRIM and Mary CONWAY.

R. H. STANDLEY died of pneumonia yesterday at his home in Fort Worth. He was a resident of Fort Worth since 1875 and was a furniture merchant. His funeral will be at the First Baptist Church with Dr. Luther LITTLE officiating.

Friday, March 4, 1904

Mrs. Harriett RECTOR, 68, widow of Judge Nelson RECTOR, died in Austin yesterday from heart failure.

Mrs. E. F. COMEGYS is dead. Her remains were sent to Gainesville, Texas for burial.

W. P. PERRY died at his home near Pope, Texas. He was an early settler of Lavaca County.

Walter L. WESTBROOK, the eldest son of J. W. WESTBROOK, died at his father's home near McDade, Texas Wednesday. He was buried yesterday.

The mother of W. P. CRAWFORD died. Her remains were sent to Denton, Texas for burial in the Flower Mound Cemetery. She was the wife of John CRAWFORD, a farmer.

Marriage licenses issued at the Tarrant County Clerk's Office: H. M. RUSSELL and Lulu SPAIN; A. L. MORRIS and Mrs. Ida COLLISTER; and H. E. WOLFORD and Mrs. Olive RAY.

Saturday, March 5, 1904

W. R. MILLER died fighting a prairie fire 9 miles northwest of Lawton, Oklahoma Territory Wednesday night.

Dr. HARMON died in a prairie fire near Lawton, Oklahoma Territory. He was a brother of John HARMON.

John BRANDON shot and killed Jow SHELTON at the BRANDON home south of Alvarado, Texas Friday night. BRANDON surrendered to authorities, telling them SHELTON came to his home, drew a gun and BRANDON was forced to kill him in self defense.

W. D. DIGGS shot and killed Tom ABERNATHY in a Dallas saloon Friday night. DIGGS was jailed for murder. The shooting happened during a quarrel between the two men.

Charles ADLER, 44, died several days ago in the Dallas City Hospital and was buried yesterday in the Hebrew cemetery. He was the son of L. ADLER, a New York City diamond and jewelry dealer.

Bettie CLAY, 66, mother of L. H. CLAY, died Thursday in Temple, Texas of paralysis.

Ethel ALEXANDER, 28, died at her home twelve miles south of Mineral Wells, Texas last Monday.

Annie HARVEY, of Acton, Texas, died March 2 and was buried Wednesday. She was a teacher in the Cresson, Texas schools.

Jeff MILFORD, 86, died at his house near Fairlie, Texas Monday. His daughter, Mrs. James MILFORD, died on an adjoining farm hours later.

Mrs. J.H. GREER died near Mineola, Texas Wednesday. She leaves a husband and three children. Burial was in Otter Lake Cemetery.

E. POPE, 65, died suddenly Thursday at his home in McKinney, Texas.

John D. BLAIR died of pneumonia on his farm three miles east of Springtown, Texas. He was a veteran of the Mexican and Civil Wars. He was born in Missouri in 1827 and came to Texas in 1837. He fought for the Confederacy in the Civil War.

The two year old son of Mr. and Mrs. Herbert BUCK died in Asher, Oklahoma Territory, and was buried in the Pecan Grove cemetery yesterday.

J. E. TERRY was found not guilty of the murder of Lawrence BATT in Marshall, Texas yesterday. BATT was killed while watching a street brawl between TERRY and E. BELL. He was struck by a shot fired by TERRY.

G. W. ROBERSON, 65, died from pneumonia Wednesday at the home of his son-in-law, Robert JOHNSON, in Greenville, Texas. He was buried in Clinton, Texas.

Gerard E. MATTHES and Mary M. EWICK were married in Lawton, Oklahoma Territory Thursday. Dr. CALVIN of the Presbyterian Church officiated.

A. J. NAVE, 79, died in Columbus, Texas Thursday. His funeral was held yesterday. Rev. W. D. WENDELL conducted. NAVE was a veteran of the Mexican War and invented the breech-loading cannon during the Civil War.

C. E. MOORE and S. E. GARRISON married in McKinney, Texas Thursday.

E. J. WILSON of Garland, Arkansas and Laura L. SAUNDERS of Leigh, Texas were married at the home of her parents Thursday. Rev. J. B. K. SPAIN officiated.

Births recorded at the Tarrant County Clerk's office: a girl to Mr. and Mrs. Rubie WALLACE, of Fort Worth, on February 23; a boy to Mr. and Mrs. W. H. FREEMAN, of Riverside, on February 27; a girl to Mr. and Mrs. Will MAYES, Jr., of near Mansfield, on February 27 and a boy to Mr. and Mrs. Guy PEYTON, of Fort Worth, on February 26.

Deaths recorded at the Tarrant County Clerk's office: Don BLIZZARD, 18, residing near Mansfield, died of pneumonia with no date given; George HENDERSON, 14, residing in Tarrant County, died of pneumonia with no date given; Vanna May GRACE, 2, residing in North Fort Worth, died of pneumonia, with no date given; and Grace FULLER, 29 days, residing in Euless, died of pneumonia with no date given.

Marriage licenses issued by Tarrant County Clerk's office: James A. BELYAN and Norine B. MCKEE; and J. W. GRIDER and Addie HUGO.

Sunday, March 6, 1904

Henderson SMITH killed his wife and then himself in Ottine, Texas yesterday.

Mrs. J. W. WILEY, 59, mother of Mrs. J. T. ESTELL of Fredericksburg, Texas, died in Kingsland, Texas Friday night. She leaves her husband, one son and three other daughters.

Tom ABERNATHY, who was recently killed by W. D. DIGGS, was a nephew of Boyd ABERNATHY of the Texas state legislature.

Bill M. SELBY died near Record Crossing of pneumonia. He was the engineer for the city waterworks. No state or territorial location could be determined.

Nelli SMITH, 20, died at her Dallas home yesterday. She overdosed on morphine.

Capt C. M. WRIGLEY died in Tishomingo, Indian Territory yesterday of an overdose of medicine. He was an attorney and a veteran of the Spanish-American War.

Mrs. Perry JONES died at Edgewood, Texas Friday.

Mrs. M.E. ANDERSON, 54, wife of the Rev A. C. ANDERSON, died at her home near Center Point, Texas. Burial was in Bethel Cemetery.

J.R. DAVIS, 66, died at his home in Springtown, Texas of Bright's disease. No date was given.

J. E. DRIVER died Thursday in McGregor, Texas. He leaves a wife but no children. He was the proprietor of the King Hotel in McGregor and a cotton buyer.

The remains of Mrs. E. F. COMEGY were brought to San Angelo, Texas and then sent to Gainesville, Texas. She died in Ozona, Texas several days ago.

Jesse KENAME died in San Angelo, Texas and was buried in the local cemetery. No date was given.

Mrs. E.W. JOHNSON died yesterday in Graham, Texas.

The body of Mrs. Kate SCHIDEL was brought to Cleburne, Texas from St. Louis, Missouri. She was the daughter of Mr. and Mrs. W. N. SMITH of Cleburne.

James MITCHELL, 40, died in San Antonio yesterday. He was a noted horseman who toured with Buffalo Bill.

W. S. JAY and Loula KENNELY of Holland were married Friday in Belton, Texas by County Judge G. M. FELTS.

Ben PEEVY and Kate KIRK were married in Abilene, Texas Wednesday. The bride was the daughter of Mr. and Mrs. Frank KIRK.

N.W. STANFORD of Greenville, Illinois, and Mattie STEVENS were married in Greenville, Texas Thursday. Rev. Lee MILLER officiated.

M. F. DAY and Catherine RODGERS married Wednesday at the home of Rev. William SPROLUE in Texarkana.

Mrs. Fannie A. CONLEY, 47, died Friday in San Antonio. She was the wife of James H. CONLEY and the sister of Judge Charles M. BARNES. She was the daughter of Dr. Frances BARNES of New Orleans. Survivors include two sons and a daughter.

R. M. SMALL, editor of the *Mabank Courier*, died in Tyler, Texas at the home of Judge James FITZGERALD. He was a Confederate veteran. Burial was in Palestine, Texas.

James Matthew HAMILTON died yesterday in Fort Worth. He was about 32. He was a musician playing piano at the Crown Theater in Fort Worth.

Marriage licenses issued by the Tarrant County Clerk's office: R. H. L. LEATHERWOOD and Florence GRAVES; W. L. ROBINSON and Annie GERTH; Sowell SLACK and Maud Cornelia OSBORN; James F. WALTERS and Lillie P. HARMON; and R. E. PERRY and Mabel COY.

Deaths recorded by the Tarrant County Clerk: Mrs. J. B. SANDERS, 40, residing in Marine, died of pneumonia on March 4; Mrs. PAGE, 40, residing in Fort Worth, died of pneumonia on February 16; Mrs. Theodore BAKASKY, 32, residing in Fort Worth, died of consumption on March 1.

Births recorded at the Tarrant County Clerk's office: a boy to Mr. and Mrs. W. S. NASH of Rendon on February 27; a girl to Mr. and Mrs. J. W. ECHALIS of Rendon on March 3; a girl to Mr. and Mrs. Joseph GIRTLEY of Fort Worth on March 5; and a boy and a girl (twins) to Mr. and Mrs. Joseph HOLLAND of Glenwood on March 4.

Miss R. TEMPLE, 18, a student at Fort Worth University, died Monday of pneumonia. Her remains were sent to Enid, Indian Territory for burial.

The funeral of DeWitt Talmadge FOWLER, 10 months, was held yesterday from the family home in Fort Worth. He was the son of Mr. and Mrs. R. J. FOWLER.

A. W. HOFFMAN, 72, died yesterday in Fort Worth.

Monday, March 7, 1904

Mrs. G. C. GRASTY, 45, died at her home in Dallas yesterday.

William KUSO, a pioneer of New Braunfels, Texas, is dead. No other information appeared in the article.

The funeral of Mrs. Harriett G. RECTOR took place in Austin yesterday.

John SMITH died in Pittsburg, Texas of a paralytic stroke.

Barney SHERRILL, 10, died in Greenville, Texas Saturday. He was the son of G. W. SHERRILL.

Mrs. Addie MCLELLAN died in Belton, Texas Saturday and was buried in the North Belton Cemetery yesterday.

Green SHRUM, 14, died Thursday near Mineral Wells, Texas. He died of hydrophobia caused by the bite of a rabid skunk.

Lonnie CROWS, 19, died near Ennis, Texas yesterday of pneumonia.

William STARLING died of pneumonia Saturday near Grapevine, Texas. Rev. MORPHUS of Grapevine preached the funeral. He was a student at Denton State Normal school. His father, J. R. STARLING, died of pneumonia last week.

Jesse L. MURRAY, 92, died in Charlottesville, Virginia. He was the father of Mrs. Albert MAVERICK and Mrs. J. L. SLAYDEN of San Antonio.

D. C. BAKER died at Keene, Texas Saturday. The funeral was yesterday under the auspices of the International Order of Odd Fellows.

The funeral of Mrs. Kate T. SCHMIDEL of Cleburne, Texas took place at the home of her parents, Mr. and Mrs. W. N. SMITH, in Cleburne.

Former Cleburne, Texas resident Mrs. Mamie LINES died in Santa Fe, New Mexico Territory February 19. She was a sister of Richard KING of Gainesville, Texas.

Horace G. MARSHALL died yesterday in Sherman, Texas . He died in a hydrophobic convulsion due to the bite of a large dog three weeks ago.

P. B. ROBERTS, a farmer living near Boyce, Texas died Saturday. His remains were brought to Waxahachie, Texas for burial. He was a member of the Woodmen of the World.

Tuesday, March 8, 1904

Marriage licenses issued at the Tarrant County Clerk's office: C. TROMPE and Miss L. HANKENS; and Charles CRABTREE and Mrs. Emma THOMPSON.

Births recorded at the Tarrant County Clerk's office: a boy to Mr. and Mrs. William CHIDESTER of Tarrant County on February 28; a girl to Mr. and Mrs. Charles BRAYULL of Fort Worth on March 6; a girl to Mr. and Mrs. H. B. BARR of Fort Worth on March 1; a girl to Mr. and Mrs. Walter EDWARDS of Tarrant County on February 2; and a boy to Mr. and Mrs. John BUFFINGTON of Bedford on February 27.

Deaths recorded at the Tarrant County Clerk's office: D. BAKER, 37, residing in Fort Worth, died of pneumonia on March 5; Judy Ann TRUE, 72, residing in Kennedale, died of dropsy on February 27.

The burial of Col. Richard Henry SMALL was held Sunday in Palestine, Texas. SMALL died Saturday at the home of his son-in-law, Judge J. W. FITZGERALD, in Tyler, Texas. He was the editor of the *Mabank Courier*. Col. SMALL was born at Fort Sam Houston near Palestine, Texas on August 12, 1841. He was a member of J. P. DOUGLASS's battery during the Civil War. He left a wife and three daughters.

The death warrant for Bosier SMITH, convicted of killing his wife, was issued yesterday. SMITH will be executed in Waxahachie, Texas on March 25.

Clarence WHITE died yesterday in Longview, Texas.

The funeral of Will STARLING in Flower Mound was well attended. STARLING was a student at North Texas State Normal School and editor of the *State Normal Journal*. He died Saturday of pneumonia.

M. P. CURRIE died at the home of Mrs. A. L. LINDSEY, his sister, in Jonesville, Texas. Burial was in the family burial ground at Concord Church.

Lois LACY, 7, daughter of Don LACY, was fatally burned while playing with matches at her home. She was blind. Don LACY is cashier of City National Bank in Ardmore, Indian Territory.

Harry COLLIGAN, 87 and John MCDONALD, 75, died Sunday in the Confederate home in Austin, Texas. Both were natives of Missouri.

Wednesday, March 9, 1904

The paper for this date did not appear on the microfilm.

Thursday, March 10, 1904

Laura SWINDELLS married Harry M. FISCHER in St. Louis, Missouri, last Monday. She was the daughter of Mrs. M. H. SWINDELLS and the late J. W. SWINDELLS. J. W. SWINDELLS served as the Texas State printer at one time and was part owner of the *Dallas Herald*.

The funeral of Frank REEVES took place yesterday in Dallas. Burial was in Greenwood Cemetery. He was the son of Reuben REEVES, a former Supreme Court of Texas justice and the brother-in-law of Jeff WARD.

The funeral of Tom B. WILLIAMS, who died Tuesday, was held yesterday in Ardmore, Indian Territory. He was a Mason and a member of the Knights of Pythias.

Gladys MILAM, 8, died yesterday in Fort Worth. She was the daughter of Dr. and Mrs. Y. M. MILAM. Burial was in Lake Charles, Louisiana.

Elizabeth ZEEK and Frank LETCHER were married by Probate Judge GOODRICH in Guthrie, Oklahoma Territory yesterday.

Births recorded at the Tarrant County Clerk's office: a girl to Mr. and Mrs. R. C. HERRING of Fort Worth on March 8; a girl to Mr. and Mrs. Will IRWIN of Fort Worth on March 3; a boy to Mr. and Mrs. A. G. HILL of Fort Worth on March 6; a girl to Mr. and Mrs. J. C. BRACKER of Dove on March 4; a boy to Mr. and Mrs. James W. NORRIS of near Euless on February 22; a boy and a girl (twins) to Mr. and Mrs. William MCCORRELL of Dove on February 24; a girl to Mr. and Mrs. John H. COOK of near Grapevine on February 23; a girl to Mr. and Mrs. Thomas J. SUTTON of Grapevine on February 18; a girl to Mr. and Mrs. S. W. WILSON of Fort Worth on February 26; a boy to Mr. and Mrs. Earl YATES on February 20 and a girl to Mr. and Mrs. George HORTON of Tarrant County on March 2.

Deaths recorded at the Tarrant County Clerk's office: Fannie MARSHALL, 68, residing in Fort Worth, died of Bright's Disease on March 6; William Mack ROGERS, 87, residing near Grapevine, died of old age on February 18; Uriah P. MARTIN, 72, residing near Grapevine, died of asthma with no date listed; and Walter M. STEPHENSON, 33, residing near Enon, died of pneumonia on March 4.

Friday, March 11, 1904

Sarah MORROW died suddenly of a heart attack at her home in Ennis, Texas yesterday.

Mrs. Penelope E. ALEXANDER, 71, died in Dallas Wednesday. She was a resident of Los Angeles but was in Dallas visiting her sons, J. P. ALEXANDER and W. M. ALEXANDER.

J. G. CASH, of Goliad, Texas, and Nellie RICE, of Alice, Texas, were married at the Magnolia Hotel in Fort Worth Monday. Justice R. H. GILLETT officiated. They will live in Alice.

Saturday, March 12, 1904

C. C. PARKER, the son of Mr. and Mrs. J. H. PARKER, and Maud OWNSBY, the daughter of Mr. and Mrs. William OWNSBY, were married in Gainesville, Texas Wednesday. Rev. EVENS, pastor of the Denton Street M.E. Church officiated. The wedding took place in the parsonage.

James Woodson STNUM (sic) and Maud Hollenback TWEED were married in Gainesville, Texas Thursday. Rev. PIERCE officiated at the home of the bride.

Perry TOWNSEND and Marie WILLIAMS married Thursday in Temple, Texas. Justice John L. WARD officiated.

Mrs. R. G. GRAGG, 53, died of typhoid in San Angelo, Texas Thursday.

M. B. BROADUS died yesterday in Belton, Texas.

Myrtle SHORT died recently at Marystown, near Cleburne, Texas.

John H. SMITH died in Cleburne, Texas Thursday. He belonged to the Pat Cleburne Camp, U.C.V.

Thomas NEAL, 48, died at his home in Commerce, Texas Thursday of pneumonia. He is survived by his wife and seven children.

The five month old son of Mr. and Mrs. C.G. BOWEN died in Ennis, Texas yesterday. His name was not given.

Mrs. Belle GREENE died at her home in North Marshall, Texas Wednesday. The funeral was from the Christian Church Thursday.

The six month old child of Mr. and Mrs. Fred STILLING died March 8 of cerebral meningitis near San Angelo, Texas. The infant's name was not listed.

Manuel RAGLAND was found guilty of murdering William RICHARDSON near Waskom, Texas and sentenced to 25 years in prison. The trial took place in Marshall, Texas.

James H. COLE died yesterday in Durant, Indian Territory. His remains were sent to Ladonia, Texas for burial.

Mrs. M. WELLS. 60, was killed in Brookshire, Texas when she was accidentally shot by a grandson. He fired a .22 rifle at her and didn't know it was loaded. Survivors include her husband, four daughter and several grandchildren.

Births recorded at the Tarrant County Clerk's office: a boy to Mr. and Mrs. William MCGILL of near Azle on February 24; and a boy to Mr. and Mrs. John MATHIN of Fort Worth on March 9.

Deaths recorded at the Tarrant County Clerk's office: James MCDUNAWAY, 2, residing near Mansfield, died of inflammation of the stomach on March 7; and Gertrude WILLIAMS, 28, died of pneumonia on March 9. There was no residence listing for Gertrude WILLIAMS.

Sunday, March 13, 1904

Henry MCNAMARA, merchant and postmaster at Leesville, Texas committed suicide yesterday. He was about 40 years old, married and despondent about ill health.

A. J. GRANT died suddenly in Graham, Texas Friday while serving on a grand jury.

A. C. COX, about 53, was found dead behind a saloon in Dallas yesterday. The cause of death was unknown.

Sarah Ann Carter YOUNG died at her home 12 miles west of Fort Worth. She came to Tarrant County in 1856. Survivors include a son, F. M. YOUNG, and a daughter, Mrs. J. P. SMITH.

Mrs. G. F. SIKES died of heart failure at Beeville, Texas yesterday.

The funeral for the infant son of Mr. and Mrs. Ed LUSTER was held Friday in Gainesville, Texas. The baby died Thursday in Gainesville from congestion.

Mrs. Debora Ann NEEDHAM, 75, died of pneumonia near Joshua, Texas Thursday and was buried in Kaddo Grove Cemetery Friday.

Dora CRAIG, 15, died of pneumonia and was buried Thursday. Her sister, Flora, 20, died the following day. They were daughters of Mr. and Mrs. T.H. CRAIG.

Mrs. J. H. CONDOR, 51, died Friday at her home in Greenville, Texas of consumption. Her husband and three children survive.

Mrs. Lulu GORDON died Thursday at her home near Cash, Texas. Her husband and four children survive.

Mrs. J. C. BAILEY, of Pittsburg, Texas, died in San Antonio Friday. Burial was in Pittsburg.

Mrs. Laurena C. BLACK, formerly Mrs. John Frank MARTIN, died in the home of her brother, the Hon. T. F. TEMPLE, in Weatherford, Texas Friday. Mrs. BLACK will be buried in Cleburne, Texas. She had lived in Glen Rose, Texas with her mother.

The wife of G. W. ERICKSON died in Cleburne, Texas Friday.

The remains of Captain Eugene HERNANDEZ were buried in San Antonio yesterday. He was a veteran of the Spanish-American war and the leader of the San Antonio Zouaves.

Monday, March 14, 1904

Mrs. A. J. COUTRET died in Temple, Texas Saturday. Her husband was a druggist.

Frank FORE, 50, died Sunday night in Dallas. He was shot Thursday night by James B. MILLER at the Delaware Hotel. His remains were sent to Duncan, Indian Territory for the funeral. He was a former US Marshall in Duncan.

H. C. MCNEMAR, the postmaster at Leesville, Texas, shot himself through the heart with a shotgun Saturday morning. He was in ill health

W. J. WHITLEY, a farmer living six miles north of Rogers, Texas, drank carbolic acid and died Saturday.

Tuesday, March 15, 1904

Lish BRADFORD, convicted in 1900 for the June 14, 1899, murder of John EVANS, is being retried on appeal in Ardmore, Indian Territory. His earlier conviction was overturned.

The remains of A. S. COX were shipped to his home in McKinney, Texas. COX was found dead on the street near a saloon on Jackson Street in Dallas Saturday. Mr. COX leaves a wife, three daughters and a son. A. J. MEDLIN, a relative, took charge of the remains. An autopsy was performed to find the cause of death. The results were not available.

The family of W. I. YOPP received word that Dr. W. T. YOPP, the father of W. I. YOPP, had died in Middleton, Tennessee.

Luther MOORE, son of G. W. MOORE, was killed when he was struck by a rock held by his friend Ottie SMITH, son of R. F. SMITH. The boys were throwing rocks at a covey of quail when the accident occurred. MOORE lived ten miles south of Graham, Texas. No charges were filed.

J. R. MESTLER, 86, died in Corpus Christi, Texas Saturday. He was a gunsmith who invented the Sharpe's Rifle, but was never paid.

Mrs. John W. GOODWIN, who died in Dallas Saturday, was buried in Ennis, Texas Sunday. Her husband couldn't attend the funeral due to a broken leg suffered in Dallas a few days earlier.

Mrs. William KILNER shot John WALKER in Cisco, Texas yesterday. WALKER killed William KLINER about a year ago.

Marriage licenses issued by the Johnson County Clerk in Cleburne, Texas: Winston TIPTON and Willie MORTON; Scott CROSBY and Mary MCCLURE; G. W. FULTON and Mary DODSON; M. G. LEATHERWOOD and Cora SANDERS.

Mrs. H.G. HENDRICK, 49, died yesterday in Rogers, Texas. She leaves a husband and six children.

Girlie BYNUM, 9, died Saturday of complications from typhoid fever. She was a daughter of Louise BYNUM. Her funeral was Sunday with burial in city cemetery (presumably Fort Worth).

John CHENNEVILLE died in Austin Sunday at his home. He was a fireman and had been a policeman. He left a wife and one son.

S.B. KIRKHAM died in Cleburne, Texas Sunday from paralysis.

John BRADFORD and Annie MURPHY married at Killeen, Texas Sunday.

Hubbard THOMPSON and Mrs. William CHARLEWOOD, of Troupe, Texas, married at the home of E. F. THOMPSON, east of Thoupe. Rev C. C. SHUTTLESWORTH officiated.

Marriage licenses issued by the Hunt County Clerk in Greenville, Texas: W. G. MCFARLAND and Bettie STRICKLAND; D. H. WILSON and Katie ROSIE; W. M. TAYLOR and Rosa B. WILLIAMS; and Albert MAYHALL and Lena PAYNE.

Lucian RUFF, of St. Louis, Missouri, received a divorce from his wife, the daughter of Thomas CRAIG of Paris, Texas. Her name was not listed.

Mrs. Emma SHAW, 23, died at her home south of Fort Worth yesterday. There were no surviving children. She had been married to W. J. SHAW for three years.

Amanda RANDOLPH, widow of H. K. RANDOLPH, died yesterday in Fort Worth. Dr. Barton B. RAMAGE will conduct the funeral. Burial will be in city cemetery in Fort Worth.

Lee DAVIS, 5, died Sunday at his home in North Fort Worth. He was the son of Andrew DAVIS.

The body of Sarah I. KNUCKOLLS, 63, who died last Sunday, was buried in Oakwood Cemetery in Fort Worth yesterday .

Wednesday, March 16, 1904

Palo D. ROBERTS and Mary COBB, both of Atoka, Indian Territory, were married in Dallas Tuesday. Rev. M. M. DAVIS of Central Christian Church officiated.

Mrs. A. J. ROGERS died in New York City. She was about 40 and from New Orleans, Louisiana. She had been married for about a year and a half. She was on a buying trip to New York City with her husband, a Dallas merchant.

Mrs. Lavonia N. WALKER, 58, died in Dallas yesterday. She was the widow of H. N. WALKER and the mother of George N. WALKER and Mrs. Bettie B. MAXWELL. She was a native of Alabama.

Births recorded at the Tarrant County Clerk's office: a girl to Mr. and Mrs. T. E. WHITE of Fort Worth on February 24; a girl to Mr. and Mrs. M. L. PARRISH of near Kennedale on March 12; a boy to Mr. and Mrs. R. MOSES of North Fort Worth on December 20; a boy to Mr. and Mrs. H. C. BENNETT of North Fort Worth on January 1; a girl to Mr. and Mrs. Lewis MACKEY of Fort Worth on March 12; a girl to Mr. and Mrs. John DALTON of Johnson Station on February 29; a boy to Mr. and Mrs. C. C. MADDEN of Fort Worth on March 6; a boy to Mr. and Mrs. Lee ANDERSON of Fort Worth on February 28; a boy to Mr. and Mrs. Walter MARTIN of Fort Worth on February 29; a girl to Mr. and Mrs. Tom BAYS of Fort Worth on March 12; a boy to Mr. and Mrs. D.H. HOCKETT of Azle on March 11 and a girl to Mr. and Mrs. Oscar HACKNEY of near Bedford on March 12.

Deaths recorded at the Tarrant County Clerk's office: Vossie GLOVER, 17, residing in Fort Worth, died of indigestion with no date listed; Albert WASHINGTON, 14, residing in Saginaw, accidentally killed on March 14; Charles TUROL, 44, residing in Fort Worth, died of pneumonia with no date listed; Norton HAMMOCK, 3, residing in Fort Worth, died of measles with no date listed; D. Frank FORE, 44, no residence listed, died of gunshot wound with no date listed; Matilda HARRIS, 69, residing in Mansfield, died of gastritis with no date listed; Amie CAPPS, 11 months, residing in Mansfield, died of pneumonia with no date listed; and Frank REED, 25, residing in Arlington, died of pneumonia with no date listed.

Lucy SHERRILL, 16, died from burns Friday neat Toto, Texas. She was the daughter of Mr. and Mrs. L. D. SHERRILL.

Oscar JONES shot and killed Albert CONLEY, his father-in-law, Monday at Texarkana. Both men had been drinking.

Mrs. S. N. FIELDS, 46, died in a fire at her home in San Antonio's West End.

Manson LEE was shot to death by Henry YEAWOOD in Austin yesterday.

Frank SCHOVER was accidentally killed in Galveston, Texas yesterday. He was a gunsmith. A parlor rifle, triggered by a pet dog, discharged and killed SCHOVER.

Fannie AMYX died Monday in Slidell, Texas and was buried in the Bolivar Cemetery.

Laura GRANT, 2, died in Denton, Texas yesterday. The funeral was in the same afternoon and burial in Oddfellows Cemetery. She was the daughter of Mr. and Mrs. A. GRANT.

Jesse Leroy SIMMONS, 15, died yesterday in Denton, Texas. The funeral was conducted by Rev. T.A. MORRIS with burial in Oddfellows Cemetery.

Henry WADLEY of Graham, Texas died Monday of cancer. He was about 62 and had formerly lived in Weatherford, Texas.

Dr. W. F. CONTES died Sunday in Wills Point, Texas. He was a Mason. Burial under the auspices of the Masons was Monday.

R. L. MCLAUGHLIN was found dead in the Newcomb settlement 12 miles east of Albany, Texas Tuesday. The cause of death was unknown. An inquest was performed by Justice of the Peace T. V. BAKER, Dr. H. L. WILDER and Deputy Sheriff W. E. WILLIAMS. MCLAUGHLIN was a Confederate veteran. He had moved to the Albany area three years ago from Hopkins County, Texas. No verdict of the inquest was reported.

Georgia NICHOLS died ten miles north of Cleburne, Texas yesterday. She was the step-daughter of Tom LOFTIN and the granddaughter of W. G. GARRETT.

Dr. Daniel MOORE, physician at the coal mines, died Monday in Laredo, Texas. He was buried there yesterday.

George COLEMAN died at his home in Kerrville, Texas Monday. He was a member of the Knights of Pythias.

Henry WEIL, 70, died at his home near New Braunfels, Texas Monday and was buried yesterday there. He was one of the oldest settlers in the area and a veteran of the Civil War.

C. M. HARRISON, 66, died at Uvalde, Texas yesterday. He was a former principal of a reformatory in Newark, New Jersey, and a former editor of a newspaper there. Survivors include his wife and three sons.

W. M. TAYLOR and Mrs. Rosa B. WILLIAMS married in Greenville, Texas Sunday. Rev. J. R. WAGES officiated.

J. M. MCCULLOM and Nellie E. CATES were married at the home of the bride's father northwest of McKinney, Texas. No date was listed.

James COX was arrested in St. Louis, Missouri and charged with murder for a crime that took place in Denton, Texas in 1883.

Ella SIMS was shot and killed by Bob SCOTT, a 13 year old boy in Palestine, Texas.

Thursday, March 17, 1904

Major J. SCOTT, 40, of Texarkana, was found dead of multiple pistol wounds. His wife was not able to be found.

James BRAZIL died of measles in Corsicana, Texas Tuesday. He was an employee of the City of Corsicana in the street department.

August CRANZ, 50, and father of two, married Mrs. L. SHUMAKER, 40, in Dallas Tuesday. Justice of the Peace W. M. EDWARDS performed the ceremony. CRANZ advertised in the *Times-Herald* for a wife. SHUMAKER answered the ad.

Lee OWENS, 17 months, died at the home of his parents, Mr. and Mrs. B. M. OWENS in Fort Worth yesterday. The funeral will be today.

W. G. FLAKE, 35, died at his home in Fort Worth yesterday. The funeral will be today.

H. V. COLLIER and Edna ELLINGTON were married in Paris, Texas Tuesday by Rev. Chase MANTON.

Richard T. HARVEY and Rachel CLARK married in Cleburne, Texas yesterday.

Cora SANDERS and Milton FEATHERWOOD married in Cleburne, Texas Sunday.

Rev. Dr. J. A. BEAGLE, 80, died in Franklin, Texas Tuesday. His remains were sent to Texarkana for burial.

Miss Mack WOODS, 75, died of the grippe (influenza) at the home of Mrs. W. B. KNIGHT, her niece, in Paris, Texas.

Mrs. J. S. HOOD, 54, died Saturday of consumption (tuberculosis) in San Angelo, Texas. Her remains were sent to Nacogdoches, Texas. She was originally from Louisiana.

Aquilla JONES, 63, of South Bosque, Texas died at his home yesterday. He was an early settler of the area and had lived here for 50 years. Burial was in McLennan Cemetery in South Bosque.

R. T. ISBELL and Lillian TOGG of Fort Worth were married at the home of Rev. A. T. COLLINS in Fort Worth yesterday.

Friday, March 18, 1904

B. C. FLOWERS, 70, died in Eagle Pass, Texas yesterday. He leaves his wife and nine children. He was a Mason.

Mrs. John W. MCKEE of Cordell, Oklahoma Territory died recently. She was the daughter of Mr. and Mrs. W. R. HOUX of Parker County, Texas.

Ward GILL, 15, was convicted of manslaughter in Federal Court in Durant, Indian Territory. GILL shot and killed G. WILKERSON near Goalgate, Indian Territory a year ago.

Sam HOUSTON, a well digger, was killed in a well-digging accident at Temple, Texas. He fell into the well while being pulled up and his neck was broken.

Annie LOFTIN died Tuesday in Joshua, Texas. She was about 19.

Louisa SELLARD, 68, widow of Eli SELLARD, died at her home six miles south of Gainesville, Texas Tuesday. The funeral was conducted by Rev. W. B. BAYLESS Wednesday.

J. H. DINGUS, about 35, died in Joshua, Texas of scrofula (a form of tuberculosis) Wednesday.

J. F. JONES, 69, died at Clinton, Texas Wednesday.

Sallie BRIGHT, 74, wife of J. M. BRIGHT, died Tuesday in Devine, Texas of heart failure.

F. M. ELLIS, 74, died Tuesday at the home of his son in Beeville, Texas. He had lived in Beeville since 1877.

Ascension PENA died Wednesday in the county jail in Corsicana, Texas. He suffered a bronchial illness. He was in jail awaiting a trail on charges of stealing cattle.

Mrs. Louis POLASKI died yesterday at her home in Corsicana, Texas.

Dr. D. F. HOUSTON and Maggie FURR married Wednesday at First Methodist Church in McKinney, Texas.

J. R. SIMS and Mrs. E. T. WOMBLE married in McKinney, Texas Wednesday.

Joe BRHUIN (sic) and Luna BRACKEN married Wednesday in Gainesville, Texas. Rev. Mr. SCHOONOVER officiated.

Mr. Leroy MOODY and Miss Nettie HARTER married yesterday in Gainesville, Texas. Rev. J. F. PIERCE officiated.

E. A. SLOUGH of Cooper and Annie MCINTOSH married Tuesday night near Italy, Texas.

Percy FALLON and Mary BELL were married Wednesday by Rev. A. J. RARSON in Corsicana, Texas.

Col. P. G. LANHAN was found not guilty in the murder of Frank HUNNICUTT yesterday. HUNNICUTT was killed last August 7 in Sherman, Texas.

Births recorded at Tarrant County Clerk's office: a boy to Mr. and Mrs. William CLARK of Handley on March 15; a girl to Mr. and Mrs. John W. DANNER of near Fort Worth on March 12; a boy to Mrs. Charles SWACKHAMMER of Polytechnic Heights on March 13 (Charles SWACKHAMMER is deceased); a girl to Mr. and Mrs. James B. HILL of Arlington on March 12; a boy to Mr. and Mrs. J. W. CROCKER of Johnson Station on March 12; a girl to Mr. and Mrs. Billy CLARK of Arlington on March 10; a girl to Mr. and Mrs.. M. V. WALLACE of Arlington on March 11; a boy to Mr. and Mrs. John DAVIS of Arlington on March 10; a girl to Mr. and Mrs. George W. PAYNE of Fort Worth on March 16; a boy to Mr. and Mrs. J. B. REA of North Fort Worth on March 6 and a girl to Mr. and Mrs. T. J. BROWN of North Fort Worth on March 8.

Deaths recorded at the Tarrant County Clerk's office: Michael Green FLAKE, 33, residing in Fort Worth, died of heart paralysis on March 16; Jewell ROY, no age listed, residing in Johnson Station, died of pneumonia on March 3; Fannie WEBB, 22, residing in Arlington Heights, died of peritonitis on March 12; and Lee DAVIS, 8, residing in North Fort Worth, died of cerebral congestion on March 13.

Marriage licenses issued at Tarrant County Clerk's office: M. L. BARRIER and Hattie L. RANDLE.

Worth HALE, the infant son of W. B. HALE, died of bronchitis in Fort Worth yesterday. His mother died a month ago.

Saturday, March 19, 1904

Jim TOMLINSON shot and killed his brother John in a quarrel over a stamped envelop near Wilburton, Indian Territory. No date was listed.

Spencer WILLIAMS was arrested yesterday in the death of Will BOSELEY. BOSELEY'S body was found on the Houston and Texas Central tracks a few miles south of Dallas about a month ago.

Mary Havier VENDRIER, assistant mother superior at the Ursuline convent, died yesterday in the convent. She had been in Dallas since 1874. She was buried in the convent.

H. H. WHITE, county judge of Donley County, Texas died Thursday at his home in Clarendon, Texas. He had been county judge since 1882 and was a member of the International Order of Odd Fellows.

John DACUS, 36, of Oklahoma Territory, died Wednesday in Mineral Wells, Texas. He leaves a widow.

Miss Lulu DAVIS, 17, died suddenly yesterday in Newlin, Texas. She was the niece of Professor and Mrs. W.J. LESLIE and was in ill health.

W. A. CONNALLY of was found dead in his buggy near his home in Graham, Texas. Death was due to natural causes. He leaves an invalid wife, but no children.

Robert RIGGINS, father of Mrs. W. A. BENNETT, died on the train between Wichita Falls and Seymour, Texas. The cause of death was blood poisoning from a gunshot wound. His remains were brought to Fort Worth for burial.

N. J. HAMMOND died Thursday at his home at Pattonville, Texas.

R. C. DUMAS, a Mexican War veteran, died yesterday in Denison, Texas.

The mother of H. J. HOWELL died in Bowie, Texas. No date was given. HOWELL is a Denton, Texas businessman.

Thomas MCCALL died suddenly Thursday and was buried in Elgin, Texas. He was a merchant.

S. CLAYTON, 23, who recently relocated from Alabama to Belton, Texas, died yesterday of consumption. He is survived by a wife and one child.

Mr. and Mrs. Jim DOBY lost an infant daughter Wednesday in Cleburne, Texas.

John C. HALFORD and Louise CLARKE were married yesterday in Fort Worth by Justice Charles ROWLAND. They will live in Fort Worth.

Sunday, March 20, 1904

J. H. SALMON, 73, a farmer, died yesterday of pneumonia at Troupe, Texas. He was a Mason.

Sallie A. TUCKER, 85, died Friday from influenza and old age at the home of her daughter, Mrs. F.M. MOORE, in Denton, Texas. The funeral and burial were yesterday in Rockwall, Texas.

Mary GIBBONS, 65, died Friday from a stroke of apoplexy at the home of her brother, John C. GIBBONS, in Paris, Texas. She suffered the stroke on Thursday.

W. L. ROBERTS, of Mineral Wells, Texas and Pearl JONES of Athens, Texas, were married in the latter place a few days ago and have located in Mineral Wells.

Joe MATHIS, 26, and Mattie CRAIG, 15, were married Wednesday in Jacksboro, Texas. She is the daughter of Mr. and Mrs. C. M. CRAIG. They eloped to get married and live in Graham, Texas.

Marriage licenses issued by the Tarrant County Clerk: John C. HALFORD and Louise CLARK, J. J. PRESCOTT and Lula WHITE, and Howard DEWITT and Lottie HARDIN.

Jim DOBBS, Will DOBBS and Jake FRYE were arrested in connection with the death of Bert CLAYPOOL at Earlboro, Indian Territory. CLAYPOOL was an innocent bystander when a fight broke out at a dance and was killed in the fracas.

Monday March 21, 1904

J. S. WAGNER, vice-president of Moreland State Bank, was killed when he fell between the wheels of a wagon and a building. No place was stated.

Walter FRENCH committed suicide at Fort Supply, Indian Territory. He was a businessman living in Woodward, Indian Territory. and was despondent over ill health. No date was listed in the article.

K. A. RAFFERTY, 81, is dead in Llano, Texas. He was a former president of the Iron City National Bank and a Mason. No date was listed for his death.

W. A. RUSSELL is dead after a long illness at Johnson City, Texas. No date or age was listed.

Luther MOORE, 16, died at Graham, Texas. He was the son of G. W. MOORE and a former resident of Mineral Wells, Texas. No date of death was listed.

J. W. WITT, 41, died of consumption Friday in Greenville, Texas. He left a wife and two children. They were not named.

Annie JOHNSON, 23, died Saturday and was buried yesterday in Austin. Her funeral was at Swedish Baptist Church there.

Nick KERD, Jr., 47, died Saturday and was buried yesterday in Austin. He was the brother-in-law of Mayor WHITE.

Albert KAWALSKI and Martin STOPAUSKI died Saturday after drinking carbolic acid in Bremond, Texas. They thought it to be whiskey.

Henry BRECHT died in Dallas Saturday night. He was born in Baden, Germany on May 24, 1834, and had lived in Dallas for 32 years.

Tuesday, March 22, 1904

William MCLAUGHLIN was killed and Mrs. W. R. CHANDLER wounded in an attack on them by W. R. CHANDLER in Temple, Texas. W. R. CHANDLER was arrested. MCLAUGHLIN and Mrs. CHANDLER were employees of the Independent Telephone Company. CHANDLER was a barber. The attack took place in the office of the Independent Telephone Company.

John MAYNARD was lynched by a mob at Montgomery Station on the Santa Fe Railroad, about 100 miles from Houston.

Mollie ROE, sister of Ollie ROE, assistant superintendent of the Houston and Texas Central Railroad in Ennis, Texas died in Dallas yesterday.

J. H. DENMORE died in Tirone, Oklahoma Territory, according to a telegram received by W. P. DENHAM in Belton, Texas. J. H. DENHAM is the third family member to die this month. Two sisters also died. They were not named.

Frank WILSON died of pneumonia on Long Creek in Parker County, Texas. He left a wife and seven children.

Mrs. L. L. JONES, 37, wife of Dr. L. L. JONES, died Sunday night in Forney, Texas. Her funeral was yesterday. Her husband and five children survive. She was a member of the Women's Christian Temperance Union and the Forney Chapter of the United Daughters of the Confederacy.

F. E. ROBINSON, 25, died of pneumonia yesterday in Ardmore, Indian Territory.

John William MURRAY, foreman of the KATY boiler shops, died yesterday in Denison, Texas.

Mrs. A. Mae FERRIS, wife of C. E. FERRIS and daughter of Mr. and Mrs. R. B. HARRIS, died of consumption at her parent's home in Denton, Texas. The funeral took place and the M. E. Church, South and burial was in the Odd Fellows Cemetery in Denton.

Rayner CARYTON died yesterday in Ennis, Texas. The cause of death was head injuries from a blow to his head Wednesday night.

H. BURG, 70, a farmer in the Bolivar Community of northwest Denton County, Texas died when a barn collapsed on him during a heavy storm Saturday. His wife had died only a short time before.

Marriage licenses issue by the Tarrant County Clerk: C. C. RUSSELL and Josephine MILLER, both of Fort Worth, Sevalio CRAWFORD and Geneva HOWARD, both of Fort Worth; R. R. KEITH and Ola WEBSTER, both of Fort Worth; and C. Webb COLLINS and Mary A. DUKE, both of Fort Worth.

The five year old son of Mr. and Mrs. J. D. FINLEY died last Saturday and was buried Sunday in Oakwood Cemetery in Fort Worth. He drank lye.

Mrs. W. L. SCOTT died yesterday at her home in Fort Worth from measles and pneumonia.

Joe D. GUMM committed suicide by drinking carbolic acid yesterday in Fort Worth. He was 28, married and the father of one child. He was an unemployed waiter.

Arthur THORNTON and Clara BROWNING married Sunday in Merkel, Texas. The ceremony took place in the residence of W. O. BROWNING, the bride's father.

The young son of John JAMISON fell under the wheels of a wagon and was killed on the Otoe Indian Reservation in Indian Territory. No date or name of the victim appeared in the article.

The 18 month old child of Robert BALL died when it fell into a tub of hot water at Hobart, Oklahoma Territory. No date was reported.

Richard FRANKLIN died Sunday night from smallpox and an old gunshot wound that caused gangrene at Corsicana, Texas.

Mrs. E. ROFF committed suicide Sunday night by jumping into a cistern at Sweden, Texas, 15 miles north of Austin.

The remains of Rev. F. I. YOAKUM were exhumed at Tyler, Texas and brought to Ennis, Texas for burial in Myrtle Cemetery. YOAKUM's widow died a few weeks ago and was buried in the Myrtle Cemetery.

The trail of J. M. CHAPEL, charged with the murder of W. C. MCCAHAN on January 14, is underway in Dallas.

Mimay POORBAY is the oldest person in Indian Territory. She is 108 years old. She was born on the Cherokee Nation east of the Mississippi in 1796 and was a slave for 70 years.

L. D. WHITAKER, an Enid, Oklahoma Territory businessman, died Sunday as a result of a blood vessel bursting in his head. He had lived until recently in Lee's Summit, Missouri.

Wednesday, March 23, 1904

R. J. POOL died Monday in Aledo, Texas. He was the *Record*'s representative there.

Mrs. W. R. CHANDLER, wounded by her husband Monday in Temple, Texas, died at King's Daughter Hospital yesterday.

Max VANDERVALT shot and killed his daughter Cora, 5, mortally wounded his daughter Eleanor, severely wounded his former wife and committed suicide in El Paso. The couple was divorced a week ago. VANDERVALT wanted to remarry and take the family to St. Louis, but his former wife refused to do so.

Mrs. George Lea CAMPBELL died of pneumonia at her home in Ennis, Texas.

Mrs. W. S. PATE, widow of W. P. PATE, sued J. A. BATESON for $20,000. BATESON killed PATE in January in Cleburne, Texas.

A. E. JOHNSON, of Guthrie, Oklahoma Territory, married Nellie ZELLIKEN of Iola, Kansas in Guthrie yesterday.

William LEVERBOUGH was killed in Kingfisher, Oklahoma Territory Monday when he was struck by a switch engine there. He lived in Salem, Missouri.

J. W. LEWIS, 68, died Sunday at his home 12 miles southwest of Vernon, Texas. He was a Confederate veteran.

Joe BLACKWELL, 16 and the son of James BLACKWELL, died of measles and pneumonia at his father's home two miles south of McKinney, Texas.

The remains of Robert RIGGINS were brought to Smithfield, Texas from Seymour, Texas and buried in the Smithfield Cemetery Saturday.

General William HUDSON, 74, died at the home of Mrs. F. A. TYLER, his daughter in Gainesville, Texas. He was a Confederate veteran. Born in Alabama, he came to Texas in 1854. Survivors include Mrs. F. A. TYLER, Mrs. Oliver HUGHES and Walter HUDSON. One other daughter survives.

A telephone message received in Cleburne, Texas announced the death of Reverend Mary C. BILLINGS in Hico, Texas. Rev. BILLINGS was a Universalist minister.

B. WILKERSON and Nora SIMMONS were married yesterday by Justice of the Peace T. E. WOODS in Justin, Texas.

Frank ROGERS and Miss Bertha ROGERS married Monday near Hallville, Texas. Despite having the same last name, they were not related.

John WILMER, 45, committed suicide yesterday in his mother's home on Bessie Street in Fort Worth. His mother had died Monday night. She was identified only as Mrs. DUBOSE. WILMER left a note for Mrs. Mary WOOD of Tullahoma, Tennessee, whom he identified as his sister.

Thursday, March 24, 1904

Santiago DE LA HOZ, a newspaper editor from Mexico City, drowned yesterday while swimming in the Rio Grande near Laredo, Texas.

A telegram received Tuesday in Marshall, Texas stated Mrs. S. RAPHAEL had died in Camptl, Louisiana. She will be buried in Natchitoches, Louisiana. Rabbi G. SCHAUMBERG of Marshall will conduct the funeral.

Dr. Edward M. WILLIAMS was buried Tuesday in Texarkana under the auspices of the Woodmen of the World.

Mrs. Joe REICHANADTER died Tuesday in Texarkana.

Mrs. L. DAWSON died Tuesday at her home in Texarkana. Her remains were shipped to Little Rock, Arkansas where she formerly lived.

Dorothy CALLICUTT, 5, died Tuesday of a cerebral hemorrhage in Corsicana, Texas. She was the daughter of Judge John S. CALLICUTT.

Miss Hubee YOUNG, 16 and daughter of Mr. and Mrs. W.H. YOUNG, died yesterday in Corsicana, Texas. She was a senior in the high school. Her death was caused by a lung affliction following measles.

Thomas R. HOCKLEY died yesterday in Denison, Texas. He was the Fannin County treasurer.

News of the death of C. R. MOORE reached Blum, Texas yesterday. MOORE died several days ago at the home of J. L. MOORE in Eldorado, Oklahoma Territory.

Miss Kitty LAMAR, 21, died Tuesday of consumption at her home in West Greenville, Texas. Her funeral was yesterday.

Henderson TAYLOR, 6, died of congestion Tuesday in Clarksville, Texas. He was the son of Reverend and Mrs. J. H. TAYLOR.

Winifred WILSON, student at Weatherford College, was married on the tenth of this month to Miss COOK of Baltimore, Maryland. The marriage took place in Baltimore.

Judge N. D. WALLACE died Saturday at his home in Pleasanton, Texas. He was born in Illinois in 1853 and came to Texas in 1870. He married Miss Johnnie IRVIN in Seguin. He served as sheriff and county judge in Atascosa County. He was survived by his wife and son Lawrence.

Bert GLENDOCK died suddenly at Cement, Oklahoma Territory according to a report received at Guthrie, Oklahoma Territory yesterday.

A marriage license was issued by the Tarrant County Clerk to W. S. STEGALL and Frieda ROSSBECK.

George C. RUTLEDGE died at his home in Fort Worth Tuesday. He was a druggist and the son of Robert H. RUTLEDGE of Tennessee. He married Elma MOORE in 1886. He was survived by his wife and two children, Grady, 13, and Lucille, 11. The funeral was today with burial under the auspices of the Knights of Pythias.

J. J. BUNCH died yesterday in Fort Worth. He is survived by his wife and four children. The funeral was today. Names of survivors were not listed.

Caroline M. WHITE, 83, died yesterday at the home of Mrs. S. M. WHITE, her daughter, in Fort Worth. The funeral was held at Keller, the former home of the deceased. She was survived by a son, two daughters, grandchildren and great grandchildren.

Friday, March 25, 1904

The newspaper for this date did not appear on the microfilm.

Saturday, March 26, 1904

Brozier SMITH was executed yesterday at Waxahachie, Texas for the 1903 murder of his wife.

The remains of R. D. GRIFFIN, who died in California Monday, will be returned to Hillsboro, Texas for burial. He was a brother of Mrs. VAUGHAN, wife of Dr. VAUGHAN. No given names for the VAUGHANs were listed.

D. F. BATTAILLE of Hillsboro and Eva MITCHELL of Fort Worth married in Fort Worth Thursday. Rev. W. B. MCGARRITY of Hillsboro officiated.

J. T. CAMPBELL died in Houston recently. He was the brother of C. M. CAMPBELL of Temple, Texas.

The funeral of William MCLAUGHLIN took place in Temple, Texas. Rev. B.A. HODGES officiated.

Marriage licenses issued by the Tarrant County Clerk: W. R. MOLIERE and Ruby BINYON; and C. W. WARD and Ada SANDS.

Births reported to the Tarrant County Clerk: a girl to Mr. and Mrs. G. D. LIGHTFOOT of Fort Worth on March 16; a girl to Mr. and Mrs. A. S. BABB of Riverside on March 21 and a girl to Mr. and Mrs. William B. MARTIN of Fort Worth on March 14.

Deaths reported to the Tarrant County Clerk: Mrs. J. D. USELTON, 37, residing in Euless, died of consumption on March 23; Mrs. Viola SCOTT, 22, residing in Fort Worth, died of pneumonia on March 21; Worth K. HALE, 7 ½ months, residing in Glenwood, died of granitian on March 17; J. J. BUNCH, 44, residing in Fort Worth, died of typhoid fever on March 24.

Sunday, March 27, 1904

Dock RATLIFFE was killed Thursday near Temple, Oklahoma Territory when he was shot by a duck hunting companion.

Mrs. T. B. HOCKLEY was appointed county treasurer of Fannin County, Texas. She will complete the term of her husband who died of consumption Tuesday.

James F. JONES, 82, died yesterday at his home in Henderson, Texas. He was a former U.S. Congressman.

Henry W. BURR married Agnes WILKINSON Thursday in Dallas. J. D. BURR of Ennis, Texas is the brother of the groom.

W. M. LACY and Ella EPPERSON married Friday in the home of the bride's parents in Clarksville, Texas. They will live in Palestine, Texas.

Sallie PHILLIPS and J. T. TERRELL married Friday in Temple, Texas. Rev. C. R. WRIGHT officiated.

Jake WATSON, charged with the murder of Ben NEALY at Purcell, Indian Territory was bound over for trial.

Albert TUCKER, 20, died Friday at the home of Bud MARDDIN near Gainesville, Texas.

John CLARKE died Thursday of pneumonia in Ringgold, Texas. He was buried by the Masons Friday. He was a pioneer of Montague County.

Mrs. Mollie GAYLORD, widow of George, died Thursday at the home of her sister, Mrs. PEEBLES, in Leesville, Texas.

H. S. THOMAS was buried yesterday at the Williams ranch near Goldthwaite, Texas.

Mrs. WOOLSEY, 54, died at the home of her son-in-law, W. W. PORTER, Thursday in Sunset, Texas.

C. A. BRAGG, a druggist in DeLeon, Texas, died of pneumonia yesterday. He was survived by his wife and two children. The survivors were not named.

Mattie E. BAKER, 70, died at the home of her sister Mrs. J. A. SHORT on the Balcones. She was taken to Karnes County, Texas for burial. No dates were listed.

Laurance Johnston CLAYTON was born to Mr. and Mrs. George CLAYTON in Fort Worth Friday. He was named in honor of Laura JOHNSTON, his grandmother, who died recently.

Marriage licenses issued by Tarrant County Clerk: Arthur A. BRACKET and Ivey EDGERMAN; S. E. FULLER and Miss K. M. PRONTISS; R. E. MEADFORD and Rosa MAYER; and J. L. GILMORE and Ida DAVEY.

Monday, March 28, 1904

O. S. STRICKLAND of Roy County, Oklahoma Territory and William SHAUL of Ponca City, Indian Territory were killed when a bridge they were working on collapsed on them. The accident happened northwest of Ponca City. The date was not reported.

Jennie E. BALLARD, 24, died yesterday in Dallas of pneumonia. She was the wife of Dr. C. B. BALLARD.

Mary Nevada HARLEY, 32, died of an accidental overdose of morphine at Ardmore, Indian Territory. She is survived by a husband and daughter aged 12. The death was announced yesterday.

William M. ELLIOTT died of heart failure in a room at the Orient Saloon in Oklahoma City, Oklahoma Territory. He was a salesman.

Robert N. RUGGLES died of pneumonia Saturday in Guthrie, Oklahoma Territory. He was a journalist and editor who had worked for newspapers in Leavenworth, Kansas; Emporia, Kansas; Topeka, Kansas; and Kansas City.

Eli L. ADMIRE and Nina BALDWIN married Saturday in Hennessey, Oklahoma Territory. They are both from Kingfisher.

R. B. MCBEE drowned yesterday in the Chickasaw Gun Club Lake near Ardmore, Indian Territory. He was the head bookkeeper of a wholesale grocery firm.

Dr. C. H. ROBERTS, 55, died Friday morning in Wolfe City, Texas. He had resided in Hunt County since the close of the war.

Carrie HUNT, 52, died last week at the home of her daughter, Mrs. Doro VICE, in Lone Oak, Texas. Other survivors are Charlie HUNT, Alvin HUNT and Mrs. Jim ELLIOTT.

Thomas DUNN, Sr. died Saturday in Decatur, Texas and was buried yesterday in the city cemetery there.

L. WATTS, 62, died Friday at his home four miles from Luling, Texas and was buried at the Clear Fork Cemetery Saturday. He was a farmer. He is survived by his wife, several children and many relatives.

Mary H. MOORE, 74, died Saturday of heart disease in Brownsville, Texas. The funeral was yesterday. She was the mother of George MOORE of Brownsville and Alex MOORE of Dallas.

Myrtle LARGECT, 29, died Saturday night at the home of Mrs. L.C. LARGECT, her mother, in McKinney, Texas.

A marriage license was granted in St. Louis, Missouri for William E. DUGDELL of Texarkana and May F. WOODS of St. Louis.

J. P. HOLLEY and Gertie CHAMBERS married Thursday in the Greenville courthouse. Squire T.W. MCDANIEL officiated.

Marriage licenses issued by the Hunt County Clerk: John ALLEN and Bertha BELLE; S. H. CLARKE and May COLE; J. P. HALLEY and Gertie CHAMBERS; A. J. CRESWELL and Lizzie VISER; and C. U. TERRY and N. A. TURNER.

Tuesday, March 29 through
Thursday, March 31, 1904

Newspapers for these dates did not appear on the microfilm.

April, 1904

Friday, April 1, 1904

The funeral of Elijah W. CAMPBELL, accidentally killed in Dallas Tuesday, was very large. Campbell was the division superintendent of the Texas and Pacific Railroad. Dr. Junius B. FRENCH conducted the funeral. Burial was in Greenwood Cemetery. CAMPBELL was a member of the Woodmen of the World.

The remains of Joseph HUEY arrived yesterday from Corsicana, Texas. Burial was in Greenwood Cemetery in Dallas.

The funeral of Harry C. WALKER took place in Dallas. He was a policeman there.

The mother of Rev. Chalmers MCPHERSON died in Chicago yesterday. She was 88. Her remains are being brought to Waxahachie, Texas. Other survivors include a daughter named Mrs. BRADLEY.

Bob TAYLOR, who lives west of Venus, Texas, confessed to killing W. W. CLEMENTS. TAYLOR struck CLEMENTS with a singletree in a field about a mile west of Venus. TAYLOR is CLEMENTS' son-in-law. TAYLOR surrendered to authorities and posted bond in Cleburne, Texas.

The little daughter of J. H. BRADLEY died Tuesday in Weatherford, Texas. Her remains were brought to Cleburne, Texas for burial.

The infant son of Mr. and Mrs. Foss GARRISON died Wednesday in Cleburne, Texas.

The funeral of Mrs. R. O. DENTIN will be held today in Gainesville, Texas. Her remains were shipped from Davis, Indian Territory. Rev. A. B. INGRAM will conduct the funeral. Burial will be in East Hill Cemetery.

T. S. BUCHANAN died Wednesday in Longview, Texas.

J. J. TWITTY and Lula M. LUNN married Wednesday in Corsicana, Texas. Rev. J. I. QUISSENBERRY officiated.

Bruce COGDELL, of Mexia, Texas, and Helen ROGERS, of McKinney, Texas, married at the home of the bride's mother, Mrs. S. A. ROGERS, near McKinney.

Marriage licenses issued by Cocke County Clerk in Gainesville, Texas: G. R. HARRIS and Mrs. Clyde BRIDGES; J. B. EVANS and Miss M. F. HALL; R. T. MCCOOL and Alma MITCHELL; K. K. KELLY and Hilda GRUSENDORF.

Marriages licenses issued by Tarrant County Clerk: H. M. HENDRIX and Jessie RIGGS; Clen JACKSON and Mrs. Willie A. WOODWARD; and L. A. COLLINS and Emma GOODWIN.

Births recorded at the Tarrant County Clerk's office: a girl to Mr. and Mrs. Joe MULLINS of Marine on January 21; a boy to Mr. and Mrs. Tom BROWN of Grapevine on February 19; a boy to Mr. and Mrs. J. P. O'DELL of Grapevine on March 23; a boy to Mr. and Mrs.. W. A. STARLING of Grapevine with no date listed; a girl to Mr. and Mrs. J. M. MANGRUM of Grapevine on March 25; a boy to Mr. and Mrs. Will WILLIAMS of near Grapevine on February 27; a girl to Mr. and Mrs.. J. H. GRUBBS of Johnson Station on March 17; a boy to Mr. and Mrs. John BEASLEY of Fort Worth on March 29; a boy to Mr. and Mrs. J. A. AESPAUGH of Johnson Station on March 17 and a boy to Mr. and Mrs. George DUPREE of Fort Worth on March 28.

Deaths recorded at the Tarrant County Clerk's office: Edgar Elihu WHITE, 2, residing in Bransford, died of whooping cough on February 29; George Thomas JOHNSON, 64, residing in Grapevine, died of pneumonia on February 25; Charles Sidney LAIDLEY, 42, residing in Grapevine, died of Bright's Disease on February 21; William MIMS, 35, residing in Fort Worth, died of tuberculosis on March 28; Penelope SHARPE, 22, residing in Grapevine, died of consumption on March 6; W. B. HENDERSON, 48, residing in Fort Worth, died of pneumonia on March 28; and Charles SCHMITZ, 80, residing in Fort Worth, died of pneumonia on March 29.

Saturday, April 2, 1904

The newspaper for this date did not appear on the microfilm.

Sunday, April 3, 1904

Ethel MARTIN, 9, died from burns Tuesday in San Angelo, Texas. She was burned on March 14 when her clothing caught fire from an open fireplace.

U.S. Marshal Ben COLBERT appointed Raymond HERZ as office deputy and J. P. IRBY as field deputy at Ardmore, Indian Territory.

Ed WALKER shot and killed Bob HARRIS, his brother-in-law, at Clarksville, Texas. HARRIS was intoxicated and threatening WALKER with a knife when the shooting took place.

Marriage licenses issued by the Tarrant County Clerk: W. L. NASH and Emma HAYSLIP, George MCCONNELL and Pearl BOARDMAN, and J. S. MOORE and Beatrice WILLIAMS.

Deaths recorded by the Tarrant County Clerk: Mary O'HARA, 8, residing in Fort Worth, died of typhoid fever on March 29; and Will DEMING, 35, residing in Fort Worth, died of hemorrhage from a gunshot on April 1.

W. T. BLEDSOE died Thursday of pneumonia. His funeral was Friday in Gainesville, Texas. Rev. Marvin NICHOLAS conducted the funeral.

Charles L. MONROE died yesterday at his home in northwest Harrison County, Texas.

Bird DOTSON, 15, died of pneumonia at the home of his father, W. C. DOTSON, near Forest Grove in Collin County, Texas.

J. L. HARROW and Ada TANNER married yesterday in Corsicana, Texas. Rev. M. C. JOHNSON officiated.

T. F. BRACH and Etta May MOORE married yesterday in Corsicana, Texas. Judge Clay NASH officiated.

H. F. FORTENBERRY and Effie LATTIMER married Friday in Clarendon, Texas.

Mrs. Mabel BONNER, 26, died at the home of Mrs. J. M. BRANNON, her sister, in Fort Worth. Mrs. BONNER lived in Kansas City but was visiting in Fort Worth.

Monday, April 4 and Tuesday, April 5, 1904

The newspapers for these dates did not appear on the microfilm.

Wednesday, April 6, 1904

William Dudley KNOWLES died yesterday in Dallas. He was born in Indiana in 1836 and had lived in Dallas since 1877. He was survived by his wife, a son Charles L. KNOWLES, of Chickasha, Indian Territory, and four daughters, Mrs. Albert MANN and Mrs. Charles WAGSTAFF of Dallas, Mrs. Charles HARNED of Omaha, Nebraska and Mrs. Fred ENGELHIFF of Weatherford, Texas.

Mark ALEXANDER died suddenly Monday in Waxahachie, Texas. He was a pioneer settler of Ellis County. He died in the home of J. L. MCCARTNEY from apoplexy. He was buried in the City Cemetery in Waxahachie.

Laura E. LANGSFORD, wife of Waxahachie Alderman S.P. LANGSFORD, died at her home yesterday. She was a sister of Mrs. George B. LOVING of Fort Worth.

The five year old son of Mr. and Mrs. Fred THOMPSON died in Blum, Texas yesterday. Cause of death was paralysis of the heart. His name was not listed.

Buck ABERNATHY died Saturday and was buried Monday in Pittsburg, Texas.

Kate WOOD died Sunday of consumption in Greenville, Texas.

Henry LORENZ died at his home in Palo Pinto, Texas. He is survived by his wife and three children. Story was datelined Fredericksburg, Texas.

Rilla ELLIOTT died in Walnut Springs, Texas on Easter morning from cerebro-spinal meningitis. The funeral was from the Methodist Church.

Lorine LIEDTKE, an infant, died Sunday in Gainesville, Texas. Her parents were Mr. and Mrs. Ed LIEDTKE. Burial was in East Hill Cemetery.

Ben PRINCE was accidentally shot and killed by Susie DENNY near Francis, Indian Territory. She was playing with a pistol thought to be unloaded. She pointed it at him and pulled the trigger.

Deaths reported to the Tarrant County Clerk on April 5, 1904: John RUSH, 53, accidental death; Ermine BISHOP, 25, tuberculosis; Rebecca MAXED, pneumonia; I. A. JONES, self-inflicted pistol shot; Archie Lee SAUNDERS, 3 months, measles; Mabel CRASS, 5, measles, J.T. THEWEATT, Coppell, Texas, cerebral apoplexy; Hannah MEADE, 25, measles; and Lucille FLORENCE, 8, measles.

Births reported to the Tarrant County Clerk: a boy to Mr. and Mrs. Jack NORMAN on March 24, a boy to Mr. and Mrs. Arthur GILES, March 24; a girl to Mr. and Mrs. M. J. WILLIAMS, Birdville, no date; a girl to Mr. and Mrs. L. W. KIMBERLING, Kennedale, March 20; a girl to Mr. and Mrs. J. W. FOSTER on March 26; a boy to Mr. and Mrs. G. W. KEATON of Grapevine on March 21; a girl to Mr. and Mrs. C. A. WALL of Grapevine on March 27; and a boy to Mr. and Mrs. T. D. MONTGOMERY of Mansfield on March 21.

Marriage licenses issued by the Tarrant County Clerk: J. H. HOWELL and Daisy BAUGH; John C. CARTRIGHT and Bettie BANTON; and Jesse BYORS and Lola DIXON.

Thursday, April 7, 1904

The body of William DUNCAN was found yesterday in Sherman, Texas. He had been dead about a week and is thought to have committed suicide.

John MCCARLEY was shot and killed yesterday near Madill, Indian Territory. The shooting happened in a dispute over a pasture. Henry PARRIS was arrested. Oscar PARRIS was still at large.

John NEWLEE of Pineville, Kentucky, died of consumption Monday at Seymour, Texas. He was 32 or 33. Survivors included two sisters in Pineville. Burial is to be in Pineville.

P. T. AUSTIN died en route to Roswell, New Mexico Territory for treatment of consumption Tuesday. His remains were buried in Crowley, Texas.

R. H. MOSELEY, about 49 and a stockman, died of blood poisoning at Llano, Texas. No date of death was listed. Death resulted from a shooting incident with Clyde YOE on March 26. Burial was to be in Loyal Valley, Mason County, Texas.

Mills County treasurer E. J. CROCKETT died suddenly at Goldthwaite after inhaling carbon gas. Another account lists the cause of death as heart failure and reports the name of the deceased as H. J. CROCKETT.

Marriage licenses issued in Tarrant County: Hugh BOREN and Kathryne HUMPHREY, B. F. TURNER and Mrs. Annie M. GREY; W. P. WEATHERFORD and Mrs. M.L. TANNAHILL.

Births recorded in Tarrant County: a girl to Mr. and Mrs. W. D. SWANK on March 27, a girl to Mr. and Mrs. John VAN ZANDT on March 31, a boy to Mr. and Mrs. George OVERSTREET on April 3 and a boy to Mr. and Mrs. J. T. WILLIAMS on March 30.

Deaths recorded at Tarrant County Clerk's office: Grace DROLL, 13, peritonitis on February 26; and Lee OWENS, 17 of pneumonia on March 16.

Friday, April 8, 1904

Eugene WILLIS, injured in a railroad handcar accident Wednesday, died at St. Paul's Sanitarium last night.

The remains of William SADLER were buried Thursday from St. Patrick's Church in Fort Worth yesterday. He died Wednesday. He was a traveling salesman for the McCord-Collins Company.

T. W. WASSON died at Snyder, Texas last Saturday. He left a wife and six children. He was buried in the Snyder Cemetery.

The remains of Milton VANMETER were returned to Era, Texas yesterday and were interred in the cemetery there. He was 32 and was killed when he fell from a moving train in New Mexico.

Edith Vale TRUAX, daughter of Mr. and Mrs. Charles TRUAX of Chicago, died in San Antonio Wednesday.

Mrs. M. HESTER died yesterday in Karnes City, Texas. She was the wife of Morgan HESTER and was an early settler of the area. She was survived by her husband and several children.

The 13 months old child of Arthur FAULKNER died Monday at its home four miles southeast of Greenville, Texas. The child's name was not listed.

Captain MYERS died at his home three miles west of Denton, Texas Wednesday. No given name was reported.

Gideon CHRISTIAN died Wednesday night in Abilene, Texas. He was the father of Mrs. W. K. JENNINGS of Ennis, Texas.

Mrs. Henry WYNAN, 45, died Wednesday in Ardmore, Indian Territory. The funeral was yesterday.

Mrs. W. C. BRYAN died Sunday at Lone Oak, Texas.

Miss Lillie WALLACE, a student at the University of Texas at Austin, died yesterday in the woman's building there. Her funeral was held in Austin with burial in San Angelo, Texas.

W. C. DODNEY died Tuesday in Texarkana.

Clara SOWARDS, 16, died Tuesday near Texarkana.

Phil BRINDSLEY, 82, died on April 5 in Ennis, Texas.

Mrs. Clara KIRKPATRICK died Wednesday in Ennis, Texas. She was the wife of Otie KIRKPATRICK.

Dr. L. A. SCOTT died Wednesday in Denison, Texas.

Mrs. C. C. CLINTON died last night of consumption in Corsicana, Texas.

Charles L. REED and Ora EDDLEMON married Wednesday in Muskogee, Indian Territory.

T. A. KOVAR and Fannie ELSIK were married Wednesday by Justice of the Peace STOVALL in Ennis, Texas.

Guy YOUNGBLOOD and Letha SILLS were married Wednesday by Justice of the Peace STOVALL in Ennis, Texas.

Leon A. MYERS and Helen NEWMAN married Tuesday in Marshall, Texas. The wedding took place at the residence of Joseph NEWMAN, the bride's father. Rabbi I. SCHOUMBERG officiated

Julia JOHNSON, 16, died of typhoid fever Monday in Hondo, Texas. She was the daughter of V. A. JOHNSON. Her funeral was Tuesday.

Elmo MALONE and Elva WHITE married Tuesday at the home of Mr. and Mrs. T. A. WHITE, the parents of the bride, in Abilene, Texas.

C. K. SPRUELL was married to Miss GODFREY in Erath County, Texas on April 2. The bride's first name was not listed.

Mr. CARTWRIGHT and Bettie BANTON were married Tuesday in Mineral Wells, Texas.

Seth LEWIS and Edna BOWLS were married Tuesday in Pecos, Texas.

Births recorded in Tarrant County: a girl to Mr. and Mrs. Mark MCKINNEY on April 6.

Deaths recorded in Tarrant County: Mrs. Lou E. SNEED, 29, died of tuberculosis on March 30; Clara T. RUTLEDGE, 3, died of measles on April 6; J. R. MARTIN, 77, died of la grippe on April 1; and Wiley CALLOWAY, 44, died of dropsy on April 5.

Marriage licenses issued in Tarrant County: K. V. JENNINGS and Cora Josephine DAGGETT.

I. M. KETCHUM, 87, died in Fort Worth at the residence of his grand-daughter, Mrs. C. T. BATTERSON. His remains were shipped to Sabine Pass, Texas for burial.

Saturday, April 9, 1904

G. CHRISTIAN died Thursday at the home of his son, G. L. CHRISTIAN, in Abilene, Texas.

Fondie CROMER, 19, died Thursday of heart disease in Ardmore, Indian Territory. His funeral was yesterday.

Hugh C. GRAFTON died Thursday of consumption in Texarkana.

Ed MURPHY, 44, died Thursday in Texarkana. He is survived by his wife and three children.

Mrs. S. I. EDWARDS, the mother of H. H. EDWARDS, died in Monroe, Louisiana, last Wednesday. Burial was in Wasson, Mississippi, Thursday. H. H. EDWARDS lives in Marshall, Texas.

Mrs. Herman FISCHER, 61, died in Fredericksburg, Texas. She leaves a husband and 11 children.

James Clayton EPPS and Myra Bradley ELLINGTON married on Thursday in Abilene, Texas. The wedding took place in the home of Mr. and Mrs. L. V. ELLINGTON, the parent's of the bride.

Fred HOPSON and Pearl REDIN married Thursday in Gainesville, Texas.

John D. TROY committed suicide in Shreveport, Louisiana. The date was not stated. A coroner ruled the death a suicide.

Deaths reported to Tarrant County Clerk: Mary MCINERRY, 11 days, died of diphtheria on April 1, 1904.

Sunday, April 10, 1904

R. S. CASTLEBERRY is on trial in Ryan, Indian Territory for the June, 1901, death of J. W. WOMBOLD. CASTLEBERRY was judged insane and sent to the asylum in Washington, Indian Territory for two years. He is now being retried.

Mrs. May E. NOLEN died in Louise, Texas according to a telegram received by W. L. NOLEN of Dallas. The date of death was not stated. She is survived by her husband, G. G. NOLEN and ten children. Her maiden name was May E. ROBERTS. She lived in Dallas until five years ago when the family moved to Louise.

A coroner's inquest ruled that W. O. WILHELM died of heart failure. The date of death was not listed. He collapsed at Main and Exchange in North Fort Worth

Marriage licenses issued in Tarrant County: Sam H. DAVIS and Sophie J. WELDT, and John SMITH and Mrs. Mary LESLIE.

Births recorded at Tarrant County Clerk's Office: a boy to Mr. and Mrs. Olin GIBBONS of Arlington on April 7; a boy to Mr. and Mrs. Charlie TIDEWATER of Arlington on April 6, and a boy to Mr. and Mrs. A. N. LOWRING of Arlington on March 30.

Deaths recorded by the Tarrant County Clerk: Lee SHEEDS, 2, died of measles on March 30.

Ira BECSON, 11, was killed yesterday in a sawmill accident at San Angelo, Texas.

G. C. MASSIE died of head injuries Friday in Hokchito, Indian Territory. The remains were sent to McKinney, Texas. MASSIE was struck with an ax by A. N. TEMPLE, his son-in-law, last Monday in Hokchito. TEMPLE was jailed at Atoka. The fight took place over $5 missing from a cash drawer.

Joseph DEGAUGH, 95, died Friday in Kansas City, Missouri. He was survived by J. A. DEGAUGH and J. O. DEGAUGH of Terrell, Texas. Deceased was a Mexican War veteran.

Miss Julia Jane WALLACE, who died Thursday at the state university in Austin, was buried in San Antonio Friday.

The funeral of Stuart WILSON, about 70, was held Friday in Gainesville, Texas. He died of injuries sustained when he fell from his horse. Rev. J. W. NICHOLS conducted the services. Burial was in East Hill Cemetery.

F. M. FOX and Mrs. C. A. GRANBURY were married yesterday in Ardmore, Indian Territory. FOX is an attorney who has practiced law for 30 years.

W. O. WILHELM died Saturday of heart failure. He collapsed at Main and Exchange in North Fort Worth. He was survived by his wife and one child. He lived in Rosen Heights and was a foreman in the hide cellar for Armour and Company. His remains were shipped to Muscatine, Iowa.

Monday, April 11, 1904

The paper for this date didn't appear on the microfilm.

Tuesday, April 12, 1904

George JORDAN, 2, son of Mr. and Mrs. C. JORDAN, was fatally burned in San Antonio. He set fire to his clothes while lighting a lamp. C. JORDAN is an engineer with the Southern Pacific Railroad.

D. E. SUDDUTH and Mrs. Ida B. MCKINNEY were married in an automobile at the head of Main Street in Fort Worth. Justice ROWLAND officiated. The bride is from Seymour, Texas and the groom employed by Texas Brewing Company.

C. E. BAILEY died yesterday in El Paso. He was married 10 years ago to Miss Ollie Ruth NOBLE of New York. His death was sudden.

Jeff D. ROBERTS died Sunday in Belton, Texas and was buried yesterday in South Belton Cemetery.

Nancy JONES, 31, of Graham, Texas, died Sunday in Ardmore, Indian Territory. Her death resulted from an operation.

S. A. MAXWELL of Salina, Texas died from consumption in Roswell, New Mexico Territory.

Mrs. Wilson PHILLIPS died Sunday in Santa Anna, Texas. She is survived by her husband.

R. B. KUTEMAN died in Fort Worth Sunday night. His remains were sent to Mineola, Texas.

Minnie KING died suddenly yesterday in Boerne, Texas. She is survived by her husband H. B. KING.

D. EDMUNDSOM was ambushed and killed Sunday at his home on the McCulloch – San Saba County line. He was killed while cooking his supper.

J. C. WARE died while working his fields near Santa Anna, Texas. No date was reported. He was buried Friday by the Masons.

Brock TOLLIVER and Emma SELF and R. D. SELF and Beulah TOLLIVER were married Sunday in a double ceremony at Belton, Texas. Rev. George W. LEE officiated.

A marriage license was granted in St. Louis yesterday to Thomas G. MULHERN of El Paso and Mrs. Ada STROTHER of St. Louis.

Leon G. BRISCOE and Pearl NEILL were married in Devine, Texas.

Births reported to the Tarrant County Clerk's office in Fort Worth: a girl to Mr. and Mrs. J. J. RUSSELL on April 8, a boy to Mr. and Mrs. Will ARNOLD on March 20, a boy to Mr. and Mrs. Lemuel TRUE on April 7, a boy to Mr. and Mrs. William LAVENDAR on March 28, a boy to Mr. and Mrs. O. D. POTTER on April 8, a girl to Mr. and Mrs. Mitch HIMES on March 30 and a boy to Mr. and Mrs. J. E. HIMES on April 6.

Deaths reported to the Tarrant County Clerk's office: infant daughter of L. A. HERMESON died of pneumonia on April 7; Floyd BALEW, 17 months, died of enterocolitis on March 28; Henry MCCOY, 5 months, died of pneumonia of April 1; and Jones HARRIS, 7 months, died of cholera infantum on March 28.

Marriage licenses issued by Tarrant County Clerk, Fort Worth: Andrew O'ROURKE and Francis M. DRUMM, D. E. SUDDUTH and Mrs. Ida B. MCKINNEY and Andrew JACKSON and Izora SHELTON.

Wednesday, April 13, 1904

Mrs. E. B. RUTLEDGE died yesterday of pneumonia in Pearsall, Texas. Her husband survives.

Mrs. James LOWE, 80, died yesterday in Pearsall, Texas. She was survived by her husband. She was an early settler of Frio County.

Evelyn GESTINE died in Cleburne, Texas Monday. She was the daughter of Mr. and Mrs. M. E. RICKS.

Boone KIMBROUGH died Monday of consumption in Gainesville, Texas. He was survived by his mother, Mrs. J. C. BURNS. The funeral was yesterday. Rev. Marvin NICHOLS officiated.

L. F. BURTON, 28, died Monday in Ardmore, Indian Territory. He was a tailor and a member of the Modern Woodmen of America. His funeral was yesterday.

John WATSON and Miss Georgie NICOLA married yesterday in Waco, Texas. Father P. J. CLANEY officiated.

Richard HOLDER, of Greenville, Texas and Katie DAVIS of McKinney, Texas were married in Greenville Sunday. The marriage took place in the home of E. C. HENLEY, the bride's uncle. Rev. F. E. FINCHER officiated.

Marriage licenses issued at Greenville, Texas: James STOKES and Amanda EMERSON, J. C. FARMER and Minnie COVINGTON, and R.G. HOLDER and Kate DAVIS.

The remains of 10 year old Willie MCDANIEL were found near Shawnee, Indian Territory. He disappeared from his home three months ago and is thought to have died of exposure.

Marriage licenses issued by Tarrant County Clerk's office: A. BROWN and Lena KATZ, and T. W. COX and Mattie BURROW.

Births reported to Tarrant County Clerk: a girl to Mr. and Mrs. C. LEE on March 21, a girl to Mr. and Mrs. Hal LOCKRIDGE on April 11, a boy to Mr. and Mrs. A. J. GIDDEN on April 2, a boy to Mr. and Mrs. E. R. BROWN on April 11 and a boy to Mr. and Mrs. V. TILLERY on April 5.

The remains of Joseph H. FERGUSON were returned to Grapevine, Texas for burial in the family burying ground. FERGUSON died in an accident at Cameron, Texas. His remains were accompanied by his brother A. J. FERGUSON. The funeral will be today.

The funeral of William HIRSCHFIELD, 35, will be today. Rev. Junius B. FRENCH will officiate. HIRSCHFIELD died last week in Boulder, Colorado from complications resulting from an appendectomy. He was the son of Mrs. Joseph H. RYAN of Arlington Heights.

Thursday, April 14, 1904

A. H. TEMPLE is jailed in Atoka, Indian Territory charged with the murder of G. C. MASSIE in Hokchito, Indian Territory on April 4. His trial will be held in October.

Cyrus A. BUTTS died yesterday in Fort Worth. He was born on October 7, 1836 in Lincoln County, Tennessee. He married Nancy A. MEADE in Troy, Tennessee. They came to Texas in 1888 and settled in Fort Worth. His widow survives. Other survivors include John T. BUTTS, of Weatherford, Texas; W. A. BUTTS of New York City; R. F. BUTTS of Houston, Mrs. D. H. JOHNSTON of Stamford, Texas; Mrs. F. D. JONES of Fort Worth; Mrs. John W. BRADLEY of Fort Worth; and Mrs. A. W. TERRELL of Sherman, Texas. The funeral will be from the Taylor Street Cumberland Presbyterian Church of Fort Worth. Rev. J. W. CALDWELL will officiate. BUTTS was an elder in the church and a Confederate veteran.

The three year old child of L. W. HAMILTON, of El Reno, Texas was scalded to death yesterday when he fell into a tub of boiling water.

Rev. N. F. LAW died yesterday in Ardmore, Indian Territory. He was the pastor of the Methodist Church there. He was a former Confederate soldier, serving in the 2nd Texas Regiment from Galveston, Texas.

Mrs. Lou CHANDLER died of measles and pneumonia Tuesday in Ardmore, Indian Territory.

John T. ALEXANDER died yesterday from injuries in a railroad accident at Granite, Oklahoma Territory. He had lived in Ardmore, Indian Territory for 14 years and was a salesman.

D. J. CALVARY died of consumption Monday in Clarendon, Texas.

Mrs. Ben S. POPE died Tuesday in Marshall, Texas.

C. H. HYDE died Tuesday in Marshall, Texas. He was a 25 year resident of Marshall and was a well-known ruler and bookbinder.

The body of Grace PRESTON, who died a few days ago in South McAlester, Indian Territory, was buried Tuesday in Texarkana.

Mrs. A. S. CREWS died yesterday of heart disease at her home in Corsicana, Texas. Her husband is the Navarro County Tax Collector.

Births recorded at the Tarrant County Clerk's office: a boy to Mr. and Mrs. T. H. TRIPLETT on April 8; a boy to Mr. and Mrs. W. H. STROMAN on April 11; a boy to Mr. and Mrs. Willie SMITH on April 10; a boy to Mr. and Mrs. Ed C. DESHAZO on April 6; and a girl to Mr. and Mrs. William GARRELL on April 12.

Marriage licenses issued by Tarrant County Clerk's office: T. D. WEST and Annie L. DOWELL, D. C. RICHARDSON and Gertrude H. BYERS.

Friday, April 15, 1904

Charles HOVERMEYER and Emma SMITH married yesterday in Rhome, Texas.

J. J. STANTON and Emma PROTSMAN married Tuesday in Clarendon, Texas.

James L. MASSENGALE and Ella TIPPETT married Tuesday at the bride's mother's home in Abilene, Texas. Rev. L. R. SCARBROUGH officiated.

Marriage licenses issued in Decatur, Texas: J. H. SAVAGE and Jennie HONEY, W. C. CANTRELL and Ethel MASSEY, W. A. BOWEN and Mary BEALL, A. J. ANDERSON and Ollie CLARK, and C. L. WILSON and Lydia MILLS.

E. E. RUMBLE died in Fort Worth early Thursday morning. He suffered respiratory troubles and stayed outside at night because he couldn't sleep in a room. His remains were taken to Aurora, Illinois. He was survived by his wife. He was a bookkeeper.

Mrs. E. B. NORMAN died Wednesday in Graham, Texas. She leaves a husband and four children. Her husband is president of the Beckham National Bank. Internment was yesterday at Oak Grove Cemetery.

E. T. TUCK was shot and killed yesterday north of St. Jo, Texas.

Kearney J. KEVLIN, Jr., of Dallas was killed in an explosion on the USS Missouri yesterday. He is survived by his father and two sisters, Nellie and Annie.

J. C. NUNN, 21, son of Bryan, Texas sheriff T. C. NUNN, was among those killed in the explosion on the USS Missouri.

Alex S. FIELD, 72, died yesterday at his home in Marshall, Texas. He was district clerk for Harrison County for 25 years and a graduate of Princeton University.

Mrs. Harry WATERS died Wednesday in Abilene, Texas. Burial was yesterday.

Mrs. Mildred SCOTT died Tuesday night in Greenville, Texas. She leaves a son and a daughter. Burial was in Jefferson, Texas.

Sam SKINNER, 45, died Wednesday of measles and pneumonia in Ardmore, Indian Territory. He formerly lived in Gainesville, Texas.

John T. ALEXANDER's remains will be buried tomorrow in Ardmore, Indian Territory. He died yesterday in Granite, Oklahoma Territory.

Mrs. W. H. MITCHELL, 54, died Wednesday of heart failure in Ardmore, Indian Territory.

W. M. CROW died Monday. He was a farmer near Clarendon, Texas.

W. S. GREEN, of Sunset, Texas lost two children to death this week. Mannie, 7, died on the 11th and an unnamed infant died Wednesday.

C. C. RATHER died Wednesday in Belton, Texas and was buried yesterday at McDowell Cemetery. He was a Mason. Rev. George W. LEE conducted the funeral.

Elmer PARKS, 14, son of Sam PARKS, died very suddenly in Clarendon, Texas a few days ago.

Mrs. Lorado MAYABB died Monday north of Greenville, Texas. She died from the effects of burns suffered 7 weeks ago. She leaves a husband and a child. The funeral was Tuesday at Money graveyard.

A. M. PUCKETT and Nellie DEER were married in Kaufman, Texas Tuesday by the Rev. E. D. SOLOMON.

Z. B. STALNER, 75, of Oswego, Kansas and Mrs. Octavia CANTWELL, 67, of Powell, Texas married Tuesday in Corsicana, Texas. They left for Kansas Wednesday.

John CUTHBERT and Mary Alice WHATLEY, both of Bryan, Texas were married Sunday by Rev. V. I. STIRMAN of Garrett, Texas. The article was datelined Ennis, Texas.

W. M. BLANKENSHIP and Miss N. A. STEELMAN were married Wednesday at the Cocke County Courthouse by County Judge WRIGHT in Gainesville, Texas.

M. B. GRISSAM and Lizzie WALLIS were married Wednesday by Justice PEARMAN in Gainesville, Texas.

Dan RATTAN and Edna LINDSAY married Wednesday at the home of her parents in Van Alstyne, Texas.

Bertha KENNEDY married Gordon MATTHEWS, of Jonesboro, Arkansas Tuesday in Bonham, Texas. She is the daughter of Dr. and Mrs. J. T. KENNEDY.

Marriage license issued by Tarrant County Clerk: H. P. LOWE and Adrian ATTWELL.

Births reported to Tarrant County Clerk's office: a boy to Mr. and Mrs. Will LUTZ and a boy to Mr. and Mrs. B. L. DIXON.

Death reported to Tarrant County Clerk's office: Capt. A. W. SCOBLE, 65, died acute nephritis on April 14.

Saturday, April 16, 1904

The remains of Kearney J. KEVLIN, Jr. will arrive in Dallas Sunday or Monday. He was killed in an explosion on the battleship U.S.S. Missouri off Pensacola, Florida.

Tom DOWD surrendered to authorities Thursday night at Montague, Texas. He is accused of the killing of E. TUCK near St. Jo, Texas Thursday.

C. J. SMITH, 64, died near Mabank, Texas Thursday from injuries suffered when he fell from a wagon and was run over. He was a farmer. His wife survives him.

John W. COLE, son of Dr. J. W. COLE of Weatherford, Texas, was killed in the explosion on the battleship USS Missouri.

Etta Maurice MCCAULEY, the baby daughter of Mrs. Lula MCCAULEY, died yesterday at her home in Fort Worth.

W. F. MOORE and Mattie TURNER were married by Justice PEARMAN Thursday in the courthouse in Gainesville, Texas.

H. B. LOCKLOOR and Ola LOTT were married last night in Rural Shade, Texas.

The internment of J. E. BUNCH, who died Wednesday near Woodbine, Texas, took place at the Oak Valley graveyard near there.

H. T. POINDEXTER, 70, died at the home of W. M. WISE near Blossom, Texas recently. He was buried at Blossom Cemetery.

Lonnie MITCHELL, about 10, was shot Thursday near Gainesville, Texas. He died Friday. The shooting resulted from an accidental discharge of a target gun an older brother was cleaning.

Marriage licenses issued at the Tarrant County Clerk's office: R. A. BENEDICT and Mary MARLOUM, C. H. CARPENTER and Lula GIFFORD, R. G. GARNETT and Mattie BENTON, James L. ZINN and Eula DENNEY, and Thomas P. PERRY and Maggie STAGLE.

Sunday, April 17, 1904

Hays GEE was acquitted yesterday of murder charges in the death of S. R. EVANS in a trial held at Guthrie, Oklahoma Territory. EVANS was killed in a hotel at Stroud, Oklahoma Territory on December 1, 1902. GEE was managing the hotel at the time EVANS was shot and killed.

J. C. PREWETT was acquitted yesterday of murder charges in a trial held at Pecos, Texas. PREWETT was accused of the October, 1903, murder of Ben I. SMITH.

The funeral of District Clerk Alex S. FIELD was Friday in Marshall, Texas.

Births recorded at Tarrant County Clerk's office: a boy to Mr. and Mrs. C. H. JONES on April 13; a girl to Mr. and Mrs. H. W. HIGHTOWER on April 8; a boy to Mr. and Mrs. Ben ROBINSON on April 7; a boy to Mr. and Mrs. H. W. THOMAS on March 28, twins (boy and girl) to Mr. and Mrs. J. W. HAWKINS on March 23; a boy to Mr. and Mrs. John R. ECHOLS on April 11; a girl to Mr. and Mrs. Charles HAAS on April 11; a girl to Mr. and Mrs. J. J. THOMAS on April 11; a boy to Mr. and Mrs. J. W. WILSON on April 14; a girl to Mr. and Mrs. N. G. PRATT on April 7; a boy to Mr. and Mrs. M.A. MORRIS on April 8; a girl to Mr. and Mrs. C. JAMISON on March 29 and a boy to Mr. and Mrs. O. H. NANCE.

Deaths recorded at the Tarrant County Clerk's office: Ora Fay HARDY, 2, of pneumonia on April 2; Elizabeth FERGUSON, 2, of pneumonia on April 10, and baby COBB, 5 days, of an abscess with no date listed.

Marriage licenses issued at the Tarrant County Clerk's office: Thomas E. CHRISTOPHER and Jana D. GILMORE; Charley HATTON and Lee Etta WALKER; J. W. JONES and Rosa BELIKEN; O. K. SMITH and Alice VANCE; and D. Z. STATEN and Mrs. Sylvia WHITE.

Mr. and Mrs. R. SNODGRASS of Rosen Heights, Texas are the parents of a baby girl born last week.

E. A. UPTON shot and killed George REED Thursday in a Big Bend mining camp near Terlingua, Texas.

James HAYNIE, 23, was killed yesterday when he fell into an abandoned well near Buffalo, Texas. He was the son of Dr. W. M. HAYNIE.

W. F. MOORE and Mattie TURNER were married at the Cocke County Courthouse in Gainesville, Texas by Justice of the Peace PEARMAN yesterday.

H. B. LOCKLEAR and Ola LOTT were married at the home of the bride's parents in Rural Shade, Texas Friday.

Helen Elder SMITH of San Antonio and Hugo Claiborne ADAMS of Fort Worth married at the home of the bride's parents in San Antonio Thursday. They will make Fort Worth their home.

Andrew O'ROURKE and Frances DRUMM were married at St. Patrick's Catholic Church in Fort Worth Wednesday. They will live in Houston.

Monday, April 18, 1904

The five year old daughter of J.M. LEFEVRE was killed when she was kicked by a horse near Hobart, Oklahoma Territory. No date was listed.

James BLAIR was shot and killed Saturday in a restaurant at Muskogee, Indian Territory. Jessie KIDD was arrested.

Albert KELTON shot and killed Anna MOORE and then took his own life at Brownwood, Texas yesterday.

Joseph Winston HUDNALL, 55, died in Dallas yesterday. He was a Confederate veteran who was among the youngest of the soldiers who fought for the Confederacy. A son lives in Austin.

Nat PARKER, 77, died Saturday at his home six miles south of Greenville, Texas. His funeral will be today at Hart Cemetery by the Masons.

Charles JONES, of Marshall, Texas died suddenly yesterday there.

Lizzie WRIGHT, a teacher, died in Valley View, Texas Saturday and was buried there yesterday.

Mrs. Burney PARKS died yesterday in Belton, Texas.

Edgar COULSON, 5, died Saturday in Frances, Indian Territory. He was the son of J. E. and Mary E. COULSON.

G. W. COTTON, a druggist, died Friday in Lawton, Oklahoma Territory. His remains were shipped to Norman, Oklahoma Territory for burial.

Mrs. W. H. JOHNSON died Friday in Paris, Texas. She had lived in the same house for 42 years.

Mrs. E. O. DAVIDSON, 87, died Friday at the home of her daughter, Mrs. William GOODING, in Paris, Texas.

W. H. STEPHENSON died Friday north of Paris, Texas. He was born in Bedford County, Tennessee, in 1830 and came to Texas in 1877. He was a Confederate veteran.

W. S. ALLEN, 94, died Friday in Marshall, Texas. He was a Mason and a Confederate veteran.

The infant child of Mr. and Mrs. James OGBURN died Friday in Greenville, Texas. The remains were buried in Dixon, Texas, the family's former home.

W. D. SCOTT, an employee of the Texas and Pacific Railroad, died Friday at his home in Marshall, Texas.

The burial of J. E. BURCH, who died in Woodbine, Texas Wednesday, took place in Oak Valley Cemetery Thursday.

H. T. POINDEXTER, 70, died near Blossom, Texas a day or two ago. He died at the home of W. M. WISE. Burial took place in Blossom.

Irma IRVING and G. W. MEACHAM married Thursday in Cleburne, Texas. The bride is the daughter of Peyton IRVING.

Marriage licenses issued in Hunt County, Texas: John ADAMS and Lonlie TICHNOR and Fithian J. BROUN and Phena HARRIS.

Tuesday, April 19, 1904

Jim JULLIN, who shot and killed his wife and sister-in-law Saturday, was found dead yesterday in Walder, Texas. He is believed to have committed suicide.

Charles WARNER, 25, killed himself in Houston yesterday. He died of a gunshot wound to his head. He was a carpenter.

Sam COE, Jr., about 25, took his own life yesterday by drinking carbolic acid. He is survived by his father and brother.

Coleman BROWN was shot and killed yesterday in Marshall, Texas. Robert COLE surrendered to police and was released on $500 bail.

Walter L. BACHTEL and Miss Willie SAMS married yesterday in Lawton, Oklahoma Territory. He is a division manager for Wells Fargo Express Company in Chickasha, Oklahoma Territory. The new couple will live there.

Robert FRANKS and Ollie MANGUM were married Sunday by Judge G. M. FELTS in Belton, Texas.

J. G. COOPER of Dallas married Edna RAMSEY in Cleburne, Texas Sunday.

Marriage licenses issued at Cleburne: E. F. BARNES and Pearly NORRIS, J. A. NICHOLS and Enzella GENRY, J. G. COOPER and Edna Pearl RAMSEY, Claude BASYE and Jennie Mae WARD, C. C. GAMBRELL and Myrtle WILLIAMSON.

Dr. Benson KNOX, a physician, was buried Sunday in Hillsboro, Texas. The funeral was from the Presbyterian Church there. Dr. KNOX was a surgeon in the Confederate Army.

Annie CELUSTKA died Sunday. She was buried yesterday in Ennis, Texas.

Lem DOWD and Ed DAVENPORT appeared at St. Jo, Texas in connection with the death of E. TUCK last Wednesday. They were released on bond.

Deaths recorded by the Tarrant County Clerk: Emma WATSON, 37, died of dropsy on April 15; and Earl JOYCE, 11, died of tubercular meningitis on April 10.

Birth recorded by the Tarrant County Clerk: a boy to Mr. and Mrs. Walter E. ROLOFF on April 10.

Wednesday, April 20, 1904

The paper for this date did not appear on the microfilm.

Thursday, April 21, 1904

Express messenger W. F. BOSTICK of El Paso was killed in a train wreck near Zectacos, Mexico.

B. T. DICK, pioneer of Erath County, died in Stephenville, Texas Tuesday and was buried yesterday. He was a member of the International Order of Oddfellows.

Maurice MCASHAN of Houston and Aileen NORRIS of Austin were married in Austin yesterday. He is the son of J. E. MCASHAN and she is the daughter of John P. NORRIS.

Louis LOUCHARD, 69, died in Dallas yesterday. He was a stone and brick mason.

Ferdinand LANUKE, 68, was found dead in his camp near the Trinity River. He was a Prussian and a recluse. He had lived in a camp near Red Bank, Texas for ten years and owned several horses.

Rigsby L. BARCLAY of Temple, Texas and Miss Louzelle ROSE of Salado, Texas were married Tuesday in Salado, Texas by Dr. W.A. WILSON of Temple.

A.D. SMELSER, of Merrimac, Oklahoma Territory, and Jessie JOHNSTON, of Valley View, Texas, married in Valley View yesterday. They left on the northbound Santa Fe train for Merrimac and their new home.

Marriage licenses issued by Tarrant County Clerk's office: Riley M. CHATMAN and Josie M. JONAS, Ben Hill MARTIN and Katherine BOLAND, and Frank A. BAER and Emma LENZEN.

Births recorded at the Tarrant County Clerk's office: a girl to Mr. and Mrs. S. MATHEN on April 19 and a boy to Mr. and Mrs. Thomas NANCE on April 16.

Friday, April 22, 1904

Note: The paper was heavily damaged on the film.

Greenville, Texas marriage licenses issued: N. F. DAGGETT and Ethel ROSE; J. M. INNIS and Mattie MCASHAN, and J. E. GOOD and Sadie RUSSEY.

Robert W. PERSONS and Heny May CHAMBLESS married in Cleburne, Texas on Wednesday.

Hunter HARDEMAN and Annetto HARDEMAN were married in Corsicana, Texas Wednesday.

J. F. MARTIN of Dallas and Annie Lou HOUSER were married Wednesday in the home of R. K. ERWIN of Waxahachie, Texas. The Rev. Chalmers MCPHERSON officiated.

J. H. CATES and Lena RUSSELL were married at the bride's home near Bardwell, Texas Wednesday. Rev. F. L. DUPONT officiated.

J. J. JENNINGS died in Austin yesterday. He was superintendent of the state asylum for colored deaf and handicapped children.

J. V. SPAIN died Wednesday in Ovilla, Texas and was buried in Ovilla Cemetery. He lived on a farm owned by Worth ROCKETT.

Taylor JOHNS, formerly of Noble County, died on the streets of Perry, Indian Territory of heart failure. His wife and three children survived him. Burial was in Winfield, Kansas.

Saturday, April 23, 1904

Charles WIRTLE, 42, committed suicide in Shawnee, Oklahoma Territory. He drank carbolic acid. He was a merchant from Orange Heights, Florida.

Nanie KEITH, 42, died in Austin Thursday. She was the wife of M. S. KEITH and an employee of the comptroller's office. She died from yellow jaundice.

The remains of S. J. JENKINS were shipped to Marlin, Texas for burial.

Mary MILLER, severely burned on March 8, died of her injuries in Louise. Her funeral was yesterday there.

C. W. BONNER, 79, died of heart failure in Chico, Texas yesterday. He was a Mason.

Deaths recorded by Tarrant County Clerk's office: Martha WATSON, 38, consumption, on April 13; Mame CHEEK, infant, on April 9; and Babe CHEEK, infant on April 8.

Births recorded by Tarrant County Clerk's office: a boy to Mr. and Mrs. W.R. BRIDGES on April 18; a boy to Mr. and Mrs. F.M. ASHCROFT on April 16, a boy to Mr. and Mrs. J.M. WEEMES on April 18, a girl Mr. and Mrs. _____ BOX on April 16, a boy to Mr. and Mrs. W.M. CUMMINGS on April 7, a boy to Mr. and Mrs. Augustus CHEEK on April 8, a boy to Mr. and Mrs. Rondo SAUNDERS on April 15, a girl to Mr. and Mrs. Bryan HARRINGTON on April 11 and a boy to Mr. and Mrs. J.N. MCLEOD on April 17.

Marriage licenses issued by Tarrant County Clerk's office: A. A. HUTSELL to Cora BIGGERS; J. O. STOCKETT and Miss M. E. ALLEN.

Sunday, April 24, 1904

Mrs. M. V. CROOM, formerly of Dallas, died in New York City and will be buried in Waco, Texas. No dates were provided.

W. E. WHITESIDES died Friday at his home in Putnam, Texas. Burial was in Putnam Cemetery yesterday. He was a Confederate veteran.

Mrs. Margaret RAWLS died Thursday in San Angelo, Texas. Her funeral was yesterday.

"Aunt Sally" JONES died in DeLeon, Texas Thursday and was buried in the city cemetery there Wednesday (sic).

The funeral of J. O. WOMACK on Thursday was the largest seen in many years in Marshall, Texas.

Virginia MORGAN, infant daughter of Mr. and Mrs. G. B. MORGAN, died Thursday in Weatherford, Texas and was buried the same day there.

Mary CHANDLER died Friday in Keene, Texas. She was the daughter of George CHANDLER of Chicago.

Mrs. S. E. HATCHETT died in Vernon, Texas Thursday after a long illness.

Marriage licenses issued in Greenville, Texas: G. B. REEDER and Nina L. HOLLIDAY, W. H. REED and Mrs. Elberta HALL, O. B. LEATH and Pearl BUSH, and H. BREWER and Beulah BAKER.

G. B. REEDER of Greenville, Texas and Nina HOLLIDAY of Kingston, Texas married at the home of the bride's parents Thursday night. Rev. S. S. FRAZIER of Greenville officiated.

Blake POWERS of Bellevue, Texas and Ollie AGROBRIGHT of Vasht, Texas were married Thursday by Rev. W. J. WALKER.

W. N. CARPENTER and Miss JENKINS of Leesburg, Texas were married in the Camp County Bank with cashier R. A. MORRIS officiating.

Lymon PRESTON, 72, of Muskogee, Indian Territory, and Julia DAVIS, 63, of Nevada, Missouri, were married Thursday in South McAlester, Indian Territory.

Judge Julius SHUTZE died in Austin yesterday. He was born in Dessau, Germany, on March 29, 1835 and came to Texas with his family in 1850. He was a music teacher and nationally active in the Sons of Herman. He was survived by his sons, Albert, Edward, Hugo, Julius, Jr., Adolph and Nono, and by daughters Mrs. H. GISSEL and Misses Henrietta, Alivinia and Clara. All resided in Austin except Hugo who lived in Dallas.

The search continues for Henry SIMMONS in connection with the death of Lula SANDBERG, 18, of Manor, Texas. SANDBERG was riding in her buggy in Austin when she was killed.

R.L. DERRICK, a railroad contractor, was killed by a laborer after quarrel near Muskogee, Indian Territory.

William RANDLE, 65, died Friday of cancer in Estelline, Texas. He will be buried by the Masons in the city cemetery.

Eva MAY, 16, died of pneumonia on April 16 and was buried the same day in San Angelo, Texas.

Allie Priscilla JOHNSON, 2, daughter of Mr. and Mrs. Dave JOHNSON, died Monday in San Angelo, Texas.

Mrs. Margaret RAWLS died Thursday from stomach trouble in San Angelo, Texas. Her burial was Friday from her daughter's home there.

Mrs. S. E. HATCHETT died Thursday in Vernon, Texas. She was buried Saturday in East View Cemetery.

T. J. REEVES, 50, died at the Terrell Asylum Friday. He was survived by a wife and four children. The funeral was held at the Bingham graveyard near Campbell, Texas.

Mrs. Belle CHAMBER died Thursday near Dumas, Texas. She was the wife of Tom CHAMBERS, who is a former county treasurer for Sherman County. Two small children also survive.

Mrs. Mattie SHOW, 73, died Wednesday in Jefferson, Texas.

Word of the death of J. H. MAJORS in St. Louis, Missouri has been received. He formerly lived in Bellevue, Texas.

J. H. DORSEY, a farmer near Byron, Texas, died Friday.

Mrs. M. J. SPLAWN died in Fort Worth Friday. She was buried at Jellico, Texas, her former home.

A. PAGE died of consumption at his home in Stonebury, Texas.

Katherine BOLAND and Ben H. MARTIN were married in the Fort Worth home of Mr. and Mrs. H. W. WILLIAMS Wednesday.

Anna John BALDWIN and William Garland BROWN were married in the Dallas home of his parents, Mr. and Mrs. W.B. BROWN on Thursday.

Miss Edna Earle PURNELL and Alexander STEWART of Fort Worth were quietly married by Rev. M. M. DAVIS in Dallas this week. The couple will live in Fort Worth. He is the son of Julia E. STEWART. She is the daughter of Mrs. L. V. PURNELL.

Births recorded in Tarrant County Clerk's Office: a girl to Mr. and Mrs. R. Y. MCFADDEN on April 12, a boy to Mr. and Mrs. Will BERLESON on April 3, and a girl to Mr. and Mrs. Frank BLEVINS on April 18.

Marriage licenses issued by Tarrant County Clerk's Office: Felix RUSSELL and Annie MCLEOD, S. M. BERNARD and Mrs. M.S. BERNARD, J. A. VAN ZANDT and Harriett CANBEL.

Monday, April 25, 1904

P. E. ENGLER was found dead about two miles northeast of Virginia Point near Galveston, Texas. He was about 35 and had been dead a week. He was employed as a timekeeper near Texas City, Texas.

Robert KETCHUM shot his wife Bertha and killed himself eight miles east of Luling, Texas.

Edward TAYLOR, 15, was killed Saturday when he was crushed under a horse near Corales, Indian Territory.

James DUNCAN, 20, was killed by the accidental discharge of a gun. The article was datelined Guthrie, Indian Territory with no date or place of Duncan's death reported.

Sam DUKE was found dead in Denton, Texas. He had been shot through the head and a pistol was found near the body. An inquest was ordered.

The funeral of George C. WARD was held at the Mulkey Memorial Church in Fort Worth. He was a former deputy district clerk. Rev. J. A. WHITEHURST and Rev. I. Z. T. MORRIS officiated. Burial was in City Cemetery.

L. T. BOWLIN, 24, died of heart failure in Abilene, Texas. The word was received last night. His funeral and burial will be in Fort Worth.

M. D. MILES, of Newport, Arkansas, and May REED married Saturday in Paris, Texas. They left for Newport.

Will P. PENNY and Sadie LEDFORD married Sunday in Paris, Texas. Rev. R. S. PERDER officiated.

Marriage licenses issued in Greenville, Texas: J. M. WISDOM and Dora NELSON, J. M. BOWDEN and Susie HUNT, H. S. LYNCH and Lula REED, W. J. LEATHEN and Mary THOMPSON.

J. W. ECHELBURGER and Dora WILSON married Sunday in Rhome, Texas. They left for home in Quanah, Texas.

May MACKENZIE died Thursday in Acme, Texas. She was a former resident of Weatherford, Texas. Her body was returned to Weatherford for burial.

George T. BOWEMAN, of Superior, Wisconsin, died Thursday of Bright's Disease in Mineral Wells, Texas.

James M. HOUSTON, 30, died of typhoid fever Saturday near Cheapside, Texas. Survivors were his wife and two children.

John T. BARTLETT, of Bartlett, Texas, died yesterday. He was a banker.

F. G. AYERS died in Roswell, New Mexico Territory of heart failure. He was a native of Winston, Vermont and will be buried there.

The two-year-old daughter of Mr. and Mrs. C. H. DIXON died Saturday in Cleburne, Texas.

Dr. James M. FLENNIKEN died in Cleburne, Texas yesterday. He was buried by the Masons the same day.

The infant child of Dr. W. J. DOSSEY died Saturday in Rhome, Texas. It will be buried in Aurora Masonic Cemetery.

Tuesday, April 26, 1904

John ABBOTT, his wife and two children were killed yesterday in a storm four miles south of Pryor Creek, Indian Territory. Also killed in the storm in the area were Albert DEALY, 6, and Lucy BITTING, 8.

Mrs. Mary LAMAR, Mrs. John LEMASTER, Arthur BROUGHT, a child of N. J. HOUCK, Elijah RUSSELL and his wife and child were all killed at Fairland, Indian Territory by a tornado yesterday.

John TRUELOVE and his child were killed yesterday in a tornado at Chouteau, Indian Territory. Mrs. John TRUELOVE was mortally injured in the same storm.

J. T. HOLLAND died yesterday in Amarillo, Texas. He was a banker and a stockman. He had lived in the Panhandle since 1887.

Pete BEST, 18, was killed yesterday in Galveston, Texas. He was thrown from a wagon.

Lewis PATTERSON, 16, was killed yesterday near Weatherford, Oklahoma Territory. He was hit by a shotgun discharge.

Minor MORRIS, 74, died Sunday of the flu at Cooper, Texas. He was the father of City Marshal Frank MORRIS, John MORRIS, Mrs. Tom LANBETH, Mrs. Virg FINLEY, and Mrs. Millard ROUNDTREE.

Dr. J. M. FLENNIKER, who died yesterday, left the following children: W. J. FLENNIKEN, B. D. P. R. FLENNIKEN, Mrs. Jack MACKENZIE, Mrs. Ed OLIVER, and Mrs. Sam BENNETT of Cleburne, Texas, J. M. and T. N. FLENNIKEN of Hill County, Texas and J. C. FLENNIKEN of Bee, Indian Territory.

Mabel BANKS, 2, daughter of Walter BANKS, died from eating matches Sunday near Joshua, Texas.

T. H. SELLERS died Friday in Cleburne, Texas. His survivors include his wife and son, his brother J. W. SELLERS and his sister, Mrs. J. M. BERRY. Burial was in Granbury, Texas.

The infant of T. C. BONNER died Sunday in Corsicana, Texas and was buried there yesterday.

The infant of A. HIGHPOTE died Sunday in Corsicana, Texas and was buried yesterday.

Mrs. A. L. GEE, of Greenville, Texas, died Sunday at the home of her daughter, Mrs. Booth CLEGG, in Oklahoma City, Oklahoma Territory.

George NOBLE, 62, of Kerens, Texas, died of consumption yesterday.

Olive CARTLIDGE died Sunday at Boyce, Texas and was buried yesterday.

F. M. VAUGHT, of Little Rock, Arkansas, and Nina RICHMOND, of Ennis, Texas, were married in Ennis Sunday by Rev. W.C. HILLBURN. They will live in Little Rock.

S. W. POTEET, of Ennis, Texas, and Cora CARTER, of Hempstead, Texas, were married in Ennis yesterday by Rev. S. H. SLAUGHTER.

Henry SULLIVAN and Naomi YOWELL were married Sunday in Ennis, Texas by Elder V.I. STIRMAN.

Colonel W. A. MADDOX died yesterday in Fort Worth. His death took place at the home of his son, E. P. MADDOX. Colonel MADDOX was born in Troupe County, Georgia, in 1825 and was a Confederate veteran. He married Mary MAY. She died in Tarrant County 25 years ago. Surviving are seven sons: Walter T., John E., R. E., A. P. Jim and Pike. J. N. MADDOX, a brother also survives. A sister, Mrs. Thomas SCOTT of Atlanta, Arkansas also survives.

Births recorded at the Tarrant County Clerk's office: a boy to Mr. and Mrs. J. D. C. SMITH on April 20, a girl to Mr. and Mrs. R. E. SPEAR on April 23, a boy to Mr. and Mrs. William CROMMER on April 24, a girl to Mr. and Mrs. G. N. HULL on April 16, a boy to Mr. and Mrs. J. N. COOPER on March 29, a boy to Mr. and Mrs. R. A. YOUNG on April 11, a boy to Mr. and Mrs. J. M. CARLISLE on April 20, and a girl to Mr. and Mrs. L. COLLINS on April 22.

Deaths recorded at the Tarrant County Clerk's office: W. P. MCGEE, 77, died of pneumonia on April 18; George C. WARD, 53, died of dropsy on April 22; Lucy THOMPSON, 46, died of consumption on April 17; Mrs. M. L. CAMPBELL, 79, died of Bright's Disease on April 5; and Ben VALENTINE, 69, died of a liver abscess on April 19.

Marriage licenses issued at the Tarrant County Clerk's office: Stephen CARRINGTOIN and Annie B. WILSON, and Andrew J. FARCHER and Grace MOTHERSHEAD.

Graham RENFRO married Elizabeth BARKSDALE Thursday in Hillsboro, Texas.

Wednesday, April 27, 1904

W. R. HALEY, 94, died Monday at his home near Fulton, Oklahoma Territory.

Former Comanche chief QUINITE, 100, died. He was buried at Fort Sill.

R. F. STOKES was arrested after A. CARBELLO died in Orange, Texas. CARBELLO was injured by STOKES last November and died of his injuries.

Mamie FORD, of Marshall, Texas, was killed in a collision between a switch engine and a street car in El Paso. No date was reported.

Dr. John B. BLANTON died Monday in Chico, Texas. He was a physician and surgeon for 44 years and a Confederate veteran. He was born in Murray County, Kentucky on February 24, 1839. He married first Fensie PEEK of Clarksville, Texas. There were no children of that marriage. He married second Emma CLARK of Coryell County, Texas. There were two sons and two daughters from that marriage: Dr. William P. BLANTON, of Crofton, Texas, Dr. J. J. BLANTON of Chico, Texas, Mrs. Delia TADLOCK of Chico, Texas and Mrs. E. A. WELLS of Wellington, Texas.

W. M. ALLEN, 79, died yesterday in Chico, Texas. His death took place at the residence of his son, A. J. ALLEN. He is also survived by a daughter, Mrs. Alex GRAY. The burial will take place in Chico Cemetery.

The funeral of Colonel W. A. MADDOX was held Tuesday in the home of E. P. MADDOX, his son.

The remains of Sam DUKE were buried in Odd Fellow Cemetery Monday. The funeral was conducted by the Knights of Pythias.

J. M. DAY died Monday in Roswell, New Mexico Territory. His survivors included a wife, three daughters and five sons. He was to be buried in Austin.

R. P. KIRK is dead at Waco, Texas. He was principal of the Waco Public Schools. No date was reported.

C. A. STRAIN died in Waxahachie, Texas yesterday.

"Aunt Marietta" PHILLIPS, 97, died Sunday in Gainesville, Texas.

T. C. MCCAIN, a farmer about 50, died Monday at his home two miles north of Milford, Texas.

The infant child of Mr. and Mrs. K. RUBY died of measles Monday in Greenville, Texas.

Mrs. Mary SANDERS died Monday in Ardmore, Indian Territory and was buried there yesterday. She was the wife of J. A. SANDERS, a grocer. The cause of death was consumption.

Tillie BLUM and Fred HABERZETTE married Sunday in Temple, Texas. Rev. P. A. HECKMAN officiated.

Marriage licenses issued by Tarrant County Clerk's office: H. A. STRABLE and Cora HARSH, Ira WILLIAMS and Mrs. Susie NICHOLSON, John B. CRADDOCK and Dona Lee CARTER, and J. H. L. PRITCHARD and Minnie PATTERSON.

Births recorded at the Tarrant County Clerk's office: a boy to Mr. and Mrs. J. D. MONROE on April 24, a boy to Mr. and Mrs. S. D. DYERS on April 14 and a boy to Mr. and Mrs. Clarence BRIDGEPATH on April 22.

Deaths recorded at the Tarrant County Clerk's office: Eddie B. KING, 1, died of unknown causes on April 22; H. C. WHITEHEAD, 42, died of meningitis on April 22 and George ROSE, 14 days, died of meningitis on April 19.

Thursday, April 28, 1904

S. A. HUNT of Fort Worth and A. WADE of Houston were killed near Winchell, Texas. They were the fireman and engineer, respectively, on a train that hit a cow. WADE was to be buried in Houston.

Howard SMITH, 5, died yesterday in North Fort Worth. His funeral was held at the family home and burial took place in Oakwood Cemetery. He was the son of Mr. and Mrs. Walter SMITH

Horace WEIR, of Durant, Mississippi, and Cornelia HOPPER of Fort Worth were married yesterday and left for Durant. Dr. Junius B. FRENCH officiated.

Rev. J. T. LONGIRO died Monday night in Mineral Wells, Texas. He will be buried today in Belton, Texas.

W. H. MORGAN died yesterday of consumption in Belton, Texas. He was buried in North Belton, Texas by the Masons the same day.

The four month old child of Mr. and Mrs. Charlie WINTERWOOD died yesterday in Ennis, Texas.

Mrs. Buck SMITH, of Kerns, Texas, died yesterday in her home.

Miss Marian Louise SIMS and Edwin Ethelhart WILSON, of Cisco, Texas, married Tuesday.

C.B. DODSON and Elsey ENION, both of Barstow, Texas, were recently married. No date was reported.

Marriage licenses issued by the Tarrant County Clerk's office: W. P. BEVANS and Mabel Clara GRANDSTAFF, and John J. FISHER and Alpha MAJORS.

Friday, April 29, 1904

John WALLACE died Tuesday in North Cleburne, Texas. Burial was in Caddo Cemetery.

Mrs. M. M. SMITH died Tuesday in Cleburne, Texas. She was buried on Wednesday.

Polly YAGER, infant daughter of Mr. and Mrs. C. E. YAGER, died Wednesday in Abilene, Texas. Burial was the same day there.

Maurice G. NEATHERY and Ethelwyn LOVE married Wednesday near Hopewell, Texas.

J. D. STEPHENSON and Hattie LYON married Wednesday west of Paris, Texas.

George GAITHER and Mamie Carrie Bell WALLACE married Wednesday in Paris, Texas. Rev. W. H. WRIGHT officiated. The bride is the daughter of Mrs. C. R. CLIFTON.

Sterling HATHAWAY and Miss PRESTON married Wednesday in Paris, Texas. Rev. J. E. VINSON of Jacksboro officiated.

Marriage licenses issued at the Hunt County Clerk's office: Will JONES and Mattie MCCAIN, and J. R. BOSS and Mrs. C. R. JOHNSON.

Stephen W. CARRINGTON and Annie B. WILSON married Tuesday near Handley, Texas.

Luke HARRISON and Abbie Lee PAYNE married near Palmer, Texas. The bride is the daughter of Capt. John A. PAYNE.

John CHAPMAN and Isabella STOKER were married in Dallas Wednesday.

Omer GIBSON and Ona INMAN married in Slidell, Texas. They left for Deming, New Mexico Territory shortly afterward. He is a cattleman. She is the daughter of Mr. and Mrs. J. M. INMAN. No date was listed.

Cleburne marriage licenses: J. S. WILLINGHAM and Florence WOLF, and W. H. MYATT and Annie DICKSON.

Jenny HOFF and William H. SERVIES received a marriage license in St. Louis, Missouri. HOFF is a Dallas resident.

Marriage licenses issued by Tarrant County Clerk's office: W. L. LYON, Jr. and Maggie Augusta MCGOWAN, George L. JOHNSON and Florence PHILLIPS, Edmund OWENS and Fannie GODBERRY.

Births recorded by Tarrant County Clerk's office: a girl to Mr. and Mrs. E. HIZER of Fort Worth on April 19; a boy to Mr. and Mrs. Bert M. ADEN of Riverside on April 23, a boy to Mr. and Mrs. G. Lee BLYTHE of Fort Worth on April 24; a girl to Mr. and Mrs. E. B. O'BRYAN of Fort Worth on April 27, and a boy to Mr. and Mrs. I. W. CHANCY on April 26.

Mrs. H. C. ARENDT died Thursday on the J. Blach and Company ranch near Albany, Texas. She was buried yesterday in the Albany Cemetery.

Births recorded by Tarrant County Clerk's office: a girl to Mr. and Mrs. John D. WHITE of Fort Worth on April 28, and a girl to Mr. and Mrs. Duncan MACRAY of Polytechnic Heights with no date reported.

Death reported to Tarrant County Clerk's Office: Beatrice RIDEOUT, 6 months, residing in Marine, died of malnutrition on April 14.

Marriage licenses issued by Tarrant County Clerk's office: O. W. RYAN and Miss Willie BROWN.

Saturday, April 30, 1904

In Austin, Henry SIMMONS pled guilty to the murder of Lula SANDBERG last week. He was sentenced to be hanged on Monday.

Kendall FARMER, about 13, died Friday in rural Tarrant County, about eight miles from Fort Worth. He died of injuries suffered when he was accidentally shot with a target gun.

G. W. BROWN, 71, died Thursday three miles north of Gainesville, Texas. His remains were shipped to Fannin, Texas for burial. He was the father of Mrs. G. W. MILLER.

Mrs. Eulalie BESSE, wife of David BESSE, died yesterday in Ennis, Texas. She will be buried in the Catholic cemetery today.

News of the death of B. P. ALEXANDER in Burleson, Texas on Wednesday reached Cleburne yesterday.

Mrs. Jennie Williams HARKEY, 63, died Thursday in West Greenville, Texas.

W. C. IMPIS and Mattie PORTER, of Hokchito, Indian Territory, married Thursday in McKinney, Texas. Dr. E. E. KING, pastor of the First Baptist Church officiated.

Mr. EVERETT and Vida FRANKEBERGER married Thursday in Gainesville, Texas. No given name of the groom was reported.

Ed MITCHELL and Lerna WALTERS, both of Wynnewood, Indian Territory, married Thursday in Pauls Valley, Indian Territory.

J. R. BASS and C. R. JOHNSON married Monday in Caddo Mills, Texas. Rev. H. B. PENDER officiated.

J. S. WILINGHAM and Florence WOLF married Thursday in Cleburne, Texas. Justice of the Peace Jim SELLARS officiated.

Tom TURNER and May NORDMAN married Thursday. The place was not legible, and the dateline on the story was Ardmore, Indian Territory.

Abe REED was sentenced yesterday to hang in South McAlester, Indian Territory for the death of a man in Hokchito, Indian Territory. Judge W. H. CLAYTON passed sentence.

The trial of Joe LAWRENCE for the murder of James WILSON is set for next week in district court in Fort Worth. It is expected to be moved on a change of venue request.

The trial of Robert "Red" BONTON for the murder of Toy MAPLE is set for next week in district court in Fort Worth.

Marriage licenses issued by Tarrant County Clerk's office: O. W. RYAN and Miss Willie BERRY.

May, 1904

Sunday, May 1, 1904

William SHEFFIELD, his wife and two daughters were killed at Valiant, Indian Territory. John WALLENBERG, son-in-law of SHEFFIELD, is being pursued. Two sons, ages 16 and 7, escaped.

A wedding reception to honor Mr. and Mrs. Ed WILSON was held in Cisco, Texas. The couple was married Tuesday in Weatherford, Texas. WILSON is the son of Mr. and Mrs. N. R. WILSON of Cisco. The bride is the former Marian SIMS.

Will FREER was thrown from his horse and killed yesterday at Weatherford, Texas.

Mrs. George R. TABOR, wife of the state health officer, died in Austin yesterday.

Adolph FRIEDLANDER died in Waco, Texas yesterday. He is survived by his wife and seven children. He was born in Germany in 1850 and came to Waco in 1873.

John MCDANIEL was convicted yesterday of burglary in Weatherford, Texas. He was sentenced to five years in the penitentiary.

Miss Minnie BRATTON, 28, died in Fort Worth yesterday. The funeral took place at her home and was conducted by Rev. R. E. CHANDLER of Cannon Avenue Cumberland Presbyterian Church. She will be buried in Mansfield, Texas.

Monday, May 2, 1904

Charley FORD committed suicide at Rosston, Texas. Word arrived Saturday at Gainesville, Texas. No date was stated.

Luther LEITCH died of typhoid fever on Thursday at Granbury, Texas.

Mrs. J.W. BUCHANAN died Saturday in Belton, Texas.

Mrs. Anastacia PERALES, 68, died Saturday in Encinal, Texas.

J. H. O'MEARA committed suicide in Fort Worth Sunday. He was despondent over the death of his wife last December. Burial will be in Martindale, Texas. He is survived by a son and a daughter.

H. B. M. WILLIAMS married Irene HODGKINS Friday in Marshall, Texas.

Miss Anna GOULD and Harry HILTON of Bridgewater, South Dakota married in El Reno, Oklahoma Territory Saturday.

Tuesday, May 4, 1904

The paper for this date did not appear on the microfilm.

Wednesday, May 5, 1904

Colonel C. M. HOBBS died Tuesday in Hope, Indian Territory. He was the former president of the failed Merchants and Planters Bank at Duncan, Indian Territory. His death is thought to be due to illness.

John MOORE was shot and killed Monday in Hughes, Indian Territory. J. M. BRYAN walked eight miles to Roosevelt, Indian Territory to surrender.

Charles E. DARNELL died Tuesday in Dallas of the gunshot wounds he received last Saturday in Dallas. Sarah GARNER was arrested and placed in Dallas County Jail.

T. F. MILLIKAN died Sunday of appendicitis in El Reno, Indian Territory. His funeral will be at Guthrie, Oklahoma Territory at the home of O. O. COOPER, the deceased's friend. T. F. MILLIKAN was the brother of E. G. MILLIKAN.

Douglas DOUGLAS was shot and killed in Moody, Texas. He was a transient painter. No date was listed.

Marriage license issued by Tarrant County Clerk's office: James J. LOUGHREN and Joan WISSELL.

Thursday, May 5, 1904

John STEVENSON and M. R. WHITE were killed in a gunfight with Deputy Sheriff Dee BURRIS, Assistant Jailer Oscar KIRK and policeman Bob PARSONS in Shawnee, Texas yesterday.

Mrs. Cordia RAGSDALE was sentenced to life in the penitentiary yesterday in Paris, Texas. She was convicted of the murder of her three year old child at Chicota, Texas last November.

Will HAWKINS was drowned when he drove his buggy into Cedar Creek near Franklin, Texas. He was the son of J. D. HAWKINS.

Dudley D. BRYAN, Houston newspaperman, died in Houston yesterday. The funeral will be tomorrow. He was also city secretary for the City of Houston.

HOCHINEY, sachem of the Apache Nation, died yesterday in Hinton, Oklahoma Territory. He was 115 years old.

Cassie O'LEARY died yesterday in Dallas. He had been shot in a saloon by a porter Sunday night.

John NUSS, an old resident of Dallas, died yesterday in that city. He was the father of Henry NUSS and six other children.

Erret DUNLAP and Eula BOWMAN married Tuesday in Ardmore, Indian Territory.

Harry SHRAVE, a Santa Fe railroad brakeman, was killed yesterday in Willmore, Oklahoma Territory. He was making a coupling when he was killed.

The four children of Peter SCHMIDT were killed when lightning struck their house near Hobart, Oklahoma Territory. They were 8, 6, 4 and 2 years old. No names were reported.

Frank BARTEK drowned Tuesday while crossing the Little Elm Bridge on the Seaton Road near Temple, Texas.

Semore KNOX was struck by lightning and killed Tuesday near Whitney, Texas.

Marriage licenses issued in Greenville, Texas N. F. BROCK and Eddie HENDERSON, and J. L. EAST and Eunice ATHERTON.

Marriage licenses issued by Tarrant County Clerk's office: J. A. SMITH and Claudia I. LANDERS, Lanson F. NASH and Mrs. Mary Anna SMITH, E. J. MARSH and Ethel M. COTTON, B. J. HINE and Pearl M. COLLUP, M. C. GRIFFIN and Luella GUFFIN, S. W. DAVENPORT and Cora WALTON, and William TITLEY and Netta McGINNIS.

Births recorded by Tarrant County Clerk's office: a boy to Mr. and Mrs. W. N. SEQUIST of North Fort Worth on April 29; a girl to Mr. and Mrs. David GREEN of Rosen Heights on April 29, a boy to Mr. and Mrs. Robert BORY of Fort Worth on May 3, a girl to Mr. and Mrs. H. F. CONNOR of Fort Worth on May 2, and a boy to Mr. and Mrs. W. P. WYNNE of Newark on April 18.

B. J. HINE and Pearl M. COLLUP married Wednesday at the home of the bride's mother in Fort Worth and departed immediately for their new home in Kansas City.

Friday, May 6, 1904

William H. JAQUITH, 67, died in Selling, Oklahoma Territory yesterday. He was a grocer.

The four year old son of C. C. STEWART died Wednesday of typhoid pneumonia in Belton, Texas. He was buried in North Belton Cemetery.

M. L. RAMSEY and Mae WILLIAMS married Wednesday in Lone Oak, Texas.

Dofe AUTREY of Georgia and Mae MOSELEY married Wednesday in Garrett, Texas. Rev. W. K. PENROD officiated.

Cora CHANCE and T. T. WILLIAMS married Tuesday in San Angelo, Texas. Rev. Jesse SILER officiated.

Cordelia WEST, spouse of P. C. WEST, died in Taylor, Texas. No date was given. She will be buried tomorrow in Cleburne, Texas. Survivors include sons Walter, Butler and Harris WEST.

A. C. TOMPKINS died yesterday in Hempstead, Texas. His funeral will be tomorrow.

Ollie BERKLEY, daughter of Mr. and Mrs. H. A. BERKELEY, died Wednesday in Marshall, Texas. Burial was in Greenwood Cemetery.

Mrs. W. B. GRAHAM, 80, died of burns received when she fell into the fire at her home in Glory, Texas.

The seven month old child of Mr. and Mrs. Lacy WEBB of Greenwood died Saturday and was buried Monday in the Mt. Carmel Cemetery.

Bessie Bowen MARTIN died Tuesday in Lexington, Mississippi. She was buried yesterday in Van Alstyne, Texas.

Mrs. Roberts BURNS, nee Jessie PACE, died Wednesday at the home of her father, Dempsey PACE,. The funeral was yesterday at city cemetery in Temple, Texas.

Capt. John LOVE died Wednesday in Corsicana, Texas. He was buried in Modrell Cemetery yesterday.

R. I. ABNEY, 52, died yesterday in Lampasas, Texas. The cause of death was Bright's disease. He was the editor of the *Granger Times*. He will be buried in Lampasas today.

Marriage licenses issued by Tarrant County Clerk's office: Reese DeWitt CUMMINGS and Addie Dean GLEAVES, William C. FARRIS and Ida B. TIMS, Alec STEWART and Willie VAUGHAN, and John SULLIVAN and Pearl THOMPSON.

Saturday, May 7, 1904

Mrs. Allen DENNIS, George W. MASON and a child of S. F. HARPER were all killed Thursday night when a storm struck Goldthwaite, Texas. Allen DENNIS, Mrs. S. F. HARPER , Joe GRIFFITH and a child of S. F. HARPER were all seriously injured.

An eight year old child of Henry WAGLEY was killed Thursday in a cyclone at Cisco, Texas. Henry WAGLEY was seriously injured.

In Pawnee, Oklahoma Territory, Elijah LENOX was acquitted Friday of murder charges in the ax murder of his stepfather, John LENOX. His mother, Mrs. Sarah LENOX, was acquitted of the same charges Thursday.

George ASHBY was shot and killed at Keystone, Oklahoma Territory Thursday. John JAMES was arrested and held without bail.

Ed LISLE, who killed U.S. Deputy Marshal JONES in the Osage country last July, was sentenced yesterday to life imprisonment in a trial at Guthrie, Oklahoma Territory.

L. Meyers CONNOR reported yesterday in Dallas that the stomach of Mrs. S. E. RICHARDSON, who died suddenly a week ago, contained enough strychnine to cause death within 20 minutes. The cause of death was ruled as poison administered by an unknown person. Z. D. BOURNE, in whose house Mrs. RICHARDSON lived, was arrested and charged with murder.

Mrs. W. M. WARD, wife of Superintendent WARD of the Oak Cliff post office, died yesterday in Dallas.

Mrs. Mary K. FLYNN died yesterday at St. Paul's Sanitarium in Dallas. She was the sister of T.G. TERRY and a resident of Fayetteville, Arkansas.

Mrs. O. H. WRIGHT, mother of Mrs. Mary HOUGHTON, died in Austin Thursday. Burial will be today in Greenwood Cemetery in Dallas.

Will SLAUGHTER was found guilty of the murder of Steve JACCIME at Krebs in the Federal Court at South McAlester, Indian Territory yesterday. He will be sentenced to life imprisonment.

William Edward BEACH, 63, died in Dallas yesterday. He was a railroad engineer.

Caleb MARRATTA, 55, was killed yesterday in Vincennes, Indiana. He attempted to board a moving train and fell beneath the wheels. He was a resident of Denison, Texas.

S. M. "Maston" NIXON shot and killed Robert W. MALONE and Colonel John L. VEAZY in Luling, Texas yesterday. MALONE and VEAZY will be buried in Luling today.

The body of escaped prisoner Albert HAWKINS was found in the Trinity River near the Commerce Street Bridge in Dallas Saturday. HAWKINS escaped from the Dallas County Courthouse and drowned in the Trinity near the Texas and Pacific Bridge Tuesday.

The wedding of Miss Donelle KEE and William T. PATTERSON was celebrated Wednesday in DeLeon, Texas. Rev. G. W. SMITH officiated. The couple will live in DeLeon.

Miss Jessie MARTIN, 13 and daughter of Mr. and Mrs. J. C. MARTIN, died early this morning of typhoid fever in Fort Worth. Burial will be Monday.

Ethel TODD, of Guthrie, Oklahoma Territory, and Thurston Dwight PEBBLE, of Toledo, Ohio, married yesterday in Guthrie. They will reside in Toledo.

Grover CLOUGH, who lived near Alma, Texas, died yesterday of pneumonia. He was a brother of J. D. KING and Lee FOSTER of Ennis, Texas. Burial will be tomorrow in Myrtle Cemetery in Ennis.

Lafayette NORMAN, 78, died yesterday in Alvarado, Texas. He was a Mexican War veteran.

The funeral of attorney Hugh FREEMAN, who died Wednesday from injuries received in a runaway, was held Friday in Carlsbad, New Mexico Territory.

Mrs. M. E. GUTHRIE died of paralysis of the brain Thursday in Waxahachie, Texas.

L. RAMSEY, of Como, Texas and May WILLIAMS, of Lone Oak, Texas, married Wednesday at Lone Oak. Rev. W. F. BONE officiated.

George A. SOUR and Frances MOLETT, of Trinidad, Colorado, were married in Greenville, Texas by Rev. F.E. FINCHER on Thursday.

F. W. BAYLOR and Nannie L. ROBERTS married Thursday in Beeville, Texas.

Former San Augustine County sheriff Krug BORDER was shot and killed by Sheriff Sneed NOBLE in Nacogdoches, Texas last night.

Jose Maria Garcia VILLAREAL, 83, died in San Antonio yesterday. He was formerly President of Mexico but had lived in San Antonio for 50 years.

The remains of Henry A. WISE, Jr., who died in Denver, Colorado, recently, arrived in Abilene, Texas and were buried there yesterday.

A telegram from Durant, Indian Territory announced the death of Fannie WALKER, wife of Robert WALKER. Her funeral will be today in Sherman, Texas.

Mrs. Wilhemina MUELLER, 77, died yesterday in San Antonio. She was a 52 year resident.

Marriage licenses issued by Tarrant County Clerk's office: E. W. BURCH and Alwilda WATSON; R. W. RAY and Myrtle MCCOGGINS, J. F. MCCARTER and Miss L. E. PRICE, T. A. MOORE and M. L. GRAHAM, S. S. COOPER and C. P. BROWN, A. F. GENTRY, T. A. RUCKER and Maude RENSHAW, and P. S. BROWN and Eveline STILK.

Births recorded by Tarrant County Clerk's office: a girl to Mr. and Mrs. W. E. BAKER of Fort Worth on May 1, a girl to Mr. and Mrs. G. C. COOK of Fort Worth on April 29, a boy to Romie WALKER of Enon on April 29 and a boy to Mr. and Mrs. Jim FULLBRIGHT of Silver Creek on April 20.

Deaths reported to Tarrant County Clerk's Office: Baby HOLLAND, 6 weeks, residing in Fort Worth, died of malnutrition on April 27 and R. L. MERRILL, 36, died of hemorrhage of the stomach on May 3.

Monday, May 9, 1904
The newspaper for this date did not appear on the microfilm.

Tuesday, May 10, 1904
Harvey BRADLEY, 26, drowned in a tank of oil at Batson, Texas yesterday. He had two brothers. His remains were sent to Canada for burial.

Al SMYTH, a horse trader, was shot and killed last night in Pilot Point, Texas. Call HICKS, of Denton, Texas, is being sought in connection with the death.

Adeline KAUFMANN, 73, died yesterday at the Dallas home of her daughter, Mrs. Jacob FRANKEL. KAUFMANN was formerly from Cincinnati, Ohio. The funeral will be tomorrow with burial in the Hebrew cemetery.

Colonel John B. WARNER was buried Saturday by the Masons in Hillsboro, Texas. His wife, shot by Colonel WARNER Saturday, remains in serious condition.

Solomon BERRIDGE and wife celebrated their fiftieth anniversary at Waukomoa, Oklahoma Territory. They were married in Rutley County, England.

Dr. E. G. SHARP was married yesterday to Mrs. Luella M. GILBERT, of Caruthersville, Missouri. They will honeymoon at the World's Fair and in Chicago.

William CLACY was found dying on the highway near Ponca City, Indian Territory. His parents live at Vinita, Indian Territory

District Judge John Young GOOCH died yesterday suddenly of heart disease at Elkhart, Texas.

Joe Lee JAMESON died in Beaumont, Texas yesterday. He was born in Marshall, Missouri on October 9, 1869. He was a former deputy county clerk in McLennan County, Texas and directed a record company. He served as secretary of the state Democratic Executive Committee. He married Anne ROUTH of Moody, Texas on March 25, 1891. They had two children: Malcolm Routh and Vida. He will be buried in Austin tomorrow

The funeral of Jack CARTER, Jr., who died in Austin Sunday, took place in Hillsboro, Texas yesterday.

The infant child of Mrs. Ike LEE died and was buried in Weatherford, Texas Saturday.

Mrs. C. M. BARCLAY died Sunday in Beeville, Texas. Mrs. BARCLAY and her deceased husband settled in Bee County in 1873.

Mrs. A. M. NEWTON, widow of Rev. W. C. NEWTON, died Sunday in Lyttle, Texas. She had lived in Atascosa County for 43 years.

Births recorded by Tarrant County Clerk's office: a girl to Mr. and Mrs. AINSWORTH on May 7, a girl to Mr. and Mrs. W. E. MCGREGOR of Fort Worth on May 2, a boy to Mr. and Mrs. William B. SMITH of Fort Worth on May 3, a boy to Mr. and Mrs. Lee BOSWELL of Mansfield on April 25, a girl to Mr. and Mrs. Jim FARRIS of Kennedale on May 5, and a girl to Mr. and Mrs. J. C. ISHAM of Mansfield on April 29.

Deaths reported to Tarrant County Clerk's Office: Christ HANSON residing in Fort Worth, died of heart failure on May 6; and Mrs. Etta BLESSING residing near Mansfield died of paralysis on May 1.

Marriage licenses issued by Tarrant County Clerk's office: J. P. MACHIN and Miss S. B. BLAINE.

W. W. WOODRUFF, 60, died Sunday in North Fort Worth and will be buried in Oakwood Cemetery.

The infant child of W. LAVENDER was buried in Oakwood Cemetery yesterday. Its mother died two weeks ago.

Wednesday, May 11, 1904

Marriage licenses issued by Tarrant County Clerk's office: Clay WOODS and Pearl PARRISH, Julian Monroe ANDREWS and Ethel WILKS, John H. GREEN and Alice Pearl LONG, R. D. CHUNN and Mrs. M. B. BARKER.

Births recorded by Tarrant County Clerk's office: a girl to Mr. and Mrs. Alf TURNER of Fort Worth on May 6, a boy to Mr. and Mrs. Will TAYLOR of Arlington on May 1, a boy to W. H. MINN of Fort Worth on May 6 and a girl to Mr. and Mrs. Jim D. DUNLAP on May 7.

Deaths reported to Tarrant County Clerk's Office: Mrs. William MILLER, 30, residing in Arlington, died from septicemia on May 2; and Floyd SMITH, 5 months, died of bronchitis on April 27.

Mrs. S. A. ROSE, 85, died yesterday in the Dallas home of her daughter, Mrs. E. G. RUST. Another daughter, Mrs. H. E. RICHES, and seven sons survive. Grandchildren in the area are Mrs. J. B. JONES, Mrs. W. P. HAYES, Mrs. S. W. ANDERSON, Mrs. W. H. CHANDLER and Mrs. M. E. RICHES.

Jim WILSON was found dead in the city reservoir at Ardmore, Indian Territory. No date was reported.

Mrs. Zena KASTON, 78, burned to death yesterday near Berlin, Texas. Her clothing caught fire as she prepared breakfast.

Thursday, May 12, 1904

Maxine HOLLENBECK and J. L. LACY married in Guthrie, Oklahoma Territory by Rev. MCDERMOTT Tuesday. The groom is from Newton, Kansas.

W. B. TURNER and Haughtie RAINES married Sunday in Montague, Texas.

J. E. LENTON and Effie NICKS married Monday in Temple, Texas. The marriage took place in the home of the groom's brother, George LENTON.

Bert SEEBER and May BOSTICK married Sunday at the home of the bride's parents three miles north of Marshall, Texas. Rev. J. B. K. SPAIN of the Methodist Episcopal Church officiated.

Elmo MYERS and Emma MOFFITT married Sunday in Texarkana.

A. J. REID and Ella PRICE married yesterday in Corsicana, Texas. Justice of the Peace H. C. NASH officiated.

Charles GAMBLE and Miss Willie SIDDONS married Tuesday night in Chico, Texas. Rev. J. T. STANFIELD officiated.

Colonel William C. BARKER, 81, died Monday at Marlow, Indian Territory. The funeral was Tuesday. He was a veteran of the War for Texas Independence, the Mexican War and the Civil War.

Magruder MCFADDEN, about 40, died Sunday at Lone Oak, Texas. Burial was Monday at Hefner Chapel.

Mrs. W. H. GRAHAM died Sunday at her home one mile west of Springtown, Texas. Burial was Monday in the Springtown Cemetery.

John WILSON, 18, died of blood poisoning at the Atkin Hospital in Paris, Texas.

Mary TRIMBLE died Monday in Greenville, Texas.

Mrs. Willie G. ROBBINS, 33, died in Fort Worth yesterday. Her funeral and burial will be in Lamonte, Missouri. She leaves a daughter about 12 years old.

Frank HOUSE was found floating in a stream of oil at Sour Lake, Texas.

The bride of S. F. JONES was killed yesterday by accidental discharge of a shotgun at Carrier, Oklahoma Territory. The gun exploded after being reloaded. They had been married only seven months. He was 18 and she was 17.

William J. HALSCHNEIDER, 24, of Humboldt, Kansas, was killed when he fell under the wheels of a passenger train.

The remains of Joe Lee JAMESON were buried in Austin yesterday. The funeral took place from the Cumberland Presbyterian Church and burial was in the city cemetery.

Friday, May 13, 1904

Mrs. J. C. ROBERTS, of Kingfisher, Oklahoma Territory, resigned the presidency of the Oklahoma Federation of Women's Clubs. She was succeeded by Mrs. A. C. SCOTT, of Stillwater, Indian Territory.

Scott HICKS was arrested in El Reno, Oklahoma Territory and returned to Watonga, Oklahoma Territory. He is charged with killing John MILLER in Watonga Saturday night with a shotgun.

Charles THOMAS drowned near Blackwell, Oklahoma Territory yesterday.

William POE, 63, died yesterday. He was a dairy farmer near Garrett, Texas. He was survived by his wife, eight sons and three daughters.

Herbert BETTES, 28, died Wednesday in Paris, Texas of consumption. He was a lifelong resident of Paris.

Mrs. J. W. ROMINE died in Dallas Wednesday and was buried in Waxahachie, Texas.

Mrs. Harry GOODMAM died from pneumonia Wednesday at her home three miles east of Greenville, Texas. Her husband, two daughters and one son survive.

The mother of Dr. Clarence FREEMAN of Belton, Texas died in Griffin, Georgia Wednesday.

Mrs. Ellen WELCH, 33, wife of M. WELCH of Lawrence, Kansas, died Wednesday in Mineral Wells, Texas.

Mrs. Dacey GRAHAM, 38, wife of Will H. GRAHAM, died in Springtown, Texas and was buried there Monday.

Josephine MOSES, infant daughter of Mr. and Mrs. Martin MOSES, died in Lampasas, Texas and was buried yesterday.

Leofilia GRYCHE died yesterday in Ennis, Texas.

The infant son of Mr. and Mrs. H. G. DAVIS, of Paris, Texas, died of measles Wednesday. He was an only child.

Charles Manton KASTER and Beulah LORANCE were married Wednesday in Paris, Texas. Rev. Charles MANTON officiated.

Arch BERRY, of McKinney, Texas, and Cora CRAG, of Campbell, Texas, married in the latter Wednesday.

A. W. MCCOMAR was found guilty of manslaughter yesterday in the death of Dr. B. F. MCCUISITION in a trial at Paris, Texas. The defendant received an eight year prison sentence.

Henry FIELDS, a stockman living 15 miles from Lampasas, Texas, died Wednesday night from injuries received while herding cattle. He was buried near his home.

Deaths reported to Tarrant County Clerk's Office: John ENGEL, 68, residing in Fort Worth, died of chronic dysentery on May 10; Mrs. Willie S. ROBINSON, 33, residing in Fort Worth, died of pulmonary tuberculosis on May 11; Rebekka DAGGETT, 34, residing near Birdville, died of consumption on May 10; Addison Ferris LEWIS, 1, residing in North Fort Worth, died of congestion of the brain with no date listed, and Allison D. SMITH, 48, residing in Fort Worth, died of opium poisoning on .May 11.

Marriage licenses issued by Tarrant County Clerk's office: J. L. CROMER and Mrs. Rosa A. THOMPSON.

Saturday, May 14, 1904

The paper for this date did not appear on the microfilm.

Sunday, May 15, 1904

Ethel WILKES and Julian ANDREWS married Tuesday at the residence of Mr. and Mrs. R. E. BUCHANAN, the bride's aunt and uncle, in Fort Worth.

John MCCOSKEY, 14, was found dead by his father Charles MCCOSKEY in Decatur, Texas. The deceased had been hanged in the barn. Foul play was suspected.

G. A. EAGLE was shot and killed in Rush, Texas. The sheriff in Gail, Texas was notified yesterday.

Herman SCHLOSS, 56, died on May 10 in Baltimore, Maryland. He was formerly a salesman in Dallas.

C. D. OGDEN died Friday in Marshall, Texas. He was a member of the International Order of Oddfellows and the Woodsmen of the World.

W. F. WILSON died Friday at his home west of Ennis, Texas. He was buried in the Myrtle Cemetery. He was the father of 16 children. Almost all of them survive.

Mrs. E. M. HIGGS died Friday afternoon in Paris, Texas. She leaves a husband and three children.

Perry MILLION died Friday in Denton, Texas. He leaves several children.

Mrs. Leonard GRAHAM died Wednesday night in Abilene, Texas. She was buried there yesterday.

Bruce FOSTER and Susie RHODES were married in Paris, Texas Friday by Justice J. W. DEWEESE.

Births recorded by Tarrant County Clerk's office: a girl to Mr. and Mrs. E. L. WHITLOCK of Birdville on May 13; and a boy and a girl to Mr. and Mrs. Joseph BROOKS of Fort Worth on May 13.

Marriage licenses issued by Tarrant County Clerk's office: A. E. LUNA and Mrs. Nellie HAWKINS.

R. E. BRATTON published a card of thanks for the illness and death of his sister, Minnie BRATTON.

Monday, May 16, 1904

James BOBB, son of J. B. BOBB, of Brock, Texas, died Friday in Weatherford, Texas. He overdosed himself on patent medicine.

The infant daughter of Mr. and Mrs. W. S. WRIGHT died Saturday in Greenville, Texas.

The two-year-old son of Mr. and Mrs. John FILGO died Saturday in Cleburne, Texas.

The baby of Mr. and Mrs. J. L. DOLLAR died Saturday in Cleburne, Texas. Burial took place in Blum, Texas.

Mrs. Al FAVIEL died suddenly Friday in Jefferson, Texas. She leaves an infant about ten days old.

L. N. WHITE died Sunday in Temple, Texas.

L. J. COX and Eula THOMASON married Wednesday night in Era, Texas. The groom is a farmer. The bride is the daughter of Dr. B. R. THOMASON.

Tuesday, May 17, 1904

F. L. GRIER, brother of Judge J. G. GRIER, was shot and killed yesterday in Del Rio, Texas. Ignacio HERNANDEZ was arrested.

Land STERLING was shot and killed Sunday near Marshall, Texas. Jim WHITE is being sought.

J. D. SMITH, 70, died of consumption Saturday night in Sanger, Texas. He was buried in Sanger Cemetery Sunday.

A one year old child of J. A. O. BROWN died of the flux Saturday in Sanger, Texas. It was buried in Sanger Cemetery Sunday.

A one year old child of Robert BREWER died Friday night in Sanger, Texas and was buried Saturday in Sanger Cemetery.

Mrs. Susan TYREE, 84, died yesterday in Van Alstyne, Texas. She was buried there the same day.

Charles H. JOHNSTON, 25, died at Channing, Texas last Friday and was buried in the Vashti Cemetery seven miles south of Bellevue, Texas. He was the son of Rev. and Mrs. J.H. JOHNSTON.

Capt. John FEELEY, 94, died Sunday in Corsicana, Texas. A niece is Mrs. M. P. CALLINAN.

Mrs. Mary STEWART, wife of W. J. STEWART, of Cleburne, Texas, died Sunday. Her husband and three daughters survive. Her daughters are Mrs. P. L. BENTON, Mrs. Jeff CAMPSEY and Miss Maude STEWART. The funeral was yesterday.

Mrs. P. C. LOFTIN died Sunday in Cleburne, Texas.

Mrs. Phil SMITH and her five year old son were killed Sunday when they struck by lightning at Abilene, Texas.

J. Marvin NEWSON, 25, who was a student at the University in Austin, died there yesterday. He was the son of Major J. E. NEWSON. Death was due to nervous prostration.

Runyan COLLINS, 5, died yesterday in Fort Worth. He was the son of Rev. A. P. COLLINS. The funeral is today with burial in Oakwood Cemetery.

Robert NEWLAND and Vina YEARBY were married Sunday by Rev. A. DAVIS in Waxahachie, Texas.

J. T. SONS and Cora GEORGE married Saturday south of Sanger, Texas.

George R. HINES died in San Antonio yesterday.

Three murder cases are scheduled for trial in Fort Worth in the next days. J. B. MILLER, charged with the murder of Frank FONE will be heard next Friday. Jeff VAN will be tried for the murder of Policeman GRIMES on Monday. Gus BADER will be tried the following Friday for the death of L. BARRETT.

Marriage licenses issued by Tarrant County Clerk's office: M. L. MCANNALLY and Mrs. R. N. PADDOCK, William W. BARCLAY and Miss M.A. KILLIAN, and G.H. MCFARLIN and L.P. FARRELL.

Births recorded by Tarrant County Clerk's office: a girl to Mr. and Mrs. S. A. KENT of Glenwood on May 15, a boy to Mr. and Mrs. James WATSON of Fort Worth on May 11, a girl to Mr. and Mrs. John MIGUS of Fort Worth on May 9, a girl to Mr. and Mrs. R. I. FISHER of Fort Worth on May 13, a boy to Mr. and Mrs. G. SHERMAN of Fort Worth on May 14, a girl to Mr. and Mrs. G. P. GOLD of Fort Worth on May 14, a girl to Mr. and Mrs. C. B. BURKHART of Fort Worth on May 9, a boy to Mr. and Mrs. Albert WILSON of Kennedale on May 11, a girl to C. M. MCRAY of Fort Worth on May 13, a girl to Mr. and Mrs. K. A. WATSON of Glenwood on May 14 and a boy to George W. INGLE of Enon on May 16.

Wednesday, May 18, 1904

Sam BRAMBELL was killed by lightning yesterday. He was a rancher living ten miles south of Rock Springs, Texas.

Ammon HUBBLE, 7, died of wounds received about three weeks ago. He was struck with a pistol ball in Houston. Henry JONES was arrested and charged with murder.

Mrs. J. E. DUNMAN died of appendicitis Sunday in Mabank, Texas.

B. F. JOHNSON, 40, died yesterday in the Physicians and Surgeons Hospital in San Antonio. He was the head of the Johnson Brothers printing house there.

Inez LADOE, of Guthrie, Oklahoma Territory, and Daniel L. WOLFE, of Kansas City, Missouri, were married in Guthrie today.

J. M. KEMP died of a heart attack yesterday in Hobart, Oklahoma Territory.

Zack A. SLOUGH, 24, was killed in an industrial accident while visiting the Cleburne Gas and Electric Company power plant in Cleburne, Texas. He was married.

Charley MORGAN was killed when he was kicked by a horse south of DeLeon, Texas. He was married and had one child. His father-in-law was James TERRY.

The 13 year old son of Mr. and Mrs. W. R. GOODMAN accidentally shot and killed himself Sunday in Weatherford, Texas.

Births recorded by Tarrant County Clerk's office: a boy to Dr. and Mrs. Ernest MCCONNELL of Fort Worth on May 14, and a boy to Mr. and Mrs. L. SIMPSON of Fort Worth on May 15.

Deaths reported to Tarrant County Clerk's Office: Mrs. William LAVENDER, 38, residing in Fort Worth on May 1 of unknown causes.

Thursday, May 19, 1904

Benito RODRIQUEZ died Tuesday night in Neuvo Laredo, Mexico He was scalded to death when he fell into a tank of hot water.

The remains of James Marvin NEWSOM were buried in Oakwood Cemetery in Fort Worth Wednesday afternoon. He was a student at the University in Austin when he died.

Friday, May 20, 1904

Miss Laura BROWDER died of appendicitis Wednesday. She lived nine miles northwest of Brownsville, Texas and was a teacher.

The remains of Charles HARRIS, who died in Dallas, arrived yesterday in Denton, Texas. He was a member of the Woodmen of the World. The date of his death was not given.

Jesse TURNER died yesterday of consumption in Brownwood, Texas. He was a brother of Joe TURNER and Will TURNER of Brownwood. His body was shipped to Atlantic City, New Jersey.

Mrs. Leonora MOREHEAD, 52, died Wednesday in Denton, Texas. Her funeral was yesterday in Denton. She was the mother of one son.

R. C. FOSTER died Monday of blood poisoning in Paris, Texas. He was survived by a wife and one child.

Lilly SULLIVAN died Monday in McKinney, Texas. She died in the home of her cousin, Mrs. C. P. HOWARD.

Ruth YOUNG, daughter of Mr. and Mrs. W. B. YOUNG, died yesterday in Cleburne, Texas. Mrs. W. B. YOUNG is the sister of William JONES of Fort Worth.

William CASEY and Miss Eva MCGEE married Sunday in Gainesville, Texas.

Lyman FLEENER and Eula LAMB married Sunday in Gainesville, Texas. The wedding took place in the home of Will JOINER. Justice of the Peace PEARMAN officiated.

Jonas MAPLES and Daisy FERGUSON married Sunday in Weatherford, Texas. Pastor WALKER of Second Baptist Church officiated.

W.H. WILKINS and Eva CAVINESS were married Sunday in Greenville, Texas.

Jesse EMON, of Princeton, Texas, and Bettie CLARK, of McKinney, Texas, were married in the latter place Tuesday. Elder John M. MCKINNEY officiated.

W. W. WALTON and Lena RICHARDSON married yesterday in Guthrie, Oklahoma Territory. Rev. ROSE of the First Methodist Church officiated.

Bob TAYLOR was allowed $2500 bond in the death of W. W. CLEMMONS near Venus, Texas.

Captain F. SLAUGHTER, 75, died yesterday in Kaufmann, Texas. He was a veteran of the Mexican War and the Civil War. He also served as county attorney for Kaufmann County, Texas.

J. N. MOYER, about 65, was found dead yesterday in the Arlington Hotel in Dallas. He was believed to have died of heart failure. He may have been from LaGrange, Texas or LaGrange, Missouri.

D. B. CORLEY, 65, died yesterday in Ardmore, Indian Territory.

Marriage licenses issued by Tarrant County Clerk's office: Lucius Earl MCBRIDE and Laura F. CUREIN, T. M. REAP and Miss R. G. PARISH, Joe L. PRITCHARD and Liddie CUNNINGHAM, Pink HINSON and Hattie WILLIAMS, and Frank BRITTON and Florence TURNER.

Births recorded by Tarrant County Clerk's office: a boy to Mr. and Mrs. J. C. HENISESSER of Arlington on April 27.

Deaths reported to Tarrant County Clerk's Office: Jesse A. MARTIN, 13, residing in Fort Worth, died of typhoid fever on May 8; William Harold MCKILLEN, 1, residing in Fort Worth, died of capillary bronchitis with no date listed; Beulah RICH, 2, residing in Fort Worth, died of typhoid fever on May 11; and Ina Zelma THROCKMORTON, 4, residing in North Fort Worth, died of typhoid pneumonia with no dated listed.

Saturday, May 21, 1904

The remains of Mrs. M. A. LEONARD were buried yesterday. She was a resident of Birdville, Texas.

The infant child of S. S. MASON, of North Fort Worth, was buried in Oakwood Cemetery yesterday. The child died Thursday night.

Marriage licenses issued by Tarrant County Clerk's office: F. M. HONEA and Mrs. Ida BERLEY; and A. B. KELLEY and Maude DALEY.

Births recorded by Tarrant County Clerk's office: a boy to Mr. and Mrs. L. F. RHODES of Condon on May 9, a girl to Mr. and Mrs. Carr SCOTT of Euless on May 14, a boy to Mr. and Mrs. R. T. WILLIAMS of Euless on May 17, a girl to Mr. and Mrs. Sam WILLIAMS of Euless on May 1, a girl to Mr. and Mrs. J. T. ALLEN of Fort Worth no date given, and a girl to Mr. and Mrs. J. O. SMITH of Kennedale on May 18.

Sunday, May 22, 1904

W. X. BARNES and Jamie SCHOULTZ married Wednesday in Marshall, Texas. He is the owner of the *Covington Eagle* and she is a teacher.

Stella HUFF and Austin BELL married last Saturday in Gainesville, Georgia.

Alice HAZEL and W. J. LINN were married Thursday by Rev. A. B. INGRAM in Gainesville, Texas. She is the daughter of Mr. and Mrs. J. T. HAZEL.

Eloise DEMPSEY died Friday at the home of her parents in Marshall, Texas.

J. W. HUFF died Thursday in Olamville, Texas.

The infant of J. G. JONES died Thursday at the home of William TAYLOR in Temple, Texas.

Tom RUSSELL, 82, died Thursday very suddenly near Poetry, Texas.

Mrs. Fred JONES died Thursday night in Cleburne, Texas.

Dr. W. W. HALL was accidentally shot and killed yesterday in a hunting accident near Osage, Texas. He was killed by the discharge of a gun handled by John BARNETT.

Capt. J. T. CLEMENTS died in Fort Worth yesterday morning. He was the commercial agent for the Texas and Pacific Railroad. His funeral will take place today at Broadway Presbyterian Church. Rev. HUGHES will officiate. Burial will be in the new cemetery.

Marriage licenses issued by Tarrant County Clerk's office: Joe HICKS and Nettie HONEYCUTT, Travis GRIDER and Nora BELLAMY, and G. M. ENEN and Helen BRALTZ.

Births recorded by Tarrant County Clerk's office: a girl to Susie GRAHAM of St. Joseph's Infirmary on May 12, a boy to Mr. and Mrs. Roy TERRELL of Stove Foundry on May 20, and a girl to Mr. and Mrs. William H. TOLBERT on May 17.

Monday, May 23, 1904

The paper for this date did not appear on the microfilm.

Tuesday, May 24, 1904

E. P. CRISWELL died Sunday of pneumonia. He was a prominent cattleman and former Fort Worth resident. He was living in Mill Creek at the time of his death.

William RICHARDS of New York and Fred TRAHAM died in a refinery accident in Port Arthur, Texas yesterday.

Harry MOORE, about 50, committed suicide by a gunshot wound to the head yesterday in Dublin, Texas He was a businessman who is survived by his wife and five children. His funeral is today in Dublin.

Sid J. OPPENHEIMER, 28, died yesterday from the flu in Yoakum, Texas. He was the son of Mr. and Mrs. M. OPPENHEIMER of Victoria, Texas.

Mrs. Isham G. HARRIS died Saturday in Mineral Wells, Texas. Her remains were interred Sunday in Abilene, Texas.

Mrs. George WESTBROOK died yesterday of blood poisoning in Ennis, Texas.

George ANDERSON died yesterday of small pox in Batson, Texas. He was buried the same day.

Marriage licenses issued by Tarrant County Clerk's office: James O. LEE and Esther BARNETT, Warren SHEPHERD and Vesta POWELL, R. X. LINDSAY and Miss Willie THURMAN, and Frank OUSLEY and Mary CARSON.

Births recorded by Tarrant County Clerk's office: a girl to Mr. and Mrs. D. HIGGINS, Fort Worth, on May 14; a boy to Mr. and Mrs. Wilmer GALLAGHER, Riverside, on May 15; a boy to Mr. and Mrs. George ST. CLAIR, Stove Foundry, on May 16; a girl to Mr. and Mrs. George M. REYER, Fort Worth, on May 21; a boy to Mr. and Mrs. Paul SCHUBERT, Fort Worth, on May 22; a boy to W. D. SEXTON, Grapevine, on May 16, a boy to Mr. and Mrs. Tom CROMWELL, Grapevine, on May 18, a girl to Mr. and Mrs. R. A. WOODS, Fort Worth, on April 22, a girl to Mr. and Mrs. Will J. AUSTIN, White's Chapel, on May 12, a girl to Mr. and Mrs. Alvis C. CORBIN, Grapevine, on May 12, a boy to Mr. and Mrs. George W. DUCKIE, near Grapevine, on May 16, a boy to Mr. and Mrs. Joe D. LIPSCOMB, Grapevine, on May 20, and a boy to Mr. and Mrs. J. R. HAWORTH, Fort Worth, on May 21.

Deaths reported to Tarrant County Clerk's Office: Fallitha MARTIN, 38, residing in Dove, death due to abscess on May 13; Edward COLLINS, no age stated, residing in Fort Worth, death due to apoplexy on May 4; Fletcher WILKERSON, 66, residing in Fort Worth, death due to skull fracture on April 21; and J. H. SECREST, 56, residing in Fort Worth, death due to dropsy on April 28.

Richard Cecil GALBRAITH, 38, died east of Fort Worth Sunday. He was the secretary of Burton-Lingo Lumber Company at the time of his death. The funeral will be Wednesday from Trinity Episcopal Church. Survivors are his wife and three children. He was the son of Rev. Richard GALBRAITH, of Kerrville, Texas, and the brother of Rev. J. E. H. GALBRAITH of Colorado, Texas.

Lester Elmo PETTY, 7 months, died yesterday in Fort Worth. He was the son of Mr. and Mrs. C. C. PETTY. Remains were sent to Marquez, Texas for burial.

Claude HUMPHREY, 13, died in St. Joseph's Infirmary Sunday. His remains were sent to Hastings, Oklahoma Territory.

Wednesday, May 25, 1904 and
Thursday, May 26, 1904

The papers for these dates did not appear on the microfilm.

Friday, May 27, 1904

Walter ALEXANDER died yesterday in Houston. He fell while unloading water pipe from a freight car. Death was caused by a broken neck.

J. N. WEBB was acquitted Wednesday in the murder of T. C. BLACK at Dalhart, Texas. The indictment of John C. STOWERS in the death of T. C. BLACK was dismissed for lack of evidence.

Marriage licenses were issued in St. Louis, Missouri to Charles WILKINSON, of Pittsburg, Texas, and Miss Prince A. GAFFNEY, of Houston, and to William F. AIKEN, of Paris, Texas, and Irene HODGE of East St. Louis, Illinois.

Marriage licenses issued by Tarrant County Clerk's office: B. F. SARGEANT and Amanda A. FARLEY, A. J. MILLER and Annie M. HELMS, J. A. WILLIAMSON and Mrs. Polly J. LAPACE.

Births recorded by Tarrant County Clerk's office: a girl to Mr. and Mrs. G. W. JENNINGS, Fort Worth, on May 17, a girl to Mr. and Mrs. William COLLINS, near Birdville, on May 25; a boy to Mr. and Mrs. M. J. BLEVINS, Keller, on May 19, and a boy to Mr. and Mrs. Abner SHINES, Bransford, on May 12.

Deaths reported to Tarrant County Clerk's Office: Mrs. Tullie LEMMONS, 41, residing in Fort Worth, died due to gastralgia on May 21; Bunyan COLLINS, 5, residing in Fort Worth, died due to bronchitis on May 17; and Mat FRETWELL, 23, residing near Birdville died of phthisis abdominalis with date not stated.

Saturday, May 28, 1904

Claud WOODS, 9, accidentally shot and killed his seven year old sister in Claremont, Texas. He was handling a rifle when it discharged.

John BRENNON and Hal MCCABE burned to death in a hotel fire in Lawton, Oklahoma Territory. BRENNON was a section foreman and MCCABE a section hand. The fire destroyed the Farmer's Hotel. Frank MOORE and John KELLEY were injured.

Marriage licenses issued by Tarrant County Clerk's office: J. D. CHAPMAN and Willie Mae STOUT; and Church SMITH and Ida WILSON.

Births recorded by Tarrant County Clerk's office: a boy to Mr. and Mrs. H. B. SNOW, Fort Worth, on May 24.

Deaths reported to Tarrant County Clerk's Office: T. F. GRANTHAM, 28, residing in Fort Worth, died of a skull fracture on May 25; Claude HUMPHREY, 11, residing on Fort Worth, died of pyemeia on May 22; and Lineal WILLIAMS, 8 months, residing in Bransford, died of chronic diarrhea with no date listed.

Sunday, May 29, 1904

Marriage licenses issued by Tarrant County Clerk's office: Harold W. LOCKE and Nellie Edith WATSON, Will GRIFFIN and Jeanette EVANS.

Births recorded by Tarrant County Clerk's office: a boy to Mr. and Mrs. G. A. SPLAWN, Fort Worth, on May 28, a girl to Mr. and Mrs. M. L. ROY, Rosen Heights, on May 25, a boy to Mr. and Mrs. J. H. MCCARTY, Fort Worth, on May 26, a boy to Mr. and Mrs. I. N. LYTLE, Fort Worth, on May 14, a girl to Mr. and Mrs. Will ROGERS, Mansfield, on May 21, a girl to Mr. and Mrs. Arthur BROWNING, Mansfield, on May 23, a boy to Mr. and Mrs. Bud WILLIAMS, Fort Worth, on May 16, a girl to Mr. and Mrs. S. W. DOLE, North Fort Worth, on May 27, a boy to Mr. and Mrs. J. D. ADAMS, North Fort Worth, on May 23 and a boy to Mr. and Mrs. N. W. SEAGRIST, North Fort Worth, on April 29.

Deaths reported to Tarrant County Clerk's Office: Mrs. Kate WAGNER, 78, living in Mistletoe Heights, died of endocarditis on May 14.

George KENNEDY was hanged near Palestine, Texas yesterday. He had been convicted of criminal assault on a four year old child last fall near Elkhart, Texas.

Osie TYREE was shot and killed yesterday east of Wilmer, Texas. Dick WEAVER surrendered to authorities. TYREE was alleged to have killed WEAVER's father last February.

Mrs. Luther POSLEY died at the family home near Waxahachie, Texas Friday. Burial was in the city cemetery yesterday.

H. E. HEAD died in Lancaster, Texas Wednesday. The burial was Thursday in Hutchins, Texas.

Kenneth MCLOUD died Friday in Kingfisher, Oklahoma Territory. His death was due to internal injuries sustained while playing with his children last Saturday.

Maude BOOTH and E. Burton FALLIS were married yesterday in Pond Creek, Oklahoma Territory.

A. H. MCCORD and Miss M. E. BROWN married Friday in Ardmore, Indian Territory.

Martin Luther LARGE and Annie Walker WEBB married Wednesday in the residence of Mrs. J.B. WEBB in Abilene, Texas. Rev. L. R. SCARBOROUGH officiated.

Monday, May 30, 1904

Four men were arrested and brought to Muscogee, Indian Territory in connection with the death of Bob SUDDETH. SUDDETH was a black farmer in the Broken Bow area. He refused to leave his land despite numerous threats. He was killed by an explosion while planting corn. The explosion resulted from a bomb. Those arrested included _____ SEYMOUR, Ed LESTER, A. J. LESTER and Lakin MCQUERRY.

Graham JONES was shot and killed yesterday in Batson, Texas. He had previously lived in Greenville, Texas.

Mrs. S. W. WILLIAMS died May 2__ [partially illegible] in Granbury, Texas. She was a resident of Cleburne, Texas. She was the oldest settler in Johnson County, having settled there in 1852. Her daughters include Mrs. ALBRIGHT, Paralee LOCKETT and Mrs. JONES of Acton, Texas. Burial was in Buchanan, Texas.

J. L. WILKINS died Saturday in Harrison County, Texas.

Andy HANCOCK died of cancer of the mouth Saturday at Kellyville, Texas. Burial was yesterday in Kellyville.

R. E. STEWART, 80, died Thursday in Kellyville, Texas. He had lived there forty years.

Lanice DEMPSEY died yesterday in North Marshall, Texas. She was the daughter of Mr. and Mrs. C. C. DEMPSEY.

Edward Leroy DICKERMON, an infant, died Saturday in Gainesville, Texas. He was the son of Mr. and Mrs. Milton DICKERMON.

Mary WHITLEY died in Austin Saturday. She was a resident of Georgetown, Texas.

M. L. STORY, 67, died Saturday at his home in Florence, Texas.

Isaac Potter SMITH, who died in Louisville, Kentucky while attending medical school, was buried Friday in San Angelo, Texas.

Arthur O. ALLEN and Miss Ollie COLLINS were married in Corsicana, Texas by Judge German WALKER on Wednesday.

J. W. BOWDEN and Miss Frankie BANKS were married at 4 a.m. in the parlor of the Clayton Hotel in Pittsburg, Texas.

John W. CULWELL and Mattie FAIN married three miles west of Weatherford, Texas. She was the daughter of Mrs. A. L. FAIN. Rev. G. S. SLOVER of Waco, Texas officiated.

Max BERBERSTADT died in Dallas yesterday.

H. DANWALTER, a barber, killed himself by drinking carbolic acid yesterday in Dallas.

Pancho GARZA was shot and killed by police in New Braunfels, Texas yesterday. GARZA was resisting arrest.

Tuesday, May 31, 1904

Henry WESLEY was jailed after he killed Henry GIVENS in Dallas yesterday. WESLEY admitted the shooting but said he acted in self-defense.

James WHEELER, of Chickasha, Indian Territory, drowned in the South Canadian River near Union City, Oklahoma Territory. No date was listed.

Daudes MCCLURE, 14, drowned in a cattle pond near Hollis, Oklahoma Territory. No date was listed.

Peter DOHL, about 40, was killed when struck by a freight train near Austin yesterday. He was a foreman on a railroad bridge gang when he was killed.

Births recorded by Tarrant County Clerk's office: a boy to Mr. and Mrs. J. A. FISHER, Fort Worth, on May 21, a boy to Mr. and Mrs. George AMANN, Fort Worth, on May 28, a boy to Mr. and Mrs. James GEBB, Fort Worth, on May 22, a boy to Mr. and Mrs. J. W. PEARSON, Riverside, on May 26, and a boy to Mr. and Mrs. P.L. KEY, Kennedale, on May 21.

Deaths reported to Tarrant County Clerk's Office: Charles G. MITCHELL, 57, residing in Fort Worth, died of peritonitis on May 21; a child of C. C. PETTY, 7 months, residing in Fort Worth, died of acute suppurative mastoiditis on May 23; and E. J. CALDWELL, 76 residing in Fort Worth, died of heart failure on May 25.

June, 1904

Wednesday, June 1, 1904
The paper for this date did not appear on the microfilm.

Thursday, June 2, 1904
James L. GAINER, 38, of Waco, Texas, was shot and killed yesterday by Policeman Vester BERG in Beaumont, Texas. BERG was a former brother-in-law of GAINER. The shooting resulted from a quarrel between the two men over custody of the children from GAINER's former marriage.

Harry GRAGER died yesterday of a self-inflicted gunshot wound to the head in Orange, Texas.

Marriage licenses issued by Tarrant County Clerk's office: W. R. POTTER and Callie SANDERS, Edward J. KERWIN and Ethel BECKHAM, and O. C. BURGESS and Ella M. CARPENTER.

Tom WILSON died yesterday of injuries he received when he was run over by a freight train near Paris, Texas.

Charles T. SCHWARZ, 85, died at the Confederate Home in Austin yesterday. He was a member of Cooks' Artillery.

Violet MICHAELSON and Phillip-Jack SANGER married in Austin yesterday. Rabbi ROSENSTEIN officiated.

Margaret Theresa BECK, wife of E. L. BECK, died Monday in Denton, Texas. Her funeral was yesterday with burial in Odd Fellows Cemetery.

G. P. LYDIS, a banker and ranchman, died in Marble Falls, Texas. No date was listed.

George IRWIN, 8, died Tuesday of lockjaw at the home of his mother in Greenville, Texas.

Mrs. Low HILL died Tuesday in Sealy, Texas. She was the daughter of Captain W. T. DAVIDSON of Belton, Texas.

W. S. MORRISON and Mamie GLADDEN married in Greenville, Texas Monday. Rev. R. G. HORSLEY officiated.

C. I. CALKINS and Miss Willie J. DAVIS were married Monday afternoon by Justice Tom MCDANIEL.

Friday, June 3, 1904
The paper for this date did not appear on the microfilm.

Saturday, June 4, 1904
Ed THOMAS and H. M. LONG were killed three miles south of Strawn, Texas when a piece of heavy timber fell on them. They were clearing away a burned tipple from a coal mine when the accident happened. No date was reported.

J. R. MCCOMB, 49, was found dead yesterday on the porch of his home in Van Alstyne, Texas. He had a bullet wound to the head. A pistol lay near the body.

Ed ARCHER was struck by lightning and killed yesterday near Whitemound, Texas.

J. S. SEALY and Mabel WILLIAMS married Thursday in Greenville, Texas. Rev. A. B. INGRAM officiated.

W. J. KIRKLAND and Bonnie PENDLETON married yesterday in Greenville, Texas

H. L. FRASHER and Clara FRANKEBERGER married Thursday in Gainesville, Texas. She was a teacher in the Gainesville schools.

Cassius Clay MARSHALL of Dallas and Florence WARE of McKinney, Texas were married in McKinney Thursday.

Dr. MAUPIN and Maggie LEDDY married in McKinney Thursday.

H. B. HARDEMAN and Pearl BRANDENBERG married Thursday in Brownwood, Texas. Rev. J.P. ROBERTSON officiated.

Professor M .L. WILLIAMS and Miss PEARSON married Thursday morning in Clarendon, Texas. They were both on the faculty of Clarendon College.

Charles L. BRADY and Grace ROCKETT married Wednesday in Waxahachie, Texas. The bride was the daughter of T. M. ROCKETT.

I. W. TINDLE and Nora SANFORD married Wednesday in Joshua, Texas. Rev. S. P. MUSSETT officiated.

Wallace HORNADAY and Ora L. GOODNER married Wednesday in Lawton, Oklahoma Territory.

Dr. L. S. DEBERRY and Mrs. Kate D. LOVE married Thursday in Clarksville, Texas. Rev. L. S. BARTON officiated.

Captain Whitt PHILLIPS, 72, died suddenly of heart failure at the home of his daughter, Mrs. Will MOREHEAD, in Sulphur Springs, Texas. No date was listed. He was a veteran of the Civil War and was wounded at the Battle of Holly Springs. He served in Company G, 3rd Texas Cavalry, Ross's Brigade. He married Virginia ALDERSON of Marion County, Texas on October 3, 1866. He had lived in Sulphur Springs for 17 years and was a former city marshal. Burial took place today in city cemetery.

Bessie HUTTON, 5, died Thursday in Alvarado, Texas. She was the daughter of Mr. and Mrs. W. J. HUTTON. She was buried yesterday.

W. G. COLLINS died Wednesday in Weatherford, Texas. Burial was Thursday by the Tom Green Camp, UCV. He was a Confederate veteran.

Vivian EVERETT died of appendicitis in Weatherford, Texas Thursday.

Scott SPROLES, of Corbin, Kentucky, and Elizabeth AYRES, of Hinton, Oklahoma Territory, married yesterday in Guthrie, Oklahoma Territory.

Mrs. M. E. BROWN, of North Fort Worth, died Thursday. Burial was in Oakwood Cemetery in North Fort Worth. She was the mother of M. O. BROWNING.

Sunday, June 5, 1904

George KANE was shot and killed in Dallas yesterday. Mrs. Lydia CLARK was jailed and charged with murder.

Monday, June 6, 1904

The funeral of Mrs. Ione GILBERT, who died Friday, was held Sunday in Gainesville, Texas. Elder C. H. SCHOONOVER and Rev. A. B. INGRAM officiated. Burial was in East Hill Cemetery in Gainesville.

Christine HODGE, 2, died Friday in Greenville, Texas. Her funeral was Sunday. She was one of the twin daughters of Mr. and Mrs. J. A. HODGE.

Zack WALKER, 34, died yesterday in Seguin, Texas. His remains were shipped to Alabama for burial.

Mrs. Katherine KEMBLE, about 80, died Saturday from a stroke. She died at the family homestead on Grove Creek in Ellis County, Texas. She was an early settler of the county.

Mrs. W. W. BAINES, 61, died Thursday in Mineral Wells, Texas. She had been in Mineral Wells for about two weeks and came from near Houston.

Erie MCKAYE, of Hillsboro, Texas and Bessie DRAKE married in Abbott, Texas Thursday. Rev. Jerome DUNCAN officiated.

Don W. SOWYER and Miss Willie BROWN married Saturday in Corsicana, Texas.

Leon H. SANSOM and Mamie LOWERY married Saturday in Alvarado, Texas. Rev. O. W. DEAN officiated.

Greenville, Texas marriages: J.W. HOLLINGSWORTH and Lula MASON, W. W. SIKES and Rhoda Pearl WILLIAMS, and G. C. ALEXANDER and Mary YOUREE.

Bud HEMPHILL killed Smith HARDEMAN Saturday near Watterson, Texas.

Mrs. J. F. SUMMERS, 44, died in St. Joseph's Infirmary yesterday. The funeral is today from her home in Fort Worth. Rev. Dr. COTTON will officiate.

The funeral of A. STEFFENS, who died Saturday night in Fort Worth, will be today. Burial will be in Polytechnic Cemetery.

Tuesday, June 7, 1904

Mrs. Lydia CLARK was released on $500 bail in Dallas. She was jailed after she killed Grace KING. Sunday's paper (see above) reported she had killed a George KANE. Grace KING was in the custody of Perry CLARK at the time of the shooting. Perry CLARK is the husband of Lydia CLARK. Perry CLARK was arrested as an accomplice but later released.

Josh IRVIN committed suicide yesterday at Corsicana, Texas. He was married and employed as a brakeman.

Mrs. J. E. STEVENS, about 75, died Saturday at her home 14 miles west of Corpus Christi, Texas. Her funeral and burial were yesterday. She was buried in the Catholic cemetery.

Mrs. Margaret C. RIGGS, 89, died yesterday in Corsicana, Texas. The funeral will be today. She was the mother of Mrs. Ruth TEAS, Mrs. W. N. KENNER, Mrs. ROBINSON and Thomas RIGGS. Mrs. ROBINSON was the mother of former sheriff W. D. ROBINSON. Thomas RIGGS was killed in Pickett's Charge at the Battle of Gettysburg in the Civil War.

S. AUSTIN died Thursday of Bright's disease in Dickens, Texas. He was a member of the County Commissioner's Court and a former resident of Eastland County.

Marriage licenses issued by Tarrant County Clerk's office: E. F. LOONEY and Lera CORPNEY; A. B. HOGLUND and Minerva E. DOUGLAS; W. S. MAY and Mrs. Jennie MCDOUGAL, and A. L. WHITE and Mrs. Jennie BAILEY.

Wednesday, June 8, 1904

Alfred LEE, about 50, and his five children drowned when their wagon overturned in a slough near Muskogee, Indian Territory. The children were 5 – 10 years old and their names were not listed in the article.

H. L. FARMERS, 74, shot and killed his 14 year old son and then himself at Lone Grove, Texas.

Abraham Lincoln AYRES, of Langston, Oklahoma Territory, was shot and killed by an unknown person Monday. He was a prominent attorney in Langston and a member of the city council. The attack took place when AYRES stepped out of the meeting. His funeral was yesterday.

J. N. EVERETT was struck by lightning and killed Sunday in Point Rock, Texas.

Blanche PERRY and J. Hamilton SAVAGE married in Houston yesterday.

Dr. A. C. PARKER and Miss Minnie Lane JONES married Sunday in Greenville, Texas. Rev. J. W. HOLSAPPLE officiated.

Rimp CROCKER and Tina DAVIS married Sunday in Chico, Texas. Rev. John STANFIELD officiated.

J. H. MAYER of New Orleans died of consumption Sunday in San Angelo, Texas. He was buried in San Angelo Monday.

James A. EARLE was shot and killed Monday night in the ticket office at Yorktown, Texas. He was the night operator. Conrad SCHWARTZ was arrested.

Marriage licenses issued by Tarrant County Clerk's office: Walton H. MCKENZIE and Fay RINTLEMAN, Joseph GRAHAM and Effie MCMUTTON, Frederick DEVEREAUX and Annie MINGS, and D. L. MCGRIFF and Fredonia TAYLOR.

Births recorded by Tarrant County Clerk's office: a boy to Mr. and Mrs. R. E. PIERCE, Grapevine, on April 15; a boy to Mr. and Mrs. Willie YATES, Arlington, on June 3; a boy to Mr. and Mrs. Joe ROBINSON, near Keller, on May 27; a boy to Mr. and Mrs. J. E. CAVENDER, Grapevine, on May 1; and a girl to Mr. and Mrs. James B. CROSS, Fort Worth, on June 5.

Deaths reported to Tarrant County Clerk's Office: Richard Cecil GALBRAITH, 38, residing in Fort Worth, due to edema of the lungs on May 22; Dorence FOSTER, 22 months, residing in Grapevine, due to iliocolitis on May 23;

Otis Wood STARLING, 1 month, residing in Grapevine, died of inanition on May 5; Eugene Furman BROOKS, 23 days, residing in Fort Worth, died of inanition on June 5; Eugena Emma BROOKS, 23 days, residing in Fort Worth, died of inanition on June 5; and Florida SKELTON, 36, residing in Fort Worth, died of dropsy on June 4.

Thursday, June 9, 1904

The paper for this date did not appear on the microfilm.

Friday, June 10, 1904

Grover MCDONALD, 17, was shot and killed by his 6 year old brother near Macy in Brazos County, Texas. The article listed no date. The accident happened while the younger MCDONALD was playing with an old gun.

Edwin BURNETT, 6, drowned yesterday in an unfinished oil tank near Beaumont, Texas. He was the stepson of F. J. LANDRY.

C. S. BUCY and Miss Johnnie MELTON married Wednesday in Lone Oak, Texas.

Anthony GHIO and Theresa LIPARI married Wednesday in the Catholic Church in Texarkana.

Major W. T. M. DICKSON and Kate BULE were married in Hillsboro, Texas.

Hillary E. CHRISMAN and Alice GARDNER married yesterday in Chico, Texas. Rev. W. J. GREGORY officiated.

Professor W. Burns HEAD and Lula O'HARA married yesterday by Rev. W. J. HEARON in Grandview, Texas.

Mrs. D. A. CARLIN, about 48, died Wednesday in Greenville, Texas. She was the mother of a large family.

S.W. JOHNSON died Wednesday near Waxahachie, Texas.

John W. HOOPER died Wednesday in North Marshall, Texas. He was a Confederate veteran and an employee of the Texas and Pacific Railroad. Burial took place in Greenwood Cemetery yesterday.

Clint GALLAGHIER was killed in a fight near South McAlester, Indian Territory. John and Frank DANIELS were arrested.

The body of Frank LANE was recovered from the South Canadian River near El Reno, Oklahoma Territory. He drowned three weeks ago.

Marriage licenses issued by Tarrant County Clerk's office: John SCHMIDT and Mary Louise BROWN; and George W. SOUSIBEE and Allie B. REDD.

Births recorded by Tarrant County Clerk's office: a boy to Mr. and Mrs. L. TURNER of Brambleton on June 3 and a boy to Mr. and Mrs. W. M. BROWN of Arlington on June 7.

Deaths reported to Tarrant County Clerk's Office: William Macon BARDON, 53, residing in Mansfield, died of tuberculosis on June 5.

Saturday, June 11, 1904

William D. OPRY was shot and killed Thursday four miles north of Cryer Creek, Texas. Peter BOONE surrendered to authorities.

William MEYERS committed suicide in Houston yesterday. He was a German immigrant who was a poet and piano player.

Grace KELLEY and Theodore HERRING married Wednesday in San Angelo, Texas.

B. E. JONES and Jesse Lee GILLILAND were married in Waxahachie, Texas by Rev. C. B. SMITH.

W. P. RAGSDALE and Thea J. MARTIN married Wednesday in Gainesville, Texas. Rev. J. A. GRAY officiated.

Mrs. Sarah C. Perry BELL, 79, widow of Galveston philanthropist George BELL, died in Fort Worth last night. Burial will be in Galveston. She was the mother of six. Only Mrs. J. C. LEAGUE of Galveston survives.

Births recorded by Tarrant County Clerk's office: a girl to Mr. and Mrs. Alex M. DYE, Grapevine, on May 30, a boy to Mr. and Mrs. James D. ALEXANDER, Grapevine, on May 23, a boy to Mr. and Mrs. Foster WARREN, Grapevine, on May 31, a girl to Mr. and Mrs. A. M. MORGAN, Grapevine, on June 6, and a girl to Mr. and Mrs. J.W. TAYLOR, Fort Worth, on June 7.

Deaths reported to Tarrant County Clerk's Office: J. C. SNOW, 76, residing in Grapevine, died on May 31 of injuries suffered when he fell from a horse; and William B. KENNEDY, 7, residing in Arlington, died of typhoid fever on June 1.

Mrs. R. H. WILSON, her baby, and Miss Fay DAVIS were killed when a water spout washed away their house near Mill Creek, Indian Territory.

The Oklahoma Supreme Court affirmed the sentence of Pink SMITH for killing William L. MITCHELL in Logan County on January 1, 1901. Both men were farmers near Mulhall at the time of the killing.

Sunday, June 12, 1904

Births recorded by Tarrant County Clerk's office: a boy to Mr. and Mrs. Ed BRACKEN, Mansfield, on June 2; a boy to Mr. and Mrs. Sam BAILEY, Mansfield, on June 10; a girl to Mr. and Mrs. D. C. CLAYPOOL, Fort Worth, on June 5; a girl to Mr. and Mrs. W.E. FISHER, North Fort Worth, on May 27; a boy to Mr. and Mrs. C. H. DANIELSON, North Fort Worth, on June 10; and a boy to Mr. and Mrs. John HARGE, North Fort Worth, on June 10.

Deaths reported to Tarrant County Clerk's Office: Mattie May JOBE, 1 month, residing in Bransford, died of diarrhea on June 2.

Marriage licenses issued by Tarrant County Clerk's office: John KENNEDY and Mrs. M. A. KENNEDY, Laurence HOLMAN and Mrs. Willie GALLEY, and W. G. HUFFMAN and Mrs. Ida CUNNINGHAM.

J. Nelson PROWCE, 29, of Austin, was shot and killed by Kate SEWNDREY, 19, of Douglas, Arizona, Friday in Austin. SENDREY admitted the killing but said she did it to protect PROWCE's family. PROWSE was threatening to kill his family.

R. B. TORRENCE was killed yesterday in a gun fight over the election of a teacher to the faculty of the public school in Elk, Texas.

Monday, June 13, 1904

The remains of George W. OLLIVER were buried Saturday in Myrtle Cemetery in Ennis, Texas. He had a brother in Palisades, Colorado but no relatives in Ennis.

W. R. FARMER, of Waxahachie, Texas, died in El Paso. A telegram was received Friday telling of the death. Burial will be today in Waxahachie.

Rosa BAKER, 19, died Wednesday night of typhoid fever near Balm, Texas. She was the daughter of Joseph BAKER. Burial was in the Hibit Cemetery Thursday.

William B. BUSH, of Fort Worth, died in Weatherford, Texas Friday night and was buried yesterday. He died at the home of his brother.

S. T. TUNNELL, 54, died Thursday night in Greenville, Texas. Death took place at the home of his son-in-law, Mr. NIX. He left several children.

Luther EWING, 4, died Friday in Van Alstyne, Texas.

Mrs. John SIMPSON died Friday in Van Alstyne, Texas.

Rev. W. L. SKINNER and Mrs. Kate BARMOSE, of Itasca, Texas, were married last week. No date or place was given. He is the pastor of the First Baptist Church in Clarendon, Texas.

J. T. BUNTION and Iva RYAN were married Wednesday in Clarendon, Texas.

Ed RIDDLE and Mary MARTIN married yesterday in Chico, Texas. Rev. J. T. STANFIELD officiated. The bride is a resident of Goodnight, Texas.

E. H. HAWPE and Laura MCKINNEY were married at midnight Saturday in Cleburne, Texas. Justice J. W. SELLERS officiated.

G. M. WOOD and Laura HARVEY were married Friday at the home of the bride's parents south of Mineral Wells, Texas. Rev. D. M. COGDALE officiated.

Mary BOZARTH and Bert CHRISTIAN married yesterday in Okmulgee, Indian Territory. She was the daughter of Mr. and Mrs. Jacob BOZARTH

The funeral of R. B. TORRENCE, killed in a gunfight Saturday in Elk, Texas, was held yesterday.

Tuesday, June 14, 1904

Dr. John GRANT, 51, died Sunday at his home in Sherman, Texas. He was ex-chairman of the Texas State Republican Committee, an ex-member of the Republican National Committee and a former U.S. Marshal for the Eastern District of Texas.

"Shiner" BROWN was shot and killed by Deputy Sheriff J. B. HOOKS in Nona, Texas Sunday. BROWN was resisting arrest and attempted to shoot Sheriff ROBERTS when HOOKS killed him.

Mrs. Louisa SCHOENFIELD, 68, was kicked by a horse and killed near Beeville, Texas Saturday.

John C. WYCHE, 24, of Dallas died in Tucson, Arizona last Wednesday. He had been ill for some time with pulmonary troubles. He was survived by his wife, his parents and three brothers.

M. H. WHALEY, 68, died in Calvin, Indian Territory Friday. Burial took place in Mountain Park Cemetery in St. Jo, Texas. He was a Confederate veteran, serving in the 11th Texas. He was survived by six children.

Capt. William Monroe RUST died at his home in Seguin, Texas Sunday. He was a Confederate veteran, serving in the 21st Texas Cavalry.

J. L. COLLINS, about 80, died in Alvarado, Texas Sunday. He was buried by the Odd Fellows.

Wednesday, June 15, 1904

B. J. RENSHAW was fatally injured when he fell into a well at the site of the Hennessey, Oklahoma Territory waterworks plant today.

Louis PEYNA killed Perferio ALMANDAREZ in Kerrville, Texas Sunday. PEYNA claimed he acted in self-defense. Bond was set at $500.

Births recorded by Tarrant County Clerk's office: a boy to Mr. and Mrs. R. O. WILEY of Azle on June 10, a girl to Mr. and Mrs. L. W. KENTON of Azle with date not given, a girl to Mr. and Mrs. Henry GREEN on June 9, and a girl to Mr. and Mrs. John ENSWILEY of North Fort Worth on June 4.

Marriage licenses issued by Tarrant County Clerk's office: D. M. ELY and Mrs. H.C. MULLINS, and T. K. BALL and May PONDER.

Thursday, June 16, 1904

J. E. JOHNSON of Fort Worth, 57, died yesterday. He had lived in Fort Worth since 1873. He was survived by his wife and three children: J. E. JOHNSON, Jr.; Robert JOHNSON; and Beulah JOHNSON.

Miss Ollie GARNER, 18, died in Ennis, Texas Sunday of consumption and was buried Tuesday in Myrtle Cemetery in Ennis.

William M. FLYNN died at his home in Weatherford, Texas yesterday of blood poisoning. He was a bridge builder and an alderman.

Mrs. J. M. PRESLER, Sr., died in Beaumont, Texas and was buried in Oakwood Cemetery in Comanche, Texas. She was the stepmother of Senator J. M. PRESLER and the widow of Capt. J. M. PRESLER, Sr.

J. M. KIRK, 80, who died Sunday, will be buried in Waxahachie, Texas tomorrow.

Mrs. Sophie SOWITZKY, 60, died in Austin Monday.

J. S. WRIGHT, who was living near Vineland, Texas, died Tuesday of tuberculosis.

E. A. HEFFNER and May FEATHERSTONE, of Arkadelphia, Arkansas, were married yesterday in Texarkana. Rev. James THOMAS officiated.

J. W. CLAYWELL and Mary E. METCALF married Tuesday at the home of C. P. METCALF, the bride's father in Greenville, Texas. Rev. J. W. HOLSAPPLE officiated.

John HOUGHTON, of Guthrie, Oklahoma Territory, and Theresa SLUGGERT were married in Oklahoma City, Oklahoma Territory Tuesday. They are living in Guthrie.

Lula CARTER and L. JAMES were married last night. No place was listed.

C. D. REYNOLD and Rettie ROWLES of Hunt County were married in McKinney, Texas Tuesday.

N. N. TWADELL and Rebecca WISE were married Tuesday in Campbell, Texas. Rev. R. F. JENKINS officiated.

S. W. MONTAGUE of El Paso and Annie BLADES of Greenville, Texas married yesterday in the home of N. O. BLADES in Greenville. Rev. R. F. JENKINS officiated.

Marriage licenses issued by Tarrant County Clerk's office: E. L. BALLARD and Myrtle MCGUIRE, Harley T. CHRISTY and Flora M. CANTERBURY, Thomas T. THOMPSON and Cass M. JOHNSTON, N. N. AKE and Jessie MILLER and Tom SCOTT and Emma SIBLEY.

Births recorded by Tarrant County Clerk's office: a girl to Mr. and Mrs. Joseph EMSKAMP, Fort Worth, with no date given, and a girl to Mr. and Mrs. Charles SALERNO, Fort Worth, with no date given.

William MCKILLIP died Monday in Marshall, Texas.

Mrs. J. E. STALLINGS died Saturday in Griffin, Georgia, while visiting her sister there. She was the mother of Mrs. J.I . CLINGMAN, M. S. STALLINGS of Moody, Texas, Henry STALLINGS of Lometa, Texas, Mrs. H. A. LEAKE of Temple, Texas and Mrs. Douglas WORLESLEY of Fort Worth.

J. P. DAVIS died Sunday at his home three miles north of Pottsboro, Texas. He was born in 1867 and was an early settler of Grayson County.

Gust MOSTROM died Tuesday at his home in Pottsboro, Texas.

Capt. S. L. SMITH died Monday in Nacogdoches, Texas and was buried at Old North Church Tuesday. He was a Confederate veteran.

Mrs. Rose RILEY, the mother of P.M. RILEY, died Monday in Columbus, Texas.

Mrs. A. J. EDWARDS died Saturday night in Cleburne, Texas.

Mrs. Annie BUTLER died Friday in Justin, Texas. She was buried in the Aiken Cemetery Monday.

Mrs. J. M. SWINDELL died of apoplexy Monday in Greenville, Texas.

The six month old son of Mr. and Mrs. B. F. HOWARD died Monday in Christian, Texas.

Mrs. Martha L. STARKS, 57, died Monday in Texarkana.

O. D. ABBOTT and Annie WAKEN married in the home of the bride in Terrell, Texas Monday.

L. A. HILL and Oma POOLE were married in North Marshall, Texas by Rev. W. W. GOLLIHUGH.

Frank DENNY and Clare FUTTER married Tuesday at St. Edward's Church in Texarkana.

Emma Lee CARPENTER and August K. LIPSCOMB married Tuesday in Seguin, Texas. He is the son of W. W. LIPSCOMB of Luling, Texas. She is the granddaughter of former Governor IRELAND.

Wade BOWIE shot and killed Mrs. J. R. GOBER and then killed himself yesterday in Amarillo, Texas. Mrs. GOBER was the daughter of W. B. PLEMMONS.

Sofia Ellen VATTER, 11, was killed by a shotgun wound to the head. Her 13-year old brother was handling the gun when it fell to the floor and discharged.

Friday, June 17, 1904

Vicente LOSANO was hanged yesterday for the murder of Cusomiro SAIS in Oakville, Texas. SAIS was killed with an ax last November 28.

Nola ELLISON and E.P. GATES married in Waco, Texas Wednesday. Rev. S. Guy INMAN of New York City officiated. The groom comes from New York City.

Phil GOLDSMITH and Grace MAYER married in Waco, Texas Wednesday. Rabbi B. WOHLBURN officiated.

Edgar TOWNS and Elsie GARRETT married Wednesday in Brenham, Texas. Rev. J. A. FRENCH officiated. The groom came from Beaumont, Texas.

J. T. BARDENAC of Pueblo, Colorado, and Belva KIZER married Wednesday in Texarkana.

Ralph NICHOLSON and Hattie Ethel CASTLEBERRY married Wednesday at the home of the bride's parents, Mr. and Mrs. J. W. CASTLEBERRY, in Greenville, Texas. Rev. R. F. JENKINS officiated.

James S. SHIVERS and Gussie WORTHINGTON married yesterday in Corsicana, Texas. Rev. G. L. BITZER officiated.

Murray BRADEN and Katie Lee WRIGHT married Wednesday in Cleburne, Texas.

The five week old baby of Mr. and Mrs. King BRADFORD died Wednesday in Ennis, Texas. Death was due to cholera infantum. The baby was buried in Waxahachie, Texas.

Capt. J. T. BELL died in Houston yesterday. Burial took place in Calvert, Texas.

Frank H. PATTERSON, killed in a train wreck Tuesday, was buried Thursday in Longview, Texas

John RING died Wednesday in Texarkana.

Births recorded by Tarrant County Clerk's office: a girl to Mr. and Mrs. Amos HUCKABEE, Arlington, on June 6; a boy to Mr. and Mrs. William W. BOYD, Fort Worth, on June 5; a boy to Mr. and Mrs. John FANNING, Arlington, on June 5; a boy to Mr. and Mrs. E. W. KRIGGER, Arlington, on May 25, and a boy to Mr. and Mrs. C. H. MCCLAIN, Arlington, on May 28.

Deaths reported to Tarrant County Clerk's Office: Catherine MOLONEY, 50, residing in Arlington, died of old age on June 15.

Saturday, June 18, 1904

J. A. MAYS, the Elk City, Oklahoma Territory banker arrested in Greenville, Texas recently, killed himself in the Dallas County Jail yesterday. He died of a self-inflicted gunshot wound to the head.

Mrs. Leroy BOGAN committed suicide by drinking carbolic acid yesterday in Dale, Oklahoma Territory. She was a recent bride.

Marriage licenses issued by Tarrant County Clerk's office: J. H. APPLEWHITE and Mrs. N. J. WATSON, J. P. PRUITT and Pearl SMITH, and James OVERTON and Lula SPENCER.

Sunday, June 19, 1904

Charles GLOVER, 56, was killed by a freight train yesterday in San Marcos, Texas.

The body of J. A. MAYS, who killed himself in the Dallas County Jail Friday, was shipped to Greenville, Texas for burial there tomorrow.

Alex HUTTON, 59, died Friday at his home five miles west of Yoakum, Texas. He was a farmer.

Gladys MILLER, 10, died of typhoid fever Thursday in Corsicana, Texas. She was the daughter of Lanty MILLER.

George W. O'NEAL died Friday at his home three miles west of Mineral Wells, Texas. He died from cancer. He was a Confederate veteran.

D. B. HALE, Jr. died Friday after a long illness in his mother's home in Jefferson, Texas

W. M. DICKERSON and Lucy HORTON married Friday night in McKinney, Texas .

Roy A. CATO and Etna TOUCHTON married Wednesday in Gainesville, Texas. Rev. A. B. INGRAM officiated.

Will MARTIN and Gussie WEST married Friday in Temple, Texas.

James R. STONE and Mabel DOTY married yesterday in Brady, Texas. She was the daughter of County surveyor W. P. DOTY.

W. L. SMALL and Mrs. Pearl A. RATCLIFF married Wednesday in Fort Worth Justice of the Peace Charles W. ROWLAND officiated.

Axtel Gustavus SOLOMON and Lola May CARNEY married in Fort Worth yesterday. Rev. B. B. RAMAGE officiated.

Sam SMITH died today in Ardmore, Indian Territory. He was in jail for the death of a man last year. Cause of death was rheumatism of the heart.

Births recorded by Tarrant County Clerk's office: a boy to C. G. KEININGHAM, Fort Worth, on June 12, a girl to Mr. and Mrs. J. M. CRABB, Fort Worth, on June 15, a boy to Mr. and Mrs. Daniel BATEMAN of Fort Worth on June 12, and a boy to Mr. and Mrs. W. E. ARMSTRONG on June 16.

Marriage licenses issued by Tarrant County Clerk's office: T. H. KING and Rhoda DAVIS, and Robert MANNING and Pearl ALEXANDER.

Monday, June 20, 1904

The newspaper for this date did not appear on the microfilm.

Tuesday, June 21, 1904

S. C. BRAKE, 65, died Monday evening in Pearsall, Texas. Myrtle BRAKE, his daughter, married earlier in the day and left for a trip to the World's Fair. Survivors also included his wife and two sons.

Mrs. L. E. HICKMAN, 44, died Sunday at her home in Hico, Texas.

Jim GENTRY, 23, died yesterday in Van Alstyne, Texas.

Alva PITTS, Jr., 6 months, died yesterday of bowel trouble in Van Alstyne, Texas.

E. K. BAKER died in South Austin last night. His funeral is today. He was the superintendent of the southern division of the Southwestern Telegraph and Telephone Company.

Henry HOPKINS collapsed and died last night on a grocery platform in Fort Worth.

James B. MAXWELL, of Baird, Texas, and his brother John MAXWELL, of Globe, Arizona Territory, and Enoch WOODWARD, of Douglas, Arizona Territory, were found dead in Sonora, Mexico recently. Robbery was believed to be the motive.

John HENNESSEY drowned in Elk Creek near Lone Wolf, Oklahoma Territory. He attempted to ford the flooded creek and was swept from his horse. His body was recovered today.

John DAVIDSON drowned in a cattle pond near Hollis, Oklahoma Territory. No date was reported.

W. C. F. LANGE was found dead near Fredericksburg, Texas. No date was provided.

Homer WILLIS was killed Saturday in Atlanta, Georgia. He was the son of A. W. WILLIS of Ennis, Texas.

Fred MORRIS and Will BIRT were arrested as suspects in the murder of Josh REAGOR last winter. They were jailed in Waxahachie, Texas.

Marriage licenses issued by Tarrant County Clerk's office: Robert BURDELL and Mrs. Mattie WILSON, Lucius POLK and Nellie SHAW, and A. W. JONES and Mrs. Stella RUMLILLY.

Births recorded by Tarrant County Clerk's office: a girl to Mr. and Mrs. Will THOMPSON, Fort Worth, on June 15; a girl to Mr. and Mrs. T. J. SIMMONS, North Fort Worth, with no date given; a girl to Mr. and Mrs. Henry CHAPPELL, Handley, with no date given; a boy to Mr. and Mrs. Ed BLACKMAN, Handley, with no date given; a girl to Mr. and Mrs. J. W. MARTIN, Handley, with no date given; a girl to Mr. and Mrs. J. H. HOOVER, Handley, with no date given; a girl to Mr. and Mrs. T. R. REDMAN, Handley, with no date given; a boy to Mr. and Mrs. L. K. SMITH, Handley, with no date given; a girl to Mr. and Mrs. L. F. LESTER, Handley, with no date given; a girl to Mr. and Mrs. Tom HART, Handley, with no date given; a girl to Mr. and Mrs. B. MORROW, Handley, with no date given; a boy to Mr. and Mrs. M. F. HINES, Handley, with no date given; a girl to Mr. and Mrs. Allen ROGERS, Handley, with no date given; a boy to Mr. and Mrs. W. T. REDMAN, Handley, with no date given; a girl to Mr. and Mrs. L. F. STRICKLAND, Handley, with no date given; a boy to Mr. and Mrs. Andrew CLARK, Handley, with no date given; a boy to Mr. and Mrs. J. BRATCHER, Handley, with no date given; a boy to Mr. and Mrs. N. N. RASBURY, Handley, with no date given; a boy to Mr. and Mrs. T. S. MAXWELL, Handley, with no date given; a girl to Mr. and Mrs. J. W. BORNE, Handley, with no date given; and a girl to Mr. and Mrs. Ed WOODS, Handley with no date given.

Wednesday, June 22, 1904

Capt. William HARRIS died in Dallas yesterday. He was a long time Dallas resident and an attorney. He was born in Alabama in 1830. He attended Union University in Murfreesboro, Tennessee, and law school in Lebanon, Tennessee. He was a Confederate veteran, serving in Good's Battery. He married Martha Alice COCHRAN in 1867. He is survived by his wife and six children. His funeral will be today from the First Methodist Church in Dallas. Burial will be in Cochran's Chapel Cemetery.

Adolphus ISOM was shot and killed near Hebron, Texas. The shooting resulted from a quarrel over a horse. Lige and Mose RENO are being sought.

Marriage licenses issued by Tarrant County Clerk's office: J. JONES and Mrs. Delia TUCKER, M. C. X. LITTLES and Mattie EVANS, and George FIELDS and Lucy BRINSON.

Births recorded by Tarrant County Clerk's office: a boy to Mr. and Mrs. Charles TITTLE, Bransford, with no date given; and a girl to Mr. and Mrs. W. G. HUFFMAN, Bransford, with no date given.

Thursday, June 23, 1904

Cicero Fullerton COGRON, 46, died in Dallas yesterday. He was an attorney born in old Springfield in Limestone County, Texas. His funeral is today from his home.

"Aunt Jemima" JONES, 80, died in Dallas yesterday. She was a recent arrival in Dallas and had previously lived in Jefferson, Texas.

C. H. CARPENTER, 90, died in Roger Mills County, Oklahoma Territory recently.

Charles L. CLARKE, a locomotive engineer, was killed in the derailment of a Houston and Texas Central train 13 miles west of Austin yesterday.

Marriage licenses issued by Tarrant County Clerk's office: J. L. CLARKSON and Sinali Ball PORTER, C. E. DINKINS and Kate THOMPSON, Joseph T. PITTS and Gussie L. BROWN, E. D. SMITH and Mrs. S. KNODE, A. L. BROOKS and Janey L. MCMILLAN, Leo BAUER and Nellie SHORTELL, Hadie E. SADLER and Lenna PETTIGREW, B. J. CONDO and Theriza E. WRIGHT, and Henry WILSON and Susie BLACK.

Births recorded by Tarrant County Clerk's office: a boy to Mr. and Mrs. Charles BRUCE, Fort Worth, on June 20; a girl to Mr. and Mrs. H. BURKE, Fort Worth, on June 21; a boy to Mr. and Mrs. Charles LITTLE, Bransford, on June 11; and a boy to Mr. and Mrs. Lee AUTRY, Smithfield, on June 13.

Deaths reported to Tarrant County Clerk's Office: Ockie KELLEY, 16 days, residing in Fort Worth, died of heart failure; and _____ BASSAHAN, 47, residing in North Fort Worth, died of cirrhosis on June 20; Baby TUCKER, 11 months, residing in North Fort Worth, died of inflammation of the stomach on June 16.

George S. BROWN and Ida HAILEY were married on June 14 in Rives, Tennessee and will make their home in Abilene, Texas.

Annie May SWEENEY and Claude LANGRAN married Monday in Cleburne, Texas.

Homer WILSON and Mrs. BOND married Monday in Clarksville, Texas. Rev. J. B. WORDEN officiated. The wedding took place and the home of Mrs. Joe SMITH.

Byrd SMITH, 59, died suddenly of heart disease yesterday in Devine, Texas. He was a merchant and was survived by his wife and several children.

The remains of Francis STONE, who died Friday of consumption in Roswell, New Mexico Territory were shipped to Martin, Tennessee.

Mrs. Charles KENNEDY died Tuesday of consumption in Roswell, New Mexico Territory.

Mrs. Julie A. BURGE, 67, died yesterday in McKinney, Texas. She was the mother of Mrs. Tom SHUMATE.

Judge F.C. BECKETT, 55, died Tuesday in Vernon, Texas. He was buried there yesterday.

Mrs. John G. KISSINGER, 38, died Tuesday of tuberculosis in McKinney, Texas. Survivors include her husband and seven children.

Mrs. Thomas J. WILSON died Tuesday in Corsicana, Texas.

Ellis MCINTOSH and Bessie MOSELEY married yesterday in Waxahachie, Texas. Rev. James N. IVEY, pastor of First Baptist Church, officiated.

Friday, June 24, 1904

Ed POLSON was accidentally shot and killed Wednesday near Covington, Texas. He was killed by a shotgun that discharged when the team POLSON was driving ran away. POLSON, with his brother B. F. POLSON, was visiting his father when the accident happened.

Marriage licenses issued by Tarrant County Clerk's office: O. M. CRAIG and Miss M. E. MACK, and G. T. JAMES and Miss O. M. GIBSON.

Births recorded by Tarrant County Clerk's office: a boy to Mr. and Mrs. Wade BROWN, Fort Worth, on June 23; a boy to Mr. and Mrs. W.B. FITZHUGH, Arlington, on June 11; a boy to Mr. and Mrs. William MOORE, Arlington, on June 16; and a boy to Mr. and Mrs. M. H. KINSMAN on June 18.

Saturday, June 25, 1904

Rev. A.P. LOWRY and Jennie Mae YOUNG married Wednesday night in Kyle, Texas.

John L. CHESTER and Isa E. NEAL were married Wednesday at the home of Mrs. Henry FRAZIER in Temple, Texas.

J. REDDING and Miss D. COWAN married Wednesday in Belton, Texas. Rev. George W. LEE officiated.

Professor Ray CROWE, a faculty member at Armour Institute in Chicago, married Florence MONROE in Guthrie, Oklahoma Territory Thursday.

George PIERCE and Nellie CLAYCOMB married Wednesday night in Lancaster, Texas. Rev. MOFFET officiated.

O. B. DUNAWAY and Helen MILLER married Wednesday at the home of Houston MILLER, her father, in Waxahachie, Texas. Rev. James N. IVY of First Presbyterian Church officiated.

Rev. John Baptist TROXLER, 69, died Wednesday in Lindsay, Texas. He was a priest.

Silas B. WELLS, a contractor, died Wednesday in Texarkana. Death was attributed to acute stomach trouble and heart disease.

H. C. MCDERMOTT died from consumption in San Angelo, Texas. He was a resident of Garland, Texas

Jason PAULK, 71, died of acute stomach trouble Wednesday at his home in Texarkana.

Ruby ADAMS, 3, daughter of J. O. ADAMS, died yesterday after she drank lye in Pecos, Texas.

HICKALACHEE, 76, and Theresa ROUBIDEAUX, 94, married near Perkins, Oklahoma Territory. Both were members of the Iowa Nation.

Miss CONWAY, of Lawton, Oklahoma Territory, filed a suit against P. C. HESS of Sioux City, Iowa for breach of promise. HESS married Effie LEWIS of Lawton soon after his discharge from the US Army at Fort Sill.

Jessie MILLER, of Texarkana, was elected as chair of the history department at Corsicana, Texas yesterday.

Ida B. CRISWELL died yesterday after taking a patent tonic containing arsenic and strychnine in Denison, Texas.

Frank R. CHAFEE was found dead of a gunshot wound to the head in Houston yesterday. The wound appeared to be self-inflicted.

Conrad SCWARTZ, 18, was found guilty yesterday of the murder of W. A. EARLE at Cuero, Texas. EARLE was killed June 7, 1904. (See above). SCHWARTZ was sentenced to die. EARLE left a wife and three children. He was a night operator at Yorktown, Texas.

County attorney O. S. LATTIMORE received a telegram affirming the death sentence of Rufus MARTIN. MARTIN was convicted in the killing of Charles SWACKHAMMER last October in Fort Worth.

Births recorded at Tarrant County Clerk's office: a boy to Mr. and Mrs. Joe CHARLES, Fort Worth, on June 21; a girl to Mr. and Mrs. Joe WALKER, Fort Worth, on June 20.

Deaths recorded at Tarrant County Clerk's office: J. E. JOHNSON, 55, residing in Fort Worth, died of Bright's disease on June 15.

Sunday, June 26, 1904

Marriage licenses issued by Tarrant County Clerk: Alvin HAUPTVOGLE and Ida GOLDKE, and Abe HANCOCK and Agre BOOTH.

Births recorded at Tarrant County Clerk's office: a girl to Mr. and Mrs. C. G. KENT, Fort Worth, on June 23; a boy to Mr. and Mrs. W. M. BRADLEY, Arlington, on June 10; a girl to Mr. and Mrs. Ben JOHNSON, Peden, on June 11; a boy to Mr. and Mrs. Wesley SEXTON, Fort Worth, on June 20 and a girl to Mr. and Mrs. John MCADAMS, Fort Worth, on June 12.

E. G. ROBERTSON, 70, died in Dallas County Jail yesterday of natural causes. He was waiting transfer to an asylum after being found insane last summer. The insanity ruling came after he killed an inmate of the County Farm.

J. E. JOHNSON died in Fort Worth on June 15. He was an early settler of Fort Worth. He married Sarah HOLDER in Missouri in 1866 and had lived in Fort Worth since 1872. Their children included Beulah JOHNSON, James JOHNSON and Robert JOHNSON.

The funeral for Father John Baptist TROXLER took place Friday in Lindsay, Texas.

William MARR was stabbed to death Friday in Conroe, Texas. D. C. RILEY was arrested and charged with murder. MARR left a widow and five children.

J. W. BECKERT committed suicide by hanging himself yesterday in Bellville, Texas. He was married and had a small son. He worked as a painter.

Miss Sinah PORTER, daughter of G. W. PORTER, married J. I. CLARKSON at the home of her parents in Fort Worth this week. Rev. C. M. COLLINS officiated.

Geraldine Powell REAGAN and Edward Robert BURNS married in Dallas on June 15. Rev. J. Frank SMITH of the Cumberland Presbyterian Church officiated.

Monday, June 27, 1904

Charley REES, 2, died Thursday in Greenville, Texas. His funeral was Saturday.

I. N. POLLARD died Friday at his home near Era, Texas.

Mrs. WATERS, 70, died Friday. She lived east of Gainesville, Texas. Her remains were sent to Weatherford, Texas.

J. M. WATTS died Thursday at his home near Blue Grove, Texas. Blue Grove is located 12 miles south of Henrietta, Texas. He was a county commissioner for many years and left a widow and six grown children.

T. C. HOLLINGSWORTH died June 18 in Snyder, Texas. He was buried in Snyder June 22 and left a large family.

O. T. SIMS, a cattleman of the Texas panhandle, died recently in Snyder, Texas. He was buried in the Snyder Cemetery.

The three year old son of Mr. and Mrs. Lee SMITH died in Mabank, Texas. His name and date of death were not listed. He was buried Friday.

C. E. BLEWETT and Ora O. CULP Wednesday married in Gainesville, Texas. Rev. R. D. WEAR officiated.

Douglas N. KING and Hallie B. HORSLEY married Thursday in Greenville, Texas. The bride is the daughter of Prof. and Mrs. R. G. HORSLEY. Rev. R. F. JENKINS officiated.

Alice CHASTAIN and J.A. BARTON married Thursday in Menardville, Texas. The bride is the daughter of James A. CHASTAIN of Maynardville, Texas. The groom resides in Denton, Texas.

Eugene HUGHES and Edna MCGILL married last Monday in Panhandle, Texas.

Dr. J. A. HUMPHREY and Emma J. BUSCHE married Saturday in Gainesville, Texas. Rev. J. F. PIERCE officiated. The groom is from Ardmore, Indian Territory

Clinton REED, 17, was arrested near Stillwater, Oklahoma Territory and charged with the 1902 death of John BRAXTON.

J. W. KINCAID committed suicide yesterday in Cleveland, Oklahoma Territory. He was despondent over the loss of his potato crop in heavy rains.

Orley STRETCH, 7, drowned today near Marshall, Oklahoma Territory. He fell into a spring.

Dr. Q. A. SHUFORD, 78, died yesterday in Tyler, Texas. He came to Texas from South Carolina in 1850. He was buried today.

Tuesday, June 28, 1904

The newspaper for this date did not appear on the microfilm.

Wednesday, June 29, 1904

F. BROSE died yesterday in Corpus Christi, Texas. He took morphine. He was a shoemaker.

A skeleton found near Eureka, Texas is believed to be that of W. H. BALDWIN, a collector for the *Daily Post*.

C. T. LOUIS of Louisiana came to Corsicana, Texas to check on his son Talmadge LOUIS and learned Talmadge had been hit be a train and killed in November. His body wasn't identified and he was buried near Corsicana. The body was removed to Louisiana.

Mrs. M. E. WALTON, wife of O. C. WALTON, died yesterday in Grandview, Texas.

W. M. PARKER died Saturday night. He had lived north of Annons, Texas.

The remains of Jerome LEVI arrived yesterday in Corsicana, Texas. They were buried from the home of his parents, Mr. and Mrs. M. LEVI.

Mrs. F. A. CONE, 75, died yesterday in Marble Falls, Texas.

Mrs. Charles SETTLE died of cancer of the stomach at her home near Prosper, Texas.

"Aunt Polly" COSTER, 70, died at her home Sunday and was buried Monday near Stony, Texas. She was the sister of Mrs. J. W. COOK of Denton. Stony is located west of Denton.

C. E. HILLER and Miss E. L. CRABTREE, of Blooming Grove, Texas, were married in Corsicana, Texas yesterday.

Richard SHIELDS and Daisy FRIOU married yesterday in Cleburne, Texas.

Marriage licenses issued by Tarrant County Clerk's office: F. E. MOON and Lizzie WHITE, Harry DANIELS and Elizabeth J. COCHRAN, and George F. THOMPSON and Mrs. Rose B. YORK.

Thursday, June 30, 1904

Harry MEYER, 17, was killed yesterday in an industrial accident in Belton, Texas. He was employed by the city power plant when the accident happened.

William T. BLEDSOE and Cora THERRELL married in Fort Worth last night.

Marriage licenses issued by Tarrant County Clerk's office: George F. THOMPSON and Rosa B. YORK; John L. NORRIS and Henrietta Louise FISMER; W.C. FELDER and Miss E.F. WILLIAMS.

July, 1904

Friday, July 1, 1904

W. E. BRIDGES was killed in Austin yesterday while installing telegraph wire for Western Union on Congress Street there.

Judge Robert Symington GOULD, 79, died at his home in Austin yesterday. He was a professor of law and justice of the Supreme Court. He was born in North Carolina, educated at Presbyterian College in Alabama and served in the Confederate Army. A nephew is Robert G. STREET of Galveston, Texas.

J. C. MANN, also known as Sam EASLY, was murdered by an unknown assailant at his home north of Texarkana.

Dessie RAMSEY and Olin HALEY married Wednesday in Cleburne, Texas.

Dr. J. W. PEARSON, of White Rock, Texas, and Sallie WHITE, of Jacobia, Texas, married in Greenville, Texas Sunday. Rev. J. G. NICHOLSON officiated.

Rev. J. P. MUSSETT united C. C. TAYLOR and Tollie CHISENHALL in marriage in Joshua, Texas last Sunday.

E. H. CASHELL and Eula EVANS married Wednesday in Greenville, Texas. Rev. H. G. HOISLEY officiated. The bride is daughter of the Honorable and Mrs. B. Q. EVANS

Ed MARCHMAN and Miss Ernie FOSTER married Wednesday five miles northeast of Greenville, Texas. Rev. R.F. JENKINS officiated. The bride is the daughter of Mr. and Mrs. Tom FOSTER.

J. E. JONES and Mrs. Cassie B. HONAKEE married yesterday in Farmersville, Texas. Rev. A. J. FAWCETT officiated.

Otis L. GOODLOE and Mertie RAGLE married yesterday in Olney, Texas. Rev. G. W. RUSHNY officiated.

Christine CHILTON and Chainault OBRIEN married Thursday in Beaumont, Texas. The marriage took place in the home of Senator and Mrs. Horace CHILTON.

"Grandma" ELLIS, 95, died June 23 in Gomez, Texas. She was the mother-in-law of Dr. GRIFFITH of Gomez.

George ROBUCK, who lived one mile east of Paradise, Texas, died of appendicitis Sunday.

J. A. RUTHERFORD died Thursday in Colorado City, Texas. He lived in Ennis, Texas.

H. L. OBERTHEER, 76, who died in Merlin, Texas, was buried Tuesday in Comanche, Texas. He was born in Virginia and served as a Confederate soldier. He left a widow, a daughter and two sons.

Mrs. W. R. HAYMES, 77, died Tuesday in San Marcos, Texas.

Judge W. A. IVES died yesterday in Beaumont, Texas. His funeral is today.

Marriage licenses issued by Tarrant County Clerk's office: W. S. SILER and Cora E. TERRELL, Fred D. FELIDA and Stella WILLIAMS, and P. A. CARR and Mary MASON.

Births recorded at Tarrant County Clerk's office: a girl to Mr. and Mrs. B. P. AVERETT, Fort Worth, on June 6; and a boy to Mr. and Mrs. J. Earle PARKS, Fort Worth, on June 27.

Deaths recorded at Tarrant County Clerk's office: Mrs. Ed TOWERS, 19, residing in Fort Worth, died of hemorrhage with no date listed; Godfrey F. MERICH, 65, residing in Kennedale, died on June 18 of heart failure; Elmira Mary CLAYTON, 11, residing in Fort Worth, died on June 20 due to typhoid; and Annie VALENTINE, 22, residing near Bedford, died on June 2 of hemorrhage.

Saturday, July 2, 1904

Charles VORHOLZER and Kate SNYDER married Thursday in Paris, Texas. Rev. Charles MANTON officiated.

C. B. BOATMAN and Mrs. C. IRVIN married Thursday in Paris, Texas.

Montie FORESTER and E. K. BAILEY married Wednesday in San Angelo, Texas.

Mrs. J. W. HEALD died Wednesday at her home on Lifan Flat, Texas. Lifan Flat was near San Angelo.

Neither district court was in session yesterday due to the death of Judge S. P. GREENE.

Marriage licenses issued in Tarrant County Clerk's office: A. J. HUNTER and Ula CHILDRESS, William H. BROWN and Lizzie GALLAGHER, and Len SMITH and Voshie BROWN.

Isaac MARTINEZ was shot and killed by Deputy Sheriff W. M. HARDWICK in an attempted escape from jail in Athens, Texas yesterday.

E. H. STARKS waived examination trial in the death of Bob SPENCE at Direct, Texas. He posted $3000 bail and was released.

The body of Robert SPENCE was brought to Paris, Texas for shipment to Sulphur Springs, Texas for burial.

Norman Lee SMITH, 12, died yesterday from injuries sustained when he fell from a tree on Thursday. He was the son of S. P. SMITH.

Dick OGLE was killed when he fell from a horse while herding cattle near Lone Oak, Texas Sunday.

Sunday, July 3, 1904

Norman B. TIERNAN was found dead of epilepsy yesterday in Galveston, Texas. He was the son of R. H. TIERNAN.

Marriage licenses issued by Tarrant County Clerk's office: J. W. LONG and Lellar VINSON, J. L. DAVIS and Lena CAREY, and R. L. YOUNG and Lora ROCKETT.

Births recorded at Tarrant County Clerk's office: a boy to Mr. and Mrs. J. C. PATTERSON, Fort Worth, on June 26; a boy to Mr. and Mrs. H. H. WILKERSON, no place or date listed; a girl to Mr. and Mrs. Oscar WHITE, Rosen Heights, on June 28; a boy to Mr. and Mrs. H. L. SMALL, Fort Worth, on June 22; a girl to Mr. and Mrs. J. F. STEEL, Fort Worth, on June 30 and a boy to Mr. and Mrs. John SIFFORD, Fort Worth, on June 21.

Deaths recorded at Tarrant County Clerk's office: the child of W. L. RICHARDSON, 7 months, residing in Arlington, died of brain congestion on June 21.

R. G. WILIAMS, 32, was shot and killed in Fort Worth last night. L. B. CURD, 30, was taken into custody immediately.

W. L. JOHNSON was shot and killed yesterday in Childress, Texas. G. A. YANTIS, well-known cattleman of the Panhandle, was held without bond. YANTIS was operating the Hotel Good in Childress.

The remains of Rev. J. A. RUTHERFORD arrived in Ennis, Texas from Colorado City, Texas. They were buried in the Myrtle Cemetery. RUTHERFORD was a traveling evangelist for the Methodist church.

J. A. PAGE and Rosie TAYLOR married Friday in Marshall, Texas. Rev. J. E. MCLEAN officiated.

Roy RUDKIN, 7, was accidentally shot and killed by his five year old brother near Edmund, Oklahoma Territory. The brother's name was not listed.

Eleanor WILLIAMS and William G. FIELDER were married Wednesday at Saint Andrews Parish House in Fort Worth.

Hattie POINDEXTER and Frank COLLINS married Thursday in Fort Worth.

Lucille SCANLON and Fred BATES married Tuesday in Dallas.

Cora Etta THERRELL and W. T. BLEDSOE married Wednesday in the Fort Worth home of her parents, Mr. and Mrs. Charles BROGDEN.

Janie COCHRAN and Harry DANIELS married Wednesday in Fort Worth. The wedding took place at the home of her parents, Mr. and Mrs. S. H. COCHRAN.

Monday, July 4, 1904

An inquest concerning the death of August HOBARTH was held Wednesday in Gonzalez, Texas. HOBART died of a gunshot wound to the head.

Mrs. AUTSEY, sister of Thomas DAVIS, died Thursday night five miles east of Gainesville, Texas.

W. F. STOVAL, 66, died Friday at his home near Jardin, Texas. He was survived by his wife and seven children.

Bennett EATIER died Wednesday night at his home east of Greenville, Texas.

John VICKERS, 37, was struck by falling scantling Saturday and died yesterday near Sour Lake, Texas. His remains were shipped to Mexia, Texas.

Charles Thomas TATUM was buried yesterday near Farmersville, Texas. Odd Fellows directed the funeral. He died Saturday. He was a Confederate veteran. Charles Thomas TATUM, Jr. and Melvinia Jones TATUM, his son and widow, survived him.

Mrs. Lee PARKER, 24, died Saturday after drinking carbolic acid in Dallas. Her remains were shipped to Roxton, Texas for burial.

William HYDER committed suicide in Guthrie, Oklahoma Territory today.

George HOWARD was killed while harvesting wheat yesterday. He lived in Osage Indian country and was caught in a binder.

Tuesday, July 5, 1904

George W. HARTSFIELD, well-known railroad man, died at his Dallas home yesterday. His funeral was today. He was a Confederate veteran.

Four people were killed when a surrey collided with a street car in Texarkana. Dead are Sybil PUGH, 15, Mrs. Ben PILLOW and her two daughters aged 20 and 6. The names of Mrs. PILLOW's daughters were not reported.

Lilliard WALLACE, 6, the son of George WALLACE, was killed yesterday when he was struck by a hack in Waco, Texas.

Mrs. Sophie K. WOODS, widow of James P. WOODS and daughter of J. P. ALFORD, died yesterday in Fort Worth. Her father died last Friday. The death was due to heart failure. Surviving children were Mrs. Elmer RENFRO, Mrs. J. A. COMER, Minnie WOODS and Claude P. WOODS.

Mrs. Julia D. RAMSEY, mother of E. P. RAMSEY of Fort Worth, died in St. Louis Sunday.

Wednesday, July 6, 1904

The paper for this date did not appear on the microfilm.

Thursday, July 7, 1904

John D. CONNELLY of San Antonio and Lollie MORRIS of Austin married Tuesday in Austin.

Albion E. BROOKS, 20, was found dead Saturday in an ice factory in Shafter, Texas. He died of a self-inflicted gunshot wound to the head.

The crew of the U.S.S. Iowa sent a silver urn to commemorate the death of W. A. POWELL of that ship.

W. M. HUNTER was killed last Monday night in Garland, Texas.

Ruby ADAMS, 3, daughter of Mr. and Mrs. J. O. ADAMS of Pecos, Texas, died after drinking lye. No date was given. The story was datelined July 6.

Marriage licenses issued by Tarrant County Clerk's office: Dewitt FRIERSON and Mrs. Jamie SHAW, Ernest HOWARD and Jessie SANDERS, and J. C. ISBELL and Mrs. W. A. FIELD.

Friday, July 8, 1904

Col. S. J. SPENCER was arrested and charged with manslaughter in the traffic deaths of Sybil PUGH and the two Misses PUGH. SPENCER was president of the street car company. (See story of July 5).

Perry SIMPSON committed suicide while visiting L. WARD near Midlothian, Texas. He lived in Cleburne, Texas. The coroner's inquest showed SIMPSON died of self-administered chloroform.

The body of Ed HALLUM was found on the Texas and Pacific Railroad tracks west of Fort Worth. He had been rundown by a train.

Mrs. Eliza GALLAGHER died at San Antonio Wednesday. She was an old settler of San Antonio.

Mrs. Sallie RIDDLE, 73, died Monday night at Palmer, Texas.

Mrs. John RODGERS died Tuesday between Sterrett and Red Oak, Texas. Burial was in Red Oak Wednesday.

J. B. THOMPSON died Tuesday afternoon. He lived four miles west of Waxahachie and was buried in Sardis, Texas.

Mrs. THORNTON, 102, died Saturday at the home of her son, Horace GIDDINGS, near Jardin, Texas.

R. H. HORN, 88, died Tuesday morning at his home in Shelby County, Texas.

A. A. BLACK died in Temple, Texas. The funeral was under the auspices of the Masons.

Dr. J. A. MORRIS, 68, died Tuesday on Belton, Texas. He was buried in North Belton Cemetery Wednesday. The funeral was under the auspices of the Masons.

Laura LIDDY, 21, died Monday in Paris, Texas. Her death was due to consumption.

Postmaster STRICKLAND died of a heart attack in Cottonwood, Texas Wednesday. He resided in Cross Plains, Texas.

D. G. RAILSBACK was stabbed to death yesterday in Mountain View, Oklahoma Territory.

Ed HELM's death was the subject of an inquest yesterday. HELMS was run over by a train on the Texas and Pacific Railroad. Tom HELM, his father, lives in Weatherford and has been notified of the death.

Marriage licenses issued by Tarrant County Clerk's office: J. B. STEVENS and Allie HAMPTON, Berry SESSIONS and Angie COLEMAN, and Abraham THOMPSON and Cora MARTICUE.

Births recorded at Tarrant County Clerk's office: a boy to Mr. and Mrs. J. L. HENDERSON, Fort Worth, on July 6; a girl to Mr. and Mrs. B. A. TYSON, Fort Worth, on June 29; a boy and a girl (twins) to Mr. and Mrs. Henry SEYSTER, Riverside, on June 29; a girl to Mr. and Mrs. Charlie ANDREWS, Birdvile, on July 4; a girl to Mr. and Mrs. R. W. SPEARMAN, Fort Worth, on July 4; a boy to Mr. and Mrs. E. C. FISK, Fort Worth, on June 6; a boy to Mr. and Mrs. L. M. CAIN, Mansfield, on June 24; a girl to Mr. and Mrs. R. G. TAYLOR, Mansfield, on July 1; and a girl to Mr. and Mrs. Milt BRISCOE, Mansfield, on July 6.

Deaths recorded at Tarrant County Clerk's office: Sophie K. WOODS, 55, residing in Arlington, died of erysipelas on June 25; Ben BALL, 10, residing in Mansfield, died of typhoid fever on June 26; Ed HELM, 21, residing in Fort Worth, died when struck by a train on July 7; Martha BROWN, 65, residing near Arlington, died of erysipelas on June 25; John BLASCO, 23, residing in Euless, died of typhoid fever on June 27; John Lawrence TOWN, 3, residing near Johnson Station, died from measles on June 30; and Claude Sanders JAY, 3 months, residing in North Fort Worth, died from chronic dysentery on July 1.

Saturday, July 9, 1904

Bill HUGHES, an old time stockman on Turkey Creek, was killed today at Mangum, Texas.

Mrs. C. M. BENNETT and a boy drowned yesterday near Coleman, Texas.

L. H. ZETZSCHE and Miss W. R. RICHARDSON married Sunday east of Paris, Texas.

P. P. CHILDERS and Beulah WATSON married Sunday in Slidell, Texas. Rev. J. H. HEATHINGTON officiated.

Attorney __.M. JONES and Elizabeth KOONTZ married Monday in Wichita, Kansas.

Raymond SCHLIGA and Carolina SCHULER married in Marshall, Texas Sunday. Rev. L. GRANGER of St. Joseph's Catholic Church officiated.

V. B. DEATON, a merchant of Brady, Texas, and Alice GREENWOOD married Tuesday in Lampasas, Texas. The bride is the daughter of B. C. GREENWOOD.

Mollie O. TURMAN and Robert SPRAGUE married Sunday in San Angelo, Texas.

Charlie HINEMAN and Bessie WHALEY married Tuesday in Longview, Texas.

J. S. CRAVENS and Rinka DELASHAW married Wednesday in Greenville, Texas. Rev. Forest SMITH, pastor of the First Baptist Church of Sherman, officiated.

"Axhandle" BROWN was shot and killed yesterday on the plantation of H. A. GRAYSON near Marquez, Texas. Kiah HAMAN surrendered to authorities.

Marriage licenses issued by Tarrant County Clerk's office: Barry SESSIONS and Angie COLEMAN.

Births recorded at Tarrant County Clerk's office: a girl to Mr. and Mrs. Luther BALLARD, North Fort Worth, on June 23; a girl to Mr. and Mrs. O. D. CLARK, Fort Worth, on July 7; a girl to Mr. and Mrs. Jeff D. BEGGS, Fort Worth, on July 6; a girl to Mr. and Mrs. F. MCNELLIS, North Fort Worth, on June 30; a boy to Mr. and Mrs. John WESROCK, Fort Worth on July 1; a girl to Mr. and Mrs. J. R. WORSHAM, Fort Worth, on June 26; a boy to Mr. and Mrs. Thomas COLOY, Fort Worth, on June 24; a boy to Mr. and Mrs. J. B. PRUITT, Fort Worth, on June 19; a boy to Mr. and Mrs. J. H. GANN, Fort Worth, on June 15; and a girl to Mr. and Mrs. Charles E. COONS, Arlington, on June 24.

Deaths recorded at Tarrant County Clerk's office: Sarah Delilia BURNEY, 18, residing in North Fort Worth, died of pneumonia on June 27; Ione MCNELLIS, infant, residing in North Fort Worth, died of inanition on June 30; and Thelma MCNELLIS, residing in North Fort Worth, died of typhoid fever on July 1.

Sunday, July 10, 1904

Marion BARTON and Naomi PIERCE married Thursday in Greenville, Texas. Squire Tom MCDANIEL officiated.

Frank MOXLEY and Nora DART married in Dallas Wednesday. Rev. I. W. CLARK officiated.

R. P. TIPPETT and Nola OAKS, both of Indian Territory, were married by Justice J.R.G. LONG in Paris, Texas.

Mrs. R. C. THOMAS died Thursday in Waxahachie, Texas. Burial was yesterday in the city cemetery.

John YOUNGER, 33, died suddenly Thursday of heart disease in McKinney, Texas.

Fred NEWCOMB died Thursday in Texarkana. He was found sick and destitute and placed in the hospital earlier in the week.

Willie BREWER, 14, died Thursday at his home near Texarkana.

Matie WILLIAMS, 31, the wife of John H. MCLAIN, died Thursday. Her remains were shipped to Fayetteville, Arkansas.

Mary CLAY, 24, died Friday in Texarkana. Her body was shipped to Bernard, Texas.

W. L. BROWNING died Thursday in Fort Worth and was buried Friday in Oakwood Cemetery. He left a widow, Jennie Lovett BROWNING. There were no children.

Monday, July 11, 1904

Henry MULLINO, of Hico, Texas, was shot and killed by Fred HICKLIN near Iron King, Arizona Territory. MULLINO was the son of F. H. MULLINO.

G. W. MORTON and Florence GIBSON married Saturday at Paris, Texas. Rev. W. W. HARRIS officiated.

S. W. WESTBROOK and Ollie Z. CAMPBELL married Friday at Paris, Texas.

S. T. BOSTICK and Mrs. Louise BREWER married in the residence of William GEEBER in Marshall, Texas.

Miss Russell PRICE died in Marshall, Texas Saturday night. She was buried in Blalock Cemetery five miles south of Marshall.

The funeral of General Thomas Baltimore HOWARD took place in Houston yesterday.

Tuesday, July 12, 1904

The paper for this date did not appear on the microfilm.

Wednesday, July 13, 1904

The five year old child of Bryant CHURCH was killed when he fell beneath the wheels of a threshing machine yesterday in Stroud, Texas.

Marriage licenses issued by Tarrant County Clerk's office: Phillips LEVINE and Mrs. Ray TOUKSFSKY, Marion H. WOOD and Mary A. CARLEY, and Hunt GARRISON and Mrs. Mattie DAVIS.

John F. ONION and Sallie Jane YOUNG married yesterday in Palestine, Texas. She was the daughter of Mr. and Mrs. John YOUNG.

Lewis PARHAM and Ruby GLASS married Sunday in Omaha, Texas.

L. V. HILBURN and Maggie WOOLDRIDGE married Sunday near Paris, Texas.

J. D. PARHAM and Alice PINKARD married Monday in Covington, Texas.

J. ARMSTRONG and Dora ROBERTSON married Monday in her home in Mineral Wells, Texas.

Walter P. TERRELL and Mary S. RICHARDSON married Tuesday in Graham, Texas. Rev. A. C. PARKER officiated.

Les_oyres GILLIAM and H. Al JOHNSON married Sunday in Rovis, Indian Territory.

Fayette NICHOLS died at his home of dropsy Monday. The remains were sent to Denton, Texas. He farmed at Krum, Texas

Mrs. John ELLIS died of consumption yesterday near Mildred, Texas. Her remains were sent to Corsicana, Texas.

George M. WATTS, 89, died Monday east of McKinney, Texas. He was a pioneer, settling in Collin County in 1855. His widow and children survive.

Mrs. E. H. BOND died and was buried Monday in Cooper, Texas.

John HALAMUDA died in Beaumont, Texas. He was injured in Loeb, Texas. His remains were sent to San Antonio.

Herman GREEN, about 13, and Alfonso FULLER, about 18, drowned in the Trinity River at Fort Worth yesterday.

Mrs. M. A. HAMMER died Saturday in Belton, Texas. She was buried in North Belton Cemetery Sunday.

Mrs. B. H. CALHOUN died in San Angelo, Texas Sunday. Her remains were sent to Temple. The funeral was from the Methodist Church.

Lota LEMMONS, 22, the daughter of T. D. LEMMONS, died suddenly Sunday in Weatherford, Texas.

Hattie BENTLEY, 20, died Sunday in Mineral Wells, Texas. She was from Bristol, Texas.

James Franklin CULP, 55, died of heart failure in Temple, Texas. He is survived by his wife and four children.

Hattie MURPHEY died Sunday in Mineral Wells, Texas. He resided in Brownwood, Texas

W. J. KEACH died Saturday at Greenville, Texas. His remains were sent to Ennis, Texas.

Mary GRAVES died Saturday morning in Tidwell, Texas.

Thursday, July 14, 1904 through
Friday, July 15, 1904

The papers for these dates did not appear on the microfilm.

Saturday, July 16, 1904

Hiram T. KEENAN died in Fort Worth yesterday. He was born in Quincy, Illinois and was the "dean of railroad officials" in Fort Worth.

The 13 year old son of John GRIMES was killed when a mule kicked him in Leon, Indian Territory.

Homer MCCLARY, 8, the son of F. C. MCCLARY, was fatally injured Thursday in Fort Worth when he fell from the family's phaeton while riding with them. Burial was in Oakwood Cemetery.

Collin SANDEL died from gunshot wounds at Brenham, Texas. Constable BURCH was charged with murder.

Laura May SHIELDS, 3, died Thursday in Roswell, New Mexico Territory. She was the daughter of Samuel SHIELDS. Burial was Friday in Southside Cemetery.

Mrs. Walter H. PARK died Wednesday at Boyce, Texas. Burial was Thursday in Waxahachie, Texas.

Dr. B. F. MCCARTHY, 76, died Thursday in Comanche, Texas. He was a Mexican War veteran and was survived by two sons and three daughters.

Mrs. J. H. CALLOWAY died Thursday in Hereford, Texas. She was a former resident of Ennis, Texas.

Henry COLLARD, 5, and Charlie COLLARD, 3, died Thursday in Alma, Texas. They were buried Friday in Rice, Texas.

F. W. LIMBAUGH and Mable SHAPP married Thursday in Roswell, New Mexico Territory. Rev. C. C. YOUNG officiated.

Jennie CARPENTER, daughter of J. J. CARPENTER, and Carl BURLEY married Tuesday in San Antonio.

Nola BENTON and R. H. POWELL married Thursday in Mineola, Texas. Rev. J. V. MAHAN officiated.

C. T. BECKNELL and Mrs. R. T. MCKAY married Tuesday in Greenville, Texas. The wedding took place at the home of the bride's brother, A. H. TURNER.

T. A. RICHEY of and Mattie LANIER married Wednesday in Marshall, Texas. Rev. J. B. K. SPAIN officiated. The groom is from Walden, Georgia. The bride is from Atlanta, Texas.

J. P. HOWELL and Willie PAYNE married Thursday in Greenville, Texas. Rev. R. F. JENKINS officiated.

Rev. J. C. MCWHIRTER and Anna DEES married Thursday in Tyler, Texas.

W. R. MULLEN and Abbie TURNER married Thursday in McKinney, Texas. She is daughter of R.B. TURNER.

Francis WILLIS, 11, was shot and killed yesterday near Cordell, Oklahoma Territory. John SMITH, 11, was arrested.

Marriage licenses issued by Tarrant County Clerk's office: S. MASERANG and Martha GALLOWAY, J. S. ZINN and Mary WEST.

Deaths recorded at Tarrant County Clerk's office: Antonio GONZALES, age unknown, residing in Fort Worth, died of mitral regurgitation on July 13.

Sunday, July 17, 1904

James DANIEL, 13, was killed when he was struck with a baseball bat during a quarrel after a game yesterday in Laredo, Texas. He was the son of J. M. DANIEL.

Ansel B. ALEXANDER, 36, died last night at the Hotel Rosen in Fort Worth.

Mrs. A. G. THOMAS died yesterday in Atlanta, Georgia. She was the mother of Mrs. H. W. FAIRBANKS and Mrs. J. F. HOWARD of Dallas.

The two year old child of Mr. TAYLOR, agent for the Frisco Road at Scullen, Indian Territory, was killed instantly yesterday when it was run over by a train. No name or gender of the child was given.

Marriage licenses issued by Tarrant County Clerk's office: W. E. GOLDRING and Emma HARRISON; R. S. ROCHESTER and Mrs. Lavina MESERANG; Stanley BOYKIN and Clota Winona TERRELL; James Henry CORD and Lula JACKSON; Jeah MEADFORD and Susie HINES; and Henry WINBUSH and Mattie C. CHAMP.

Births recorded at Tarrant County Clerk's office: a boy to Mr. and Mrs. A. J. SCOTT, near Grapevine, on July 5; a girl to Mr. and Mrs. J. A. FOWLER, near Grapevine, on July 15; a boy to Mr. and Mrs. E. BATEMAN, Grapevine, on July 14; a girl to Mr. and Mrs. Marcus FULFORD, Fort Worth, on July 13; a girl to Mr. and Mrs. W. G. MILLER, Grapevine, on June 26; and a girl to Mr. and Mrs. Robert KEYS, Benbrook, on July 9.

Deaths recorded at Tarrant County Clerk's office: Jessie CARLILES, 9 months, residing in Arlington, died of hydroencephalitis on July 10; Sena ROSS, 50, residing in North Fort Worth, died of congestion on July 8; Bettie AUSTIN, 76, residing near Grapevine, died of old age on July 7; Edith TRANTHAM, 2, residing in Fort Worth, died of inflammation of the bowels on July 14; and Homer MCCLAREY, 8, residing in Fort Worth died from an accident on July 14.

Monday, July 18 through Tuesday, July 19, 1904
The papers for these dates did not appear on the microfilm.

Wednesday, July 20, 1904
Jack CANE seriously wounded his wife and killed himself yesterday with a revolver at Earlboro, Oklahoma Territory.

John GOUGH died yesterday in Fort Worth at the home of Mrs. W. S. WALTON, his daughter. He was a Confederate veteran and was survived by his widow, four sons and two other daughters. Remains were shipped to Mexico, Missouri.

Marriage licenses issued by Tarrant County Clerk's office: H. P. SWAIN and Edith L. ADAMS; Nedom R. TISDAL and Virginia BALL; J. C. ELSON and Etna G. GRIER; J. H. FARIS and Mrs. Lena SCHITZER.

Births recorded at Tarrant County Clerk's office: a girl to Mr. and Mrs. HERDINGER (no other name), Fort Worth on July 1; a boy to Mr. and Mrs. Isaac KELLER, Keller, on July 18; a boy to Mr. and Mrs. James SMITH, Keller, on July 17; a girl to Mr. and Mrs. Arthur DAVIS, Fort Worth, on July 17; and a boy to Mr. and Mrs. T. C. HOWARD, North Fort Worth, on July 15.

Deaths recorded at Tarrant County Clerk's office: E. H. WILSON, no age listed, residing in Fort Worth, died of strychnine poisoning on July 18.

Thursday, July 21, 1904
The paper for this date did not appear on the microfilm.

Friday, July 22, 1904
Charley SCOTT was killed yesterday at Antlers, Indian Territory. A loaded shotgun accidentally discharged and struck him.

The five year old son of Francisco AVELARE was killed when he was run over by a Wells Fargo express wagon in Alamagordo, New Mexico Territory.

William Kenneth DAVIS, 2, the son of Mr. and Mrs. J. H. DAVIS, died Tuesday in Fort Worth. The cause of death was pleural pneumonia.

The remains of Mrs. C. G. STATTS were buried in Oakwood Cemetery yesterday. She lived in Arlington Heights before her death.

John A. KENNEDY and Mrs. Rosa E. NEWBY married in Fort Worth yesterday. Rev. Luther LITTLE officiated.

George W. TODD died yesterday in St. Louis, Missouri. He was the father of George W. TODD, Jr. of Waco, Texas. The senior TODD died of apoplexy. He was a long time steward on Mississippi River steam boats.

Mrs. A. O. MCBRIDE died of consumption yesterday in Roswell, New Mexico Territory. She was the daughter of Mr. and Mrs. Joseph BELL and the mother of a three month old child.

J. P. ADAMS, 60, died Wednesday at the home of W. H. ADAMS, his son, in Greenville, Texas. He was a Union veteran and left two others sons and a daughter.

G. W. LABOR, 66, died yesterday in Hico, Texas.

Mrs. George PERKINS, of Taylor's Valley, Texas, died at the home of her parents Wednesday. Burial was in North Belton Cemetery. Rev. William HAY officiated.

Postmaster WARSON died Wednesday at his home in Leland, Texas.

Mrs. Beverly L. ROGERS, 69, died Wednesday at her home near Frisco, Texas. She lived in Collin County for more than fifty years.

Mayor John REICHSTETTER died last Thursday of Bright's disease in Granbury, Texas.

Clemmie SCOTT, the daughter of Hixie SCOTT, married Raymond ROGERS Sunday in DeLeon, Texas.

L. E. BARRICK and Ida DODSON married at the home of her brother in Antelope, Texas Sunday. Rev. W.H. MARTIN officiated. The groom is from Fort Worth.

Grover ELDER and Ethel C. ALEXANDER married Wednesday in Greenville, Texas. The marriage took place at the home of Mrs. J. F. SOCKWELL, the bride's aunt. Rev. R. F. JENKINS officiated. Following the wedding, the couple left for their new home in Amarillo, Texas.

Jane RINEHART, daughter of former sheriff Frank RINEHART, married Wendall P. PHELPS at Guthrie, Oklahoma Territory. No date was indicated. The groom is from Columbus, Ohio.

R. W. SIMS and Lola GUYTON married Wednesday afternoon on the public square in Cleburne, Texas.

Frank REYNOLDS and Jane MERCER married Wednesday in Tarpon, Texas. After the wedding, they left for a trip to Corpus Christi, Texas.

Marriage licenses issued by Tarrant County Clerk's office: John A. KENNEDY and Mrs. Rose E. NEWBY, W. H. DEKEY and Laura Luckett ALLEN; G. R. BARRY and Myrtle May RECTOR; W. A. R. DAVIS and Miss M. Wootie YATES; W. M. SHOCKLEY and Amanda MEDFORD; C. D. SHANTEAN and Eva CLAYBORN; and Joe EVANS and Mamie WEAR.

Births recorded at Tarrant County Clerk's office: a girl to Mr. and Mrs. William DOWDY, Fort Worth, on July 20; a boy to Mr. and Mrs. Luther WILLIAMS, Birdville, on July 18; a girl to Mr. and Mrs. J. H. NOBLE, Arlington, on July 5; and a boy to Mr. and Mrs. D. H. BIGGUS on July 11.

Deaths recorded at Tarrant County Clerk's office: A. R. ALEXANDER, 39, residing in Fort Worth, died of renal failure on July 16; George Ernest DUKE, 91, residing in Fort Worth, died of an intestinal obstruction on July 20.

Saturday, July 23, 1904

An old man named PERRY was found dead in his bed at Blum, Texas Wednesday. His remains were sent to Meridian, Texas.

Cleve HILBURN, 20, died yesterday in an explosion in a coal mine at Alba, Texas.

John HAMBLIN died in Gabriel, Texas. His niece, Mrs. R. W. BARTON, who lived in Temple, Texas, went to Gabriel for the funeral. HAMBLIN had lived in Gabriel since 1833.

Luther MAXWELL, the son of Mrs. R. W. MAXWELL of Waco, Texas, died Thursday there. His remains were shipped to Temple, Texas.

"Grandma" HIMIL, 85, died yesterday in Kaufman, Texas. She was the mother of W. H. HAMIL of Kaufman.

The remains of S. B. LONG arrived in Cleburne, Texas from Houston yesterday. Survivors included A. Z. LONG and S. D. LONG.

Lula CRISP, 16, died Thursday in Clarendon, Texas. She was daughter of Mr. and Mrs. J. E. CRISP.

J. F. MCMANUS and Cora ANDERSON married Thursday in Belton, Texas. Judge G. M. FELTS officiated.

J. N. BARFIELD and Nora MCCLAIN married Thursday in Belton, Texas.

G. R. BOHANNON and Effie ROBBINS married Thursday in Belton, Texas. Rev. C. W. DANIELS officiated.

E. S. SAMFERS and Helen TEAGARDEN married yesterday in Mineola, Texas.

Jap NAY and Nola YATES were married in Terrell, Texas Wednesday. The groom is from Pentel, Texas. The bride is from Poetry, Texas.

Marriage licenses issued by Tarrant County Clerk's office: S. O. JOHNSON and Miss C. B. L. COKE.

Births recorded at Tarrant County Clerk's office: a girl to Mr. and Mrs. G. W. HAZLETT, Handley, on July 17; a girl to Mr. and Mrs. R. J. REDFORD, Fort Worth, on July 19; a boy to Mr. and Mrs. Fred WILKINSON, Fort Worth, on July 13; a boy to Mr. and Mrs. W. H. MAUPIN, Fort Worth, on July 14; a girl to Mr. and Mrs. Doc ESTES, Fort Worth, on July 11; a boy to Mr. and Mrs. M. P. RUSSELL, Handley, on June 20; a girl to Mr. and Mrs. J. N. DRAGO, Handley, on June 21; a boy to Mr. and Mrs. M. HART, Handley, on June 23; a boy to Mr. and Mrs. Jack CARROLL, Handley on June 25; a girl to Mr. and Mrs. J. T. MCNELLIS, Handley, July 14; a boy to Mr. and Mrs. J. L. SINN, Handley, on July 4; and a boy to Mr. and Mrs. Wil WILLIAMS, Handley, on July 3.

Deaths recorded at Tarrant County Clerk's office: John GROUGH, 62, residing in Fort Worth, died of congestion of the bowels on July 19; Mrs. Mollie STAATS, 30, residing in Arlington Heights, died of tuberculosis with no date listed.

Sunday, July 24, 1904

J. R. KNAUP, 21, died of typhoid at the residence of his brother in Fort Worth yesterday. His remains were sent to Waco, Texas.

Frank MILLER shot and killed himself in San Antonio yesterday. He wounded Elizabeth SCOTT and Jack JONES before killing himself.

John WHITE was killed with a shotgun in his home yesterday in Liberty, Texas.

Marriage licenses issued by Tarrant County Clerk's office: O. P. HEADLAND and Esther BRATT, Harry E. JOHNS and Christina MEYERS, and J. F. KERLEE and Alice GILLEAN.

Births recorded at Tarrant County Clerk's office: a girl to Mr. and Mrs. J. S. BOND, Fort Worth, on July 23; a boy to Mr. and Mrs. J. M. BILLINGTON, Fort Worth on July 21 and a boy to Mr. and Mrs. W. L. SWEARINGEN, Fort Worth, on July 21.

Harrison WILLIAMS, 70, died yesterday of consumption in Alsdorf, Texas.

Mrs. Millie HUGHES died yesterday in Crisp, Texas. Her death was caused by consumption of the bowels.

Mrs. Florence Ann KELLY died Friday night in Gainesville, Texas. Her remains will be buried in Collinsville, Texas.

A. J. POSTON died of typhoid Friday night at his home in Silvia Bend, Cocke County, Texas.

Ben MITCHELL and Callie SANDERS were married in Ennis, Texas by Father J. E. MALONE yesterday.

Edith Lyle ADAMS and Henry P. SWAIN married Tuesday at the home of Mr. and Mrs. J. W. ADAMS, her parents, in Fort Worth.

Virginia BALL and Nedom B. TISDAL married Tuesday in Fort Worth's First Methodist Church.

John MENDEZ was shot and killed yesterday in Brownwood, Texas. Rupert BRUMFIELD surrendered to authorities.

Wallace ERICKSON drowned yesterday near Watonga, Oklahoma Territory.

Monday, July 25, 1904

Burt KIRKPATRICK, 26, was killed by T. F. HENDRICKS in Dallas yesterday. HENDRICKS surrendered to police. He said he killed KIRKPATRICK to avenge a wrong done to his sister by KIRKPATRICK.

Mrs. Lydia GRISCOM, 38, died yesterday of consumption in Ardmore, Indian Territory.

The funeral of Mary FAULKNER took place in Austin yesterday. She died in Houston and was the sister of Capt. Andy FAULKNER.

Rosie May CLARK, 2 months, died yesterday in Fort Worth. She was the daughter of Mr. and Mrs. O. D. CLARK. Burial was in Oakwood Cemetery.

C. C. NIFONG arrived in Fort Worth to attend the funeral of his brother F. C. NIFONG, who died Sunday in Oklahoma City, Oklahoma Territory.

The remains of J. R. KNAUP were shipped to Waco, Texas for burial.

Charles E. QUINN, of Toledo, Ohio, committed suicide in El Paso yesterday.

Jack SOZIER died in San Antonio yesterday.

Ross SILVER died last night in Mangum, Oklahoma Territory. He was injured in an explosion earlier in the day.

Tuesday, July 26, 1904

Joyce MALONE was killed Sunday ten miles south of Sequin, Texas. Chester MALONE was jailed. Chester was a half-brother of the deceased.

Richard WEITSTRUCK, about 20, was killed yesterday when he was hit with a brick near Bellville, Texas. Sam CUMMINGS, about 20, was arrested and charged with throwing the brick.

Mrs. H. L. EKLINS died yesterday in Beaumont, Texas. Her remains were sent to Temple for burial. She was survived by two daughters and one son. She was an early settler of Temple.

The infant son of Mr. and Mrs. Charles DOUGLAS died Sunday of dysentery five miles west of Mineral Wells, Texas.

The remains of Rubye WHEELIE, who died in Baltimore, Maryland, arrived yesterday in Marshall, Texas. The funeral was from the home of her parents, Mr. and Mrs. Z. T. HILL. Interment was in Greenwood Cemetery in Marshall.

The small son of Mr. and Mrs. John BAILEY died yesterday in Belton, Texas. Burial was in South Belton Cemetery.

Floy CURREY, the daughter of C. D. CURREY, died yesterday in Omaha, Texas. Burial was in Spring Hill Cemetery.

Allen MCCLINTOCK was killed yesterday near Minton, Texas. James MOBLEY surrendered to authorities in Paris, Texas. The duel between the two men resulted from a dispute over a house.

Robin SULLIVAN, Sr. was killed Sunday near New Caney, Texas.

The four year old son of George DAUGHTERY was killed yesterday near Hugo, Indian Territory.

Rosa BOYER was struck by lightning and killed yesterday near Jefferson, Oklahoma Territory.

Marriage licenses issued by Tarrant County Clerk's office: A. L. APPLEWHITE and Bettie FINLEY, Thomas JORDAN and Hattie KNOWLES; L. J. MANTAUX and Bessie BRACKNEY, W. R. WILSON and Maggie WILLIAMS, and S. E. KELLER and Effie May GARNER.

Births recorded at Tarrant County Clerk's office: a boy to Mr. and Mrs. M. N. HENDERSON, Arlington, on July 15; a girl to Mr. and Mrs. L. DOORKY, Fort Worth, on July 15; a boy to Mr. and Mrs. R. C. SHARP, Mansfield, on July 10; a boy to Mr. and Mrs. John J. WILLIAMS, Mansfield, on July 11; a boy to Mr. and Mrs. J. A. NIXON, Mansfield, on July 17; a girl to Mr. and Mrs. Edward KEMPER, Fort Worth, on July 24; a girl to Mr. and Mrs. G. W. FORD, Mansfield, on July 11; a boy to Mr. and Mrs. T. W. FRENCH, Kennedale, on July 18 and a boy to Mr. and Mrs. Joe CHANDLER, Fort Worth, on July 24.

Deaths recorded at Tarrant County Clerk's office: Mildred BACON, 1, residing in Fort Worth, died of inanition on July 21; John JOHNSON, 33, died of malarial congestion on July 20. No residence was listed for John JOHNSON.

Wednesday, July 27, 1904
The paper for this date did not appear on the microfilm.

Thursday, July 28, 1904
Gustave WILKENING and his son Carl, 12, died in Houston yesterday when the street car they were riding was hit by a train.

Annie Lee CRAWFORD drowned in the Brazos River Tuesday night near Marlin, Texas. She was the daughter of Mr. and Mrs. M. C. CRAWFORD.

T. W. FOX, 65, of Ole, Texas, died Tuesday of heart failure. Burial was in the Fox Cemetery near his home.

John KENNEDY, Jr. and Stella ARNOLD married Tuesday in Fort Worth. Thomas J. FORGY officiated.

Rev. W. F. CLEMMONS was killed Wednesday near Bartlesville, Indian Territory. A wagon ran over him.

Births recorded at Tarrant County Clerk's office: a girl to Mr. and Mrs. Henry AMMONS, Fort Worth, on July 24; a girl to Mr. and Mrs. Robert COUNTS, Fort Worth, on July 25; a girl to Mr. and Mrs. W.R. WILLIS, Fort Worth, on July 22; a girl to Mr. and Mrs. Dave RANLEY, White Settlement, on July 23; a girl to Mr. and Mrs. John L. JOHNSON, Fort Worth, on July 24; and twin boys to Mr. and Mrs. John Lawrence TEVIS, Fort Worth, on July 26.

Clyde Beaufort HAIRE, 12, died yesterday at the home of his parents in Fort Worth.

Friday, July 29, 1904
Nannie JOHNSON, 18, was found guilty of second degree murder yesterday in McKinney, Texas. She killed Della WRIGHT last Christmas at Farmersville, Texas. JOHNSON was sentenced to seven years in the penitentiary.

Lizzie Cleo MCDOWELL, 6 months, died Wednesday in Fort Worth. She was daughter of D. S. MCDOWELL. Her remains were sent to Grapevine, Texas.

The funeral of Mrs. J. H. B. HOUSE, who died last week in North Carolina, took place Tuesday in Houston.

Nona BYRNE, of Houston, died in Weatherford, Texas from typhoid fever Sunday. She was a student and died at the home of Mr. and Mrs. J. H. HARRIS. She was the daughter of P. C. BYRNE.

Mrs. M. L. ELKINS died Monday in Beaumont, Texas. The funeral took place at the Episcopal Church in Temple, Texas. Her burial was in Waco, Texas.

The infant child of Mr. and Mrs. C. L. PHILLIPS died Monday in Texarkana.

The infant child of Mr. and Mrs. Ben SORABY died Sunday in Texarkana.

Lee BILLINGSLEY and Hope SESSIONS married in Rice, Texas Wednesday. The groom lives in Dallas.

J. E. RAYNOR and Flora ROCKWELL married Wednesday in Albany, Texas. She was the daughter of Mrs. Mary ROCKWELL.

Editor Leopold MORRIS of the *Victoria Advocate* and Rosa MURPHY married Wednesday in Catholic Church at Corpus Christi, Texas.

Edward SINGLETON and Mabel KILLINGSWORTH married Wednesday in Allen, Texas.

J. T. HIGGINS and Rosa Lee WALLACE married Wednesday in the Blue Ridge Community near McKinney, Texas.

Marriage licenses issued by Tarrant County Clerk's office: William R. HOWARD and Birdie SPAULDING, and Jeff HAINES and Mrs. Mattie TURNER.

Births recorded at Tarrant County Clerk's office: a girl to Mr. and Mrs. M. F. QUAYLE, Grapevine, on July 17; a girl to Mr. and Mrs. M. E. JORDAN, Grapevine, on July 6; a girl to Mr. and Mrs. J. Ike MCPHERSON, Grapevine, on June 22; a boy to Mr. and Mrs. William H. ROUSSEAU, Fort Worth, on July 26; a girl to Mr. and Mrs. Frank SHEPARD, Grapevine, on July 19; and a boy to Mr. and Mrs. John W. KOONCE, Grapevine, on June 23.

Deaths recorded at Tarrant County Clerk's office: Witten CAVENDER, 2, residing in Grapevine, died of blood poisoning with no date listed; Pearl Tucker LOYD, 1, residing in Grapevine, died of indigestion with no date listed; Thomas HAMBY, 73, residing in Grapevine, died of heart disease with no date listed.

Saturday, July 30, 1904 through Sunday, July 31, 1904

The papers for these dates did not appear on the microfilm.

August, 1904

Monday, August 1, 1904

Rogue GARCIA committed suicide Saturday in Brownsville, Texas. He was an officer in the Mexican Army.

J. H. CONKLIN was killed yesterday at Fort Hancock, Texas. He was run over by a hand car. He was a bridge carpenter.

Alex SUFERSTEIN and Etta PERGMAN married yesterday in Fort Worth. Dr. A. GORDON officiated. The bride was a niece of Max HORSCHOW.

Minnie PITTMAN died Saturday at Ennis, Texas. Rev. S. H. SLAUGHTER conducted the funeral yesterday at Alma, Texas.

Mrs. Dick MURRAY (nee Bettie GARRETT) died of consumption Saturday in Milford, Texas. She was buried in Hillsboro, Texas.

The funeral for Charles PUCKETT was held yesterday in Shreveport, Louisiana.

M. D. BROWN, 76, died Saturday in Ardmore, Indian Territory. His remains were sent to Cumby, Texas. He was the father of Dr. W. J. BROWN.

Mrs. Edna MCCOGHERN died Saturday in Cleburne, Texas.

Samuel ATKINSON and Mary H. WEBER married Saturday in Roswell, New Mexico Territory.

Harlow TAYLOR and Mrs. Ella HOWARD married Friday in Temple, Texas. Rev. C. R. WRIGHT officiated.

C. C. AYERS posted $5000 bond and was released from custody in Bernalillo County, New Mexico Territory. AYERS was arrested and charged with killing Henry HARRISON.

The funeral of Sam CLAYPOOL was conducted yesterday in Fort Worth. Dr. Luther LITTLE officiated. The remains were shipped to Marble Falls, Texas.

Tuesday, August 2, 1904

A. P. SMITH was shot and killed by Coke County Sheriff GREEN and Deputy DAVIS Sunday near San Angelo, Texas. SMITH was resisting arrest for refusing to do road work in Coke County. There was a dispute about his residence.

Will JOHNSON was shot and killed yesterday near Frost, Texas. William HARRIS was arrested by Deputy Sheriff E. C. SCOTT.

A memorial for Captain T. W. WINSTON was held in Marshall, Texas Sunday. He was president of the Scottsville Holiness Camp Meeting Association for 17 years.

Assistant postmaster Lyman KNIGHTON and Jessie MCPHERSON married yesterday in Guthrie, Oklahoma Territory.

G. Walter REED and Mattie HALL married in McGregor, Texas. Rev. J. Will KENT officiated.

W. B. LEWIS and Olan MCLAUGHLIN Sunday married in Abilene, Texas. . MCLAUGHLIN lives in Stith, Texas.

Bessie LOCKETT and Hiram MITCHELL married Monday in Pittsburg, Texas. She was the daughter of Mr. and Mrs. M. G. LOCKETT.

E. SANSING died yesterday in Goldthwaite, Texas.

W. M. DICK died of heart trouble Sunday in Milsap, Texas. He was buried yesterday in Newberry, Texas.

G. E. SCOTT, 87, died Sunday in Mineral Wells, Texas. He was buried yesterday in the city cemetery. He was the father of George SCOTT.

W. H. BYRNE died Sunday in San Angelo, Texas. He fell from a transfer wagon while riding to the train to go his home in McKinney, Texas.

Marriage licenses issued by Tarrant County Clerk's office: E. W. KEITH and Lula ISAAC.

Births recorded at Tarrant County Clerk's office: a boy to Mr. and Mrs. Louis H. WHITLEY, Fort Worth on July 29; a boy to Mr. and Mrs. J. D. HAMER, Fort Worth, on July 24; a girl to Mr. and Mrs. R. A. RITCHIE, Rosen Heights, on July 27; a boy to Mr. and Mrs. W. E. CHAPMAN, Glenwood, on July 24; a girl to Mr. and Mrs. C. H. KEITH, Fort Worth, on July 25; a girl to Mr. and Mrs. John HARPER, Fort Worth, on July 25; a girl to Mr. and Mrs. W. H. HILL, Glenwood, on July 29; and a boy to Mr. and Mrs. R. L. MOTLE, Fort Worth, on July 29.

Deaths recorded at Tarrant County Clerk's office: Charles WEAVER, 66, residing in Fort Worth, died of chronic asthma on July 25; Denton WHITAKER, 16, residing in Euless, died of congestion on July 20; Clyde HAVRE, 12, residing in Fort Worth, died of typhoid on July 23; Rosie May CLARK, 18 days, residing in Fort Worth, died of inflammation of the stomach on July 24.

Wednesday, August 3, 1904

The remains of W. H. BYRNE, 58, were buried in Pecan Grove Cemetery.

Mrs. L. S. TURNER died recently in Cloudcroft, New Mexico Territory. She was the mother of Mrs. R. S. TIPTON and a former resident of Mineral Wells, Texas.

Mrs. Voorhies P. BROWN died yesterday in San Antonio, Texas. She suffered a stroke.

Robert H. TURNER died in Dallas Monday. He was buried in Waxahachie, Texas. He was an old resident of Waxahachie and was married to the daughter of Major F. W. ROGERS, who founded Waxahachie.

Mrs. Alice JOHNSON died Monday in Marshall, Texas. She was buried in Marshall. Survivors include her husband and five children.

Editor L. H. MILLER of the *Alvord Budget* and Lucy FREE married on July 18 in Chico, Texas.

Charley WAKELAND and Lula TRULL married Saturday in Waxahachie, Texas.

Homer ADAMS and Alma POWELL married Sunday in Temple, Texas. Rev. P. E. BURROUGHS officiated. ADAMS is from Cleburne, Texas

Thomas DURRETT was killed in Dallas County by a Missouri, Kansas and Texas Railroad switch engine about 5 a.m. today. The body will be sent to Lisbon, Texas. Foul play is suspected.

Harry BALL, 35, was struck by lightning and killed yesterday near Jacksboro, Texas.

Marriage licenses issued by Tarrant County Clerk's office: Odie GOBLE and Rosa LANCE, H.W. BUSBY and May WISE, and John WALLER and Florence WARD.

Births recorded at Tarrant County Clerk's office: a boy to Mr. and Mrs. M. GRABER, Fort Worth, on July 28; and a girl to Mr. and Mrs. H. M. STINSON, Fort Worth, on July 31.

Deaths recorded at Tarrant County Clerk's office: Mary A. CREED, 76, residing in Fort Worth, died from anemia on August 1.

Thursday, August 4, 1904

The paper for this date did not appear on the microfilm.

Friday, August 5, 1904

Joe ROSSI was killed yesterday in Marshall, Texas. He was shot while he slept. His wife and another man were arrested.

Mrs. Joseph JENKINS died yesterday at her home near Gallatin, Texas. She apparently died of severe fright when a calf chased her while she walked home with her baby.

Dr. MCWHITHERS died from a broken neck after he fell from a railroad trestle yesterday near Athens, Texas. No given name was reported.

John CARPENTER died of a gunshot wound to the head in Dallas yesterday. The funeral will be tomorrow with burial in Greenwood Cemetery. Masons and Knights of Pythias will be in charge of the funeral.

Clarence IRWIN killed Mrs. John JAMES, 46, his mother-in-law, and then himself yesterday in Ponca City, Indian Territory.

The body of Fred WESTHAUSEN, 63, was found in San Antonio yesterday. He had been dead from several days. Because of the advanced state of decomposition of the remains, they were buried where they were found.

Mrs. Ruby HENRY and Elmer VAN NATTAN married Wednesday in Alamagordo, New Mexico Territory.

Douie Lenora HUNTER and Way Manvers PARK married yesterday in Alamagordo, New Mexico Territory.

Helen STEWART and Frederico VALASCO married in Alamagordo, New Mexico Territory. Rev. E. QUINONE officiated.

Edna Bell WISE, 19 months, died this morning in Fort Worth. She was the daughter of Mr. and Mrs. W. P. WISE.

Charles STEWART was killed yesterday near Medford, Oklahoma Territory. He was hit by a Rock Island train.

Marriage licenses issued by Tarrant County Clerk's office: R. C. KELLAN and Mrs. Lula SHELTON, J. O. HASSELL and Minnie DAVIS, and Louis HOYT and Lucinda HUBBARD.

Births recorded at Tarrant County Clerk's office: a boy to Mr. and Mrs. J. C. PHILLIPS, Riverside, on July 14; and a boy to Mr. and Mrs. Vester SUTHERLAND, Avondale, on July 31.

Saturday, August 6, 1904

Rev. J. S. BLEDSOE, 94, died Wednesday in Waxahachie, Texas. He was a Baptist minister for 60 years and the father of Mrs. A. H. BUNKLEY.

Mrs. Mary Ann TOWNSON, 58, the wife of L. Jasper TOWNSON, died in Lampasas, Texas yesterday. Born in Teppa (Tippah) County, Mississippi on April 9, 1846, she was the mother of 11 children. Eight of her children survived her death as well as two brothers and three sisters survived her. She was buried in the family burying ground near Adamsville, Texas.

Captain J. H. DEGAN was found dead Thursday in Denton, Texas. His funeral was yesterday.

Mrs. N. G. RICE died Tuesday in North Marshall, Texas. Her funeral was Wednesday. Burial was in Greenwood Cemetery.

Mrs. M. J. PRESLEY, sister of W. R. and J. P. RUSSELL, died Tuesday in Terrell, Texas. She was also survived by Maggie PRESLEY of Dallas and Annie RASERA of San Francisco, California.

J. J. JAYROE died Wednesday in Paris, Texas. He was a Confederate veteran. His funeral was Thursday.

Mrs. W. C. HOWARD, 59, died Thursday in Garner, Texas. Her remains went to Lampasas, Texas. Another report stated her remains were sent to Alabama.

Richard STRAYHORN died yesterday in San Antonio.

Mrs. M. BAKER was buried Thursday in Atlanta, Texas.

In a double ceremony Wednesday Luther MAUNEY married Della SHOWVER while James WEBB married Lela GATLIN. Rev. J. M. HART did the double duty in Weatherford, Texas.

W. L. EDMUNDSON and Edna MEWSHAW married yesterday, possibly in Garland, Texas. She was a teacher in the Roscoe schools last term.

A. C. RALPH and Mattye GRAY married Wednesday in Greenville, Texas. Rev J. L. PIERCE officiated.

Foy BARCLAY and Marguerite MCGREGOR married Wednesday in Temple, Texas.

George C. SUTHERLAND, the son of Tom SUTHERLAND, was killed in a horse race near Uvalde, Texas recently. He struck a tree limb when his horse ran away.

Charles B. MCCHESNEY, 13, was killed in Houston yesterday. He was the son of Mr. and Mrs. Pierce BUTLER. Death resulted from being kicked by a horse.

Sunday, August 7, 1904

M. A. BROWN died Friday in Mineral Wells, Texas. He had been a resident of Mineral Wells since 1886.

Mrs. Olin LUMPKIN, 60, died Wednesday in Tupelo, Mississippi. She was the mother of W. H. LUMPKIN of Ennis, Texas.

John BROWN died from blood poisoning yesterday near Weatherford, Texas. He was a farmer living in the Carter community.

L. E. EDWARDS, 70, died from Bright's disease Friday at his home in Greenville, Texas.

Marriage licenses issued by Tarrant County Clerk's office: C. W. MCGOWAN and Lelia DAVIS; Claude HARMON and Callie TRIBBLE, Marian WILLSHIRE and Estella THOMPSON, A. E. CANNON and Mrs. Dona SOUDER, E. D. WILSON and Celia BROWN, Willie YOUNG and Sallie E. DAVENPORT, Monroe PHILLIPS and Bessie WASHINGTON, and Ben WYATT and Louvada CHATMAN.

Births recorded at Tarrant County Clerk's office: a child to Mr. and Mrs. HIGHTOWER, Riverside, on August 3; a girl to Mr. and Mrs. W. K. FELLS, North Fort Worth, on August 4; a boy to Mr. and Mrs. Fred CRESBY, Fort Worth, on August ____; a boy to Mr. and Mrs. George MACK, Fort Worth, on July 30; a girl to Mr. and Mrs. D. DALE, Fort Worth, on August 4; a girl to Mr. and Mrs. E. L. REDFORD, Fort Worth, on August 4; and a boy to Mr. and Mrs. Ernest JOHNSON, Fort Worth, on August 3.

Deaths recorded at Tarrant County Clerk's office: Mrs. Homer CASTOR, 33, residing in Azle, died on July 26 with no cause reported; Russ RAWLINSON, 6, residing in Azle, died of typhoid on July 27; A. MOORE, 18, residing in Fort Worth, died of peritonitis on July 30; John BLACK, 45, residing in Fort Worth, died of tuberculosis on July 31; and Annie Belle WISE, 1, residing in Fort Worth, died of whooping cough on August 5.

Monday, August 8, 1904

Mrs. Mary E. DICKEY, wife of Nat DICKEY, died Saturday. She was survived by her husband and several children.

T. M. TANNER, about 30, drowned yesterday near Ennis, Texas. The boat in which he was riding capsized on the city lake. He was a railroad machinist.

The two month old son of Mr. and Mrs. Lum FURR was scalded to death Saturday near McKinney, Texas. No name was reported.

W. B. HILL, aka M. L. KIMBALL, died in Fort Worth yesterday. His wife, Irene HILL, survived him. He was a painter. She lived in Kemp, Indian Territory.

Tuesday, August 9, 1904

A man named GRAY and his 18 year old son were shot and killed from ambush yesterday near Tyler, Texas.

Mrs. A. F. DURPERTHUS committed suicide by drowning herself in a cistern at the Halsell Ranch in Jack County, Texas.

Mrs. HOETLING died yesterday of a gunshot would she received from a section foreman at Aransas Pass, Texas.

Clarence PACE, 17, drowned while boating near Darden yesterday. (The compiler was not able to locate this town).

Preston DAVENPORT, 24, drowned yesterday near Shawnee, Indian Territory. He was swimming with friends in a cattle pond.

John TYLER, 20, was killed in New Braunfels, Texas when he fell beneath a train. He lived in Temple, Texas.

Wallace FRANK, 20, was convicted Friday of the murder of Will GALLOWAY last spring near Blevins, Texas. Frank received a sentence of 25 years in the penitentiary.

Miss Maxmillan LUNA, daughter of Major and Mrs. A. S. B. LUNA, married Howard ANDERSON in San Diego, California recently. No date was reported.

Charles CRAVEN of Anson, Texas and Ada GAMBLE were married in Merkel, Texas yesterday.

Samuel MORRIS and Daisy CAMPBELL married at the home of Mr. and Mrs. W. T. CAMPBELL, the bride's parents, in Slidell, Texas yesterday. Rev. John BALTHROP officiated.

Thomas A. HARVEY and Mary STEEN married yesterday in Slidell, Texas. Rev. W. F. BURTON officiated. HARVEY lives in Valley View, Texas.

Reagan B. STILL and Mattie EUBANK married yesterday in Mabank, Texas. Rev. F. F. BLEDSOE officiated.

Algie FRANKLIN and Maggie LITTLEFIELD, who live in the Pringle community four miles north of Chico, Texas, married Sunday. Rev. Melvin PLEASANT officiated.

Rev. W. B. STONE and Mrs. Samuel BOWDEN married last Saturday at the residence of the bride near Crofton, Texas.

State Senator J. R. WILSON died of typhoid fever Sunday in New Boston, Texas.

Frank CHILES died of typhoid fever Sunday in Roswell, New Mexico Territory. He was a railroad conductor and was survived by his wife.

Rev L. S. NELSON died Saturday at the home of Mrs. C. N. HAMPTON, his daughter, in Forreston, Texas. He was buried in Waxahachie, Texas.

Theodore BERRING, 81, died in New Braunfels, Texas. He was a pioneer settler of New Braunfels. Survivors included a wife and a daughter.

Mrs. Sarah YORK, 91, died Sunday near Terrell, Texas. Her remains were buried yesterday at College Mound, Texas.

The 18 month old son of Russell SMITH, who lived a few miles south of Kaufman, Texas, died Saturday.

Mrs. Lenny E. LOONEY applied in Tarrant County Court for guardianship of her husband's estate on behalf of minors John S. and Henry C. LOONEY.

Marriage licenses issued by Tarrant County Clerk's office: R. O. PERRY and Augusta MONIGIN, J. D. USELTON and Mary MORROW, and J. W. ALEXANDER and Lalla HILL.

Births recorded at Tarrant County Clerk's office: a boy to Mr. and Mrs. W. E. BASS, Arlington, on July 25; a girl to Mr. and Mrs. L. L. KENNEDY, Arlington, on July 24; a girl to Mr. and Mrs. W. F. MCDONALD, Arlington, on July 31; and a girl to Mr. and Mrs. S. S. RAINS, Kennedale, on August 6.

Deaths recorded at Tarrant County Clerk's office: R. A. WILLIAMS, 32, residing in Fort Worth, died of a gunshot wound on July 2; Sam CLAYPOOL, 28, residing in Fort Worth, died from an accident on July 30; and M. B. COULTER, 73, residing in Arlington, died on July 27 with no cause stated.

Wednesday, August 10, 1904

S. G. JOHNSON, 33, died in Fort Worth yesterday. Internment was in Oakwood Cemetery under the auspices of the bricklayer's union.

Holly B. BELL, 24, shot himself through the heart yesterday in Beaumont, Texas.

The child of Mr. and Mrs. William SEABURN was killed Monday near Springtown, Texas. The child was thrown from a wagon when the mules ran away. The article didn't mention name, age or gender of the child.

Marriage licenses issued by Tarrant County Clerk's office: Sam DAVIS and Annie LOWE, W. O. HARRIS and Helen MASSIE, and James WOODS and Jessie ROSS.

Deaths recorded at Tarrant County Clerk's office: Rev. A. D. BOURLAND, 65, residing in Keller, died of paralysis caused by dropsy on August 1.

Thursday, August 11, 1904

Charles LANGSDON, 16, died yesterday near Andarko, Oklahoma Territory. He was thrown from his horse while driving cattle and died of a skull fracture a few hours later.

John TANICEK and Albina MAYER married Tuesday in Temple, Texas.

J. Arthur TAYLOR and Gervis FALTON married yesterday in Sherman, Texas.

T. C. MCGAUGH and May GARRISON married in Corsicana, Texas yesterday. Judge H. Clay NASH officiated.

Paul MOMAND, formerly of Dallas and Waxahachie, Texas, married Clevia BALLARD on July 25 in Montgomery, Alabama.

W. J. YOUNG and Edith DEAVERS married August 1 in Taylor County, Texas.

E. B. HERNDON and Willie NORWOOD married Tuesday in Abilene, Texas.

Captain Frank S. BOCKER and Stella H. GILBERT married Sunday in Stephenville, Texas.

Watt WELLMAN and Mary MIDDLETON married Sunday in Terrell, Texas.

R. PATTERSON and Maude LABONTY, of Kerens, Texas, married Tuesday at the home of the bride's mother.

Dr. W. E. RATLIFF and Mrs. Lilly May WILSON married Tuesday in Marshall, Texas. Rev. J. B. K. SPAIN officiated.

Donna TURNER and Herman BOOCH married Tuesday in Marble Falls, Texas. She is the daughter of Mr. and Mrs. Don TURNER.

Lee MARTIN died recently in Apalachicola, Florida. His remains were shipped to Terrell, Texas.

Mrs. Virginia LADD, 81, died Tuesday in Oran, Texas.

"Aunt Sarah" RICHARDSON, 93, said to be the oldest black person in Navarro County, Texas, died in Corsicana yesterday.

Jess CLOUD died of heart failure Monday near Olney, Texas.

Clark MCQUEEN died Saturday in Marystown, Texas. Marystown is located near Cleburne.

S. W. CLOUD died Monday in western Young County, Texas. He was a rancher and former resident of Fort Worth.

Sam HOUSTON died recently in Shreveport, Louisiana. The remains were shipped to Longview, Texas. His funeral was held Tuesday at Pine Tree, Texas.

Mrs. J. L. LINDSAY committed suicide Monday in Whitt, Texas. She was the wife of Dr. J. L. LINDSAY.

Ederbijen CORDAJO died yesterday in Floresville, Texas. He was wounded July 17. Thomas REYES surrendered to authorities.

Marriage licenses issued by Tarrant County Clerk's office: J. A. APPLETON and Mary JOHNSON, and E. A. LAWRENCE and Florence MIDDLETON.

Births recorded at Tarrant County Clerk's office: a boy to Mr. and Mrs. C. R. BROILES, Fort Worth, on August 3; a girl to Mr. and Mrs. Will MOSS, Fort Worth, on August 7; a boy to Mr. and Mrs. Walter DAVID, Mansfield, on July 31; a girl to Mr. and Mrs. W. W. NORMAN, Fort Worth, on August 9; a girl to Mr. and Mrs. W. M. AYLOR, North Fort Worth, on August 1; a girl to Mr. and Mrs. C. L. BAKER, Mansfield, on August 7; and a girl to Mr. and Mrs. J. A. KEMP, Mansfield, on August 9.

Friday, August 12, 1904

Miss Fannie HERSCOVIT jumped from a moving train west of Dallas yesterday and died of her injuries. She was from Shreveport, Louisiana.

Thomas T. WALNE, 24, died yesterday in Dallas. He fell from a bridge Monday night. He was blind. Funeral will be tomorrow with burial in Oakwood Cemetery.

The trial of W. B. CHANDLER at Belton, Texas is scheduled to begin today. He is accused of killing his wife and William MCLAUGHLIN last spring in Temple, Texas. (See March 22, 1904).

Edward Gideon HORNE, 78, died Wednesday in Durant, Indian Territory. Survivors are wife and three daughters. He was a pioneer peach grower.

Dr. M. C. COTY, 46, died in New York City. He was a resident of Shreveport and the parish coroner.

J. W. STEPHENSON, 81, died of heart failure Wednesday in Comanche, Texas. His funeral was held yesterday.

John LEDBETTER died yesterday in Quanah, Texas.

Louise MCKAY, 11 months, died and was buried yesterday in Marshall, Texas. She was the daughter of Mr. and Mrs. H. MCKAY.

Scott KEARNEY, 26, died Wednesday in Ardmore, Indian Territory. He was the son of T. M. KEARNEY. Burial was yesterday under the auspices of the Elks.

William BENDER, the youngest son of Mr. and Mrs. W. B. BENDER, died Wednesday north of Marshall, Texas.

Mrs. Hollie JACKSON died Wednesday in Temple, Texas. Her burial was yesterday.

Price ANGEL, 9, died yesterday in Midlothian, Texas. He was the son of Mr. and Mrs. E. M. ANGEL

The baby of Mr. and Mrs. Frank DELOR died Wednesday in Ennis, Texas.

E. D. HICKS and Fannie SORRELS married yesterday in Corsicana, Texas. Judge H. Clay NASH officiated.

Will A. NEWSOM and Challie BANKS married yesterday in Midlothian, Texas. Rev. M. K. LITTLE officiated.

Lewis HUDSON and Ethel PERRY married Wednesday in Seymour, Texas. The groom lives in Oklahoma City, Oklahoma Territory. The bride is the daughter of Captain and Mrs. T. H. C. PERRY.

Frank ADAMS and Allie BRANN married Wednesday in Temple, Texas.

Alice REED and W. L. THOMAS married Wednesday in Holand, Texas. Rev C. R. WRIGHT officiated. She was daughter of Vol REED.

W. H. TAYLOR, the editor of the *Strawn Enterprise*, and Bessie WARREN married Wednesday in Strawn, Texas.

Jim BIRDSONG, about 12, drowned Wednesday near Longview, Texas.

Marriage licenses issued by Tarrant County Clerk's office: John MORRIS and Emma POWELL.

Deaths recorded at Tarrant County Clerk's office: Mrs. Ira F. OSBORNE, residing in Fort Worth, died of Bright's disease on August 10; and T. L. MAURICE, 74, residing in Fort Worth, died of heart failure on August 5.

Saturday, August 13, 1904

The paper for this date didn't appear on the microfilm.

Sunday, August 14, 1904

R. G. LEE returned to Denton, Texas from a lengthy trip to Europe to study the anatomy of the different races.

C. J. ERWIN, 48, died last night at St. Joseph's Infirmary in Fort Worth. He left a wife and family.

W. B. HOLLAN, 71, was found dead Friday in Mineral Wells, Texas. His remains were shipped to Waco, Texas. He was the father of two sons and employed at the post office in Waco.

Roy MAJOR, 12, died in Ryan, Indian Territory. He was buried there Friday. He was the son of Mr. and Mrs. L. D. MAJOR.

Nona ALBEROS and Charles SITTLER, both of Kansas City, Missouri, married Friday in Guthrie, Oklahoma Territory. Rev. J. T. OGLE officiated.

L. H. KUCKER and Mrs. C. HAMIL married last Friday in Guthrie, Oklahoma Territory. KUCKER is a local merchant and HAMIL lives in West Guthrie.

Near Lather, W. H. KENNEDY, 58, formerly of Deep Water, Missouri, fell dead of sunstroke while operating a mowing machine. No state or territory was specified or could be determined as the location for Lather.

John MCFARLAN petitioned for an absolute divorce from Nancy MCFARLAN in Beaumont, Texas.

Helen MASSIE, daughter of Mr. and Mrs. R. M. MASSIE, and William Oscar HARRIS married Tuesday in Fort Worth. Rev. J. A. WHITEHURST officiated.

Marriage licenses issued by Tarrant County Clerk's office: W. F. KAHLER and May TICE; Terrell COLLINS and Zellah MURRAY; S. CAPLIN and Gertrude SHANBLUM; G. W. RONE and Eller NEEL; J. W. COX and Rosa PIERCE; and J. J. SWENSON and Nettie CONBON.

Births recorded at Tarrant County Clerk's office: a girl to Mr. and Mrs. Samuel SPARGER, county, on August 9; a boy to Mr. and Mrs. A. A. HUNT, Fort Worth, on August 9; a girl to Mr. and Mrs. Charles WHITE, Keller, on August 12; a boy to Mr. and Mrs. W. L. KOWLSEY, Fort Worth, on August 12; a boy to Mr. and Mrs. Charles HALEY,

Fort Worth, on August 11; a girl to Mr. and Mrs. Howard FOGG, Stove Foundry, on August 11; and a boy to Mr. and Mrs. D. F. PUMMEL, Fort Worth, on August 10.

Deaths recorded at Tarrant County Clerk's office: Emma SAYLES, 59, residing in Fort Worth, died of acute gastroenteritis on August 9.

Monday, August 15, 1904

J. W. KEMP, 26, charged with the killing of W. J. PERKINS, 31, surrendered to Deputy Sheriff CRAIG Saturday at Boyd, Oklahoma Territory. The crime took place near Boyd. Both men were recent homesteaders in Beaver County.

Medric BESSE, 18, a musician, drowned yesterday near Lake Arthur, Louisiana. He was survived by his parents, four brothers and two sisters.

Preston TANKERSLEY, accused of killing his wife, was arrested Saturday near Georgetown, Texas.

Rev. T. W. CONNOR, former minister of the Cumberland Presbyterian church in Weatherford, Texas, died Wednesday in Greenville, Tennessee.

Mrs. Ada BACKALOUPE died Saturday in Ennis, Texas. She was the wife of Lon BACKALOUPE. Her remains were shipped to Navasota, Texas.

John BOYLEN, about 42, died of heart failure yesterday in Mineral Wells, Texas. He was married. He worked as a conductor on the International and Great Northern Railroad. His remains were shipped to Taylor, Texas.

Mrs. Rosalie SANTANGELO, 33, died Saturday near Spindletop, Texas. She was a recent immigrant from Italy.

Mrs. Mollie JONES, the wife of Paul JONES, died Saturday in Marshall, Texas. She was a Methodist.

The infant child of Mr. and Mrs. C. B. JUNGAN died Friday night at their home in Greenville, Texas.

Captain John A. LILLEY, 79, died Sunday in Wortham, Texas. He was a veteran of the Mexican War.

The marriage of S. CAPLAN and Gertie SHANBLUM was solemnized in Fort Worth Sunday.

Tuesday, August 16, 1904

The paper for this date didn't appear on the microfilm.

Wednesday, August 17, 1904

Harry RUSSELL and Mamie MILLER, daughter of H. L. MILLER, married Monday in Fruitland, Texas. Rev. Junius B. FRENCH officiated.

Judge W. I. MARTIN and Willie J. MCCREARY married in Fort Worth yesterday. County judge R. F. MILLER officiated.

Madeline Adelaide TOLKSDORF and Mr. CRIMMINGS (no first name given) married yesterday in Fort Worth.

William EARNEST, a restaurateur in San Antonio, died there yesterday.

W. A. BRYANT died last Sunday. His remains were shipped to MacGregor, Texas.

Owen TUMELTY, a farmer, died of cancer at his home in Decatur, Texas. He was buried in the city cemetery there yesterday.

Lewis PATE and Pearl SPENCER married Tuesday in Decatur, Texas.

George SHORT and Maude MINCEY married last Sunday near Gainesville, Texas.

R. L. LONG and Emma I. MCCASKILL married today in Marshall, Texas. Rev. J. B. K. SPAIN officiated.

Jefferson Davis BRYAN died in San Antonio today.

James BOYLE, 89, died today near Stroud, Oklahoma Territory.

Mary BENNETT, 8 months, died yesterday in Fort Worth. She was the daughter of Annie BENNETT. Her remains were shipped to Sherman, Texas.

Marriage licenses issued by Tarrant County Clerk's office: W. F. MARTIN and Willie I. MCCREARY; and O. H. BRYANT and Florence L. KIRKER.

Births recorded at Tarrant County Clerk's office: a boy to Mr. and Mrs. J. A. EAKIN, Kennedale, on August 12 and a boy to Mr. and Mrs. F. E. BELEW, Azle, on August 12.

A body believed to be that of John PARKER was found near the Trinity River in Fort Worth yesterday. PARKER had been missing for six weeks. Frank E. MANLEY was arrested and charged with PARKER's murder. The body was found by Lib PARKER.

The report of the death of George E. JOHNSON near Crowley was wrong. Johnson was shot by Bruce GRIFING but did not die. GRIFFING surrendered to Johnson County authorities and is free on bail.

Thursday, August 18, 1904

The paper for this date did not appear on the microfilm.

Friday, August 19, 1904

Frank KIRBY committed suicide yesterday in Roswell, New Mexico Territory. He was a well-known and wealthy sheep man.

Mrs. Leonora GALLINGTON was re-arrested in Dallas for the murder of George GALLINGTON. She was returned to Marshall, Texas.

Mrs. J. N. WITHERS, of Amarillo, Texas, the mother of Dr. I. A. WITHERS of Fort Worth, died Wednesday. Her remains have been shipped to Fort Worth for today's funeral.

Florence COLE, the 15 months old daughter of Mr. and Mrs. J. A. COLE, died Wednesday. Her remains were shipped to Garrett, Texas.

E. B. LANE died of appendicitis at his ranch near Millett Station in Bexar County, Texas. He was a lawyer and a Confederate veteran.

Mrs. Sallie BENSHOW, 77, died Tuesday night in Decatur, Texas. She left four sons and four daughters. Her funeral was Wednesday with burial in city cemetery.

Z. H. KING died Wednesday in Ennis, Texas.

Mrs. W. M. CROW, 31, the daughter of Judge W. D. IRVINE, died Wednesday in Terrell, Texas. Her burial was Thursday.

Mrs. E. M. SPARKS died Tuesday near Springtown, Texas. Burial was in Springtown Cemetery.

Mrs. Julia MAYNARD died Wednesday in Corsicana, Texas.

Felix PARKER, 76, died of typhoid fever Wednesday in Crisp, Texas.

Tom PRUETT and Clara NELSON married Wednesday in Comanche, Texas.

E. BULLOCK and Lorraine TURNER married yesterday in Marshall, Texas. The bride was the daughter of Major and Mrs. James TURNER. The groom is from Little Rock, Arkansas. Rev. R. W. THOMPSON and Rev. J. B. K. SPAIN officiated.

Annie NEWTON and I. GASSENHEIMER married yesterday in Belton, Texas. Dr. W. A. NELSON officiated.

Roy GILLILAND and Bertie GOSE married Tuesday in Fort Worth. The bride is the daughter of John GOSE.

W. J. BERRY and Lola MCLENDON married Tuesday in Greenville, Texas. Justice Tom M. MCDANIEL officiated.

Thomas R. LEWIS and Mattie Ella THREADGILL married yesterday in Sherman, Texas.

Jim MABRY and Leola HOWARD married Wednesday in Mineral Wells, Texas.

Marriage licenses issued by Tarrant County Clerk's office: M. T. WRIGHT and Lucy URESTE, R. C. MATHERSON and Mrs. Pearl HARWELL, J. KLOPNER and Miss E. LONGTUTH, James DAWSEY and Lena RAFFORD.

Births recorded at Tarrant County Clerk's office: a girl to Mr. and Mrs. G. W. SWEARINGTON, Fort Worth, on August 9; a boy to Mr. and Mrs. J. W. ADAMS, Fort Worth, on August 1; and a boy to Mr. and Mrs. J. B. PARKER, Euless, on August 15.

Saturday, August 20, 1904

Ed L. COLE, 28, died Thursday in Dallas. He was the son of Mark COLE and a former newspaperman. He was unmarried.

Henry WILSON shot and killed John BLUDSO Thursday night in Marshall, Texas.

W. W. GAVIN, 83, died yesterday in Fort Worth. The funeral will be today.

Mrs. Elizabeth EDER, 71, died yesterday near Handley, Texas. Burial was in Handley.

Ben LEWIS was killed by Manuel CHAVEZ yesterday near El Paso. LEWIS was a ranchman who accused CHAVEZ of committing depredations. A gun fight ensued and LEWIS was killed.

The coroner's inquest into the death of Bert MORGAN ruled he died of heart failure in Sunset, Texas. MORGAN was found dead in bed yesterday.

James FROST drowned in a canal yesterday at Galveston, Texas.

Marriage licenses issued by Tarrant County Clerk's office: William J. MADIGAN and Mrs. C. WINNINGHAM, Stewart MCMECHLE and Laura MORRELL, Willie HOLT and Etta SILK, S. K. REYNOLDS and Maude HUDGINS, and Charles ROBERSON and Edna GORE.

Birth recorded at Tarrant County Clerk's office: a boy to Mr. and Mrs. James MILLER, county, on August 16.

Sunday, August 21, 1904

Roger P. SANDERSON was killed by William LACEY in Dallas last night. SANDERSON was superintendent of the street department. LACEY was a police officer. The two men argued over some lumber left near a police station. LACEY is reported to have acted in self-defense after SANDERSON attacked him.

Seven people were killed in flood at Globe, Arizona Territory. Dead were M. N. MITCHELL and wife, O. D. WILSON, Charles SIMS, John EPLEY, Mrs. HURD and Miss MOODY.

Mrs. Heber PAGE received word Friday of the death of her mother, Mrs. HIGHLYMAM, in Sedalia, Missouri.

Thomas MCMAHAN, 74, committed suicide by drinking carbolic acid in Parker County, Texas.

A posse pursued John BROWN, who is wanted in connection with the death of Esau ROBERTSON at Boynton, Indian Territory Saturday.

Charles CHRISWELL, 10, drowned in a cattle pond near Tonkawa, Indian Territory.

G. C. YOUNG was found dead in the Golden Hotel in Dallas yesterday. He was a traveling salesman for Wheelock China Company.

Hugh STANFIELD was arrested and charged with the criminal assault of Ida MONK, 17, near San Antonio.

Mrs. Elizabeth WILLIAMS, 83, died Friday morning at Riverside, Texas. Burial was in Oakwood Cemetery. She was the mother of Mrs. M. J. REES.

Clyde CONNELL and Florine PATTERSON married yesterday morning in Fort Worth. Rev. Luther LITTLE officiated. The groom is the son of W. E. CONNELL and the bride is the daughter of A. K. PATTERSON.

Thomas Frederick CRIMMINS and Madeline Adelaide TOLKSDORF married Tuesday in Fort Worth. The bride is the daughter of Mr. and Mrs. H. P. TOLKSDORF.

F. C. WHITE and Annie PITTMAN married Thursday in Pittsburg, Texas. Rev. R. A. MORRIS officiated.

J. S. CROWDER, 50, died Friday in Waco, Texas. He was a businessman.

Charles YOST died Friday in Albany, Texas. His remains were returned to Troy, Ohio.

Mrs. Mary A. Kuhlman REICHART died in Houston Friday. She was born near Houston March 4, 1848 and married William REICHART on July 20, 1865. Seven children survive.

F. EDWARDS, 66, died Thursday in Greenville, Texas. He was a Union veteran. His funeral was Friday.

Dr. C. C. WALKER, 55, died Monday at his home two miles north of Pickens, Texas. He was a Mason and a member of Woodsmen of the World.

E. W. LUKENS died of heart failure yesterday in Bodson, Texas. His body was shipped to Houston.

Births recorded at Tarrant County Clerk's office: a girl to Mr. and Mrs. E. V. GORDON, Handley, on August 6; a girl to Mr. and Mrs. L. N. BAILEY, county, on July 29; a girl to Mr. and Mrs. G. F. DAY, Grapevine, on August 10, a girl to Mr. and Mrs. C. M. TUCK, county, on August 6; a girl to Mr. and Mrs. Iva SEXTON, county, on July 31; a boy to Mr. and Mrs. J. B. DYER, county, on July 28; a girl to Mr. and Mrs. P. A. FARRELL, Handley, on August 11; a boy to Mr. and Mrs. T. M. TALBOTT, no place listed, on August 11; a boy to Mr. and Mrs. B. C. DRAGO, Handley, on July 27; a girl to Mr. and Mrs. D. E. PHILLIPS, Handley, on July 29; a girl to Mr. and Mrs. Walter WATTS, Mansfield, on August 19; a boy to Mr. and Mrs. H. G. MALONE, Handley, on August 18; a girl to Mr. and Mrs. J. F. WARRINER, no place listed, on August 11; a boy to Mr. and Mrs. A. G. ROSSER, Handley, on August 5; a boy to Mr. and Mrs. W. W. HARBISON, Handley on August 17; a girl to Mr. and Mrs. Ed FINLEY, Handley, on August 7; and a girl to William and Otta SMITH, no place, on August 19.

Deaths recorded at Tarrant County Clerk's office: Elizabeth WILLIAMS, 83, residing in Riverside, died on August 19 with no cause listed.

Marriage licenses issued by Tarrant County Clerk's office: Clyde CONNELL and Florine PETERSON, N. A. GREER and Lizzie WALLER, P. S. GOODMAN and Mrs. P. F. BALLINGER, R. H. HERD and Docia ADAMS, and Albert AHLES and Hannah WEEKS.

J. R. LINDSAY died Friday in Wills Point, Texas. He was a farmer.

Monday, August 22, 1904

Dr. L. P. JONES attacked and killed his wife while she slept yesterday morning in Benjamin, Texas. The couple had separated and Mrs. JONES was seeking divorce. Dr. JONES also attacked County attorney BROOKSON, who represented Mrs. JONES. Mrs. JONES was the daughter of H. M. MCCELVEY and the sister of Dr. J. S. MCCELVEY of Temple, Texas. The body was sent to Temple for burial. Dr. and Mrs. JONES were the parents of two boys, 14 and 9, and a girl 12.

W. L. ASHE, of Navasota, Texas died Friday in Ennis, Texas. He was buried there Saturday with Masonic honors. Mrs. Rebecca NEAL was his mother.

Mrs. Minerva S. ALLEN, the wife of Dr. J. S. ALLEN, died Friday in Ennis, Texas. She was buried in Myrtle Cemetery Saturday.

Mrs. Dove WILSON died yesterday in Snyder, Texas.

French-born A. COIRET, 84, died in Dallas Saturday. He was the father of Mrs. J. P. GOETSEELS and Mrs. A. W. COPY. His funeral was yesterday.

J. A. HUGGINS, 23, died Saturday in Winona, Texas.

Emma SANDEFER died of typhoid fever Saturday in Winona, Texas. She was an orphan living with her uncle W. A. HILL.

Normal GIRDWOOD and Hattie NICHOLSON married recently in Garden City, Texas. Rev. Malcolm BLACK officiated.

Henry THOMPSON and Corine WILSON married Thursday in Garden City, Texas. Rev. F. T. POLLARD officiated.

Claude HARRISS, 3, fell from a windmill tower and was killed Saturday in Deming, New Mexico Territory. He was the son of G. H. HARRISS. No date was reported.

Tuesday, August 23, 1904

The funeral of Roger P. SANDERSON took place in Dallas yesterday. William E. LACEY was remanded to jail after waiving preliminarily examination. LACEY was accused of killing SANDERSON on Saturday.

Columbus WILEY was accidentally shot and killed yesterday near Texanna, Indian Territory. He was mistaken for a thief by two of his companions who were seeking the thief.

Charles D. MADDUX was killed yesterday in Corsicana, Texas. He was a police officer escorting Walter EARL of Wortham to jail when EARL fired a shot that killed MADDUX. EARL fled the scene but was soon recaptured.

Mrs. H. B. STODDARD, wife of General H. B. STODDARD, died Sunday in Bryan, Texas. Mrs. E. F. BEAUCHAMP, sister of the deceased, left Fort Worth to attend the funeral.

The six year old daughter of W. M. WITTS was killed near Mountain Park, Oklahoma Territory recently. She was thrown from a runaway wagon. Her name was not listed.

Ellen ARMISTEAD and H. W. BROWN married Sunday in Weatherford, Texas.

R. E. MAYS and Cleo GREER married Friday in Greenville, Texas.

Frank PETER and Hermina DOSTAL married Sunday in Ennis, Texas.

R. H. BANNISTER and Sida ROBBINS married last Thursday in Ennis, Texas. Rev. H. T. MCKAY officiated.

William CORY, infant son of Mr. and Mrs. T. S. CORY, died in North Marshall, Texas Sunday. He was buried in Greenwood Cemetery yesterday.

George LANCASTER, son of B. C. LANCASTER, died Saturday in Holdenville, Indian Territory. His remains were shipped to Waxahachie, Texas.

Don Juan ARMANDIAZ died in El Paso yesterday.

Marriage licenses issued by Tarrant County Clerk's office: Sam CORBIN and Della FOSTER, O. J. STEPHENS and Stella TUCKER, Fitzhugh LEE and Elsie Joseph HUYHURST, and George SANDERS and Fannie DAWSON.

Births recorded at Tarrant County Clerk's office: a boy to Silas S. and Mary R. H. KING; a boy to Frank and Minnie TAYLOR; and a boy to J. A. and Minnie QUINN. No dates or places of residence were reported.

Deaths recorded at Tarrant County Clerk's office: Amy HUDGENS, 14; Arle REED, 18. No dates or causes of death were reported.

Wednesday, August 24, 1904

The body of Mrs. L. P. JONES was buried yesterday in Temple, Texas.

The body of Charles D. MADDUX was buried yesterday in Corsicana, Texas.

W. J. BELL, father of Mrs. S. E. MORRISON, died yesterday in Arlington, Texas. His funeral will be today.

Thursday, August 25, 1904

Dr. L. P. JONES, accused of killing his wife in Benjamin, Texas last Sunday morning, committed suicide while jailed in Benjamin yesterday.

Capt. John EVANS died yesterday at his home on Wolf Ridge near Gainesville, Texas.

J. H. GRIFFITHS, living six miles northeast of Gainesville, Texas died Tuesday.

L. M. SEAMAN died Tuesday at his home in the southeast portion of Harrison County, Texas.

Julian GARVIN died of Bright's disease Tuesday in Greenville, Texas.

Mrs. Margaret LOVE, 86, died Tuesday in Sherman, Texas.

Miss GALAPKA and V. SHEHLOK married Tuesday in Ennis, Texas.

Alphonso MAPLES and Sadie HICKS married Sunday in Temple, Texas.

O. J. BENDEL and Katherine FEHRENSTEIN married Sunday in Temple, Texas. The groom lives in Burgess, Texas.

Jule HOPKINS and Minnie MCLAIN married in Kaufman, Texas Tuesday. The bride is from Ashworth, Texas.

George JONES and Eula MAYFIELD married Saturday in Chico, Texas.

J. K. WINFREY and Maggie STARNES married Tuesday in Sherman, Texas. Elder J. H. BAXTER officiated.

T. H. FOGG and Nannie FULLMAN married Tuesday in Greenville, Texas. Judge F. M. NEWTON officiated.

Ollie T. BERRY and Maggie MESSER married in Belton, Texas. Rev. S. G. TOWNSEND officiated.

C. L. ADCOCK and Nannie FESTERDON of Louisiana married Tuesday in Texarkana.

W. H. LUMMINS and Fannie BROWN married Tuesday in Texarkana The bride is from Ida, Louisiana.

Lilly BOGEN and Louis MARROS married Tuesday in Texarkana. The bride was the daughter of Rabbi BOGEN.

The remains of F. H. GRINNAN, about 26, who died in Fort Worth Tuesday, reached Terrell, Texas Wednesday. He was the son of Major J. S. GRINNAN. His funeral will be today. His death was due to gunshot wounds received in Beaumont, Texas on June 29. Those wounds were received in a duel with Claude ROBERTS, the brother of Felix ROBERTS, who was killed in Terrell three years ago.

Adam BATISTE died in Fort Worth yesterday.

Eugene GINTON, alleged to have killed his wife in Benton, Texas Tuesday, is still at large.

Marriage licenses issued by Tarrant County Clerk's office: Tom BINKLEY and Emma THREADWELL, Joe MCGENTLIE and Mrs. Annie MEDLIN, and James E. HENDERSON and Belle Vida MCBRIDE.

Deaths recorded at Tarrant County Clerk's office: A. C. BATISTE, 27, residing in Fort Worth, died of heart failure with no date listed.

Friday, August 26, 1904

Bert WATSON, 15, was arrested after killing his father, John WATSON, yesterday in Oak Grove, Texas.

Marriage licenses issued by Tarrant County Clerk's office: Verder WARE and Leila BAKER.

Births recorded at Tarrant County Clerk's office: a boy to H. N. and Ada DAVIS, Mansfield, with no date listed; a girl to Mr. and Mrs. H. N. HOGLER, Fort Worth, with no date listed.

Deaths recorded at Tarrant County Clerk's office: Glen MATTHEWS, residing in Fort Worth, with no date listed; the infant of Mr. and Mrs. STANLEY with no place or date listed.

Saturday, August 27, 1904

F. G. "Pete" WOOTEN died Thursday in Texarkana. He was a Confederate veteran and a newspaperman.

Patrick NOONAN, 52, fire captain, died in Fort Worth yesterday.

Marriage licenses issued by Tarrant County Clerk's office: W. L. PLUMBE and Bertha M. LINHORST, and Neil ROWLA and Eva Belle SMITH.

Births recorded at Tarrant County Clerk's office: a girl to Mr. and Mrs. C. A. LANIER, Fort Worth; a boy to Mr. and Mrs. J. N. REVILLE, Riverside; a girl to Mr. and Mrs. George R. TURNER, Fort Worth; a boy to Mr. and Mrs. W. BLACK, Fort Worth; a boy to Mr. and Mrs. George COKE, Arlington. (Dates were not listed for any of the births).

Sunday, August 28, 1904

Colonel C. BAKER, 75, died of apoplexy at his home near Marlin, Texas. He left five daughters and two sons.

Charles MORRIS was killed Friday in Woodward County, Oklahoma Territory. He was thrown from his horse.

Mr. and Mrs. W. J. BOOZ of Fort Worth are the parents of a baby boy weighing 10 pounds.

W. T. STEPHENS and Vendetta HITCHINS were married in Fort Worth yesterday by Rev. R. R. HAMBLIN. The ceremony was performed while the couple sat in a buggy.

William A. BAILEY and Veva FULLINGTON married Friday in Sherman, Texas. Rev. P. C. ARCHER officiated.

Monday, August 29, 1904

Joseph FORBES, 35, died yesterday near Byron, Oklahoma Territory. He was kicked by an unbroken colt.

Three children of Mr. and Mrs. Jim FRANKLIN and a son of Mrs. Emma GOODLOE drowned Wednesday in a lake near Burleson, Texas. Burial was in Bethesda Cemetery Thursday. The names of the children were not listed.

Miss Mabel LEAGEY died in Fort Worth yesterday.

T. H. WALTER and Annie May RENNIE were married yesterday in Fort Worth. Rev. J. D. YOUNG officiated.

E. C. CAMPBELL, 80, died Saturday near Alvarado, Texas. He was the father of Dr. Peyton CAMPBELL and Ed CAMPBELL.

Hamp RATTON, 45, died yesterday near Melissa, Texas.

Harry FAGENT, 14, died yesterday in McCoy, Texas. Burial was in Ables Springs.

Mrs. M. J. MCCULLOUGH died yesterday in Marshall, Texas. Burial was in Greenwood Cemetery.

News of the death of Colonel Edward Russell NORTON in Winchester, Massachusetts was received in San Antonio yesterday.

John O. PEEBLES, 46, died Saturday near Cheapside, Texas. He was a wealthy stockman. He was survived by his mother, his sister, Mrs. W. H. BOYD, and several children.

Tuesday, August 30, 1904

John S. HORNBEAK committed suicide in El Paso yesterday. He was a salesman with Mine and Smelter Supply Company.

William STOCKERT was thought to be the man who committed suicide yesterday under the name of W. S. CRAWFORD in Jackson, Mississippi. He was a brother of Mrs. Y. A. SUMMERS of Houston. STOCKERT lived in Rusk, Texas.

Word of the death of Will F. GORDON in Monette, Missouri was received in Belton, Texas. GORDON was a railroad fireman. Burial was in Garden City, Kansas.

Rev. J. B. BUCHANAN died yesterday near Sherman, Texas. He was the father of W. B. BUCHANAN.

James AINSWORTH died yesterday in Paris, Texas. He was a porter in a saloon. The cause of death was a broken neck.

Births recorded at Tarrant County Clerk's office: a girl to Mr. and Mrs. W. L. BOSTICK, Arlington, on August 9; a girl to Mr. and Mrs. Fritz HAHN, Fort Worth, on August 21; a boy to Mr. and Mrs. S. D. HARDIN, Fort Worth, on August 24; and a girl to Mr. and Mrs. C. S. MCCARVER, Polytechnic Heights, on August 23.

Deaths recorded at Tarrant County Clerk's office: W. J. BELL, 55, residing in Arlngton, died of asthma on August 23; and Samuel N. HUTCHINS, 49, residing in Fort Worth, died of anemia on August 24.

Marriage licenses issued by Tarrant County Clerk's office: Edward C. LEBEL and Annie DAUGHTERY, W. T. STEPHENS and Vindetta HUTCHINS, T. H. WALTER and Annie Mae RENNIE, S. I. STURGIS and Cora MURRAY, L. W. SWANEY and Beulah SMITH, J. H. CURRY and Mrs. Pearle ESTES.

Mr. and Mrs. J. A. MEISLOHN became the parents of a boy in Fort Worth last night.

Mable LEAKY, 12, was buried in Oakwood Cemetery yesterday.

Richard REYNOLDS died Sunday in Kaufman, Texas.

Mary Susan BROWN died yesterday in Heloise, Texas.

John RYAN, 60, died Friday in Terrell, Texas.

Wednesday, August 31, 1904

Oscar HAZLETON, about 30, was found dead in Beaumont, Texas Tuesday morning.

Bert SMITH was killed yesterday on the Pat SOLOMON farm north of Garland, Texas. Richard IVY was jailed in connection with the killing.

W. Ross HARRIS and Lucille WITHERS, daughter of J. N. WITHERS, married in Fort Worth last night. Rev. R. R. HANLIN officiated.

James E. QUARLES, 41, died in Mineral Wells, Texas yesterday. He was a cousin of James Hays QUARLES of Fort Worth. He was also a son of Mrs. R. L. QUARLES and a brother of Mrs. J. L. RIGGINS of Weatherford, Texas. His wife and a son survived him.

Births recorded at Tarrant County Clerk's office: a girl to Mr. and Mrs. P. BAILEY, North Fort Worth, on August 20; a girl to Mr. and Mrs. E. L. BROWN, North Fort Worth, on August 25; a girl to Mr. and Mrs. W. W. MCFARLAND, county, on August 27; and a girl to Mr. and Mrs. C. G. MITCHELL, Station A, on August 26.

Marriage licenses issued by Tarrant County Clerk's office: W. J. PULLEY and Nannie MCNATT, R. C. DUNHAM and Mrs. Loretta TRENT, Frank MOORE and Daisy ARTHUR, and Allen DAVIS and Fanny ODOM.

John STICE and Mrs. Mattie BRAZLETON married Sunday in Gainesville, Texas.

Joe ULK and Mabry MENECK married Tuesday in Ennis, Texas.

May V. MCKINLEY married yesterday Rolla J. BROWN in Kingfisher, Oklahoma Territory. The bride was a cousin of Willie MCKINLEY.

Mrs. P. L. WHITTENBERG died Monday in Waco, Texas. Her remains were shipped to Temple, Texas.

Marion Simeon COVINGTON died Monday in Ennis, Texas. She was buried there Tuesday. She was an infant of Mr. and Mrs. Sid COVINGTON.

Mrs. Lee MOSS died Monday near Gainesville, Texas.

September, 1904
Thursday, September 1, 1904
The paper for this date did not appear on the microfilm.

Friday, September 2, 1904
Sam REEDUS and Erna STAPP married Tuesday in Greenville, Texas. Rev R. P. JENKINS officiated. The bride lives in Tishomingo, Indian Territory.

Earl LAND and Della HANSLEY married Sunday in College Mound, Texas.

G. D. DANNER and Murtle MONTGOMERY married Tuesday in Waxahachie, Texas. The bride was the daughter of John MONTGOMERY. Rev. J. C. SMITH officiated.

W. L. DOUGHDRILL and Mabel HANKS married Wednesday in Lawton, Oklahoma Territory.

Charles WATKINS and Emma DUNCAN married Wednesday in Floydada, Texas. He is the editor of the *Crosby County News*. She is the daughter of A. B. DUNCAN.

Emma RICKEL died Wednesday in Waxahachie, Texas.

Fred BENSON, 12, died Wednesday in Corsicana, Texas. He was the son of N. L. BENSON.

D. D. MYERS, 73, died Wednesday in Gainesville, Texas. He was a Confederate veteran.

W. C. HOWARD died Tuesday in Garner, Texas.

Charles BEATY died Wednesday in Laredo, Texas. He underwent an operation last week. He was a railroad conductor.

Mrs. Leola Lawrence MAUPIN died Wednesday in Oklahoma City, Oklahoma Territory. Her remains were shipped to Corpus Christi, Texas. She was the daughter of T. M. LAWRENCE and married in 1902 in Corpus Christi.

Mrs. Ben INGRAM, 37, died Tuesday from appendicitis in Greenville, Texas. Her husband and three children survived her.

Dr. T. MCDONALD died Monday in Celeste, Texas. His remains were sent to Calvert, Texas.

Barney M. HOBBY, a brother of Colonel A. M. HOBBY, died in Dallas yesterday. He was a Confederate veteran. He was born April 1, 1846, in Jacksonville, Florida. He was survived by his widow.

Harvey V. LOWENSTEIN, brother of James W. LOWENSTEIN of Fort Worth, died yesterday in Cameron, Texas. He was to be buried in either Waco, Texas or St. Joseph, Missouri.

Birth recorded at Tarrant County Clerk's office: a girl to Mr. and Mrs. Wilson CHILCUTT, Fort Worth, on August 29.

Marriage licenses issued by Tarrant County Clerk's office: J. W. DEWEES and Mrs. L. C. YOAKUM, George W. MYERS and Nora JAGUA, Jake SALERNO and Mary PASSALAGUA, and Jerry COLE and Elizabeth BOATMAN.

Saturday, September 3, 1904
Captain Christobal BENAVIDES died yesterday at his home in Laredo, Texas. He was a Confederate veteran and left a widow and several children.

John BLASSINGAME, 68, died Thursday in Van Alstyne, Texas. He was buried yesterday.

Mrs. George STOVALL, a resident of Jackson, Texas, died Thursday in Terrell, Texas. Her remains were buried in the city cemetery.

J. M. "Bud" JONES, 38, died Wednesday in Terrell, Texas. His remains were buried in Ables Springs Cemetery. He was a resident of Poetry, Texas.

Mrs. M. U. WILSON of Childress, Texas died in Minerals Wells, Texas yesterday. Her remains were returned to Childress.

William MISER died yesterday at his home on Wolf Ridge in Cocke County, Texas.

Clark BRADY, 12, died Thursday of typhoid in Waxahachie, Texas. He was the son of Mr. and Mrs. C. M. BRADY.

Dr. M. S. KABLE received word of the death of his sister, Mrs. S.A. ROBERTSON, in Roanoke, Virginia. Dr. KABLE lives in Cleburne, Texas.

Lillie WATKINS and Charles MORRISON married Thursday in Guthrie, Oklahoma Territory.

Mont HALEY and Ella MILLER married yesterday in Cleburne, Texas.

Walter WATSON and Doll TAYLOR married Wednesday in Palo Pinto, Texas.

Annie DOODY, 12, died yesterday of burns received when her clothing caught fire at St. Patrick's Academy in Paris, Texas.

The infant child of Mr. and Mrs. John ANDREWS died in Fort Worth yesterday. Burial was in city cemetery.

Fayette HOLLAND was found dead Wednesday in his home near Pottsboro, Texas.

Word has been received in Sherman, Texas of the death of Albert CHEATHAM near Day, Texas. He died soon after taking a dose of quinine.

Mrs. Isabelle CATES, 85, died Thursday in Ennis, Texas.

J. B. PINSON, 50, died Wednesday at the North Texas Insane Asylum in Terrell, Texas. His remains were shipped to Forney, Texas.

T. S. HALL, 76, died Thursday in Pecos, Texas. He formerly lived in Troup, Henderson and Jacksonville, Texas.

James PONDER died of dropsy Wednesday at his home near Millsap, Texas.

T. H. TAYLOR and Nettie BRAZEALE married Wednesday in Ashland, Texas.

Paul HENSON and Ollie HARTMAN married Wednesday east of Marshall, Texas. Justice H. B. MCWILLIAMS officiated.

Professor Ernest T. CROFT and Lilla Belle SMITH married Thursday in Corsicana, Texas. Rev. H. C. JOHNSON officiated.

Harbert ESTES was shot and killed yesterday near Mansfield, Texas. Sid HEARD, his brother-in-law, surrendered to authorities.

John BARNES, 42, died Thursday in Dallas. He was a traveling man. His funeral was yesterday with burial in Oak Cliff Cemetery. His wife and several siblings, including Mrs. Ruth PETERS survived him. PETERS is from Bonham, Texas.

Robert COLE was yesterday acquitted of the murder of Coleman BROWN last April. The trial was held in Marshall, Texas.

Births recorded at Tarrant County Clerk's office: a girl to Mr. and Mrs. E. C. PEERCE, Fort Worth, on August 31; and a girl to Mr. and Mrs. Dave RICHARDSON, Diamond Hill, on September 1.

Marriage licenses issued by Tarrant County Clerk's office: D. C. ROOS and Etta M. ACKERMAN, and J. E. D. DICKERSON and Lena C. FREDERICK.

Sunday, September 4, 1904

Charles H. SCHRODER, 24 and his wife, 37, were found dead of gunshot wounds in their home in Houston Friday. It was believed the deaths were a murder-suicide by Charles SCHRODER.

Mr. and Mrs. L. L. HAWES rejoiced at the birth of a son in Fort Worth yesterday.

Mrs. Margaret BLACKWELL, 81, died Friday at her home near Vineland in Collin County, Texas. She was buried at Walnut Grove Cemetery.

Lawrence Lee RUCKER, the son of Max RUCKER, died Friday in Belton, Texas.

Perry O. SHELBY died yesterday in Oklahoma City, Oklahoma Territory. His funeral is today.

Ed MCCAIN, son of R. A. MCCAIN died Friday near Milford, Texas.

A. C. JUSTAVUS and Erma NUNNALLY married Thursday in Greenville, Texas. Justice Tom MCDANIEL officiated.

Arthur BOUNDS and Fannie SINGLTEON married Thursday in Milford, Texas. Rev. A. D. BROOKS officiated.

H. F. CROSBY and Lillian TUMLIN married Thursday in Sulphur Springs, Texas. Rev. J. P. KINCAID officiated.

Logan BILLINGSLEY shot and killed C. W. WHEATLEY Friday in Andarko, Indian Territory. WHEATLEY was the father-in-law of BILLINGSLEY.

Births recorded at Tarrant County Clerk's office: a boy to Mr. and Mrs. L. L. HAWES, Fort Worth, on September 3; a girl to Mr. and Mrs. Q. S. ADAMS, Riverside, on September 3; a boy to Mr. and Mrs. F. L. WILKERSON, Fort Worth, on August 27; a girl to Mr. and Mrs. Fred HOLDER, Diamond Hill, on August 25; and a girl to Mr. and Mrs. G. L. WALKER, Fort Worth, on September 2.

Deaths recorded at Tarrant County Clerk's office: Edward ROBERTS, 15, residing in Tarrant County, died of malaria with no date reported.

Marriage licenses issued by Tarrant County Clerk's office: D. T. MORROW and Maggie L. WILLIAMS, K. T. SCOTT and Vivian BEYETT, W. T. HOLT and Essie M. WILLIAMS, Walter STUBBLEFIELD and Amanda HICKS, Wesley COSBY and Minnie Belle KELLEY, B. T. PRINE and Mrs. Della FORD, and T. T. BLAND and L. V. CLAITH.

Monday, September 5, 1904

M. M. BENNETT committed suicide Saturday in Tehuacana, Texas. He was believed to be despondent over ill health.

Dr. David H. ARMSTRONG, 74, died at his home in Austin Saturday and was buried there yesterday.

Mr. and Mrs. W. L. SHIELD of Fort Worth are the parents of a baby girl born last night.

Emlie MAYER died in Fort Worth last night. The funeral will be today.

Eugene MONTGOMERY and Alice PASSONS married Friday in Greenville, Texas. The bride is the daughter of J. H. PASSONS. Rev. F. E. FINCHER officiated.

Mrs. C. E. DUBBS died last week in Clarendon, Texas.

Tuesday, September 6, 1904

Mathey Walker CORBITT, 68, died suddenly in Dallas Sunday. Burial was in Oak Cliff Cemetery yesterday. He was a native of Capetown, South Africa, and was survived by his wife. Mrs. Cecil ROGERS of Dallas is a niece of the deceased.

Holloway BRITTON was killed in a knife duel with Sam BARNES Saturday night near Waxahachie, Texas.

W. R. CHANDLER was acquitted Saturday in Belton, Texas of charges of killing his wife. He was given a habeas corpus hearing in the death of Manager MCLAUGHLIN the same day. It was thought the latter case would never come to trial. (See March 21, 1904).

Ed MADISON, 25, was found dead yesterday on the Katy tracks two miles east of Denison, Texas.

Jesus CANTU and Juan MORALES, wounded by Germion MARTINEZ Sunday, died in a San Antonio hospital Monday.

D. H. JOHNSTON will be inaugurated today as governor of the Chickasaw Nation in Ardmore, Indian Territory.

Marriage licenses issued by Tarrant County Clerk's office: M. BECKHAM and Frances WHEELER.

Fred BRENNAN, a member of J. B. BRENNAN and Son, died yesterday in Sherman, Texas.

Mrs. CHAPMAN, 65, died of congestion Sunday night in the house of Lon ROSSON in Crisp, Texas. No given name was reported for the deceased.

Manard ROOPE and Emma HIGGS married Sunday at the Baptist Church in Slidell, Texas.

T. H. FIELDS and Vessie YAGER married Sunday in Sunset, Texas.

Henry MOSELEY shot and killed Matthew CAMPOR near Bryan, Texas Sunday night. MOSELEY was arrested and jailed.

Wednesday, September 7, 1904

Births recorded at Tarrant County Clerk's office: a boy to Mr. and Mrs. J. A. TODD, Fort Worth, on September 2; a boy to Mr. and Mrs. H. ELLOTSON, Birdville, on September 3; a girl to Mr. and Mrs. W. E. BROWN, Fort Worth, on September 1; a girl to Mr. and Mrs. H. P. HAYES, North Fort Worth, on September 3; a girl to Mr. and Mrs. John LEATH, Mansfield, on August 26; a girl to Mr. and Mrs. C. N. FRY, Mansfield, on September 27 (sic); a girl to Mr. and Mrs. H. J. SMITH, Fort Worth, on August 30; a boy to Mr. and Mrs. Lige ADMIRE, Azle, on August 28; a boy to Mr. and Mrs. J. P. SMITH, Fort Worth, on August 29; a girl to Mr. and Mrs. J. L. JOHNSON, Fort Worth, on September 1; a boy to Mr. and Mrs. T. W. PHILLIPS, Fort Worth, on September 4; a boy to Mr. and Mrs. C. HOLMBERG, North Fort Worth, on August 24; and a boy to Mr. and Mrs. A. M. WRIGHT, Fort Worth on August 25.

Deaths recorded at Tarrant County Clerk's office: William J. HOPPER, 69, residing in Fort Worth, died of a blood clot on the brain on August 22; J. G. BOWMAN, 23, residing in Fort Worth, died of typhoid fever on August 3; and Patrick NOONAN, 52, residing in Fort Worth, died of typhoid fever with no date listed.

Marriage licenses issued by Tarrant County Clerk's office: Willie YOUNG and Nellie HILLIARD, F. N. T. CATUDAL and Mrs. Hattie E. LANNIER, F. BUCHANAN and Lizzie ADAMS, J. T. STRIBLING and Elizabeth F. GIBSON, E. G. HOFFMAN and Nettie DICKIE, Wallace PRATER and Etta LYONS, T. J. PANNELL and Nellie DUNLAVEY, T. F. HALE and Mrs. H. M. ADKINS, and E. H. CRENSHAW and Alice A. REYNOLDS.

Thursday, September 8, 1904

Henry J. LANG, a blacksmith at Fort Sill, died yesterday in Lawton, Oklahoma Territory. He was shot by a man named NEAL Sunday. NEAL was to be tried by civil authorities.

Robert M. CARLEY, postmaster at Golden, New Mexico Territory, was killed from ambush Tuesday.

Joe COLLINS, aka Jack FISHER, was arrested and charged with murder Tuesday. He is accused of beating his wife to death last Monday.

J. L. MILLER of Indianapolis, Indiana, and Dolla BEAL of Wichita, Kansas, married yesterday in Lawton, Oklahoma Territory.

Juana GARZA was killed Sunday at Santa Rosalito, Texas.

Orrin MCCARTHY, 28 and son of G. P. MCCARTHY, died of tuberculosis yesterday at the home of T. D. DILL in Austin.

The remains of Mrs. J. W. DAVIDSON, who died Tuesday in Grand Saline, Texas, arrived in Weatherford, Texas for burial.

Mrs. M. N. WILSON, 50, died last Friday in Mineral Wells, Texas.

Mrs. M. N. DUNCAN of Houston died of heart failure yesterday in Mineral Wells, Texas.

The funeral of Fred C BRENNAN, who died Monday, occurred yesterday in Sherman, Texas.

W. H. HOLMES died Sunday at his home five miles west of Frisco, Texas.

Mrs. Jennie GREEN died of cancer in Overbrook, Indian Territory. She was the wife of William Lea GREEN.

Mrs. Sarah MITCHELL, 75, died Tuesday near Ennis, Texas. Her remains were buried yesterday in Waxahachie, Texas.

The infant of Mrs. Lee C. SPRINGER died Tuesday on a train en route to Cleburne, Texas.

Laura DEVORTEX and A. Stanley CHRISTENBERRY married Monday in Sherman, Texas. Elder J. H. FULLER officiated.

Pietro RIALO and Rosa SCARCELLO married Sunday in Temple, Texas.

D. J. DODD and Maud HARVEY married Sunday in Oak Branch, Texas. Rev. C. A. CLARK officiated.

Olen TURNER and Nettie ELLIS married Sunday in Oak Branch, Texas. Rev. Manson KILLETT officiated.

Ella HEATH and Capt. W. R. BOUDS married Sunday in Cleburne, Texas.

Ahta GRIFFIN and Dr. Ben TURNER married Sunday near Cleburne, Texas.

L. D. KELLEY and Cary MCCULLOUGH married Tuesday in Longview, Texas.

R. E. DURNING and Eilene HACKETT married Tuesday in Sherman, Texas. Rev Ed NEILL, of Texarkana officiated. The bride was the daughter of the late S. P. HACKETT.

Gussie REYNOLDS and Hodge CRENSHAW married in Fort Worth yesterday. Rev. Chalmers MCPHERSON of Waxahachie, Texas officiated.

Births recorded at Tarrant County Clerk's office: a girl to Mr. and Mrs. F. R. YANCEY, North Fort Worth, on September 5.

Marriage licenses issued by Tarrant County Clerk's office: Willie YOUNG and Nellie HILLIARD, and John EASTMAN and Deshie ANGLEY.

Friday, September 9, 1904

W. R. STEPHENS and Miss Vernon LONG married in Rusk, Texas. The bride is the daughter of Congressman John B. LONG.

Ernest KEEN and Mattie SANDERS married Monday in Terrell, Texas. The groom lives in Royse, Texas. The bride lives in Heath, Texas.

Harvey BRYANT and Miss SHORT married Sunday in Heath, Texas.

Charlotte GALLEHER and Alexander Gilpin BLACKLOCK of Dallas married yesterday in Sewanee, Tennessee. The bride is the daughter of Bishop J. N. GALLEHER.

J. O. BLAKE and Edna HILL married yesterday in Sherman, Texas. Dr. E. E. MULKEY officiated. Dr. MULKEY was a physician who attended the birth of the groom 23 years ago.

Mrs. J. T. BUFORD, 60, died in Greenville, Texas. Survivors included a husband and six children.

George Lawler WILDER died Wednesday in Weatherford, Texas. He was buried there yesterday. He was the son of Dr. and Mrs. H. L. WILDER of Granbury, Texas.

A baby girl was born to Mr. and Mrs. Ernest BAILEY of Houston yesterday. Mrs. BAILEY is the daughter of Mrs. Frank DEBEQUE of Fort Worth.

Elizabeth GIBSON and T. P. STRIPLING married near Fort Worth yesterday. The bride is the daughter of T. L. GIBSON.

Births recorded at Tarrant County Clerk's office: a girl to Mr. and Mrs. J. W. MCDONALD, Fort Worth, on September 2.

Saturday, September 10, 1904

A young man named THORNTON was killed yesterday when he was hit by a train in Winfield, Texas. He was asleep on a cross-tie when the train hit him. A brother was with him, but wasn't hurt. No other names were given.

Claude A. BEALL, 34, was shot and killed yesterday by Harry P. ROSS in Fort Worth. ROSS was an engineer and BEALL a fireman on the Fort Worth and Rio Grande Railroad. The two men argued after arriving in Fort Worth. ROSS defended himself after BEALL attacked him with an air brake coupling. ROSS was released on $3000 bail.

John ROTLEY killed C. H. LYSTER with a blow to the head from a chair a few days ago in the Confederate home in Austin. ROTLEY is now prostrate with heart trouble and may die.

Judge ROWLAND held an inquest yesterday into the death of John O'HARA, 60, in Fort Worth. The verdict was death from natural causes.

Marriage licenses issued by Tarrant County Clerk's office: C. A. CORNETT and Catherine MOREY.

Births recorded at Tarrant County Clerk's office: a boy to Mr. and Mrs. W. B. CROWELL, Bransford, on August 30; a girl to Mr. and Mrs. J. L. LITTLE, Bransford, on September 6 and a boy to Mr. and Mrs. _____ HAYES, Fort Worth on September 4.

Deaths recorded at Tarrant County Clerk's office: John O'HARA, 60, residing in Fort Worth, died of throat trouble on September 9.

Sunday, September 11, 1904

Philo H. GOODWYN, 43, died in San Antonio yesterday. His funeral was scheduled for Monday. He was the general freight agent for the Santa Fe Railroad. He was survived by his wife, Isadore Cantrell GOODWYN and two sons, Philo H., Jr. and William Cantrell.

The body of Thomas J. TREDWELL was found near Monterrey, Mexico. He was a railroad contractor in Mexico and was believed to be from Little Rock, Arkansas.

On WEBB and Alice BOTCHER, both of Ardmore, Indian Territory, married Thursday in Sherman, Texas. Rev. P. C. ARCHER officiated.

Hattie JENKINS and A. J. O'NEAL married Thursday in Greenville, Texas. Rev D. W. JESSE officiated.

Allyne Percy HOLT and Bertha GIBSON married Wednesday in Gainesville, Texas. Rev. Percy KNICKERBOCKER officiated.

Rev. Jarrett FINNEY, 74, died Friday near Luella, Texas.

Mrs. J. P. HAYES, 54, of Omaha, Texas died Tuesday and was buried in Spring Hill, Texas. Her husband and a son, W. Z. HAYES, survive.

Prof. B. H. THORNTON, 74, died Thursday in Hunter, Texas. Burial was Friday in San Marcos, Texas. He was the postmaster in Hunter and was survived by his wife, a son and two daughters.

The little child of J. A. NEAL died Thursday on the Green Demonstration Farm near Terrell, Texas.

Mrs. Mary WILLIAMS died Thursday night near Rockett, Texas.

Charles BUSTER, 14, died Friday in Weatherford, Texas. He was the son of Mr. and Mrs. C. W. BUSTER of Waggoner, Indian Territory. He was buried in Weatherford Saturday.

Marvin ELLIOTT died Thursday in Greenville, Texas. He was son of Mr. and Mrs. Wright ELLIOTT.

Thomas E. VOSS, 84, died Thursday in Corsicana, Texas.

Maggie WASHINGTON died of burns in Dallas yesterday. She was injured when Georgia HOLLEY threw a lamp at her. HOLLEY was arrested.

John B. DENTON was killed Friday in Gilmer, Texas. He was a brakeman on the Texas Southern Railroad. He was run over by freight cars.

The remains of Elon VIRGIL were found near Vici, Indian Territory. No date was reported. VIRGIL had wandered from his home and had been missing for several days when the remains were found.

Charles A. CORNETT and Catherine MOREY married in Fort Worth Thursday.

The mother of Dr. T. S. RIGGS died Wednesday in Kingston, Louisiana. Dr. RIGGS lives in Ennis, Texas.

George A. BENEDICT, 42, died Friday in Sherman, Texas.

J. S. MILLS died yesterday at his home seven miles west of Gainesville, Texas.

Joe LOVE, 21, died Tuesday at the home of his father, Dr. Thomas B. LOVE, in Dickens, Texas. The cause of death was rheumatism and indigestion.

Mrs. H. N. C. DAVIS died Wednesday in Milford, Texas. She was survived by her husband and an adopted daughter.

W. D. WILLIAMS died Thursday in Mason, Texas. He was a farmer living near Fredonia, Texas.

Porter C. MARK, a Pullman car conductor on the Missouri, Kansas and Texas Railroad (Katy) died of heart trouble on the train north of Dallas yesterday.

George BEARDON overdosed on strychnine and died near Annona, Texas. His body was found yesterday.

Nellie DUNLAVY of Fort Worth and F. J. PANNELL married in Fort Worth Tuesday. The couple will live in Mineo, Texas. Dr. Junius. B. FRENCH officiated.

Monday, September 12, 1904

Paul LAGA and Annie MOTT were married in Temple, Texas Saturday. Justice WARD officiated. The bride lived near Seaton, Texas.

News reached Marshall, Texas yesterday of the marriage of Ethel PRESTON and Ernest ILSHMER in Beaumont, Texas. PRESTON was a resident of Marshall while ILSHMER was from Port Arthur, Texas.

The funeral of Philo H. GOODWYN will take place in San Antonio today. His burial will be in Anchor Lodge Masonic Cemetery under Masonic auspices.

Charles A. LEWIS died Friday in La Rosen, Louisiana. Howell LEWIS and J. B. LEWIS were brothers of the deceased.

John A. WARE died of heart failure Saturday night in Longview, Texas.

E. C. BARKLEY died yesterday in Oklahoma City, Oklahoma Territory. He was a traveling salesman for the Moline Plow Company.

Edward DAUGHTERY died of a stroke Saturday in Kenney, Texas. He was the oldest living native Texan at the time of his death. He was born on October 20, 1825 in San Augustine County, Texas and married Antoinette DIXON in 1857. There were 16 children born to the couple. Twelve of them were alive at the time of Edward DAUGHTERY's death.

Tuesday, September 13, 1904

The baby of Mr. and Mrs. NUGENT died of malarial fever yesterday in Terrell, Texas. It was 15 months old. Its remains were buried in College Mound, Texas.

W. T. SMITH, the founder of Blanket, Texas, died there yesterday.

May JOHNSON, 18, died Saturday in McKinney, Texas. The cause of death was tuberculosis. She was the daughter of John JOHNSON.

Rev. B. A. COPASS and Crickett KEYS married yesterday in Waxahachie, Texas. Rev. A. J. COPASS, brother of the groom, officiated.

E. M. LAFOY and Minnie TAYLOR married Saturday near Sherman, Texas. Elder J. H. BAXTER officiated.

Claude COLE, 17, and Arthur LAMPER, 17, were killed in South McAlester, Indian Territory when they were run over by a train yesterday. They were asleep on the tracks. Another report said the two were killed 12 miles north of Denison, Texas and named the victims as COLE and Fred MILLS of Muskogee, Indian Territory.

Charley BEVERS was shot and fatally wounded in Dexter, Texas yesterday. Sam MCKINGLE surrendered to authorities.

John READY was shot and killed yesterday at Howith Station, five miles north of Hempstead, Texas.

Births recorded at Tarrant County Clerk's office: a girl to Mr. and Mrs. J. A. CAMPBELL, Arlington, on August 28; a boy to Mr. and Mrs. T. W. MITCHELL, Fort Worth, on September 6; a boy to Mr. and Mrs. H. HOFFMAN, Fort Worth, on September 10; a boy to Mr. and Mrs. J. BOYD, Riverside, on September 9; a girl to Mr. and Mrs. E. G. BAYLEY, Fort Worth, on September 8; a boy to Mr. and Mrs. A. P. WILKERSON, Arlington, on August 29; a boy to Mr. and Mrs. C. J. HOFFMAN, Arlington, on August 30; a boy to Mr. and Mrs. J. L. JOHNSON, Johnston Station, on September 3; a girl to Mr. and Mrs. J. L. SHIELDS, Fort Worth, on August 12; a boy to Mr. and Mrs. C. KILLEN, Fort Worth, on August 18; a boy to Mr. and Mrs. T. L. SORRELLS, Fort Worth, on August 15; a girl to Mr. and Mrs. J. W. TUCKER, Fort Worth, on September 2; a girl to Mr. and Mrs. J. L. MCCLURG, Fort Worth, on September 1; a girl to Mr. and Mrs. S. W. RAY, Fort Worth, on August 21; a boy to Mr. and Mrs. C. CAHOON, Fort Worth, on August 7; and a boy to Mr. and Mrs. J. THUMELL, Fort Worth, on August 31.

Deaths recorded at Tarrant County Clerk's office: Johnson KILLMAN, 75, residing in Fort Worth, died of pneumonia on September 9; Claude A. BEALL, 26, died of a gunshot wound on September 9; J. L. BAGWELL, 45, died of heart failure on September 8; and Mattie LEWIS, 40, died of heart failure on September 10. There was no residence listed for the final three people.

Marriage licenses issued by Tarrant County Clerk's office: H. E. KNIGHT and Mrs. Lurah ARMSTRONG, H. B. SEIFFERT and Myrtle FLORY, J. M. DRIVER and Ethel STEPHENS, James WORTHAM and Maggie BANKS.

Mrs. D. H. CRAVENS, 45, of Arlington, died in Illinois Sunday. Her funeral will be today in Arlington. She was the wife of Dr. CRAVENS.

John BOYL of Riverside announced a new baby in his house.

Wednesday, September 14, 1904

Mrs. Margaret A. NORTON sued the Houston and Texas Central Railroad for the death of her husband November 18, 1903. He was killed while disembarking from the train at Ferris, Texas. He fell between the train and the platform and was crushed.

D. T. BEVIS was shot and killed near Quinlan, Texas. H. D. WILSON surrendered and was taken to Greenville, Texas. WILSON is a farmer on whose land BEVIS was seeking cotton pickers.

Guy LOWERY died yesterday in Terrell, Texas. He was an attendant in the state insane asylum. An inmate of the asylum struck him.

John ROTLEY was released on bond in the death of C. H. LYSTER.

Mrs. Mattie MILLS died Monday in the home of H. C. CASE, her son-in-law, in Hyde Park, near Austin. She died of typhoid fever. She was buried yesterday.

Births recorded at Tarrant County Clerk's office: a boy to Mr. and Mrs. L. P. ALEXANDER, Mansfield, on September 10; a girl to Mr. and Mrs. James BROWNING, Keller, on September 9; and a boy to Mr. and Mrs. W. M. ROSS, Fort Worth, on September 10.

Marriage licenses issued by Tarrant County Clerk's office: Charles DAVIDSON and Irene WOOD; and S. D. HOWK and Clara BURLESON.

Thursday, September 15, 1904

The paper for this date did not appear on the microfilm.

Friday, September 16, 1904

Henry WILSON was convicted of second degree murder in Marshall, Texas. He killed John BLEDSOE last August 18. WILSON was sentenced to 20 years in prison.

The case of the state v. Joe COLLINS, aka Joe FIFER, began yesterday in Marshall, Texas. COLLINS stands accused of killing his wife several weeks ago near Jonesville, Texas.

Laura INGRAM was indicted in Marshall, Texas for the death of her six weeks old son. She was released on $750 bond.

Robert KINDCAID died in Houston yesterday of injuries sustained Monday when he fell through an elevator shaft. His remains will be sent Cleburne, Texas.

Howard A. WHITE and Anna L. TODD married Wednesday in Corsicana, Texas. Rev. H. Z. WHITESIDE officiated. The couple is from Powell, Texas.

Ivy RENFRO and Effie BURRIS married Sunday near Cleburne, Texas.

J. Gary FLOWERS and Lillie MOORE married yesterday in Kaufman, Texas.

J. S. FUNDERBURK, 52, and Mrs. Elizabeth DAVIS, 51, married yesterday in Waxahachie, Texas.

Miss Eva MCCAMPBELL and Dr. Thomas Albert ANDERSON, married Wednesday in Corpus Christi, Texas. Rev. A. H. P. MCCURDY officiated. The bride is the daughter of Judge and Mrs. J. S. MCCAMPBELL. The groom is from Saltillo, Mexico.

Silas PELL and Florence MCNEIL married Wednesday in McKinney, Texas.

Samuel MCDOWELL died of black jaundice Tuesday in his home in Blooming Grove, Texas.

Mrs. S. M. N. MARRS, 41, died Tuesday in Terrell, Texas. Her husband is superintendent of schools in Terrell.

W. E. DAILEY died Tuesday night at his home in Mineral Wells, Texas. He left a wife and child.

James A. PRICE, 79, died of old age Wednesday in Del Rio, Texas. He lived in Del Rio over 20 years.

Births recorded at Tarrant County Clerk's office: a boy to Mr. and Mrs. S. O. JOHNSON, Mansfield, on September 13.

Marriage licenses issued by Tarrant County Clerk's office: B. F. FOREMAN and Minnie M. CRAIG; Charles NANCE and Willie SHIVERS; and J. D. POWELL and Mrs. M. H. CARTER.

Saturday, September 17, 1904

Tom JONES, a railroad porter, was shot and killed by an unknown man Thursday. JONES attempted to put the man off the train for not paying his fare. In the ensuing fight, JONES was shot. The story was datelined Texarkana, but the location of the shooting wasn't stated.

In Hempstead, Texas Louis HENSON posted $2500 bond in the death of John READY several days ago at Howith, Texas.

J. W. HELMS, living north of Marlin, Texas, died Thursday night from poisoning caused by eating preserved fruit.

J. G. HUGHES, of Coleman, Texas, was killed Thursday when he was thrown from his buggy. He was seeking medicine for an ill grandchild when the accident happened. The child died Friday. HUGHES's remains were shipped to Comanche, Texas.

Mrs. Sabrina E. CARLE, mother of Norman E. NELSON, died yesterday in Fort Worth. Her remains were shipped to Clinton, Illinois.

Ira O. WYSE, about 45 and a resident of Greenville, Texas, died Thursday in Delafield, Wisconsin. He was an oilman and left a wife and three daughters.

Oscar BEATY, 26, died of consumption in Oak Grove, located near Ennis, Texas. He was born in Grayson County, Kentucky.

John STEWART, 19, died of malarial congestion Wednesday in Paris, Texas. He lived in the territory and was visiting relatives when he died.

W. E. WATKINS, 55, died Thursday in Kaufman, Texas. He was a former resident of Terrell, Texas.

Mrs. Mittie JARRED, wife of John JARRED, died Tuesday near Pine Ridge, Texas.

Wardie TAYLOR, 18 and daughter of Mr. and Mrs. George TAYLOR, died Wednesday in Harleton, Texas.

The remains of Sam MONTGOMERY, killed when he tried to board a moving Cotton Belt railroad freight train near Pollock, Texas, were shipped to Elkhart, Texas.

Births recorded at Tarrant County Clerk's office: a boy to Mr. and Mrs. J. J. L. BELL, North Fort Worth, on September 12; a girl to Mr. and Mrs. William MCNATT, Arlington, on September 15; and a boy to Mr. and Mrs. R. M. HARKEY, Arlington, on September 11.

Marriage licenses issued by Tarrant County Clerk's office: F. K. PROCTOR and Mrs. Hallie M. ROBERTSON; and J. D. HILL and Nettie GREEN.

Sunday, September 18, 1904

Lewis WOOD, 14 and the son of A. G. WOOD, was killed at the Fin and Feather Club Lake 12 miles north of Dallas yesterday. He died in Hutchens. He was injured by a fowling piece that misfired and struck him in the knee.

C. S. "Red" STUART was murdered in his sleep Friday night at Velasca, Texas.

Ed MOORE, aka Tuck MCCOY, fell from his wagon in Fort Worth and was instantly killed yesterday.

Esther FORBERG, 25, died of typhoid fever Thursday in Mineral Wells, Texas.

M. B. HUMPHRIES died of meningitis Wednesday in Abilene, Texas. He was buried there the same day.

Mrs. Robert FILGO died Friday in Cleburne, Texas.

Robert J. KINCAID died in Houston. His remains were brought to Cleburne, Texas.

Ralph GURLEY, 2, died Thursday in Greenville, Texas. Internment was in Rockwall, Texas.

Mrs. M. E. JENKINS, died Thursday in Belton, Texas. She was buried Friday in North Belton Cemetery. Her son is Dr. S. M. JENKINS.

The 18 months old child of Mr. and Mrs. Sam BEDINGFIELD died yesterday in McCoy, Texas. Burial is in Ables Springs.

Mrs. S. MOUNTS died Friday near Vernon, Texas. Her remains were taken to Bellevue, Texas.

J. B. ADAMS, an inmate of the county jail, died Thursday night in Gainesville, Texas.

Ely NORRIS died Thursday south of Burleson, Texas. He was buried at Marystown Cemetery the same day. He was a pioneer of Johnson County.

Frank R. PUTMAN and Emma HARRISON married Wednesday in Fort Worth. Rev. George OAKLEY officiated.

F. A. DOBBS, tax assessor of Donley County, Texas, and Maggie HODGES married Thursday in Clarendon, Texas.

S. M. MCCLANAHAN and Mollie JESSEE married Wednesday in Greenville, Texas.

H. A. BURCH and Jennie DEMOREE married Wednesday in Cleburne, Texas.

J. A. NORTON and Rodessa STRAWN married Thursday in Greenville, Texas. Rev. W. B. MCDANIEL officiated.

Sam COLLINS, aka Sam FIFER, was found guilty of the murder of his mistress near Jonesville, Texas. He was sentenced to death.

N. D. STRONG was killed Friday near Bonham Junction, Texas. He was run over by freight cars.

Births recorded at Tarrant County Clerk's office: a boy and a girl to Mr. and Mrs. _____ KEEL, Euless, on September 11; and a girl to Mr. and Mrs. J. HUFFMAN, Euless, on September 15.

Deaths recorded at Tarrant County Clerk's office: Emma Ferris CONDON, 5, died of congestion on September 7; Dave HOBBS, 46, residing in Fort Worth, died of phthisis on September 4; and Mrs. S. S. CARLE, 71, residing in Fort Worth, died of typhoid on September 16. No residence was listed for Emma CONDON.

Marriage licenses issued by Tarrant County Clerk's office: B. B. WHITEHEAD and M. S. MOBLEY, W. T. WILSON and Hattie CLOWERS, B. R. CHAPPELL and Florence V. TANT, Hierson LEWIS and Leona BRYANT, W. A. UTIS and Bertha TOMLIN, E. B. GOULD and Emlie L. PRESTON, P. L. PENDERGRASS and Lettie B. THOMAS, C. C. SHOFFITT and Grace L. GRAHAM, and W. J. COLBERT and Della MOSLEY.

Monday, September 19, 1904

Tom ROSE, 14, was struck by lightning and killed yesterday in Marietta, Indian Territory.

The body of Ben JOHNSON, 20, was found yesterday on the Texas and Pacific Railroad tracks west of Big Spring, Texas. He apparently ad been hit by a train. His father, Frank JOHNSON, who lives at Glade Water, Texas, was notified.

Henry MINK, about 22, was shot and killed Saturday near Smithville, Texas. A warrant was issued for Lord FOXWELL. MINK and FOXWELL had a dispute prior to the shooting.

Ruth STERNS, 2, died of lockjaw south of McKinney, Texas. No date was reported. She was the daughter of J. B. STERNS.

Mrs. J. Emma BEDECARRAX, 53, died Friday in Minerals Wells, Texas. She was the mother of Mrs. E. H. MCCRACKEN.

C. W. HAWKINS died at his home Saturday in Harrison County, Texas.

The funeral of D. MASSIE, who dropped dead in Sherman, Texas Thursday, was held there yesterday.

Justice of the Peace Tom MCDANIEL died Saturday in Greenville, Texas. He left a wife and several children.

Mrs. T. A. MOUNTS died Saturday near Vernon, Texas. She was buried in Bellevue, Texas. She was an early settler of Bellevue, living there 25 years. She was survived by a husband and several grown children.

Dr. B. B. WHITEHEAD and Mrs. M. S. MOBLEY married six weeks ago. No date or place was reported. The groom is from Rising Star, Texas. The bride is from Mineral Wells, Texas.

Ernest J. BREWER and Mary F. PERKINS married yesterday in Temple, Texas. Rev. T. J. SLOAN officiated.

Tuesday, September 20, 1904

Mike WHITE died of consumption Sunday in Ardmore, Indian Territory. He had been jailed on an arson charge.

J. F. YATES jailed at Mangum, Oklahoma Territory for the murder of William HUGHES in July, was released on $20,000 bond posted by 49 farmers in Greer County.

Henry HOLMES was sentenced to death yesterday in Columbus, Texas. HOLMES killed Emil BELL in Eagle Lake last winter. The execution was scheduled for November 25.

O. E. HEAD, 35, died in Fort Worth last night. He was a traveling salesman and the son of Captain W. O. HEAD. He is survived by his parents, wife, three children and siblings Walter, Porter, Robert and Maggie. The funeral will be today with burial in Oakwood Cemetery.

Julian Raymond STRAUGHON, an infant, died Sunday in Ennis, Texas. He was buried here yesterday. He was the son of Alderman J. R. STRAUGHON.

Mrs. L. R. LONGLEY, 53, died in Austin Sunday. Her funeral was yesterday.

Essie VARDEMAN, telephone manager at Plaster, Texas, died Sunday of typhoid. Her funeral was yesterday. The story was datelined Weatherford.

Wesley SANDERS, 22 and son of W. B. SANDERS of Mt. Calm, Texas, died August 17 in the Philippine Islands. He was killed while on duty with Company B, 17th Infantry, U.S. Army.

S. P. GREEN, 78 and a San Antonio resident, died in Victoria, Texas yesterday. He was the father of Ed GREEN of San Antonio, Will GREEN of Houston and Tom GREEN of Victoria.

J. S. DAVENPORT and Leada LOWE were married in Weatherford by Rev. W. M. BUNCH. The groom is from Thurber, Texas. The bride is from Parker County, Texas.

Henry HAYNES and Bessie NICHOLS married Sunday in Sherman, Texas. Elder J. H. BAXTER of the Christian Church officiated.

Charlie CARTER and Mabel MOORE married Sunday in Terrell, Texas. Rev. W. B. KENDALL officiated.

Dr. A. A. TERHUNE and Mrs. F. E. WHITSETT married in North Marshall Sunday. Justice of the Peace S. F. PERRY officiated.

Marriage licenses issued by Tarrant County Clerk's office: Robert M. CURRIE and Zue GULLEDGE, W. L. CORNWELL and Maggie HOWE, Henry P. MULER and Mary O'CONNOR, and R. B. BROWN and Lois SHIRLEY.

E. R. WOODWARD, 20, was killed in St. Louis, Missouri when he fell trying to get off a streetcar there. His remains will be shipped to his family Waco, Texas.

Wednesday, September 21, 1904

The paper for this date didn't appear on the microfilm.

Thursday, September 22, 1904

R. COOPER, F. N. LAWRENCE, W. M. GLOFF, D. F. MCDONALD and J. W. SAILS were killed in Port Arthur, Texas when lightning struck an oil storage tank causing an explosion and fire. COOPER, GLOFF, and LAWRENCE were each survived by a wife and three children. SAILS was from Dubuque, Iowa. MCDONALD lived in Beaumont and was survived by a wife and child.

George MEYER, 27, died of an overdose of morphine in Dallas yesterday.

Henry MERRITT was killed Tuesday in Belton, Texas when a sandbank collapsed on him. Dr. John MERRITT, his brother was also trapped but managed to escape. The funeral was yesterday in Hasley graveyard.

A baby boy weighing 10 ½ pounds was born to Mr. and Mrs. F. D. IRVING in Fort Worth Sunday. Mrs. IRVING is a daughter of Judge F. B. STANLEY.

B. P. MCCARTHY, 25, died in Fort Worth yesterday of lung disease. He was a brother of J. E. MCCARTHY. His body was sent to St. Louis.

Isom HAYES was sentenced to life in prison yesterday in Angleton, Texas. HAYES killed M. L. MIMPHER. MIMPHER kept a store near the county farm in Brazos County, Texas.

John MOTEN was jailed yesterday and charged with killing Tom LEE in a fight at Waco, Texas.

Julius ROBERTSON pled guilty in 17th District Court in Fort Worth yesterday to manslaughter for the death of Clark PEARY. ROBERTSON was sentenced to two years in prison.

Births recorded at Tarrant County Clerk's office: a girl to Mr. and Mrs. E. J. LAWRENCE, Fort Worth, on September 18; a boy to Mr. and Mrs. H. A. ZABEL, Fort Worth, on September 16; a girl to Mr. and Mrs. Clarence

BOYER, Fort Worth, on September 13; a girl to Mr. and Mrs. E. W. BOYER, Fort Worth, on September 12; a girl to Mr. and Mrs. S. MCHAM, Fort Worth, on September 14; a girl to Mr. and Mrs. J. G. ROGERS, Arlington, on September 19; a boy to Mr. and Mrs. O. R. ANDERSON, Fort Worth, on September 18; a boy to Mr. and Mrs. J. C. NINING, Fort Worth, on September 19; a girl to Mr. and Mrs. R. L. CRAFTON, Fort Worth, on September 17.

Marriage licenses issued by Tarrant County Clerk's office: R. C. BALDWIN and Miss L. M. MAYFIELD, E. L. HUFF and Mattie PURL, and Ben JOHNSON and Mattie ALDRIDGE.

The two years old daughter of Mr. and Mrs. M. V. HUDMAN died Monday southwest of Mineral Wells, Texas.

Mrs. Letha WARD, 81, died Monday in Temple, Texas. She was the mother of John WARD and an early settler in the city.

M. GOWEN, 75, died Monday in Peede, Texas.

Captain Thomas J. WILEY died Monday in Tyler, Texas. Burial was Wednesday in Oakwood Cemetery. He was a Confederate veteran and a Mason. He was survived by a wife and two grown sons.

Mrs. James CLARRY and her son Ross, 5, died of typhoid fever Sunday in Putnam, Texas. They died within 40 minutes of each other.

Gertrude SIMMONS, daughter of L. N. SIMMONS, died Sunday in Merkel, Texas. Her remains were shipped to Putnam, Texas. Her funeral was held Monday with burial in Putnam Cemetery.

The funeral for Amanda BULE, who died Monday, was held Tuesday in Hillsboro, Texas. She was buried in Milford.

Mrs. Orville T. BUNDY (nee Helen MCDANIEL), 22, died Monday in Milford, Texas. Her infant daughter died earlier in the day. Helen BUNDY was the elder daughter of J. K. MCDANIEL. Orville BUNDY is the son of Dr. Z. T. BUNDY.

Pearl NEWSOMS, 15, died of typhoid near Chambersville, Texas. She was the daughter of S. NEWSOMS.

W. B. SCOTT, 55, died of a stroke near Luela, Texas. The deceased was a farmer and native of Kentucky.

Mrs. Signora IRWIN, 54, died Tuesday in Sherman, Texas. Her funeral was conducted Wednesday by Rev. P. C. ARCHER.

The remains of Mrs. S. O'BANNON were buried in West Hill Cemetery in Sherman, Texas. She died Monday. Rev P. C. ARCHER officiated.

Miss Vesta JOHNSON, daughter of F. M. JOHNSON, died of appendicitis Tuesday. She was buried Wednesday in Milsaps, Texas.

Mrs. A. A. MURPHY, 72, died in Weatherford, Texas Wednesday. Her burial was yesterday in Cox Cemetery.

J. W. BAKER and Dollie BURROUGHS married Sunday south of Caddo Mills, Texas. Dr. H. B. PENDER officiated.

C. M. MOURSUND and Evelyn SMITH married in Longview, Texas Wednesday. Rev. W. R. HUDSON officiated.

Rudolph PATEK and Annie DELABOJ, both of Crisp, Texas, married in Ennis, Texas Tuesday.

Alanson WARNER, 71, and Mrs. Luca MCFARLAND, 59, married in Chandler, Indian Territory.

Zella SWANSCRAFT and J. L. BUEL married in San Marcos, Texas Tuesday.

Friday, September 23, 1904

Henry RUCKER, Thomas BROWNING and Ray MOORE were killed and Rufus BLEVINS, Charles WILSON and Lee CAREY fatally injured when a scaffold on which they were working collapsed three miles west of Siloam Springs, Arkansas in Indian Territory yesterday. They were among forty men on the scaffold when it collapsed. The men were working on a bridge across the Grand River. Most of the workmen lived in Grove, Indian Territory.

Charles D. HENRICHSON committed suicide in Laredo, Texas Wednesday night. He took strychnine. He was a brother of George E. HENDRICHSON.

Two children of Mat EDWARDS were struck by lightning and killed while picking cotton near Athens, Texas Wednesday. The children were a boy aged 6 and a girl aged 8. Neither child was named in the article.

Lillian Belle BARFIELD, 13 months, died of catarrhal fever in Ensign, Texas Wednesday.

Mrs. H. C. ANDERSON died in Dallas Monday night.

W. H. PATTON died recently in Hereford, Texas. He was a former resident of Mineral Wells, Texas.

Mrs. John WOODS, 58, died in Terrell, Texas Wednesday.

Maggie MINGS, 26, of Cedar Grove, Texas, died in Terrell, Texas yesterday. Her remains were shipped to Cedar Grove for burial.

William A. PHILLIPS, 20, died from dropsy in Texarkana Wednesday.

J. R. ELAM died near Cleburne, Texas Wednesday.

The little daughter of Mr. and Mrs. T. M. DOWNEY died in Cleburne, Texas Wednesday.

John COOK, son of A. B. COOK, died in Ardmore, Indian Territory yesterday.

Cyrus G. KEEN, 38, of Wynnewood, Indian Territory, died Wednesday. He was buried there yesterday under the auspices of the Masons. He was the chairman of the Republican Executive Committee.

Walter GOLDSTON and Burlie JACKS married Sunday in Clarendon, Texas.

Professor William GREEN, of Denton, Texas, and Lucy MELTON, of Allen, Texas, married Wednesday in McKinney, Texas.

J. L. STEAKLEY and Nora E. CROZIER married in Cleburne on September 14.

Will PRICE and Ouida WILLIAMSON married in Temple, Texas Wednesday. The bride is the daughter of Mr. and Mrs. P. D. WILLIAMSON.

Harry DOISON, of New York City, and Mae MORRIS, of Greenville, Texas, married in Dallas Tuesday.

J. P. MATTOX and Irene YOUNG, daughter of Rev. F. E. YOUNG, married by Greenville, Texas Wednesday. Rev. F. L. YOUNG officiated.

The re-trial of J. H. DENT, charged with the murder of John WILSON two years ago, is underway in Fort Worth.

Births recorded at Tarrant County Clerk's office: a boy to Mr. and Mrs. M. WALDRUP, Tarrant County, on September 4; a girl to Mr. and Mrs. D. S. WINDLE, Fort Worth, on September 17; a girl to Mr. and Mrs. J. B. EARL, Arlington Heights, on September 19 and a boy to Mr. and Mrs. A. CHAUCHAU, no place listed, on September 14.

Marriage licenses issued by Tarrant County Clerk's office: J. H. STONE and Nona MULLIGAN; W. RATLIFF and Lizzie GRAHAM; Hugh WILBANKS and Mae Alberta THOMAS; J. R. FRANKLIN and Cyrena POTTS; and Perry WHITE and Annie GLOVER.

Saturday, September 24, 1904

Tom WOOD was convicted yesterday in Pond Creek, Indian Territory of killing Herman KIERSTING in Enid, Indian Territory last fall.

Enid SHERMAN was killed in Houston when he fell from the McKee Street Bridge yesterday.

Conductor W. O. SORRELLS was killed when he fell between two moving freight cars between El Paso and Lordsberg, Texas. He planned to meet his wife, who was returning from a trip, in Lordsberg.

The body of J. R. ANDERSON, 28, was found on the Texas and Pacific Railroad tracks near Dallas yesterday. He sustained a massive head injury which caused his death. It was thought he had been hit by a train.

Rev. Charles LAXTON, 87, died in McKinney, Texas Thursday. He was a pioneer Methodist minister.

The two years old baby of Otey KIRKPTRICK died yesterday in Ennis, Texas. Its remains will be shipped to Telico, Texas to be buried beside its mother who died a few weeks ago.

Mrs. W. L. DAVIS died at her home in Marshall, Texas yesterday.

Mrs. N. E. HALL, 43, died Thursday at the residence of J. J. A. SAUNDERS, her father, near Greenville, Texas. She left a husband and three children.

Charles K. COLLUM and Lillie RANDOLPH married Tuesday in Greenville, Texas. Rev. J. F. JENKINS officiated.

Mat EASON and Ellen REEVES, both of Boyce, Texas, married in Ennis, Texas yesterday. Rev. J. S. ELLIOTT officiated.

Will NOBLES and Katie MCGRATH married in Youngstown, Ohio last Monday. Both lived in Marshall, Texas before the wedding.

Thomas CATON and Ida GOLDEN married in Corsicana, Texas Thursday. Rev. G. C. TAYLOR officiated.

Roy CONNALLY and Clara EDWARDS married in Waxahachie, Texas Thursday. Rev. J. C. SMITH officiated.

J. H. DENT was found guilty of second degree murder for killing John WILSON about two years ago. He was sentenced in Fort Worth to five years in prison yesterday. The sentence was the shortest one possible for the crime committed. DENT had previously been convicted of the crime and sentenced to forty years; however, that conviction was overturned by the Court of Criminal Appeals.

The marriage of C. B. BALDWIN and Miss L. M. MAYFIELD took place Tuesday in Fort Worth. Rev. J. D. YOUNG officiated.

Births recorded at Tarrant County Clerk's office: twin boys to Mr. and Mrs. B. MASTERS, Tarrant County, on September 15; and a boy to Mr. and Mrs. T. J. GEE, North Fort Worth, on September 11.

Deaths recorded at Tarrant County Clerk's office: Verner LASTER, 3, residing in Grapevine, died on September 12 with no cause listed.

Marriage licenses issued by Tarrant County Clerk's office: E. A. FERNANDEZ and Fay JAEGER.

Sunday, September 25, 1904

City Marshal Wesley TRAYLOR of Texarkana was indicted and jailed Friday for the murder of Tom JONES on the Iron Mountain train last week.

Tom ANGLES was killed in Weir, Indian Territory, according to a telephone message received by the US Marshal in Muskogee, Indian Territory.

Mrs. H. E. NORTH died last Friday at her home in Fall River, Kansas. She was a sister of W. F. BECK, a merchant in Marshall, Texas.

Mrs. Ella ADKINS, of Trimble, Tennessee, died in Texarkana Friday night. Her remains were shipped to Trimble.

D. E. NORCROSS and Mrs. Amelia J. WADE married Friday night in Marshall, Texas. Rev. J. B. K. SPAIN officiated.

Hobart FRONHOFF, of College Hill, Texas, and Texana BEARD, of San Augustine, Texas, married in Texarkana Friday.

Monday, September 26, 1904

Bossie GARRETT, 13, died in Smithfield, Texas yesterday. She was daughter of W. M. GARRETT. Burial will be today in Smithfield Cemetery.

John A. DANKIEFS, 53, died in Handley, Texas yesterday. He left a wife, a daughter, and two sons. His burial will be today in the cemetery near Handley.

Lizzie BECK, 22, died Saturday in the asylum in Terrell, Texas. Her remains were shipped to Timson, Texas.

Oscar Eugene HEAD, 34, died last Monday in Fort Worth. Survivors included Lulu Cox HEAD, his wife, and sons, Carroll, Eugene and Adrian. He was a traveling salesman who became ill in Galveston, just a week before his death.

Tom WOOD was declared guilty of manslaughter in Pond Creek, Indian Territory. The trail resulted from the death of Herman KIERSTING in Enid, Indian Territory, about a year ago.

Mrs. W. F. BENNETT, visiting her father, C. C. BROWN, in Yukon, Oklahoma Territory, received word that her husband had been killed by a burglar in their home in Thompson, Illinois.

Tuesday, September 27, 1904

Louis BROWN, charged with the murders of Walter RICHARDSON and Moses PETTIGREW in Ada, Indian Territory secured a change of venue to Paris, Texas.

Abner LAMBERT, 65, was found dead in El Paso, Texas yesterday.

Ernest Beverly CLAYPOOL, 8 months, died yesterday in Fort Worth. The funeral will be today. Rev. R. R. HAMLIN will officiate.

E. W. LEWIS, of Deming, New Mexico Territory, and Mabel BONNER, of Weatherford, Texas, married in Fort Worth last night. Dr. Alonzo MONK officiated. Mrs. R. B. CRAFT of Fort Worth is the bride's sister. The couple left for Deming and their new home last night.

T. A. BRYSON and Miss Jimmie HANKS married Sunday in Terrell, Texas. Rev. W. B. KENDALL officiated.

O. S. ANDERSON and Ollie BRACKEN married in Dallas a few days ago.

Abb SMITH and Ola WILLIAMSON, of Coolidge, Texas, married in Corsicana, Texas Sunday. Judge A. B. GRAHAM officiated.

Mrs. Sallie CHERRY, wife of H. H. CHERRY, died in Weatherford, Texas yesterday. Burial will be tomorrow.

Frank STANSEL, 72, died near Ennis, Texas Sunday.

The infant daughter of Mr. and Mrs. J. G. WALKER died in Marshall, Texas Sunday.

Mrs. M. M. HALL, 74, died in Elmo, Texas Sunday.

Mrs. Willie Hill STOVALL, 23, died in Terrell, Texas Sunday.

Aaron DAVIS died in Palestine, Texas recently. He left a wife and four daughters, including Mrs. Jake COHEN of Cleburne, Texas.

Births recorded at Tarrant County Clerk's office: a girl to Mr. and Mrs. C. N. WEBB, Fort Worth, on September 23; a boy to Mr. and Mrs. Thomas O'DONNELL, Fort Worth, on September 24; a boy to Mr. and Mrs. J. L. GODFREY, Kennedale, on September 22; and a boy to Mr. and Mrs. J. E. WILSON, Kennedale, on September 20.

Deaths recorded at Tarrant County Clerk's office: Harvey TUCKER, infant, residing in Fort Worth, died of diphtheria on September 25.

Marriage licenses issued by Tarrant County Clerk's office: H. L. WAGONER and Mary HARRIS; L. E. TURPEN and Ella YERBY; W. H. R. MCFADIN and Ida BIRDSONG; C. R. VOSS and Lillie B. WATSON; Ralph STINSON and Miss S. H. BRAZELTON; Henry F. PERKINS and Alma BROWNE; E. W. LEWIS and Mabel BONNER.

Wednesday, September 28, 1904

Dick BELL was charged with killing Boots GARDNER in a fight in Smith County, Texas. BELL was jailed.

Mercario ALOCORN was convicted in Coleman, Texas of second degree murder in the death of Horace JARRETT last October.

Mrs. Jessie MUMPOWER committed suicide in Elk City, Oklahoma Territory Monday. She was the wife of Bart MUMPOWER.

Howard MCDONALD died in Oklahoma City, Oklahoma Territory Saturday. He left a wife and six children.

Luther RAY, a small boy, was smothered to death near his home in Pleasant Mound, Indian Territory. He was in a cotton wagon when a load of cotton was accidentally dumped on him.

William SCOTT died in Fort Worth yesterday morning. Born in Kent, England in 1844, he was the brother of Fred T. SCOTT of Fort Worth, Henry SCOTT of Topeka, Kansas, and Charles SCOTT of Kent, England. The funeral was yesterday with burial in Oakwood Cemetery.

Ed NICHOLS was killed when he was overcome with fumes and fell to the bottom of a newly dug well yesterday. The story was datelined Guthrie, Oklahoma Territory but no place of death was reported.

B. C. MCCLELLAN and Pearl THORNTON married in McKinney, Texas Monday.

Miss Del BAILEY and A. H. COUNTS married in Pittsburg, Texas Sunday.

Robert J. MASSEY and Vicie ALREAD married in Terrell, Texas Monday. Rev. J. J. COOK officiated.

Edgar W. JONES and Frances KAUFMAN married in Guthrie, Oklahoma Territory yesterday. Jones is a recent Congressional candidate recovering from a serious illness.

George J. PARKS, brother of Harry PARKS, and Johnnie GILBERT married in Waxahachie, Texas Monday. Rev. J. C. SMITH officiated.

C. A. BRUTON and Ella MCCORD, of Italy, Texas, married in Waxahachie, Texas yesterday.

J. W. WILLIS and Willie REEVES married in Ennis, Texas Sunday. Justice of the Peace H. R. STOVALL officiated.

Dr. H. R. MCMULLINS, of Green, Texas, and Willie STIRMAN married in Ennis, Texas yesterday. Rev. R. R. STRIMAN, brother of the bride, officiated.

John E. ELLIS died of appendicitis yesterday in Paris, Texas. He was a former journalist currently employed as a bookkeeper.

The infant of Mr. and Mrs. J. L. MEADLEY died in Texarkana Monday.

Charles HOLDEN, 42, died in Glenn Monday. He was brother of Albert HOLDEN and Mrs. W. D. BRANNON of Fort Worth. (Note: the complier couldn't determine the location of Glenn)

Births recorded at Tarrant County Clerk's office: a girl to Mr. and Mrs. W. I. BIGGERS, Grapevine, on August 15; a girl to Mr. and Mrs. W. T. POWELL, Grapevine, on September 10; a boy to Mr. and Mrs. R. W. PATTON, Grapevine, on August 20; a girl to Mr. and Mrs. G. H. MCPHERSON, Shiloh, on August 9; a girl to Mr. and Mrs. C. W. WOOLSEY, North Fort Worth, on August 3; a girl to Mr. and Mrs. George FETTERS, Enon, on September 22; a boy to Mr. and Mrs. J. W. JOHNSON, Enon, on September 19; a girl to Mr. and Mrs. D. SMALLEY, Hurst, on September 17; a girl to Mr. and Mrs. W. R. MOLIERE, North Fort Worth, on September 14; a boy to Mr. and Mrs. Charles BISHOP, Fort Worth, on September 25; a girl to Mr. and Mrs. J. A. COLE, Fort Worth, on September 26; a girl to Mr. and Mrs. J. E. DUKE, Grapevine, on September 5; and a boy to Mr. and Mrs. J. W. MCMURRAY, Grapevine, on August 16.

Deaths recorded at Tarrant County Clerk's office: Viola TOMBLIN, 1, residing in Grapevine, died of inanition on August 22; James MOONEY, 47, residing near Grapevine, died of a ruptured aneurism on September 13; and an infant of Mr. and Mrs. SMALLEY residing in Hurst, died on September 21 with no cause listed.

Marriage licenses issued by Tarrant County Clerk's office: H. C. COLEMAN and Alice VINCENT.

Thursday, September 29, 1904

Captain A. A. HUTCHINSON, 70 was killed in Mullen, Texas Tuesday night. He was hit by a train at the depot there. He was an old settler of Brown County.

Frank SWEET died in Tahlequah, Indian Territory yesterday.

Hirschel MAPLES died in Tahlequah, Indian Territory Tuesday.

John FICKE, 14, was killed in Chandler, Oklahoma Territory when his horse fell on him.

E. L. GREENE and Lorean SEAY married in Dallas Tuesday.

Births recorded at Tarrant County Clerk's office: a boy to Mr. and Mrs. Andre FOURNIER, Fort Worth, on September 26; a boy to Mr. and Mrs. Tom DICKSON, Hurst, on September 21; and a girl to Mr. and Mrs. A. H. JOHNSON, Fort Worth, on September 25.

Deaths recorded at Tarrant County Clerk's office: William SCOTT, 60, residing in Fort Worth died of cerebral anemia with no date listed.

Marriage licenses issued by Tarrant County Clerk's office: E. J. GRAY and Lettie GRAVES; L. E. ROBERTS and Mrs. T. H. COOK; Rufus PUTMAN and Jennie BILSON; S. K. GRAMMER and Pierce RIDGEWAY; A. A. HARPER and Maola BUTLER; John NELSON and Alice MITCHELL.

Mary Alice VINCENT and Harry COLEMAN married in Fort Worth yesterday. Rev. S. G. INMAN officiated. The bride is the daughter of Mr. and Mrs. J. M. VINCENT. The couple left for Dalhart, Texas, their new home.

Friday, September 30, 1904

News of the death of Lem STEWART reached Cleburne, Texas yesterday. STEWART was a merchant in Rainbow, Texas who was killed by an unknown man there. S. W. (Shirley) STEWART was wounded by an unknown man in Rainbow, Texas. The shooting took place when STEWART tried to settle a dispute between Lem STEWART and a man who was working for him.

R. K. MURPHEY died of lockjaw near Nursery, Texas Wednesday. He was a farmer.

Capt. E. P. JERVEY of the US Army and Katherine Weagley GRANT married in Oklahoma City, Oklahoma Territory Wednesday.

Frank ZAPLETAL and Fannie BROWN married in Waxahachie, Texas Wednesday.

S. R. BRINSON, a railroad engineer, and Miss Willie DANIEL married in Longview, Texas Wednesday. Rev. C. JACKLEY officiated.

T. B. WILLIAMS and Bertha MERDUTH married Wednesday in Sherman, Texas. Rev. Dr. E. S. CLYIC, president of Austin College, officiated.

Ernest HEAD and Edith C. WYLIE, both of Fort Smith, Arkansas, married in Sherman, Texas yesterday. Rev. J. H. FULLER officiated.

Asa S. MATTHEWS and Daisy NEAL married in Weatherford, Texas yesterday. Rev. A. P. SMITH officiated. The bride is the daughter of Mr. and Mrs. W. K. NEAL.

Joseph HERALD and Rebecca NOSSEK married Sunday in Greenville, Texas. The marriage took place in the home of Ed SCHIFF.

Otis MAYFIELD and Jennie CULLUM married in Mount Lebanon, Tennessee recently and are now living in Ennis, Texas.

R. S. STYLES and Vera VANSICKLE married Sunday morning in Greenville, Texas. Rev. H. T. MONEY officiated.

Joe JECNESMEC and Mary BELL married in Temple, Texas Wednesday.

William K. WARD, about 45, died in Mineral Wells, Texas Wednesday. The cause of death was dropsy. His remains were shipped to San Saba, Texas for burial.

J. M. ELLER died Tuesday in Parker, Texas. His funeral will be tomorrow. Knights of Pythias will conduct the funeral. He was a brother of J. A. ELLER of Tennessee and the postmaster of Parker.

Mrs. John BROWN died in childbirth near Weatherford, Texas Wednesday. She was a widow. John BROWN died six weeks ago due to blood poisoning.

Willie BAXTER, 11, died of congestion in Telico, Texas yesterday.

Joe WILSON, 15, died near Burleson, Texas Tuesday. Burial was in Marystown Cemetery. He was the son of Mr. and Mrs. Tyler WILSON.

Tom COX, 9, died Monday night in Greenville, Texas. He was the son of Mr. and Mrs. E. M. COX.

John L. BELL and Dorothy ROGERS, of Dallas, married in Fort Worth last night. Dr. Luther LITTLE officiated.

Dr. J. H. KEENER and Mrs. Jessie SHAW, both of Dallas, married in Fort Worth. Dr. Luther LITTLE officiated.

Mary JACKSON, 10, was struck by lightning and killed while picking cotton near Georgetown, Texas Wednesday. She was buried in Austin.

Births recorded at Tarrant County Clerk's office: a boy to Mr. and Mrs. M. T. CLOWDUS, near Mansfield, on September 16; a girl to Mr. and Mrs. C. A. MCMEANS, near Mansfield, on September 15; a girl to Mr. and Mrs. E. W. KEITH, Fort Worth, on September 26; a boy to Mr. and Mrs. W. F. ALBRITTON, Birdville, on Sept 27; a girl to Mr. and Mrs. J. L. DUNLAP, Fort Worth, on September 27; and a boy to Mr. and Mrs. W. H. LOGAN, Fort Worth, on September 28.

Deaths recorded at Tarrant County Clerk's office: Ira WHITEHURST, 8 months, residing in Fort Worth, died of enterocolitis on September 27; and Emil MAYER, no age listed, residing in Fort Worth, died from diabetes on September 4.

October, 1904

Saturday, October 1, 1904

P. G. ROSE, a freight brakeman on the Texas and Pacific Railroad, was killed Thursday when he fell from a train between Greenwood and Easkom, Texas. He was run over by the train after the fall. His wife and child will arrive tonight in Marshall, Texas.

C. A. FRAZIER and Annie STUART married in Lone Oak, Texas.

John H. WADLEY and Hallie BOYCE married Thursday in Boyce, Texas. The bride is the daughter of Captain W. A. BOYCE. The groom is from Massey, Indian Territory.

W. L. FOREMAN and Miss Eddie ALEXANDER married in Temple, Texas yesterday.

Bessie CHILSOM and Harry HUNTINGTON married in El Reno, Oklahoma Territory yesterday. The groom is from Alexandria, Nebraska.

J. H. HIGHSMITH, from Hunt County, and Mrs. Edna ROWLETTE, of Carthage, Texas, married Thursday in Longview, Texas.

John BELL, of Weatherford, Texas, and Dorothy ROGERS, of Sulphur Springs, Texas, married in Fort Worth Thursday.

Mrs. Virginia E. BAERTICHT died Thursday in North Marshall, Texas. She was the wife of Al G. BAERTICHT and the mother of two small children. She was the daughter of Mrs. V. E. COLEMAN.

Bob STANLEY was buried in the Cleburne Cemetery yesterday. He died in Del Rio, Texas.

Al G. MOSELEY died yesterday near Corsicana, Texas. He was a carpenter and a member of the Woodmen of the World.

Pedro CASTRO drowned in a railroad oil tank in San Antonio yesterday.

Colonel Ed SACRA, Sr., died in Purcell, Indian Territory on September 19. He was the father of Mrs. Duke GOODMAN of Fort Worth.

Samuel Edward FLYNN, Jr., 6 months, died Thursday in Fort Worth. His funeral was yesterday in Fort Worth. Immediately afterward, his parents left for Altheimer, Arkansas, their former home.

R. A. BLACKWELL died in Bloomington, Illinois. He was the father of Mrs. H. H. FAVER of Fort Worth. The date of death was not reported.

Word was received in Seguin that Andreas ROBLES has been killed by a gunshot wound on a farm outside Seguin, Texas.

The infant child of W. A. BROWN, of Fishville, Texas, was found dead in its bed near Georgetown, Texas. The child smothered while the parents picked cotton.

Sunday, October 2, 1904

Don F. TURNER was shot and killed yesterday in Marble Falls, Texas. Ed FARMER, an employee of Farmer's cotton gin, was believed to be the killer.

Marriage licenses issued by Tarrant County Clerk's office: Arthur BROCK and Dezar ISHAM; James E. SKINNER and Ruth BARNETT; A. L. WHITE and Miss E. D. ROGERS; B. G. SCHMIDT and Anna MILLIKEN; Jessie I. FIELDS and Mary L. SULLIVAN; and H. ALBERT and Sarah WOLF.

Births recorded at Tarrant County Clerk's office: a boy to Mr. and Mrs. C. V. WILLIE, Grapevine, on September 14; a girl to Mr. and Mrs. Noah V. GUESS, Grapevine, on September 14; a boy to Mr. and Mrs. J. H. WILLIAMS, Dove, on September 15; a girl to Mr. and Mrs. G. W. EVANS, Grapevine, on September 23; a boy to Mr. and Mrs. Harry P. MCINTIRE, near Grapevine, on September 29; a boy to Mr. and Mrs. Bose FILLEY, Grapevine, on

September 13; a girl to Mr. and Mrs. Ewing HUDDEN, Grapevine, on September 14; a girl to Mr. and Mrs. John MCCRORY, Grapevine, on September 30; a boy to Mr. and Mrs. Lee WILSON, Grapevine, on September 29; and a boy to Mr. and Mrs. J. MARTIN, Grapevine, on September 11.

Deaths recorded at Tarrant County Clerk's office: Robert MCCARVER, 50, residing in Grapevine, died of uremic poisoning on September 29.

John DOWITY, a farmer, was shot and killed yesterday in a saloon in Marshall, Texas.

Miss Berta JONES, North Fort Worth, died Thursday and was buried that afternoon. She was daughter of Mr. and Mrs. J. W. JONES.

William H. ROSS, of Roland, Texas, was found dead on the porch of his father's home Thursday.

Frances GORDON and C. J. SUTTON married Thursday in Texarkana.

Monday, October 3, 1904

J. H. STONE, and Nona MILLIGAN married yesterday in Poetry, Texas. The bride was a resident of Poetry while the groom lived in Elmo, Texas.

F. B. JORDAN and Mrs. S. J. POSEY married yesterday in Ennis, Texas. The bride is a resident of Ennis while the groom comes from Terrell, Texas.

W. E. AYERS and Gussie NORTHCRAFT married yesterday in San Antonio. Rev. A. J. HARRIS officiated.

J. G. GILLESPIE and Mary ERWIN married yesterday in Ennis, Texas. The bride lived in Ennis while the groom was a resident of Dallas.

James HUNTER and Marie LINDSAY married Saturday in Terrell, Texas. They both lived in College Mound, Texas.

Sam COPE died Saturday in Abilene, Texas. He died after an operation for appendicitis. His remains were taken to the Lawn community in Taylor County.

Mrs. James WILLIAMS died yesterday in Corsicana, Texas. A husband and five children survive her.

Dr. MCLENAHAN, 67, died Saturday in Ocnaville, Texas. He was a pioneer settler of Bell County. His given name was not reported.

John ROBBINS, 22, died yesterday in Texarkana.

Willis E. BELL, 28, died from swamp fever Saturday in Texarkana. He was a section foreman on the Kansas City Southern Railroad at Witton, Texas. His wife survives him.

J. H. DIXON, 79, was hit by a train and instantly killed yesterday in Daughter, Indian Territory.

Tommy WOODS, 12, accidentally shot himself Friday in Handley, Texas. He died the next day. He was a brother of William WOODS.

S. W. STEWART, who was shot in Rainbow, Texas, last Tuesday, died Saturday. Mose ARNOLD, the alleged killer, was arrested in Bosque County and jailed.

Gilbert BERCOW, 32, died in Houston yesterday. He fell from a crowded streetcar and was run over by the trailer on the car.

The funeral of Don F. TURNER, who was killed Saturday, was held in Marble Falls, Texas. Ed FARMER, the accused killer, escaped.

W. G. BARNHILL, wounded Wednesday by Bill ANDERSON in Walter, Oklahoma Territory, died of his injuries Sunday. ANDERSON is in jail.

Tuesday, October 4, 1904

John LYONS, 35, was killed yesterday in a boiler explosion at the Swift and Company plant in North Fort Worth. He was a steamfitter. His remains will be buried in the Catholic cemetery. He is survived by a wife and several children.

H. Parker BLAIN and Eula FUGATE married Sunday in Terrell, Texas. Rev. J. J. CLARK, pastor of First Methodist Church, officiated.

Thomas KILGORE and Ruth CRAWFORD married Sunday in Burleson, Texas.

John MOWLAND and Vida Maude ALLEN married Sunday in Ennis, Texas. Rev. S. H. SLAUGHTER officiated.

H. C. SMITH and Mary OWENRev. married Sunday in Waxahachie, Texas. Chalmers MCPHERSON officiated.

Hollis MILLER, who lives in Weatherford, Texas, and Grace ROBERTSON, who lives in Sulphur Springs, Texas, married in Fort Worth on October 19 [sic]. Rev. Alonzo MONK officiated.

Alonzo WILLIAMS, a farmer living near Carter, six miles west of Springtown, Texas, died last week.

W. A. HODGE, a former constable in Waxahachie, Texas, died Saturday in Maypearl, Texas. He was buried Sunday in Auburn, Texas.

Mrs. W. P. ALEXANDER died Sunday in Hillsboro, Texas. She was burned Saturday there. Rev. W. B. MCGARITY preached her funeral yesterday. She was buried in the new city cemetery.

A body found several days ago in St. Louis was identified yesterday as being that of Mark ADAMS of Fort Worth.

Births recorded at Tarrant County Clerk's office: a girl to Mr. and Mrs. Charles HYSMITH, Keller, on October 2; a girl to Mr. and Mrs. J. H. CROFT, Fort Worth, on September 29; a boy to Mr. and Mrs. William SCOTT, Fort Worth, on September 26; a boy to Mr. and Mrs. E. ANDREWS, Fort Worth, on September 30; a girl to Mr. and Mrs. William DAVIS, Fort Worth, on September 29; and a boy to Mr. and Mrs. Henry BORDERS Weatherford, Fort Worth, on September 30.

Marriage licenses issued by Tarrant County Clerk's office: H. H. MILLER and Grace ROBERTSON, Tom HARGROVES and Tennie MCMASTERS, and Daniel WYRICH and Maude Stanley MOFFITT.

Wednesday, October 5, 1904

J. A. STREET and Lula EMERY married Monday in Mineral Wells, Texas. The groom is from Tucumcari, New Mexico Territory.

James DOUGLAS and Florence FIORE, both of Wetumpka, Indian Territory, married Monday in Sherman, Texas. Elder J. H. BAXTER officiated.

John H. ROBERTSON and Viola HARRISON married Sunday in the KATY Depot in Greenville, Texas. Rev. J. W. HOLSAPPLE officiated.

Eulalie Blanche AVERITT, 10, died Sunday in Concord, Texas. She was daughter of Mr. and Mrs. D. C. AVERITT.

Short CLARK died of black jaundice yesterday at his home in Birdston, Texas.

Conductor PATTERSON, injured in a wreck on the Cotton Belt near Pittsburg, Texas, died Monday at the company hospital in Texarkana. No given name was reported.

F. H. MANNING killed A. RIDDLE in a Dallas saloon yesterday. RIDDLE worked as a bartender and MANNING as a porter in the saloon.

Word has been received in Dallas of the death of Mrs. Irene McFadden WESTERVELT in Tacumbara, Mexico. She was a former Dallas resident.

Barnett GIBBS died in Dallas yesterday. He was a prominent business and political leader in Texas. His death resulted from stomach, kidney and liver conditions. Rev. Percy R. KNICKERBOCKER will conduct the funeral services today. Pall bearers will be W. H. GASTON, W. ILLINGSWORTH, B. C. AYERS, Byron T. BARRY, A. J. BROWN, J. H. TRAYLOR, Jules E. SCHNEIDER, Royal A. FERRIS, John N. SIMPSON, T. J. FREEMAN, Alex SANGER, and J. B. WILSON. Burial will be in Oakwood Cemetery. GIBBS was born in Yazoo City, Mississippi on March 12, 1850. He came to Texas in 1872 and served as Dallas City Attorney, Texas State Senator and Lieutenant Governor of Texas. He is survived by his wife Mrs. Sallie Haynes GIBBS, son G. Wiley GIBBS, daughters Mrs. S. E. MILLIKAN and Dorsey GIBBS, age 4, brother General W. B. GIBBS of Yazoo City. He was the son of Judge O. D. GIBBS and Sallie Dorsey GIBBS.

S. P. LEWIS, a resident of Lovena, Texas, was killed Tuesday in Waco, Texas. He was a victim of a runaway accident.

The two year old child of Baxter NEAL, living in Lovena, Texas, died yesterday of scalds. The child pulled a plate of boiling cabbage from a table onto itself.

Mrs. B. S. MUMPOWER took her own life in Elk City, Oklahoma Territory. She was despondent over ill health since the birth of her child two years ago. No date was reported.

Miss Louise NOBLE, 60, living near Chandler, Texas, took her own life this week. She took strychnine.

A. H. ANDERSON was shot and killed by one of his renters in Sinclair, Texas Saturday.

Robert E. MORGAN and Mabel MAIER married yesterday in Fort Worth. Rev. R. R. HAMLIN performed the ceremony. The couple left immediately for Decatur, Texas, where they will make their home.

The trial of Andrew CROWS of Elk City for the murder of Hedricks LONG is underway in 17th District Court in Fort Worth. It is expected to go to the jury today.

Births recorded at Tarrant County Clerk's office: a girl to Mr. and Mrs. W. E. HANKINS, Fort Worth, on September 16; a boy to Mr. and Mrs. William PORTER, Riverside, on September 30; a boy to Mr. and Mrs. T. J. ELKINS, Haslet, on September 10; a girl to Mr. and Mrs. L. RINGOLD, Fort Worth, on September 25; a girl to Mr. and Mrs. W. R. MITCHELL, Rosen Heights, on September 29; a girl to Mr. and Mrs. Chancy COROS, Glenwood, on September 27; a boy to Mr. and Mrs. Charles SMALL, Fort Worth, on September 6.

Deaths recorded at Tarrant County Clerk's office: W. W. SMITH, 35, residing in Arlington, with no cause listed, on September 28.

Marriage licenses issued by Tarrant County Clerk's office: E. MOORE and Mabel MAIER, James E. RICHARDS and Mary W. COPELAND, E. G. MARTIN and Anna E. BENNETT.

Thursday, October 6, 1904

The case of the State of Texas v. T. E. BELL, charged with the murder of N. T. SHATLEY, in Collin County, is underway in McKinney, Texas.

Mrs. Louise SMITH died Tuesday in Dallas. She was a sister of Dr. E. G. PATTON. Three sons survive her.

W. W. JONES testified at an inquest in San Antonio about the death of H. S. ELWELL. He stated the death of ELWELL resulted from a quarrel in the courthouse over a business deal between ELWELL and G. M. CHITTIM. ELWELL's body may be shipped to Sheboygan, Wisconsin. R. ELWELL, the deceased's brother lives there.

J. W. BARR, 58, died Tuesday at his home in Kingston, Texas. His wife and five children survive.

Ada CROUCH died yesterday near Heldenheimer, Texas. She was the daughter of Mr. and Mrs. Wade CROUCH.

Mary TERRELL, 53, died yesterday at her home in Seguin, Texas. She was the widow of Henry TERRELL. Survivors include sons Ed TERRELL of San Marcos, and James of Los Canera, Mexico, daughters Mrs. CAROLAN of San Marcos and Mrs. LANGLOIS of Waelder. Mary TERRELL was daughter of D. C. BLEDSOE. She was buried in san Geronimo Cemetery today.

Mrs. Patrick GLENNING, 70, died Tuesday in Tarpon, Texas. She was buried in Rockport, Texas yesterday. She formerly lived in Aransas Pass, Texas.

Dr. W. F. SEALE, 75, died yesterday in Corsicana, Texas. Funeral services will be today with Masonic honors.

Kirby SMITH, 1, died Sunday in Haley, Texas. He was the son of Mr. and Mrs. A. K. SMITH.

F. E. MCLARTY and Bessie SMITH married yesterday in Whitney, Texas. The bride is a sister of Mrs. W. T. HERRICK.

F. E. WILLIAMS, of Baird, Texas, and Camille TOWNSEND, of Ennis, Texas, married in Waxahachie, Texas. Rev. J. C. SMITH, pastor of the Cumberland Presbyterian Church, officiated.

Milton FORE and Alise ROBERTS married Sunday in Gilmer, Texas.

Marriage license issued by Tarrant County Clerk's office: A. H. DAVIDSON and Grace E. BRECKENRIDGE.

Births recorded at Tarrant County Clerk's office: a girl to Mr. and Mrs. J. B. MORGAN, North Fort Worth, on October 4; a boy to Mr. and Mrs. J. W. REDDY, Mansfield, on October 3; a boy to Mr. and Mrs. C. C. PEFFER, Fort Worth, on October 2; and a girl to Mr. and Mrs. Lee HOLVICK, Mansfield, on October 2.

Anna BENNETT and Edward MARTIN married in Fort Worth yesterday. The bride is a daughter of Mr. and Mrs. G. E. BENNETT. The couple will live in Amarillo.

Alfred DAVIDSON and Grace E. BRECKENRIDGE, a resident of Port Huron, Michigan, married in Fort Worth yesterday. The groom is a son of Mr. and Mrs. Sam DAVIDSON. The couple will live in Chickasha, Indian Territory.

Friday, October 7, 1904

The trial of H. F. MANNING, accused of killing A. RIDDLE, will begin in Dallas next Thursday.

H. C. WATSON, between 55 – 60 years of age, was shot and killed Wednesday in Prairieville, Texas. His son, Ben WATSON, was arrested. The two men fought over a debt and the division of a crop. WATSON's remains were sent to Seagoville for burial.

The citizens of Kaufman are gathering a reward for information about the murder of Joe SPENCE there last Friday.

Marriage licenses issued by Tarrant County Clerk's office: William F. REMINGTON and Mrs. Catherine B. BROWN, J. W. AUSTIN and Mrs. Sarah MONNEY, George L. DuB_____ and Helen F. CLARK, M. E. WRIGHTS and Minnie KNOX, Thomas COUGHLIN, Jr. and Anna HUTCHINSON.

Births recorded at Tarrant County Clerk's office: a boy to Mr. and Mrs. William DUNCAN, Fort Worth, on September 30; a girl to Mr. and Mrs. C. E. DOTSON, Fort Worth, on October 4; a boy to Mr. and Mrs. Harry DUKE, Fort Worth, on October 2; a girl to Mr. and Mrs. William L. SYKES, Fort Worth, on September 24; a boy to Mr. and Mrs. William R. LITSEY, Fort Worth, on October 24; a boy to Mr. and Mrs. Clarence WOLF, Fort Worth, on September 22; a boy to Mr. and Mrs. William W. PATE, Fort Worth, on September 24 and a boy to Mr. and Mrs. J. C. WALKER, Fort Worth, on September 30.

James COUGHLIN and Anna HUTCHINSON married last night in Fort Worth. Rev. R. R. HAMLIN officiated.

J. GREEN of Marine was killed by a train in Georgetown, Georgia Thursday. A letter from there advised of his death. He was a meat cutter.

O. E. TURNER and Mrs. Jennie SHRADER married Wednesday in Ennis, Texas. Rev. W. K. PENROD officiated.

H. W. WINN and Louisa SALMON married Wednesday on the train between Commerce and Greenville, Texas. Justice of the Peace J. W. MANNING officiated.

James C. LANDON and Mai N. FOREMAN married Wednesday in San Angelo, Texas. Rev. W. W. WOOSTER officiated.

Saturday, October 8, 1904

R. J. HASKETT, living near Stillwater, Oklahoma Territory, was fatally burned Thursday night. He was attempting to rescue four horses from his burning barn. Arson is suspected.

John LOUPAT, 70, died at his home west of Dallas Thursday night. He was a native of France who came to the U.S. in 1857. He was a founder of the French colony located five miles west of Dallas and lived on his homestead nearly 50 years. He is survived by a wife, three sons and two daughters.

E. E. MOSSMAN, 34, died in Natchez, Mississippi, Thursday. His body is expected to arrive in Dallas tomorrow.

Arden RIDDLE was buried in Crowley, Texas Thursday. He was killed in Dallas earlier this week. His father, W. N. RIDDLE, was an early settler of the area.

John MAY, a farmer living near Garven, Indian Territory, was killed by his half-brother Frank SHIELDS yesterday. The two men fought over stock getting into MAY's field. SHIELDS surrendered to authorities.

The funeral of Mrs. James A. TODD was held in Fort Worth. Burial was in Oakwood Cemetery.

The body of Mark ADAMS will arrive in Fort Worth from St. Louis today. His funeral will be held this afternoon at Broadway Presbyterian Church. Burial will be in the old cemetery.

Bessie BURNEY, 38, died of paralysis in the county jail in Fort Worth yesterday.

Births recorded at Tarrant County Clerk's office: a boy to Mr. and Mrs. G. N. STONE of Mansfield, a boy to Mr. and Mrs. Charles MURPHY of near Mansfield, a girl to Mr. and Mrs. James HUFF with place garbled, a girl to Mr. and Mrs. C. D. FOSTER of Mansfield, a boy to Mr. and Mrs. E. T. WILLIAMS of Mansfield. No dates were listed.

Marriage licenses issued by Tarrant County Clerk's office: Thomas COUGHLIN, Jr. and Anna HUTCHINSON, J. T. MCKEON and Jean WHITLEY, and M. E. WRIGHT and Emma KNOX.

Sunday, October 9, 1904
The paper for this date did not appear on the microfilm.

Monday, October 10, 1904
C. W. JONES was killed in Houston Saturday. Major H. N. SWAIN was arrested and charged with murder.

Reis URIPIA died in San Antonio of lockjaw yesterday. Tebocio GARZA, Jr. was arrested and charged with murder. GARZA is aid to have struck URIPIA with a rock several days ago causing the injury that led to death.

Lydia GREEN died in Brenham, Texas yesterday. She had been struck over the head with a garden hoe wielded by Jennie PERKINS last week. PERKINS was arrested on a complaint of Constable R. H. BURCH. She was charged with murder. PERKINS' house was destroyed by fire yesterday morning.

Ernest SCHILLING, Sr. and Herman OTTMAN were killed in Houston yesterday.

Sam GLASSAWAY and Ella SPLAWN married Friday in Thockerville, Indian Territory.

Charles A. AUSTIN and Della LOVE married Wednesday in Marshall, Texas. Rev. W. B. MILLER, of First Baptist Church, officiated.

Pressley B. COLE and Maude WINTER married Friday in Wynnewood, Indian Territory. He is an attorney.

D. P. JONES and Lucy JONES married Wednesday in Sherman, Texas. He is from Greenville, Texas and she from Alderson, Indian Territory.

J. M. SPURLOCK and Ophelia BOYD married Thursday in Greenville, Texas. The bride is the daughter of Dr. and Mrs. W. E. BOYD. Rev. E. L. SPURLOCK officiated. He is the groom's brother.

J. R. MACE, Jr. and Althea BOWLIN married Saturday in Clarendon, Texas.

Robert BLOCK, 35, was buried Friday in Cooper, Texas. He died of a fit of apoplexy while unloading cotton. Survivors include his wife and four children.

Athleen PATTERSON, 14, was buried Friday in Cooper, Texas. She was daughter of Elmer PATTERSON.

The child of Lee PERRY, living near Cooper, was buried Friday.

George KIRKPATRICK died in Cordell, Oklahoma Territory Tuesday and was buried in Weatherford, Oklahoma Territory. He formerly lived in Ennis, Texas.

"Grandma" KIDDY: died Friday in her home south of Burleson, Texas. She was buried in Bethesda Cemetery that afternoon. She was an aged pioneer of Johnson County.

Mrs. E. BULWER, 76, died Friday in Yoakum, Texas.

Edna Mae KAUFFMAN died Friday in Fort Worth. She was buried Saturday in the city cemetery. She was daughter of Mr. and Mrs. Frank KAUFFMAN.

Miss Lucy CARR, 21, died Saturday of typhoid fever in Pecos, Texas. Her home was in St. Charles County, Virginia.

Mrs. George W. WASHINGTON, 49, died in Clarendon, Texas yesterday.

Thurmond WOOD, 18, died Friday of black jaundice in Elmo, Texas.

Judge Charles MERRIMAN, 67, died yesterday in Pecos, Texas. Death was due to heart failure. He was a confederate veteran and a former merchant in Houston. The funeral was in Pecos Tuesday. His son and daughter will arrive from Palestine, Texas today.

Marie GRAHAM, 17, died yesterday in Waxahachie, Texas from typhoid fever. Burial will be in city cemetery tomorrow. She was the daughter of Mr. and Mrs. L. T. GRAHAM.

The remains of Mrs. Annie WENTZEL, who died recently in Clay Center, Kansas, will arrive in Fort Worth for burial Wednesday.

Tuesday, October 11, 1904

Jeff VANN will be retried in 48th District Court in Fort Worth for the death of A. J. GRIMES about two years ago. VANN was previously convicted but the sentence was overturned on appeal.

E. M. JOHNSON, charged with killing A. ROBINSON 18 months ago, will be retried in 48th District Court in Fort Worth this term.

Births recorded at Tarrant County Clerk's office: a boy to Mr. and Mrs. R. H. BILLINGSLEA, Fort Worth, on September 30; a boy to Mr. and Mrs. Sam A VERELLO, Fort Worth, on September 28; a boy to Mr. and Mrs. Sam LORELL, Handley, on October 4; a girl to Mr. and Mrs. J. L. DIESMAN, county, on October 5; and a boy to Mr. and Mrs. P. J. BAILEY, Arlington, on September 26.

Deaths recorded at Tarrant County Clerk's office: Mrs. Florence TODD, 36, residing in Fort Worth on October 6 with no cause listed; and the infant of Mr. and Mrs. Sam AVERELLO, residing in Fort Worth, on September 30 with no cause listed.

Marriage licenses issued by Tarrant County Clerk's office: L. G. SMITH and Ellen MCCULLOCH; and Charles WATKINS and Eliza THOMPSON.

J. P. POWELL, about 50, was killed yesterday when he fell from the roof of the sanitarium in Marlin, Texas. He lived in Waco, Texas.

Jay WHITAKER died Wednesday in Christoval, near San Angelo, Texas. He was buried there. His residence was Fort Worth.

Mary A. PAYNE died yesterday in Fort Worth. She was a resident of Fort Worth for thirty years. She will be buried today in the city cemetery. Her husband and several children survive.

Mary A. SUIT died Saturday in Windom, Texas. She is survived by four children.

Wednesday, October 12, 1904

Births recorded at Tarrant County Clerk's office: a girl to Mr. and Mrs. David H. MCGEE, Fort Worth, on October 10; a boy to Mr. and Mrs. Thomas B. HILLERON, Fort Worth, on October 10; a boy to Mr. and Mrs. T. J. P. NESBITT, Riverside, on September 29; and a boy to Mr. and Mrs. Will CONNELLY, Glenwood, on October 9.

Mary WRIGHT, 10, was killed by a runaway horse at a street fair in Bonham, Texas Monday night. She was the daughter of C. WRIGHT.

Dr. E. L. HANN was killed yesterday in Denton, Texas by the accidental discharge of a gun he was cleaning. An inquest was held. He was a dentist and the son of Robert HANN.

Woodford P. POPE, a bookstore proprietor, died of heart failure in Houston yesterday.

The bond of Frank SHIELDS, accused of the death of John MAY in Garvin, Indian Territory, was set at $2000.

The funeral of Mary A. PAYNE took place yesterday. Rev. Alonzo MONK officiated.

Thursday, October 13, 1904

Will COCHRANE killed his wife, aged 31, his mother-in-law and then himself west of Plano, Texas yesterday. COCHRANE's mother-in-law was Mrs. James SKELTON, 73. She was the widow of old Joe SKELTON. COCHRANE was blind.

Dr. E. L. HANN was buried in Denton, Texas yesterday.

Dr. J. J. TOBIN died in Austin yesterday. He left a large family of grown children.

Mrs. Elizabeth EWING, 82, died in Houston yesterday. She was the widow of Judge George EWING and had been a resident of Texas since 1836.

Charley SHULTZ died in Fort Smith, Arkansas on Saturday.

Mrs. Ann GIBBS died Monday in her home near Rosston, Texas.

Louis Foster WILLCHECK died Monday in Belton, Texas. He was son of Mrs. Beatrice WILLCHECK. His funeral was yesterday with burial in Corn Hill Cemetery.

Mrs. F. I. DAVIS died Saturday in Greenville, Texas. She was a resident of Floyd, Texas and the mother of Mrs. W. F. HARRIS.

Minnie MORAN died in Dallas Tuesday. She formerly lived in Ennis, Texas.

Sallie HUTCHINS, 82, died Saturday in Bardwell, Texas.

Mrs. Della SENSABAUGH died in Telico, Texas. No date was reported. He husband died August 23.

A small child of Mr. and Mrs. A. W. DAUGHTERY died in Faulkner, Texas. No date was reported.

The baby of Mr. and Mrs. J. L. LAND died in Ensign, Texas with no date reported.

Mrs. John ELLIOTT died Tuesday in Ovilla, Texas.

Thomas W. WITHERSPOON died yesterday a few miles east of Waxahachie, Texas.

G. W. LANEY died Monday in Vernon, Texas and was buried with Masonic honors.

Rufus GILES was buried Monday in Marshall, Texas.

The infant son of Mr. and Mrs. Walter AKERS died Saturday in Sherman, Texas and was buried Monday in Akers Cemetery south of Sherman.

Mrs. A. P. MORGAN died in Fort Worth Monday. She was the daughter of J. S. MCDUFFIE.

Louise HYMANS died Tuesday in Del Rio, Texas. She was the youngest daughter of Jose HYMANS.

Eugene TALLMADGE, 14, died Tuesday in Marshall, Texas. He was the son of Mr. and Mrs. J. W. TALLAMDGE. He was buried yesterday in Greenwood Cemetery.

Henry MYERS, 18 months, died Tuesday in Sherman, Texas and was buried yesterday in West Hill Cemetery. He was the son of Mr. and Mrs. J. T. MYERS.

W. H. DAVIS died Sunday near Cleburne, Texas.

Mrs. Ben HODGES died Tuesday in Terrell, Texas.

Mrs. Frank DONOVAN died Sunday from congestion in Lampasas, Texas.

Jack CHANDLER, 27, died of typhoid Monday near Elmo, Texas. He was buried Tuesday there.

Mrs. Fannie Barrett WHERRY died in Chicago recently. She was a former resident of Marshall, Texas.

Frank B. HEALY, 50, died Monday. He was the registrar of government land in Woodward, Oklahoma Territory. No place of death was stated.

Thomas B. RECORDS and Bertha CARR married Tuesday in Lawton, Oklahoma Territory. Rev. T. J. IRVIN officiated.

Frank OATS and Myrtle LEE married Tuesday in Weatherford, Texas.

Lee BLAINE and Laura HART married in College Mound, Texas Tuesday. Rev. H. W. ARANT officiated.

Walter DATTON and Cecil SARTIN married Tuesday in Palo Pinto, Texas. The marriage took place in the home of Ed DATTON.

B. J. NELSON and May COLLINS married Sunday in Fort Calm, Texas. Rev. J. C. DANIEL officiated.

O. A. MULLINS and Florence SIMPSON married in Ardmore, Indian Territory Tuesday.

Thomas CHRISTIANSEN and Amelia HAWLOWRITZ married Tuesday in Sherman, Texas. The groom lives in Sulphur Springs, Texas. Father BLUM officiated.

Ancel BAKER and Carrie DUKES married Tuesday in Sherman, Texas. Rev. P. C. ARCHER, pastor of Travis Street Methodist Church, officiated.

William MCCLANAHAN and Ellen TAULBEE married in Dallas Tuesday.

Walter BURGESS and Kate MOLDER married in Corsicana, Texas Tuesday. Rev. George L. BITZER officiated. BURGESS is the city auditor for Corsicana.

C. E. REASONER and Kate MCDONALD married in Corsicana, Texas Wednesday. Rev. M. C. JOHNSON officiated.

R. L. CALDWELL and Fannie CLARY married yesterday in Grape Creek, six miles south of Corsicana, Texas. The bride is the daughter of Mr. and Mrs. Sidney J. CLARY and the groom is from South Carolina.

Marriage licenses issued by Tarrant County Clerk's office: W. G. MUSTA and Mrs. A. A. GILLESPIE, J. T. WISE and Mrs. Mary PUCKEL, C. M. BRIGGS and Ethel SCROGGINS, J. A. WEATHERLY and Josie LINTON, and Steve PAYTON and Polly THOMPSON.

The remains of Mrs. WENDT were buried in Oakwood Cemetery yesterday. She died on her way to visit Mrs. J. GREVE in Fort Worth. She was from Iowa.

Joe ROWE killed Clark DANNENBERG, his brother-in-law, near Sallisaw, Indian Territory Saturday. Both men were members of the Cherokee Nation.

Joe CORDERY is on trial in Muskogee, Indian Territory for the murder of George BROWN, his brother-in-law, last summer.

J. K. SMITH, city marshal of Wynnewood, Indian Territory, died of injuries in Shawnee, Oklahoma Territory. He was hit with a meat clever thrown by Jack JORDAN in a restaurant. SMITH was survived by a wife and three children in Wynnewood.

F. M. TERRY was shot by Bud TEEL in Saratoga, Texas Tuesday. TEEL shot TERRY three times with a revolver while TERRY was sitting in a barber chair.

George FRANKS, 70, died at his home ten miles west of Corpus Christi, Texas Monday. He was buried in Neuces, Texas that day. He was a pioneer of Neuces County.

Friday, October 14, 1904

The paper for this date was not on the microfilm.

Saturday, October 15, 1904

F. H. MANNING was found guilty in Dallas yesterday of the murder of Arden RIDDLE on October 4. MANNING was sentenced to die. The verdict is expected to be appealed.

Thomas JOHN, 92, died in Roswell, New Mexico Territory yesterday. He was a former resident of Eastland, Texas and a Civil War veteran. He served in the 12th Louisiana.

Mrs. E. J. HARRIS, 74, died in McKinney, Texas Thursday. Her death took place in the home of her son, former state senator J. R. GOUGH. She was a pioneer of Collin County.

S. RICHARDSON, 65, died Wednesday in Terrell, Texas.

John BARGSLEY, 74, died near Austin yesterday. He was a veteran of the Mexican War.

Z. T. COUCH, of Chief, Texas, died Wednesday.

R. A. JUDGE and Adele OXFORD married in Sherman, Texas Wednesday. Rev P. C. ARCHER officiated. The groom is from Haleville, Indian Territory.

J. B. BLAFFNER and Byrde BULLARD married Wednesday in Waxahachie, Texas. The bride is the daughter of Mr. and Mrs. D. B. BULLARD. The groom is from Shreveport, Louisiana.

T. M. KERBO and Helen WEBB married Wednesday in Greenville, Texas. The bride is the daughter of Mrs. L. J. WEBB. Rev. J. L. PRICE officiated.

Roy LARGEANT and Bessie HAMILTON married Wednesday in McKinney, Texas. Rev. J. L. MORRIS of Paris, Texas officiated.

Nellie MCKAMY and Dr. Walter H. ROWAN married in Plano, Texas Wednesday. The groom is from Wiggins, Mississippi.

R. C. MONTGOMERY and Lille RIKE married Thursday in Haskell, Texas. He was formerly the cashier of the First National Bank of Munday.

E. F. SCOTT, of Center Mills, and Jeannie NORRY, of Spring Creek, married Wednesday in Weatherford, Texas. Rev. W. M. BUNCH officiated.

Lucien LINCOLN shot and killed Willie HUGHES in Davilla, Texas Thursday. LINCOLN mistook HUGHES for a burglar and shot him in the store where LINCOLN clerked and slept. LINCOLN's father, Rev. John LINCOLN, owned the store.

Bill HARDISON was convicted of second degree murder yesterday in McKinney, Texas. HARDISON killed Levi YOUNG and was sentenced to seven years in prison.

Judge R. B. LEVY will hear a bail application from Arthur FISHER in Longview, Texas later this month. FISHER is charged with the death of John DORRITY.

Guy BREWER, of Prairieville, Texas, died of hydrophobia Wednesday. He was bitten by a rabid dog in July.

Births recorded at Tarrant County Clerk's office: a boy to Mr. and Mrs. John CAYWOOD, Fort Worth, on October 8; a boy to Mr. and Mrs. J. O. CHENNEY, Mansfield, on October 9; and a boy to Mr. and Mrs. C. C. DENNEY, Fort Worth, on October 12.

Deaths recorded at Tarrant County Clerk's office: Mrs. WILLIAMS of Henryetta, Texas, died in Fort Worth of acute peritonitis on October 10.

Marriage licenses issued by Tarrant County Clerk's office: Henry J. BLESSE and Mrs. Julia KILLERMAN, John CAPPS and Emma GRANTLAND, T. W. LOWE and Roxy SMITH, W. C. BARTON and Ella LEWIS, J. L. PENDER and Dora CRABB, and Andrew ANDERSON and Sallie JONES.

Sunday, October 16, 1904

Births recorded at Tarrant County Clerk's office: a boy to Mr. and Mrs. Walter WILLIE, Handley, on October 11; a girl to Mr. and Mrs. M. GRAHAM, Polytechnic Heights, on October 13; and a boy to Mr. and Mrs. T. E. NEWBY, Fort Worth, on October 5.

Marriage licenses issued by Tarrant County Clerk's office: W. A. FOX and Lizzie YEAGER, W. F. CLODUS and Nellie GARRETT, W. O. FARRELL and E. O. FOGLE, J. H. BLACK and Laura BRUMMETT, M. W. MARLET and Leona Maude PRUETT, W. A. CHILDRESS and Bessie FOGELBERG, L. L. ARNOLD and Lizie May WARD, Herman BRAND and Ethel Bertha EVANS, Lee SMITH and Annie JACKSON, and Fred CONNOR and Mary ALEXANDER.

Monday, October 17, 1904

The daughter of Judge T. R. JOHNSON, office assistant for the attorney general, died in Llano, Texas yesterday. Her funeral is today in Austin. Her name was not reported.

George BEAVERS died Friday in Graford, Texas. He was an early settler and a prominent farmer.

James PALMER, 88, died Friday at his home near Argus, Texas.

Mrs. Nathaniel FUTRELL, 30, died Friday in Heath, Texas.

Emma WILLIAMS died Wednesday near Haskell, Texas. She was the daughter of T. L. WILLIAMS. Her remains were sent from Stamford to Forney, Texas for burial.

Nellie DARDEN died in Terrell, Texas Friday.

Frederick SCHARF died in Kennedale, Texas yesterday. He was visiting his son, Charles SCHARF, when he died. He lived in Cleveland, Ohio.

Frank JOHNSON died Thursday in Anson, Texas. He was severely injured two weeks ago when his horse fell on him. He never regained consciousness after the accident. He was buried in Anson Cemetery.

Mary NIX, 72, died Friday in her home in South Greenville, Texas. She was buried in the home graveyard Saturday.

Mrs. J. E. EASTERWOOD died Saturday in Italy, Texas. She was buried yesterday in Waxahachie, Texas.

Louis PARHAM, 7, died Saturday in Blum, Texas. He was buried the same day. He was the son of Mrs. Lula PARHAM. Their husband and father died less than a year ago.

Martin G. RAGLY and Mabel L. WISE married in Jefferson, Texas Wednesday. Father MCGUINN officiated.

W. A. MCLENDON and Floy MOORE married south of Kennedale, Texas yesterday.

Emma TIERCE, 39, died in Fort Worth last night. She suffered heart failure. She was a widow and is survived by a sister in Fort Worth and a daughter in Sherman, Texas.

Ethel A. FOGLE and William O'FARRELL married yesterday in Fort Worth. The couple left for St. Louis. He is a foreman in the meat cutting department at Swift and Company.

Tuesday, October 18, 1904

Arthur M. FIELDS committed suicide at his home north of Livingstone, Texas Sunday.

A. J. WILSON was arrested in Amarillo, Texas yesterday. He is charged with the death of Lon O'REILLY last August.

Lucy TURNER and Walter CRANE married in Smithfield, Texas on October 9.

Clemmie SKAGGS and Sam SMITH married in Marble Falls, Texas Sunday. The bride is daughter of L. H. SKAGGS.

F. J. MILLETT and Nellie ROBINSON married Sunday in Frost, Texas.

Clifford MORRIS and Nora MELINAM married Sunday in Terrell, Texas.

J. G. BANKSTON, 69, died Sunday in Hillsboro, Texas. He was on a journey to San Antonio when he died.

May HARRIS died Sunday east of Sherman, Texas. She was the daughter of Mr. and Mrs. O. D. HARRIS. She was buried in Stony Point Cemetery.

Epsie WILLIAMS died Friday in Hallville, Texas. She was daughter of Mr. and Mrs. F. C. WILLIAMS. Burial was Sunday in Cave Springs Cemetery, nine miles south of Marshall, Texas.

Allie TROUPE, 8, died yesterday of diphtheria in Marshall, Texas. He was the son of Charles TROUPE.

J. W. DAUGHTERY, 28, died near Ennis, Texas Sunday. One of his children died a week ago.

Annie BETIK, 66, died of cancer Sunday in Ennis, Texas.

Maggie GALLIMORE, 17, died of fever near Iowa, Texas yesterday.

Mollie Clough ARDEN, wife of J. C. ARDEN, died Sunday in Ennis, Texas. She was buried in Myrtle Cemetery.

A. A. SCHAFFER was struck and killed by a train while walking on the Texas and Pacific Railroad tracks east of Minneola, Texas.

The funeral of Martha JOHNSON was held in Austin yesterday. She was the daughter of Judge T. S. JOHNSON. The funeral took place at the Tenth Street Methodist Church.

Funeral services for Emma TIERCE will be this morning. Her body will be shipped to Millsap, Texas for burial.

Births recorded at Tarrant County Clerk's office: a girl to Mr. and Mrs. F. C. BOORMAM, Fort Worth, on October 8 and a boy to Mr. and Mrs. Henry V. HEAD, Fort Worth, on October 19 (sic).

Marriage licenses issued by Tarrant County Clerk's office: M. V. WALLACE and Myrtle E. COOPER, Ed GRAHAM and Rhelda SPENCER, Will LEACH and Mrs. Julia TATE, Herman BRANDT and Ethel Bertha EVANS, L. L. ARNOLD and Lizie (sic) May WARD:, W. A. CHILDRESS and Bessie FOGELBERG, M. W. MARILETT and Leonora Maud PRUITT, Fred CONNOR and Mary ALEXANDER, and J. H. BLACK and Laura BRUMMETT.

Wednesday, October 19, 1904

Charles L. JOHNSON, 15, was found dead of consumption in Corpus Christi, Texas. He was from Houston and the son of G. D. JOHNSON.

Marriage licenses issued by Tarrant County Clerk's office: John BROWN and Ida MICHEL, Harvey ALLEN and Martha WOOD, Otto A. LISCHKE and Lora E. LETCHWORTH.

Births recorded at Tarrant County Clerk's office: a boy to Mr. and Mrs. Robert TANNAHILL, Azle, on October 8; a girl to Mr. and Mrs. G. J. LEDFORD, Arlington, on October 3; a boy to Mr. and Mrs. Albert HENRY, Arlington, with no date reported; a girl to Mr. and Mrs. Charles H. HICKS, Arlington, on October 8; and a boy to Mr. and Mrs. A. M. HUTT, Johnson Station, on October 4.

Thursday, October 20, 1904

W. L. MILAM, about 25, was killed in Wichita Falls, Texas yesterday. He was hit by a falling steel beam while he worked building a bridge over the Wichita River. He lived in Weatherford, Texas.

C. WILHITE was killed Tuesday when he was run over by a hay bailer seven miles north of Weatherford, Texas.

G. SCHWEITZER, about 60, committed suicide by drinking carbolic acid Tuesday at his home near Okarche, Oklahoma Territory.

John PETITT, of Olney, Texas, was killed in Stonewall County, Texas. He was buried alive when a bank collapsed, trapping him. He had sought shelter from a thunderstorm there. PETITT's remains were to arrive in Olney Monday for burial in Olney Cemetery Tuesday. No date for the death was reported.

A young son of James MAXWELL died Sunday after he drank a quart of whiskey Saturday night near Sanger, Texas.

Metsa HALE, of Canton, Texas, and Alice SLAUGHTER, of Edgewood, Texas, married Monday in Edgewood. Rev E. B. EAKIN officiated.

Cecil JONES and Maud HERDON married in Temple, Texas Monday. They are both employees of Southwestern Telephone Company in Belton, Texas.

Jud MCCARTHY and Willie CARROLL married Sunday in Comanche, Texas.

Benjamin F. WILSON, of Fort Worth, and Alice WARNOCK, of Eagle Pass, Texas, married in the latter location yesterday.

Oliver GILLILAND and Alice MORRIS, both of Woodville, Indian Territory, were married in Sherman, Texas Tuesday. Elder J. H. BAXTER officiated.

Mrs. G. H. CLIFTON, of Pilot Point, Texas, died in Fort Worth yesterday. Her remains were shipped to Pilot Point for burial.

H. B. CUSHMAN, 84, died in Greenville, Texas Tuesday. He was a Confederate soldier.

Lem MYERS died yesterday in Alvarado, Texas. He was the son of J. W. MYERS and is survived by a wife and two children.

George FRANKS died of typhoid fever in MacGregor, Texas Tuesday.

George W. HELM, 96, died Saturday in Charleston, Texas.

B. J. GRANT died in Dallas Monday.

Nina Fay AKERS died in Sherman, Texas and was buried in West Hill Cemetery there. The date was not legible.

James K. MERCHANT died in Austin and his remains were sent to Sour Lake, Texas. The date was not legible.

Marriage licenses issued by Tarrant County Clerk's office: James G. LOWDON and Kathleen NORRIS, W. H. IRWIN and Helen ZANE-CETTI, H. CARR and Sallie MURPHEY, R. H. HARKEY, Jr. and Miss R. M. POTTER, Juman WOODS and Anna REED, Alonso CAMPBELL and Mattie HINDEN and Tom FLOY and Frankie SASSEY.

Friday, October 21, 1904

Les HODGKINSON was shot and killed in Gainesville, Texas yesterday. Henry PATTERSON was arrested.

Judge J. T. FREEMAN and Mrs. Josephine B. KENNEDY married in Austin yesterday.

Mrs. Isabelle PRATER, 70, was fatally burned in Temple, Texas yesterday. She was attempting to start a fire.

Marriage licenses issued by Tarrant County Clerk's office: W. H. IRWIN and Helen ZANE-CETTI, L. L. CARR and Sallie MURPHEY, R. H. HARKEY, Jr. and Katherine Martin PORTER, C. M. ALLCORN and Jennie STEWART, Alonzo CAMPBELL and Mattie HENDERSON.

Births recorded at Tarrant County Clerk's office: a boy to Mr. and Mrs. William E. BRUNER, Fort Worth, with no date listed; a girl to Mr. and Mrs. F. C. MCCARY, Glenwood, with no date.

Deaths recorded at Tarrant County Clerk's office: Mrs. G. H. CLIFTON, 52, residing in Pilot Point, with no cause or date listed; Tom HOPE, 57, with no residence, cause or date listed.

Saturday, October 22, 1904

Deputy Sheriff Tom MOORE killed Dan F. KING yesterday in Longview, Texas.

Walter H. EARLE was allowed bond of $5000 in the death of Corsicana policeman Charles D. MADDUX on August 22, 1904.

Alexander ALLMAN died Thursday south of Temple, Texas.

Lemiel MYERS died of consumption in Alvarado, Texas Thursday. He was buried yesterday in Alvarado Cemetery. He was a former Justice of the Peace.

Milton A. LASATER, Jr. died in Weatherford, Texas Thursday and was buried there Friday. His parents live in Pauls Valley, Indian Territory.

Mrs. J. S. ROY died in Dallas yesterday. Her remains were shipped to Ennis, Texas for burial.

Russell THODE, 6, died Monday in Mason, Texas. He was the son of H. THODE, a merchant.

Maggie KELLEY, 44, died yesterday of black jaundice in Telico, Texas.

Lewis SHACKLEFORD and Love DU BOSE married Thursday in Waxahachie, Texas. Rev. J. G. PUTNAM officiated. The bride is the daughter of Mr. and Mrs. E. A. DU BOSE.

J. B. SMOTHERMAN and Amy PATTERSON, both of Ennis, Texas, married yesterday in Waxahachie, Texas.

C. H. DUFFAN and Herberta BLISS married Wednesday in Sherman, Texas.

George L. MCMILLAN and Mary LANE married in Hillsboro, Texas Wednesday. Rev. J. G. LANE, the father of the bride, officiated.

J. C. BROUSE, of Mulberry Grove, Illinois, and Ethel MCCANS, of Troupe, Texas, married in the latter location Thursday. Rev. L. H. MCGEE officiated. The couple will live in Illinois.

Oscar W. WALKER of Stockton, California and Carrie SNOW married Wednesday in Melissa, Texas.

Sam J. TAYLOR and Nannie PURYEAR married Thursday in Corsicana, Texas.

Jessie MITCHELL and Maggie BECK married Tuesday near Mason, Texas.

The infant son of C. C. BISHOP died in Fort Worth last night. The remains will go to Cleburne, Texas for burial.

The funeral of Amos Edward CHOUCHON, Jr., 5 months, was held yesterday in Fort Worth. He was buried in Oakwood Cemetery.

George W. FLEENER died in Fort Worth last night. His funeral will be tomorrow. He is survived by a wife and four children.

Mrs. Ella LYONS filed suit against Swift and Company for the death of her husband, John LYONS, two weeks ago. He was killed in a boiler explosion.

Marriage licenses issued by Tarrant County Clerk's office: Howard L. AGEE and Nora L. SISK, Tom HARRVEL and Mae CAPPS, C. R. RATHBURN and Elizabeth ROBE, and Rhodes PERKINS and Mary LOGAN.

Births recorded at Tarrant County Clerk's office: a boy to Mr. and Mrs. S. S. CHAPEL, Marine, on October 19.

Sunday, October 23, 1904

Note: Only section 3 appeared on the microfilm for this date.

Anna Lee CATE and Arthur Blackburn MAYHEW, of Paris, Texas, married in Fort Worth Wednesday. The bride is the daughter of Mr. and Mrs. M. L. CATE. The couple will live in Paris.

Katherine Martin PORTER and Robert Harrison HARKEY married in Fort Worth Wednesday. Rev. J. B. FRENCH officiated. The wedding took place in the residence of Mr. and Mrs. George W. PORTER, the parents of the bride.

Helen Emma ZANE-CETTI and William D. IRWIN married Wednesday in Fort Worth. The wedding party included the bride's siblings: Louise, Marion and Carl ZANE-CETTI.

W. O'FARRELL and Ethel Audrey FOGLE married last Sunday in Fort Worth. Father GUYOT officiated. The ceremony took place in the rectory of St. Patrick's Church.

Monday, October 24, 1904

Leon FRANKLIN was killed by Will SMITH Saturday near Beaver, Oklahoma Territory. SMITH was freed on a verdict of justifiable homicide. FRANKLIN entered a tent and began shooting. SMITH fired in self-defense.

Claude MARTIN was stabbed to death Saturday night at a dance near Buda, Texas. MARTIN killed Pedro BALINSUELO in a fight before he was killed by unknown parties.

Jep SULLIVAN and A. C. KAUFMAN were charged Saturday with the murder of Oclanda CONTRADA near Norwood, Texas ten days ago.

Louis BLANKENSHIP, 26, was killed when he was hit by a train while walking on the tracks near Faulkner, Texas. The date was not stated. BLANKENSHIP was deaf. His body was sent to Bardwell, Texas for burial. He recently lost his wife.

Alice SLOAN and R. L. SMITH married Saturday in Crescent City, Oklahoma Territory.

Henry MONTGOMERY and Ella CRUMP, of Venus, Texas, married in Cleburne, Texas Friday.

Dr. William Wilson PHILLIPS and Bess Leland MCDONALD married in Roswell, New Mexico Territory Saturday.

W. P. SCOTT died in Elgin, Texas yesterday. He was an old resident of the town.

"Grandpa" SHERLY, 90, died last night. The place wasn't stated. He was a resident of Providence and a pioneer in Indian Territory.

Chin SOOU, 52, died in Ardmore, Indian Territory yesterday from paralysis. He was a restaurateur.

Mrs. Joe BREEDLOVE died in Pecos, Texas of heart failure yesterday. Her husband and two children survive her. Her parents live in Troy, Texas.

Nathan SKIPPER was shot and killed allegedly by Joe MITCHELL near Navasota, Texas Saturday.

Wesley SMITH, 21, accidentally shot and killed himself while hunting near his home on Cedar Creek near Bastrop, Texas.

R. W. ATKEISON, about 25, was found dead in his bed in Houston yesterday morning. Ed DOBARD was jailed pending investigation. The two men fought in the market square Saturday night.

The infant son of Mr. and Mrs. W. C. HATHAWAY died in Fort Worth Saturday night. He was buried in Oakwood Cemetery Sunday.

Bert G. MARTEL and Nannie M. MCALLISTER married in Fort Worth yesterday.

The funeral of William J. ELLIS, who drowned in a lake south of Fort Worth Saturday, will be held today from the residence of James M. ELLIS. Burial will be in the new cemetery.

Mrs. R. S. WOOTEN died in LaFayette, Kentucky yesterday of typhoid fever. She was the daughter of Mr. and Mrs. B. M. BARKSDALE of Fort Worth. Survivors include her parents, husband and a ten months old child.

Mrs. E. T. FURMAN died Saturday night in Fort Worth of heart failure. Her funeral will be today from the Catholic Church with burial in the Catholic cemetery.

E. J. HOOKS died yesterday of bronchial pneumonia in Fort Worth. He leaves a wife and six children. The youngest child is 11 years old. Burial will be under Masonic auspices. Rev. WHITEHURST of Mulkey Methodist Church will officiate.

Jennie LELA died Saturday night of cancer in Fort Worth. She was born in Italy on November 1, 1839 and immigrated to America on November 13, 1902. Her funeral will be today from the home of her daughter, Mrs. AVRILLA. Father GUYOT will officiate.

Mary SWACKHAMMER, 3, died of typhoid yesterday. She was the daughter of the late Charles SWACKHAMMER, who was killed near Handley several months ago.

Tuesday, October 25, 1904

S. W. HARVEY will be buried today in Dallas. He died a week ago, but no relative could be located. His father finally saw a news account and telegraphed instructions that the deceased be buried in Dallas.

The year old child of William DERRICK, left in a wagon to play while the parents picked cotton, entangled itself in the reins and was killed yesterday near Guthrie, Indian Territory.

R. W. ATKEISON's cause of death was a fractured skull. He died Sunday in Houston after a fight Saturday night with Ed DOBARD. ATKEISON's remains were sent to Atkeison, Alabama for burial.

R. H. MOORE was granted a change of venue to Delta County, Texas in the re-trial of his conviction for the death of A. MCLAUGHLIN two years ago.

Funeral services for William J. ELLIS were held yesterday in Fort Worth. They took place at the home of his brother, James M. ELLIS. Jere ELLIS and Mrs. L. H. DU BOSE, siblings of the deceased, were in the city for the funeral.

William JENKINS, 88, died Sunday at the county farm near Sherman, Texas.

Mrs. M. E. GIBBONS, the wife of J. M. GIBBONS, died Sunday in Sherman, Texas. She was buried in West Hill Cemetery yesterday.

Bennett A. MAY died in Dallas Sunday. He is survived by his wife, two sisters and three brothers. He was buried yesterday in Masonic Cemetery.

Mrs. J. J. ROACH died in Oklahoma City, Oklahoma Territory Sunday. She was the sister of Mrs. T. H. WILSON of Dallas. The remains will be sent to Dallas for burial.

Marriage licenses issued by Tarrant County Clerk's office: R. S. TALIFERRO and Eugenia BRIGGS, G. C. MCCOLLUM and Dodie BARLIOUR, J. M. WIGGLESWORTH and Udell Regina RHOMBURG, A. T. STRONG and Annie L. CONNOR, Bascom CLARDY and Novilla Pearl NORTON, Paul TOWNSEND and Della PERRY, J. D. SMITH and Mrs. Fannie NELSON, Andrew GAGE and Viola HEWETT, and R. J. HOUSTON and Alice DAVIS.

Births recorded at Tarrant County Clerk's office: a girl to Mr. and Mrs. Edwin W. BUSH, Fort Worth, on October 22; a girl to Mr. and Mrs. W. L. SLADE, Riverside, on October 14; a girl to Mr. and Mrs. Will ROSE, Arlington, on October 15; a girl to Mr. and Mrs. A. W. BUCHANAN, Arlington, on October 11; and a boy to Mr. and Mrs. C. W. GRIDER, Arlington, on October 10.

Wednesday, October 26, 1904

Henry COX died Monday after a hunting accident near Lampasas, Texas. His horse collided with another horse, throwing COX to the ground.

R. R. MCDADE shot and killed W. H. LEHMAN in Halletsville, Texas Monday. MCDADE was jailed.

W. A. WHITLOCK, of Crisp, Texas, died yesterday of black jaundice.

The funeral of Ed SMITH, killed Friday in Mart, Texas, took place in Timpson, Texas yesterday.

Judge J. R. BROWNE died in San Marcos, Texas last night.

The mother of Judge E. R. SINKS died in Alvin, Texas yesterday.

W. T. BLANKENSHIP and Ida BROWN married Sunday east of Greenville, Texas. Rev. G. P. SIMPSON officiated.

G. B. WARNER and Willie MCDANIEL married in Austin yesterday.

The funeral of Mrs. Hannah HADDLE, who died Sunday in Fort Worth, will be held this morning.

Births recorded at Tarrant County Clerk's office: a girl to Mr. and Mrs. C. E. RIVERS, Fort Worth, on October 21; a girl to Mr. and Mrs. William H. NEWBERRY, with no place listed, on October 21; a boy to Mr. and Mrs. Guy S. RALL, Fort Worth, on October 21 and a girl to Mr. and Mrs. George LUNN, Rosen Heights, on October 22.

Thursday, October 27, 1904

Tom ROBERTS shot and killed Dan CABLE near Wichita Falls, Texas Tuesday. ROBERTS surrendered to authorities and was released on bond of $500. CABLE was buried by county authorities.

Henry JOHN brought the body of John HAMMOND to Paris, Texas last week. JOHN indicated he had killed the man in self-defense and wanted to stand trial for the offense.

The funeral of Mrs. Hannah HADDLE was postponed Tuesday because of inclement weather. It was held Wednesday.

Harry P. SAYRE and Mrs. Mary J. NEWKIRK married in Fort Worth last night.

Mrs. A. B. STREET, 79, died last night in Fort Worth. She was the mother of Mrs. Emmons ROLFE of Fort Worth. Mrs. STREET's body was shipped to Nebraska City, Nebraska for burial.

Judge J. M. RICHARDS, of Weatherford, Texas, and Mrs. Mary Florence LEACH married in Fort Worth last night. Rev. WHITEHURST officiated. Due to the recent death of the bride's mother, the ceremony was very small. The couple will live in Weatherford.

W. R. PEACHER, 39, died in Fort Worth of dropsy yesterday. He lived in Handley, Texas. His funeral will be today.

Marriage licenses issued by Tarrant County Clerk's office: Harry P. SAYRE and Mrs. Mary G. NEWKIRK, P. GROUPTON and Mrs. Myra MILLIGAN, J. M. RICHARDS and Mrs. Mary Frances LEACH.

Births recorded at Tarrant County Clerk's office: a boy to Mr. and Mrs. Honore MANN, Enon, on October 17; a girl to Mr. and Mrs. T. J. HORTON, Enon, on October 16; a boy to Mr. and Mrs. John ROSS, Arlington, on October 17; and a boy to Mr. and Mrs. W. E. POLLOCK, Glenwood, on October 21.

Deaths recorded at Tarrant County Clerk's office: Clyde YOUNGBLOOD, 6, residing in Fort Worth, died from an accident on October 26; Infant TAYLOR, 1, residing in Arlington, died of diphtheria with no date listed; and John C. MATTHEWS, 64, residing in Fort Worth, died of heart failure on October 21.

Clyde YOUNGBLOOD, 6, was killed yesterday in Fort Worth when he was run over by a streetcar. He was the son of Mrs. Silas YOUNGBLOOD. His funeral will be today.

Knox A. ANDERSON and Josephine ISBELL married in Fort Worth yesterday. Rev. J. W. GILTON officiated.

Friday, October 28, 1904

Dick WEBBER died of heart failure yesterday in Lexington, Oklahoma Territory. He was a sewing machine salesman and resided at Lindsay, Indian Territory.

Addison SMITH, 21, was found guilty of murder in Waco, Texas yesterday. He killed Sheriff GRUBBS in Bell County in August, 1902. SMITH was sentenced to 25 years in prison. SMITH's parents, Catherine and T.E. SMITH, were also charged in the death of GRUBBS, and will be tried next month.

Mrs. Margaret BRAWLEY died Monday at her home five miles north of Weatherford, Texas. She was buried Tuesday. She was a pioneer citizen of Parker County.

H. F. DAWSON died at his home in Weatherford, Texas Tuesday. He was buried the next day.

The remains of Mrs. Hattie CASTEEL reached Marshall, Texas from Terrell Monday. They were buried from the residence of her sister, Mrs. W. C. FIELD, the same day.

Will ELLIOTT of Marion, Illinois, died in Texarkana Tuesday of appendicitis. His remains were shipped to his old home for internment.

The death of Senora Anastasia BANDONAO occurred Saturday in San Angelo, Texas. Funeral services were conducted Sunday by Father MOLINE. Burial was in Knickerbocker Cemetery. She was a pioneer of Tom Green County, settling there two decades ago. She was the mother of Mrs. R. F. TANKERSLEY.

Roscoe SIMMONS, 7, died Sunday of blood poisoning in Hillsboro, Texas. The funeral was conducted by Rev. Jerome DUNCAN. Burial was in the old cemetery that afternoon. He was the son of Mr. and Mrs. H. H. SIMMONS.

L. W. SHAPPARD and Susie TALLEY married Sunday in Temple, Texas.

George H. WARREN and Arta PRINCE, of Nolan Valley, married in Belton, Texas Sunday. Rev. George W. LEE officiated.

William VIDLER, of Taylor, Texas, and Annabelle GOTT married SUNDAY in Belton, Texas. The bride is the daughter of Mr. and Mrs. R. W. GOTT. Rev G. W. LEE officiated.

J. Walter WILSON and Candace RANDOLPH, both of Fort Worth, married in Weatherford, Texas Tuesday. Rev. B. F. FRONABARGER officiated.

John ALMONS and Stella PAULK, both of College Hill, a suburb of Texarkana, were married at her home Sunday.

Mr. And Mrs. M. B. HARRIS are the parents of a daughter born Wednesday in Fort Worth.

Mrs. Matilda GLENN, about 60, died in Fort Worth yesterday. Her funeral will be today from St. Paul's Methodist Church.

Mrs. Marie GORDON, 26, died Wednesday in Fort Worth. She was a widow. Her funeral will be today from her late home.

Charles LAST, 76, died in Fort Worth Wednesday night. He was buried in Oakwood Cemetery Thursday. He was survived by his wife and three children.

Joseph FILLIP was found dead at his home near Schulenberg, Texas yesterday. Neighbors investigated when his children aged 1-8 begged for food. It was believed FILLIP died Saturday.

Ernest MAXEY, charged with the murder of Dayton MADDOX, waived examination in Justice TERRELL's court. His bond was set at $2000.

Marriage licenses issued by Tarrant County Clerk's office: R. C. PHILLIPS and Mrs. Lena MCPHERSON.

Births recorded at Tarrant County Clerk's office: a girl to Mr. and Mrs. Ed WILKERSON, Glenwood, on October 24; a boy to Mr. and Mrs. Ben GRIMSLEY, Rendon, on October 21; and a boy to Mr. and Mrs. George LOFTON, Rendon, on October 17.

Saturday, October 29, 1904

Mrs. B. E. WEBB died in Boyce, Texas Wednesday. Her remains were buried in Waxahachie, Texas yesterday.

Judge L. H. BROWN died Tuesday in San Marcos, Texas. His funeral was Wednesday. He was a native of Madison County, Arkansas and came to Texas in 1867. He was a state senator as well as a judge. Seven children survive. Four of them were named in the story: J. L. BROWN of Karnes City, Texas; N. H. BROWN of Goliad, Texas; L. H. BROWN, Jr., of San Marcos and W. W. BROWN of Helena, Arkansas.

Mrs. W. W. WOLFE died in Cresson, Texas Tuesday.

Mrs. Jennie OLDHAM, wife of Ed OLDHAM, died Tuesday in Waxahachie, Texas.

J. B. SHELTON, about 75, died Thursday in Decatur, Texas.

Clifford B. HALEY and Sallie COLEMAN married Tuesday in Corsicana, Texas. Rev. J. B. BERRY officiated.

Mamie HYNSON and J. L. BOWSER, of Franklin, Pennsylvania, married in Texarkana Wednesday. Rev. Percy T. FENN officiated. The marriage took place in St. James Episcopal Church.

Morgan JONES and Jessie WILDER married in Weatherford, Texas Thursday. Rev. J. W. ROWLETT officiated. JONES is the general superintendent of the Wichita Valley Railroad.

Lola MARTIN and David HUNTER married in Guthrie, Oklahoma Territory Thursday.

John JOHNSON and Polina CORNWELL married in Denton, Texas Wednesday. The marriage took place in the home of T. F. HILL. JOHNSON is a farmer in Brazoria County.

A baby girl was born to Mr. and Mrs. C. HEIRX in Fort Worth Thursday.

Paul ENGELKING was accidentally shot and killed by Richard WARD in Sealy, Texas Thursday. WARD was handling a revolver, which discharged. The bullet passed through a wall and struck ENGELKING in an adjoining barber shop. ENGELKING was the brother of Johanna ENGELKING, a teacher in Brenham, Texas. WARD is a cousin of Mrs. Green MORGAN.

Marriage licenses issued by Tarrant County Clerk's office: K. L. NASH and Mrs. Lou CASSELMAN, W. R. MCDONALD and Mainel M. WACKER.

Births recorded at Tarrant County Clerk's office: a girl to Mr. and Mrs. C. PHENIX, Fort Worth, on October 27; a boy to Mr. and Mrs. L. WILLIAMS, Fort Worth, on October 23; a boy to Mr. and Mrs. C. R. MILLER, Keller, on

October 20; a girl to Mr. and Mrs. Ambrose RYAN, Fort Worth, on October 18; a girl to Mr. and Mrs. A. L. SUGGS, Fort Worth, on October 25; and a boy to Mr. and Mrs. J. P. CHAPMAN, Fort Worth, on October 25.

Deaths recorded at Tarrant County Clerk's office: Mrs. M. A. PAYNE, residing in Fort Worth, died of cerebral hemorrhage on October 10.

Charles PIERCE died of kidney trouble in Tarrant County Jail in Fort Worth yesterday. He was buried at county expense.

Sunday, October 30, 1904
The paper for this date did not appear on the microfilm.

Monday, October 31, 1904
W. E. LEHEW and Miss M. L. SHOEMAKER married Saturday in Waxahachie, Texas.

Charles T. WEBB and Rosa STALLINGS married Wednesday in Clarendon, Texas.

Henry C. NICHOLS and Lola R. STONEBACK, both of Comanche County, Oklahoma Territory, married in Vernon, Texas Sunday. J. R. ROTHMAN, justice of the peace, officiated. The couple will live in Frederick, Oklahoma Territory.

Elsie BERRY and J. W. DWYER married in Pawnee, Indian Territory Saturday. She is assistant cashier at Pawnee First National Bank. He is a railroad man from St. Louis.

Dan BOWEN and Lavonia AULT, both of Preston, Texas, married in Sherman, Texas yesterday. Justice J. Frank TOWERS officiated.

Norris WATKINS arrived in Guthrie, Oklahoma Territory among a group of prisoners from Pawnee, Indian Territory. WATKINS was indicted for the murder of Joseph HAIGLER two weeks ago in the Osage Indian country.

Mildred CLIFTON was convicted Saturday of manslaughter in the death of Ab PATTERSON. She was sentenced to four years in prison. An appeal is expected.

November, 1904

Tuesday, November 1, 1904

Two small children of J. F. EVANS, residing near Tea Cross, Oklahoma Territory, burned to death in a house fire Sunday. Tea Cross is near Lawton, Oklahoma Territory. The children's names were not reported. They were home alone.

Shell HAROLSON, 20, died of hydrophobia near Tecumseh, Oklahoma Territory. The date was not specified.

William REGNIER was convicted in Guthrie, Oklahoma Territory of the murder of William ROWAN two years ago. REGNIER was sentenced to 15 years in prison.

James B. WYCHE, a brakeman, was killed west of Oklahoma City, Oklahoma Territory on his run. The date was not specified.

Clara RILEY, 14, died of burns she received Sunday when her clothes caught fire from a heating stove. The date or place was not specified.

Lee BURNETT shot and mortally wounded S. E. PRATZ in Marshall, Texas yesterday.

Mrs. James LOUGHRAY, 49, died yesterday in Glenwood. Her funeral is today from her former residence.

D. B. HAYES and Dorothy DOLLY married in Gainesville, Texas Sunday. Rev. J. F. PIERCE officiated.

H. T. LIVINGSTON and Mary JONES married Sunday in Marshall, Texas. Rev. J. B. K. SPAIN officiated.

Mary A. CRAVENS and R. C. WILCOX married in Austin Sunday. The bride is the daughter of Judge and Mrs. N. A. CRAVENS.

Word was received in Temple, Texas yesterday that R. L. HOLLINGSWORTH died of consumption in Veracruz, Mexico. He was a former resident of Temple and Fort Worth.

The infant daughter of Mr. and Mrs. E. MARR died east of Sherman, Texas on Sunday. She was buried yesterday in the local cemetery.

Mrs. J. F. MARSHALL, of Dexter, Texas was found dead in bed yesterday. Her death was attributed to heart failure.

A baby child of Mr. and Mrs. Robert WHITE died Saturday in Temple, Texas.

Chin Lee GOWN died in Gainesville, Texas Sunday.

Claude BOGGES died in Ennis, Texas yesterday. He left a wife and some children.

A. S. HODGE, 81, died at his home in Cuero, Texas yesterday. He was a physician.

James T. WILCOX, 38, died in Calvert, Texas last night.

Mrs. Eugene WILSON, wife of Judge WILSON, died in Brazoria, Texas on Sunday.

Monroe TEEL died of pneumonia in Tiger, Texas on Saturday.

Mrs. Maria MILLER, 92, died in Gainesville, Texas on Sunday. Her remains were shipped to Sedalia, Missouri. She was the mother of Mrs. H. B. FLETCHER.

Joe LAMPKIN shot and killed Miles ROSS near Cameron, Texas on Sunday. LAMPKIN surrendered.

Births recorded at Tarrant County Clerk's office: a girl to Mr. and Mrs. James CULPEPPER, Mansfield, on October 14; a boy to Mr. and Mrs. Ed NICHOLS, Mansfield, on October 26; a girl to Mr. and Mrs. Joe EDGERMAN, Mansfield, on October 27; a girl to Mr. and Mrs. John WHALEY, Mansfield, on October 1; a boy to Mr. and Mrs. R. H. ARMSTRONG, Tate Springs, on October 27; a boy to Mr. and Mrs. Thomas LOUCHARD, Fort Worth, on October 21; and a boy to Mr. and Mrs. George H. SWIFT, Fort Worth, on October 27.

Wednesday, November 2, 1904

Clarence HOFF and Jack BRUMLEY were killed and John RIDER and Bert HOLT fatally injured in an explosion near Batson, Texas yesterday.

John HANCOCK committed suicide west of Greenville, Texas on Monday.

S. P. PRICE, of Anna, Texas, was robbed and murdered near Ogden, Arkansas, yesterday.

Elizabeth PROVINE, 15, died of typhoid fever yesterday in Fort Worth. She was daughter of Mr. and Mrs. E. W. PROVINE.

A. J. COMPTON died in Galveston, Texas yesterday. He was the county treasurer.

Mrs. Annie CLOTT, 74, died of asthma near Alma, Texas yesterday.

The son of George GRAY died of cholera infantum yesterday in Union Hill, Texas yesterday. He was 11 months old.

An infant grandchild of J. A. WEBB died in Union Hill, Texas yesterday.

Mrs. Katherine HILL, 73, died Sunday night in Greenville, Texas.

The 11 months old child of Mr. and Mrs. COOK died in Mt. Calm, Texas on Sunday. No other names were reported.

Mrs. N. J. COLLINS, who died Tuesday in Texarkana, was buried in State Line Cemetery yesterday.

Alexander F. DANNER died in Dallas yesterday. He was a son-in-law of G. O. HAMBRICK. He left a wife and daughter.

M. D. L. HARMON, 71, died Monday of pneumonia northeast of Sherman, Texas. He was buried yesterday at Friendship, Texas.

H. T. MEEKS and Aggie HILLIARD, of Campbell, Texas, married yesterday in Greenville, Texas. The bride is daughter of Mr. and Mrs. S. G. HILLIARD.

C. L. TANNER and Lula THOMPSON married in Sherman, Texas Tuesday. Rev. J. H. FULLER officiated.

A. C. MYERS and Nellie MURRAY married Sunday near McKinney, Texas.

C. L. DANIELS and Lovie GARRETT married yesterday north of Mineral Wells, Texas. Squire G. C. GREEN officiated.

Robert STAULTS and Annie MARTIN married Sunday south of Marshall, Texas. Rev. J. L. STEVENSON officiated.

Marriage licenses issued by Tarrant County Clerk's office: James CHILDS and Mrs. Arthur PHILLIPS, J. T. EUSTACE and Cora SMITH, R. W. CALLAHAN and Mrs. Mary T. VAN WINKLE, and Nick WITZER and Mrs. Mahala WENCE.

Births recorded at Tarrant County Clerk's office: a girl to Mr. and Mrs. James CULPEPPER, Mansfield, on October 14; a boy to Mr. and Mrs. W. T. STEWART, Mansfield, on October 31 and a boy to Mr. and Mrs. A. STINSON, Fort Worth, on October 29.

Deaths recorded at Tarrant County Clerk's office: S. A. DAVIS, residing in Birdville, died of diabetes on October 29; Nona SWACKHAMMER, 3, residing in Fort Worth, died of peritonitis on October 23.

The state health office closed Monday in respect of the death of Dr. Arthur WOLFF, the state quarantine officer at Brownsville, Texas.

Thursday, November 3, 1904

Sid WILLIAMS, a constable of Brown Township, was shot and killed by Nep BRADY, a deputy constable in Brown Township, in a saloon in Lawton, Oklahoma Territory yesterday. BRADY was severely injured.

The funeral of Elizabeth PROVINE, who died Tuesday, will be held at the Cumberland Presbyterian Church in Fort Worth this afternoon.

Walter KING and Juni STEWART married yesterday in Fort Worth.

James Alexander WRIGHT, 61, died in Austin Tuesday. He was a former member of the Travis County Commission.

John BURNETT, 56, died Tuesday on his farm west of Maypearl, Texas.

Marriage licenses issued by Tarrant County Clerk's office: Joel Angus MCGUIRE and Ethel FANTY, J. B. DAVIS and Mrs. Mary GILBERT, D. COWAN and Verna May HOVEY, and J. R. SCHOONFIELD and Mrs. Ruth ERWIN.

Births recorded at Tarrant County Clerk's office: a girl to Mr. and Mrs. Lorin HUNTER, Saginaw, on October 27; a child to Mr. and Mrs. Wallace WOLDRUP, Newark, on October 25; a girl to Mr. and Mrs. R. H. MCDUFFIE, Fort Worth, on October 28.

A United States District Court jury in Paris, Texas found Major F. REED guilty of manslaughter for causing the death of John RILEY, his father-in-law, on January 19, 1904, in Durant, Indian Territory.

Verna HOVEY, the daughter of Mr. and Mrs. W. W. HOVEY, and D. COWAN, the son of Mr. and Mrs. Andrew COWAN, married in Fort Worth last night. Rev. Junius B. FRENCH officiated.

Friday, November 4, 1904

Marriage licenses issued by Tarrant County Clerk's office: E. L. THERRELL and Mrs. Inez WHITLEY, John DANIEL and Dovie SIMS, J. L. BRAY and Josie EVANS, Willie ADAMS and Allie STONE, L. D. HUSKEY and Sarah WALTERS, and G. H. THOMAS and Mrs. B. F. MCDANIEL.

Births recorded at Tarrant County Clerk's office: a girl to Mr. and Mrs. Jefferson Davis RICE, Enon, on October 26; a boy to Mr. and Mrs. John PATTON, Enon, on October 30; a girl to Mr. and Mrs. J. W. HUGHES, Enon, on November 2; and a girl to Mr. and Mrs. Albert BROWN, Fort Worth, on October 30.

Deaths recorded at Tarrant County Clerk's office: Emma TRINE, 39, residing in Fort Worth, died of gastritis, on October 16; and Sidney STEPHENSON, 28, residing in Enon, died of appendicitis, on October 23.

Mary Hilda KEY, infant daughter of A. W. KEY, died yesterday in Fort Worth and will be buried today.

E. L. THERRELL and Mrs. Inez WHITLEY married yesterday in Fort Worth. Rev. Luther LITTLE officiated. The couple will live in Fort Worth.

Herbert WRIGHT, 2, died in Fort Worth yesterday. His funeral will be today.

Gus ROBERTSON, of Colorado City, Texas, and Gertie Grace GRIGSBY married in Elkhart, Texas. Rev. N. B. READ officiated.

Elihu A. SANGER and Evelyn Warene BECKMAN married in Natchez, Mississippi yesterday. Rabbi S. G. BOTTINGHEIMER officiated. The couple will live in Dallas.

E. E. LAWSON and Mamie EAST married Wednesday in Sherman, Texas. Rev. Forrest SMITH officiated.

Thorst DYSART, of Anna, Texas, and Hattie HORY, of Vineland, Texas, married in McKinney, Texas Tuesday. The marriage took place at the home of the bride's grandfather, Capt. E. R. STIFF.

Adam HILLHOUSE of Colorado Springs, Colorado, and Annie MCKEMIE married Wednesday in Gainesville, Texas.

Howard NORRIS and Emma Lena DOYLE married Tuesday in Ennis, Texas. Father J. E. MALONE officiated.

Charles JONES and Ida WEBB married Monday near Ennis, Texas. Rev. V. I. STIRMAN officiated.

John NEFF and Katie DOPHEID married Wednesday in Sherman, Texas. Father BLUM officiated.

Orson F. CALDWELL, of Parsons, Kansas, and Pearl KELLEY, of Orongo, Missouri, married Wednesday in Sherman, Texas. Elder J. T. BAXTER officiated.

F. W. STAHL and Lillie WILSON married Tuesday in Clarksville, Texas. The bride is the sister of Mrs. J. B. SHAW of Clarksville.

A. E. LEWIS, of Louisville, Kentucky, and Miss J. M. LEACH, of Weatherford, Texas, married Monday in the Texas and Pacific Railroad station in Weatherford. Rev. K. G. TENNISON officiated.

John HIBBDON, of Mineral Wells, Texas, and Willie CHAMBERS married in Stephenville, Texas on October 23. The bride is the daughter of Frank CHAMBERS.

John KELLER and Emma ROBERTS married Tuesday in Terrell, Texas.

L. E. HUGHES and Mrs. Laura FORBERN married Wednesday in Cleburne, Texas.

Sallie ADKINS and W. D. CANNON married in Henrietta, Texas on October 27.

J. T. BRYANT, of New Braunfels, Texas, and Lillian TATUM married Tuesday in Belton, Texas.

Anne KEEN and C. E. BEANLAND married in Prosper, Texas. The date was not legible.

R. H. HOWARD and Hattie BALL married in Clarksville, Texas. The date was not legible.

T. A. JOHNSON and Ella Willie WOMACK married Tuesday in Marshall, Texas. The bride is the sister of Mrs. J. H. POPE.

James P. EBERHEART and Nell ARNOLD married Wednesday in Sherman, Texas. The bride is the daughter of Mr. and Mrs. E. ARNOLD. Rev. W. J. MILLER of St. Steven's Episcopal Church officiated.

H. E. PIERCE and Allie COLEMAN married Wednesday in McKinney, Texas. The bride is the daughter of Mr. and Mrs. T. A. COLEMAN.

W. F. PIERCE, 100, died in Houston yesterday. He was a native of South Carolina and a Civil War veteran.

The remains of Scrap WILSON arrived yesterday in Stephenville, Texas from Indian Territory for burial.

Nick SHERMAN, 63, died in Sherman, Texas Wednesday. He was buried in West Hill Cemetery.

B. R. BAGWELL died Wednesday in the eastern part of Harrison County, Texas. He was buried in Scottsville Cemetery yesterday.

The remains of Mrs. Alice WINCHESTER, who died in Sherman, Texas yesterday, were shipped to Morgantown, Indiana, for burial.

Frank NAUGHTON died yesterday in Waxahachie, Texas. He was a traveling salesman for McCormick Harvester Company.

Captain J. W. TODD died Wednesday in Terrell, Texas. He was born in Tennessee on June 24, 1828 and was a veteran of the Mexican War.

Mrs. J. F. MOSER: died Tuesday near Chico, Texas. She was buried yesterday in Green Elm Cemetery.

H. P. HELBERT died Tuesday near Rogers, Texas. Burial was yesterday in the McKann graveyard.

Logan HARRIS, 30, died Monday near Rogers, Texas. He died in the home of his brother-in-law, Todd SHIPP.

The four year old son of Mr. and Mrs. W. F. FOWLER: died of diphtheria in Greenville, Texas. The date was not legible.

The body of Mrs. George H. ADAMS arrived Wednesday in Brownwood, Texas for burial.

John MCCARTY died of consumption in Ennis, Texas and was buried in Telico, Texas. The dates were not legible.

Mrs. Charles SCHULER died in Marshall, Texas. The date was not legible.

Rube CONNOR, 6, died yesterday in Chico, Texas. He was the son of Judge T. H. CONNOR. Rube will be buried in Eastland, Texas. He had four sisters (Maggie, Annie, Frances and Elsie) and one brother (George) at the time of his death.

Saturday, November 5, 1904

John NESBITT was struck by a train and killed Friday near Lampasas, Texas.

H. L. THOMPSON was indicted for murder in the second degree in San Antonio yesterday. He is accused of causing the death of Delores MORAN by frightening her to death two weeks ago. He supposedly entered her room with a drawn pistol shortly after she had given birth.

Mark HATLEY, 60, died Thursday at his home twenty miles north of Lampasas, Texas. He was a lifelong resident of Lampasas County.

Mrs. D. MCCLOUD, 50, died in Fort Worth yesterday. Her funeral will be today.

Mrs. Sue BONNER, 51, died yesterday in Fort Worth. She was the wife of M. J. BONNER and the mother of several children. Her funeral will be today.

Births recorded at Tarrant County Clerk's office: a girl to Mr. and Mrs. Ben BELLOWS, North Fort Worth, on November 3; and a girl to Mr. and Mrs. M. B. HARRIS, Fort Worth, on October 26.

Sunday, November 6, 1904

Marriage licenses issued by Tarrant County Clerk's office: William MILLS and Jennie HARP, V. L. PIRKLE and Annie WISROCK, Paul Allen TOWNSEND and Tommie CRAWFORD, and Sam BRANDON and Mrs. Annie TOMAMICHEL.

Deaths recorded at Tarrant County Clerk's office: Laura LOUGRAY, 41, residing in Glenwood, died on October 31 with no cause listed; and Bessie M. STEWART, 3 months, residing in North Fort Worth, died on October 22 with no cause listed.

Births recorded at Tarrant County Clerk's office: a girl to Mr. and Mrs. J. W. CARNES, Fort Worth, on November 4 and a boy to Mr. and Mrs. H. SOLSBERG, Fort Worth, on November 4.

R. H. HOWARD and Hallie BALL married Wednesday in Clarksville, Texas. The groom was seriously ill and wanted to marry before he died. He died the following morning. Rev. S. M. TEMPLETON officiated. The remains of R. H. HOWARD were shipped to Culpepper, Virginia.

Major F. REED was sentenced to five years in prison yesterday. He was convicted of the murder of his father-in-law, John RILEY.

Monday, November 7, 1904

S. M. NIXON, charged with the murder of John L. VEASEY and Robert W. MALONE, surrendered in San Antonio. He is presently confined to the hospital in San Antonio.

Captain Edgar W. JONES, 34, died in Guthrie, Oklahoma Territory, Saturday. He recently married Frances KAUFFMAN of St. Louis. He died of ptomaine poisoning and was a veteran of the Spanish-American War.

The remains of Michael DIMAND, 67, who died Thursday, arrived in Corpus Christi, Texas Saturday en route to Brooklyn, New York for burial. He was a merchant and a Mason.

T. J. MURPHY, a traveling salesman, died in Brownwood, Texas Thursday. His wife died three months ago in Mineral Wells, Texas. He was visiting his two small sons when he died.

The remains of Pearl BRISTOL, 19, who died in the home of her brother, Dr. W. A. BRISTOL in Denison, Texas were brought to McKinney, Texas and buried Thursday.

A. A. MORRIS, 63, died in Harrold, Texas Thursday. He was buried by his Masonic brethren.

Mrs. Lon C. HILL died Friday in Brownsville, Texas. Her burial was Saturday. She was survived by her husband and eight children.

Ollie DICKERSON died Thursday near Sherman, Texas. She was the daughter of Mr. and Mrs. James DICKERSON. She was buried Friday in Cedar Church Cemetery.

Susan SPRADLIN, 34, died Saturday in Ardmore, Indian Territory.

Ezra JENNINGS died Friday in Temple, Texas. He suffered a broken back several days ago when he fell from a pecan tree in Eagle Lake.

Charles WALSH, 9, died Friday in Mineral Wells, Texas. He was the son of Mr. and Mrs. R. C. WALSH.

Mrs. Kalazler BLACKWELL, 74, died Friday in Gainesville, Texas.

Lucia BOWEN, 8, died of pneumonia in Mineral Wells, Texas. She was the daughter of Mr. and Mrs. C. H. BOWEN.

Mrs. Mattie BOMAR, 54, died Saturday in Sherman, Texas. She was buried Sunday in West Hill Cemetery.

B. B. BELL, 61, died in Aberdeen, Texas last Thursday. The funeral was held on Saturday. Rev. C. E. MILLS officiated.

Bell BILES died in Bourne, Texas Friday and was buried in Pittsburg, Texas Saturday.

James Earl BOND died Saturday in Marshall, Texas. He was the son of Mr. and Mrs. E. H. BOND. His remains were shipped to Pine Bluff, Arkansas for burial.

Frances COPPAGE, 12, died Saturday in Temple, Texas. She was the daughter of Mr. and Mrs. T. B. COPPAGE.

Herbert GALLOWAY, 16, was buried Friday in Sulphur Springs, Texas. The public school students and teachers attended his funeral as a group.

A. M. WHITELEY died Friday near Belton, Texas. He was a farmer in the Youngblood community and was buried yesterday.

Mrs. George NASH, 29, died east of Weatherford, Texas Wednesday.

Earl S. VINCENT and Phoenie Belle MCCOWN married Saturday in Marshall, Texas. Rev. J. E. MCLEAN officiated.

D. W. FAIN and Mary BARBER, both of Greenwood, married Saturday in Weatherford, Texas. Rev. T. M. NEELY officiated.

E. M. LANGFORD and Annie NEVIL married Saturday in Weatherford, Texas.

Joe SPARRA and Miss A. M. SAVINGER married Saturday in Belton, Texas.

C. F. GOBLE, of Ferris, Texas, and Fannie HICKS married Saturday in Ennis, Texas.

V. B. SUTTON and Mrs. E. E. MATTHEWS married in Ennis, Texas Saturday. Rev. H. T. MCKAY officiated.

Gay BROILES and Ollie SPENCER married Wednesday in Cedar Grove, Texas. Rev. Cam WRIGHT officiated.

Porter KIRCHNER and Minnie VANNOY married in Belton, Texas Friday. The marriage took place in the residence of Henry KIRCHNER. Rev. George W. LEE officiated.

Joe FAWCETT and Annie FISH married in Hillsboro, Texas yesterday. Rev. Jerome DUNCAN officiated. The groom is the son of Mr. and Mrs. John FAWCETT.

E. GOLDSTEINE and Zora HUFFMASTER married in Dallas yesterday. They are residents of Minneola, Texas.

Edward BRADON, 75, died in San Antonio Sunday. He was an immigrant from Germany in 1850 and is survived by two sisters and six children. He was a builder.

John HOPSON stabbed and killed Mat BROWN near La Grange, Texas last night.

R. D. JAMES, 9, died yesterday in Fort Worth.

Mrs. Salah LE LISLE, 74, died yesterday in Fort Worth. Her funeral will be today. She is survived by two daughters, Mattie and Kate LE LISLE.

J. F. DOUTHIT died in Guthrie, Oklahoma Territory of injuries sustained when he was shot three times by his wife last April. He exonerated her before his death. The date wasn't stated.

The four year old son of John VITALIA burned to death yesterday in Leigh, Indian Territory.

Albert BENKE was killed in Castroville, Texas yesterday. He was hit by a piece from a broken flywheel while drilling a well and died of a fractured skull.

Tuesday, November 8, 1904

G. H. STEVENS and Eula ANDERSON married Sunday in Gainesville, Texas.

J. H. BUCHANAN and Bell WOODFORD married Sunday in Terrell, Texas. Rev. W. B. KENDALL officiated.

Newt BELL and Mabel LONGHAM married Sunday in Rice, Texas.

Thomas MARSHALL and Alice COLEMAN married in Marshall, Texas Sunday.

B. C. MCELROY and Bessie Y. UTZ, of Shreveport, Louisiana, married in Marshall, Texas Sunday. Rev. Dean Herbert E. BOWERS officiated.

Robert F. HODGES and Lizzie LaBaun JOHNSON married Sunday in Paris, Texas.

The eight year old son of J. E. GILBERT was killed by a dynamite explosion near Hillsboro, Texas Wednesday.

P. J. MALONE, 60, died Sunday in Fort Worth. His remains will be buried in Danville, Illinois. He was a former resident of Fort Worth, but was living in Gainesville at the time of his death.

Captain Albert G. FIELDS died in Victoria, Texas yesterday. He was a Confederate veteran.

Mrs. Harley CADWELL died in Salida, California Sunday. She was a resident of Gainesville, Texas and will be buried there today.

Mrs. Sarah WHITWORTH, 69, died near Quinlan, Texas Sunday.

V. V. CAVER, 81, died Sunday in Atlanta, Texas. He was buried in Law's Chapel yesterday.

J. B. VESPER died in Corsicana, Texas Sunday.

J. H. WARREN, 69, of Sour Lake, Texas, died in Houston yesterday. His remains will be shopped to Austin where he lived for 50 years.

Marriage licenses issued by Tarrant County Clerk's office: H. C. KOENIG and Mrs. Ethel May PAYNE, S. E. COLEMAN and Ruby HARRISON, D. E. GORDON and Louise MOSZON, H. G. MARTIN and Miss L. HERBERT, Mack THOMPSON and Mollie GLAZE, Allen WOODS and Annie BRUCE, Ed TUCKER and Mariah SMITH, and J. W. JORDAN and Alice M. LAWRENCE.

Births recorded at Tarrant County Clerk's office: a boy to Mr. and Mrs. Eugene WHITWORTH, Arlington, on October 27; a girl to Mr. and Mrs. W. D. DEVORE, Arlington, on October 18; a girl to Mr. and Mrs. C. C. ARCHER, Arlington, on October 20; a girl to Mr. and Mrs. W. N. MILLER, Arlington, on October 20; a girl to Mr. and Mrs. George PERRETT, Arlington, on October 22; a boy to Mr. and Mrs. George G. MOSIER, Arlington, on October 30 and a girl to Mr. and Mrs. Abe SCHNIDER, Fort Worth, on November 1.

Deaths recorded at Tarrant County Clerk's office: Mrs. Mattie GORDON, 26, residing in Fort Worth died on October 26 with no cause listed; and Mrs. Elizabeth RUSHING, no age listed, residing in Arlington, died on November 3 with no cause listed.

Wednesday, November 9, 1904

Luke WARREN was killed yesterday in an explosion in the naphtha house at Trinity Cotton Oil Company in Dallas.

Mrs. Fannie PAYNE, 68, died in Oak Cliff, near Dallas, yesterday. She was an old settler of Dallas. She was a daughter of A. W. MORTON. Survivors include her daughter, Mrs. FREEMAN, who lives in Indian Territory, and her son John PAYNE, who lives in Oak Cliff.

Mrs. Julia M. TABER, wife of John C. B. TABER, died in Dallas yesterday. She was born in Norwich, Connecticut on November 16, 1843. She was the mother of ten children. Seven of them survive her: Ben, Sam, Alfred, Rock, Oak, Martin and Alma. Her funeral will be today with burial in Oakwood Cemetery.

Walter H. EARLE was convicted of the murder Charles D. MADDUX on August 22, 1904 and sentenced to twenty years in prison yesterday.

Charley LEWIS, the son of W. S. LEWIS, is reported to have burned to death in a hotel fire in Sour Lake, Texas. The date of the fire was not reported. His remains were shipped to Moody, Texas for burial.

Births recorded at Tarrant County Clerk's office: a boy to Mr. and Mrs. Percy S. BLACK, Fort Worth, on November 5; and a girl to Mr. and Mrs. W. E. BOSWELL, Saginaw, on October 28.

Deaths recorded at Tarrant County Clerk's office: Mrs. Martha BONHAM, Fort Worth, on November 5. No cause or age was reported.

Marriage licenses issued by Tarrant County Clerk's office: N. C. WHITE and Pauline F. FEHLERSON, and Porter KING and Georgia A. SHERLOCK.

Rev. J. M. ZIMMERMAN, 82, died in Kurten, Texas yesterday. He had lived in Brazos County since 1858 and was a Confederate veteran. He was also a Royal Arch Mason and an Odd Fellow.

J. W. HARRISON, 62, died yesterday in Oak Grove, Texas. He will be buried in Ennis, Texas today. He was a Catholic.

W. W. HALL and May FLORES married yesterday in Hillsboro, Texas. Rev. Z. T. HUBBARD officiated.

J. H. BUCHANAN and Bell WOODFORD married Monday in Terrell, Texas.

Four people died in a hotel fire in Sour Lake, Texas yesterday. Dead are Lee HANSON, C. E. LEWIS, Jack W. SMITH and Clara SMITH. The fire destroyed the Silver Queen Hotel. Sam KINDRED and his wife were arrested and charged with arson.

Hence POE, 62, a pioneer of Tarrant County, died yesterday at his home near Mansfield, Texas. He was a Confederate soldier and a farmer. His funeral will be today. Burial will be in Johnson Station.

Thursday, November 10, 1904

George W. MCADAMS, 66, died in Dallas. He was the father of Charles R. MCADAMS. The date was not legible.

The funeral of Julia M. TABER was held in the Cathedral of the Sacred Heart yesterday in Dallas.

Ada Louise WALKER died of pneumonia Tuesday in Ballard, Texas. She was the sister of Thomasine WALKER of Dallas.

George BROWN, 50, of Acme, Texas, was run over and killed by a Rock Island Railroad train at El Reno, Indian Territory yesterday.

Will STARLINK was shot and killed by City Marshal Bud MORRISON in Clarksville, Texas Monday.

Albert P. SAUNDERS committed suicide yesterday in Guthrie, Oklahoma Territory. He was a defeated candidate for county commissioner in Tuesday's election.

Mrs. Ruth Matthews RATLIFF died in Fort Worth yesterday. The funeral will be today from the Mulkey Memorial Church. She was the daughter of W. R. MATTHEWS.

F. J. GATES, of Gainesville, Texas, and Mrs. J. E. SCULLEY married yesterday in Fort Worth. Rev Luther LITTLE performed the ceremony in the home of Mrs. Robert NOBLE.

Fred ABERNATHY, 13, was run over by a wagon and killed yesterday in Jacksonville, Texas.

J. P. DWYER drowned in San Jacinto Bay several days ago. His body was recovered yesterday at La Porte, Texas. He left a wife and two children in Houston.

A man believed to be J. A. MURRAY was struck and killed by a Southern Pacific train in San Antonio yesterday. Only a bank deposit slip with the name J. A. MURRAY could be found on his body.

Marriage licenses issued by Tarrant County Clerk's office: F. J. GATES and Mrs. E. C. SCULLEY, J. W. ABBOTT and Ethel SPARKS, B. A. SADDLER and Fannie W. MILLER, William VAUGHAN and Bessie BRIGGINS, and Zachary T. ANDERSON and Helen C. INGERSEN.

Births recorded at Tarrant County Clerk's office: a boy to Mr. and Mrs. Cecil MORROW, Glenwood, on November 6; a boy to Mr. and Mrs. Tom TAYLOR, Kennedale, on November 6, a girl to Mr. and Mrs. I. I. ELROD, Kennedale, on November 8 and a boy to Mr. and Mrs. J. N. MCCARTY, Kennedale, on November 5.

Friday, November 11, 1904

William GEATON is standing trial in Roswell, New Mexico Territory for the murder of Henry JONES, formerly of Cleburne, Texas. JONES's body was found near Roswell on October 25, 1903. The two men were well drillers.

Josie ROGERS, 5 months, died of whooping cough on October 31 in Weatherford, Texas.

Mrs. Margaret BRAWLEY, 56, died in the home of her daughter, Mrs. Oscar HILL, in Roberts, Texas on October 29. Her body was taken to Haskell, Texas for burial.

Mary BISH, 45, died Monday. She was buried Tuesday in Brock, Texas, where she lived.

Mrs. W. N. CLEMENS, 26, died of typhoid fever at her home in Peaster, Texas last Friday.

Mrs. Susan JAMES, 26, died of typhoid fever at her home near Brock, Texas Saturday.

Jimmy EDGEMAN, 13, died of heart failure Saturday at his home south of Weatherford, Texas.

Mrs. R. L. HUNTER, an aged lady, died at her home in Weatherford, Texas Wednesday.

Captain Ben A. VANSICKLE, 96, died at his home in Vansickle, ten miles south of Greenville, Texas Tuesday. He was born in San Augustine, Texas. His wife, aged 90, and numerous children and grandchildren survive him.

Mrs. Dan SULLIVAN died of meningitis in San Antonio Wednesday. She is survived by her husband, four sons (Daniel, Will, Walter and John) and three daughters (Mrs. John CLEM, Mrs. J. R. COLLINS, and Annie SULLIVAN). Dan Sullivan is a banker. Daniel recently married. Mrs. Clem and Annie are in the Philippines.

Mrs. Edna NIRDLINGER died in Denver Tuesday. She was the sister of Mrs. Sam GROSS of Marshall, Texas. Her remains were shipped to Leavenworth, Kansas, for burial.

D. C. SCARBOROUGH died in Alba, Texas Tuesday. He was a physician.

E. D. BUTLER died Wednesday in Temple, Texas. He was the father of Mrs. F. H. MERRILL, Kate BUTLER and Mrs. NETTLETON.

Mrs. John PORTER died yesterday of black jaundice near Telico, Texas.

Bob LEVERITT, 35, died Wednesday of congestion at Village Bend, near Mineral Wells, Texas.

Mrs. J. C. HUTCHINGSON died in Hico, Texas Wednesday. She was buried in the city cemetery yesterday.

The three year old child of Mr. and Mrs. Andy BRUMBELOW died near Terrell, Texas Wednesday. Burial was in Kemp, Texas.

Luther CARPENTER died Wednesday of typhoid fever in Elmo, Texas.

R. H. HARRISON, a music teacher living near Nash, Texas, died Wednesday afternoon.

Alfred Harmon LEWIS died at Chisholm, Texas Wednesday of typhoid fever.

J. B. DAVENPORT and Annie May HARBERGER married in Peaster, Texas last Sunday. Rev. B. F. FRONBARGER officiated.

Roe LIDE and Salevia HEMPHILL, both of Millsap, married in Weatherford, Texas Sunday.

D. A. REEVES and Mattie TAYLOR married Tuesday in Weatherford, Texas.

W. C. AKARD and Clyde Fay CULWEL, both of Springtown, Texas, married there Wednesday.

H. B. BARKER and Lillie AMES married in Greenwood, Texas Monday.

M. L. DANIELS, of Cleburne, Texas, and Etta HARELL of Grandview, Texas, married in the latter Wednesday. The bride is the daughter of G. A. HARRELL. Rev. D. I. SMYTH officiated.

H. P. VARLEY and Vera HICKS married Tuesday in Gainesville, Texas.

J. A. BLAIR and Miss I. E. WARD married yesterday in Gainesville, Texas.

Rev. W. E. MORGAN and Zudie COLEMAN married in Hallville, Texas Sunday. Rev. E. TATUM officiated. The bride is the daughter of D. E. COLEMAN.

T. H. BLOCK and Florence SEARS married in Belton, Texas yesterday. Rev. George W. LEE officiated.

Wilmotte S. CURTIS and Edith PURYEAR married in Corsicana, Texas yesterday.

Henry YOUNG was found guilty of first degree murder in Waxahachie, Texas yesterday. He killed Atherton MOORE. YOUNG will be hanged.

Mrs. Cy LANE shot and killed Bob HILL, who was her brother-in-law, in Carrollton, Texas Wednesday night.

Mrs. T. C. PHILLIPS, 34, died at St. Joseph's Infirmary in Fort Worth yesterday. Her remains were shipped to Hillsboro, Texas.

Sid BOULWARE, 51, was found dead in his home in Fort Worth yesterday. He died of heart failure. A three year old boy is the only surviving relative in Fort Worth.

Marriage licenses issued by Tarrant County Clerk's office: M. F. GRAHAM and Minnie May GATHING, William COX and Lillie HARONG, T. J. ANDERSON and Mrs. E. G. LUND, and R. R. DAVIS and Mary Ellen MORRIS.

Births recorded at Tarrant County Clerk's office: twin boys to Mr. and Mrs. M. D. MIMS, Glenwood, on November 2.

Saturday, November 12, 1904

J. R. EDWARDS was acquitted yesterday of manslaughter charges in Waxahachie, Texas. He was accused of the death of Sam RICSMAN, in Ennis, Texas last December. The jury ruled EDWARDS acted in self-defense.

The infant daughter of Mr. and Mrs. Auburn CHEEK died today of burns she received Thursday in Cleburne, Texas.

J. A. HOLBROOK, 60, died yesterday near Sunset, Texas.

Marriage licenses issued by Tarrant County Clerk's office: C. L. MADISON and Mrs. Henry DEE, William THOMAS and Tennie BLACKBURN.

John C. ROY died last night in Arlington, Texas. His funeral will be today in Arlington. He was the father of R. E. L. ROY.

Walter ARCHDALE and Antoine GUERICK were killed in a coal mine explosion near South McAlester, Indian Territory yesterday.

Sunday, November 13, 1904

The four year old son of Philip ROE, of Pond Creek, Oklahoma Territory burned to death yesterday. He was playing with matches.

The remains of J. C. THOMAS, who died in Dallas Friday, were shipped to Louisville, Kentucky for burial. He was a salesman.

The infant child of Mr. and Mrs. E. F. CASSIDY died in Fort Worth Friday night. Its remains will be buried in the Catholic cemetery this afternoon.

Sarah F. ALLEN, 70, died in Benbrook, Texas Friday night and will be buried today.

Marriage licenses issued by Tarrant County Clerk's office: W. C. MCPHERSON and Eula KELLEY, Charles F. WATT and Rosa HUKILL, Fred BILBERRY and Cora CAKE, Max KING and Cora JORDAN, S. P. WOLFF and Effie MAXEY, Joe HAYDEN and Alomella ZANONE, and Dr. E.E. MOORE and Bessie PLATT.

Births recorded at Tarrant County Clerk's office: a boy to Mr. and Mrs. W. E. MELTON, Fort Worth, on November 11; and a girl to Mr. and Mrs. Pat DOYLE, North Fort Worth, on November 11.

Deaths recorded at Tarrant County Clerk's office: Mrs. Ruth Matthews RATLIFF, 27, residing in Fort Worth, died on November 9 with no cause listed.

Bessie MCLEAN and Dr. Lloyd POLLOCK married Saturday in Fort Worth. Rev. B. B. RAMAGE officiated. The bride is the daughter of Judge and Mrs. W. P. MCLEAN. The groom is the son of Dr. J. R. POLLOCK.

Virginia HARP and William MILLS married in Fort Worth last Sunday. Rev. J. W. WHITEHURST officiated.

Monday, November 14, 1904

James L. REDPATH, 33, was found dead in Water Valley, near San Angelo, Texas yesterday. His remains were sent to Martin, Michigan.

Steve HIGGINS was run over and killed by a train near Laredo, Texas Saturday night.

Henry BELL was allegedly shot and killed by Bob BONNER at a dance near Tyler, Texas Saturday. BONNER is still at large.

E. W. SEWELL and Mrs. Frances W. CALHOUN of San Antonio married in St. Louis Saturday. The couple will live in Houston.

Joseph C. STAULTS and Maggie FOGLE married in Gill, Texas Sunday.

W. E. MULLINS and Edna SCALES married in Ardmore, Indian Territory Thursday. The bride is the daughter of Bob SCALES.

W. E. TURNER and Rosela BANTLEY married Thursday in Temple, Texas. Rev. C. R. WRIGHT performed the ceremony.

William C. HAMILTON and Nellie Louise DONOHO married in Clarksville, Texas Wednesday. The bride is the daughter of Captain and Mrs. J.B. DONOHO.

Russell M. HAMILTON and Charlotte P. SMALLWOOD married in San Angelo, Texas Saturday.

Louise ESTES and A. B. ROBERTS married Wednesday in Texarkana.

William CARL and Ida ROSS married Saturday in Gainesville, Texas.

H. L. HODGE and Mary WILLIARD married Sunday in Greenville, Texas. Dr. J. J. COPPEDGE officiated.

O. H. STIFF and Marie EMERSON married at the First Presbyterian Church in McKinney, Texas Wednesday.

S. P. WOLFF and Effie MAXIE married in Watauga, Texas last night. They will live on Clark's Ranch north of Fort Worth. WOLFF is the ranch manager.

Mrs. Daniela MILLER, wife of G. S. MILLER, died Sunday in Fort Worth. Her funeral will be today. She is survived by her husband and five children.

Martin J. MCDONOUGH, 37, died in Fort Worth Sunday. His funeral will be today. He is survived by his wife, a daughter and a brother.

William WARD, 23, died in Peaster, Texas Friday.

Mrs. L. T. DAVIS died in Elk City, Oklahoma Territory Thursday and was buried in Weatherford, Texas the following day.

Mrs. Bettie RUTLEDGE, 21, died in Whitt, Texas on October 30.

Johnnie G. LINDSAY, 4, died of diphtheria near Garner, Texas a week ago today.

Willie Wray WRIGHT, 2, died of erysipelas near Whitt, Texas a week ago today.

Mrs. F. A. SIMMONS, 25, died of tuberculosis at Rock Creek, Texas on November 1.

Amp MACAULEY, of Brown's Valley, Texas, died Thursday and was buried in Bazette, Texas Friday.

Henry M. PULE, of Weches, Texas, died near Barry, Texas Saturday. Barry is six miles from Corsicana. His body was sent to Weches.

Mrs. Miles BIRDSONG, 41, died Friday in Greenville, Texas. She is survived by her husband and six children.

Floyd GREEN, 4, died in Sunset, Texas Friday. He was son of W. S. GREEN.

Christina BERG, 80, died in Corpus Christi, Texas Friday. Her funeral was that afternoon.

Ben F. CARVER died at his home in Gordonsville, Texas Friday.

Elizabeth MCCLURE, 82, died west of Paris, Texas Saturday. She was the widow of Captain Jack MCCLURE.

Lucy WORTHAM died in Dallas Friday. Her body was shipped to Temple, Texas for burial. She was the mother of Dr. E. F. WORTHAM.

Mary L. JOHNSON, 75, died in Forney, Texas Friday. She was the widow of Telephus A. JOHNSON and had lived in Waco, Texas for forty years. She was buried Saturday in Forney.

Charlotte M. SIDBURY, 75, died in Corpus Christi, Texas Saturday.

William SLATER died yesterday in Leigh, Indian Territory. His remains were shipped to Austin for burial.

W. H. TILLEY died on a train yesterday morning near Houston. He was en route from Bremond, Texas.

John HARDIN died in Terrell, Texas Friday. His funeral was yesterday in Terrell. He was a Confederate veteran who had lived in Kaufman County since 1857.

Tuesday, November 15, 1904

Rufugio SALINAS was killed Sunday in a billiard and gambling room in Carrizo, Texas. Two soldiers of the U. S. 26th Infantry, Company H, were implicated in the death. They were surrendered to civilian authorities.

Francis W. B. RUBY, 13, died yesterday in San Antonio. He was shot while playing with other boys in a game Sunday.

James CRUTCHFIELD committed suicide yesterday in Gastana, Mexico.

William WADE, about 32, was shot and killed yesterday in a saloon in Waco, Texas. Tom CASEY is in custody. WADE is survived by his wife and two children.

Marriage licenses issued by Tarrant County Clerk's office: A. W. JACKSON and Laura JOHNSON, Phillip Lloyd POLLOCK and Bess MCLEAN, Ross SETSER and Edna FOSTER, T. C. HUTSON and Ollie JOHNSON, W. R. RUTHERFORD and Miss D. E. R. MATTHEWS, and W. D. HARRIS and Sadie B. GRAY.

Births recorded at Tarrant County Clerk's office: a boy to Mr. and Mrs. John KING, North Fort Worth, on November 10 and a boy to Mr. and Mrs. T. M. ROBERTSON, North Fort Worth, on October 28.

Deaths recorded at Tarrant County Clerk's office: Gilmore HIMES, 2 months, residing in North Fort Worth, died on November 13 with no cause listed.

Wednesday, November 16, 1904

Mack SUMMERLIN and Ethel POOL married Sunday near Burleson, Texas. The bride is the daughter of Mr. and Mrs. J. T. POOL.

Ernest WOODSON and Bettie LANKFORD married Sunday south of Burleson, Texas. Rev. C. M. WOODSON performed the ceremony.

W. C. ROGERS and Lila GRIGGS married Sunday in Ennis, Texas. The ceremony was performed by Rev. W. C. HILBURN in the Methodist church.

Thomas DUNLOP died Saturday in Jefferson, Texas.

Susie BOWEN, about 9, died MONDAY in Mineral Wells, Texas. She was the daughter of Mr. and Mrs. C. H. BOWEN.

J. H. G. FORD, about 50, died Monday in Mineral Wells, Texas.

Mrs. A. B. WHILBECK, 45, died Sunday in Creechville, Texas. She was buried in Telico, Texas the next day.

Mrs. William WOOD died suddenly Saturday of heart disease at her home three miles from Jefferson, Texas. Her husband was a prosperous farmer.

Daniel M. GREEN was found dead yesterday in a boarding house in Saint Louis, Missouri. He was a druggist from Gainesville, Texas. Police are investigating. GREEN was found fully clothed, lying on his bed with a revolver in his hand and a gunshot wound to the temple.

Dr. EDDLEMAN, 81, died Sunday in his home in Pilot Point, Texas. He was buried Monday in Pilot Point Cemetery. Elder F. L. YOUNG preached the funeral. Dr. EDDLEMAN had been a resident of Pilot Point since 1851. He was a physician. No given name was reported.

Mr. O. M. PUTNAM died Saturday night in Lovelace, Texas. She was buried in Prairie Dale Cemetery. Her husband is the postmaster in Lovelace.

W. M. UNDERWOOD:, 47, died yesterday in Roscoe, Texas. His body was shipped to Navarro County for burial.

W. T. LANGSTON, 27, died of pneumonia yesterday in his home near Melissa, Texas. He is survived by his wife and two children.

Mrs. Hugh HARRIS died Sunday near Temple, Texas.

Will RAMSEY, 27, died yesterday of typhoid fever in Terrell, Texas.

Mrs. J. W. BRADLEY, Sr., died yesterday in Goldthwaite, Texas.

Mrs. Will EMMONS died yesterday in Byron, Texas.

Dessie GRIFFIN and Robert HARRIS married Sunday in Pittsburg, Texas. The bride is the daughter of Mr. and Mrs. W. A. GRIFFIN.

Dr. Joe SLAUGHTER and Grace HENDERSON married yesterday in Van Alstyne, Texas. Rev. J. E. VINCON officiated.

J. R. REED and Donna MCDONALD married Sunday in Temple, Texas. Rev A. V. ATKINS officiated.

Albert D. KERNODEL and Mrs. Alice DOOL married Monday in Belton, Texas. Rev. George W. LEE officiated.

George CARVER and Bettie GARRETT married Sunday in Temple, Texas. Rev. C. R. WRIGHT officiated.

Asa MAJORS and Fannie MCCANDLESS married Sunday in McKinney, Texas.

Arthur REEVES and Maude BOON married Sunday in the home of F. M. REEVES in Pittsburg, Texas.

Annie FAULKNER, 73, died in Fort Worth yesterday. Her funeral is today at St. Patrick's Church. Burial will be in Oakwood Cemetery.

Nettie PRATT, wife of Wells PRATT, died at St. Joseph's Infirmary in Fort Worth yesterday. Her remains will be shipped to Jackson, Michigan for the funeral and burial.

T. J. MAY, 69, was killed yesterday in Terrell, Texas. He was hit by a Texas and Pacific train while crossing the tracks.

Jim WOODS was arrested in El Reno, Indian Territory and charged with the November 4, 1903, murders of Mrs. Sophronia AMES and A. J. JACKSON near Davenport, Oklahoma Territory.

Thursday, November 17, 1904

"Grandma" SILVERS, 94, burned to death Tuesday in Winsboro, Texas. Her clothing caught fire from the stove. She was the mother of J. F. SILVERS.

John ANDERSON, 18, burned to death yesterday in Muskogee, Indian Territory. He was blind and unable to escape his burning dwelling. His grandmother and little brother were severely burned, but managed to escape.

Will PRICE was murdered Tuesday at his home near Bryan, Texas.

M. C. PIERCE was killed yesterday in a fall in the mines of the Central Coal Company in McDade, Texas.

Colonel Alexander SHIPLEY, 74, died in Austin Tuesday. His remains were sent to San Antonio for burial in a national cemetery. He was a retired U.S. Army officer.

William RIDLEY and Walter TUCKER are on trial in Lawton, Oklahoma Territory for the killing of Munsey VAUGHN last November. VAUGHN was the son-in-law of RIDLEY. VAUGHN and his wife had separated. VAUGHN was visiting his wife when he was killed. (See November 26, 1903).

Marriage licenses issued by Tarrant County Clerk's office: W. I. MAYS and Ruby HAYWOOD, and S. H. PATTERSON and Annie L. MCDONALD.

Friday, November 18, 1904

William GLEATON was convicted yesterday of second degree murder in Roswell, New Mexico Territory. He was convicted for the murder of Henry JONES his partner in October, 1903.

W. F. TURNELL died in Dallas yesterday. His funeral will be today with burial in Oakland Cemetery. He was a Confederate veteran, serving in the 3rd Georgia Infantry.

Lucy CARTER, 13, died in Dallas yesterday after a fall from the second story of the school she attended.

Hattie Howell DELAY and Robert E. HARRIS married Wednesday in Comstock, Texas. Rev. C. H. WARY officiated.

Gyp FREEMAN died Wednesday from an accidentally self-inflicted gunshot wound in Meeker, Texas.

Births recorded at Tarrant County Clerk's office: a boy to Mr. and Mrs. John DUNN, Azle, on November 9; a girl to Mr. and Mrs. J. T. JAMES, North Fort Worth, on November 6; a boy to Mr. and Mrs. J. B. CLARK, North Fort Worth, on November 29 (sic); and a girl to Mr. and Mrs. M. E. LERPIN, Mansfield, on November 16.

Marriage licenses issued by Tarrant County Clerk's office: C. D. GREGORY and Cora SMALL, William TAYLOR and Maggie WEIGHT.

Saturday, November 19, 1904

Marriage licenses issued by Tarrant County Clerk's Office: R. L. LEWIS and Essie HILL and John WILSON and Sudie LEWIS.

W. T. ELDRIDGE is on trial or the shooting death of a Captain DUNAVANT, which took place August 11, 1902. The trial is being held in Richmond, Texas.

Bert THOMASON married Essie MCCOSTIN in Fort Worth on Thursday morning. The groom is a Fort Worth Police officer. They will live in Fort Worth.

Every Name Index

The index contains the name of every person mentioned. Space considerations caused the omission of the names of wives in birth records. *The Fort Worth Record* listed, with only rare exceptions, only births occurring when the parents were a married couple. In those cases, the listing was usually in the form of "a boy to Mr. and Mrs. John SMITH of Glenwood on May 2". Therefore only the name of the husband was listed in those entries. In cases where the mother's name was listed, her name was reported.

Similarly, only the names of the individuals are reported in the eindex. Titles such as military ranks, positions in the clegy, political offices or marital designators are omitted for space considerations.

As is the custom in genealogical reporting, surnames are in all capital letters. Original spellings have been left as they appeared in the news stories.

ABBOTT
 J. W., 192
 John, 88
 Maggie L., 30
 O. D., 113
 Thorpe, 28
ABERNATHIE
 Frank, 18
ABERNATHY
 Boyd, 59
 Buck, 76
 Fred, 192
 Tom, 58, 59
ABNEY
 R. I., 95
ABRAM
 James, 21
ABSLOR
 H. L., 18
ABSTON
 Mattie, 18
ACKERMAN
 Etta M., 150
ADAIR
 George, 31
 James H., 31
 W. A., 32
ADAMS
 C. M., 7
 Docia, 143
 Edith, 128
 Edith Lyle, 130
 Frank, 139
 George H., 188
 Gono, 45
 Homer, 134
 Hugo Claiborne, 83
 J. B., 157
 J. D., 104
 J. O., 117, 123

J. P., 128
J. W., 130
James, 8
John, 84
Lizzie, 152
Mark, 169, 171
Phil, 55
Q. S., 151
Ruby, 117, 123
Vernon, 11
W. H., 128
Willie, 187
ADAMSON
 Fannie, 28
 Jennie, 43
 Larkin, 41
ADCOCK
 C. L., 145
ADDINGTON
 Effie Robertson, 20
 Parks, 20
ADDISON
 Lora, 32
ADELBERG
 L., 17
ADEN
 Bert M., 91
ADKINS
 Ella, 162
 H. M., 152
 Sallie, 188
ADLER
 Charles, 58
 L., 58
ADMIRE
 Eli L., 72
 Lige, 152
AESPAUGH
 J. A., 75
AGEE

Howard L., 179
AGROBRIGHT
 Ollie, 86
AHLES
 Albert, 143
AIKEN
 H. J., 31
 William F., 104
AIKENS
 Si, 29
AIKIN
 Mary, 28
AINSWORTH, 97
 James, 146
AKARD
 W. C., 193
AKE
 N. N., 113
AKERS
 Nina Fay, 178
 Walter, 174
ALBEROS
 Nona, 139
ALBERT
 H., 167
ALBERTHAL
 W. A., 55
ALBRIGHT, 105
 A. S., 32
ALBRITTON
 W. F., 165
ALDERSON
 Virginia, 108
ALDREDGE
 George N., 32
 Will, 32
ALDRIDGE
 Mattie, 160
ALEXANDER
 A. R., 129

Ansel B., 127
B. P., 91
David, 32
Eddie, 167
Ethel, 58
Ethel C., 129
G. C., 108
George, 52
J. P., 62
J. W., 137
James D., 110
John T., 81
L. P., 156
Mark, 76
Mary, 176, 177
Pearl, 115
Penelope E., 62
R. E., 52
Richard, 46
W. M., 62
W. P., 169
Walter, 103
ALEXANDER's
 John T., 82
ALFORD
 J. P., 123
ALLAN
 Manual, 14
ALLCORN
 C. M., 178
ALLEN
 A. J., 89
 Alta, 53
 Arthur O., 105
 Dud, 25
 G. M., 36
 Harvey, 177
 J. S., 143
 J. T., 102
 James, 10

John, 73
Laura Luckett, 129
M. E., 86
Minerva S., 143
Sarah F., 194
Vida Maude, 169
W. H., 51
W. M., 11, 89
W. S., 84
ALLMAN
  Alexander, 179
ALMANDAREZ
  Perferio, 112
ALMONS
  John, 183
ALOCORN
  Mercario, 163
ALREAD
  Vicie, 163
ALTENBERG
  John, 49
  Mary, 49
  Walter, 49
ALVIS
  Hattie, 7
AMACKER
  Charlie, 24
AMANN
  George, 105
AMES
  Lillie, 193
  Sophronia, 197
AMMER
  J. A., 7
AMMONS
  Henry, 131
AMYX
  Fannie, 65
ANDAY
  Andrew, 56
ANDERSON
  A. C., 59
  A. H., 170
  A. J., 81
  Andrew, 176
  Bertha, 34
  Bill, 168
  Cora, 129
  Eula, 190
  George, 103
  H. C., 161
  H. N., 51
  Harry L., 42
  Howard, 136
  J. P., 11
  J. R., 161
  John, 197
  Knox A., 182
  Lee, 65
  M. E., 59

Mattie, 30
N., 18
O. R., 160
O. S., 163
S. W., 97
T. J., 193
T. R., 19
Thomas Albert, 156
Zachary T., 192
ANDREWS
  Charlie, 124
  Daisy, 41
  E., 169
  E. L., 10
  Ernest, 11
  John, 150
  Julian, 99
  Julian Monroe, 97
ANGEL
  E. M., 139
  Price, 139
ANGLES
  Tom, 162
ANGLEY
  Deshie, 153
APPLEBY
  Edward, 41
APPLETON
  J. A., 138
APPLEWHITE
  A. L., 131
  Eliza, 31
  J. H., 114
  Stephen, 31
  T. C., 31
ARANT
  H. W., 174
ARCHDALE
  Walter, 194
ARCHER
  C. C., 191
  Cleveland, 15
  Ed, 107
  P. C., 145, 154, 160, 174, 175
  Walter, 15
ARDEN
  Annie, 20
  J. C., 177
  Mollie Clough, 177
ARENDT
  H. C., 91
ARMANDIAZ
  Juan, 144
ARMISTEAD
  Ellen, 144
ARMSTRONG
  David H., 151
  E. L., 23
  F. E., 41

Frances, 15
Ike, 10
J., 126
Lurah, 155
R. H., 185
S. A., 17
W. E., 114
ARNAPEIGER
  John, 18
ARNOLD, 32
  E., 188
  Frank, 13
  Fred, 13
  L. L., 176, 177
  Mose, 168
  Nell, 188
  Stella, 131
  Will, 80
  William, 13
ARP
  R. W., 18
ARTHUR
  Daisy, 147
ASHBY
  George, 95
ASHCROFT
  F. M., 86
ASHE
  W. L., 143
ATCHESON
  James, 57
ATHERTON
  Eunice, 94
ATKEISON
  R. W., 180, 181
ATKINS
  A. V., 196
ATKINSON
  Samuel, 133
ATTWELL
  Adrian, 82
AULT
  Lavonia, 184
AUSTIN
  Bettie, 127
  Charles A., 172
  J. P., 16
  J. W., 171
  P. T., 77
  S., 109
  Will J., 103
AUTREY
  Cora, 17
  Dofe, 94
AUTRY
  L. A., 15
  Lee, 116
  Scottie B., 13
AUTSEY, 123
AVELARE

Francisco, 128
AVERELLO
  Sam, 173
AVERETT
  B. P., 121
AVERITT
  D. C., 169
  Eulalie Blanche, 169
  James, 45
AVINGER
  M. R., 24
AVRILLA, 180
AXE
  Ludwig, 56
AXELROD
  J., 36
AYERS
  B. C., 169
  C. C., 133
  F. G., 88
  Jonah, 47
  W. E., 168
AYLOR
  W. M., 138
AYRES
  Abraham Lincoln, 109
  Elizabeth, 108
  Katie, 46
BABB
  A. S., 71
BACHTEL
  Walter L., 84
BACKALOUPE
  Ada, 140
  Lon, 140
BACKE
  John, 55
BACON
  Mildred, 131
BADER
  Gus, 50, 100
BAER
  Fran A., 85
BAERTICHT
  Al G., 167
  Virginia E., 167
BAGGS
  R. J., 25
BAGLEY
  W. M., 39
BAGWELL
  B. R., 188
  J. L., 155
BAILEY
  C. E., 79
  Del, 163
  E. K., 122
  Ernest, 153
  J. C., 63
  J. F., 33

Jennie, 109
John, 131
L. N., 143
P., 147
P. J., 173
R. H., 24
Sam, 111
William A., 145
BAINES
   W. W., 108
BAKASKY
   Theodore, 60
BAKER
   Ancel, 174
   Beulah, 86
   C., 145
   C. L., 138
   Collins, 46
   D., 61
   D. C., 61
   E. K., 115
   J. H., 46
   J. W., 160
   James B., 57
   Joseph, 111
   Leila, 145
   Leve, 34
   M., 135
   Mattie E., 72
   Ola, 42
   R. G., 51
   Rosa, 111
   T. V., 65
   W. E., 96
   Willie, 51
BALCH
   Sallie, 9
BALDWIN
   Anna John, 87
   C. B., 162
   Nina, 72
   R. C., 160
   W. H., 119
BALEW
   Floyd, 80
BALINSUELO
   Pedro, 180
BALL
   Ben, 124
   Hallie, 189
   Harry, 134
   Hattie, 188
   O. D., 33
   Robert, 69
   T. K., 112
   Virginia, 128, 130
BALLARD
   C. B., 72
   Clevia, 137
   E. L., 113

Jennie E., 72
Luther, 125
BALLINGER
   P. F., 143
BALTHROP
   John, 136
BANDONAO
   Anastasia, 182
BANKS
   Challie, 139
   Frankie, 105
   Mabel, 88
   Maggie, 155
   S. K., 45
   Walter, 88
BANKSTON
   J. G., 177
BANNER
   Ernest, 53
BANNISTER
   R. H., 144
BANTLEY
   Rosela, 194
BANTON
   Bettie, 77, 78
BARBER
   John, 42
   Mary, 190
BARBOOZA
   Tom, 34
BARCLAY
   C. M., 97
   Foy, 135
   Rigsby L., 85
   William W., 100
BARDENAC
   J. T., 113
BARDON
   William Macon, 110
BARFIELD
   J. N., 129
   Lillian Belle, 160
BARGSLEY
   John, 175
BARKER
   "Aunt Sue", 54
   Charles H., 54
   H. B., 193
   M. B., 97
   William C., 98
BARKLEY
   E. C., 155
BARKSDALE
   B. M., 180
   Elizabeth, 89
BARLIOUR
   Dodie, 181
BARLOW
   Grace, 55
BARMOSE

Kate, 111
BARNARD
   George, 31
BARNES
   B. O., 43
   Charles M., 60
   E. F., 85
   Frances, 60
   John, 150
   Sam, 151
   W. X., 102
BARNETT
   Esther, 103
   John, 102
   Kid, 50
   M. A. V., 55
   Ruth, 167
BARNHILL
   W. G., 168
BARNWELL
   R. E., 29
BARR
   G. W., 35
   George W., 33
   H. B., 61
   J. W., 170
BARRETT
   L., 100
   Louis Sherwood, 52
BARRICK
   L. E., 128
BARRIER
   M. L., 67
BARROW
   Lillie, 24
BARRY
   Byron T., 169
   G. R., 129
BARTEK
   Frank, 94
   J. E., 10
BARTELS
   G. A., 55
BARTHOLD
   C. C., 54
BARTLETT
   John T., 88
   S. T., 29, 31
   Walton G., 51
BARTON
   J. A., 118
   Marion, 125
   R. W., 129
   W. C., 176
BASS
   Dana, 41
   J. R., 91
BASSAHAN, 116
BASYE
   Claude, 85

BATEMAN
   Daniel, 114
   E., 127
BATES
   Fred, 122
   J. L., 34
   James, 36, 39
BATESON
   J. A., 70
   John, 43
   John A., 23
BATISTE
   A. C., 145
   Adam, 145
BATT
   Lawrence, 59
BATTAILLE
   D. F., 71
BATTERSON
   C. T., 78
BATTLE, 8
   Rofe, 8
BAUER
   Leo, 116
BAUGH
   Daisy, 77
BAXTER
   J. H., 144, 155, 159, 169, 178
   J. T., 187
   Willie, 165
BAYLESS
   W. B., 66
BAYLEY
   E. G., 155
BAYLOR
   F. W., 96
BAYS
   Tom, 65
BEACH
   William Edward, 95
BEACHUM
   Frank A., 54
BEAGLE
   J. A., 66
BEAL
   Dolla, 152
BEALE
   Dona, 44
   Jack, 50
BEALL
   Claude A., 153, 155
   Mary, 81
BEAN
   F. M., 30
BEANLAND
   C. E., 188
BEARD
   Johnnie, 21
   Texana, 162

BEARDON
  George, 154
BEASLEY
  John, 75
  Rebecca H., 15
BEATY
  Charles, 149
  John, 42
  Oscar, 157
BEAUCHAMP
  E. F., 144
BEAUMONT
  R. W., 44
BEAUREGARD
  P. G. T., 49
  Richard T., 49
BEAVERS
  George, 176
BECHTOLD
  H., 11
BECK
  E. L., 107
  Lizzie, 162
  Maggie, 179
  Margaret Theresa, 107
  W. F., 162
BECKERT
  J. W., 118
BECKETT
  F. C., 116
BECKHAM
  Ethel, 107
  M., 151
  T. J., 24
BECKMAN
  Evelyn Warene, 187
BECKNELL
  C. T., 127
  Maggie, 7
BECSON
  Ira, 79
BEDECARRAX
  J. Emma, 158
BEDINGFIELD
  Sam, 157
BEGGS
  Christine, 7, 8
  Jeff D., 125
BELCHER
  M. A., 47
BELDEN
  Ashton, 24
BELEW
  F. E., 141
BELIKEN
  Rosa, 83
BELL
  Austin, 102
  B. B., 189
  Carrie, 57
  Dick, 163
  Dora, 14
  Emil, 159
  Frank, 19
  George, 110
  George W., 10
  Henry, 194
  Holly B., 137
  J. L. L., 157
  J. T., 114
  John, 9, 167
  John L., 165
  Joseph, 128
  Mary, 67, 165
  Newt, 190
  Sam, 36
  Sarah C. Perry, 110
  T. E., 170
  W. J., 144, 146
  Willis E., 168
BELLAMY
  Nora, 102
BELLE
  Bertha, 73
BELLOWS
  Ben, 188
BELYAN
  James A., 59
BENAVIDES
  Christobal, 149
BENDEL
  O. J., 144
BENDER
  W. B., 139
  William, 139
BENEDICT
  George A., 154
  R. A., 83
BENKE
  Albert, 190
BENNETT
  Anna, 171
  Anna E., 170
  Annie, 140
  C. M., 124
  Charles, 18
  Dan, 46
  E., 49
  Ernie, 50
  Ethel, 51
  G. E., 171
  H. C., 65
  M. M., 151
  Mary, 140
  Sam, 88
  W. A., 67
  W. F., 162
BENSHOW
  Sallie, 141
BENSON
  Fred, 149
  N. L., 149
  Samuel, 26
BENTLEY
  Hattie, 126
BENTON
  Mattie, 83
  Nola, 127
  P. L., 100
  W. S., 47
BERBERSTADT
  Max, 105
BERCOW
  Gilbert, 168
BERG
  Christina, 195
  Vester, 107
BERKELEY
  H. A., 94
BERKLEY
  Ollie, 94
BERLESON
  Will, 87
BERLEY
  Ida, 102
BERNARD
  M. S., 87
  S. M., 87
BERNER
  George, 13
BERRIDGE
  Solomon, 96
BERRIER
  Minnie, 30
BERRING
  Theodore, 137
BERRY
  Anna, 19
  Arch, 99
  Ella, 49
  Elsie, 184
  Fannie, 28
  George, 36
  J. B., 29, 183
  J. M., 88
  Ollie T., 145
  W. J., 141
  Willie, 91
BESSE
  David, 91
  Eulalie, 91
  Medric, 140
BEST
  Edward, 49
  G. M., 49
  James, 49
  P. K., 49
  Pete, 88
  Robert, 49
  W. E., 49
  Willie, 49
  Zoe, 49
BETIK
  Annie, 177
BETTES
  Herbert, 98
  O. H., 57
BEVANS
  W. P., 90
BEVERS
  Charley, 155
BEVIS
  D. T., 156
BEYETT
  Vivian, 151
BIDAUT
  A., 50
BIGGERS
  Cora, 86
  W. I., 164
BIGGUS
  D. H., 129
BIGHAM
  C. R., 18
  G. M., 17
  May, 16
BILBERRY
  Fred, 194
BILES
  Bell, 189
BILLINGS
  Mary C., 70
BILLINGSLEA
  R. H., 173
BILLINGSLEY
  A. E., 42
  Lee, 132
  Logan, 151
BILLINGTON
  J. M., 130
BILSON
  Jennie, 164
BINCON
  Rufus, 9
BINGHAM
  Catherine, 27
  John, 28
BINKLEY
  Tom, 145
BINYON
  Ruby, 71
BIRDSONG
  Ida, 163
  Jim, 139
  Miles, 195
BIRT
  Will, 115
BISH
  Mary, 192
BISHOP

"Uncle Johnnie", 49
C. C., 179
Charles, 49, 164
Emma, 77
H. G., 14
Mattie, 14
BITTING
Lucy, 88
BITZER
G. L., 114
George L., 174
BLACK
A. A., 124
J. B., 30
J. H., 176, 177
John, 136
Laurena C., 63
Malcolm, 143
Oscar, 43
Percy S., 191
Susie, 116
T. C., 103
W., 145
BLACKBURN
Tennie, 193
BLACKFORD
J. B., 16
BLACKLOCK
Alexander Gilpin, 153
BLACKLOUPE
Lon, 34
BLACKMAN
Ed, 115
BLACKMON
Thomas L., 14
BLACKWELL
James, 70
Joe, 70
Kalazler, 189
Margaret, 150
R. A., 167
Thomas H., 15
BLADES
Annie, 113
N. O., 113
BLAFFNER
J. B., 175
BLAIN
H. Parker, 168
BLAINE
Lee, 174
S. B., 97
BLAIR
J. A., 193
James, 84
John D., 59
Will, 51
BLAKE
J. O., 153
BLAKELEY

Lettie, 12
BLAKEMOORE
T. M., 52
BLAKER
A., 54
BLALOCK
Della, 11
BLAND
T. T., 151
BLANKENSHIP
Louis, 180
W. M., 82
W. T., 181
BLANTON
J. J., 89
John B., 89
William P., 89
BLASCO
John, 124
BLASSINGAME
John, 149
BLASSO
J. A., 44
BLEDSOE
D. C., 170
F. F., 137
J. S., 135
John, 156
W. T., 76, 122
William T., 119
BLESSE
Henry J., 176
BLESSING
Etta, 97
BLEVINS
Frank, 87
M. J., 104
Rufus, 160
BLEWETT
C. E., 118
BLEWITT
C. H., 17
Nancy, 17
BLISS
Herberta, 179
BLIZZARD
Don, 59
BLOCK
Robert, 172
T. H., 193
BLUDSO
John, 142
BLUM, 174, 187
Tillie, 89
BLUNT
Patrick, 58
BLYTHE
G. Lee, 91
BOARDMAN
Pearl, 76

BOATMAN
C. B., 122
Elizabeth, 149
BOATWICK
Lucy, 28
BOBB
J. B., 99
James, 99
BOBO
J. F., 34
R. A., 34
BOCK
Birtle, 14
BOCKER
Frank S., 138
BOGAN
Leroy, 114
BOGEN
Lilly, 145
BOGGES
Claude, 185
BOHANNON
G. R., 129
BOID
A. M., 36
BOLAND
Katherine, 85, 87
BOLLETER
Lillian, 47
T. J., 47
BOMAR
Mattie, 189
BOND, 116
E. H., 126, 189
James Earl, 189
William, 17
BONE
W. F., 96
BONHAM
Martha, 191
R. H., 19
BONNER
Bob, 194
C. W., 86
John, 15
M. J., 188
Mabel, 76, 163
Mitch, 45
Pearl, 45
Sue, 188
T. C., 88
BONTON
"Red", 91
Robert, 91
BOOCH
Herman, 138
BOOE
D. J., 45
BOOKER
H. V., 24

BOON
Maude, 196
BOONE
Tony, 58
BOORMAM
F. C., 177
BOOTH
Agre, 117
C. F., 30
J. H., 34
Maude, 104
BOOTHE
J. H., 35
BOOZ
W. J., 145
BORDER
Krug, 96
BORDERS
Henry, 169
BORDIN
C. H., 35
BOREN
Hugh, 77
BORNE
J. W., 115
BORY
Robert, 94
BOSELEY
Will, 67
BOSLEY
Lilly, 54
Will, 54
BOSS
J. R., 90
BOSTICK
May, 98
S. T., 125
W. F., 85
W. L., 146
BOSWELL
Lee, 97
W. E., 191
BOTCHER
Alice, 154
BOTFO
Tony, 46
BOTHA
John, 56
BOTTINGHEIMER
S. G., 187
BOUDS
W. R., 152
BOULWARE
Sid, 193
BOUNDS
Arthur, 151
William, 26
BOURLAND
A. D., 137
BOURNE

Z. D., 95
BOUTON
  Ernest, 12
BOWDEN
  J. M., 88
  J. W., 105
  Samuel, 137
BOWEMAN
  George T., 88
BOWEN
  C. G., 62
  C. H., 189, 196
  Dan, 184
  Lucia, 189
  Susie, 196
  T. C., 55
  W. A., 81
BOWERS
  Herbert E., 190
BOWIE
  Wade, 113
BOWLIN
  Althea, 172
  L. T., 87
BOWLS
  Edna, 78
BOWMAN
  Eula, 94
  J. G., 152
BOWSER
  J. L., 183
BOX, 86
BOXTER
  Bennah, 34
BOYCE
  Hallie, 167
  W. A., 167
BOYD
  J., 155
  J. A., 15
  Ophelia, 172
  W. E., 172
  W. H., 146
  William W., 114
BOYER
  Clarence, 160
  E. W., 160
  Robert, 25
  Rosa, 131
BOYKIN
  Stanley, 127
BOYL
  John, 155
BOYLE
  George, 23
  Gertrude, 44
  James, 140
BOYLEN
  John, 140
BOZARTH

Grace, 40
Mary, 111
BRACH
  T. F., 76
BRACKEN
  Dick, 52
  Ed, 111
  Luna, 67
  Ollie, 163
BRACKER
  J. C., 62
BRACKET
  Arthur A., 72
BRACKNEY
  Bessie, 131
BRADEN
  Murray, 114
BRADFORD
  John, 64
  King, 114
  Lish, 63
BRADLEY, 75
  Harvey, 96
  J. H., 75
  J. W., 196
  John W., 81
  Minnie, 20
  Nannie, 34
  W. H., 29
  W. M., 117
  Walter C., 17
BRADON
  Edward, 190
BRADY
  C. M., 150
  Charles L., 108
  Clark, 150
  Nep, 186
  W. W., 28
BRAGG
  C. A., 72
BRAKE
  Myrtle, 115
  S. C., 115
BRALTZ
  Helen, 102
BRAMBELL
  Sam, 100
BRAMLETT
  Lawrence, 41
BRAND
  Herman, 176
BRANDENBERG
  Pearl, 108
BRANDON
  John, 58
  Sam, 189
BRANDT
  Herman, 177
BRANN

Allie, 139
BRANNON
  J. M., 76
  W. D., 164
BRANYON
  W. D., 18
BRATCHER
  J., 115
BRATT
  Esther, 130
BRATTON
  R. E., 99
BRAWLEY
  Margaret, 182, 192
  Mrs., 13
BRAXTON
  John, 118
BRAY
  J. L., 187
BRAYULL
  Charles, 61
BRAZEALE
  Nettie, 150
BRAZELTON
  S. H., 163
BRAZIL
  James, 66
BRAZLETON
  Mattie, 147
BRECHT
  Henry, 68
BRECKENRIDGE
  Grace E., 170
BREEDLOVE
  Joe, 180
BRENNAN
  Fred, 151
  Fred C., 152
BRENNON
  John, 104
BRESSLER
  G. A., 53
BREWER
  Ernest J., 158
  Guy, 176
  Louise, 125
  Robert, 100
  Willie, 125
BREWSTER
  Alma Kate, 44
BRHUIN
  Joe, 67
BRIDGEPATH
  Clarence, 90
BRIDGES
  Clyde, 75
  W. E., 121
  W. R., 86
BRIGGINS
  Bessie, 192

BRIGGS
  C. M., 175
  Eugenia, 181
BRIGHT
  J. M., 66
  Sallie, 66
BRIM
  T. J., 58
BRINDSLEY
  Phil, 78
BRINSON
  Lucy, 116
  S. R., 165
BRISCOE
  Leon G., 80
  Milt, 124
BRISTOL
  Pearl, 189
  W. A., 189
BRISTOW
  Harris, 16
BRITTON
  Eva, 50
  Frank, 102
  Holloway, 151
BROADKEY
  H., 18
BROADUS
  M. B., 62
BROCK
  Arthur, 167
  C. M., 23
  N. F., 94
  Rebecca, 10
  Robert, 30
BROGDEN
  Charles, 122
BROILES
  C. R., 138
  Gay, 190
  Sallie Anne, 46
BROOKE, 47
BROOKS
  A. D., 151
  A. L., 116
  Albion E., 123
  Eugena Emma, 110
  Eugene Furman, 110
  George D., 26
  J. M., 28
  Joseph, 99
  M. D., 27
  M. J., 47
BROOKSON, 143
BROSE
  F., 119
BROUGHT
  Arthur, 88
BROUN
  Fithian J., 84

BROUSE
   J. C., 179
BROWDER
   Florence H., 46
   Laura, 101
   W. W., 46
BROWN
   "Axhandle", 125
   "Shiner", 112
   A., 80
   A. J., 169
   A. T., 58
   Albert, 187
   Allen, 8
   B. L., 49
   C. C., 162
   C. P., 96
   Cart, 52
   Catherine B., 171
   Celia, 136
   Charles, 36
   Charles F., 25
   Charles T., 25
   Charley, 9
   Coleman, 84, 150
   E. B., 49
   E. F., 27
   E. L., 147
   E. R., 80
   Emma, 7
   Fannie, 145, 165
   G. W., 91
   George, 175, 192
   George S., 116
   Gussie L., 116
   H. F., 27
   H. W., 144
   Hugh F., 34
   Ida, 181
   J. A. O., 100
   J. F., 34
   J. H., 30
   J. L., 183
   Jacob, 47
   John, 13, 136, 142, 165, 177
   L. H., 33, 183
   Louis, 162
   Louise, 110
   M. A., 135
   M. D., 133
   M. E., 104, 108
   Martha, 124
   Mary Susan, 146
   Mat, 190
   N. H., 183
   P. S., 96
   Rolla J., 147
   T. J., 67
   Tee, 56
   Tom, 75
   Voorhies P., 134
   Voshie, 122
   W. A., 167
   W. B., 87
   W. E., 152
   W. J., 133
   W. L., 30, 31
   W. M., 110
   W. W., 183
   Wade, 117
   Walter, 40
   William Garland, 87
   William H., 122
   Willie, 91, 108
BROWNE
   Alma, 163
   J. R., 181
BROWNING
   Arthur, 104
   Clara, 69
   E. G., 49
   James, 156
   Jennie Lovett, 125
   M. O., 108
   Samuel, 10
   Thomas, 160
   W. L., 125
   W. O., 69
BRUCE
   Annie, 191
   C. F., 12
   Charles, 116
   D. C., 12
   E. L., 20
BRUMBELOW
   Andy, 193
BRUMFIELD
   Rupert, 130
BRUMLEY
   Jack, 186
BRUMMETT
   J. F., 27
   Laura, 176, 177
BRUNER
   William E., 178
BRUTON
   C. A., 164
BRYAN
   Dudley D., 94
   J. M., 93
   Jefferson Davis, 140
   W. C., 78
BRYANT
   Annie, 35
   D. K., 48
   Daisye, 40
   George W., 46
   H. A., 35
   Harvey, 153
   J. M., 41
   J. T., 188
   John, 35
   Leona, 158
   Nancy Jane, 36
   O. H., 141
   Oscar, 15
   Sam, 35
   W. A., 140
   Wallace, 35
   Witt, 35
BRYSON
   T. A., 163
BUCHANAN
   A. W., 181
   F., 152
   J. B., 146
   J. H., 190, 191
   J. W., 93
   R. E., 99
   T. S., 75
   W. B., 146
   W. H., 15
BUCK
   Herbert, 59
BUCY
   C. S., 110
BUDDE
   Henry, 20
BUEL
   J. L., 160
BUFFINGTON
   John, 61
BUFORD
   J. T., 153
BUGG
   B. N., 33
BULARD
   A. A., 25
   Lurinda, 25
BULE
   Amanda, 160
   Kate, 110
BULLARD
   Byrde, 175
   D. B., 175
   G. C., 14
   George H., 44
   M., 44
BULLOCK
   E., 141
BULWER
   E., 172
BUMPUS
   Levi, 42
BUNCH
   J. E., 83
   J. J., 71
   W. M., 159, 175
BUNDY
   Orville T., 160
   Z. T., 160
BUNKLEY
   A. H., 135
BUNTION
   J. T., 111
BURCH
   E. W., 96
   H. A., 158
   J. E., 84
   Myrtle, 15
   R. H., 172
BURDELL
   Robert, 115
BURDEN
   C. C., 23
BURG
   H., 69
BURGE
   Julie A., 116
BURGESS
   O. C., 107
   Walter, 174
BURGHER
   Lee, 31
BURKE
   H., 116
   William Hamey, 47
BURKHALTER
   A. P., 28
BURKHART
   C. B., 100
BURLESON
   Clara, 156
BURLEY
   Carl, 127
BURNETT
   Edwin, 110
   Irma, 10
   Jerry, 54
   John, 187
   Lee, 185
   S. R., 10
BURNEY
   Bessie, 171
   Sarah Delila, 125
BURNS
   Edward Robert, 118
   J. C., 80
   John H., 51
   Lizzie, 26
   Roberts, 95
BURR
   Henry W., 72
   J. D., 72
BURRAGE
   Virgie, 35
BURRIS
   Effie, 156
BURRIS

Dee, 94
BURROUGHS
    Dollie, 160
    P. E., 134
BURROW
    Mattie, 80
BURTON
    George, 16
    Jennie, 34
    Jim, 53
    L. F., 80
    W. F., 137
BUSBY
    H. W., 134
BUSCHE
    Emma J., 118
BUSH
    Edwin W., 181
    Maud, 19
    Pearl, 86
    William B., 111
BUSHEY
    Elizabeth, 14
    Joseph, 14
BUSTER
    C. W., 154
    Charles, 154
    Minnie, 30
BUTCHER
    Mattie, 24
BUTLER
    Annie, 113
    Charlie, 53
    E. D., 193
    Kate, 193
    Maola, 164
BUTTS
    Cyrus A., 81
    John T., 81
    R. F., 81
    W. A., 81
BYARS
    William, 36
BYAS
    Lucinda, 10
BYERS
    Gertrude H., 81
BYNUM
    Girlie, 64
    Louise, 64
BYORS
    Jessie, 77
BYRD
    Minnie, 49
BYRNE
    Nona, 132
    P. C., 132
    W. H., 134
BYRNES
    John F., 25

L. G., 36
CABINES
    Charles, 14
CABLE
    Dan, 181
CADE
    Vera, 45
CADWELL
    Harley, 190
CAGE
    Cotany, 17
CAHN
    August, 29
CAHOON
    C., 155
CAIN
    L. M., 124
CAKE
    Cora, 194
CALBERT
    A. M., 18
CALDWELL
    D. C., 24
    E. J., 106
    Ellen, 34
    J. W., 81
    Orson F., 187
    R. B., 10
    R. L., 175
CALHOUN
    B. H., 126
    Frances W., 194
CALKINS
    C. I., 107
CALLAHAN
    R. B., 52
    R. C., 18
    R. W., 186
CALLAWAY
    A. A., 26
CALLICUTT
    Dorothy, 70
    John S., 70
CALLINAN
    M. P., 100
CALLOWAY
    J. H., 127
    M., 44
    Wiley, 78
CALVARY
    D. J., 81
CALVIN, 59
CAMERON
    R. H., 40
CAMMACK
    A. I., 10
    W. W., 27
CAMPBELL
    Alonso, 178
    Alonzo, 178

C. M., 71
Daisy, 136
Elijah W., 75
Forrest, 13
George Lea, 70
J. A., 155
J. T., 71
M. L., 89
Ollie Z., 125
Peyton, 146
R. B., 40
R. E., 35
R. H., 7
W. T., 136
CAMPOR
    Matthew, 152
CAMPSEY
    Jeff, 100
CANBEL
    Harriett, 87
CANE
    Jack, 128
CANNON
    A. E., 136
    Ida, 25
    James H., 46
    Lee, 45
    W. D., 188
    W. G., 39
    W. S., 36
    Walter, 55
CANTERBURY
    Flora M., 113
CANTRELL
    Luke, 32
    W. C., 81
CANTU
    Jesus, 151
CANTWELL
    Jess, 10
    Lee, 11
    Octavia, 82
CAPERTON
    J. F., 19
CAPLAN
    S., 140
CAPLIN
    S., 139
CAPPS
    Amie, 65
    John, 176
    Mae, 179
CARBELLO
    A., 89
CAREY
    Lee, 160
    Lena, 122
CARL
    William, 194
CARLE

S. S., 158
Sabrina E., 157
CARLETON
    D. J., 49
CARLEY
    Mary A., 126
    Robert M., 152
CARLILES
    Jessie, 127
CARLIN
    D. A., 110
CARLISLE
    J. M., 89
CARNES
    J. W., 189
CARNEY
    Lola May, 114
CAROLAN, 170
CARPENTER
    C. H., 83, 116
    Ella M., 107
    Emma Lee, 113
    J. J., 127
    Jennie, 127
    John, 134
    Joy, 23
    Luther, 193
    S. P., 23
    W. N., 86
CARR
    Bertha, 174
    Bessie Joel, 20
    Christine, 20
    H., 178
    L. L., 178
    Lucy, 172
    P. A., 121
CARREL
    Sam, 19
CARRINGTOIN
    Stephen, 89
CARRINGTON
    Stephen W., 90
CARROLL
    Jack, 129
    Willie, 178
CARSON
    Mary, 103
CARTER
    Charlie, 159
    Cora, 88
    Dona Lee, 89
    Jack, 97
    Lucy, 197
    Lula, 112
    M. H., 156
    W. C., 8
CARTLIDGE
    Olive, 88
CARTRIGHT

John C., 77
CARTWRIGHT, 78
CARVER
   Ben F., 195
   George, 196
   Maggie H., 16
CARYTON
   Rayner, 69
CASE
   H. C., 156
CASEY
   H. A., 54
   Tom, 195
   William, 101
CASH
   J. G., 62
CASHELL
   E. H., 121
CASKEY
   T. C., 27
CASSELMAN
   Lou, 183
CASSIDY
   E. F., 194
CASTEEL
   Hattie, 182
CASTLEBERRY
   Hattie Ethel, 113
   J. W., 113
   R. S., 79
   W. N., 19
CASTOR
   Homer, 136
CASTRO
   Pedro, 167
CATE
   Anna Lee, 179
   Clarence, 10
   M. L., 179
CATES
   Isabelle, 150
   J. H., 85
   Nellie E., 65
CATNER
   M., 39
   S. C., 39
CATO
   Lula C., 7
   Roy A., 114
CATON
   Thomas, 162
CATUDAL
   F. N. T., 152
CAVENDER
   J. E., 109
   Witten, 132
CAVER
   V. V., 191
CAVINESS
   Eva, 101
CAWTHRONE
   Talmadge, 53
CAYWOOD
   John, 176
CEFFERTY
   Daisy, 48
CELLUM
   Thomas H., 20
CELUSTKA
   Annie, 85
CENDER
   Robert, 33
CHAFEE
   Frank B., 117
CHAMBER
   Belle, 87
CHAMBERS
   A. L., 10
   Frank, 9, 187
   Gertie, 73
   Pearl, 53
   Tom, 87
   Willie, 187
CHAMBLESS
   Henry May, 85
CHAMP
   Mattie C., 127
CHANCE
   Cora, 94
CHANCY
   I. W., 91
CHANDLER
   ___. E., 30
   Jack, 174
   Joe, 131
   Joe L., 51
   Lou, 81
   Mary, 86
   R. E., 93
   W. B., 138
   W. H., 97
   W. R., 68, 70, 151
CHAPEL
   J. M., 69
   S. S., 179
CHAPMAN, 151
   George W., 43
   J. D., 104
   J. P., 184
   John, 90
   W. E., 134
CHAPPELL
   B. R., 158
   Henry, 115
   J. M., 28
   J. W., 30
CHARLES
   Joe, 117
CHARLESVILLE
   Myrtle, 24
CHARLEWOOD
   William, 64
CHASE
   Turner, 24
CHASTAIN
   Alice, 118
   James A., 118
CHATMAN
   Louvada, 136
   Riley M., 85
CHAUCHAU
   A., 161
CHAVEZ
   Manuel, 142
CHEATHAM
   Albert, 150
   Edna, 18
   Eliza Y., 17
   Ned, 30
CHEEK
   Auburn, 193
   Augustus, 86
   Babe, 86
   Mame, 86
CHENAULT
   Felix, 32
CHENNEVILLE
   John, 64
CHENNEY
   J. O., 176
CHERRY
   H. H., 163
   Josephine, 53
   Sallie, 163
CHESTER
   John L., 117
CHIDESTER
   William, 61
CHILCUTT
   Wilson, 149
CHILDERS
   P. P., 124
   W. E., 19
CHILDRESS
   Jessie, 51
   Ula, 122
   W. A., 176, 177
   Z. J., 10
   Zack J., 10
CHILDS
   James, 186
   Morris, 12
CHILES
   Frank, 137
CHILSOM
   Bessie, 167
CHILTON
   Christine, 121
   Horace, 121
CHISENHALL
   Tollie, 121
CHITTIM
   G. M., 170
CHOUCHON
   Amos Edward, 179
CHRISMAN
   Hillary E., 110
CHRISTENBERRY
   A. Stanley, 152
CHRISTFER
   Mary, 9
CHRISTIAN
   Bert, 111
   Fred, 34
   G., 78
   G. L., 78
   Gideon, 78
   J. K., 50
   Jacob, 111
   John W., 34
CHRISTIANSEN
   R. B., 42
   Thomas, 174
CHRISTMAN
   Mary A., 33
CHRISTOPHER
   Lillie, 19
   Thomas E., 83
CHRISTY
   Harley T., 113
CHRISWELL
   Charles, 142
CHUNN
   R. D., 97
CHURCH
   Bryant, 126
   Jasper, 15
CLACY
   William, 97
CLAITH
   L. V., 151
CLANEY
   P. J., 80
CLARDY
   Bascom, 181
CLARK
   Al, 26
   Andrew, 115
   Bettie, 101
   Billy, 67
   Emma, 89
   H. M., 47
   Helen F., 171
   Homer, 10
   I. W., 125
   J. ___., 35
   J. B., 197
   J. J., 168
   John, 53
   L. W., 50

Lydia, 108, 109
Marshall, 25
O. D., 125, 130
Ollie, 81
Perry, 109
Rachel, 66
Rosie May, 130, 134
S. N., 50
Short, 169
Toyra, 48
Visnie, 35
W. F., 50
William, 67
CLARKE
  Charles L., 116
  John, 72
  Louise, 68
  S. H., 73
  Willis, 35
CLARKSON
  J. I., 118
  J. L., 116
CLARRY
  James, 160
  Ross, 160
CLARY
  Fannie, 175
  Sidney J., 175
CLAUNCH
  Lee, 48
CLAY
  Bettie, 58
  L. H., 58
  Mary, 125
CLAYBORN
  Eva, 129
CLAYCOMB
  Nellie, 117
CLAYPOOL
  Bert, 68
  D. C., 111
  Ernest Beverly, 163
  Sam, 133, 137
CLAYPOOLE
  L. J., 32
CLAYTON
  Elmira Mary, 121
  George, 72
  George R., 36
  George Root, 36
  Jane, 33
  Laura Johnston, 36
  Laurence Johnston, 72
  Lilly B., 36
  S., 67
  W. H., 91
CLAYWELL
  J. W., 112
CLEGG
  Booth, 88

CLEM
  John, 192
CLEMENS
  W. N., 192
CLEMENT
  Dasie, 19
CLEMENTS
  J. T., 102
  Kate, 19
  W. W., 75
CLEMMONS
  W. F., 131
  W. W., 101
CLIFTON
  C. R., 90
  G. H., 178, 179
  Mildred, 184
CLINER
  Will, 39
CLINGMAN
  J. I., 113
CLINTON
  C. C., 78
CLODUS
  W. F., 176
CLOTT
  Annie, 186
CLOUD
  James, 44
  Jess, 138
  S. W., 138
CLOUGH
  Grover, 96
  R. A., 20
CLOWDUS
  M. T., 165
CLOWERS
  Hattie, 158
CLYIC
  E. S., 165
CLYMER
  J. M., 35
COATS
  S. B., 29
COBB
  Carl Schwartz, 9
  Howell, 28
  Mary, 64
  R. E., 9
COBLE
  Blanche, 18
COCHRAN
  Elizabeth J., 119
  Harry, 50
  Harry T., 51
  Janie, 122
  Martha Alice, 115
  Ruby, 21
  S. H., 122
COCHRANE

  Will, 173
COCKRELL
  Effie, 9
COCOANUT
  Jack, 8
COE
  C. A., 19
  Sam, 84
COFFEE
  America, 44
COFFEY
  Minnie, 9
COFFMAN
  Jack, 54
COGDALE
  D. M., 111
COGDELL
  Bruce, 75
COGRON
  Cicero Fullerton, 116
COGSDELL
  Robert R., 36
COIRET
  A., 143
COKE
  C. B. L., 129
  George, 145
COKER
  Richard, 24
COLBERT
  Ben, 76
  W. J., 158
COLCLAZER
  H. H., 47
COLDBERG
  Eva, 8
COLE
  Claude, 155
  Ed L., 142
  Florence, 141
  J. A., 141, 164
  J. W., 83
  James H., 62
  Jerry, 149
  John W., 83
  Mark, 142
  May, 73
  Pressley B., 172
  Robert, 84, 150
COLEMAN
  Alice, 190
  Allie, 188
  Angie, 124, 125
  D. E., 193
  George, 65
  H. C., 164
  S. E., 191
  Sallie, 183
  T. A., 188
  V. E., 167

  Zudie, 193
COLES
  Earl, 42
  J. C., 42
COLLARD
  Charlie, 127
  Henry, 127
COLLIER
  H. V., 66
COLLIGAN
  Harry, 61
COLLINS
  A. P., 100
  A. T., 66
  Bunyan, 104
  C. M., 118
  C. Webb, 69
  Dan, 21
  Edward, 103
  Frank, 122
  J. L., 112
  J. R., 192
  Joe, 152, 156
  L., 89
  L. A., 75
  Luther, 30
  May, 174
  N. J., 186
  Nrs. D. H., 8
  Ollie, 105
  Runyan, 100
  Sam, 158
  Terrell, 139
  W. G., 108
  William, 104
COLLISTER
  Ida, 58
COLLOM
  Mary E., 24
COLLUM
  Charles K., 161
COLLUP
  Pearl M., 94
COLOY
  Thomas, 125
COMEGY
  E. F., 59
COMEGYS
  E. F., 58
COMER
  C. H., 41
  E. P., 41
  H. M., 41
  J. A., 123
COMPTON
  A. J., 186
CONBON
  Nettie, 139
CONDO
  B. J., 116

CONDON
  Emma Ferris, 158
CONDOR
  J. H., 63
CONE
  Charles C., 51
  F. A., 119
CONFAR
  John, 10
CONIGLIO
  Mariano, 54
CONKLIN
  J. H., 133
  R. M., 18
  Robert, 18
CONLEY
  Albert, 65
  Fannie A., 60
  James H., 60
CONNALLY
  Roy, 162
  W. A., 67
CONNELL
  Clyde, 142, 143
  W. E., 142
CONNELLY
  John D., 123
  Will, 173
CONNOLLY
  Owen, 17
CONNOR
  Annie, 188
  Annie L., 181
  D. H., 52
  Elsie, 188
  Fannie, 48
  Frances, 188
  Fred, 176, 177
  George, 188
  H. F., 94
  L. Meyers, 95
  Maggie, 188
  Rube, 188
  T. H., 188
  T. W., 140
CONRAD
  John B., 49
CONSTABLE
  J. A., 34
CONTES
  W. F., 65
CONTRADA
  Oclanda, 180
CONWAY, 117
  Mary, 58
COODY
  Dan, 29
COOK, 71, 186
  A. B., 161
  Amos, 34

Fannie Bell, 33
  G. C., 96
  J. J., 163
  J. W., 119
  John, 161
  John H., 62
  Nannie, 11
  T. H., 164
  William, 39
COONRAD
  J. C., 52
COONS
  Charles E., 125
COOPER
  A. B., 7, 44
  D. W., 26
  J. G., 84, 85
  J. N., 89
  Myrtle E., 177
  O. O., 93
  R., 159
  S. S., 96
COOT
  Robert, 47
COPASS
  A. J., 155
  B. A., 155
COPE
  Sam, 168
COPELAND
  Mary W., 170
COPING
  F. D., 18
COPPAGE
  Frances, 189
  T. B., 189
COPPEDGE
  J. J., 194
COPY
  A. W., 143
CORBIN
  Alvis C., 103
  Sam, 144
CORBITT
  Mathey Walker, 151
CORD
  James Henry, 127
CORDAJO
  Ederijen, 138
CORDERY
  Joe, 175
CORLEY
  D. B., 102
CORNER
  John W., 39
CORNETT
  C. A., 153
  Charles A., 154
CORNWELL
  Nellie, 15

Polina, 183
  W. L., 159
COROS
  Chancy, 170
CORPNEY
  Lera, 109
CORY
  T. S., 144
  William, 144
COSBY
  Wesley, 151
COSTER
  "Aunt Polly", 119
COTHER
  Enos, 32
COTTON, 109
  Ethel M., 94
  G. W., 84
COTY
  M. C., 138
COUCH
  Z. T., 175
COUGHLIN
  Thomas, 171, 172
COULSON
  Edgar, 84
  J. E., 84
  Mary E., 84
COULTER
  M. B., 137
  Mariah, 40
COUNTS
  A. H., 163
  Robert, 131
COUTRET
  A. J., 63
COVINGTON
  C. Steele, 9
  L. B., 33
  Marion Simeon, 147
  Minnie, 80
  Rezi, 36
  Sid, 147
COWAN
  Andrew, 187
  D., 117, 187
COWLEY
  W, J,, 46
COX
  A. C., 63
  A. S., 63
  D. R., 27
  E. M., 165
  E. V., 48
  Henry, 181
  Ida, 20
  J. W., 139
  James, 65
  L. J., 99
  Myranndy, 49

R. V., 29
  T. W., 80
  Tom, 165
  W. C., 41
  William, 193
  Willie S., 46
COY
  Mabel, 60
CRABB
  Dora, 176
  J. M., 114
CRABTREE
  Charles, 61
  E. L., 119
CRADDOCK
  John B., 89
CRAFT
  R. B., 163
CRAFTON
  R. L., 160
CRAG
  Cora, 99
CRAIG, 140
  C. M., 68
  Dora, 63
  Mattie, 68
  Minnie M., 156
  O. M., 116
  T. H., 63
  Thomas, 64
  William D., 25
CRAIGO
  Ruby, 7
CRANE
  Walter, 177
CRANZ
  August, 66
CRASS
  Mabel, 77
CRAVEN
  Charles, 136
CRAVENS
  D. H., 155
  J. S., 125
  Mary A., 185
  N. A., 185
CRAWFORD
  Annie Lee, 131
  Bert, 53
  J. R., 36
  J. W., 28
  John, 58
  M. C., 131
  Nancy C., 28
  P. S., 53
  Ruth, 169
  Sevalio, 69
  Tommie, 189
  W. B., 13
  W. P., 58

CREED
　Mary A., 134
CRENSHAW
　E. H., 152
　Hodge, 153
CRESBY
　Fred, 136
CRESWELL
　A. J., 73
CREWS
　A. S., 81
CRIMM
　E. A., 19
CRIMMINGS, 140
CRIMMINS
　Thomas Frederick, 142
CRISMAN
　Lon, 29
CRISP
　J. E., 129
　Lula, 129
　R. __., 35
CRISWELL
　E. P., 103
　Ida B., 117
CROCKER
　J. W., 67
　Rimp, 109
CROCKETT
　Avery, 16
　Davy, 16
　E. J., 77
　H. J., 77
CROFT
　Ernest T., 150
　J. H., 169
CROMER
　Fondie, 78
　J. L., 99
CROMMER
　William, 89
CROMWELL
　Tom, 103
CROOM
　M. V., 86
CROSBY
　H. F., 151
　Scott, 64
CROSS
　James B., 109
CROUCH
　Ada, 170
　Wade, 170
CROW
　W. M., 82, 141
CROWDER
　J. S., 142
CROWE
　Ray, 117

CROWELL
　W. B., 153
CROWS
　Andrew, 170
　Lonnie, 60
CROZIER
　Nora E., 161
CRUMP
　Ella, 180
CRUTCHFIELD
　James, 195
　May, 8
CULLEN
　Edward F., 25
CULLUM
　Jennie, 165
CULP
　James Franklin, 126
　Ora O., 118
CULPEPPER
　James, 185, 186
CULWEL
　Clyde Fay, 193
CULWELL
　John W., 105
　M. T., 53
CUMMINGS
　Reese DeWitt, 95
　Sam, 130
　W. M., 86
CUNNINGHAM
　Ida, 111
　Liddie, 102
　R., 55
　W. M., 42
CURD
　L. B., 122
CUREIN
　Laura F., 102
CURREY
　C. D., 131
　Floy, 131
CURRIE
　M. P., 61
　Robert, 159
CURRY
　J. H., 146
　Lena, 28, 29
　Mary, 40
CURTIS
　Wilmotte, 193
CUSHMAN
　Alonzo R., 26
　H. B., 178
CUTHBERT
　John, 82
CYRUS
　Jim, 24
DACUS
　John, 67

DADNEY
　Albert, 54
DAGGETT
　Cora Josephine, 78
　N. F., 85
　Rebekka, 99
DAILEY
　W. E., 156
DALE
　D., 136
DALEY
　Maude, 102
DALTON
　Blanche, 17
　John, 65
DAMRON
　Jack, 46
DANIEL
　A. J., 35
　Ernest, 45
　J. C., 174
　J. M., 127
　James, 127
　John, 187
　Robert S., 40
　Willie, 165
DANIELS
　C. L., 186
　C. W., 129
　D., 19
　Frank, 110
　Harry, 119, 122
　John, 110
　M. L., 193
　Mary, 14
　Will, 31
DANIELSON
　C. H., 111
DANKIEFS
　John A., 162
DANNENBERG
　Clark, 175
DANNER
　Alexander F., 186
　G. D., 149
　John W., 67
DANWALTER
　H., 105
DARBY
　J. Ad, 51
DARDEN
　Nellie, 176
DARNELL
　Charles E., 93
DART
　Nora, 125
DATO
　Willie, 29
DATTON
　Ed, 174

Walter, 174
DAUGHTERY
　A. W., 174
　Annie, 146
　Edward, 155
　George, 131
　J. W., 177
DAVENPORT
　Ed, 85
　F. J. R., 53
　Inez, 53
　J. B., 193
　J. S., 159
　Preston, 136
　S. W., 94
　Sallie, 136
DAVEY
　Ida, 72
DAVID
　Walter, 138
DAVIDSON
　A. H., 170
　Charles, 156
　Clara, 45
　E. O., 84
　Emma, 11
　J. W., 152
　John, 115
　R. L., 56
　Sam, 171
　W. T., 107
　Walter, 55
　Z. W., 56
DAVIS, 133
　A., 100
　Aaron, 163
　Ada, 145
　Albert, 19
　Albert A., 18
　Alice, 181
　Allen, 147
　Andrew, 64
　Arthur, 128
　Elizabeth, 156
　F. I., 174
　Fay, 111
　H. G., 98
　H. N., 145
　H. N. C., 154
　Ida, 16
　Iva, 28
　J. B., 187
　J. H., 128
　J. L., 122
　J. M., 49, 51
　J. P., 113
　J. R., 59
　Jeff, 42
　John, 67
　Julia, 86

Kate, 80
Katie, 80
L. T., 195
Lee, 64, 67
Lelia, 136
Lulu, 67
M. M., 64, 87
Mattie, 126
Minnie, 135
Oscar, 40
Peter, 26
R. R., 193
Rhoda, 115
S. A., 186
Sam, 137
Sam H., 79
Thomas, 123
Tina, 109
W. A. R., 129
W. H., 174
W. I., 46
W. L., 161
Wallace, 20
William, 169
William Kenneth, 128
Willie J., 107
DAWSEY
　James, 141
DAWSON
　Fannie, 144
　H. F., 182
　John, 10
　L., 70
DAY
　G. F., 143
　J. M., 89
　M. F., 60
　Mary Ellen, 39
DE LA HOZ
　Santiago, 70
DEALY
　Albert, 88
DEAN
　H. W., 49
　O. W., 108
DEARING
　J. L., 47
DEATON
　Laura, 28
　V. B., 124
DEAVERS
　Edith, 138
DEBEQUE
　Frank, 153
DEBERRY
　L. S., 108
DECKER
　J. C., 28
　Lizzie, 49
DEDMON
　Charles, 9
　Eva, 9
DEDRICK
　N. V., 41
DEE
　Henry, 193
DEER
　Nellie, 82
DEES
　Anna, 127
DEGAN
　J. H., 135
DEGAUGH
　J. A., 79
　J. O., 79
　Joseph, 79
DEKEY
　W. H., 129
DELABOJ
　Annie, 160
DELASHAW
　Rinka, 125
DELAY
　Hattie Howell, 197
DELK
　Dick, 13
DELOR
　Frank, 139
DEMING
　Will, 76
DEMOREE
　Jennie, 158
DEMPSEY
　C. C., 105
　Eloise, 102
　Lanice, 105
DENARDS
　J., 34
DENHAM
　W. P., 69
DENMORE
　J. H., 69
DENNEY
　C. C., 176
　Eula, 83
DENNIS
　Allen, 95
　Minnie, 57
　Robert H., 20
DENNY
　A. D., 50
　Frank, 113
　Susie, 77
DENT
　J. H., 161, 162
DENTIN
　R. O., 75
DENTON
　Ike, 51
　John B., 154
DERRICK
　Eva, 9
　R. L., 87
　William, 181
DESHAZO
　Ed C., 81
DEUTSCHNER
　Adele, 9
　David, 9
DEVEREAUX
　Frederick, 109
DEVLIN
　Fannie, 55
DEVORE
　W. D., 191
DEVORTEX
　Laura, 152
DEWEES
　J. W., 149
DEWEESE
　J. W., 99
DEWITT
　Howard, 68
DICK
　B. T., 85
　W. M., 133
DICKENS
　William, 39
DICKERMON
　Edward Leroy, 105
　Milton, 105
DICKERSON
　J. E. D., 150
　James, 189
　Ollie, 189
　W. M., 114
DICKEY
　C. L., 20
　Mary E., 136
　May, 36
　Nat, 136
DICKIE
　Nettie, 152
DICKINSON
　Rebecca, 27
DICKSON
　Annie, 90
　Tom, 164
　W. T. M., 110
DIEGEE
　David, 43
DIEHL
　John, 34
DIESMAN
　J. L., 173
DIGGS
　W. D., 58, 59
DILL
　T. D., 152
DIMAND
　Michael, 189
DINGUS
　J. H., 66
DINKINS
　C. E., 116
DIXON
　Antionette, 155
　B. L., 82
　C. H., 88
　J. H., 168
　Lola, 77
　W. A., 18
DOBARD
　Ed, 180, 181
DOBBS
　F. A., 158
　Jim, 68
　Will, 68
DOBY
　Jim, 67
DODD
　D. J., 152
DODDS
　Elsie, 23
DODNEY
　W. C., 78
DODSON
　C. B., 90
　Ida, 128
　Mary, 64
　Sam, 8
DOHL
　Peter, 105
DOISON
　Harry, 161
DOKE
　Ethel, 10
DOLAN
　Ed, 31
DOLE
　S. W., 104
DOLLAR
　J. L., 99
DOLLY
　Dorothy, 185
DONALDSON
　Claude, 25
DONAN
　Nona, 47
DONIHOO
　Nannie, 32
DONNEY
　C., 45
DONOHO
　J. B., 194
　Lou, 18
　Nellie Louise, 194
DONOVAN
　Frank, 174
DOODY

Annie, 150
DOOL
　Alice, 196
DOOR
　J. W., 36
DOORKY
　L., 131
DOPHEID
　Katie, 187
DORR
　J. W., 39
DORRIS
　James, 47
DORRITY
　John, 176
DORSEY
　J. H., 87
DOSSEY
　W. J., 88
DOSTAL
　Hermina, 144
DOTSON
　Bird, 76
　C. E., 171
　W. C., 76
DOTY
　B. S., 48
　Mabel, 114
　W. P., 114
DOUGHDRILL
　W. L., 149
DOUGLAS
　A. M., 28
　Charles, 131
　Douglas, 93
　James, 169
　Minerva E., 109
DOUGLASS
　J. P., 61
DOUTHIT
　J. F., 190
DOWD
　Lem, 85
　Tom, 82
DOWDEN
　William H., 36
DOWDY
　Fred H., 15
　William, 129
DOWELL
　Annie L., 81
　Lon, 28
DOWITY
　John, 168
DOWNEY
　T. M., 161
DOYLE
　Emma Lena, 187
　Pat, 194
　Zebbie, 47

DRAGO
　B. C., 143
　J. N., 129
DRAKE
　Bessie, 108
DRESSER
　Ben P., 57
DREW
　Byron, 25
DRISKELL
　Wright, 50
DRISTELL
　W. L., 50
DRIVER
　J. E., 59
　J. M., 155
DROLL
　Grace, 77
DRUMM
　Frances, 83
　Francis M., 80
DU BOSE
　E. A., 179
　L. H., 181
　Love, 179
DuB＿＿＿＿
　George L, 171
DUBBS
　C. E., 151
DUBOSE, 70
DUCKIE
　George W., 103
DUFF
　Noah, 15
DUFFAN
　C. H., 179
DUGAN
　James, 26
DUGDELL
　William E., 73
DUKE
　George Ernest, 129
　Henry, 171
　J. E., 164
　Sam, 87, 89
DUKES
　Carrie, 174
DUMAS
　R. C., 67
DUNAVANT, 197
DUNAWAY
　O. B., 117
DUNBAR
　Ed, 58
DUNCAN
　A. A., 44
　A. B., 149
　Boaz, 34
　Callie, 34
　Emma, 149

James, 87
Jerome, 34, 108, 182, 190
M. N., 152
Stark, 34
T. J., 12, 34
William, 77, 171
DUNHAM
　Branch B., 45
　D. O., 40
　R. C., 147
DUNLAP
　Erret, 94
　J. L., 165
　Jim D., 97
DUNLAVEY
　Nellie, 152
DUNLAVY
　Nellie, 154
DUNLOP
　Thomas, 196
DUNMAN
　J. E., 100
DUNN
　John, 197
　Mary, 56
　Thomas, 72
DUNNICA
　A. A., 31
DUNWOODY
　Lizzie M., 19
DUPONT
　F. L., 85
DUPREE
　George, 75
DURIER
　Antoine, 55
DURNING
　R. E., 153
DURPERTHUS
　A. F., 136
DURRETT
　Ed, 43
　Thomas, 134
DUWELL
　Lonnie, 29
DWYER
　J. P., 192
　J. W., 184
DYE
　Alex M., 110
DYER
　J. B., 143
DYERS
　S. D., 90
DYSART
　John, 29
　Thomas, 187
EAGER
　Bud, 54

EAGLE
　G. A., 99
EAKIN
　E. B., 178
　J. A., 141
EARL
　J. B., 161
　Walter, 144
EARLE
　James A., 109
　W. A., 117
　Walter H., 179, 191
EARLEY
　A. L., 33
　Ruth, 33
EARNEST
　W. E., 17
　William, 140
EARP
　Alex, 55
　H. H., 55
EASLY
　Sam, 121
EASON
　Mat, 161
EASOY
　Beatrice, 24
EAST
　J. L., 94
　Mamie, 187
EASTERMAN
　Will, 14
EASTERWOOD
　J. E., 176
　J. S., 16
EASTMAN
　John, 153
EATIER
　Bennett, 123
EATON
　Lou, 9
EBERHEART
　James P., 188
ECHALIS
　J. W., 60
ECHELBURGER
　J. W., 88
ECHOLS
　John R., 83
EDDLEMAN, 196
　Addie, 29
　H. B., 29
EDDLEMON
　Ora, 78
EDER
　Elizabeth, 142
EDGEMAN
　Jimmy, 192
EDGERMAN
　Ivey, 72

Joe, 185
EDMUNDSOM
  D., 80
EDMUNDSON
  W. L., 135
EDWARDS
  A. J., 113
  Clara, 162
  F., 142
  F. E., 14
  H. H., 78
  J. B., 21
  J. R., 193
  J. V., 16
  L. E., 136
  Lola, 16
  M. E., 45
  Mat, 160
  S. I., 78
  W. M., 66
  Walter, 61
EKLINS
  H. L., 130
ELAM
  J. R., 161
ELDER
  Grover, 129
ELDRIDGE
  W. T., 197
ELKINS
  M. L., 132
  T. J., 170
ELLER
  J. A., 165
  J. M., 165
ELLINGTON
  Edna, 66
  L. V., 78
  Myra Bradley, 78
  W. A., 52
ELLIOTT
  J. S., 161
ELLIOTT
  H. C., 24
  J. S., 30
  Jim, 72
  John, 174
  Marvin, 154
  Rilla, 76
  Will, 182
  William E., 72
  Wright, 154
ELLIS
  "Grandma", 121
  Cash, 41
  F. M., 66
  james M., 180
  James M., 181
  Jere, 181
  John, 126

John E., 164
Nettie, 152
William J., 180, 181
ELLISON
  Nola, 113
ELLOTSON
  H., 152
ELMO
  George F., 21
  May, 23
ELROD
  Hugh, 57
  I. I., 192
ELSIK
  Fannie, 78
ELSON
  J. C., 128
ELWELL
  H. S., 170
  R., 170
ELWICK
  Frank, 29
ELY
  D. M., 112
  Sarah, 49
EMBRY
  J. W., 19
EMERSON
  Amanda, 80
  Marie, 194
EMERY
  Lula, 169
EMIN
  A. J., 25
EMMA
  eduardo, 28
EMMINS
  Will, 9
EMMONS
  Will, 196
  William, 44
EMON
  Jesse, 101
EMSKAMP
  Joseph, 113
ENEN
  G. M., 102
ENGEL
  John, 99
ENGELHIFF
  Fred, 76
ENGELKING
  Johanna, 183
  Paul, 183
ENGLER
  P. E., 87
ENGLISH
  Sadie, 27
ENION
  Elsey, 90

ENSWILEY
  John, 112
ENTRIKEN
  H. L., 34
EPERSON
  S. M., 18
EPLEY
  John, 142
EPPERSON
  Ella, 72
EPPS
  James Clayton, 78
EPSON
  Stella, 18
ERBY
  J. H., 20
ERICKSON
  G. W., 63
  Wallace, 130
ERNEST
  George, 36
ERWIN
  C. J., 139
  Mary, 168
  R. A., 53
  R. K., 85
  Ruby, 53
  Ruth, 187
ESTELL
  J. T., 59
ESTES
  Carrie L., 19
  Doc, 129
  Harbert, 150
  Jesse, 7
  Louise, 194
  Mr., 14
  Pearl, 146
EUBANK
  Mattie, 137
EUSTACE
  J. T., 186
EVANS
  B. Q., 121
  Ethel Bertha, 176, 177
  Eula, 121
  F. J., 8, 9
  G. W., 167
  George B., 33
  Hers, 21
  Hez, 41
  J. B., 75
  J. F., 185
  James H., 12
  Jeanette, 104
  Joe, 129
  John, 63, 144
  Josie, 187
  Laura, 30
  M. N., 41

Mattie, 116
S. R., 83
Thomas, 36
William A., 19
EVENS, 62
EVERETT, 91
  J. N., 109
  Vivian, 108
EVETTS
  H. V., 46
EWICK
  Mary M., 59
EWING
  Elizabeth, 173
  George, 173
  Jennie, 14
  Luther, 111
FAGENT
  Harry, 146
FAIN
  A. L., 105
  D. W., 190
  J. A., 49
  Mattie, 105
FAIR
  R. S., 52
FAIRAMA
  John W., 7
FAIRBANKS
  H. W., 127
FAIRCHILD
  A. L., 41
FALLIS
  E. Burton, 104
FALLON
  Percy, 67
FALTON
  Gervis, 137
FANNING
  John, 114
FANTY
  Ethel, 187
FARCHER
  Andrew J., 89
FARIS
  J. H., 128
FARLEY
  Amanda, 104
FARMER
  Ed, 167, 168
  J. C., 80
  Kendall, 91
  M. R., 36
  W. R., 111
FARMERS
  H. L., 109
FARQUHAR
  R. C., 55
FARRELL
  Alec, 16

Charlie, 16
L. P., 100
P. A., 143
W. O., 176
FARRIS
  A. M. Clayton, 8
  Jim, 97
  William C., 95
FARRISH
  Rosa, 47
FAULK
  M. F., 35
  Royal, 52
FAULKNER
  Andy, 130
  Annie, 196
  Arthur, 77
  Green, 46
  Mary, 130
FAVER
  H. H., 167
FAVIEL
  Al, 99
FAWCETT
  A. J., 121
  Joe, 190
  John, 190
FEATHERSTONE
  May, 112
FEATHERWOOD
  Milton, 66
FEELEY
  John, 100
FEHLERSON
  Pauline F., 191
FEHRENSTEIN
  Katherine, 144
FELDER
  W. C., 119
  W. D., 31
FELIDA
  Fred D., 121
FELLS
  W. K., 136
FELTS
  G. M., 60, 84, 129
FENN
  Percy T., 12, 183
FERGUSON
  A. J., 80
  C. H., 19
  Daisy, 101
  Elizabeth, 83
  Joseph H., 80
  S. M., 55
FERNANDEZ
  E. A., 162
FERRELL
  Eunice, 24
FERRIS
  A. Mae, 69
  C. E., 69
  Charles E., 17
  Royal A., 169
FESTERDON
  Nannie, 145
FETTERS
  George W., 164
FICKE
  John, 164
FIELD
  Alex S., 82, 83
  W. A., 123
  W. C., 182
FIELDER
  William G., 122
FIELDS
  Albert G., 190
  Arthur M., 177
  George, 116
  Henry, 99
  Jessie, 167
  S. N., 65
  T. H., 152
FIFER
  Joe, 156
  Sam, 158
FILGO
  John, 99
  Robert, 157
FILLEY
  Bose, 167
FILLIP
  Joseph, 183
FINCHER
  F. E., 14, 20, 80, 96, 151
FINLEY
  Bettie, 131
  Ed, 143
  J. D., 69
  John, 51
  Myrtle, 26
  Virg, 88
FINNEGAN
  M., 36
FINNEY
  Jarrett, 154
FIORE
  Florence, 169
FISCHER
  Henry M., 61
  Herman, 78
  J. W., 61
  M. H., 61
FISH
  Annie, 190
FISHER
  Arthur, 176
  J. A., 105
  Jack, 152
  John, 30
  John J., 90
  R. I., 100
  W. E., 111
FISK
  E. C., 124
FISMER
  Henrietta, 119
FITE
  Frank, 33
FITZGERALD
  B. S., 34
  Bessie, 19
  J. W., 61
  James, 60
  Nancy, 7
FITZHUGH
  W. B., 117
FITZPATRICK
  Annie, 13
FLAKE
  Michael Green, 67
  W. G., 66
FLANNERY
  Kate May, 18
FLEENER
  George W., 179
  Lyman, 101
FLEET
  Clarence, 15
FLEITMAN
  Joseph, 26
FLENNIKEN
  B. D. P. R., 88
  J. C., 88
  J. M., 88
  James M., 88
  T. N., 88
  W. J., 88
FLENNIKER
  J. M., 88
FLETCHER
  H. B., 185
  Luther L., 46
FLORENCE
  J. H., 49
  Lucille, 77
FLORES
  May, 191
FLORY
  Myrtle, 155
FLOWERS
  B. C., 66
  J. Gary, 156
FLOY
  Tom, 178
FLOYD
  J. H., 54
FLYNN
  John, 10
  Lucian, 45
  Mary K., 95
  Samuel Edward, 167
  William M., 112
FOGELBERG
  Bessie, 176, 177
FOGG
  Howard, 140
  T. H., 144
FOGLE
  E. O., 176
  Ethel A., 177
  Ethel Audrey, 180
  Maggie, 194
FONE
  Frank, 100
FOOTE
  Clide, 42
  Corrinne, 24
FORBERG
  Esther, 157
FORBERN
  Laura, 187
FORBES
  Joseph, 145
FORD
  Charley, 93
  Della, 151
  G. W., 131
  J. H. G., 196
  Mamie, 89
  S. D., 48
FORE
  D. Frank, 65
  Frank, 63
  Milton, 170
FOREMAN
  B. F., 156
  Mai N., 171
  W. L., 167
FORESTER
  Montie, 122
FORGEY
  Mary, 27
FORGY
  Thomas J., 131
FORTENBERRY
  H. F., 76
FOSTER
  Bruce, 99
  C. D., 172
  Della, 144
  Dorence, 109
  Edna, 195
  Ernie, 121
  J. W., 77
  Jones, 23
  Lee, 96
  R. C., 101

Tom, 121
FOURNIER
   Andre, 164
   Annie, 31
FOWLER
   DeWitt Talmadge, 60
   Frank, 17
   J. A., 127
   R. J., 60
   W. F., 188
FOX
   F. M., 79
   Mary, 30
   T. W., 131
   W. A., 176
FOXWELL
   Lord, 158
FRANCES
   R. C., 33, 35
FRANCIS
   R. C., 34
FRANK
   H., 56
   Lillian, 27
   Wallace, 136
FRANKEBERGER
   Clara, 107
   Viola, 91
FRANKEL
   Jacob, 96
FRANKLIN
   Algie, 137
   J. R., 161
   Jim, 145
   Leon, 180
   Robert, 69
FRANKS
   George, 175, 178
   Robert, 84
   Tucker, 28
FRASHER
   H. L., 107
FRAZIER
   C. A., 167
   Helen, 43
   Henry, 117
   John H., 44
   Mach, 16
   Minnie, 17
   S. S., 86
   Sam, 42
   William, 32
FREDERICK
   Lena C., 150
FREE
   Lucy, 134
FREEMAN, 191
   Clarence, 98
   E. P., 35
   Gyp, 197
   H. S., 9
   Hugh, 96
   Judge J. T., 178
   T. J., 169
   W. H., 59
FREER
   Will, 93
FRENCH, 44
   J. A., 113
   Junius, 187
   Junius B., 52, 75, 81, 90, 154, 179
   T. W., 131
   Walter, 68
FRETWELL
   Mat, 104
FRIEDLANDER
   Adolph, 93
FRIERSON
   Dewitt, 123
FRIOU
   Daisy, 119
FRONABARGER
   B. F., 183
FRONBARGER
   B. F., 193
FRONHOFF
   Hobart, 162
FROST
   James, 142
   Thomas Clayton, 8
FRY
   Belle, 12
   C. N., 152
FRYE
   Jake, 68
FUGATE
   Eula, 168
FUGETT
   Henry, 46
FUGITT
   John P., 24
FULFORD
   Marcus, 127
FULLBRIGHT
   Jim, 96
FULLER
   Alfonso, 126
   Grace, 59
   J. H., 165, 186
   S. E., 72
   Willie, 24
FULLINGTON
   Veva, 145
FULLMAN
   Nannie, 144
FULTON
   G. W., 64
FUNDERBURK
   J. S., 156
FUNK
   I. M., 49
FURGUSON
   Oscar, 15
FURMAN
   Albert G., 11
   E. T., 180
FURR
   Lum, 136
   Maggie, 66
FUSTON
   Isaac M., 13
FUTRELL
   Nathaniel, 176
FUTTER
   Clare, 113
GAFFNEY
   Prince A., 104
GAGE
   Andrew, 181
GAIL
   Annie, 20
GAINER
   James L., 107
GAINES
   Albert, 15
GAITHER
   George, 90
GALAPKA, 144
GALBRAITH
   H., 53
   J. E. H., 103
   Richard, 103
   Richard Cecil, 103, 109
   T. S., 53
   W. Fred, 48
GALBREATH
   Fred, 12
   G. W., 49
   R. C., 36
GALLAGHER
   Eliza, 124
   Jack W., 36
   Lizzie, 122
   W. D., 7
   Wilmer, 103
GALLAGHIER
   Clint, 110
GALLEHER
   Charlotte, 153
   J. N., 153
GALLEY
   Willie, 111
GALLIMORE
   Maggie, 177
GALLINGTON
   George, 141
   Lenora, 141
GALLOWAY
   Herbert, 189
   Martha, 127
   Will, 136
GAMBLE
   Ada, 136
   Charles, 98
GAMBRELL
   C. C., 85
   J. H., 44
GANN
   J., 27
   J. H., 125
GARCIA
   Rogue, 133
GARDNER
   Alice, 110
   Boots, 163
   L. C., 23
   R. S., 52
GARNER
   Effie May, 131
   John, 27
   Ollie, 112
   Sarah, 93
GARNETT
   R. G., 83
GARRELL
   William, 81
GARRETT
   Bettie, 133, 196
   Bossie, 162
   Elsie, 113
   Jessie, 17
   Lovie, 186
   Nellie, 176
   W. G., 65
   W. M., 162
GARRISON
   Eva, 33
   Foss, 75
   Hunt, 126
   May, 137
   S. E., 59
GARVIN
   Julian, 144
GARZA
   Antonio, 27
   Ideifonso, 27
   Juana, 152
   Pancho, 105
   Rosa, 27
   Sturino, 57
   Tebocio, 172
GASSENHEIMER
   I., 141
GASTON
   Larren T., 27
   W. H., 169
GATES
   E. P., 113

F. J., 192
W. E., 50
GATHING
  Minnie May, 193
GATLIN
  Lela, 135
GATTON
  William O., 19
GAUYTON
  J. S., 46
GAVIN
  W. W., 142
GAY
  Dave, 24
  George B., 32
GAYLORD
  Mollie, 72
GEATON
  William, 192
GEBB
  James, 105
GEE
  A. L., 88
  Hays, 83
  T. J., 162
GEEBER
  William, 125
GENICARTO
  Josie, 7
GENRY
  Enzella, 85
GENTRY
  A. F., 96
  Jim, 115
GEORGE
  Albert C., 45
  Cora, 100
GERTH
  Annie, 60
GESTINE
  Evelyn, 80
GETSINGER
  Annie, 47
GHALESON
  Bessie, 18
GHIO
  Anthony, 110
GIBBONS
  J. M., 181
  John C., 68
  M. E., 181
  Mary, 68
  Olin, 79
GIBBS
  Ann, 173
  Barnett, 169
  Dorsey, 169
  G. Wiley, 169
  O. D., 169
  Sallie Dorsey, 169

Sallie Haynes, 169
W. B., 169
GIBSON
  Bertha, 154
  Bessie, 47
  Elizabeth, 152, 153
  Florence, 125
  Myrtle, 32
  O. M., 116
  Omer, 90
  T. L., 153
GIDDEN
  A. J., 80
GIDDINGS
  Horace, 124
GIFFORD
  Lula, 83
GILBERT
  Harry, 48, 50
  Ione, 108
  J. E., 190
  Johnnie, 164
  Luella M., 97
  Mary, 187
  Mrs. Simon, 14
  Stella H., 138
GILES
  Arthur, 77
  Rufus, 174
GILL
  W. C., 19
  Ward, 66
GILLEAN
  Alice, 130
GILLESPIE
  A. A., 175
  J. G., 168
GILLETT
  R. H., 62
GILLHAM
  May, 11
GILLIAM
  Les_oyres, 126
GILLILAND
  Jesse Lee, 110
  Oliver, 178
  Roy, 141
GILMORE
  J. L., 72
  Jana D., 83
  Louisa, 56
  Mary, 57
GINTON
  Eugene, 145
GIRDWOOD
  Normal, 143
GIRTLEY
  Joseph, 60
GISSEL
  H., 86

GIVENS
  Charles, 15
  Henry, 105
GIVING
  David, 41
GLADDEN
  Mamie, 107
GLADSON
  M., 40
GLASGOW
  A. C., 42
  A. J., 42
  W. C., 42
GLASS
  Ruby, 126
GLASSAWAY
  Sam, 172
GLAZE
  Mollie, 191
GLEATON
  William, 197
GLEAVES
  Addie Dean, 95
GLENDOCK
  Bert, 71
GLENN
  BiJone, 53
  Matilda, 183
  William, 54
GLENNING
  Patrick, 170
GLINK
  Charles, 42
GLOFF
  W. M., 159
GLOVER
  Annie, 161
  Charles, 114
  Mary Magdalene, 54
  Vossie, 65
  W. D., 35
GLOZE
  Martin, 53
GOBER
  J. R., 113
GOBLE
  C. F., 190
  Odie, 134
GODBERRY
  Fannie, 90
GODFREY, 78
  J. L., 163
GODSOE
  John, 11
GOETSEELS
  J. P., 143
GOLD
  G. P., 100
GOLDEN
  Claud, 16

Ida, 162
GOLDKE
  Ida, 117
GOLDRING
  W. E., 127
GOLDSMITH
  Phil, 113
GOLDSTEINE
  E., 190
GOLDSTON
  Walter, 161
GOLLIHUGH
  W. W., 113
GONZALES
  Antonio, 127
GOOCH
  John Young, 97
GOOD
  J. E., 85
GOODING
  William, 84
GOODLOE
  Emma, 145
  Otis L., 121
GOODMAM
  Harry, 98
GOODMAN
  Duke, 167
  P. S., 143
  W. R., 101
GOODNER
  Ora L., 108
GOODNIGHT
  Maude, 18
GOODRICH, 62
GOODWIN
  Emma, 75
  J. L., 29
  John W., 64
  W. H., 57
GOODWYN
  Isadore, 154
  Philo H., 154, 155
  William Cantrell, 154
GOOLSBY
  Horace, 48
GORDON
  A., 133
  Claud, 8
  Claud O., 7
  D. E., 191
  E. V., 143
  Frances, 168
  Jesse, 35
  Lulu, 63
  Marie, 183
  Mattie, 191
  W. J., 24
  Will F., 146
GORE

Edna, 142
GOREE
  R. E., 43
GOSE
  Bertie, 141
  John, 141
GOSS
  Jenny, 8
GOSSERT
  A., 27
GOTT
  Annabelle, 182
  R. W., 182
GOUGH
  J. R., 175
  John, 128
GOULD
  Anna, 93
  E. B., 158
  Robert Symington, 121
GOWEN
  M., 160
GOWN
  Chin Lee, 185
GRABER
  M., 134
GRACE
  G. W., 27
  Vanna May, 59
GRAFTON
  Hugh C., 78
GRAGER
  Harry, 107
GRAGG
  R. G., 62
GRAHAM, 24
  A. B., 163
  Beatrice, 24
  C. G., 36
  Dacey, 98
  E. M., 39
  Ed, 177
  Evaline, 20
  Grace L., 158
  Joseph, 109
  L. T., 172
  Leonard, 99
  Lizzie, 161
  M., 176
  M. E., 14
  M. F., 193
  M. L., 96
  Marie, 172
  Susie, 102
  W. H., 98
  W. B., 95
  Will H., 98
GRAMMER
  S. K., 164

GRANBURY
  C. A., 79
GRANDSTAFF
  Mabel Clara, 90
GRANDSTOFF
  Gertie, 50
GRANGER
  Fletcher D., 28
  L., 124
GRANT
  A., 65
  A. J., 63
  B. J., 178
  John, 112
  Katherine Weagley, 165
  Laura, 65
GRANTHAM
  J. D., 47
  Lewis, 47
  T. F., 104
GRANTLAND
  Emma, 176
GRASON
  W. G., 52
GRASTY
  C. G., 60
GRAVES
  B. J., 30
  Florence, 60
  Lettie, 164
  Mary, 126
GRAY, 136
  Alex, 89
  Alice, 7
  B. O., 23
  E. J., 164
  G. W., 55
  George, 186
  J. A., 110
  J. D., 55
  Mattye, 135
  Rastburn, 11
  Sadie B., 195
GRAYSON
  H. A., 125
GREEN, 133
  C. G., 19
  Daniel M., 196
  David, 94
  Ed, 159
  Floyd, 195
  Henry, 112
  Herman, 126
  J., 171
  Jennie, 152
  Jimmie, 8
  John H., 97
  John L., 7
  Lydia, 172

Mannie, 82
Myrtle, 26
Nettie, 157
Polly Ann, 8
Ross, 30
S. P., 159
Tom, 159
W. S., 82, 195
Will, 159
William, 161
William Lea, 152
GREENE
  Belle, 62
  E. L., 164
  S. P., 122
GREENLEIGH
  Amanda, 46
GREENWOOD
  Alice, 124
  B. C., 124
  David, 13
GREER
  Cleo, 144
  F. M., 19
  J. H., 58
  N. A., 143
  Robert, 48
GREGORY
  C. D., 197
  W. J., 110
GRESHAM
  Ada, 34
  Iva Dan, 40
GREY
  Annie M., 77
GRIDER
  C. W., 181
  J. C., 16
  J. W., 59
  Travis, 102
GRIER
  Etna G., 128
  F. L., 100
  J. G., 100
GRIFFIN
  Ahta, 153
  Dessie, 196
  James A., 15
  John, 47
  M. C., 94
  Maude, 52
  R. D., 71
  W. A., 196
  Will, 104
GRIFFITH, 121
  Joe, 95
  Martha J., 41
GRIFFITHS
  J. H., 144
GRIFING

Bruce, 141
GRIGGS
  Benjamin, 23
  Lila, 196
GRIGSBY
  Gertie Grace, 187
GRIMES, 100
  A. J., 173
  John, 126
  L. F., 27
GRIMSLEY
  Ben, 183
GRINNAN
  F. H., 145
  J. S., 145
GRISCOM
  Lydia, 130
GRISSAM
  M. B., 82
GROGAN
  James, 27
GROSS
  Sam, 192
GROUGH
  John, 129
GROUPTON
  P., 182
GROVES
  Carrie, 11
  Ethel, 24
GROW
  J. P., 15
GRUBBS, 182
  J. H., 75
GRUSENDORF
  Hilda, 75
GRYCHE
  Leofilia, 98
GUERICK
  Antoine, 194
GUESS
  Noah V., 167
GUFFEE
  John, 11
GUFFIN
  Luella, 94
GULLEDGE
  Zue, 159
GUMM
  Joe D., 69
GURLEY
  Ralph, 157
GUTHRIE
  M. E., 96
GUYOT, 180
GUYTON
  Lola, 129
HAAS
  Charles, 83
HABERZETTE

Fred, 89
HACKENBERG
  George P., 25
HACKETT
  Eilene, 153
  S. P., 153
HACKNEY
  Oscar, 65
HADDLE
  Hannah, 181
HADDON
  Effie, 29
HAGGARD
  Ethel, 40
HAGOOD
  Sallie, 19
HAHN
  Fritz, 146
HAIGLER
  Joseph, 184
HAILEY
  Ida, 116
HAINES
  Jeff, 132
HAIRE
  Clyde Beaufort, 131
HALAMUDA
  John, 126
HALBURT
  W. C., 26
HALE
  C. B., 45
  D. B., 114
  Ellen, 53
  Josie, 41
  Metsa, 178
  T. F., 152
  W. B., 67
  Worth, 67
  Worth K., 71
HALEY
  Charles, 139
  Clifford B., 183
  M. T., 17
  Mont, 150
  Olin, 121
  W. R., 89
HALFORD
  John C., 68
HALK
  John, 27
HALL
  C. E., 19
  Charles B., 13
  Elberta, 86
  Fannie, 50
  H. P., 14
  M. F., 75
  M. M., 163
  Mattie, 133

N. E., 161
T. S., 150
W. J., 40
W. T., 33
W. W., 102, 191
HALLUM
  Ed, 124
HALSCHNEIDER
  William J., 98
HALTON
  F. S., 20
HAMAN
  Kiah, 125
HAMBLIN
  John, 129
  R. R., 145
HAMBRICK
  G. O., 186
HAMBY
  Thomas, 132
HAMER
  J. D., 134
HAMIL
  C., 139
  Mattie, 32
  W. H., 129
HAMILTON
  Bessie, 175
  James Matthew, 60
  L. W., 81
  Russell M., 194
  William C., 194
HAMLETT
  John, 42
HAMLIN
  R. R., 10, 163, 170, 171
HAMMACH
  N. A., 16
HAMMER
  M. A., 126
HAMMOCK
  Norton, 65
HAMMOND
  John, 182
  N. J., 67
HAMPTON
  Allie, 124
  C. N., 137
  John M., 9
HANCOCK
  Abe, 117
  Andy, 105
  John, 186
  Willie, 40, 41
HANEY
  O. P., 42
  Vick, 25
HANKENS
  L., 61

HANKS
  Jimmie, 163
  Mabel, 149
HANLIN
  R. R., 146
HANN
  E. L., 173
  Robert, 173
HANNA
  Sam, 8
HANSLEY
  Della, 149
HANSON
  Christ, 97
  Lee, 191
HARBERGER
  Annie May, 193
HARBISON
  W. W., 143
HARDEMAN
  Annetto, 85
  H. B., 108
  Hunter, 85
  Smith, 109
HARDIE
  Ed, 14
HARDIN
  Joe, 55
  John, 195
  Lottie, 68
  M. J., 30
  S. D., 146
  W. J., 31
HARDING
  J. G., 35
HARDISON
  Bill, 176
HARDWICK
  W. M., 122
  W. P., 42
HARDY
  Ora Fay, 83
HARE
  Amanda, 50
HARELL
  Etta, 193
HARGE
  John, 111
HARGIS
  N. C., 33
HARGRAVE
  Mel, 52
HARGRAVES
  John, 25
  Ruth, 24
HARGREAVE
  Bertha, 26
HARGROVES
  Tom, 169
HARKEY

R. H., 178
HARKEY
  Jennie Williams, 91
  John, 44
  R. H., 178
  R. M., 157
  Robert Harrison, 179
HARLAN
  John R., 36
HARLEY
  Mary Nevada, 72
HARMON, 58
  Claude, 136
  Elizabeth A., 27
  John, 58
  Lillie P., 60
  M. D. L., 186
  Maggie, 25
HARNED
  Charles, 76
HARNEY
  J. T., 54
HAROLSON
  Shel, 185
HARONG
  Lillie, 193
HARP
  Jennie, 189
  Virginia, 194
HARPER
  A. A., 164
  John, 32, 134
  S. F., 95
HARRELL
  G. A., 193
  Nora, 9
  W. W., 37
HARREMAN
  Earl, 53
HARRINGTON
  Bryan, 86
HARRIS
  A. J., 48, 168
  Bob, 76
  Charles, 101
  E. J., 175
  Ella, 57
  Emma, 28
  G. R., 75
  Hugh, 196
  Isham G., 103
  J. H., 132
  J. N., 53
  Joe, 48
  Jones, 80
  Logan, 188
  M. B., 183, 188
  M. J., 53
  Mary, 163
  Matilda, 65

May, 177
O. D., 177
Phena, 84
R. B., 69
Robert, 19, 196
Robert E., 197
Thomas, 28
W. D., 195
W. F., 174
W. O., 137
W. Ross, 146
W. W., 125
Will, 32
William, 115, 133
William Oscar, 139
HARRISON
C. M., 65
Emma, 127, 158
Henry, 133
J. W., 191
Joseph, 19
Luke, 90
R. H., 193
Ruby, 191
Viola, 169
W. B., 26
HARRISS
Claude, 143
G. H., 143
HARROW
J. L., 76
HARRVEL
Tom, 179
HARSH
Cora, 89
HART
J. M., 135
Laura, 174
M., 129
Rosa, 44
Tom, 115
HARTER
Nettie, 67
HARTLEY
Emma, 10
HARTMAN
Ollie, 150
HARTNESS
John H., 14
HARTNETT
C. D., 43
Con D., 43
HARTSFIELD
George W., 123
HARVEY
Annie, 58
Courtland G., 12
Ed, 31
Laura, 111
Mary R., 52

Maud, 152
N. J., 31
Peter, 43
Richard, 52
Richard T., 66
S. W., 181
Thomas A., 137
HARWELL
Pearl, 141
HASKETT
R. J., 171
HASSELL
J. O., 135
HATCHER
J. H., 36
HATCHETT
S. E., 86, 87
HATHAWAY
Sterling, 90
W. C., 180
HATLEY
Mark, 188
HATTON
Charley, 83
HAUPTVOGLE
Alvin, 117
HAVRE
Clyde, 134
HAWES
L. L., 150, 151
HAWKINS
Albert, 95
C. W., 158
Edwin R., 25
J. D., 94
J. W., 83
Nellie, 99
Will, 94
HAWLOWRITZ
Amelia, 174
HAWORTH
Eliza May, 18
J. A., 19
J. R., 103
HAWPE
E. H., 111
J. R., 31
Nannie, 31
HAY
William, 128
HAYES, 153
D. B., 185
D. O., 50
H. P., 152
Isom, 159
J. P., 154
Phillips, 9
Rose, 10
W. P., 97
W. Z., 154

HAYMES
W. R., 121
HAYNES
Henry, 159
HAYNIE
James, 83
W. M., 83
HAYS
G. R., 53
John, 29
HAYSELE
Nellie May, 40
HAYSLIP
Emma, 76
HAYWOOD
Ruby, 197
HAZEL
Alice, 102
J. T., 102
HAZLETON
Oscar, 146
HAZLETT
G. W., 129
HEAD
Adrian, 162
Carroll, 162
Ernest, 165
Eugene, 162
H. E., 104
Henry V., 177
Lulu Cox, 162
Maggie, 159
O. E., 159
Oscar Eugene, 162
Porter, 159
Robert, 159
W. Burns, 110
W. O., 159
Walter, 159
HEADLAND
O. P., 130
HEADON
W., 27
HEALD
J. W., 122
HEALY
Frank B., 174
HEARD
Sid, 150
HEARON
W. J., 110
HEATH
C. L., 12
Ella, 152
HEATHINGTON
J. H., 124
HECKMAN
P. A., 89
HEDGES
Reuben, 54

HEFFNER
E. A., 112
Harry M., 48
HEIMER
J. F., 32
HEIRX
C., 183
HELBERT
H. P., 188
HELD
J. A., 9
HELM
Ed, 124
George W., 178
J. N., 16
James, 27
Tom, 124
HELMS
Annie M., 104
J. W., 157
HEMPHILL
Bud, 109
Salevia, 193
HENDERSON, 8
"Uncle Billie", 8
Eddie, 94
George, 59
Grace, 196
J. L., 124
James F., 145
M. N., 131
Mattie, 178
Sam, 8
W. B., 75
W. W., 27
HENDRICK
M. G., 64
HENDRICKS
Cora, 36
N. R., 52
T. F., 130
Will, 15
HENDRIX
H. M., 75
HENISESSER
J. C., 102
HENLEY
E. C., 80
HENNESSEY
John, 115
HENRICHSON
Charles D., 160
George E., 160
HENRY
Albert, 177
J., 46
Lula, 7
Ruby, 135
HENSHAW
J. W., 20

HENSLEY
  "Uncle John", 14
HENSON
  Louis, 157
  Paul, 150
HERALD
  Joseph, 165
HERBERT
  L., 191
HERD
  R. H., 143
HERDINGER, 128
HERDON
  Maud, 178
HERMAN
  J. A., 40
HERMESON
  L. A., 80
HERNANDEZ
  Apolicario, 44
  Eugene, 63
  Ignacio, 100
HERNDON, 36
  E. B., 138
HERRICK
  W. T., 170
HERRING
  R. C., 62
  Theodore, 110
HERRINGTON
  M. V., 10
HERRON
  Minnie, 24
HERSCOVIT
  Fannie, 138
HERZ
  Raymond, 76
HESS
  P. C., 117
HESTER
  M., 77
  Morgan, 77
HEWETT
  Viola, 181
HEWITT
  David, 36
HIBBDON
  John, 187
HICKALACHEE, 117
HICKERSON
  James, 57
HICKLIN
  Fred, 125
HICKMAN
  L. E., 115
HICKS
  Amanda, 151
  B. C., 28
  Call, 96
  Charles H., 177

E. D., 139
Fannie, 190
Hubert, 39
Joe, 102
R. C., 52
Sadie, 144
Scott, 98
Vera, 193
HIGGINS
  B. E., 48
  D., 103
  J. T., 132
  Steve, 194
  W. B., 51
HIGGS
  E. M., 99
  Emma, 151
HIGHLYMAM, 142
HIGHPOTE
  A., 88
HIGHSMITH
  J. H., 167
HIGHTOWER, 136
  H. W., 83
HILBURN
  Cleve, 129
  L. V., 126
  W. C., 196
HILL, 44, 49
  A. G., 62
  Blanche, 46
  Bob, 193
  Carl, 26
  Edna, 28, 153
  Ella, 15
  Irene, 136
  J. D., 157
  J. M., 46
  J. W., 42
  James B., 67
  Katherine, 186
  L. A., 113
  Lalla, 137
  Lon C., 189
  Low, 107
  Oscar, 192
  T. F., 183
  W. A., 143
  W. B., 136
  W. H., 134
  Z. T., 131
HILLARD
  Lottie, 36
  William, 32
HILLBURN
  W. C., 88
HILLER
  C. E., 119
HILLERON
  Thomas B., 173

HILLGER
  Daisy, 48
HILLHOUSE
  Adam, 187
HILLIARD
  Aggie, 186
  Nellie, 152, 153
  S. G., 186
HILTON
  henry, 93
HIMES
  Gilmore, 195
  J. E., 80
  Lula, 17
  Mitch, 80
HIMIL
  "Grandma", 129
HINDEN
  Mattie, 178
HINE
  B. J., 94
HINEMAN
  Charlie, 125
HINES
  George R., 100
  M. F., 115
  Susie, 127
HINSDALE
  Carrie, 31
HINSON
  Pink, 102
HIRGLE
  Fred G., 15
HIRSCHFIELD
  William, 81
HIRST
  Will, 34
HITCHINS
  Vendetta, 145
HITT
  Henry Randall, 25
HIX
  Donaho, 56
  Howard, 56
  Ollie, 56
  Roscoe, 56
HIXSON
  John, 19
HIZER
  E., 91
HOBARTH
  August, 123
HOBBS
  C. M., 93
  Dave, 158
  W. C., 20
HOBBY
  A. M., 149
  Barney, 149
HOBSON

Jane, 39
HOCHINEY, 94
HOCKETT
  D. H., 65
HOCKLEY
  T. B., 71
  Thomas R., 70
HOCKNEY
  Elmo, 50
HODGE
  A. S., 185
  Christine, 108
  H. L., 194
  Irene, 104
  J. A., 108
  W. A., 169
HODGES
  B. A., 71
  Ben, 174
  Maggie, 158
  Robert F., 190
HODGKINS
  Irene, 93
HODGKINSON
  Les, 178
HOENY
  J. Clifford, 47
HOETLING, 136
HOFF
  Clarence, 186
  Jenny, 90
HOFFMAN
  A. W., 60
  C. J., 155
  E. G., 152
  H., 155
  J. H., 34
HOGETT
  Cyril, 52
HOGLER
  H. N., 145
HOGLUND
  A. B., 109
HOIGWOOD
  Walter, 53
HOISLEY
  H. G., 121
HOLBROOK
  J. A., 193
HOLDEN
  Albert, 164
  Charles, 164
HOLDER
  Fred, 151
  R. G., 80
  Richard, 80
  Sarah, 118
HOLLABAUGH
  O. S., 20
HOLLAN

W. B., 139
HOLLAND
  Baby, 96
  Fayette, 150
  H. E. P., 41
  J. T., 88
  Joseph, 60
  W. R., 52
HOLLENBECK
  Maxine, 97
HOLLEY
  Georgia, 154
  J. P., 73
HOLLIDAY
  Nina L., 86
  Oralndo Steen, 12
HOLLINGSWORTH
  J. W., 108
  Mary, 17
  R. L., 185
  T. C., 118
HOLLINS
  Taylor, 29
HOLLIS
  Rosa L., 34
HOLMAN
  Laurence, 111
HOLMBERG
  C., 152
HOLMES
  Bishop, 36
  Henry, 159
  J. F., 52
  J. P., 36
  W. H., 152
HOLSAPPLE
  J. W., 35, 109, 112, 169
HOLT
  Allyne Percy, 154
  Bert, 186
  W. T., 151
  Willie, 142
HOLVICK
  Lee, 170
HONAKEE
  Cassie B., 121
HONEA
  F. M., 102
HONEY
  Jennie, 81
HONEYCUTT
  Nettie, 102
HOOD
  J. S., 66
HOOKS
  E. J., 180
  J. B., 112
  W. B., 44
  Warren, 44

HOOPER
  John W., 110
HOOT
  Nome, 30
HOOVER
  Carrie, 37
  J. H., 115
  M. V., 37
HOPE
  Tom, 179
HOPKINS
  Henry, 115
  Jule, 144
HOPPER
  Comelia, 90
  Nannie, 47
  William J., 152
HOPSON
  Fred, 78
  John, 190
HORD
  Elizabeth P., 18
HORN
  R. H., 13, 124
HORNADAY
  Wallace, 108
HORNBEAK
  John S., 146
HORNE
  Edward Gideon, 138
HORSCHOW, 133
HORSELEY
  R. G., 20
HORSLEY
  Hallie B., 118
  R. G., 107, 118
HORTON
  George, 62
  John R., 39
  Lucy, 114
  T. J., 182
HORY
  Hattie, 187
HOSKINS
  Brice, 30
HOTUBBY
  Solomon, 56
HOUCK
  N. J., 88
HOUGHTON
  John, 112
  Mary, 95
HOUSE
  Frank, 98
  J. H. B., 132
HOUSER
  Annie Lou, 85
HOUSTON
  D. F., 66
  James M., 88

R. C., 18
R. J., 181
Sam, 66, 138
W., 15
W. H., 51
HOUX
  W. R., 66
HOUZELL
  H. P., 19
HOVERMEYER
  Charles, 81
HOVEY
  Verna, 187
  Verna May, 187
  W. W., 187
HOVINGHORST
  John, 55
HOWARD
  B. F., 113
  C. H., 51
  C. P., 101
  Ella, 133
  Ernest, 123
  Geneva, 69
  George, 123
  J. F., 127
  Leola, 141
  Murray, 47
  R. H., 188, 189
  T. C., 128
  T. H., 48
  Thomas Baltimore, 125
  V. B., 14
  W. C., 135, 149
  William R., 132
HOWE
  Maggie, 159
HOWELL
  Charles, 29
  Frank, 27
  H. J., 67
  J. H., 77
  J. P., 127
  James T., 14
HOWK
  S. D., 156
HOYL
  Lem, 8
HOYT
  Louis, 135
HUBBARD
  E. T., 11
  Lucinda, 135
  Tom, 12
  W. W., 23
  Z. T., 191
HUBBLE
  Ammon, 100
HUCKABEE

Amos, 114
HUDDEN
  Ewing, 168
HUDDLESTON
  Gus, 28
HUDDLO
  Willie, 15
HUDELSON
  William, 53
HUDGENS
  Amy, 144
  Arle, 144
HUDGINS
  Maude, 142
HUDMAN
  M. V., 160
HUDNALL
  Joseph Winston, 84
HUDSON
  Alice, 47
  C. A., 15
  John, 45
  Lewis, 139
  W. R., 160
  Walter, 70
  William, 70
HUEY
  Joseph, 75
  L., 36
  William, 56
HUFF
  E. L., 160
  J. W., 102
  James, 172
  John B., 26
  Stella, 102
  Thomas H., 54
HUFFMAN
  J., 158
  J. J., 15
  W. G., 111, 116
HUFFMASTER
  Zora, 190
HUGGINS
  J. A., 143
HUGHES
  Bert, 31
  Bill, 124
  Ed, 20
  Edna, 51
  Eugene, 118
  F. E., 13
  J. G., 157
  J. W., 187
  L. E., 187
  Mary E., 13
  Millie, 130
  Oliver, 70
  P. T., 26
  William, 158

Willie, 176
HUGO
  Addie, 59
HUKILL
  Rosa, 194
HULL
  G. N., 89
HULLY
  W. G., 39
HUMPHREY
  Claude, 103, 104
  J. A., 118
  Kathyrne, 77
HUMPHREYS
  Bird, 50
HUMPHRIES
  M. B., 157
HUNLEY
  Marie, 48
HUNNICUTT
  Frank, 67
HUNT
  A. A., 139
  Alvin, 72
  Carrie, 72
  Charlie, 72
  George W., 14
  Minnie, 39
  S. A., 90
  Suzie, 88
HUNTER
  A. J., 122
  David, 183
  Doucie Lenora, 135
  E. C., 14
  Edgar E., 34
  Edith Gail, 31
  Edith Gale, 30
  G. O., 14
  J. S., 42
  James, 168
  John, 7
  Lorin, 187
  Odus, 37
  R. L., 192
  V. R., 32
  W. M., 123
HUNTINGTON
  Harry, 167
HURD, 142
  Mamie, 9
HURDS
  Minnie, 34
HURLEY
  George, 52
  W. J., 52
HUSBAND
  Vinius, 18
HUSKEY
  L. D., 187

HUTCHINGSON
  J. C., 193
HUTCHINS
  Sallie, 174
  Samuel N., 146
  Vindetta, 146
HUTCHINSON
  A. A., 164
  Anna, 171, 172
  Mettie, 41
HUTSELL
  A. A., 86
HUTSON
  T. C., 195
HUTT
  A. M., 177
  Joe, 15
HUTTON
  Alex, 114
  Bessie, 108
  W. J., 108
HUYHURST
  Elsie, 144
HYDE
  C. H., 81
  C. R., 42
  T. W., 46
HYDER
  William, 123
HYMANS
  Jose, 174
  Louise, 174
HYNSON
  George W., 16
  Mamie, 183
HYSMITH
  Charles, 169
ILLINGSWORTH
  W., 169
ILSHMER
  Ernest, 155
IMPIS
  W. C., 91
INGERSEN
  Helen C., 192
INGRAM
  A. B., 75, 102, 107, 108, 114
  Ben, 149
  Charles V., 34
  Henry, 20
  James M., 10
  Laura, 156
INMAN
  J. M., 90
  Ona, 90
  R. W., 25
  S. G., 164
  S. Guy, 113
INNIS

J. M., 85
IRBY
  J. P., 76
IRELAND, 113
IRVIN
  C., 122
  Johnnie, 71
  Josh, 109
  Lena Bell, 19
  T. J., 174
IRVINE
  W. D., 141
IRVING
  F. D., 159
  Irma, 84
  Peyton, 10, 84
IRWIN
  Clarence, 135
  George, 107
  Signora, 160
  W. H., 178
  Will, 62
  William D., 179
ISAAC
  Lulua, 134
ISBELL
  Claud, 11
  J. C., 123
  Josephine, 182
  Lillian, 10
  R. T., 66
ISHAM
  Dezar, 167
ISOM
  Adolphus, 115
ISOMS
  William, 33
IVES
  W. A., 121
IVEY
  Bailey, 9
  J. N., 14
  J. O., 32
  James N., 116
IVY
  James N., 117
  Richard, 146
JACCIME
  Steve, 95
JACK
  Charlie, 19
JACKS
  Burlie, 161
JACKSON
  A. J., 197
  A. W., 195
  Andrew, 80
  Annie, 176
  Clen, 75
  H. W., 41

Hollie, 139
James, 17
Louis, 18
Lula, 42, 127
Mary, 165
JACO
  Harry, 26
JAEGER
  Fay, 162
JAGUA
  Nora, 149
JAMES
  G. T., 116
  J. T., 197
  John, 95, 135
  L., 112
  Oaka, 40
  R. D., 190
  Susan, 192
  W. H., 33
JAMESON
  Joe Lee, 97, 98
  Malcolm Routh, 97
  Vida, 97
JAMISON
  C., 83
  John, 69
JANUARY
  F. B., 49
  J. E., 49
JAQUITH
  William H., 94
JARRED
  John, 157
  Mittie, 157
JARRETT
  Horace, 163
JARVIS
  D. T., 17
  Fred, 35
  John E., 19
JAY
  Claude Sanders, 124
  W. S., 60
JAYROE
  J. J., 135
JEAN
  J. I., 20
JECNESMEC
  Joe, 165
JEFFERSON
  Willis, 15
JEFFRIES
  J. H., 28
  Sallie, 28
JELINE
  C. C., 30
JENKINS, 86
  Hattie, 154
  J. F., 161

J. W., 48
Joseph, 134
M. E., 157
R. F., 113, 118, 121, 127, 129
R. P., 149
S. J., 86
S. M., 157
William, 181
JENNINGS
Ezra, 189
G. W., 104
J. J., 85
K. V., 78
Mattie, 14
W. K., 78
JERVEY
E. P., 165
JESSE
D. W., 154
JESSEE
Mollie, 158
JOBE
Mattie May, 111
JOEKEL
H. C., 34
JOHN
Henry, 182
Thomas, 175
JOHNS
Harry E., 130
Taylor, 86
JOHNSON
A. E., 70
A. H., 164
Alice, 45, 134
Allie Priscilla, 87
Annie, 68
B. F., 100
Ben, 117, 158, 160
Beulah, 112, 118
C. R., 90, 91
Charles L., 177
Dave, 87
E. M., 173
E. W., 59
Ernest, 136
F. J., 49
F. M., 160
Frank, 158, 176
G. D., 177
George E., 141
George L., 90
George Thomas, 75
Gertie May, 8
H. Al, 126
H. C., 150
Harry, 17
J. E., 112, 117, 118
J. L., 152, 155

J. T., 51
J. W., 164
Jake, 47
James, 118
John, 47, 131, 155, 183
Julia, 78
K. W., 15
Lem, 17
Linda, 195
Lizie LaBaun, 190
Lizzie, 18
M. A., 47, 54
M. C., 47, 76
Mary, 10, 138
Mary B., 10
Mary L., 195
Matha, 177
May, 155
Mike, 16
Nannie, 131
Nora, 57
Ollie, 195
Perthenia, 35
Robert, 59, 112, 118
S. G., 137
S. O., 129, 156
S. W., 110
Sid, 15
T. A., 188
T. R., 176
T. S., 177
Telephus A., 195
Toby, 25
V. A., 78
Vesta, 160
W. A., 28
W. H., 84
W. K., 53
W. L., 122
Will, 23, 133
JOHNSTON
Cass M., 113
Charles H., 100
D. H., 81, 151
Elmira Laura, 41
J. H., 100
James C., 28
Jennie, 15
Jessie, 85
Joseph, 34
Laura, 72
Lela, 15
JOINER
C. S., 32
Will, 101
JOLINE
Charles O., 30
JOLLY
Sallie Lee, 26

JONAS
Josie M., 85
JONES, 95, 105
"Aunt Jemima", 116
"Aunt Sally", 86
__. M., 124
A. E., 21
A. F., 51
A. G., 17
A. W., 115
Aquilla, 66
B. E., 110
Berta, 168
Bertha, 7
C. H., 83
C. W., 172
Cecil, 178
Charles, 84, 187
Collier, 27
D. P., 172
Edgar W., 164, 189
F. D., 81
Fred, 102
G. C., 25
George, 144
Graham, 105
H. G., 17
Henry, 12, 18, 100, 192, 197
I. A., 77
Iron Mountain, 17
J., 116
J. B., 97
J. E., 121
J. F., 51, 66
J. G., 102
J. M., 149
J. W., 83, 168
Jack, 130
James, 57
James F., 71
Jim, 10
John, 35, 39
L. L., 69
L. P., 143, 144
Lucy, 172
Mary, 185
Minnie Lane, 109
Mollie, 140
Morgan, 183
Mrs. C. A., 12
Nancy, 79
Oscar, 65
Paul, 140
Pearl, 68
Perry, 59
R. F., 52, 53
Ruby, 43
S. F., 98
Sallie, 176

T. H., 18
Tom, 157, 162
W. W., 170
Walter, 53
Will, 90
William, 13, 101
JORDAN
C., 79
Cora, 194
F. B., 168
George, 7, 79
H. T., 14
J. W., 191
Jack, 175
M. E., 132
Thomas, 131
JOURDAN
J. A., 48, 50
W. T., 48
JOYCE
Earl, 85
JUDGE
R. A., 175
JUHLIN
Jospehine, 24
JULLIN
Jim, 84
JUNGAN
C. B., 140
JUSTAVUS
A. C., 151
JUSTIN
Charlie, 28
KABLE
M. S., 150
KAHLER
W. F., 139
KAKEN
W. P., 11
KANE
Charles H., 26
George, 108
KARY
Mortimer L., 9
KASTER
Charles Manton, 98
KASTON
Zena, 97
KATZ
Lena, 80
KAUFFMAN
Edna Mae, 172
Frances, 189
Frank, 172
KAUFMAN
A. C., 180
Frances, 164
Otto, 19
KAUFMANN
Adeline, 96

KAWALSKI
    Albert, 68
KEACH
    Estelle, 44
    W. J., 126
KEARNEY
    Scott, 139
    T. M., 139
KEATON
    G. W., 77
KEE
    Donelle, 95
KEEBEL
    J. W., 28
KEEL, 158
KEEN
    Anne, 188
    Cyrus G., 161
    Ernest, 153
KEENAN
    Hiram T., 126
KEENER
    J. H., 165
KEININGHAM
    C. G., 114
KEITH
    C. H., 134
    E. W., 134, 165
    M. S., 86
    Nanie, 86
    R. R., 69
KELLAN
    R. C., 135
KELLER
    Isaac, 128
    John, 187
    S. E., 131
KELLEY
    A. B., 102
    Eula, 194
    Grace, 110
    J. A., 10
    Joe, 24
    John, 104
    L. D., 153
    Maggie, 179
    Minnie Belle, 151
    Ockie, 116
    Pearl, 187
    W. F., 33
KELLY
    Dora Elizabeth, 55
    Florence Ann, 130
    K. K., 75
    Nancy, 16
KELTON
    Albert, 84
KEMBLE
    Katherine, 108
KEMP
    Cain, 36
    J. A., 138
    J. M., 101
    J. W., 140
KEMPER
    Edward, 131
    W. H., 48
KENAME
    Jesse, 59
KENDAL
    kelley, 33
KENDALL
    Kelly, 51
    S. K., 54
    W. B., 159, 163, 190
KENNARD
    Nora, 11
KENNEDY
    Bertha, 82
    Charles, 116
    George, 104
    J. T., 82
    John, 111, 131
    John A., 128, 129
    Josephine B., 178
    L. L., 137
    M. A., 111
    W. H., 139
    William B., 111
KENNELY
    Loula, 60
KENNER
    W. N., 109
KENNEY
    John, 53
KENT
    C. G., 117
    J. Will, 133
    John, 28
    S. A., 100
KENTON
    L. W., 112
KERBE
    Maude, 19
KERBO
    T. M., 175
KERBY
    Beulah, 16
KERD
    Nick, 68
KERLEE
    J. F., 130
KERNODEL
    Albert D., 196
KERR
    G. C., 46
    Nellie, 45
KERWIN
    Edward J., 107
KETCHUM
    Bertha, 87
    I. M., 78
    Robert, 87
KEUHN
    Oscar, 14
KEVLIN
    Kearney J., 82
KEY
    A. W., 187
    Hilda, 187
    P. L., 105
KEYS
    Crickett, 155
    J. E., 26
    Robert, 127
KIDD
    Jessie, 84
KIDDY
    "Grandma", 172
KIERSTING
    Herman, 161, 162
KILGORE
    Thomas, 169
KILLEN
    C., 155
KILLERMAN
    Julia, 176
KILLETT
    Manson, 152
KILLIAN
    Leona, 41
    M. A., 100
KILLINGSWORTH
    Mabel, 132
KILLMAN
    Johnson, 155
KILLOUGH
    Lillie M., 45
KILNER
    William, 64
KIMBALL
    M. L., 136
KIMBERLAIN, 57
KIMBERLING
    L. W., 77
KIMBROUGH
    Boone, 80
KINCAID
    J. P., 151
    J. W., 118
    Robert J., 157
KINCAIDE
    T. R., 16
KINDCAID
    Robert, 156
KINDRED
    Sam, 191
KING
    A. K., 46
    Dan, 20
    Dan F., 179
    Douglas N., 118
    E. E., 9, 91
    Eddie B., 90
    Grace, 109
    H. B., 80
    J. D., 96
    John, 195
    L. P., 8
    Mary R. H., 144
    Max, 194
    Minnie, 80
    Porter, 191
    Richard, 61
    Silas S., 144
    T. H., 115
    W. C., 19
    Walter, 186
    Will, 55
    William, 40
    Z. H., 141
KINSLOE
    H. E., 48
KINSMAN
    M. H., 117
KIRBY
    "Aunt Patsy", 48
    Edgar, 50
    Frank, 141
    J. C., 50
KIRCHNER
    Henry, 190
    Porter, 190
KIRK, 89
    Frank, 60
    J. M., 112
    Kate, 60
    Oscar, 94
    R. P., 89
KIRKER
    Florence L., 141
KIRKHAM
    S. B., 64
KIRKLAND
    Obie, 26
    W. J., 107
KIRKPATRICK
    Burt, 130
    Byron, 36
    Clara, 78
    George, 172
    Otie, 78
    S. S., 36
KIRKPTRICK
    Otey, 161
    Van, 35
KISSINGER
    John G., 116
KITTERMAN
    Ruby, 50

KIZER
  Belva, 113
KLOPNER
  J., 141
KNAUP
  J. R., 130
KNICKERBOCKER
  Percy, 154
  Percy R., 169
KNIGHT
  Ben, 33
  Katherine, 31
  Knight, 66
  Ludie, 27
KNIGHTON
  Lyman, 133
KNODE
  S., 116
KNOWLES
  Charles L., 76
  Hattie, 131
  W. D., 56
  William Dudley, 76
KNOX
  Benson, 85
  Emma, 172
  Sam, 20
  Semore, 94
KNUCKOLLS
  Sarah I., 64
KOENIG
  H. C., 191
KOONCE
  DeMoore, 46
  John W., 132
  Lula, 46
KOONTZ
  Elizabeth, 124
KOVAR
  T. A., 78
KOWLSEY
  W. L., 139
KRIGGER
  E. W., 114
KUCKER
  L. H., 139
KUSO
  William, 60
KUTEMAN
  R. B., 80
KYLE
  T. C., 43
LABAUNE
  G. A., 21
LABONTY
  Maude, 138
LABOR
  G. W., 128
LACEY
  William, 142

William P., 143
LACY
  Don, 61
  J. L., 97
  Lois, 61
  W. M., 72
LADD
  G. A., 13
  Virginia, 138
LADOE
  Inez, 101
LAFOY
  E. M., 155
LAGA
  Paul, 154
LAIDLEY
  Charles Sidney, 75
LAIR
  H. T., 20
LAMAR
  Kitty, 71
  Mary, 88
LAMB
  Eula, 101
  J. T., 43
  M. R., 43
  Marie, 35
  R. W., 43
LAMBERT
  Abner, 163
LAMBRIGHT
  Addie, 54
LAMPER
  Arthur, 155
LAMPKIN
  Joe, 185
LANBETH
  Tom, 88
LANCASTER
  B. C., 144
  George, 144
LANCE
  Rosa, 134
LAND
  Earl, 149
  J. L., 174
LANDERS
  Claudia, 94
LANDON
  James C., 171
LANDRUTH
  Cora, 27
  Walter, 23
LANDRY
  F. J., 110
LANE
  Cy, 193
  E. B., 141
  F. A., 24
  Frank, 110

J. G., 9
J. G., 179
Mary, 179
S. H., 28
LANEY
  C. H., 28
  G. W., 174
LANG
  Henry, 44
  Henry J., 152
  J. R. G., 33
LANGDON
  Rosa, 19
LANGE
  J. S., 20
  W. C. F., 115
LANGFORD
  E. M., 190
  Mattie, 29
LANGLEY
  Julia Mae, 51
LANGLOIS, 170
LANGRAN
  Claude, 116
  Joe C., 24
LANGSDON
  Charles, 137
LANGSFORD
  Laura E., 76
  S. P., 76
LANGSTON
  W. T., 196
LANHAN
  P. G., 67
LANICCA
  Wieland Burwell, 11
LANIER
  C. A., 145
  Mattie, 127
LANKFORD
  Bettie, 196
  C. A., 48
LANKLORD
  C. L., 48
LANNIER
  Hattie E., 152
LANUKE
  Ferdinand, 85
LAPACE
  Polly J., 104
LARGE
  Martin Luther, 105
LARGEANT
  Roy, 175
LARGECT
  L. C., 73
  Myrtle, 73
LASATER
  Frances, 41
  Milton A., 179

LASKEY
  Ida, 17
LASNER
  A., 42
LASSATER
  G. M., 19
LAST
  Charles, 183
LASTER
  Verner, 162
LATTIMER
  Effie, 76
LATTIMORE
  O. S., 117
LAUDERDALE
  John T., 55
LAVENDAR
  William, 80
LAVENDER
  W., 97
  William, 101
LAW
  N. F., 81
LAWLESS
  J. T., 19
LAWLING
  Tom, 11
LAWRENCE
  Alice M., 191
  D. C., 18
  E. A., 138
  E. J., 159
  F. N., 159
  Joe, 91
  Lillian, 11
  T. M., 149
LAWS
  Owen, 34
LAWSON
  E. E., 187
  Emma, 11
LAXTON
  Charles, 161
LAYFIELD
  J. D., 40, 45
  Will, 27
LE LISLE
  Kate, 190
  Mattie, 190
  Salah, 190
LEACH
  J. M., 187
  Mary Florence, 182
  Will, 177
LEAGEY
  Mabel, 145
LEAGUE
  J. C., 110
LEAKE
  H. A., 113

LEAKY
    Mable, 146
LEAR
    Jim, 21
LEATH
    John, 152
    O. B., 86
LEATHEN
    W. J., 88
LEATHERS
    William, 35
LEATHERWOOD
    M. G., 64
    R. H. L., 60
LEBEL
    Edward C., 146
LEBEN
    William, 13
LEDBETTER
    John, 138
LEDDY
    Maggie, 108
LEDFORD
    G. J., 177
    Sadie, 87
LEE
    Alfred, 109
    Birdie, 14
    C., 80
    D. W., 33
    Fitzhugh, 144
    George W., 80, 82,
        117, 182, 190, 193,
        196
    Ike, 97
    J. K., 9
    James O., 103
    Lucia E., 32
    Manson, 65
    Myrtle, 174
    R. G., 139
    Rosa Yet, 9
    Tom, 159
LEECROFT
    S. E., 25
LEFEVRE
    J. M., 84
LEGTERS
    L. L., 20
LEHEW
    T. J., 20
    W. E., 184
LEHMAN
    W. H., 181
LEITCH
    Luther, 93
LELA
    Jennie, 180
LEMASTER
    John, 88

LEMMON
    Seymour, 47
LEMMONS
    Lota, 126
    T. D., 126
    Tullie, 104
LENGEL
    Adolph J., 21
LENOX
    Elijah, 95
    John, 95
    Sarah, 95
LENTON
    George, 97
    J. E., 97
LENZEN
    Emma, 85
LEONARD
    M. A., 102
LERPIN
    M. E., 197
LESLIE
    Mary, 79
    W. J., 67
LESTER
    A. J., 105
    Ed, 105
    L. F., 115
LETCHER
    Frank, 62
LETCHWORTH
    Lora E., 177
LETTER
    Nina, 15
LEVERBOUGH
    William, 70
LEVERITT
    Bob, 193
LEVI
    Jerome, 119
    Leo M., 27
LEVINE
    Phillips, 126
LEVINSON
    Harriet, 34
LEVY
    R. B., 176
LEWIS
    A. E., 187
    Addison Ferris, 99
    Al, 32
    Alfred Hammon, 193
    Ben, 142
    Charles A., 155
    Charley, 191
    Doug, 36
    E. W., 163
    Effie, 117
    Ella, 176
    Henry, 36, 39

    Hierson, 158
    Howell, 155
    J. B., 155
    J. W., 70
    Martin L., 41
    Mattie, 155
    R. F., 55
    R. L., 197
    S. D., 55
    S. P., 169
    Seth, 78
    Sudie, 197
    Thomas R., 141
    W. B., 133
    W. S., 191
LIDDY
    Laura, 124
LIDE
    Roe, 193
LIDESTER
    Thomas W., 10
LIEDTKE
    Lorine, 76
LIEL
    W. M., 33
LIGHTFOOT
    A. H., 40
    G. D., 71
LILLARD
    Will, 33
LILLEY
    John A., 140
    Maude Gertrude, 11
LIMBAUGH
    F. W., 127
LINCOLN
    John, 176
LINDSAY
    Charles, 33
    Edna, 82
    J. L., 138
    John G., 195
    Marie, 168
    R. X., 103
    Samuel, 29
LINDSEY
    A. L., 61
LINES
    Mamie, 61
LINHORST
    Bertha M., 145
LINN
    W. J., 102
LINTHICUM
    Elizabeth, 8
LINTON
    A. D., 29
    Josie, 175
LIPARI
    Theresa, 110

LIPSCOMB
    August K., 113
    Joe D., 103
    M. L., 39
    Tom, 20
    W. W., 113
LISCHKE
    Otto A., 177
LISLE
    Ed, 95
LITSEY
    William R., 171
LITTLE
    Charles, 116
    H. P., 47
    J. L., 153
    Luther, 33, 41, 54, 58,
        128, 133, 142, 165,
        187, 192
    M. K., 139
    N. C., 40
    William, 19
LITTLEFIELD
    M., 11
    Maggie, 137
LITTLES
    M. C. X., 116
LITTLETON
    Charley, 19
    Mace, 19
    Sanford, 19
LIVINGSTON
    H. T., 185
LOCHMAN
    Henry A., 16
    John Henry, 16
LOCKE
    Harold W., 104
LOCKETT
    Bessie, 133
    Mrs. C. J., 14
    Paralee, 105
LOCKHARD
    Julian T., 47
LOCKLEAR
    H. B., 83
LOCKLOOR
    H. B., 83
LOCKMAN
    John T., 31
LOCKRIDGE
    Hal, 80
LOFTIN
    Annie, 66
    P. C., 100
    Tom, 65
LOFTON
    George, 183
LOGAN
    Mary, 179

W. H., 165
LOGSDEN
　Claud, 31
LONG
　A. C., 40
　A. Z., 129
　Alice Pearl, 97
　H. M., 107
　Hendricks, 170
　J. R. G., 125
　J. W., 122
　John B., 153
　R. L., 140
　S. B., 129
　S. D., 129
　S. E., 56
　Vernon, 153
　W. J., 40
LONGENEUKER
　Nannie, 20
LONGHAM
　Mabel, 190
LONGIRO
　J. T., 90
LONGLEY
　L. R., 159
LONGTUTH
　E., 141
LOOMIS
　Mary E., 19
LOONEY
　E. F., 109
　Henry C., 137
　John S., 137
　Lenny E., 137
　M. R., 36, 48
LOPES
　Albert, 18
LORANCE
　Beulah, 98
LORELL
　Sam, 173
LOREN
　W. F., 26
LORENZ
　Henry, 76
LOSANO
　Vicento, 113
LOSEY
　Mary E., 48
LOTT
　Ola, 83
LOUCHARD
　Louis, 85
　Thomas, 185
LOUGHRAY
　James, 185
LOUGHREN
　James J., 93
LOUGRAY

Laura, 189
LOUIS
　C. T., 119
　Talmadge, 119
LOUPAT
　John, 171
LOVE
　Della, 172
　Ethelwyn, 90
　Joe, 154
　John, 95
　Kate D., 108
　Margaret, 144
　Ray, 16
　Thomas B., 154
LOVELESS
　J. L., 31
LOVING
　George B., 76
　Joseph L., 42
　Roy S., 12
　Royal S., 10
LOWDON
　James G., 178
LOWE
　Annie, 137
　G. T., 10
　H. P., 82
　James, 80
　Leada, 159
　T. W., 176
LOWENSTEIN
　Harvey V., 149
　James W., 149
LOWERY
　Guy, 156
　Mamie, 108
LOWRING
　A. N., 79
LOWRY
　A. P., 117
LOYD
　Pearl Tucker, 132
LUCAS
　Josie, 19
　Mrs. Sam, 8
LUCCACHE
　Eugene, 15
LUCE
　T. Z., 53
LUKENS
　E. W., 143
LUMMINS
　W. H., 145
LUMPKIN
　Olin, 136
　W. H., 136
LUNA
　A. E., 99
　A. S. B., 136

Maxmillan, 136
LUND
　E. G., 193
LUNK
　W. R., 35
LUNN
　George, 181
　Lula M., 75
LUSTER
　Ed, 63
LUTHER
　J. F., 19
LUTT
　C. W., 18
LUTTERELL
　Thomas, 55
LUTTLE
　L., 19
LUTZ
　Will, 82
LYDIS
　G. P., 107
LYNCH
　H. S., 88
LYNN
　Roy J., 55
LYON
　Hattie, 90
　W. L., 90
LYONS
　Ella, 179
　Etta, 152
　Jack, 179
　John, 168
　R. E., 37
LYSTER
　C. H., 153, 156
LYTLE
　I. N., 104
MABRY
　Jim, 141
　Willie, 13
MACAULEY
　Amp, 195
MACE
　J. R., 172
MACGREGOR
　T. A., 24
MACHIN
　J. P., 97
MACK
　George, 136
　M. E., 116
MACKENZIE
　Jack, 88
　Josephine, 27
　May, 88
MACKEY
　John, 29
　Lewis, 65

MACMURRAY
　S. H., 26
MACON
　Mayne, 42
MACRAY
　Duncan, 91
MADDEN
　C. C., 65
MADDOX
　A. P., 89
　Dayton, 183
　E. P., 89
　J. N., 89
　Jim, 89
　John E., 89
　Pike, 89
　R. E., 89
　W. A., 89
　Walter T., 89
MADDUX
　Charles D., 144, 179, 191
MADIGAN
　William J., 142
MADISON
　C. L., 193
　Ed, 151
MAGEL
　Charles, 39
　Henry, 39
MAHAFFEY
　Mike, 28
MAHAN
　J. V., 127
MAHANEY
　J. P., 57
MAIER
　Mabel, 170
MAINS
　W. J., 40
MAJOR
　L. D., 139
　Roy, 139
MAJORS
　Alpha, 90
　Asa, 196
　J. H., 87
MALKEY
　Annie Laura, 54
　W. D., 54
MALLOY
　John, 10
MALONE
　Chester, 130
　Elmo, 78
　Files, 7
　H. G., 143
　J. E., 130, 187
　Joyce, 130
　Leland, 11

P. J., 190
Robert W., 95, 189
MANAHAN
   Charlie, 48
   Willie T., 48
MANGRUM
   J. M., 75
MANGUM
   Ollie, 84
MANLEY
   Frank E., 141
MANN
   Albert, 76
   Honore, 182
   Horace, 15
   J. C., 121
   J. M., 16
MANNING
   E. R., 29
   F. H., 169, 175
   H. F., 171
   J. W., 171
   Robert, 115
MANTAUX
   L. J., 131
MANTON
   Charles, 24, 98, 122
   Chase, 19, 66
MAPLE
   Toy, 91
MAPLES
   Alphonso, 144
   Hirschel, 164
   Jonas, 101
MARCHMAN
   Ed, 121
MARDDIN
   Bud, 72
MAREN
   L. P., 45
MARILETT
   M. W., 177
MARION, 49
MARK
   Porter C., 154
MARLER
   Reuben, 41
MARLET
   M. W., 176
MARLOUM
   Mary, 83
MARR
   E., 185
   William, 118
MARRATTA
   Caleb, 95
MARROS
   Louis, 145
MARRS
   S. M. N., 156

MARSH
   E. J., 94
MARSHALL
   Cassius Clay, 108
   F. W., 41
   Fannie, 62
   Horace G., 61
   J. F., 185
   Thomas, 190
MARTEL
   Bert G., 180
MARTICUE
   Cora, 124
MARTIN
   Alta, 19
   Annie, 186
   Ben H., 87
   Ben Hill, 85
   Bessie Bowen, 95
   C. E., 11
   Claude, 180
   E. G., 170
   Edward, 171
   Ethel, 76
   Fallitha, 103
   H. G., 191
   J., 168
   J. C., 96
   J. F., 85
   J. M., 42
   J. R., 78
   J. W., 115
   Jesse A., 102
   Jessie, 96
   John Frank, 63
   Lee, 138
   Lola, 183
   Marcella, 19
   Mary, 111
   Rufus, 29, 117
   Thea J., 110
   Uriah P., 62
   W. F., 35
   W. H., 128
   W. I., 140
   W. L., 25
   Walter, 65
   Will, 114
   William B., 71
MARTINEZ
   Germion, 151
   Isaac, 122
MASERANG
   S., 127
MASON
   George W., 95
   Lula, 108
   Mary, 121
   S. S., 102
MASSENGALE

James L., 81
MASSENGILL
   William, 20
MASSEY
   Albert, 14
   Ethel, 81
   G. M., 14
   Robert J., 163
MASSIE
   D., 158
   G. C., 81
   G. G., 79
   Helen, 137, 139
   R. M., 139
MASTERS
   B., 162
MATHEN
   S., 85
MATHERSON
   R. C., 141
MATHIN
   John, 63
MATHIS
   J. S., 28
   Joe, 68
MATTHES
   Gerard E., 59
MATTHEWS
   Asa, 165
   Bill, 19
   D. E. R., 195
   E. E., 190
   Glen, 145
   Gordon, 82
   Ivey, 16
   John C., 182
   W. R., 192
MATTOX
   J. P., 161
MAUNEY
   Luther, 135
MAUPIN, 108
   Leola Lawrence, 149
   W. H., 129
MAURICE
   T. L., 139
MAVERICK
   Albert, 61
MAXED
   Rebecca, 77
MAXEY
   Effie, 194
   Ernest, 183
   W. T., 19
MAXIE
   Effie, 194
MAXWELL
   Bettie B., 64
   Enoch, 115
   James, 178

James B., 115
John, 115
Luther, 129
R. W., 129
S. A., 80
T. S., 115
MAY
   Bennett A., 181
   Eva, 87
   John, 171, 173
   Mary, 89
   T. J., 196
   W. S., 109
MAYABB
   Lorado, 82
MAYDEN
   C. C., 8
MAYER
   Albina, 137
   Emil, 165
   Emlie, 151
   Grace, 113
   J. H., 109
   Joseph, 11
   Rosa, 72
MAYES
   Will, 59
MAYFIELD
   Eula, 144
   L. M., 160, 162
   Otis, 165
MAYHALL
   Albert, 64
MAYHEW
   Arthur Blackburn, 179
   M., 35
MAYNARD
   John, 68
   Julia, 141
   Laura, 20
MAYS
   J. A., 114
   R. E., 144
   W. I., 197
MAYTON
   A. J., 47
MCADAMS
   Charles R., 192
   George W., 192
   John, 117
MCAFEE
   John, 24
MCAFFEE
   S. T., 32
MCALLISTER
   Harry, 41
   Nannie M., 180
MCANALLY
   Jefferson A., 54
MCANNALLY

M. L., 100
MCASHAN
　J. E., 85
　Mattie, 85
　Maurice, 85
　S. M., 23
MCBEE
　R. B., 72
　Robert, 27
MCBRAYER
　J. E., 44
MCBRIDE
　A. O., 128
　Belle Vida, 145
　Lucius, 102
　M. E., 21
　R. A., 21
　Wilson, 32
MCCABE
　Hal, 104
MCCAHAN
　James, 30
　John, 30
　Sarah, 30
　W. C., 69
MCCAIN
　Ed, 151
　Grace, 20
　Mattie, 90
　R. A., 151
　T. C., 89
MCCALL
　Elsie, 29
　George H., 54
　J. L. L., 54, 56
　J. M., 54
　John N., 54
　Thomas, 67
MCCALLUM
　W. C., 51
MCCAMPBELL
　Eva, 156
　J. S., 156
MCCANDLESS
　Fannie, 196
MCCANS
　Ethel, 179
MCCARLEY
　John, 77
MCCARTER
　J. F., 96
MCCARTHY
　B. F., 127
　B. P., 159
　G. P., 152
　J. E., 159
　Jud, 178
　Leila, 18
　Orrin, 152
MCCARTNEY
　J. L., 76
　Larry, 39
MCCARTY
　J. H., 104
　J. N., 192
　John, 188
MCCARVER
　C. S., 146
　L. V., 9
　Robert, 168
MCCARY
　F. C., 178
MCCASKILL
　Emma I., 140
MCCAULEY
　Etta Maurice, 83
　Lula, 83
MCCELVEY
　H. M., 143
　J. S., 143
MCCHAN
　Anna, 30
　William C., 30
MCCHESNEY
　Charles B., 135
MCCLAIN
　Nora, 129
MCCLANAHAN
　S. M., 158
　William, 174
MCCLAREY
　Homer, 127
MCCLARY
　Adam, 49
　F. C., 126
　Homer, 126
MCCLELLAN
　B. C., 163
　Paul, 56
MCCLINTOCK
　Allen, 131
MCCLOUD
　D., 188
MCCLURE
　Daudes, 105
　Elizabeth, 195
　Mary, 64
　S. H., 9
　W. V., 45
MCCLURG
　J. L., 155
MCCOGGINS
　Myrtle, 96
MCCOGHERN
　Edna, 133
MCCOLLUM
　G. C., 181
MCCOMAR
　A. W., 99
MCCOMB
　J. R., 107
MCCONNELL
　Carrie, 21
　Ernest, 101
　George, 76
MCCOOL
　R. T., 75
MCCORD
　A. H., 104
　Ella, 164
MCCORMICK
　Anita, 10
MCCORRELL
　William, 62
MCCOSKEY
　Charles, 99
　John, 99
MCCOSTIN
　Essie, 197
MCCOWEN
　Gus, 43
MCCOWN
　Phoenie, 190
　Phoenie Bell, 190
MCCOY
　Albert, 10
　Henry, 80
　Ola May, 28
　Tuck, 157
MCCRACKEN
　E. H., 158
MCCRARY
　W. A., 33, 34
MCCREARY
　Willie I., 141
　Willie J., 140
MCCREIGHT
　R. L., 45
MCCRORY
　John, 168
MCCUISITION
　B. F., 99
MCCULLOCH
　A. C., 10
　Ellen, 173
MCCULLOM
　J. M., 65
MCCULLOUGH
　Carry, 153
　M. J., 146
　R. N., 57
MCCURDY
　A. H. P., 156
MCDADE
　R. R., 181
MCDANIEL
　B. B., 34
　B. F., 187
　Helen, 160
　J. K., 160
　John, 93
　N. B., 35
　Russell G., 10
　T. W., 73
　Tom, 19, 46, 50, 107, 125, 141, 151, 158
　W. B., 158
　Willie, 80, 181
MCDERMOTT, 97
　H. C., 117
MCDONALD
　Alex, 40
　Annie L., 197
　Bess Leland, 180
　Bill, 40
　D. F., 159
　Donna, 196
　George, 40
　Grover, 110
　Howard, 163
　J. W., 153
　John, 61
　Kate, 174
　Sarah, 26
　T., 149
　W. F., 137
　W. R., 183
MCDONOUGH
　Martin J., 195
MCDOUGAL
　Jennie, 109
MCDOWELL
　D. S., 131
　John, 19
　Lizzie, 131
　Sam, 23
　Samuel, 156
　W. F., 7
MCDUFFIE
　J. S., 174
　R. H., 187
MCDUNAWAY
　James, 63
MCELROY
　B. C., 190
MCFADDEN
　Magruder, 98
　R. Y., 87
MCFADIN
　W. H. R., 163
MCFARLAN
　John, 139
　Nancy, 139
MCFARLAND
　C., 52
　Luca, 160
　W. G., 64
　W. W., 147
MCFARLANE
　J. S, 25

MCFARLIN
  G. H., 100
MCGARITY
  W. B., 169
MCGARRITY
  W. B., 71
MCGAUGH
  T. C., 137
MCGEE
  David H., 173
  Eva, 101
  H. L., 179
  Mary, 24
  Sam, 19
  W. P., 89
MCGENTLIE
  Joe, 145
MCGILL
  Edna, 118
  William, 63
MCGINNIS
  Netta, 94
MCGOWAN
  C. W., 136
  Maggie Augusta, 90
MCGRATH
  Katie, 162
MCGREGOR
  Marguerite, 135
  W. E., 97
MCGRIFF
  D. L., 109
MCGUINN, 176
MCGUIRE
  Joel Angus, 187
  Myrtle, 113
MCHAM
  S., 160
MCHANEY
  J. H., 11
MCINERRY
  Mary, 79
MCINTIRE
  Harry P., 167
MCINTOSH
  Annie, 67
  Ellis, 116
MCKAMY
  Nellie, 175
MCKAY
  H., 138
  H. T., 144, 190
  Louise, 138
  R. T., 127
MCKAYE
  Erie, 108
MCKEE
  J. L., 57
  John W., 66
  Norine B., 59

MCKELLAR
  H. N., 16
MCKEMIE
  Annie, 187
MCKENZIE
  Walton H., 109
MCKEON
  J. T., 172
MCKIBBEN
  Annie, 51
MCKILLEN
  William Harold, 102
MCKILLIP
  William, 113
MCKINGLE
  Sam, 155
MCKINLEY
  May V., 147
  Willie, 147
MCKINNEY
  ida B., 79
  J. W., 21
  John M., 101
  Laura, 111
  Mark, 78
  T. E., 49
  T. F., 30
MCLAIN
  John H., 125
  Minnie, 144
MCLARREN
  J. R., 44
MCLARTY
  F. E., 170
MCLAUGHLIN, 151
  A., 181
  Olan, 133
  R. L., 65
  William, 68, 71, 138
MCLEAN
  Bess, 195
  Bessie, 194
  J. E., 122, 190
  W. P., 194
MCLELLAN
  Addie, 60
MCLENAHAN, 168
MCLENDON
  Lola, 141
  W. A., 176
MCLEOD
  Annie, 87
  J. N., 86
MCLOUD
  Kenneth, 104
  Neer, 35
MCLYNN
  Carl, 48
MCMAHAN
  Thomas, 142

MCMANUS
  J. F., 129
MCMASTERS
  Tennie, 169
MCMEANS
  C. A., 165
MCMECHLE
  Stewart, 142
MCMILLAN
  George L., 179
  Janey L., 116
  W. P., 45
MCMULLINS
  H. R., 164
MCMURRAY
  J. W., 164
MCMUTTON
  Effie, 109
MCNAMARA
  Henry, 63
MCNATT
  Nannie, 147
  William, 157
MCNEIL
  C. M., 34
  Florence, 156
MCNELLIS
  F., 125
  Ione, 125
  J. T., 129
  Thelma, 125
MCNEMAR
  H. C., 63
MCPHERSON
  Chalmers, 75, 85, 153, 169
  G. H., 164
  J. Ike, 132
  Jessie, 133
  Lena, 183
  Lydia Starr, 14
  T. W., 14
  W. C., 194
MCQUEEN
  Clark, 138
MCQUERRY
  Lakin, 105
MCRAY
  C. M., 100
MCTEER
  G. S., 43
MCWHIRTER
  Alice, 41
  J. C., 127
MCWHITHERS, 134
MCWILLIAMS
  H. B., 150
  Kettler, 43
MEACHAM
  G. W., 84

MEADE
  Hannah, 77
  Nancy A., 81
MEADFORD
  Jeah, 127
  R. E., 72
MEADLEY
  J. L., 164
MEADOR
  Valley, 12
MEADOWS
  Audrey, 11
MEASURALL
  D. D., 12
MECHEN
  E., 20
MEDFORD
  Amanda, 129
MEDLEY
  Austin P., 11
MEDLIN
  A. J., 63
  Annie, 145
MEEKS
  H. T., 186
MEISLOHN
  J. A., 146
MELINAM
  Nora, 177
MELTON
  Johnnie, 110
  Lucy, 161
  W. E., 194
MENDEZ
  John, 130
MENECK
  Mabry, 147
MENTON
  W. D., 12
MERCER
  Jane, 129
  Myrtle, 16
MERCHANT
  James K., 178
MERDUTH
  Bertha, 165
MERICH
  Godfrey F., 121
MERRILL
  F. H., 193
  R. L., 96
MERRIMAN
  Charles, 172
MERRITT
  Belle, 20
  Henry, 159
  John, 159
  W. A., 10
MESERANG
  Lavina, 127

MESSENGER
  J. W., 26
MESSER
  Maggie, 145
MESTLER
  J. R., 64
METCALF
  C. P., 112
  Mary E., 112
METZGER
  Harriett Josephine, 33
MEWSHAW
  Edna, 135
MEYER
  George, 159
  Harry, 119
MEYERS
  Christina, 130
  Elsie, 18, 19
  Ernest, 27
  Tom, 27
  William, 110
MICHAELSON
  Violet, 107
MICHEL
  Ida, 177
MIDDLETON, 47
  Florence, 138
  Mary, 138
MIERS
  Rosa, 27
MIGUS
  John, 100
MILAM
  Gladys, 62
  John, 41
  Scott, 31
  W. L., 178
  Y. M., 62
MILES
  J. S., 20
  M. D., 87
MILFORD
  James, 58
  Jeff, 58
MILLER
  A. J., 104
  Albert, 25
  Annie J., 10
  C. R., 36, 183
  Daniela, 195
  Ella, 150
  F. O., 8
  Fannie W., 192
  Frank, 130
  G. S., 195
  G. W., 91
  Gladys, 114
  H. H., 169
  H. L., 140

Helen, 117
Hollis, 169
Houston, 117
J. B., 100
J. L., 152
James, 142
James B., 63
Jessie, 113, 117
John, 98
Josephine, 69
L. H., 134
Lanty, 114
Lee, 60
Lucille, 24
Mamie, 140
Maria, 185
Mary, 44, 86
R. F., 140
W. B., 172
W. G., 127
W. J., 188
W. N., 191
W. R., 58
William, 97
MILLETT
  F. J., 177
MILLIGAN
  Lillie, 33, 34
  Nona, 168
MILLIKAN
  E. O., 93
  S. E., 169
  T. F., 93
MILLIKEN
  Anna, 167
MILLION
  Perry, 99
MILLS
  Fred, 155
  J. S., 154
  Lydia, 81
  Mattie, 156
  William, 189, 194
MILLSAP
  Ross, 27, 30
MIMPHER
  M. L., 159
MIMS
  M. D., 193
  William, 75
MINCEY
  Maude, 140
MINGS
  Annie, 109
  Maggie, 161
MINK
  Henry, 158
MINN
  W. H., 97
MISER

William, 150
MITCHELL
  Alice, 164
  Alma, 75
  Ben, 130
  C. G., 147
  Charles G., 106
  Ed, 91
  Emmett, 8
  Eula, 29
  Eva, 71
  Fred, 11
  Hiram, 133
  Howard, 18
  James, 60
  Jessie, 179
  Joe, 180
  Lonnie, 83
  M. N., 142
  R., 30
  Samuel, 10
  Sarah, 152
  T. A., 28
  T. W., 155
  W. H., 82
  W. R., 170
  William L., 111
MOBLEY
  James, 131
  M. S., 158
  S., 158
MOFFET, 117
MOFFITT
  Emma, 98
  Maude Stanley, 169
MOLDER
  Kate, 174
MOLETT
  Frances, 96
MOLIERE
  W. R., 71, 164
MOLINE, 182
MOLONEY
  Catherine, 114
MOMAND
  Paul, 137
MONAGHEN
  John, 45
MONEGHAN
  John, 45
MONEY
  H. T., 165
MONIGIN
  Auguste, 137
MONK, 49
  Alonzo, 163, 169, 173
  Ida, 142
MONNEY
  Sarah, 171
MONROE

Charles L., 76
Florence, 117
J. D., 90
MONTCASTLE
  W. D., 42
MONTGOMERY
  Eugene, 151
  Henry, 180
  John, 149
  Margaret, 53
  Murtle, 149
  R. C., 175
  Sam, 157
  T. D., 77
MOODY, 142
  John, 16
  Leroy, 67
  Willie, 50
MOON
  F. E., 119
MOONEY
  James, 164
MOORE
  A., 136
  Alex, 72
  Anna, 84
  Annie, 25
  Atherton, 193
  C. E., 59
  C. R., 70
  Daniel, 65
  E., 170
  E. P., 51
  Ed, 157
  Elma, 71
  Etta May, 76
  F. M., 68
  Floy, 176
  Frank, 104, 147
  G. W., 64, 68
  George, 72
  Harry, 103
  J. L., 70
  J. S., 76
  John, 25, 93
  Lillie, 156
  Luther, 64, 68
  Mabel, 159
  Mary H., 72
  R. H., 181
  Ray, 160
  Robert F., 8
  S. V., 25
  T. A., 96
  Tom, 179
  W. C., 55
  W. F., 83
  W. T., 8
  William, 15, 117
MOORHEAD

J. M., 24
MOORMAN
  Maud, 30
MORALES
  Juan, 151
MORAN
  Delores, 188
  Minnie, 174
MORARITY
  Timothy, 56
MOREHEAD
  Leonora, 101
MOREY
  Catherine, 153, 154
MORGAN, 35
  A. M., 110
  A. P., 174
  Bert, 142
  Charley, 101
  Ed, 28
  G. B., 86
  Green, 183
  Hortense, 56
  J. B., 170
  J. T., 56
  Robert E., 170
  Virginia, 86
  W. E., 193
  W. H., 90
MORPHUS, 60
MORRELL
  Laura, 142
MORRIS
  Mae, 161
MORRIS
  A. A., 189
  A. L., 58
  A. R., 28
  Alice, 178
  Beulah, 33
  Charles, 145
  Clifford, 177
  Frank, 88
  Fred, 115
  Gertrude, 30
  I. Z. T., 87
  J. A., 124
  J. E., 9
  J. L., 35, 175
  James G., 45
  John, 88, 139
  L., 17
  Leopold, 132
  Lollie, 123
  M. A., 83
  Mary Ellen, 193
  Minor, 88
  R. A., 86, 142
  Samuel, 136
  T. A., 65
MORRISON
  Bud, 192
  Charles, 150
  Henry B., 57
  S. E., 144
  W. S., 107
MORROW
  B., 115
  Cecil, 192
  D. T., 151
  J. C., 36
  Mary, 137
  Nora, 57
  Sarah, 62
MORTON
  A. W., 191
  G. W., 125
  Willie, 64
MOSELEY
  Al G., 167
  Bessie, 116
  Georgia Mae, 94
  Henry, 152
  R. H., 77
  Theodore, 20
MOSER
  J. F., 188
MOSES
  Josephine, 98
  Martin, 98
  R., 64
MOSIER
  George G., 191
MOSKEY
  Will, 17
MOSLEY
  Della, 158
MOSS
  Al, 29
  H. D., 24
  Lee, 147
  Mr., 26
  W. C., 29
  Will, 138
MOSSMAN
  E. E., 171
MOSTROM
  Gust, 113
MOSZON
  Louise, 191
MOTEN
  John, 159
MOTHERSHEAD
  Grace, 89
MOTLE
  R. L., 134
MOTT
  Annie, 154
  Matilda, 10
MOUNTS
  S., 157
  T. A., 158
MOURSUND
  C. M., 160
MOWLAND
  John, 169
MOXLEY
  Frank, 125
MOYER
  J. N., 102
MUCKLEROY
  J. D., 55
MUELLER
  wilhemina, 96
MULHERN
  Thomas G., 80
MULKEY
  Abe, 31
  E. E., 153
  Royal R., 31
MULLEN
  W. R., 127
MULLIGAN
  Nona, 161
MULLINO
  F. H., 125
  Henry, 125
MULLINS
  Annie, 39
  F. F., 48
  H. C., 112
  Joe, 75
  O. A., 174
  W. E., 194
MUMPOWER
  B. S., 170
  Bart, 163
  Ernest, 7
  Jessie, 163
MUNZESHEIMER
  Max, 20
MURCHISON
  Jim, 32
MURDOCK
  James B., 12
MURPHEY
  Hattie, 126
  R. K., 165
  Sallie, 178
MURPHREE
  J. D., 13
MURPHY
  A. A., 160
  Annie, 64
  Charles, 172
  Ed, 78
  Rosa, 132
  T. J., 189
MURRAY
  Cora, 146
  Dick, 133
  G. T., 57
  J. A., 192
  Jesse L., 61
  John William, 69
  Nellie, 186
  Tobe, 11
  Zellah, 139
MURRELL
  Delos, 52
MUSSETT
  J. P., 34, 121
  S. P., 108
MUSTA
  W. G., 175
MYATT
  W. H., 90
MYERS, 78
  A. C., 186
  D. D., 149
  Elmo, 98
  George W., 149
  Henry, 174
  J. H., 11
  J. T., 174
  J. W., 178
  Joseph S., 27
  Lem, 178
  Lemiel, 179
  Leon A., 78
MYRICK
  J. R., 55
NADRY
  Lovella, 16
NAGLE
  Annette A., 41
  J. W., 41
NANCE
  Charles, 156
  O. H., 83
  Thomas, 85
NASH
  Clay, 76
  George, 190
  H. C., 98
  H. Clay, 137, 139
  J. M., 12
  John, 44
  K. L., 183
  Lanson F., 94
  W. L., 76
  W. S., 60
NAUGHTON
  Frank, 188
NAVE
  A. J., 59
NAY
  Jap, 129
NEAL, 152
  Baxter, 170

Daisy, 165
Isa E., 117
J. A., 154
Thomas, 62
W. K., 165
NEALY
　Ben, 72
NEATHERY
　Maurice G., 90
NEEDHAM
　Debora Ann, 63
NEEL
　Eller, 139
NEELY
　T. M., 190
NEFF
　J. C., 27
　John, 187
NEILL
　Ed, 153
　Pearl, 80
NELSON
　B. J., 174
　C. F., 30
　Clara, 141
　Dora, 88
　Fannie, 181
　John, 164
　L. S., 137
　Norman E., 157
　Roy, 42
　W. A., 141
NESBITT
　John, 188
　T. J. P., 173
NETTLETON, 193
NEUMEGEN
　Mary, 8
NEVIL
　Annie, 190
NEVITT
　James, 11
NEWBERRY
　William H., 181
NEWBILL
　Ethel A., 10
NEWBY
　Rosa, 128
　Rose E., 129
　T. E., 176
NEWCOMB
　Fred, 125
NEWKIRK
　Mary J., 182
NEWLAND
　Robert, 100
NEWLEE
　John, 77
NEWLIN
　Nancy, 50

NEWMAN
　H. W., 27
　Helen, 78
　Joseph, 78
NEWSOM
　James Marvin, 101
　Will A., 139
NEWSOMS
　Pearl, 160
　S., 160
NEWSON
　J. E., 100
　J. Marvin, 100
NEWTON
　A. M., 97
　Annie, 141
　F. M., 144
　W. C., 97
NIBLING
　Fred, 26
NICHOLAS
　Marvin, 76
NICHOLS
　Bessie, 159
　Ed, 163, 185
　Fayette, 126
　Georgia, 65
　Henry C., 184
　J. A., 85
　J. W., 79
　Jim, 12
　Louis, 24
　Marvin, 80
　William, 10
NICHOLSON
　Hattie, 143
　J. G., 121
　J. M., 47
　Ralph, 113
　Susie, 89
　W. A. J., 39
NICKERSON
　J. R., 39
NICKS
　Effie, 97
NICOLA
　Georgie, 80
NIFONG
　C. C., 130
　F. C., 130
NINING
　J. C., 160
NIOUS
　Albert, 29
NIRDLINGER
　Edna, 192
NIX, 111
　Mary, 176
NIXON
　"Maston", 95

J. A., 15, 131
S. M., 95, 189
NOATON
　Simpson, 24
NOBLE
　J. H., 129
　Louise, 170
　Ollie Ruth, 79
　Robert, 192
　Sneed, 96
NOBLES
　Will, 162
NOLEN
　G. G., 79
　Mary E., 79
　W. L., 79
NOONAN
　Patrick, 145, 152
NORCROSS
　D. E., 162
NORDMAN
　May, 91
NORMAN
　E. B., 81
　J. B., 16
　Jack, 77
　Lafayette, 96
　W. W., 138
NORRIS
　Aileen, 85
　Arthur, 41
　Ely, 158
　Howard, 187
　James W., 62
　John L., 119
　John P., 85
　Kathleen, 178
　Mattie, 20
　Pearly, 85
NORRY
　Jeannie, 175
NORTH
　H. E., 162
NORTHCRAFT
　Gussie, 168
NORTHINGTON
　Roe, 24
NORTON
　Edward Russell, 146
　J. A., 158
　J. K., 32
　Margaret, 156
　Novilla Pearl, 181
NORWOOD
　Willie, 138
NOSSEK
　Rebecca, 165
NOVICH
　Tobia, 11
NUGENT, 155

Joseph, 15
NULL
　Lee Andrew, 34
NUNN
　J. C., 82
　T. C., 82
NUNNALLY
　Erma, 151
NUSS
　Henry, 94
　John, 94
O'BANNON
　S., 160
O'DONNELL
　Thomas, 163
O'FARRELL
　W., 180
　William, 177
O'NEAL
　A. J., 154
O'REILLY
　Lon, 177
OAKES
　Frances C., 32
OAKLEY
　George, 158
OAKS
　Nola, 125
OATS
　Alice, 17
　Frank, 174
O'BANION
　Clara, 20
OBERTHEER
　H. L., 121
OBRIEN
　Chainault, 121
O'BRIEN
　William, 17
O'BRYAN
　E. B., 91
OBST
　Frank, 43
O'CONNOR
　Mary Elizabeth, 35
ODEKIRK
　Dora, 27
O'DELL
　J. P., 75
ODOM
　Fanny, 147
OGBURN
　James, 84
OGDEN
　C. D., 99
OGLE
　Dick, 122
　J. T., 139
　Jim, 34
O'HARA

John, 153
Lula, 110
Mary, 76
OLDENBERG
  Paul, 28
OLDHAM
  Ed, 183
  Jennie, 183
O'LEARY
  Cassie, 94
OLENBUSH
  Stella, 55
OLIVER
  Ed, 88
  G. A., 48
  Mary L., 49
OLLIVER
  George W., 111
O'MEARA
  J. H., 93
O'NEAL
  A. H., 19
  George W., 114
  William, 21
ONION
  John F., 126
ONVER
  Annie, 52
OPPENHEIMER
  M., 103
  Sid J., 103
OPRY
  William D., 110
O'ROURKE
  Andrew, 80, 83
ORR
  Charles, 9
ORRICK
  B. L., 10
ORTIS
  Gregorio, 57
OSBORN
  A. C., 44
  Maud Cornelia, 60
OSBORNE
  Ira F., 139
  J. D., 30
  J. P., 30
  Jonathan, 8
  Julia, 30
OTT
  James H., 57
OTTMAN
  Herman, 172
OTTO
  Herman, 43
OTWAY
  Isabell, 49
OUSLEY
  Frank, 103
OVERALL
  Edwin Elias, 9
OVERSTREET
  George, 77
  Hattie Lois, 32
OVERTON
  James, 114
OWEN
  Mary, 169
  R. D., 40
OWENS
  B. M., 66
  Edmund, 90
  James, 57
  Jeff, 51
  Lee, 66
OWENSBY
  J. M., 36
OWNSBY
  Maud, 62
  William, 62
OXFORD
  Adele, 175
PACE
  Clarence, 136
  Dempsey, 95
  James T., 54
  Jessie, 95
PADDOCK
  R. N., 100
PAGE, 60
  A., 87
  Heber, 142
  J. A., 122
PAINE
  Angie, 18
PALMER
  E. J., 19
  James, 176
PANNELL
  F. J., 154
  T. J., 152
PARHAM
  J. D., 126
  Lewis, 126
  Louis, 176
  Lula, 176
PARISH
  R. G., 102
PARK
  Lake Em, 17
  Walter H., 127
  Way Manvers, 135
PARKER
  A. C., 109, 126
  C. C., 62
  Charles Chandler, 8
  Edward S., 44
  Felix, 141
  J. H., 62
John, 141
Josie, 9
Lee, 123
Lib, 141
Lillian S., 10, 12
Minter H., 33
Nat, 84
R. L., 9
W. M., 119
PARKS
  Archer, 16
  Burney, 84
  Elmer, 82
  George, 164
  Harry, 164
  J. Earle, 121
  J. P., 14
  Sam, 82
PARLIER
  John, 16
PARNELL
  Alvis, 26
PARRIS
  Henry, 77
  Oscar, 77
PARRISH
  M. L., 64
  Pearl, 97
PARROTT
  R. B., 16
PARSONS
  Bob, 94
  J. W., 32
  Ora, 47
PARVIN
  Florence, 24
PASSALAGUA
  Mary, 149
PASSONS
  Alice, 151
  J. H., 151
PATE
  Lewis, 140
  W. M., 9
  W. S., 23, 43, 70
  William W., 171
PATEK
  Rudolph, 160
PATTERSON, 169
  A. K., 142
  Ab, 184
  Amy, 179
  Athleen, 172
  Ed, 9
  Elmer, 172
  Florine, 142
  Frank H., 114
  Henry, 178
  Hiram R., 10
  J. C., 122
  Kathy, 49
  Lewis, 88
  Minnie, 89
  Mollie, 40, 41
  R., 138
  S. H., 197
  William T., 95
PATTON
  E. G., 170
  John, 187
  R. W., 164
  W. H., 161
PAUL
  J. W., 40
  Jimmie W., 41
PAULK
  Jason, 117
  Stella, 183
PAXTON
  Mary, 19
PAYNE
  Abbie Lee, 90
  Brant, 44
  C. R., 21
  Ethel May, 191
  Fannie, 191
  George W., 67
  John, 191
  John A., 90
  Lena, 64
  Leonard, 7
  M. A., 184
  Mary A., 173
  W. C., 45
  W. M., 30
  Willie, 127
PAYTON
  Steve, 175
PEACHER
  W. R., 182
PEACOCK
  Mittie, 28
PEARCE
  J. E., 31
PEARMAN, 50, 82, 83, 101
PEARSON, 108
  Gertrude, 17
  J. W., 105, 121
PEBBLE
  Thurston Dwight, 96
PECKHAM
  G. W., 19
  George W., 18
PEEBLES, 72
  John O., 146
PEEK
  Fensie, 89
PEERCE
  E. C., 150

PEEVY
  Ben, 60
PEFFER
  C. C., 170
PELL
  Silas, 156
PELS
  William, 26
PENA
  Ascension, 66
PENDER
  H. B., 91, 160
  J. L., 176
PENDERGRASS
  P. L., 158
PENDLETON
  Bonnie, 107
PENICK
  Trisie, 16
PENNEWELL
  Harry, 52
PENNINGTON
  Lawrence, 49
PENNY
  Will P., 87
PENROD
  W. K., 26, 94, 171
PERALES
  Anastacia, 93
PERDER
  R. S., 87
PERGMAN
  Etta, 133
PERKINS
  Bertie, 51
  George, 128
  Henry F., 163
  Jennie, 172
  Lou, 27
  Mary F., 158
  Rhodes, 179
  W. J., 140
PERNET
  J. L., 42
PERRETT
  George, 191
PERROTT
  George, 16
PERRY, 129, 139
  Blanche, 109
  Della, 181
  Lee, 172
  R. E., 60
  R. O., 137
  T. H. C., 139
  Thomas P., 83
  W. P., 58
PERSON
  L. B., 55
PERSONS
  Robert W., 85
PERTIE, 39
PETER
  Frank, 144
PETERS
  Ruth, 150
PETERSON
  Florine, 143
PETITT
  John, 178
PETRIL
  John, 44
PETTERS
  George, 57
PETTIGREW
  Lenna, 116
  Moses, 162
PETTIS
  Juan, 13
PETTY
  C. C., 103, 106
  Lester Elmo, 103
PEYNA
  Louis, 112
PEYTON
  Guy, 59
PHELPS
  Wendall P., 129
PHENIX
  C., 183
  C. L., 34
PHILLIPS
  "Aunt Marietta", 89
  Arthur, 186
  C. L., 132
  D. E., 143
  Florence, 90
  J.C., 135
  Monroe, 136
  R. C., 183
  R. T., 10, 24
  Sallie, 72
  T. C., 193
  T. W., 152
  W. D., 50
  Whitt, 108
  William A., 161
  William Wilson, 180
  Wilson, 80
PHIPPS
  William B., 20
PIERCE, 62
  Charles, 184
  Clarence, 49
  George, 117
  H. E., 188
  J. F., 67, 118, 185
  J. L., 135
  J. S., 40, 41
  M. C., 197
  Naomi, 125
  R. E., 109
  Rosa, 139
  W. F., 188
PIERSON
  George F., 58
PILARD
  Dave, 47
PILARSOTO, 20
PILLOW
  Ben, 123
PINEOD
  D. P., 57
PINKARD
  Alice, 126
PINSON
  J. B., 150
  J. T., 32
PINTO
  James, 32
PIRKLE
  V. L., 189
PITTMAN
  Annie, 142
  Ella, 29
  Minnie, 133
  N. B., 36
PITTS
  Alva, 115
  Joseph T., 116
PITTUCK
  A. A., 23
PLATT
  J. W., 11
PLEASANT
  Melvin, 137
PLEMMONS
  W. B., 113
PLUMBE
  W. L., 145
PLUMMER
  Jennie, 17
  O. T., 17
  Vera, 8
POE
  Hence, 191
  William, 98
POINDEXTER
  H. T., 83, 84
  Hattie, 122
POINTER
  J. L., 54
POLASKI
  Louis, 66
POLK
  C., 18
  C. W., 39
  Lucius, 115
POLLARD
  F. T., 143
  Frank, 35
  I. N., 118
POLLOCK
  J. D., 45
  J. R., 194
  Lloyd, 194
  Phillip Lloyd, 195
  W. E., 182
POLSON
  B. F., 116
  Ed, 116
POND
  U. J., 18
PONDER
  James, 44, 150
  May, 112
POOL
  Ethel, 196
  J. T., 196
  R. J., 69
POOLE
  Oma, 113
POOR
  T. W., 39
POORBAY
  Mimay, 69
POPE
  Ben S., 81
  E., 58
  J. H., 188
  Woodford P., 173
PORTER
  G. W., 118
  George W., 179
  J. W., 29
  John, 193
  Katherine Martin, 178, 179
  Maggie, 27
  Mattie, 91
  N. B., 47
  Sinah, 118
  Sinali Ball, 116
  W. W., 72
  William, 170
PORTMAN
  Jesse P., 30
POSEY
  J. A., 46
  S. J., 168
POSLEY
  Luther, 104
POSTON
  A. J., 130
POTEET
  S. W., 88
POTTER
  A., 9
  O. D., 80
  R. M., 178

Robert, 46
W. R., 107
POTTS
　Cyrena, 161
POWELL
　Alma, 134
　C. R., 19
　Emma, 139
　J. D., 156
　J. P., 173
　Lawrence, 28
　Mary E., 41
　R. H., 127
　S. C., 39
　Vesta, 103
　W. A., 123
　W. T., 164
POWERS
　Blake, 86
PRATER
　Isabelle, 178
　Wallace, 152
PRATHER
　A. L., 53
PRATT
　N. G., 83
　Nettie, 196
　Susan E., 18
　Wells, 196
PRATTLER
　Florence, 11
PRATZ
　S. E., 185
PRESCOTT
　J. J., 68
PRESLER
　J. M., 112
PRESLEY
　M. J., 135
　Maggie, 135
PRESTON, 90
　Emlie L., 158
　Ethel, 155
　Grace, 81
　Lymon, 86
PREWETT
　Charles, 27
　J. C., 83
PRICE
　Ella, 98
　Emma, 11
　Etta, 51
　Henry, 11
　James A., 156
　L. E., 96
　L. L., 24
　Russell, 125
　S. P., 186
　Will, 161, 197
PRIDDY

A. M., 46
PRIDY
　Otis, 44
PRIGMORE
　R. Y., 47
PRINCE
　Arta, 182
　Ben, 77
PRINE
　B. T., 151
PRITCHARD
　J. H. L., 89
　Joe L., 102
PROCTOR
　Angie, 7
　F. K., 157
PRONTISS
　K. M., 72
PROTSMAN
　Emma, 81
PROUTY
　C. T., 16
PROVINE
　E. W., 186
　Elizabeth, 186
PROWCE
　J. Nelson, 111
PRUE
　W. M,, 19
PRUETT
　Leona Maude, 176
　Tom, 141
PRUITT
　J. B., 125
　J. P., 114
　Leonora Maud, 177
　Thomas, 43
PUCKEL
　Mary, 175
PUCKETT
　A. M., 82
　Charles, 133
PUGH
　H. H., 52
　Sybil, 123
PULE
　Henry M., 195
PULLEN
　J. C., 37, 39
PULLEY
　W. J., 147
PUMMEL
　D. F., 140
PURL
　Mattie, 160
PURNELL
　Edna Earle, 87
　L. V., 87
PURYEAR
　Edith, 193

Nannie, 179
PUTMAN
　Frank R., 158
　Rufus, 164
PUTNAM
　J. G., 179
　O. M., 196
QUARLES
　Henry, 29
　James E., 146
　James Hays, 29
　James Hays., 146
　R. L., 146
QUAYLE
　M. F., 132
QUINITE, 89
QUINN
　Angie, 19
　Charles E., 130
　Dora, 19
　J. A., 144
　J. J., 28
　Minnie, 144
　Reba, 30
QUINONE
　E., 135
QUISSENBERRY
　J. I., 75
RAFFERTY
　K. A., 68
RAFFORD
　Lena, 141
RAGAN
　J. B., 45
　John W., 29
　Leah, 45
RAGLAND
　Manuel, 62
RAGLE
　Mertie, 121
RAGLY
　Martin G., 176
RAGSDALE
　Cordia, 94
　W. P., 110
RAILSBACK
　D. G., 124
RAINES
　Haughtie, 97
　W. D., 20
RAINEY
　Cynthia R., 19
　J. H., 24
RAINS
　S. S., 137
RAINWATER
　Dave, 29
RALL
　Guy S., 181
RALPH

A. C., 135
RALSTON
　John, 40
RAMAGE
　B. B., 194
　Barto B., 24, 114
　Barton B., 64
RAMSAY
　J. J., 43
　John, 43
　Sam, 43
　W. F., 43
RAMSEY
　Dessie, 121
　E. P., 123
　Edna, 84
　Edna Pearl, 85
　Frederick E., 30
　Julia D., 123
　L., 96
　M. L., 94
　Will, 196
RANDLE
　Hattie L., 67
　William, 87
RANDOLPH
　Amanda, 64
　Candace, 183
　H. K., 64
　Lillie, 161
RANKIN
　J. V., 41
RANLEY
　Dave, 131
RANSOM
　Harry A., 34
RAPHAEL
　S., 70
RARSON
　A. J., 67
RASBURY
　N. N., 115
RASERA
　Annie, 135
RATCLIFF
　Pearl A., 114
RATHBURN
　C. R., 179
RATHER
　C. C., 82
RATLIFF
　Richard, 15
　Ruth Matthews, 192, 194
　W., 161
　W. E., 138
RATLIFFE
　Dock, 71
RATTAN
　Dan, 82

RATTON
  Hamp, 146
RAWLINSON
  Russ, 136
RAWLS
  Margaret, 86, 87
RAY
  Luther, 163
  Olive, 58
  Philip, 17
  R. W., 96
  S. W., 155
RAYNOR
  J. E., 132
REA
  J. B., 67
READ
  N. B., 11, 187
READY
  John, 155, 157
REAGAN
  Geraldine Powell, 118
REAGIN
  Leonard C., 18
REAGOR
  Josh, 115
REAP
  T. M., 102
REARDON
  W. E., 49
REASONER
  C. E., 174
REAVES
  David, 23
  Della, 31
REAVIS
  Watt, 25
RECORDS
  Thomas B., 174
RECTOR
  Harriett, 58
  Harriett G., 60
  Myrtle May, 129
  Nelson, 58
REDD
  Allie B., 110
REDDEN
  Fate, 57
REDDING
  J., 117
REDDY
  J. W., 170
REDFORD
  E. L., 136
  R. J., 129
REDIN
  Pearl, 78
REDINE
  Lizzie, 57
REDMAN
  Emmel, 17
  T. R., 115
  W. T., 115
REDPATH
  James L., 194
REED
  Abe, 91
  Alice, 139
  Anna, 178
  Charles L., 78
  Clinton, 118
  Elva, 19
  Frank, 65
  G. Walter, 133
  George, 83
  J. R., 196
  K., 11
  Lula, 88
  Major F., 187, 189
  May, 87
  O. E., 11
  S. H., 34
  Vol, 139
  W. H., 86
REEDER
  G. B., 86
REEDUS
  Sam, 149
REES
  Charley, 118
  M. J., 142
REESE
  J. W., 29
REEVER
  Homer, 46
REEVES
  Arthur, 196
  D. A., 193
  E. R., 45
  Ellen, 161
  Ethel, 52
  F. M., 196
  Frank, 61
  Henry, 47
  Homer L., 45
  Reuben, 61
  S. W., 48
  T. J., 87
  Willie, 164
REGNIER
  William, 185
REICHANADTER
  Joe, 70
REICHART
  Mary A. Kuhlman, 142
  William, 142
REICHSTETTER
  John, 128
REID
  A. J., 98
  Frank F., 7
REILLY
  James, 37
REISMANNET
  Sam, 21
RELATOR
  "Grandpa", 7
RELFE
  G. P., 27
REMINGTON
  William F., 171
RENFRO
  Elmer, 123
  Graham, 89
  Ivy, 156
  W. T., 24, 47
RENNIE
  Annie Mae, 146
RENSHAW
  B. J., 112
  Maudie, 96
REUTER
  Edward, 42
REVES
  Bessie, 16
REVILLE
  J. N., 145
REYER
  George M., 103
REYES
  Thomas, 138
REYMERSHOFFER
  Gus, 7
REYNA
  Margareta, 15
REYNOLD
  C. D., 112
REYNOLDS
  Alice A., 152
  Frank, 129
  Gussie, 153
  J. H., 20
  Minnie, 8
  Pearlie, 53
  Richard, 146
  S. K., 142
RHODES
  J. W., 9
  L. F., 102
  Susie, 99
RHOMBURG
  Udell Regina, 181
RIALO
  Pietro, 152
RICE
  A. E., 27
  Hamp, 44
  James, 28
  Jefferson Davis, 187
  Lena, 16
  N. G., 135
  Nellie, 62
  P. B., 29
RICH
  Beulah, 102
RICHARDS
  Charlie, 49
  Ivey, 9
  J. M., 182
  James E., 170
  William, 103
RICHARDSON
  "Aunt Sarah", 138
  D. C., 81
  Dave, 150
  Henry E., 26
  Lena, 101
  Mary S., 126
  R. B., 53
  S., 175
  S. E., 95
  W. L., 122
  W. R., 124
  Walter, 162
  William, 41, 62
  William H., 9
RICHES
  H. E., 97
  M. E., 97
RICHEY
  T. A., 127
RICHMOND
  G. B., 20
  Nina, 88
RICKEL
  Emma, 149
RICKS
  M. E., 80
RICSMAN
  Sam, 193
RIDDLE
  A., 169, 171
  Arden, 175
  Ed, 111
  Sallie, 124
  W. N., 171
RIDE
  M. D., 31
RIDEOUT
  Beatrice, 91
RIDER
  John, 186
RIDGEWAY
  Pierce, 164
RIDLEY
  Bill, 11
  William, 197
RIGGINS
  J. L., 146

Robert, 67, 70
RIGGS
    Jessie, 75
    Margaret C., 109
    T. S., 154
    Thomas, 109
RIKE
    Lillie, 175
RILEY
    Clara, 185
    D. C., 118
    James, 39
    John, 187, 189
    P. M., 113
    Rose, 113
RINEHART
    Frank, 129
    Jane, 129
RING
    John, 114
RINGOLD
    L., 170
RINTLEMAN
    Fay, 109
RISER
    George, 33
RISTON
    Lizzie, 36
RITCHIE
    R. A., 134
RIVERS
    C. E., 181
ROACH
    Adaline, 14
    J. J., 181
    Phillip, 25
ROBBINS
    Effie, 129
    John, 168
    Sida, 144
    Willie G., 98
ROBE
    Elizabeth, 179
ROBERSON
    Charles, 142
    G. W., 59
ROBERTS, 112
    A. B., 194
    Alise, 170
    C. H., 72
    Claude, 145
    Edward, 151
    Emma, 187
    Felix, 145
    J. C., 98
    Jeff D., 79
    L. E., 164
    Mary E., 79
    Moselle, 19
    Nannie L., 96

Nellie, 45
P. B., 61
Palo D., 64
S. Morton, 54
Tom, 181
W. L., 68
ROBERTSON
    Dora, 126
    E. G., 118
    Esau, 142
    Grace, 169
    Gus, 187
    Hallie M., 157
    J. C., 7
    J. P., 108
    Joe, 57
    John H., 169
    Julius, 159
    Kate, 26
    L. G., 20
    L. P., 26
    Lou, 16
    Mary, 46
    S. A., 150
    T. M., 195
    W. A., 57
ROBINSON, 109
    A., 173
    Ben, 83
    F. E., 69
    Florence, 17
    Joe, 109
    Lena B., 32
    Maggie, 8
    Mittie, 7
    Nellie, 177
    W. D., 109
    W. L., 60
    Willie S., 99
ROBLES
    Andreas, 167
ROBUCK
    George, 121
ROCHESTER
    R. S., 127
ROCKETT
    Grace, 108
    Lora, 122
    T. M., 108
    Worth, 85
ROCKWELL
    Flora, 132
    Mary, 132
RODGERS
    Catherine, 60
    Effie Montrose, 20
    John, 124
RODRIQUEZ
    Benito, 101
ROE

Mollie, 69
Ollie, 69
Philip, 194
ROEWE
    Annie, 26
    Katie, 26
ROFF
    E., 69
ROGERS
    A. J., 64
    Allen, 115
    Bertha, 70
    Beverly L., 128
    Cecil, 151
    Dorothy, 165, 167
    E. D., 167
    Eula, 47
    F. W., 134
    Frank, 70
    George B., 33
    Hattie, 14
    Helen, 75
    Henry, 15
    J. G., 160
    Josie, 192
    Mattie, 53
    Raymond, 128
    S. A., 75
    W. C., 53, 196
    Will, 104
    William Mack, 62
ROLFE
    Emmons, 182
ROMINE
    J. W., 98
RONE
    G. W., 139
ROOPE
    Manard, 151
ROOS
    D. C., 150
ROSE, 101
    A. J., 17
    C., 45
    Daniel M., 9
    Ethel, 85
    George, 90
    Louzelle, 85
    P. G., 167
    S. A., 97
    Tom, 158
    V. L., 34
    Will, 181
ROSEBOROUGH
    Jennie, 12
ROSENSTEIN, 107
ROSENTHAL
    M. A., 8
ROSIE
    Katie, 64

ROSPESIL
    John, 26
ROSS
    Harry P., 153
    Henry, 25
    Ida, 194
    Jessie, 137
    John, 182
    L. S., 31
    Miles, 185
    Sena, 127
    W. M., 156
    Will, 9
    William H., 168
ROSSBECK
    Frieda, 71
ROSSER
    A. G., 143
ROSSI
    Joe, 134
ROSSON
    Lon, 151
ROTAN
    C. A., 11
    Ed, 54
ROTHMAN
    J. R., 184
ROTLEY
    John, 153, 156
ROUBIDEAUX
    Theresa, 117
ROUNDTREE
    Millard, 88
ROUSSEAU
    William H., 132
ROUTH
    Anne, 97
ROWAN
    Walter H., 175
    William, 185
ROWE
    Joe, 175
ROWELL
    T. D., 19
ROWLA
    Neil, 145
ROWLAND, 79, 153
    Charles, 68
    Charles W., 114
ROWLETT
    J. W., 183
ROWLETTE
    Edna, 167
ROY
    J. S., 179
    Jewell, 67
    John C., 194
    M. L., 104
    R. E. L., 194
ROYSTER

C. E., 25
Jack, 11
RUBY
   Frances W. B., 195
   K., 89
RUCKER
   Henry, 160
   Lawrence Lee, 150
   Max, 150
   T. A., 96
RUDKIN
   Roy, 122
RUDOLPH
   Lena, 18
RUFF
   Lucian, 64
RUGGLES
   Robert N., 72
RUMBLE
   E. E., 81
RUMLILLY
   Stella, 115
RUNGE
   George Lewis, 58
   Julius, 58
RUSH
   John, 77
RUSHING
   Dillard, 34
   Elizabeth, 191
RUSHNY
   G. W., 121
RUSSELL
   C. C., 69
   Elijah, 88
   Fannie, 45
   Felix, 87
   George T., 23
   H. M., 58
   Henry, 140
   J. J., 80
   Lena, 85
   M. P., 129
   Rachel, 57
   Tom, 102
   W. A., 68
RUSSEY
   Sadie, 85
RUST
   E. G., 97
   Willaim Monroe, 112
RUTHERFORD
   C., 32
   J. A., 121, 122
   W. R., 195
RUTLAND
   J. H., 17
RUTLEDGE
   Bettie, 195
   Clara T., 78

E. B., 80
George C., 71
Grady, 71
Lucille, 71
Robert H., 71
RYAN
   Ambrose, 184
   Iva, 111
   John, 146
   Joseph H., 81
   O. w., 91
   O. W., 91
SABINO
   John, 54
SACRA
   Ed, 167
SADDLER
   B. A., 192
SADLER
   Hadie E., 116
   William, 77
SAILS
   J. W., 159
SAIS
   Cusomiro, 113
SALERNO
   Charles, 113
   Jake, 149
SALINAS
   Rufugio, 195
SALMON
   J. H., 68
   Louisa, 171
SAMFERS
   E. S., 129
SAMS
   Willie, 84
SANCHEZ
   Antonio, 36
SANDBERG
   Lula, 87, 91
SANDEFER
   Emma, 143
SANDEL
   Collin, 126
SANDERS
   Callie, 107, 130
   Cora, 64, 66
   George, 144
   J. A., 89
   J. B., 60
   Jessie, 123
   Katie, 14
   Mary, 89
   Mattie, 153
   Mattie A., 11
   P. F., 10
   Solomom W., 11
   W. B., 159
   Wesley, 159

William, 54
SANDERSON
   Roger P., 142, 143
SANDS
   Ada, 71
SANFORD
   Nora, 108
SANGER
   Alex, 169
   Elihu A., 187
   Phillip-Jack, 107
SANSING
   E., 133
SANSOM
   Leon H., 108
   Winfred, 40
SANTANGELO
   Rosalie, 140
SARGEANT
   B. F., 104
SARTIN
   Cecil, 174
SASSEY
   Frankie, 178
SAUNDERS
   Albert P., 192
   Archie, 77
   J. J. A., 161
   Laura L., 59
   Rondo, 86
SAVAGE
   J. H., 81
   J. Hamilton, 109
SAVINGER
   A. M., 190
SAWYERS
   Ida, 52
SAXTON, 8
SAYLES
   Emma, 140
SAYRE
   Harry P., 182
SCALES
   Bob, 194
   Edna, 194
SCANLON
   Lucille, 122
   R. G., 20
SCARBOROUGH
   D. C., 192
   L. R., 105
SCARBROUGH
   L. R., 81
SCARCELLO
   Rosa, 152
SCHAFFER
   A. A., 177
SCHARF
   Charles, 176
   Frederick, 176

SCHAUMBERG
   G., 70
SCHIDEL
   Kate, 60
SCHIFF
   Ed, 165
SCHILLING
   Ernest, 172
SCHITZER
   Lena, 128
SCHLIGA
   Raymond, 124
SCHLOSS
   Herman, 99
SCHMIDEL
   Kate T., 61
SCHMIDT
   B. G., 167
   John, 110
   Peter, 94
SCHMITZ
   Charles, 75
SCHNEIDER
   Jules E., 169
SCHNIDER
   Abe, 191
SCHOENFIELD
   Laura, 112
SCHOONFIELD
   J. R., 187
SCHOONOVER, 67
   C. H., 108
SCHOULTZ
   Jamie, 102
SCHOUMBERG
   I., 78
SCHOVER
   Frank, 65
SCHRODER
   Charles H., 150
SCHUBERT
   Paul, 103
SCHULER
   Carolina, 124
   Charles, 188
SCHULTZ
   W. O., 40
SCHWACKHAMMER
   Charles, 29
SCHWARTZ
   Conrad, 109
SCHWARZ
   Cahrles T., 107
SCHWEITZER
   G., 178
SCOBLE
   A. W., 82
SCOONOVER
   Frank, 24
SCOTT

A. C., 98
A. J., 127
Al, 31
Albert, 41
Bessie, 32
Bob, 66
Carr, 102
Charles, 163
Charley, 128
Clemmie, 128
E. C., 133
E. F., 175
Elizabeth, 130
Fred T., 163
G. E., 133
Henry, 163
Hixie, 128
J., 66
J. H., 51, 52
J. P., 45
J.M., 17
K. T., 151
L. A., 78
Mattie, 14
Mildred, 82
Thomas, 89
Tom, 113
Viola, 71
W. B., 160
W. D., 84
W. L., 69
W. P., 180
William, 163, 164, 169
SCROGGINS
Brice, 27
Ethel, 175
Mary, 15
SCROGIN
W. R., 17
SCULLEY
J. E., 192
SCURLOCK
H. H., 49
SCWARTZ
Conrad, 117
SEABURN
William, 137
SEAGRIST
N. W., 104
SEALY
J. S., 107
SEAMAN
L. M., 144
SEARS
Florence, 193
SEAY
Bennie, 16
J. D., 23
Lorean, 164

SECREST
J. H., 103
SEE, 52
George J., 42
SEEBER
Bert, 98
SEIFFERT
H. B., 155
SELBY
Bill M., 59
SELF
Emma, 80
F. M., 17
P. D., 15
R. D., 80
T. N., 17
SELKIRK
Lutie, 51
William, 51
SELLARD
Eli, 66
Louisa, 66
SELLARS
Jim, 91
SELLE
R. L., 57
SELLERS
Bertha, 14
J. W., 9, 88, 111
T. H., 88
SENSABAUGH
Della, 174
SEQUIST
W. N., 94
SERVIES
William, 90
SESSIONS
Barry, 125
Berry, 124
Hope, 132
SETSER
Ross, 195
SETTLE
Charles, 119
SEVERT
A. F., 16
SEVIER
J. P., 53
SEWELL
E. W., 194
Geraldine, 33
J. L., 41
SEWNDREY
Kate, 111
SEXTON
Iva, 143
W. D., 103
Wesley, 117
SEYMOUR, 105
SEYSTER

Henry, 124
SHACKLEFORD
Katie, 20
Lewis, 179
SHANBLUM
Gertie, 140
Gertrude, 139
SHANTEAN
C. D., 129
SHAPP
Mable, 127
SHAPPARD
L. W., 182
SHARP
E. G., 97
Kathleen, 30
R. C., 131
Walter B., 30
SHARPE
M. B., 19
O. R., 27
Penelope, 75
SHATLEY
N. T., 170
SHAUL
William, 72
SHAW
Emma, 64
George, 48
Harvey L., 17
J. B., 187
Jamie, 123
Jessie, 165
Nellie, 115
W. J., 64
SHAY
T. D., 35
SHEA
Mat, 18, 19
Pat, 50
SHEEDS
Lee, 79
SHEFFIELD
Paul, 53
William, 93
SHEGOG
J. M., 21
SHEHLOK
V., 144
SHELBY
Perry O., 150
SHELLENBARGER
Frank, 43
SHELTON
A. L., 47
Izora, 80
J. B., 183
John, 19
Jow, 58
Lula, 135

SHEPARD
Frank, 132
SHEPHARD
W. S., 41
SHEPHERD
Warren, 103
SHERIDAN
George, 33
SHERLOCK
Georgia A., 191
Sue, 9
SHERLY
"Grandpa", 180
SHERMAN
Enid, 161
G., 100
Nick, 188
SHERRILL
Barney, 60
G. W., 60
L. D., 65
Lucy, 65
SHIELD
W. L., 151
SHIELDS
Carrie E., 51
E. L., 9
Frank, 171, 173
Fred, 51
Henry, 25
J. L., 155
Laura May, 127
Richard, 119
samuel, 127
SHINER
H. H., 31
SHINES
Abner, 104
SHIPLEY
Alexander, 197
SHIPP
Todd, 188
SHIVERS
James S., 114
Willie, 156
SHOCKLEY
W. M., 129
SHOEMAKER
M. L., 184
SHOFFITT
C. C., 158
SHORT, 153
George, 15, 140
J. A., 72
Myrtle, 62
SHORTELL
Nellie, 116
SHOW
Gus, 24
Mattie, 87

SHOWVER
  Della, 135
SHRADER
  Jennie, 171
SHRAM
  Paul D., 35
  Paul P., 33
SHRAVE
  Harry, 94
SHRUM
  Green, 60
SHUCKEY
  James, 8
SHUFERT
  Clyde, 20
SHUFORD
  Q. A., 118
SHULER
  Morand, 41
SHULTZ
  Charley, 173
SHUMAKER
  L., 66
SHUMAN
  O. K., 50
SHUMATE
  Tom, 116
SHUTTLESWORTH
  C. C., 64
SHUTZE
  Adolph, 86
  Albert, 86
  Alivinia, 86
  Clara, 86
  Edward, 86
  Henrietta, 86
  Hugo, 86
  Julius, 86
  Nono, 86
SIBLEY
  Emma, 113
SIDBURY
  Charlotte M., 195
SIDDONS
  Willie, 98
SIDES
  J. H., 53
SIFFORD
  John, 122
SIKES
  G. F., 63
  W. W., 108
SILER
  Jesse, 94
  W. S., 121
SILK
  Etta, 142
SILLS
  Letha, 78
SILVER
  Ross, 130
SILVERS
  "Grandma", 197
  J. F., 197
SIMINGTON
  Mose, 47
SIMMLER
  John, 13
SIMMONS
  C. E., 40
  F. A., 195
  Gertrude, 160
  H. H., 182
  Henry, 87, 91
  Jesse Leroy, 65
  L. N., 160
  M. L., 40
  Nora, 70
  Roscoe, 182
  Roy, 39
  T. J., 115
SIMPSON
  C. P., 24
  Florence, 174
  G. P., 181
  John, 111
  John N., 169
  L., 101
  Oscar, 10
  Perry, 124
  William, 57
SIMS
  B. H., 52
  Charles, 142
  Dovie, 187
  Ella, 66
  J. R., 66
  Marian, 93
  Marian Louise, 90
  O. T., 118
  R. W., 129
SINGLETON
  Edward, 132
SINGLTEON
  Fannie, 151
SINKS
  E. R., 181
SINN
  J. L., 129
SISK
  Nora L., 179
SITTLER
  Charles, 139
SKAGGS
  Clemmie, 177
  L. H., 177
SKEEN
  Virgil, 35
SKELTON
  Florida, 110
  J. M., 28
  James, 173
  Joe, 173
SKIFFLETT
  "Grandma", 35
SKILLERN
  Ed, 31
SKINNER
  James F., 167
  Sam, 82
  W. L., 111
SKIPPER
  Nathan, 180
SLACK
  Sowell, 60
SLADE
  W. L., 181
SLATER
  Laura, 27
  R. R., 12
  Robert, 11
  William, 195
SLATURNE
  Gordon, 43
SLAUGHTER
  Alice, 178
  Dale, 30
  Eliza, 18
  F., 101
  Joe, 196
  S. H., 9, 34, 36, 88, 133, 169
  Will, 95
SLAVEN
  M. B., 20
  Tom, 20
SLAYDEN
  J. L., 61
  T. Bailey, 18
  T. J., 41
SLOAN
  Alice, 180
SLOCUM
  Charles, 27
SLOUGH
  E. A., 67
  Zack A., 101
SLOVER
  F. H., 29
  G. S., 105
SLUDER
  W. H., 21
SLUGGERT
  Theresa, 112
SMALL
  Charles, 170
  Cora, 197
  Elsie, 36
  H. L., 122
  R. M., 60
  Richard Henry, 61
  W. L., 114
SMALLEY
  D., 164
SMALLWOOD
  Charlotte P., 194
  Thomas, 47
SMART
  Louis, 52
SMELSER
  A. D., 85
SMITH
  J. C., 164
SMITH
  A. K., 170
  A. P., 133, 165
  Abb, 163
  Addison, 182
  Allison D., 99
  Ben I., 83
  Bert, 146
  Bessie, 170
  Beulah, 146
  Bosier, 61
  Brozier, 71
  Buck, 90
  Byrd, 116
  C. B., 110
  C. J., 82
  Catherine, 182
  Church, 104
  Clara, 191
  Cora, 186
  E. D., 116
  Ed, 181
  Emma, 81
  Eulalia, 45
  Eva Belle, 145
  Evelyn, 160
  Floyd, 97
  Forest, 125
  Forrest, 187
  G. W., 95
  Gabe, 10
  H. C., 169
  H. J., 152
  Hannah, 57
  Helen Elder, 83
  Henderson, 59
  Henry E., 40
  Henry Richard, 48
  Howard, 90
  Isaac Potter, 105
  J. A., 57, 94
  J. C., 30, 149, 162, 170
  J. D., 100, 181
  J. D. C., 89
  J. Frank, 118
  J. K., 175

J. O., 102
J. P., 63, 152
J. T., 51
Jack W., 191
James, 8, 128
Jesse, 9
Joe, 116
John, 60, 79, 127
John H., 62
Joseph, 23
Kirby, 170
L. G., 173
L. K., 115
Lee, 118, 176
Len, 122
Lilla Belle, 150
Louise, 170
M. M., 90
Malissa, 29
Mamie, 14
Mariah, 191
Mary Anna, 94
Minton, 40
Nelli, 59
Norman Lee, 122
O. K., 83
Otta, 143
Ottie, 64
P. B., 47
Paerl, 114
Phil, 100
Pink, 111
R. F., 64
R. L., 180
Roxy, 176
Russell, 137
S. L., 113
S. P., 122
Sam, 114, 177
T. E., 182
Tennie, 18
W. L., 36
W. N., 60, 61
W. T., 155
W. W., 170
Walter, 90
Wesley, 180
Will, 180
William B., 97
Willie, 81
SMOTHERMAN
  J. B., 179
SMYTH
  Al, 96
  D. I., 193
SNEE, 45
SNEED
  John, 7
  Lou E., 78
SNODGRASS
  Esther, 10
  R., 83
SNOW
  Carrie, 179
  H. B., 104
  J. C., 111
  Lulu, 35
SNYDER
  Kate, 122
SOCKWELL
  J. F., 129
SOLOMON
  Axtel Gustavus, 114
  E. D., 82
SOLSBERG
  H., 189
SONS
  J. T., 100
SOOU
  Chin, 180
SORABY
  Ben, 132
SORRELLS
  T. L., 155
  W. O., 161
SORRELS
  Fannie, 139
SOUDER
  Dona, 136
SOUR
  George A., 96
SOUSIBEE
  George W., 110
SOUSTRON
  Eunice, 23
SOUTHERN
  Edna Eugene, 43
SOWARDS
  Clara, 78
SOWITZKY
  Sophie, 112
SOWYER
  Don W., 108
SOZIER
  Jack, 130
SPAIN
  J. B. K., 59, 98, 127,
    138, 140, 141, 162,
    185
  J. V., 85
  Lulu, 58
SPANN
  L. L., 15
SPARGENBURG
  J. W., 48
SPARGER
  Samuel, 139
SPARKS
  Charles D., 14
  E. M., 141
Ethel, 192
L. B., 14
SPARRA
  Joe, 190
SPAULDING
  Birdie, 132
SPEAR
  R. E., 89
SPEARMAN
  Dan, 42
  E. C., 17
  R. W., 124
SPENCE
  Bob, 122
  Jason, 15
  Joe, 171
SPENCER
  Ollie, 190
  Pearl, 140
  Rhelda, 177
  S. J., 123
  Sallie Mae, 34
SPLAWN
  Ella, 172
  G. A., 104
  M. J., 87
SPOONAMOORE
  Eugene, 52
  J. L., 52
SPRADLIN
  S. E., 44
  Susan, 189
SPRADLING
  Lelia, 52
SPRAGUE
  Robert, 124
SPRATT
  Jim, 15
SPRINGER
  Lee C., 152
SPROLES
  Scott, 108
SPRUELL
  C. K., 78
SPURLOCK
  E. L., 172
  J. M., 172
SQUIRES
  J. W., 18
  William, 11
ST. CLAIR
  George, 103
STAATS
  Mollie, 129
STABB
  F. R., 20
STAGGS
  P. B., 7
  Preston, 32
STAGLE
Maggie, 83
STAGNER
  E. L., 18
STAHL
  F. W., 187
STALCUP
  E. C., 46
STALLCUP
  Naomi, 8
STALLINGS
  Henry, 113
  J. E., 113
  M. S., 113
  Rosa, 184
STALNER
  Z. B., 82
STANDIFER
  Charles, 30
  Charles A., 31
  L. E., 31
  Margaret Eleanor
    Armstrong, 31
  W. A., 31
STANDLEY
  R. H., 58
STANFIELD
  Hugh, 142
  J. T., 98, 111
  John, 109
STANFORD
  N. W., 60
STANLEY, 145
  Addie, 49
  Bob, 167
  F. B., 159
STANSEL
  Frank, 163
STANTON
  J. J., 81
STAPP
  Erna, 149
STARKS
  E. H., 122
  Martha L., 113
STARLING
  J. R., 60
  Otis Wood, 110
  W. A., 75
  Will, 61
  William, 60
STARLINK
  Will, 192
STARNES
  Maggie, 144
STASTNEY
  Mattie, 56
STATELER
  Charles, 7
STATEN
  D. Z., 83

STATTS
  C. G., 128
STAULTS
  Joseph C., 194
  Robert, 186
STEAKLEY
  J. L., 161
STEDHAM
  Arie, 14
STEEL
  J. F., 122
STEELMAN
  N. A., 82
STEEMPF
  Charles, 10
STEEN
  Mary, 137
STEFFENS
  A., 109
STEGALL
  Teresa, 35
  W. S., 71
STEIN
  W. H., 35
STEPHENS
  Ethel, 155
  G. W., 14
  John, 27
  L. H., 42
  Mattie Belle, 20
  O. J., 144
  W. R., 153
  W. T., 146
STEPHENSON
  Baker, 43
  C. C., 40
  J. D., 90
  J. H., 44
  J. W., 138
  Sidney, 187
  W. H., 84
  Walter M., 62
STERLING
  Land, 100
STERNS
  Ruth, 158
STEVENS
  Belle, 14
  C. W., 14
  Caroline Ellis, 14
  Carrie, 14
  F. A.., 55
  Frank., 30
  G. H., 190
  Henry G., 17
  J. B., 124
  J. E., 109
  J. W., 14
  L. B., 23
  Luellen, 35

  Luellen., 33
  Mattie, 60
  Zenah, 14
STEVENSON
  Charles T., 32
  J. L., 186
  John, 94
  T. B., 11
STEWART
  A. R., 53
  Alec, 95
  Alexander, 87
  Bessie M., 189
  C. C., 94
  Charles, 135
  Helen, 135
  Jennie, 178
  John, 157
  Julia E., 87
  Juni, 186
  Lem, 164
  Mary, 100
  Maude, 100
  R. E., 105
  S. W., 164, 168
  W. E., 23
  W. J., 100
  W. T., 186
STICE
  John, 147
STIFF
  E. R., 187
  O. H., 194
STILK
  Eveline, 96
STILL
  Reagan B., 137
STILLING
  Fred, 62
STILLWELL
  R. R., 45
STINSON
  A., 186
  H. M., 134
  Ralph, 163
STIRMAN
  V. I., 82, 89, 187
  Willie, 164
STNUM
  James Woodson, 62
STOCKERT
  William, 146
STOCKETT
  J. O., 86
STODDARD
  H. B., 144
STOKER
  Isabella, 90
STOKES
  James, 80

  R. F., 89
STONE
  Allie, 187
  Ellen, 19
  Francis, 116
  G. N., 172
  J. H., 161, 168
  James R., 114
  W. B., 137
STONEBACK
  Lola R., 184
STOPAUSKI
  Martin, 68
STORY
  Charles, 50
  M. L., 105
STOUT
  Willie Mae, 104
STOVAL
  W. F., 123
STOVALL, 78
  George, 149
  H. R., 164
  Willie Hall, 163
STOWE
  Ed, 42
STOWERS
  John C., 103
STRABLE
  H. A., 89
STRAIN
  C. A., 89
  Jim, 28
STRANGE
  J. A., 9
  Latha, 47
STRAUGHON
  J. R., 159
  Julian Raymond, 159
STRAWN
  Rodessa, 158
STRAYHORN
  Richard, 135
STREET
  A. B., 182
  J. A., 169
  Robert G., 121
STRETCH
  Orley, 118
STRIBLING
  F. M., 31
  J. T., 152
  Mrs., 31
STRICKLAND, 124
  Bettie, 64
  Ira, 13
  L. F., 115
  O. S., 72
  Will, 14
STRIMAN

  R. R., 164
STRINGER
  J. Cullen, 53
STRIPLING
  T. P., 153
STROMAN
  W. H., 81
STRONG
  A. T., 181
  L. J., 23
  N. D., 158
STROTHER
  Ada, 80
STROUD
  W. D., 54
STUART
  Annie, 167
  C. S., 157
  Carrie, 20
  Wade, 15
STUBBLEFIELD
  Rosa, 13
  Walter, 151
STUBBS
  Minnie, 16
STURGIS
  S. I., 146
STYLES
  R. S., 165
SUDDETH
  Bob, 105
SUDDUTH
  D. E., 79
SUFERSTEIN
  alex, 133
SUGART
  Gussie, 50
SUGGS
  A. L., 184
SUIT
  Mary A., 173
SULLIVAN
  Annie, 192
  C. B., 25
  Dan, 192
  Daniel, 192
  Henry, 89
  Jep, 180
  John, 95, 192
  Lilly, 101
  Mary L., 167
  Robin, 131
  W. P., 19
  Walter, 192
  Will, 192
SUMMER
  J. M., 35
SUMMERLIN
  Mack, 196
SUMMERS

243

J. F., 109
Y. A., 146
SUMNER
　Wesley, 7
SURGNOR
　Dan, 39
SUTHERLAND
　George C., 135
　Tom, 135
　Vester, 135
SUTTON
　C. J., 168
　Maggie, 19
　Thomas J., 62
　V. B., 190
SWACKHAMMER
　Charles, 67, 117
　Mary, 180
　Nona, 186
SWAIN
　H. N., 172
　H. P., 128
　Henry P., 130
SWANEY
　L. W., 146
SWANK
　W. D., 77
SWANN
　Abe, 35
SWANSCRAFT
　Zella, 160
SWEARINGEN
　Allen, 25
　W. L., 130
SWEAT
　John, 47
SWEENEY
　Annie May, 116
SWEET
　Frank, 164
SWENSON
　J. J., 139
SWIFT
　George H., 185
SWINDELL
　J. M., 113
SWINDELLS
　Laura, 61
SWINEHART
　William, 17
SWINK
　H. H., 23
　Sidney, 46
SYKES
　William L., 171
TABER
　Alfred, 191
　Alma, 191
　Ben, 191
　John C. B., 191

Julia M., 191
Martin, 191
Oak, 191
Rock, 191
Sam, 191
TABOR
　George R., 93
TADLOCK
　Delia, 89
TALBOTT
　T. M., 143
TALIFERRO
　R. S., 181
TALLAMDGE
　J. W., 174
TALLEY
　Susie, 182
TALLMADGE
　Eugene, 174
TANICEK
　John, 137
TANKERSLEY
　Preston, 140
　R. F., 182
TANNAHILL
　M. L., 77
　Robert, 177
TANNER
　Ada, 76
　C. L., 186
　T. M., 136
TANT
　Florence V., 158
TARWATERS
　James, 33
TATE
　Ed, 57
　Julia, 177
　Tom, 57
TATUM
　Charles Thomas, 123
　E., 193
　H. W., 44
　Lillian, 188
　Lou, 27
　Melvinia Jones, 123
　Virginia, 29
TAULBEE
　Ellen, 174
TAVE
　Emma, 57
TAYLOR, 127, 182
　A. L., 55
　Bob, 75, 101
　C. C., 121
　Doll, 150
　Edward, 87
　Frank, 144
　Fredonia, 109
　G. C., 162

G. W., 39
George, 157
Harlow, 133
Henderson, 71
J. Arthur, 137
J. H., 71
J. Hillary, 8
J. J., 9
J. W., 110
James M., 55
M. A., 41
Mattie, 193
Minnie, 144, 155
R. G., 124
Rosie, 122
Roxie, 16
Sam J., 179
T. H., 150
T. R., 16
Tom, 192
W. H., 139
W. M., 64, 65
Wardie, 157
Will, 97
William, 102, 197
Young, 43
TEAGARDEN
　Helen, 129
TEAGUE
　E. E., 44
　Minnie, 36
　W. S., 42
TEAL
　B. I., 45
TEAS
　Ruth, 109
TEDLEY
　J. F., 28
TEEL
　Monroe, 185
TEMPLE
　A. H., 81
　A. N., 79
　Arthur L., 54
　R., 60
　T. F., 63
　W. C., 54
TEMPLETON
　S. M., 189
TENNERY
　Fannie Kou, 20
TENNISON
　K. G., 187
TERHUNE
　A. A., 26, 159
TERRELL, 183
　A. W., 81
　Clotha Winona, 127
　Cora E., 121
　Ed, 170

Henry, 170
J. T., 72
James, 170
Mary, 170
R. D., 24
Roy, 102
Walter P., 126
TERRY
　C. U., 73
　F. M., 175
　J. E., 59
　James, 101
　Maude, 48
　T. G., 95
TEVIS
　John Lawrence, 131
THALEN
　Tullie, 50
THAYER
　Manie, 43
THERRELL
　Cora, 119
　Cora Etta, 122
　E. L., 187
THETFORD
　W. H., 9
THEWEATT
　J. T., 77
THIESL
　F. W., 14
THODE
　H., 179
　Russell, 179
THOMAS
　A. G., 127
　Charles, 98
　Claudy, 25
　D. M., 42
　Ed, 107
　G. H., 187
　H. S., 72
　H. W., 83
　J. C., 194
　J. J., 83
　James, 112
　Lettie B., 158
　Mae Alberta, 161
　R. C., 125
　Richard, 45
　W. L., 139
　William, 193
THOMASON
　B. R., 99
　Bert, 197
　Eula, 99
　Z. B., 44
THOMPSON
　Abraham, 124
　E. F., 64
　Eliza, 173

Emma, 61
Estella, 136
Ethel, 48
Fred, 76
George F., 119
H. L., 188
Henry, 143
Hubbard, 64
J. B., 124
Kate, 116
Lillian, 8
Lillian B., 9
Lucy, 89
Lula, 186
Mack, 191
Mary, 88
Mona, 23
Pearl, 95
Polly, 175
R. W., 141
Thomas T., 113
Will, 115
THOMSON
　Frank, 34
THORNTON, 124, 153
　A. H., 26
　Arthur, 69
　B. H., 154
　Octavia, 13
　Pearl, 163
THREADGILL
　Mattie Ella, 141
THREADWELL
　Emma, 145
THROCKMORTON
　Ina Zelma, 102
THUMELL
　J., 155
THURMAN
　E. R., 55
　Willie, 103
THWEATT
　Whitley, 36
TIBBS
　Jack, 34
TICE
　May, 139
TICHNOR
　Lonlie, 84
TIDEWATER
　Charlie, 79
TIDWELL
　Lizzie, 57
　S. J., 18
TIERCE
　Emma, 177
TIERNAN
　Norman B., 122
　R. H., 122
TIERRY

Frank, 42
TILLERY
　A. S., 7
　V., 80
TILLEY
　W. H., 195
TIMS
　Ida B., 95
TINDLE
　I. W., 108
TIPPETT
　Ella, 81
　R. P., 125
TIPTON
　R. S., 134
　Winston, 64
TIREE
　Oso, 39
TISDAL
　Nedom B., 130
　Nedom R., 128
TITLEY
　William, 94
TITTLE
　Charles, 116
TITUS
　Henry, 28
TOBIN
　J. J., 173
TODD
　Anna L., 156
　Ethel, 96
　Florence, 173
　George W., 47, 128
　J. A., 152
　J. W., 188
　James A., 171
　O. C., 13
　Wilburn, 29
TOGG
　Lillian, 66
TOLAS
　W. R., 56
TOLBERT
　William H., 102
TOLER
　W. R., 8
TOLES
　Emily, 10
TOLKSDORF
　H. P., 142
　Madeline Adelaide, 140, 142
TOLLIVER
　Beulah, 80
　Brock, 80
TOM
　Dudley, 11
　Mattie Sue, 11
TOMAMICHEL

Annie, 189
TOMBLIN
　Viola, 164
TOMLIN
　Bertha, 158
　J. W., 36
　Sam, 14
TOMLINSON
　Henry, 21
　Jim, 67
TOMPKINS
　A. C., 94
TONNALE
　J. W., 32
TORRENCE
　R. B., 111
TOUCHTON
　Etna, 114
TOUKSFSKY
　Ray, 126
TOWERS
　Ed, 121
　J. Frank, 184
TOWN
　John Lawrence, 124
TOWNE
　Perry, 43
TOWNS
　Edgar, 113
TOWNSEND
　Annie, 52
　Camille, 170
　J. H., 57
　Paul, 181
　Paul Allen, 189
　Perry, 62
　S. G., 145
TOWNSHEND
　G. W., 18
TOWNSON
　L. Jasper, 135
　Mary Ann, 135
TRAHAM
　Fred, 103
TRAMMEL
　J. S., 57
TRAMMELL
　W. M., 42
TRAMPTON
　Adalin Lillian, 23
TRANTHAM
　Edith, 127
TRAVIS, 47
TRAYLOR
　J. H., 169
　Wesley, 162
TREDWELL
　Thomas J., 154
TRENT
　Loretta, 147

TRIBBLE
　Callie, 136
TRICE
　Ira, 19
　J. C., 25
TRIMBLE
　Mary, 98
　W. M., 50
TRINE
　Emma, 187
TRIPLETT
　Sam D., 26
　T. H., 81
TROGLE
　William, 42
TROMPE
　C., 61
TROUPE
　Allie, 177
TROXLER
　John Baptist, 117, 118
TROY
　John D., 79
TRUAX
　Charles, 77
　Edith Vale, 77
TRUE
　Judy Ann, 61
　Lem H., 50, 52
　Lemuel, 80
TRUELOVE
　John, 88
TRULL
　Lula, 134
TRUMAN
　H.J., 15
TUBBS
　Ed, 16
TUCK
　C. M., 143
　E., 82, 85
　E. T., 82
TUCKER
　Albert, 72
　Baby, 116
　Delia, 116
　Ed, 191
　Harvey, 163
　J. W., 155
　James F., 56
　Sallie A., 68
　Stella, 144
　Walter, 197
TUGWELL
　Charley, 44
TUMELTY
　Owen, 140
TUMLIN
　Lillian, 151
TUNNELL

C. V., 16
S. T., 111
TUNNERY
   Marvin, 13
TUNNEY
   Martin, 14
TURLEY
   Clota, 29
TURMAN
   Mollie O., 124
TURNBO
   John, 37
TURNELL
   W. F., 197
TURNER
   A. H., 127
   Abbie, 127
   Alf, 97
   Alfred, 26
   B. F., 77
   Ben, 153
   Don, 138
   Don F., 167, 168
   Donna, 138
   Florence, 102
   George R., 145
   Hubbard, 31
   J. E., 52
   James, 141
   Jesse, 101
   Joe, 101
   L., 110
   L. S., 134
   Lorraine, 141
   Lucy, 177
   Mattie, 83, 132
   N. A., 73
   O. E., 171
   Olen, 152
   R. B., 127
   Robert H., 134
   Tom, 91
   W. B., 97
   W. E., 194
   W. M. J., 9
   W. T., 29
   Will, 101
TUROL
   Charles, 65
TURPEN
   L. E., 163
TWEED
   Maud Hollenback, 62
TWITTY
   J. J., 75
TYLER
   F. A., 70
   John, 136
TYREE
   Osie, 104

   Susan, 100
TYSON
   B. A., 124
   W. H., 57
ULK
   Joe, 147
UNDERHILL
   Edward M., 43
UNDERWOOD
   W. M., 196
UPSHUR
   Stephen, 37
UPTON
   E. A., 83
URESTE
   Lucy, 141
URIPIA
   Reis, 172
URQUHART
   Allen, 53
USELTON
   J. D., 71, 137
   R. E., 51
UTIS
   W. A., 158
UTT
   Millie E., 52
UTZ
   Bessie Y., 190
VALASCO
   Frederico, 135
VALENTI
   Hannah, 36
VALENTINE
   Annie, 121
   Ben, 89
VAN
   Jeff, 100
VAN NATTAN
   Elmer, 135
VAN NEEF
   A. M., 7
VAN WINKLE
   Mary T., 186
VAN ZANDT
   J. A., 87
   John, 77
   T. L., 42
   W. L., 10
VANCE
   Alice, 83
VANDERVALT
   Cora, 70
   Eleanor, 70
   Max, 70
VANLANDINGHAM
   W. C., 35
   W. T., 35
VANMETER
   Milton, 77

VANN
   Jeff, 173
VANNOY
   Minnie, 190
VANSICKLE
   Ben A., 192
   Vera, 165
VARDEMAN
   Essie, 159
VARIAN
   Charles, 17
VARLEY
   H. P., 193
VARNELL
   Allie, 21
   Tom P., 15
VATTER
   Sofia Ellen, 113
VAUGHAN, 71
   A. M., 19
   Munsey, 11
   W. H., 29
   William, 192
   Willie, 95
VAUGHN
   Munsey, 197
VAUGHT
   F. M., 88
VEASEY
   John L., 189
VEAZY
   John L., 95
VENABLE
   Paul C., 13
VENDRIER
   Mary Havier, 67
VERELLO
   Sam A., 173
VERNON
   Ernest, 11
   T. F., 34
VESPER
   J. B., 191
VICE
   Doro, 72
VICK
   Edith, 41
VICKERS
   John, 123
   Perry, 7
VIDLER
   William, 182
VILLALON
   Esmeregilda, 57
VILLAREAL
   Jose Mara Garcia, 96
VILLE
   Juan, 20
VILLELA
   Valentine, 43

VINCENT
   Alice, 164
   Earl S., 190
   J. M., 164
VINCON
   J. E., 196
VINSON
   J. E., 90
   Lellar, 122
VIOLETTE
   Gay, 13
   Gaye, 14
VIRGIL
   Elon, 154
VISER
   Lizzie, 73
VITALIA
   John, 190
VORHOLZER
   Charles, 122
VOSS
   C. R., 163
   Thomas E., 154
VOTAW
   Millie, 18
WACKER
   Mainel M., 183
WADE
   A., 90
   Amelia J., 162
   E. W., 57
   William, 195
WADLEY
   Henry, 65
   J. H., 167
   T. J., 31
WAFAER
   Frank, 43
WAGES
   J. R., 45, 65
WAGGOMAN
   B. L., 31
WAGLEY
   Henry, 95
WAGNER
   J. S., 68
   Kate, 104
   Lena G., 12
WAGONER
   C. C., 45
   H. L., 163
   L. O., 40
WAGSTAFF
   Charles, 76
WAKELAND
   Cahrley, 134
WAKEN
   Annie, 113
WALCOTT
   James T., 45

WALDEN
　Delta, 20
　Sam A., 45
WALDRUP
　M., 161
WALKER, 101
　Ada Louise, 192
　Anna, 32
　Bob, 25
　C. C., 143
　Charles W., 21
　Dora, 13
　Ed, 76
　Fannie, 96
　G. L., 151
　George N., 64
　German, 105
　Green, 13
　H. N., 64
　Harry C., 75
　J. C., 171
　J. G., 163
　Joe, 15, 117
　John, 39, 64
　Johnny, 41
　Lavonia N., 64
　Lee Etta, 83
　Mary, 29
　Mike, 13
　Oscar W., 179
　Robert, 96
　Romie, 96
　S. H., 32
　T. O., 32
　Thomasine, 192
　W. J., 86
　Zack, 108
WALKUP
　D., 19
WALL
　C. A., 77
WALLACE
　George, 123
　Henry, 46
　John, 90
　Julia Jane, 79
　Laura, 39
　Lilliard, 123
　Lillie, 78
　M. V., 67, 177
　Mamie Carrie Bell, 90
　Mollie, 50
　N. D., 71
　Rosa Lee, 132
　Rubie, 59
　T. C., 16
WALLENBERG
　John, 93
WALLER
　John, 134

　Julia, 18
　Lizzie, 143
WALLIS
　Lizzie, 82
　Marie, 20
WALNE
　Thomas T., 138
WALSH
　Charles, 189
　Mary A., 42
　R. C., 189
WALTER
　T. H., 146
WALTERS
　G. W., 19
　James F., 60
　Lema, 91
　Sarah, 187
WALTON
　Cora, 94
　G. W., 15
　M. E., 119
　O. C., 119
　W. S., 128
　W. W., 101
WANSLEY
　R. S., 53
WARBLOM
　A. J., 7
WARD, 56, 154
　C. W., 71
　Florence, 134
　George C., 87
　George W., 89
　I. E., 193
　J., 44
　Jeff, 61
　Jennie, 85
　John, 160
　John L., 62
　Justice, 10
　L., 124
　Letha, 160
　Lizie May, 176, 177
　Ricahrd, 183
　W. M., 95
　William, 195
　William K., 165
WARE
　Florence, 108
　J. C., 80
　John A., 155
　Verder, 145
WARNER
　Alanson, 160
　Charles, 84
　G. B., 181
　John, 49
　John B., 96
WARNOCK

　Alice, 178
WARREN
　Albert, 27
　Bena A., 34
　Bessie, 139
　F. E., 13
　Foster, 110
　Frank W., 13
　George H., 182
　J. H., 191
　Luke, 191
WARRICK
　Zola, 58
WARRINER
　J. F., 143
WARSON, 128
WARY
　C. H., 197
WASHBURN
　Jack, 50
WASHINGTON
　Albert, 65
　Bessie, 136
　George W., 172
　Maggie, 154
WASSON
　T. W., 77
WATERS, 118
　Harry, 82
WATKINS
　Alice, 10
　Charles, 149, 173
　J. T., 47
　Lillie, 150
　Norris, 184
　W. E., 157
WATSON
　Alvin, 7
　Alwilda, 96
　Ben, 171
　Bert, 145
　Beulah, 124
　Emma, 85
　H. C., 171
　J. H., 57
　Jake, 72
　James, 100
　John, 17, 80, 145
　K. A., 100
　Lillie B., 163
　Linda, 15
　Martha, 86
　N. J., 114
　Nellie Edith, 104
　Walter, 150
　William H., 28
WATT
　Charles F., 194
WATTS
　George M., 126

　J. M., 26, 118
　L., 72
　Walter, 143
WAUL
　Mary Simmons, 26
　T. N., 26
WEAKLEY
　Fannie, 43
WEAR
　Mamie, 129
　R. D., 118
WEATHERBY
　J. E., 50
WEATHERFORD
　A. W., 24, 51
　D. M., 49
　May, 51
　Temp, 50
　W. P., 77
WEATHERLY
　J. A., 175
WEATHERS
　H. T., 56
WEAVER
　C. W., 10
　Charles, 134
　Charlie, 10
　D. H., 39
　Dick, 104
　Houston, 36
　Mary, 46
　Myrtle, 20
WEBB
　Annie Walker, 105
　B. E., 24, 183
　Bonnie Mattie, 20
　C. N., 163
　Charles T., 184
　Charley, 48
　Etta, 20
　Fannie, 67
　Helen, 175
　Ida, 187
　J. A., 186
　J. B., 105
　J. N., 103
　James, 135
　Lacy, 95
　On, 154
WEBBER
　Dick, 182
WEBER
　Mary H., 133
WEBSTER
　I. N., 26
　Maud J., 45
　Ola, 69
WEEKS
　Hannah, 143
WEEMES

J. M., 86
WEIGHT
  Maggie, 197
WEIL
  Henry, 65
WEIR
  Horace, 90
WEITSTRUCK
  Richard, 130
WELCH
  E. L., 20
  Ellen, 98
  M., 98
  W. L., 14
  William, 45
WELDT
  Sophie L., 79
WELL
  A., 51
WELLMAN
  Watt, 138
WELLS
  E. A., 89
  Elizabeth, 41
  George W., 41
  M., 63
  Samuel, 28
  Silas B., 117
  Willie, 57
WENCE
  Mahala, 186
WENDELL
  W. D., 59
WENDT, 175
WENTZEL
  Annie, 173
WESLEY
  Henry, 105
WESROCK
  John, 125
WEST
  Butler, 94
  Cordelia, 94
  George, 31
  Gussie, 114
  Harris, 94
  Ike, 31
  John Q., 39
  Katherine, 8
  Mary, 31, 127
  P. C., 94
  Sol, 31
  T. D., 81
  Walter, 94
WESTBROOK
  George, 103
  H., 27
  S. W., 125
  Walter L., 58
WESTERVELT
  Irene McFadden, 169
WESTHAUSEN
  Fred, 135
WHALEY
  Bessie, 125
  John, 185
  M. H., 112
WHATLEY
  Mary Alice, 82
WHEATLEY
  C. W., 151
  H. H., 20
WHEELER
  Bessie, 40
  Frances, 151
  James, 105
  W. A., 55
WHEELIE
  Rubye, 131
WHERRY
  Fannie Barrett, 174
WHILBECK
  A. B., 196
WHISENANT
  Laura, 9
  M. F., 26
WHISTON
  Henry, 15
WHITAKER
  Denton, 134
  Jay, 173
  L. D., 69
WHITBECK
  Pearl, 36
WHITE, 68
  A. F., 11
  A. L., 109, 167
  Alice, 25
  Caroline M., 71
  Charles, 139
  Clarence, 61
  Edgar Elihu, 75
  Elva, 78
  Ethel, 16
  F. C., 142
  G. B., 15
  George, 16
  George C., 8
  George R., 16
  H. H., 67
  Howard A., 156
  J. B., 34
  Jim, 100
  John, 130
  John D., 91
  L. G., 51
  L. N., 99
  Lizzie, 47, 119
  Lois, 8
  Lula, 68
  M. R., 94
  May, 16
  Mike, 158
  N. C., 191
  Oscar, 122
  Perry, 161
  Robert, 185
  Ruby, 47
  S. M., 71
  Sallie, 121
  Sylvia, 83
  T. A., 78
  T. E., 64
  W. P., 16
  Will, 52
  William, 16
WHITEHEAD
  B. B., 158
  H. C., 90
WHITEHURST, 180
WHITEHURST, 48, 182
  Ira, 165
  J. A., 87
WHITELEY
  A. M., 190
WHITESIDE
  H. Z., 156
WHITESIDES
  W. E., 86
WHITLEY
  Inez, 187
  Jean, 172
  Louis H., 134
  Mary, 105
  W. J., 63
WHITLOCK
  E. L., 99
  W. A., 181
WHITLOW
  "Sporty", 49
WHITNER
  J. H., 17
WHITNEY
  A. P., 33
  Albert, 34
WHITSELL
  J. A., 14
WHITSETT
  F. E., 159
WHITTEN
  Albert, 35
WHITTENBERG
  P. L., 147
WHITTY
  Ivy, 19
WHITWORTH
  Annie, 37
  Eugene, 191
  Sarah, 191
WHOLTTEN
  Sallie, 23
WIGGLESWORTH
  J. M., 181
WILBANKS
  Hugh, 161
WILBOURN
  J. W., 43
WILCOX
  James T., 185
  R. C., 185
WILDER
  George Lawler, 153
  H. L., 65, 153
  Jessie, 183
WILEY
  Columbus, 143
  J. L., 36
  J. W., 59
  R. O., 112
  Thomas J., 160
WILFORD
  S. H., 53
WILHELM
  W. O., 79
WILHITE
  C., 178
WILIAMS
  R. G., 122
WILINGHAM
  J. S., 91
WILKENING
  Carl, 131
  Gustave, 131
WILKERSON
  A. P., 155
  B., 70
  Ed, 183
  F. L., 151
  Fletcher, 103
  G., 66
  H. H., 122
  W. Z., 48
WILKES
  Ethel, 99
WILKINS
  Charles, 27
  Emory, 27
  J. L., 105
  W. H., 101
WILKINSON
  Agnes, 72
  Charles, 104
  Fred, 129
WILKS
  Ethel, 97
WILLARD
  Frances, 49
WILLCHECK
  Beatrice, 174
  Louis Foster, 174

WILLIAMS, 176
  Ada, 19
  Alonzo, 169
  Beatrice, 76
  Belle, 10
  Bud, 104
  C. B., 30
  Charles, 18
  Claudie, 45, 46
  E. F., 119
  E. T., 172
  Ed, 30
  Edward M., 70
  Eleanor, 122
  Elizabeth, 142, 143
  Ella, 33
  Emma, 176
  Epsie, 177
  Essie M., 151
  F. C., 177
  F. E., 170
  Fauchon, 17
  George B., 42
  Gertrude, 63
  Grant, 31, 41
  H. A., 34
  H. B. M., 93
  H. W., 87
  Harrison, 130
  Hattie, 102
  Ida, 42
  Ira, 89
  J. H., 167
  J. T., 77
  James, 168
  John, 47, 52
  John J., 131
  L., 183
  Leatine, 19
  Lineal, 104
  Luther, 129
  M. J., 77
  M. L., 108
  Mabel, 107
  Mae, 94
  Maggie, 131
  Maggie L., 151
  Marie, 62
  Mary, 32, 154
  Matie, 125
  May, 96
  R. A., 137
  R. T., 102
  Rhoda Pearl, 108
  Rosa B., 64, 65
  S. W., 105
  Sam, 102
  Sid, 186
  Spencer, 67
  Stella, 121
  Susie, 17
  T. B., 165
  T. L., 176
  T. T., 94
  Tom B., 62
  Velma, 26
  W. D., 154
  W. E., 65
  Will, 75
WILLIAMSON
  J. A., 104
  John M., 9
  Myrtle, 85
  Ola, 163
  Ouida, 161
  P. D., 161
WILLIARD
  Mary, 194
WILLIE
  C. V., 167
  Lee, 51
  Walter, 176
WILLINGHAM
  J. S., 90
WILLIS
  A. W., 115
  Eugene, 77
  Francis, 127
  Homer, 115
  J. W., 164
  W. E., 9
  W. R., 131
WILLMON
  Edgar, 8
WILLSHIRE
  Marian, 136
WILMER
  John, 70
WILSON
  A. J., 177
  Albert, 100
  Annie B., 89, 90
  Benjamin F., 178
  C. L., 81
  Cap, 21
  Charles, 160
  Corine, 143
  D. H., 64
  D. M., 30
  Dora, 88
  Dove, 143
  E. D., 136
  E. H., 128
  E. J., 59
  Ed, 93
  Edwin Ethelhart, 90
  Eugene, 185
  Frank, 69
  George W., 39
  H. D., 156
  Henry, 116, 142, 156
  Homer, 116
  Ida, 104
  J. A., 14
  J. B., 169
  J. E., 163
  J. R., 137
  J. W., 83
  J. Walter, 183
  James, 91
  Jim, 97
  Joe, 165
  John, 19, 98, 161, 162, 197
  Lee, 168
  Lennie, 30
  Leonard, 17
  Lillie, 187
  Lilly May, 138
  Lucille, 34
  M. N., 152
  M. U., 150
  Mattie, 115
  May, 44
  N. R., 93
  O. D., 142
  R. H., 111
  S. W., 62
  Scrap, 188
  Stuart, 79
  T. H., 181
  Thomas J., 116
  Tom, 15, 107
  Tyler, 165
  W. A., 24, 85
  W. F., 99
  W. R., 131
  W. T., 158
  William T., 52, 53
  Winifred, 71
WIMBLEY
  Sally, 34
WINBUSH
  Henry, 127
WINCHESTER
  Alice, 188
WINDLE
  D. S., 161
WINFREY
  J. K., 144
WINKLER
  Ida, 12
WINN
  H. W., 171
WINNINGHAM
  C., 142
  G. F., 18
WINSTON
  T. W., 133
WINTER
  Maude, 172
WINTEROWD
  C. W., 23
  Gertrude, 29
  Sarah, 23
WINTERWOOD
  Charlie, 90
WIRTLE
  Charles, 86
WISDOM
  J. M., 88
WISE
  Annie Belle, 136
  Edna Bell, 135
  Henry A., 96
  J. T., 175
  Mabel L., 176
  May, 134
  W. B. (or W. R.), 48
  W. M., 83, 84
  W. P., 135
WISELEY
  Pearl, 23
  W. G., 23
WISEMAN
  Claudia, 10
  Delia, 18
WISROCK
  Annie, 189
WISSELL
  Joan, 93
WITHERS
  I. A., 141
  J. N., 141, 146
  Lucille, 146
WITHERSPOON
  Thomas W., 174
WITHROW
  E. T., 50
  Hettie, 14
WITT
  Frank, 18
  Grover, 32
  J. W., 68
  John, 32
WITTS
  W. M., 144
WITZER
  Nick, 186
WOHLBURN
  B., 113
WOLDRUP
  Wallace, 187
WOLF
  Clarence, 171
  Florence, 90, 91
  Sarah, 167
WOLFE
  Bert, 40
  Daniel L., 101

249

M. M., 40
W. W., 183
WOLFF
  Arthur, 186
  S. P., 194
WOLFORD
  H. E., 58
WOMACK
  Ella Willie, 188
  J. O., 86
WOMBLE
  E. T., 66
WOMBOLD
  J. W., 79
WOOD
  A. G., 157
  G. M., 111
  Irene, 156
  J. H., 30
  J. N., 52
  Kate, 76
  Lewis, 157
  Marion H., 126
  Martha, 177
  Mary, 70
  Thurmond, 172
  Tom, 161, 162
  W. L., 42
  William, 196
WOODFORD
  Bell, 190, 191
WOODMANSEE
  Winfield, 55
WOODRUFF
  W. W., 97
WOODS
  Alberta E., 19
  Allen, 191
  Claud, 104
  Claude P., 123
  Clay, 97
  Ed, 115
  James, 137
  James P., 123
  Jim, 197
  John, 161
  Juman, 178
  Laura, 14
  Mack, 66
  May F., 73
  Minnie, 123
  R. A., 103
  Sophie K., 123, 124
  T. E., 70
  Tommy, 168
  William, 168
WOODSON
  C. M., 196
  Ernest, 196
  R. F., 7
WOODWARD
  E. R., 159
  W. F., 50
  Willie A., 75
WOOLDRIDGE
  Maggie, 126
WOOLSEY, 72
  C. W., 164
WOOSTER
  W. W., 171
WOOTEN
  F. G., 145
  R. S., 180
WORDEN
  J. B., 116
WORLESLEY
  Douglas, 113
WORSHAM
  J. R., 125
WORTHAM
  E. F., 195
  James, 155
  Lucy, 195
WORTHINGTON
  Gussie, 114
WORTHY
  M. C., 16
WOTIPKA
  Antoine, 44
WRIGHT, 82
  A. M., 152
  Abbie, 40
  C., 173
  C. B., 15
  C. R., 72, 133, 139, 194, 196
  Cam, 190
  Della, 131
  F. A., 10
  Henry, 25
  Herbert, 187
  J. M., 17, 24
  J. S., 112
  James Alexander, 186
  Katie Lee, 114
  Lillie, 33, 35
  Lizzie, 84
  M. E., 172
  M. T., 141
  Mary, 173
  Mary Anne, 19
  Myrtle, 15
  O. H., 95
  Rose, 12
  S. A., 10
  Theriza E., 116
  W. H., 90
  W. S., 99
  Willie Wray, 195
WRIGHTS
  M. E., 171
WRIGLEY
  C. M., 59
WYATT
  Ben, 136
WYCHE
  James B., 185
  John C., 112
WYLIE
  Edith C., 165
WYNAN
  Henry, 78
WYNNE
  A. M., 8
  H. M., 8
  Sam, 24
  W. P., 94
WYRICH
  Daniel, 169
WYSE
  Ira E., 157
YAGER
  C. E., 90
  Polly, 90
  Vessie, 152
YANCEY
  Emma, 27
  F. R., 153
YANKEY
  Dan, 25
YANTIS
  G. A., 122
  G. R., 17
YARBROUGH
  Beatrice, 24
YATES
  Earl, 62
  Henry, 47
  J. F., 158
  M. Wootie, 129
  Nola, 129
  Willie, 109
  Zada, 18
YEAGER
  Lizzie, 176
YEARBY
  Vina, 100
YEARWOOD
  R. L., 31
YEAWOOD
  Henry, 65
YERBY
  Ella, 163
YOAKUM
  B. F., 52
  F. I., 69
  L. C., 149
  R. E., 52
YOE
  Clyde, 77
YOPP
  W. I., 64
  W. T., 64
YORK
  Rose B., 119
  Sarah, 137
YOST
  Charles, 142
YOUNG
  C. C., 127
  Clarence, 53
  F. E., 161
  F. L., 18, 20, 161, 196
  F. M., 63
  G. C., 142
  Henry, 193
  Hubee, 70
  Irene, 161
  J. D., 10, 51, 146, 162
  J. T., 30
  Jennie Mae, 117
  John, 126
  Levi, 176
  Mary, 25
  Matha, 34
  R. A., 89
  R. L., 122
  Ruth, 101
  Sallie Jane, 126
  Sarah Ann Carter, 63
  Sud, 35
  W, T,, 46
  W. B., 101
  W. H., 70
  W. J., 138
  W. T., 45
  William C., 17
  Willie, 136, 152, 153
YOUNGBLOOD
  Clyde, 182
  E. Lucille, 35
  Guy, 78
  Silas, 182
YOUNGER
  John, 125
YOUNGS
  Annie, 7
YOUREE
  Mary, 108
YOWELL
  Naomi, 89
ZABEL
  H. A., 159
ZANE-CETTI
  Carl, 179
  Helen, 178, 179
  Louise, 179
  Marion, 179
ZAPLETAL
  Frank, 165

ZEEK
   Elizabeth, 62
ZELLIKEN
   Nellie, 70
ZETZSCHE
   L. H., 124
ZIMMERMAN
   J. M., 191
ZINN
   J. S., 127
   James L., 83

www.ingramcontent.com/pod-product-compliance
Lightning Source LLC
Chambersburg PA
CBHW080430230426
43662CB00015B/2231